P9-DIF-875

A Touchstone Book

RENÉ A. WORMSER

The Story of the LAW

AND THE MEN WHO MADE IT—

From the Earliest Times to the Present

REVISED AND UPDATED EDITION OF *THE LAW*

A Touchstone Book Published by
Simon and Schuster • New York

A TOUCHSTONE BOOK
PUBLISHED BY SIMON AND SCHUSTER
ROCKEFELLER CENTER, 630 FIFTH AVENUE
NEW YORK, N. Y. 10020

REVISED EDITION

FOURTH PAPERBACK PRINTING

SBN 671-21333-4
LIBRARY OF CONGRESS CATALOG CARD NUMBER: 62-10325
MANUFACTURED IN THE UNITED STATES OF AMERICA

To

E. W. W., A. B. W., *and* E. W. W.

To

R.V.W. A.B.W. and E.W.W.

Contents

PART THREE: The Romans

PART FOUR: The German Barbarians and the Feudal System

PART FIVE: The Churchmen

PART SIX: The Western Europeans

PART SEVEN: The English

PART NINE: The Internationals

Preface

The original version of this book was born of a suggestion once made by Wendell Willkie. He felt the need for a book—written for laymen—which would give some idea of how the law which governs us today came into being: how it had its beginning in ancient civilizations, how it developed, what great personalities helped give it shape and substance, and some of its major past and present problems.

I soon found that the greatest difficulty in organizing such a project was the selection of material. The law spreads out into all sorts of fields (philosophy, history, anthropology, religion, ethics, and many others), and the volume of written material is staggering. So I have selected as I thought best, and I undoubtedly should tender apologies to many jurists, statesmen, and writers who have been excluded because others seemed more vital to the story.

It has been my intention to make this the story of our *law, and therefore I have also excluded sources that seemed not too directly concerned with the growth of American legal institutions and legal philosophy. In some cases it has even seemed preferable to by-pass what is usually regarded as standard source material. I have made, for example, only fleeting reference in this book to the famous Babylonian Code of Hammurabi. For the ancient Israelites borrowed liberally from this code of their neighbors, and it was these borrowed portions, rather than Hammurabi's work itself, that survived to influence our law.*

Moreover, I have had to confine myself, necessarily, largely to secondary sources and I cannot, therefore, hold this book out as an authoritative work. Indeed, some of my material may well be disputed by technicians in the field. But I have sought to approach the monumental material involved in a history of the law with as much care as possible.

And instead of plodding in detail along the entire weary way up from the habits and customs of our prehistoric ancestors (about which, in any event, we can only guess), I have for the most part begun my story with the three great classical civilizations from which we have inherited so much—Jewish, Greek, and Roman—and then pursued the law through Europe, across the Channel to England (our most direct legal ancestor), and to our own country. I have added some material on international law as well, since that has become, in effect, a part of our own law.

I hope, with the late Wendell Willkie, that this book may give Americans a better understanding of the law, its development, processes and problems.

* * * * *

To acknowledge all the help and assistance I have had in the preparation of this book, in critical readings, criticisms and suggestions, would require a long list, indeed. I do express my sincere gratitude to these kind and helpful people, particularly to Albert Leventhal (who prompted the project while at Simon and Schuster); Henry Simon of Simon and Schuster (who promoted its rebirth); my partner, Venan J. Alessandroni; my associate, William Ruffa; Abraham Guterman of the New York Bar; the late Dr. Oskar Samek, formerly of the Vienna Bar; Philip B. Frere, Solicitor of London; General John Foster, Barrister of London; the late Professor Edwin Borchard of Yale; and the many correspondents who have made constructive suggestions.

RENÉ A. WORMSER

New York
August 31, 1961

PART ONE

THE JEWS

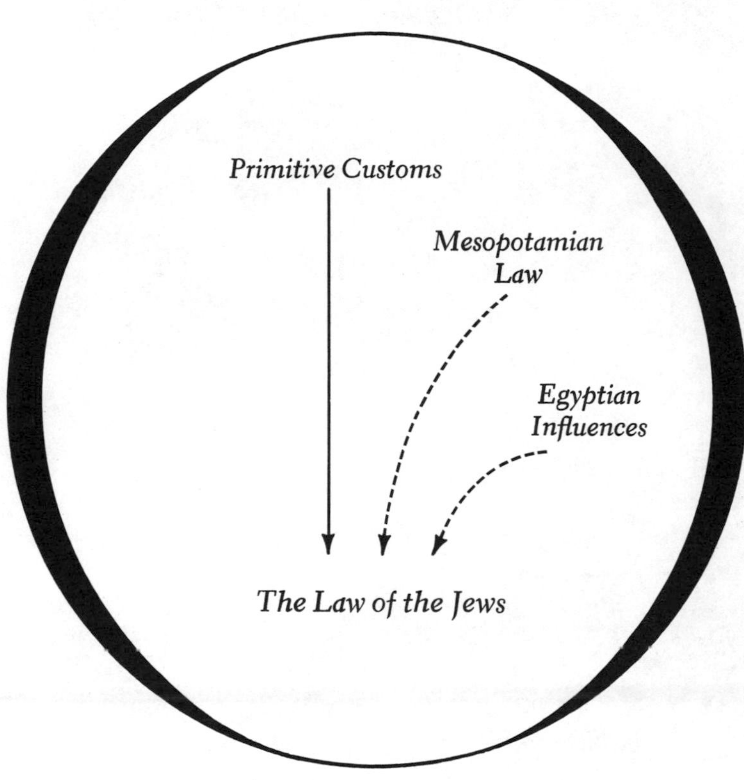

THE CHIEF BASIC SOURCES

CHAPTER 1

Moses

"And Moses came and called for the elders of the people, and laid before their faces all these words which the Lord commanded him." EXODUS, XIX, 7

I: How the Law Began

IT WAS a long time before anybody made any law. For ages man's conduct was governed by nothing more than the accumulated experience of his forefathers, which he followed unconsciously. We call such ways of conduct "folkways," and they are distinguishable from customs, which came into being very late in man's career. Customs were then followed consciously, even though men might have no idea why a custom had originated or what purpose it served. Many were devised to suit life in the peculiar circumstances in which a particular group found itself. Others were set by psychical factors or by any one of a number of other determining causes. Great numbers were merely accidental in their origin, and customs have a way of persisting long after their origin has been lost and even after their usefulness has completely disappeared.

Primitives seem to have been extraordinarily well-behaved; they needed no policemen, but there was one thing which compelled proper conduct. The word "taboo" is of Polynesian origin (*tapu*), but expresses something common to almost all primitive peoples. Religion declared certain things taboo, meaning either "sacred" or "unclean" and, therefore, "untouchable." Some taboos were wholly religious, such as the Jewish taboo of not using the name of the Lord in vain; others were hygienic, such as the Jewish rule against eating pork in a country where meat spoiled rapidly and pigs were probably infested anyway. There were social taboos, many probably invented by women, such as those prohibiting intercourse with a woman during her menstrual period or while she was nursing a child; and there were also taboos of legal significance, such as those which regulated selection in marriage. The wrath of the gods, conjured up by some terrifying medicine man, was not to be incurred lightly, nor was it wise to get into the bad graces of the headman; but the most important deterrent was fear of getting in wrong with the whole group. A small boy will sometimes rather face his angry parents than violate one of the taboos of his gang.

Modern dictators have learned the value of training children early in an ideology, but primitive groups knew all about this thousands of years ago. The primitive youth was initiated into the mysteries of his own group in such a manner as to impress him with the necessity of conforming to the tribal customs. He had some of his front teeth knocked out with a club; or they were filed down to points without benefit of Novocain or he was circumcised with a not-too-sharp shell; or incisions were made in his back into which something was rubbed to retard healing and thus produce the scars which would advertise his hardiness. Experiences such as these, accompanied by the hocus-pocus of ceremonial and magic, were certain to make the boy a conformer; he was impressed with the importance of passing into adult membership in his tribe, and he took pride in its customs.

Each people built up its set of customs, and many of these customs developed into law. I might put it that the customs turned into "customary law," and from that into "law." These are admittedly confusing terms, very difficult to define technically. Many different definitions of "law" have been offered but not one has been found wholly satisfactory. However, as in the case of many semantic problems, the term generally is understandable enough in whatever its context happens to be. "Customary law" is also difficult to define technically. But I can give some indication of its meaning by stating that it is custom which has the force of law. Our own courts recognize that certain customs in trades and professions are so vital and intrinsic a part of our social and economic system that they are treated as though they were laws.

II: How the Law Grew

AMONG primitive peoples, religious and secular laws were usually inextricably mixed. That is understandable enough, because of the religious nature of the taboo system, in which so much legal custom was solidified. It was natural that law should, at first, be in the custody of the priests; but an abrupt change usually took place when the laws were written down. Then they ceased to be the monopoly of a privileged class and became common knowledge. Lay jurists arose, who developed a philosophy of law, in actuality or in practice, which reflected changes in social and economic conditions, and the jurists and the people could then use such a philosophy gradually to emancipate the law from the religious chains which confined it.

There is an end to spontaneous development in the law, however, when it is written down. There then comes to be a certain rigidity about it, but human groups managed to escape from these rigidities and mold the law to suit changing circumstances. Sir Henry Maine, in his *Ancient Law,* noted three methods. The most modern is *legislation,* which quickly reflects the wishes of the dominating power, which, in a democracy, is the people. An older method is *equity,* used primarily in the Roman and English legal systems, but also used to some extent by the Jews. This consists of setting alongside the rigid law a set of principles of supposedly higher authority to which appeal can be made when the existing law does not seem just. The oldest method is the use of *fictions,* and here the ancient Jewish jurists excelled. Maine's definition of a fiction is an "assumption which conceals, or affects to conceal, the fact that a rule of law has undergone alteration, its letter remaining unchanged, its operation being modified." He gives, as an example, the institution of adoption, which "permits a family to be artificially created."

Perhaps no other people have been so adept at taking a sentence, a phrase, or even a word and rationalizing upon it a substantial and intricate structure of law as the ancient Jews. It was a precept of the Jewish system that "the law" must stand unchanged; yet the Jewish jurists managed to use all sorts of fictions to justify new rules which would otherwise seem to violate an existing rule. The same system was used by the Romans in changing their law, and it is used to this day by our own judges. It is one method by which the law is kept alive and adjusted to change in public opinion without having to resort to the difficulties of legislative reform.

III: Moses, the Lawgiver

WHATEVER the merits of the Arab case in the Palestine controversy, the issue was a simple one to the Jews. They wanted home, after living for so long in lands where they were rarely more than tolerated, usually discriminated against, and often slaughtered. And that is an old story. The Israelites who migrated to Egypt, long, long ago, came to want home dearly. They had prospered for a while, until a new Pharaoh, so reports the Bible, told his people that the Israelites must be "dealt wisely" with. He directed a series of persecutions against them and finally decreed that no male Israelite child might be permitted to live. But God took pity on these persecuted people and appointed Moses to lead them out of captivity. After the waters of the Red Sea had closed over the pursuing Egyptian host, the long trek to the Promised Land began. It took forty years of privation and hardship, says the Bible, and all this time Moses led, encouraged, and judged his people. From "morning unto evening" he sat and judged them, and so hard did he labor that his father-in-law suggested that he appoint others to help him in his work.

"So Moses hearkened to the voice of his father-in-law, and did all that he had said.

"And Moses chose able men out of all Israel, and made them heads over the people, rulers of thousands, rulers of hundreds, rulers of fifties, and rulers of tens.

"And they judged the people at all seasons: the hard cases they brought unto Moses, but every small matter they judged themselves." *

Three months after their departure from Egypt, the Israelites arrived at the wilderness of Sinai. It was there that the Lord revealed the law to Moses, who transmitted it to the people. The law is to be found in the Pentateuch, the first five books of the Old Testament. *Pentateuch* is a Greek word meaning "the five rolls." The Jews call these five books the *Torah*, meaning "the law" or, literally, "direction" or "guidance."

The Bible gives Moses no credit for having devised any law. It was all revealed to him by God, and that is a story frequently found among Eastern peoples. The Babylonians believed that the Sun God had given their law to Hammurabi; the Egyptians, that theirs had come from Thoth; the Persians, that theirs had come from Ahura Mazda by way of Zoroaster. Such stories are not uncommon even in the modern era: witness the alleged revelation of the *Book of Mormon* to Joseph Smith. If Moses did not devise the law but merely reported what God had given him, did he actually write the law

* Exodus, xviii.

down, was he the author of the Pentateuch or Torah? Opinions on this subject, many of them violent, run the gamut from a belief that Moses wrote the whole five books to the conviction that Moses was himself a legendary character. Orthodox Jewish opinion is that Moses wrote the whole thing except for the last eight verses, which were added by Joshua. Roman Catholic opinion is that Moses was the original author of the whole, but that transcribers have altered the text to such an extent that it is not entirely reliable and is open to some criticism.

The Torah is the "constitution" of the Jewish law. All other sources of Jewish law are based upon or dependent on it, and a great mass of such auxiliary law has grown up. The *Talmud*, a remarkable compound of poetry, mysticism, dialectic, and realism, contains a complete compilation of this additional law, which bears somewhat the same relation to the Torah as English common law does to the constitutional and statutory law. The Jews have been governed by the laws of the Torah and the Talmud during all these intervening years, except to the extent that they have strayed from the ways of their ancestors, and the extent to which a foreign yoke has prevented them from governing themselves. Even until very recently in many parts of Europe Jews within their ghettos, or within their own limited communities, have subjected themselves to their own law of the Torah and the Talmud, even when other law was available to them. Few such communities now remain. Some were exterminated through concentration camps and gas chambers. Yet the Jewish law is not dead. The communities in Palestine have preserved it in part, and Jews everywhere still on occasion submit a dispute to a rabbi for adjudication or arbitration under Jewish law.

But the law of Moses has not been law for the Jews alone. It has played a direct and vital part in the creation of our own legal system. Some of our early colonial communities were ruled under the exact and precise law of the Old Testament; moreover, the law of the Jews became one of the chief root sources of both the law of the Continent of Europe and the English law upon which ours is directly based.

IV: The Ten Commandments

The most important set of laws in the Pentateuch is, of course, the Ten Commandments. They are taught to every Christian as well as

Jewish child, and the secular rules of conduct which they contain are among the foundation stones of the systems of law of the so-called Christian nations. Yet there is some dispute as to exactly what the "Ten" Commandments are. They are found, in somewhat different language, in both Exodus xx and Deuteronomy v, and it is difficult to determine where one Commandment begins and another ends. They are not listed as ten commandments, nor numbered in any way. Probably they came to be called by the number ten because of the convenience of counting off with the fingers of two hands. At any rate, Jews, Catholics, and Protestants disagree as to the wording of the Ten Commandments. The Catholics even disagree with the other two about which Commandments are which; the Catholic ten vary in substance from the ten recognized by the Jews and the Protestants. In the following discussion, the Jewish (and Protestant) listing will be referred to.

The first four Commandments are purely religious, but the remainder have secular significance. And it is not only in the case of the Ten Commandments that religious and secular rules of conduct are mixed together; when a Jew spoke of the law he meant not merely the rules of secular law but the religious law as well. One further comment before discussing the Ten Commandments, upon which a great body of law was based: the Torah or Pentateuch contains not only fine ethical principles but also some very crude law of a distinctly primitive character. The conclusion is inevitable that a great part of the law was merely Jewish tribal law written down at a time when the Jews were still in a state not very far advanced from the primitive; and some was assimilated from contemporary peoples.*

The *Fifth Commandment* orders the honoring of father and mother, thus sanctifying the family. No other people centered life around the family unit more than did the Jews, and their family was essentially a clan family. It is no mere coincidence that almost all the primitive people of whom we have any knowledge organized themselves on the tribal-clan pattern. The most difficult problem which man had to solve when he began to live in groups was the mating problem. He generally found that it was wise not to permit

* In using the term "Jews" in this chapter, I have not always been strictly accurate but have done so for convenience. Strictly speaking, the "Jews" were originally only one of the tribes of Israel, the descendants of Judah. References to "Jews" are to be found only in the latter parts of the Old Testament. Eventually, the term came to be applied to all the Israelites.

the young men to select their mates from within their own immediate group, and yet to make them stay within the larger group so that the manpower of the larger group would not decline. From this principle the common form of tribal-clan organization must have followed. The larger group, the tribe, is composed of clans, each actually an enlarged family. The tribe is *endogamous,* while the clan is *exogamous:* one *must* marry within one's own tribe but *cannot* marry within one's own clan.

It is probable that the earliest tribal-clan pattern was matriarchal, relationships being traced through female descent only. In the days before formal mating, when a woman could consort with as many men as she pleased, it was a wise child who could know his own father; and there have been primitive tribes, even in our own day, who did not know the connection between sexual intercourse and the production of children. The Egyptians retained a somewhat matriarchal system even into the highest point of their civilization, but this was most unusual. By the time a group has advanced to the state in which we find the Jews in the early parts of the Old Testament, it has generally shifted to a patriarchal form of organization.

In a patriarchal society, in its classic state, relationships are traced through the father, and you are related only to those who are related to your father. Our system of relationships is called the *cognatic,* every person of one's own blood being considered a relative. The matriarchal form of relationship is called the *enatic,* every person of one's mother's family (even those not of her blood) being deemed related. The patriarchal form is the *agnatic,* every person of one's father's family being related. Something of this system remains in our society when a woman takes her husband's name when she marries, but in the old patriarchal form of society the woman was virtually ejected from her own family and became a member of her husband's family, as though born into it.

While there were tribal gods, each clan also had its own family deities. When the woman was ready to marry, she was divorced from her own family religion and joined that of her husband, and in many other ways it was made clear that she had nothing further to do with her old family. Therefore, as all relationship between the woman and her own family was severed, the primitive could not understand how her children could be related to her former family.

We know the Jews of the Old Testament as a people with one God, but it is probable that they had formerly lived a more or less typical patriarchal clan life, for many characteristics of this pattern still remained.

In a clan the power of the chief or headman is usually somewhat limited by the right of the adult males to act as a sort of clan assembly, to be consulted on the most important matters. But in the individual family there was no limitation on the power of the father of the family. Among the Jews, the father was king in his home, able to rule his wife, descendants, and slaves with an iron hand. He could even sell his daughter if he so desired, or give her in marriage without her consent. And he had the right to punish his family and to direct the use of its property; these were almost completely arbitrary rights.

Since the Jews were few in numbers and were originally an agricultural and pastoral people, large families were desirable, for they constituted labor for the father's use and manpower for the state. Fecundity in women was therefore considered of extraordinary importance and the duty of women to bear children emphasized. A woman who could not produce children often provided her handmaiden for that purpose, so that the family might be continued. Thus Sarah gave her handmaiden Hagar to Abraham, but such a practice was hardly necessary among the early Jews, for polygyny was not forbidden, nor was concubinage. In later periods, the practice of plural marriage passed into disuse, and then it became illegal by custom.

Marriage was generally by purchase from the bride's father or male relatives, and the wife left her family completely, joining that of her husband in the agnatic pattern. If the husband died and there were no children, then his brother—or, if there was no brother, the nearest male relative—was obliged to marry the widow. So, Boaz of the Bible, after a closer relative had violated this custom by refusing to marry Ruth when her husband died, took her himself. This custom of widow-marriage, frequently found in primitive and semiprimitive societies, was later ameliorated among the Jews by the procedure called *Chelitza*, through which the woman and her brother-in-law could be released from the obligation to marry, and she would then be free to marry one of her own choice.

There is some scientific and logical basis for intelligent speculation about the customs of early primitive peoples, but much of it is pure guessing. What the prehistoric marriage customs of the Jews and of our other cultural ancestors were is by no means clear, nor was there necessarily a uniform pattern of development. All kinds of marriage came into existence, some of them most curious. Monogamy was by no means the universal rule, nor was a simple form of polygamy. The Urabunna of Australia, for instance, had a form of group marriage. A group of males consorted with a specific group of females and no others. Even under this interesting system the endogamous-clan principle prevailed. One had to be *nupa* (technically unrelated) to all the women of the group in order to cohabit with them.

There were temporary marriages. In some of the Malaccan tribes each girl made the rounds of the men of the tribe, staying with each for a time and then passing on to the next. Frequent shifting of spouses was common among the Tahitians, the ancient Hawaiians, and many other peoples. Polyandry was not unusual. Some of the Tibetans to this day practice it, a girl marrying one man but being considered also the wife of his brothers. And polygyny, of course, was a very popular institution. Even when monogamy was in vogue, men were generally permitted to have concubines.

There was also great variety in the method of marriage. Sometimes there was much formality, sometimes there was little or none. One of the oldest forms of marriage, marriage by duel, man saw in operation all around him in nature. Two men fought for the girl whom each wanted. There was also marriage by capture. A young man from one clan might have little opportunity to woo a girl from another clan openly. So, in order to get himself a wife, he kidnaped a girl and took her home to his own family. There were probably occasional marriages by elopement, even in violation of tribal taboos; but, if the couple had a child, they were generally forgiven and deemed legitimately married.

The Kaffirs of Africa had an interesting form of marriage by purchase. The suitors bid for the girl, and the father was usually avaricious enough to give her to the man who offered the largest number of cattle, the medium of exchange. But this system was not wholly heartless, for the cattle were shared with some of the father's male relatives and remained as a sort of security for the bride.

Marriage by purchase was common among primitives, and it often led to difficulties for a groom. If he could not get the price together, he sometimes had to go into service in his father-in-law's or mother-in-law's household to work off his debt. There was even a form of marriage among the Malays called "abillatory," in which the poor husband sometimes was bought by the wife's family and became little more than a servant to his mother-in-law. In another variety of Malayan marriage the bride and groom stayed with their respective families. In a third, the bride went to her husband's family. The fourth kind was more in line with our ideas. The bride and groom established their own household.

Varying social and geophysical factors may have determined some of the odd forms of matrimony. Certainly where there was a shortage of men polygyny might have been expected, and where the reverse, then polyandry. In the case of the Jews, the religious-clan base of society seems to have determined the form of the marriage, but that may not be the whole explanation. The form of religious and social organization was frequently determined by the necessities of life as a group of men found it. I can give no further historical explanation than that the Jews presumably developed along what might be called the "common," patriarchal pattern.

A new body of legal custom came into existence when marriage became a socially recognized and controlled institution. For a man began to consider his wife a valuable property. Not only did he often pay something to get her, or, at least, go to some trouble to marry her, but she had value to him as a laborer. To have a wife who does not work is entirely a modern idea. So the primitive devised legal customs to protect his property right in the family which helped him till the soil or herd the cattle, constructed utensils for him and generally contributed to his limited wealth.

Among the Kaffirs the husband might demand from one to four head of cattle from the man who committed adultery with his wife. There was no sense of morals behind this, but a strong feeling that the victim's property had been used or interfered with. In the same manner, if a Kaffir's virgin daughter was seduced and a child produced, the father could ask compensation from the seducer. The compensation was paid to the father and not to the daughter. And here is the strangest part of it. The child became the property of the seducer if he paid the fine. If he did not, then the child became the property of the parents or guardians of the girl.

The double standard of morality seems to have existed in most societies. The reason for it is not only that a woman had to be chaste in order to assure her husband that her children were his also. A more important reason may be that, as I have said, men began to regard women as property. Much law has been based on the necessity which men felt for protecting this peculiar and valuable property right.

The *Sixth Commandment* says, "Thou shalt not kill," but it is not to be taken literally. The Lord of the Old Testament enjoyed seeing his enemies, foreign and domestic, slaughtered in great numbers, and many of the Biblical heroes, such as Solomon, slew their own private enemies and did not lose any of the Lord's grace for it. So we may take it that the Jewish law, like ours, prohibited only unjustified killing, leaving it to the sages to determine when a killing was justified. Men have differed, in various places and various generations, about what kind of killing is justified.

The *Seventh Commandment* enjoins adultery and thus is another basic precept intended to sanctify and protect the family. It is not directed against sex relations before marriage, yet laws were rationalized from it which demanded virginity of a bride. Virginity was not, however, demanded of a bridegroom. Indeed, prostitution was a prosperous trade among the Jews, and no one seemed concerned about it except an occasional reformer; and it was a rare reformer, for that matter, who made any objection at all to professional relations with an alien woman.

The *Eighth Commandment* prohibits stealing. It is thus the great protector of the institution of private property, and a mass of property law has been built upon it. While the owning of slaves was universal in Biblical times, it is somewhat distressing to find it countenanced by the Lord in the Old Testament.

In some respects, however, Jewish slavery laws were exceptionally benign. In Chapter xxi of Exodus, the Lord ordains that, if a Jewish servant (slave) is bought, he must be freed after six years of service. But there follows a strange rule, which ignores the feelings of the human heart and the sacredness of the parental relationship: "If his master have given him a wife, and she have borne him sons or daughters; the wife and her children shall be her master's and he shall go out by himself."

The *Ninth Commandment* enjoins perjury and establishes a religious basis for legal procedure. Perjury was heavily punished; sometimes a perjurer was even made to suffer whatever penalty his victim would have suffered.

The *Tenth Commandment* proscribed covetousness, and from this also a great body of law has been derived. This Commandment seems to indicate that women were treated by the ancient Jews as a form of property: "Thy neighbor's wife" is included among such items as "thy neighbor's house," his ox, his ass, and his slaves.

The origins of the property concept are obscure, but whatever rudimentary property idea man had in his early stages, it seems certain that the development of agriculture on an intensive scale always carried a growth of property-consciousness with it.

Except in the most extremely communal societies, one felt that one "owned" the agricultural tools which one used, the animals which became essential to husbandry, and even the produce of the land. Agriculture also attached an owership idea to human property, for slavery grew more popular as agriculture developed. Even before slavery became an adjunct of agriculture, man had partially enslaved his family. For his wife and children could be made to till the fields, increase the productivity of the lands, and thereby increase the materials which the father could barter for whatever small luxuries existed, including more wives and, therefore, more children. Barter itself brought with it a more definite property concept. Trading arrowheads for fishhooks or spears for cabbages began to give some idea of absolute ownership of property.

A society's attitude toward theft is a good indication of just how seriously property rights are regarded. In some very early societies, theft was punished severely. In others, theft was not condemned at all, and a successful thief was thought clever. A distinction was often made between a thief caught in the act and one who was not discovered until afterwards. The former was considered much more reprehensible, because the act might have caused personal violence or conflict. A trace of this idea persisted in early English law; in the twelfth century a thief caught red-handed could be hanged summarily, while one who got away with the goods could only be subjected to a fine of twice the value of the goods taken. A similar rule obtained in the Book of the Covenant, which is the name by which the set of laws in Exodus immediately following the Ten Commandments is called. As society grew more complex and trade expanded, private property was more likely to be protected. A moral idea attached to property right, and the thief was not merely subjected to personal vengeance, or restitution and penalty, but to public prosecution as a violator of a moral rule.

The Ten Commandments illustrate the difficulty which lawyers and judges have in interpreting the law. The Commandments cannot always be taken literally. It is clear that Jehovah did not disapprove of all killings, and the injunction to "honor" a father would undoubtedly be properly ignored if the father were an unmitigated scoundrel. Thus the Jewish jurists have been obliged to take the Ten Commandments and the other parts of the Mosaic law and to interpret, clarify, and make exceptions. We continue to do the same thing with our own laws, which, however lengthy they may seem, are yet brief in relation to the subject matter which they attempt to cover. Judges must read into the law the detail which its unavoidable brevity makes necessary. One method of interpreting a law is to determine its fundamental purpose, in order to set reasonable limits to its practical application. But many rules of law developed without any well-defined purpose, and the reasons for which they originated may have disappeared. Therefore, we often ascribe a purpose to a rule which did not attach to it when it was first made.

V: Vengeance

MAN did not develop legislative machinery until comparatively recently. There was no need for doing so. Legal customs accommodated themselves easily enough to change in social views. This is illustrated most readily by the changes in the treatment of vengeance. In the Bible, in Exodus xxi, the chapter following that containing the Ten Commandments, is the following:

> ". . . thou shalt give life for life,
> Eye for eye, tooth for tooth, hand for hand, foot for foot,
> Burning for burning, wound for wound, stripe for stripe,"

indicating that, when these words were written, the Jews were in a state of primitive tribal law and yet at least one stage from barbarism.

At first the group had had no interest at all in the problem of revenge; if someone put out your eye, you went off and waylaid him and knocked his brains out, or kidnaped his wife, or stole his children. But there came a time when it was felt that revenge should not be allowed to go too far. If your eye was put out, you had a right to put out the eye of the offender but not to hack off his arm in addition. It is this stage in development which the eye-for-an-eye rule of the Old Testament reflects. About this time we find the beginnings of a judicial system, for there had to be some way of determining how much revenge you were entitled to. Then chiefs and headmen began to make an effort to reduce the slaughter within the group and prevent manhunts and clan feuds. They would get the disputants together and try to induce a compromise, a voluntary form of arbitration in which the matters at issue were the right to get personal revenge, and how that revenge should be satisfied.

There was another factor in revenge which developed some law. It is almost a reflex action to want revenge on the object which hurt you. If you stumble over a chair, you kick it. The primitive felt this sort of urge clearly, and he wanted revenge not only against the man who did him an injury but also against the *thing* which did it. He was often willing, strange as it may seem, to forgo revenge against the person if he could get revenge against the thing. In the Old Testament if an ox gored a man to death the ox must be stoned to death, and his flesh might not be eaten. Under the Roman law an animal who did an injury must be given up and the owner was then not responsible for damages. In England, under Edward I, if a man fell out of a tree the tree was made *deodand*—in the language of Blackstone, "an accursed thing." If he was drowned in a well, the well had to be filled up, as *deodand*. The *deodand* concept carried on into modern law, for, in British criminal cases, even in this century, the article with which a man was killed was appraised in the indictment and forfeited to the king. The thing which did the deed was accursed, and the injured party (or the king in his stead) had the right to revenge against it. And so, in our own admiralty law, if a ship does you an injury, you "libel" or attach, and actually sue, the ship.

Our system of granting damages probably came about through this idea of revenge against the object which did the damage. Instead of delivering that object, the owner made a stipulated payment, either in money or in cattle or some other medium of exchange, buying off the right of revenge. Regular scales of payment became the vogue. But there were limitations on this composition system. Certain injuries—murder and rape, for instance—could not be settled by payment of a fine; the family was still entitled to its personal revenge.

Obviously, with damages some sort of court became necessary. This was not yet a true court in our sense, deciding facts and applying law. It was merely a medium for limiting the right of blood feud; the court was just a peacemaker; it might still be ignored and its decision violated, but it became more and more difficult to repudiate the decision of a peacemaking court. As the chief, who usually acted as the court or presided over it, grew more powerful, it became less likely that his judgment would be ignored. Moreover, the idea of the "king's peace" came along. The chief or king had the right to have peace in his tribe or in his domain, and he could impose a fine on anyone who broke the peace. The chief could even impose a more dreaded penalty, banishment, or outlawry. Thus the group, acting through its executive, began to protect itself against breaches of the peace; but it was still not "punishing" a wrongdoer, in the sense that we punish a criminal. At least, it was not conscious of doing punishment.

Sometimes a feud was ended by leaving it to the gods to decide who was right. Trial by battle was one method. The theory was that the righteous would win. Another method was to make the disputants take a fearful oath; everybody was satisfied that the perjurer would be punished from on high. Often "compurgators" were sworn as well, members of the family or friends of the litigants, who would also be subject to the revenge of the gods if they swore falsely. Trial by ordeal had behind it the same idea, that the gods would save the righteous and punish the evildoer. If the accused succumbed to the ordeal—if his hand burned in the fire, or if he drowned (or didn't) when thrown into the water—that proved his guilt.

There is a most interesting form of trial by ordeal in Numbers v, available to any husband who thinks his wife has been unfaithful. The husband is directed to take his wife to a priest and to bring him a specially prepared "offering of jealousy." The priest sets the woman "before the Lord" and takes holy water and mixes it with the dust "that is in the floor of the tabernacle." He then asks her to drink this concoction, charging her:

"If no man have lain with thee, and if thou hast not gone aside to uncleanliness with another instead of thy husband, be thou free from this bitter water that causeth the curse:

"But if thou hast gone aside to another instead of thy husband, and if thou be defiled, and some men have lain with thee beside thine husband," then the Lord shall make her a curse: "And this water that causeth the curse shall go into thy bowels to make thy belly to swell, and thy thighs to rot."

The woman drinks the water; if her belly swells, she is guilty; but if her belly swells not, then she is innocent of the imputation, and her husband must be satisfied.

It took a long while, in the development of society, for courts to be established which were impartial agencies for trying cases, relying on evidence and testimony, and for the mandates of such courts to be executed by some public agency. Yet the roots of public action, in cases of wrongdoing, are very deep. Perhaps the very first use of force or coercion by society was in outlawry. When a primitive violated an important taboo or ran amok with tribal custom, he might face ostracism. That was unpleasant enough, but, if the group went further and made him an outlaw, his fate might be a terrible one. In primitive societies it was not easy to get along by oneself in the wilderness, particularly if one were free game for anyone's arrow or spear. But, whenever the very primitive group acts so summarily and so consciously, it is not from a matured sense of justice. It simply protects itself as a group. Punishment is not involved. Punishment or revenge is left to the individual. Self-protection is the motivating cause of the group action.

Perhaps the final stage in the early development of law was the birth of the idea that the chief or leader of the group should attempt to prevent wrongdoing and should punish it when done. So began the legislative function, marked at its beginnings by the harshness and cruelty deemed necessary to effect peaceful human relations. As society became more stable and more secure, harshness could give way to reason, both in legislation and in punishment. But that took a long while!

Man has had so much to learn—and has so much more to learn, perhaps, before he grows up fully. Many social and legal concepts which are so obvious to us now came into the consciousness of man only very late in his career. That there might be a difference between an accidental killing and one which was intended, for example, is an advanced concept. The Jews did make a distinction between an intended and an unintended killing, but they did not protect the accidental killer fully. They expected that an avenger from the family of the deceased would pursue the unfortunate killer and try to kill him in turn, and his only protection was that certain "cities of refuge" were established to which he could flee for sanctuary. If he was caught before he reached one of them, that was just his bad luck, and the avenger was not punished.

Much of the law of the Torah is taken up with torts, as might be expected in any primitive or semiprimitive system. A tort is an injury to a person or his property for which he may sue. You commit a tort when you hit someone in the jaw. If you walk over another's land without his permission, or beat his dog, that is a tort. And if you libel or slander a man, that is a tort also. As the Jews were pastoral and agricultural, many of the rules of tort law had to do with domesticated animals and with the fields. For example, "If a man shall steal an ox or a sheep, and kill it, or sell it; he shall restore five oxen for an ox, and four sheep for a sheep." * Or, "If a man shall cause a field or vineyard to be eaten, and shall put in his beast, and shall feed in another man's field: of the best of his own field, and of the best of his own vineyard, shall he make restitution."†

All the tort law in the Torah is not primitive. It is provided that, if an ox gore a man or woman, "the ox shall be surely stoned, and his flesh shall not be eaten; but the owner of the ox shall be quit." However, "if the ox were wont to push with his horn in time past, and it hath been testified to his owner, and he hath not kept him in," then, if the ox gore someone to death, the owner, as well as the ox, is to be put to death.‡ Note that the ox is put to death. This may be a hangover of some superstitious idea—that the offending animal is a thing possessed—or it may derive merely from the simple primitive desire for revenge against things which injure. Such explanations have been given by jurists. On the other hand, the ox may have been killed just as a vicious dog might now be exterminated. Note that a man is not held responsible if he does not know that his ox is dangerous; but if a man has an ox which is known to be likely to gore, he is held accountable for anything that happens. It took most of humanity a long while to understand the concept of negligence, and here we have it stated in an Old Testament law.

VI: The Land and the Family

WHEN the white man first came to our shores, most of the Indians he encountered roamed from place to place and would have thought it ridiculous for anyone to claim ownership of a particular piece of land. The land was free as the air or the sea. And this was the opin-

* Exodus, xxii, 1.
† Exodus, xxii, 5.
‡ Exodus, xxi, 28, 29.

ion of all migratory peoples. You defended the land upon which you happened to have stopped; but, when the seasons changed, or the hunting got bad, or the grass deteriorated, or the corn did not seem to grow well any more, you packed up your meager belongings and moved elsewhere.

We have no record of the life of the Jews in very ancient times, but we believe them to have been migratory, and it is not likely that they could have had any concept of ownership in land until they learned to cultivate the fields intensively, for that seems to have been the history of all migratory peoples. But even intensive agriculture did not necessarily bring the idea of landownership with it. A great many of the earliest agricultural societies, if not all of them, were communal in organization; we come to this conclusion partly by observing the primitive societies which remained in the historical era. A Samoan, for illustration, before he was spoiled by civilization, would not have permitted some to starve while others had full larders; and the American Indian, the Hottentot, and the Eskimo would have found it just as impossible to understand a civilization in which one man could hoard food while another went without. Jean Jacques Rousseau, the French philosopher, maintained that primitive societies were far more ethical, kindly, and moral than our so-called civilized ones, and there is much to be said for his proposition.

The Jews of the Old Testament were still in a semicommunal condition, and one which had been interwoven with their religious ideas. All the land was owned by God, and he merely permitted those to hold it who worked it. The growth of a landlord class, living on rents, was frowned upon; and usury was forbidden because it endangered the economic independence of the borrower of money and fostered landlordism. "Usury" today means lending money at excessive interest, but the lending of money at any interest was "usury" to the Jews, a concept which was carried over into the Middle Ages in Europe by the Christian Church.

While the theory that God owned the land persisted, it was in fact held by the tribes, and these divided it up among the constituent clans, which, in turn, made distributions among the families. The family plot was usually worked under patriarchal direction, the eldest son succeeding to the management of the property, but for the benefit of the entire family. When there was a division among the sons, the first-born got a double share. Thus, private ownership of land was recognized, within the general communal scheme, and the abuses of a private-property system were to be found in Palestine as anywhere else. Mortgages were given and foreclosed, and unscrupulous men frequently accumulated vast acreage by this method. But the unique, semicommunal system of the Jews included a method of righting such wrongs periodically. The Sabbath, as we know it, had its counterpart in the sabbatical year. In that seventh year, the Jews were forbidden to engage in agriculture, and two reasons have been given for this custom. The rest gave the land a chance to lie fallow and to restore itself to fertility, and the pause in labor gave the people an opportunity to study the law and generally to acquire learning. But then came the year of jubilee, the year of correction, the bad year for the landlords. In that seven-times-seventh year, all leases fell simultaneously and the land was redistributed, regardless of the industry of one or the indolence of another. This rule applied only to farms; a town house might be purchased by the original owner. Perhaps the most interesting feature of the year of jubilee was that all slaves were freed.

VII: The Talmudists Interpret Moses

In the sixth century B.C. Nebuchadnezzar conquered Judah and thought that he would have an easy time ruling his new Jewish subjects. But the Jews resented the foreign yoke; the country was in a constant state of ferment, and Nebuchadnezzar finally decided to solve his "Jewish problem" by a mass expulsion to Babylon. The "Babylonian captivity" does not seem, however, to have been a very unpleasant experience. One gets the impression that the Jews liked the lush life in the "Land between the Rivers." Certainly when Cyrus of Persia conquered Babylon and gave the Jews permission to leave, even assisting them with their emigration finances, only a small group departed. The rest stayed on, and descendants of these eventually scattered all over the Near East.

Those who returned to Palestine were the Zionists of their day, and the return to the homeland was marked by a strong wave of puritanism. A new interest in the literature of the race, a renaissance of concern with Jewish culture and history, accompanied the homecoming; and the best Jewish minds, for many generations, turned to an intensive study of the scanty remnants of folk and religious history which remained. Study of the Scriptures, and particularly of the law of Moses, became the ruling passion of the Hebrew intellect, and it was about this time that the Talmud began to be compiled. There were, finally, two separate and distinct Talmuds. One, the Palestine or Jerusalem version, eventually disappeared almost entirely from use. The so-called Babylonian version is far more comprehensive, and it is the one generally referred to when the Talmud is cited or mentioned. The Talmud contains some alien matter. In it may be traced borrowings from the Greek philosophers, and from the culture of Mesopotamia and from current religions; no one will ever know the extent to which it has absorbed materials from outside sources. But its compilation is original, and the work, to which in the course of perhaps a thousand years so many sages contributed, bears the stamp and the character of the people who produced the Old Testament and who produced Jesus.

It had its basis in the *Midrash,* the name given to the searching of the Scriptures which began after the period of Babylonian exile. Several distinct methods of study arose, and the four most important of them are associated with the word "Paradise," which, as the Hebrew alphabet contains no vowels, is spelled "PRDS." Actually the word designated by the consonants is *Pardas,* meaning "Garden of Groves." The word "Paradise" is probably derived from it, but the Hebrew word for Paradise is *Gan Aden,* or "Garden of Eden." Each of the letters "PRDS" designates a method of Midrash. One is *peshat* and consisted of the simple interpretation of words and things. Another is *remes,* meaning "to hint," which sought to find meanings hidden in apparently superfluous or meaningless words and signs. The third, *derush,* was a homiletic, prophetical, sermon-like approach somewhat similar to that of the New Testament. The fourth, *sod,* was a mysterious, metaphysical, theosophical approach, into the intricacies of which few were initiated.

Midrash produced the Talmud—Midrash in all its types. Therefore, while the Talmud contains a compilation of laws, it is not a code set forth in the simple logical manner of modern codes, but one interspersed with, and sometimes apparently beclouded by, poetical, religious, and philosophical digressions, by prophesy, and by other obscuring results of the several methods of Midrash study of the Scriptures. The logical exposition of the legal content of the Scriptures (largely from Exodus, Leviticus, and Deuteronomy) was called *Halachah* (meaning "rule" or "norm"). The prophetical, religious, historical, and ethical aspects of the Talmud are called *Haggadah* (meaning "legend" or "song").

The Talmud is divided into two parts. One is the *Mishnah,* the exposition of the laws of Moses. The other is the *Gemara,* a further exposition of the Mishnah. The Torah was the constitution of the Hebrews, their "written" law. The Mishnah and the Gemara are sometimes referred to as the "unwritten" law. The origin of the detailed rules of the law in the Mishnah and the Gemara is obscure. Tradition traces their compilation in substance to Moses himself, who is supposed to have laid down these rules along with the basic code of the Torah. It is more likely that these rules began with primitive customs, grew through the determination of tribal councils, and found early expansion in the rulings of the tribal judges. In the long lapse of time between Moses and the beginnings of Talmudic writing, many new conditions had appeared, and new laws must constantly have been required by new circumstances. In order to satisfy Hebrew religious feeling, it was necessary that new laws be inspired or commanded by God, and it was for this reason that the Hebrew "common law" developed by a system of interpretation or exposition of the Mosaic law. The wise men, the commentators, were permitted to interpret with the use of collateral material such as tradition, lore, historical incident, and previously existing comment; but they were required to found their reasoning on the ultimate source of law, the constitution, the Mosaic code.

It was the so-called scribes who did the work of Talmudic compilation from the time of the return from Babylon (perhaps 530 B.C.) to about 220 B.C. Ezra and Nehemiah were the supposed founders of this school of compilators. The scribes taught in the schools, preached in the synagogues, and instructed the people. A later school of commentators, called the "learners" or "repeaters" or "master builders," did their part from about 220 B.C. to about A.D. 220. During this period the Jews were ruled by Persians, Egyptians, Syrians, and Romans. It was the period in which took place the revolt of the Maccabees, the birth of Jesus, the destruction of the Temple at Jerusalem by Titus, the later destruction of Jerusalem itself, and the final expatriation of the Jews. Nothing, however, was permitted to interfere with the schools of the repeaters. No degree of persecution, no amount of martyrdom, stopped this flow of Jewish learning. The law throve and grew.

The Babylonian Talmud, as we know it today, was completed in about A.D. 500, under the supervision of four famous rabbis, Ashi, Rabina bar R, Huna, and Jose. Prior to that time the Talmud had been in oral form, for the most part, owing to a religious prohibition against writing the Halachah. This prohibition was finally disregarded in order to preserve the great mass of material for posterity.

The repeaters were led by a President (called *Nasi*, "Prince") and a Vice-President (called *Ab-Beth-Din*, "Father of the House of Judgment"). These were the presiding officers of the highest legal assembly, the *Sanhedrin*. The Sanhedrin was the highest tribunal, both civil and religious. Where the New Testament mentions the "priests, elders, and the scribes," what is referred to is the Great Sanhedrin, consisting of seventy-one members chosen from among the scribes (who may be called the lawyers) and from the heads of the great families and from among the priests.

These men had to be learned in the law. That did not mean, however, that they needed only the learning of lawyers. They were required to know the whole body of Jewish learning, religious, legal, and lay, and all there had been of previous Talmudic "science." It was the theory of Talmudic interpretation that a full understanding of all "law," religious and social as well as legal (that is, really an understanding of all learning), was necessary to a proper comprehension of rules to govern human conduct. Nor was the member of the Sanhedrin permitted to confine his knowledge to things Jewish. He was required to be a linguist and to know the history, geography, and languages of the important neighboring nations, like Babylon, Persia, and Greece. He was required to have an encyclopedic knowledge of every phase of contemporary learning. That was what was meant by being learned in the law.

Wisdom and the intellect were highly respected and revered by the Jews. It is safe to say that there were more schools, and that there was more general learning, among the Jews of ancient times than among any other contemporary peoples, excepting, possibly, the Greeks. There were schools of various grades, including universities of higher learning. The teaching in the universities was not of the modern kind. A method somewhat Socratic in its mechanism was used. Instead of merely lecturing, the teachers posed questions to the students, and then debated and discussed them. The discussion method used by some present-day law schools is somewhat similar; and in the New Testament may be found many examples of this quasi-Socratic method of instruction.

Several attempts had been made to codify the Mishnah. Hillel I, who was President of the Sanhedrin when Jesus was born, attempted it. He was appalled at the fact that there were then some six hundred separate fragments of Mishnah scattered about. But Hillel died before he could complete his proposed compilation. A hundred years later Akiba, a learned shepherd, also failed to complete the job, for he fell victim to a Roman executioner. Finally, Jehudah the Saint, in about A.D. 200, did complete the stupendous undertaking, which required not only the collection but also the reconciliation of the many separate schools of thought and comment. The completed Mishnah became the accepted code of the Jews, even the obsolete sections having historical and supplemental value.

The regulations established by the Mishnah are various in form and intent. Some are apparently categorically applicable laws; others are merely preceptory. Some are only temporary in effect; others are intended to be permanent. No distinction was made between ancient and modern laws. Whatever had been once firmly received or established as a genuinely extracted rule was included. It was left to later authorities to reconsider or abrogate what was obsolete or inconsistent with current life.

The general approach of the Mishnah was practical and not metaphysical, and it is in actuality a code for practical human guidance and government. While there is some harshness, its general tenor is humane and its general intent liberal. The law is not always meant to be observed to the letter, particularly when the rights of one man against another are involved. If the spirit of humanity moves a man to disclaim an advantage given to him by law, he is "beloved of God and man." Equitable dealing is praised. Reward for fair acts is promised in the world to come. Nor is the Jew expected to live in complete fulfillment of the law. "The law had been given to men, and not to angels," meaning that it is too much to expect perfection or entire observance.

The Mishnah made sharp distinction between administration of the civil law and that of the criminal law. No more than three judges were required to decide a civil case, but in a criminal case at least twenty-three judges were necessary. This court of twenty-three judges was known as the Small Sanhedrin. In a civil case a majority verdict of one decided the case. In a criminal case, however, a majority of one acquitted the defendant; it took a majority of two to convict. In civil cases anyone could act as a witness, provided he were not in certain limited prescribed classes, such as gamblers, usurers, and slaves. In criminal cases, however, witnesses for the prosecution were carefully scrutinized, and it was only for the defense that the generality of witnesses could appear. Witnesses for the prosecution were carefully admonished and even awed, and cross-examination of witnesses was strictly controlled.

Criminal punishments were stern, from our modern point of view, but not in comparison with those of contemporary civilizations. The literal interpretation of an "eye for an eye" advocated by the Sadducees failed before the insistence of the Pharisees that bodily injuries might be redeemed in money. By the same token, the harsh punishments established by the Mosaic code were often ignored in practice. Lashing was limited to thirty-nine strokes, and if there was any danger to the life of the convicted man the number was reduced. Only one punishment could be dealt out, no matter how many crimes the criminal had been convicted of simultaneously.

Eventually, capital punishment was denied the Jewish courts by the Roman government of Palestine, and was taken over by Roman judges. Before that, however, capital punishment had come to be so gravely considered that the judges in a capital case were required to fast a full day before rendering judgment. Every opportunity was given to the defendant to show additional evidence. At the entrance to the court where judgment had been rendered a signalman was stationed, after a capital sentence had been uttered and the execution was to take place. Within sight was a horseman ready to take to the executioners the message that a new witness had appeared or that new evidence had been discovered, so that the execution might be stayed. The convicted criminal himself was permitted to stop four times on the way to the place of execution to offer new arguments in his defense or to produce new evidence. A herald preceded the criminal on his way, shouting the name of the convicted, the crime of which he had been declared guilty, and the names of the witnesses against him, and asking anyone who knew anything in the criminal's favor to come forth and proclaim it. The convict was treated with sympathy and compassion, and the women of Jerusalem provided him with a drink compounded of myrrh and vinegar which acted as an opiate to dull his sensibilities at the execution.

There were four methods of execution: stoning, burning, slaying with the sword, and strangling. Crucifixion was not known to Jewish law. It was Roman. The stoning method of execution consisted of throwing the culprit from a two-story "house of stoning" to break his neck, the chief witness being required to give him the fatal push. If he did not die immediately, the second witness was obliged to cast a stone on the victim's heart. Only if that did not kill were the people entitled to cast further stones until the criminal died.

The method of strangling consisted of embedding the criminal in mud to his waist. Two men then strangled him with a cord wrapped in a soft cloth. The execution by burning was similar, except that a burning wick was cast down the criminal's throat as he opened his mouth for his last breath.

After an execution the family of the deceased, by strange but reasonable custom, visited the judges and witnesses to assure them that no hard feelings existed and that no malice was borne for a just verdict.

The fact is that, even before capital punishment was taken out of the hands of the Sanhedrin by the Romans, it had been practically abolished. For witnesses for the prosecution were so awed by the admonitions of the judges that they were usually reluctant to testify. The cross-examination of the prosecution's witnesses grew more and more rigorous; and, if everything else failed and a conviction seemed inevitable, a flaw in the proceedings was generally found and the sentence was commuted to life imprisonment. Akiba and other doctors of a later period openly and strongly advocated the abolition of capital punishment. Evidence of the limited extent to which capital punishment was actually carried out is found in a reference in the Talmud to a certain Sanhedrin which had condemned one man to death over a period of seventy years.

VIII: The Direct Dispersion of the Laws of Moses

No PEOPLE in history have been as widely scattered as the Jews. And no people have clung as closely to their identity. Many times in history they have been carried off into slavery; and each time some have gone home to Palestine and others have remained to establish a closely knit colony in a foreign land. At a very early date, substantial Jewish colonies were to be found in all the great Mediterranean cities; and eventually the Jews wandered as far as China, deep into Africa, and indeed all over the world. Their greatest dispersion came after the Romans ejected large masses of them from Palestine. These Jews traveled far and wide within the Empire, and wherever the Roman arms penetrated it was likely that Jewish traders would follow.

In the course of their wanderings the Jews always took with them their law as well as their customs. It is impossible to trace the exact, direct effect of the Jewish law on that of other peoples, but it is probable that there was a strong effect in relation to commercial law. For the Jews were so frequently restricted from owning land and engaging in the ordinary pursuits of their host nations that they took to trading and banking as a necessary means of livelihood. They were among the first commercial bankers of Europe. And they were the middlemen, the traveling merchants, who had so close a communion among themselves that they were able to transact international business often far better than their competitors. It is not surprising that they were the authors of many financial and trading mechanisms, and midwives to others. It is possible that many of our commercial rules of law came out of decisions of the Talmudists.

But the most important contribution of the Jews to our legal system was the very existence of the Torah, the Pentateuch, adopted by Christianity as part of its basic law. Even Mohammed, creator of a new faith, built it frankly upon the Old Testament and upon the Jewish prophets, calling Jesus one of them. Though it differs from the Old Testament in much detail, yet the Koran has most of its roots in Old Testament moral reasoning; and large parts of the Moslem law, ruling many millions today, are difficult to distinguish from the parent Jewish law.

Similarly, many of the moral and ethical principles which underlie the laws of the Western nations are those which are found in the Pentateuch, and were taken from it. But it was not only in an assimilation of Jewish principles that the Western nations borrowed from the Jewish law. Unfortunately, much medieval legal reasoning was based on a literal acceptance of harsh sections of the law of Moses, a pitfall into which some of our New England ancestors fell as easily.

Was the tribal law of the Jews wholly self-generated? Obviously not. When they arrived in Mesopotamia from Arabia they found there a civilization higher than their own. When they moved on from Mesopotamia to Canaan, they found a well-developed culture among the people whom they only partially displaced. In their long sojourn in Egypt they were subjected to still further and highly organized influences. It is difficult to believe that the Jews did not borrow here and there, in matters of law as well as in other fields of culture.

The only substantially complete pre-Hebrew code of law which has been discovered is the famous *Code of Hammurabi,* King of Babylon. Were this the story of law in general, rather than the story of *our* law, Hammurabi would more than merit a chapter, but suffice it here to say that a comparison of the Jewish law with the Code of Hammurabi discloses many similarities—so close, indeed, that one may well infer that substantial borrowings were made by the Jews from their Babylonian neighbors, perhaps during the Babylonian captivity.

CHAPTER 2

Jesus

"And if any man will sue thee at the law, and take away thy coat, let him have thy cloak also."

MATTHEW, V, 40

ONE MIGHT NATURALLY ASK why Moses has been given so much space in this book and Jesus so little. Jesus was certainly a far more important character in the law than Moses. But it was because of his religious teaching rather than his lawgiving. The religion built upon the life and teachings of Jesus rushed over the Western world like wildfire, making it inevitable that the Western systems of law be deeply affected by the ethical principles which Jesus taught; and it was inevitable also that much of the detail of the law in which Jesus believed would be adopted by the Christian nations. Actually, however, the ethical principles which Jesus taught were the ethical principles enunciated by Moses, the principles of the Torah. And Jesus' law was "the law," the conventional law of the Jews, with only a few differences of interpretation.

He himself said in his Sermon on the Mount: "Think not that I am come to destroy the law, or the prophets; I am not come to destroy, but to fulfill. For verily I say unto you, Till heaven and earth pass, one jot or one tittle shall in no wise pass from the law, till all be fulfilled. Whosoever therefore shall break one of these least commandments, and shall teach men so, he shall be called the least in the kingdom of heaven. . . ." *

So Jesus preached and upheld the Jewish law, and we may conclude that by "the law" he meant that term as commonly used, including the whole Jewish law, both secular and religious. For, as I have said, the Jews made no sharp distinction between religious and civil ordinances and rules—they were all one or all part of one coordinated system.

Jesus began his legal studies early. Even when he was twelve he astounded the "doctors" with whom he discussed the law. The doc-

* Matthew, v, 17, 18, 19.

tors were, of course, the rabbi-jurists. Luke tells us that when Jesus' family was returning from celebrating the Passover feast at Jerusalem, they missed the boy and went back to find him. "And it came to pass, that after three days they found him in the temple, sitting in the midst of the doctors, both hearing them, and asking them questions. And all that heard him were astonished at his understanding and answers." We may infer that Jesus pursued his studies of the civil as well as the religious laws of the Jews, for the Gospels record frequent mention of them. And though Jesus, in the Sermon on the Mount, professed that he did not intend to change the law, we must take this as meaning that he did not mean to change the basic law but not that he would always agree with the classic or current interpretation of the law; we find him, on several occasions, differing with some accepted, detailed interpretation of civil law.

For example, the Pharisees came to him and asked him whether it were "lawful for a man to put away his wife," and, upon being asked by Jesus what the law of Moses was, the Pharisees replied that Moses had permitted a "bill of divorcement." But Jesus then said that Moses had written this law "for the hardness of your heart," and went on to say, "Whosoever shall put away his wife, and marry another, committeth adultery against her. And if a woman shall put away her husband, and be married to another, she committeth adultery." * And other times he inferentially supported a rule of law but asked that it be tempered with kindness or humility. For example, the scribes and Pharisees brought to Jesus a woman caught in an act of adultery, and quoted Moses as saying that such a woman should be stoned. "What sayest thou?" asked the man. And Jesus made his oft-quoted reply, "He that is without sin among you, let him first cast a stone at her." †

However, his variances from the strict interpretation of the Mosaic law were, for the most part, only in the direction of kindness, tolerance, and brotherhood. His attitude may be summarized in his words "if ye forgive not men their trespasses, neither will your Father forgive your trespasses."‡ But even here Jesus was not preaching something new. His "do unto others" had already been enunciated as an old principle by Rabbi Hillel in the words "What you wish not to be done to you, do not do unto others," and several sects

* Mark, x, 2 *et seq.*
† John, viii, 3 *et seq.*
‡ Matthew, vi, 15.

of Jews had been advocating a gentle approach to life and a liberal interpretation of the law. There is good reason to believe that Jesus came under the influence of one of these sects, the Essenes, who preached humility, kindness, charity, self-abnegation, and self-imposed poverty. I think it is not well understood by Christians generally that the moral and ethical teachings of Jesus had already been propounded by other Jews before him and that he merely preached what Jewish "liberals" had taught. Perhaps it is because the New Testament makes so much of the opposition of the Jewish upper classes to Jesus that the impression has been left that all contemporary Jews were formal and rigid in their interpretation of the law. Perhaps it is also because few Christians realize that the harsh rules and precepts which often appear in the Old Testament date from an era when the Jews were in a state only just emerged from the primitive. By Jesus' time much water had gone over the dam and, however stern and unbendingly fundamentalist many of the upper-class Jews may have remained, Jewish liberal thought had already produced the fine flowering of ethics which we know best from Jesus' lips.

While the Christian world has not always followed these teachings of Jesus, they have been of gigantic importance in guiding the course of development of modern law. It remains astounding that so much persecution of the Jew has taken place in the name and often under the direction of a religion which worships a Jew, a faith whose first teachers were Jews and whose ethical basis is Jewish.

PART TWO

THE GREEKS

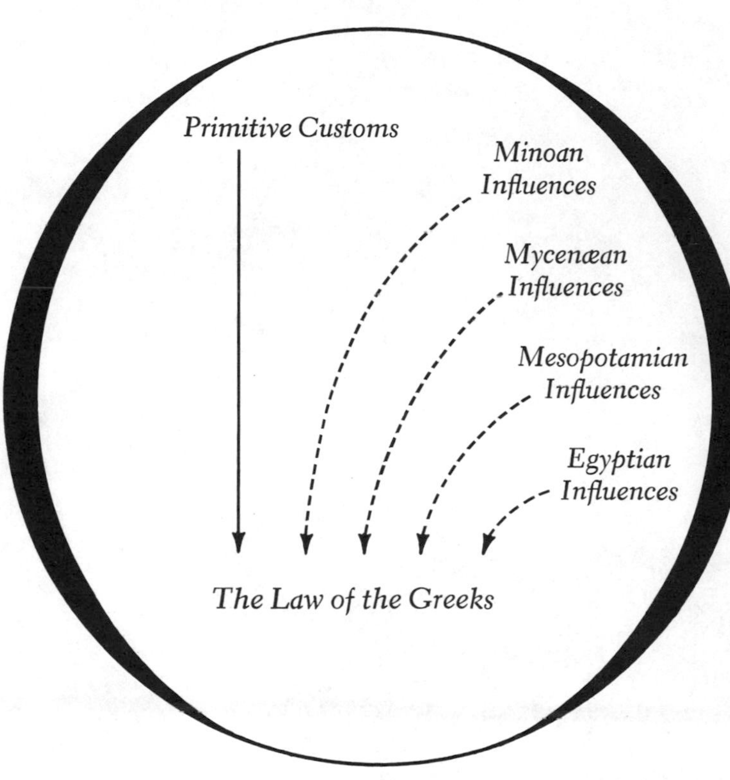

THE CHIEF BASIC SOURCES

CHAPTER 3

Homer

"Sing, goddess, the wrath of Achilles Peleus' son, the ruinous wrath that brought on the Achaians woes innumerable, and hurled down into Hades many strong souls of heroes, and gave their bodies to be a prey to dogs and all winged fowls; and so the counsel of Zeus wrought out its accomplishment from the day when first strife parted Atreides king of men and noble Achilles."

HOMER: ILIAD

I: The Greek Law Reporter

THE FIRST PARAGRAPH of the *Iliad* of Homer hardly reads as though one might expect it to be a serious source book for Greek law. Yet, beyond a few scraps to be found elsewhere, most of our knowledge of ancient Greek law comes from the *Iliad* and the *Odyssey*. It is for this reason that I list Homer among the immortals of the law. He did not presume to be a lawmaker or a lawgiver or even the mouthpiece of some deity granting laws to men. He had a tale to tell, and in the course of it he gave us historical material which is precious and singular.

There is no evidence that Homer was anything more than a legend himself. Several "lives" of Homer have been written, but they are not very convincing, nor are the illustrations in children's schoolbooks which show him as a blind bard wandering about and reciting his verses. There is nothing credible to substantiate any personal history or description of the great poet. We do not even know when he lived, for speculations run from 1044 to 685 B.C., and this spread indicates some wild guessing. Regardless of all this, it is now generally accepted that, interspersed with romantic and fanciful material, the *Iliad* and the *Odyssey* contain a great deal of authentic historical material. Some of the most valuable of these data are in the field of the law.

II: The Homeric Greeks

When you meet a Belgian or a Spaniard or a Frenchman and ask him what his nationality is, he doesn't often say, "I am a European." Similarly, if you had met a citizen of ancient Athens and asked him what his nationality was, he would not have replied "Greek" but "Athenian"; and had you asked him by what laws he was governed, he would have given the same reply. Yes, he might have stretched "Athenian" to "Attic," for Attica was the tiny state of which Athens was the capital, but the word "Greek" (or, rather, "Hellene") would have meant to him only a general classification of people in a certain geographical area, not more cohesive politically than present-day Europe. The Greeks had the same general culture, the same religion, and the same language, and they usually, though not always, felt closer to each other than to non-Greeks, but they had no real sense of national unity. Greece was composed of numerous small city-states, squabbling with each other a great part of the time, each so jealous of its own sovereignty that local political independence was more important than almost anything else. But the history of virtually all European peoples related by race, custom, and even religion is a history of similar, endless, internecine quarreling.

One reason for the Greek disunity was geographic. The rocky Greek peninsula is crisscrossed by many mountain ranges and hills, and is further broken up by inlets, bays, and watercourses. It consists of countless tiny pockets—little valleys of not too fertile land bounded by the fortifications of nature. The Greeks, divided into tribes, subdivisions of tribes, and clans, broke into even smaller sections when they settled in some of these naturally isolated divisions; and, as communication by land was sometimes very difficult, "isolationism" became the rule. The Greeks spread far and wide; they occupied almost all of Sicily and most of the southern coast of Italy, and they made the Black Sea practically a Greek lake. Plato said of his people, the Greeks, that they settled around the Mediterranean like frogs around a pond. They established so many separate communities that to tell the history of Greece would be like telling the history of a myriad of nations. I shall concentrate on Athens and Sparta, for these two states and their legal institutions and conceptions influenced later civilizations far more than all the other Greek states combined.

When the Greeks came down from the north and arrived in their eventual homeland, they brought with them the common inheritance of the Aryan language group, which was not essentially different from that of the Semitic peoples and many others. They were grouped into patriarchal tribes and clans, and some of the clans were associated in "phratries," or fraternities or brotherhoods, for religious purposes. As the members of a clan presumed that they were descended from a common ancestor, the clan bore his name.*

The concept of kinship through clan membership was so firmly fixed in the Greek mind that it precluded naturalization as we know it. If you were a Megaran, you could live in Athens as long as you wished, provided you behaved yourself, and you could produce children there and raise them there. But neither you nor your children, even those born in Athens, could become Athenians. You could be an Athenian only if you belonged to an Athenian or Attic clan, and these clans were so clannish that they would not permit the adoption of anyone but an Athenian. There was one process by which an outlander could be adopted by the Athenian state itself, but this was used very rarely.

There was a certain uniform pattern of government among most of the peoples who adopted the patriarchal clan system, and the Greeks followed this pattern. The head of the clan might be a strong and forceful character, yet the adult males of the clan constituted a sort of lower assembly, the consent of which had to be obtained for various measures and proposals, and this consultative assembly is the spiritual ancestor of our lower legislative house. Comparable to our upper house was the council, composed of the heads of families and the other important men of the clan, with whom the chief discussed matters which did not require consent of the whole clan. In the Homeric age the clan chief had already become a monarch, but the two legislative or consultative bodies still existed.

There was, however, no common pattern of legal development. In

* A system which is in contrast to matriarchal tribes, in which the clan bore the name of the clan totem, which might be Fish or Pig or Wind. But it is not always possible to recognize the nature of the system by clan names. Sometimes a clan acquired a nickname which stuck; there were amusing clan names of this kind among the Blackfoot Indians, such as Liars, Patched Moccasins, and Buffalo Dung.

Greece, each petty state had its own treasured localisms of law and custom. Nevertheless, there were many similarities among the multitude of separate legal systems in Greece. For one thing, the Greeks loved trade, and it was necessary for them to agree upon rules of doing business, just as it became necessary in modern Europe for the highly differentiated peoples to find a commercial law common to them all. Moreover, the clan customs were brought into the cities by the invading tribes, and here there was a basic, common inheritance from which grew most of the law of the family and of property, so that we do find much uniformity in these fields.

The clan customs had a distinctly democratic base, but we must stop here to discuss that difficult term "democratic." It derives from *demos,* meaning "the people." "Democracy," very plainly, signifies government by the people. The Greeks, whose language gave us the word, considered their system "democratic" because sovereignty was in the people. But we must understand that Greek democracy was a qualified institution. Democracy existed for the clan members, who were the citizens. Under them, in the structure of the state, were large disenfranchised classes: aliens who could not acquire citizenship even if born in the state; semisubordinated peoples and classes; and a huge population of slaves. Many Greek states might be called aristocratic democracies, for in them a minority ruled absolutely, but with democracy applying within the ruling class.

In the ruling group, democracy was theoretically complete. Among the clan members there were nobles and commoners, but there was usually little distinction between these two classes as far as political voice was concerned. The idea was never lost in Greece that the "citizens" should have equal rights, and that these rights should be exercised in open meetings. Such meetings, or assemblies, were the true *demos.* There were times when the nobles managed to assume almost complete direction of the state, but the concept of ultimate sovereignty in the assembly of the citizens was never lost. Certain important decisions were always left to the people: the declaration of war or peace, the banishment of citizens and the sentence of death —these were functions of the assembly.

There was also a common religious basis to Greek law, and in the hierarchy of Greek gods there were deities whose jurisdiction was the field of the law. There was Themis, a consort of Zeus, whose territory was moral law and harmony. Themis's two daughters had detailed jurisdiction: Dike over morality and divine law; and Eunomia over law and order. The Greek word *themis* has the significance of a "rule of life." It was probably used in Greece in that sense before it was assigned to the name of a goddess in the later pantheon of Greek gods. It also had the meaning of "judgment." *Dike* also had a theocratic-legal significance, for it too meant "judgment" as well as "custom" and "usage." *Themis* is our word "doom" (presumably from the same Aryan root), in the sense of "judgment." On the Isle of Man, "deemster" or "doomster" is still the word for "judge."

In the course of time, the Greeks ceased to consider that their laws were given by the gods—or at least they grew indifferent to the theory. Nevertheless, a mass of law had developed upon a base of religious ideas. The Greek religion was polytheistic, and each tribe had its own gods. The gods were generally the same throughout Greece, but there were countless others as well, for each family had its own personal gods, which were worshiped in the household. The father of the family was its chief priest, and priesthood was hereditary, the duties of family worship passing to the sons. As the sons could not conduct their office without having the family property, which was so closely identified with the family gods, the daughter was disinherited except for a dowry* and the right to be maintained while she was single. Everything else went to the sons, to enable them to fulfill their priestly duties, but the sons had to assume the family debts and obligations when they took over the property.

If there was no son, the inheritance passed to the brother and, if there was no brother, then to the brother's son; for religious custom demanded that the nearest male continue the family worship, and he must own the property in order to do so. Upon the same logic, if a son was emancipated by his father and adopted by another family, he lost all right of inheritance from his father's family, for the property must be preserved to enable some related male to continue the family worship, and the emancipated son no longer belonged to the family. So firm was this system that wills were not permitted in Athens until Solon allowed them, and then they were allowed only if there were no male descendants.

* This word "dowry" is often confused with "dower." The "dowry" is the marriage portion given by the father or the family when a daughter marries. "Dower" is a special right or interest in real estate given by law to a widow upon the death of her husband.

III: Greek Marriage

THE RELIGIOUS BASIS of the Greek family was deep, and its members had no choice of religion. The tribal and clan gods of the Greek were his gods, and he could have no other except certain deities also worshiped by his entire nation or city. Today a Baptist girl may marry a Methodist and remain a Baptist. Such a thing was impossible in Greece. When a girl married she left her own clan and its gods behind her. As was the case among other primitive peoples, she joined her husband's family and worshiped his gods at his altar.

This shift to new gods, which, as far as the bride was concerned, accompanied every marriage, was no light matter. So the marriage had three parts, all of which had serious religious import. First the bride had to stand before her own family hearth, before the altar of the gods whom she had worshiped her whole life, and there her father solemnly divorced her from adherence to them. When this was done, the second part of the ceremony took place; she was conducted to the house of her prospective bridegroom, either by the groom himself or by some special herald. She was dressed in white, the color of the vestments used in religious worship, and she wore a crown and a veil which also had religious significance. The white gown, the crown, and the veil are all continued customs in our own times.

After the marriage ceremonies, many grooms still carry their wives over the threshold of the home. This comes from the Greeks, but it was a far different performance for them; it was a required part of the second stage in the marriage ceremony. The Greek groom carried his bride over the threshold with a simulation of force, and she gave a show of resistance, for this procedure was necessary in order to appease the husband's family gods, to whose worship the young lady was to be brought. She could not enter the gods' house presumptuously and of her own motion. She could be brought in only by the force of her man, who was already a communicant of these gods. Then came the third part of the ceremony, which took place before the groom's family altar. There the bride was inducted into the religion of the family, a serious performance in which she was first introduced to the formulas, rituals, and rites with which she would have to become familiar.

We inherit another marriage custom from the Greeks: after the bride had joined the family religion and the wedding was over, the bride and groom shared a cake together. Now merely a custom, this had religious significance to the Greeks, for in some way the eating of the cake supposedly made the two as one.

IV: The Gods and the Land

THE PECULIAR religious ideas of the Greeks reflected themselves in the customs and laws which arose in connection with property in land. There was a belief that their gods liked to stay put and disliked being moved about. Their gods were attached to the hearth; the hearth was attached to a particular piece of ground; and the family was, therefore, attached to that particular piece of ground also. Moreover, as the gods wanted privacy, they insisted on their own enclosure, and the Greeks therefore built their houses apart from one another. As some of the family gods were ancestors, the burial places were deemed holy; and from this it was just a short jump to the idea that the whole field was sacred. So private property in land was a concept which arose among the Greeks far earlier than among many other people whose religions did not attach them so closely to specific pieces of real estate. Religion itself guaranteed the right to the family plot of soil. The fields were surrounded by unused neutral strips upon which boundary stones, or "termini," were fixed; and reckless was he who disturbed these stones or transgressed upon the sacred boundaries of the field. Land became almost inalienable —in fact, transfers usually could be made only with religious sanction and ceremony.

So important was the identification of a Greek with the land that foreigners could not own land in a Greek state, and a landless Greek had little standing in the community. Therefore, primogeniture rarely appealed to the Greeks, and each son was usually given an equal part of the family land.

The government of the state had a religious face, too. In later Athens there were nine archons or governors. One of them had the title of king, but his title had far more religious than civil significance. The Athenian archon with the title of king was essentially the chief priest of the national hearth. He wore a crown; and, though the crown came later to have kingly significance, it originally denoted the presiding priest. All magistrates were religious officials as well as civil, and were entitled to perform certain ritualistic sacrifices. Much of the character of these religious factors in government was later lost, but the forms were usually continued.

So the Greeks started with divine law and converted it into secular law, as was the course with many other peoples.

V: Torts

WE GATHER from Homer that the Greeks of his day had not advanced much from the system of self-help as a remedy for injuries. There was some justice available through the clan assembly, which acted not only as a legislature but also as a court of justice. The following description of a popular trial by assembly is given by Homer in the *Iliad:* "But the folk were gathered in the assembly place; for there a strife was arisen, two men striving about the blood-price of a man slain; the one claimed to pay full atonement, expounding to the people, but the other denied him and would take naught; and both were fain to receive arbitrament at the hand of a daysman. And the folk were cheering both, as they took part on either side. And heralds kept order among the folk, while the elders on polished stones were sitting in the sacred circle, and holding in their hands staves from the loud-voiced heralds. Then before the people they rose up and gave judgment each in turn. And in the midst lay two talents of gold, to be given unto him who should utter among them the most righteous doom."

But if a Greek was injured, he usually took it upon himself to get personal revenge or satisfaction. Originally, the whole family was made responsible for the acts of its members, a principle from which it took centuries for the innocent individual to be emancipated. Often a son was banished because his father had done a wrong.

From the absolute right of self-help, the Greeks followed a common pattern of growth. In order to escape feuds a system of commutation was instituted. "Blood money" was given in order to avoid personal vengeance. Then came the next step: arbitration was forced on the disputants. The compulsory arbitration often consisted of subjecting the parties to a trial by ordeal; this seemed logical enough to all primitive and semicivilized people, for they had faith that the gods would determine innocence or guilt. Determining the merits of a controversy by oath was also a religious procedure. The oath was formal and prescribed by the priests, and the Greeks, like the Jews, could not imagine anyone taking a sacred oath and not being punished from on high if the oath were false.

VI: Development

Gradually, and after Homer's time, a more elaborate system of law-giving and of justice developed. *Thesmothetai* (lawmen) collected and co-ordinated the early customs and put them into writing; and these *thesmoi* (sacred usages) then became *nomoi* (man-made laws). In a later period, revisions of the legal system were often made by a committee of citizens chosen for the purpose from among the general assembly courts. When repeal of an old law was suggested, an advocate was appointed to defend that law, and the resulting popular debate determined whether revision was to be made.

Hundreds of local codes developed but no "common law" in the sense in which we used the word. One of the best known of the law codifiers was Zaleucus of the Greek colony of Locri, on the sole of the toe of the Italian boot. Legend had it that the people of Locri (Aristotle tells us that they were runaway rascals) asked an oracle for advice, and were told to get themselves some laws. Zaleucus, a shepherd slave by origin, produced these laws for them, in about 664 B.C., asserting that the goddess Athena had dictated them to him in a dream. Though not the first divinely ordained one, this was the first written code of the Greeks, and it was so well liked that anyone who proposed a new law had to do so with a rope around his neck. The laws of Zaleucus treated personal injuries on the eye-for-an-eye system and contained many restrictions on social conduct, including regulation of dress and ornament. There is a legend that, when Zaleucus found that he had inadvertently violated one of his own laws, he committed suicide.

But the two most renowned Greek lawgivers were Solon of Athens and Lycurgus of Sparta.

CHAPTER 4

Solon

"To make an empire durable, the magistrates must obey the laws, and the people the magistrates."

SOLON

I: The Depression in Athens

A TERRIBLE DEPRESSION struck Athens in the seventh century B.C. The political situation had become unbearable. The great mass of people, the slaves and disenfranchised classes, had no part in government at all, and the middle classes, the *demiurgoi* (skilled workmen) and the *georgoi* (farmers), had very little power. Government was almost entirely in the hands of the *eupatrids*, or "sons of noble fathers." They controlled the state through their Council of the Areopagus. This was the chief criminal court, which appointed the magistrates and most of the major officers of the government, and ran the state about as it pleased. All too often this was for the benefit of the upper class, whose private instrument the Council of the Areopagus was. The lower classes had no relief because the laws had not yet been written down; they reposed in the convenient memories of the aristocrats and their priests, and it was therefore impossible for an ordinary citizen to point to page and paragraph and say, "There are my rights."

The political injustices might have been suffered without too much complaint had it not been for the economic distress. A New Deal was really needed to stave off revolution. The class of free farmers was disappearing rapidly. The old patriarchal system of landholding had long since gone out of use, and frequent subdivisions of land had left most of the peasants with so little acreage that they could not support themselves on their farms. Like all poor farmers in such a situation, they borrowed from wealthier landowners and capitalists, who took mortgages on the land for security and sometimes even accepted the pledge of the borrower's person as security. When the debts could not be paid, the unfortunates who had given their persons as security were sold into slavery, sometimes with their entire families. Those who were fortunate enough only to have borrowed upon their lands lost them through foreclosure and drifted into the cities, where they were exploited by the *demiurgoi*. Still other farmers just gave up the struggle voluntarily and moved to town, where they joined the mass of the discontented.

The breaking point came by about 620 B.C. To quiet the state, the aristocrats commissioned a man named Draco to make new laws and to have all the laws written down for the first time. Draco's lawmaking had considerable merit. He substituted legal procedure for the old custom of getting justice through personal revenge, and he extended the right to vote. However, he is not known for his constructive legislation but for his extremely harsh criminal code. His name has been used to coin the word "Draconian," which means "cruel" or "severe." His Draconian laws prescribed the death penalty for almost any crime, even for stealing a cabbage. When he himself was asked why he imposed the death penalty on small offenses, he answered: "Small ones deserve that, and I have no greater penalty for the greater crime."

It soon became clear that Draco was no true reformer. His laws were directed chiefly at protecting persons of wealth and their property rights. He did nothing to relieve the poor of their overburdening debts; on the contrary, he was interested in seeing that the poor did their duty by the rich. He provided that idleness should be punished by disenfranchisement; and if the idler were not a citizen he would be punished with death.

So the poor remained as poor, and the oppressed just as oppressed, and Draco's harsh laws did not decrease the general discontent. Revolution was again about to boil when the *demiurgoi*, the tradesmen and middle-class capitalists, decided that they would have to do something to save the state from destruction. About 594 B.C. they looked around for a man who might be made dictator to reorganize the law and to do a better job than Draco had. They selected a man who seemed suitable and got the aristocrats to approve him. The man selected was Solon (c. 638-558 B.C.), and it was agreed that he could handle the reformer's job, if anyone could, without sacrificing the rights of property.

II: Solon's New Deal

IT WAS EASY enough to enjoy yourself in Athens if you had money. While his improvident father's money lasted, young Solon had plenty of fun, but when the bottom of the barrel was reached, Solon decided he would go to work. He went into trade and devoted himself to it intensively and intelligently and not only built up a large fortune but also made himself a wide reputation for honesty and fair dealing. He did not confine himself to business alone. He participated actively in public affairs and took advantage of his many travels to study the government and laws of other countries. So goes Solon's story as we have it from the ancients. Actually, we do not know whether he ever lived. Historians have doubted it, as they have doubted the existence of Homer and of Draco and of Moses; but in Solon's case, so many stories have come down to us about him that it may well be that he is no legendary character but really one of the great men of history.

One of the most interesting of stories about Solon is told by Plutarch. The island of Salamis had been conquered from Athens by the Megarans, and the Athenians were so ashamed of their defeat that they passed a law making it a crime to promote an expedition to retrieve their loss. But Solon thought that a recapture could be accomplished and that there were plenty of Athenians who would welcome a rescuing expedition. The problem was to get around the law which prevented discussion of a Salamis project; and Solon found the answer. He had his family spread the rumor that he had gone out of his mind, while he sat quietly at home and composed a hundred verses ("very elegantly written," says Plutarch) for a poetical oration intended to incite an expedition to Salamis.

When he had finished his verses he ran out into the market place and dashed around acting like a madman. A crowd collected, which was what Solon wanted, and he then read them his verses. These were so well composed that the crowd listened to them, and they were so well devised that he aroused their enthusiasm. By the time he had finished, the group which had listened to his inspired reading began to clamor for an expedition to rescue Salamis, and the voice of the people grew so loud that the authorities had to relent and rescind the law which prohibited discussion of a Salamis project.

Once it could be discussed openly, it was not long before an expedition was authorized and organized.

Plutarch recounts a ruse which Solon is reputed to have used in recapturing Salamis. He sent some beardless youths ashore at Colias, dressed in female apparel but armed with daggers. In the meantime, he had sent to Salamis a man posing as an Athenian renegade, who spread the rumor that the chief Athenian women were collected for religious purposes at Colias and could easily be captured there. The Megaran garrison at Salamis was gullible enough to listen to this story, and sailed off enthusiastically. When they arrived at Colias, they were delighted to see the women gathered on the shore, and they hastened to land to seize their prizes; but they found out quickly enough that they were dealing not with defenseless women but with warriors armed with daggers. It was all over quickly, and the Athenians were then able to retake Salamis without substantial opposition.

Whether this particular story is true or not, the Athenians attributed unusual shrewdness and soundness to Solon, and his counsel was always deemed wise and practical. It was partly for this reason that he was selected as the man to save the day, when conditions in Athens were near the breaking point and when it had become apparent that Draco's laws had not even approached solving the problems of the state. Plutarch says that the rich approved of Solon because he was wealthy, and the poor because he was honest.

The rich soon concluded that they had made a terrible mistake in acquiescing in Solon's appointment as archon with dictatorial powers, and the poor knew that they had at last found a champion, for one of Solon's first acts was to attack the burden of debt which weighed heavily on all but the wealthy in Attica. He debased the currency, and some say that he abolished all debts, public and private; others say that he merely cut down the debts. But it seems clear that he made a radical assault on the pockets of the creditor class. However, after a first reaction of anger, the rich came to understand that Solon was actually saving the Attic state from social disintegration. At least, though they might not have liked everything he did, the wealthy classes ceased the bitter criticism with which they greeted the early stages of his administration. After all, they said, it was better to lose a few drachmas than to have revolution.

Solon's chief concern being the necessity of restoring the disenfranchised classes to independent livelihood and keeping them there, he proclaimed that there could no longer be any borrowing upon the security of the person of the debtor. He freed those who had been enslaved, and even redeemed Athenians who had been sold into foreign slavery and brought them home. But freeing slaves was no solution to the general problem, for the land was largely in the hands of great landlords. So Solon decreed that no man might hold more than a limited acreage; and thus land was opened up for the freedmen to acquire and farm. There was still the problem of tiding the new farmers over a transitionary period until they had food from their own farms. To this end, Solon prohibited the export of any foodstuffs, except olive oil, of which there was a surplus.

One of his first acts was to abolish all the laws of Draco except those relating to murder; and he declared an amnesty and a restoration of civil rights for all who had lost them, except in instances of murder or tyranny.

In the field of private or civil law his reforms were many. He legislated against slander (unsuccessfully, because you could not stop the Greeks from slandering each other) and abolished some of the old patriarchal system, partly by enacting the first Athenian law of wills, which permitted the disposition of an estate outside of the family if there were no sons. "Yet," according to Plutarch, "he allowed not all sorts of legacies, but those only which were not extorted by the frenzy of a disease, charms, imprisonment, force, or the persuasions of a wife; with good reason thinking that being seduced into wrong was as bad as being forced, and that between deceit, flattery, and compulsion there was little difference, since both may equally suspend the exercise of reason."

Solon could not have been too popular with the Athenian women. In the first place, he legalized prostitution. But what may have annoyed the women more was that he decreed rules for their behavior which restricted their freedom and offended their sensibilities. They were permitted only three articles of apparel when they walked abroad (which hardly seems enough for the modesty which he was trying to introduce). And he regulated their walks and feasts and mourning. On the other hand, he gave them additional social protection, for he provided that a daughter or sister could not be sold into slavery unless she were an unmarried wanton; and he prescribed new fines for rape and seduction, unless the woman were a harlot. If a man caught another in an adultery, he was permitted to kill the adulterer forthwith, but this rule was less a protection of women than of the proprietary masculine prerogative.

He decreed that the sons of those who died in battle should be educated by the state. This seems to be a highly desirable measure which even we, in our presumed enlightenment, do not have. He permitted any citizen to indict another for a crime, so that the people should become more conscious of their civil responsibilities; and he went so far as to deprive of their civil rights all who remained neutral when the state was in danger. He also had his own odd ideas about certain questions of public policy or morality. For instance, he did not like the frequency with which men married heiresses merely to enjoy their wealth. So he permitted an heiress, whose husband failed her, to turn to his nearest kinsman. But if a child were born of such an extramarital union, it was credited to the legally cuckolded husband. Plutarch reports further that there was a law "that the bride and bridegroom shall be shut into a chamber, and eat a quince together; and that the husband of an heiress shall consort with her thrice a month; for though there be no children, yet it is an honor and due affection which a husband ought to pay to a virtuous, chaste wife; it takes off all petty differences, and will not permit their little quarrels to proceed to a rupture."

There seems no end to the detail to which Solon addressed himself in his reform laws. He produced almost as many laws as did Franklin Delano Roosevelt. He did not neglect the peculiar physical conditions of his country. There were few rivers and there was little fresh water, so he established rules as to the use of wells. If there was a public well within four furlongs, one was obliged to use that; but if there was none so close, one was obliged to dig a well of one's own; then, if one dug ten fathoms deep and found no water, one was entitled to draw four gallons and a half daily from a neighbor's well. He even made rules as to the planting of trees. There was so little arable land in Attica that he wanted to make sure that the planting of trees did not take away any substantial part of the earth's nourishment. So one could not plant a tree within five feet of his neighbor's ground, and if it was a fig or an olive, which spread their roots farther, not within nine feet.

What was perhaps his most interesting reform was his reconstruction of the social classes. He established what has been called the first graduated income tax system, though it was not quite that. He divided the Atticans into classes by the amount of property they had, and thus by the taxes they had to pay; and he distributed civil honors and privileges according to this classification. This still left the top offices in the hands of the men of wealth, but it gave some participation in government to the classes of moderate means. Those who were worth five hundred measures of fruit were eligible to all of the highest offices of the army and the state. Those who could keep a horse or were worth three hundred measures could serve in the cavalry and could occupy the lower offices in the state and the army. Those who were worth two hundred measures could serve in the heavy armed infantry; and those who were poorer than this could serve only as common soldiers and had no chance for any civil office but could, nevertheless, participate in the common assembly. This plutocratic system which Solon installed became popular in various Greek states in the following two centuries.

Solon also reorganized the mechanics of the state. He restored the old Senate, the Council of the Areopagus, shorn of many powers. He also brought back the old Assembly, or *ekklesia*,* open to all citizens, and gave it the power to elect the archons or governors. In between, he created a new body, a *boulê*, or Council, of four hundred members, one hundred elected by each of the four Attic tribes. This Council acted as a clearinghouse for legislation, for no business could be brought before the Assembly until it had the consent of the Council. Solon also opened the jury lists to the common citizenry; and, as the popular courts were not only courts for litigation but also had a political significance, this gave the mass of the citizenry an opportunity to participate in affairs of state; and the progress of democracy was accelerated.

It is unlikely that all these new laws which have been described, and so many more which have not been mentioned, were the sole invention of Solon. Most of the old codes of ancient peoples were merely collections of existing laws, even those that have come down to us as the assumed work of one man. Possibly much of what is attributed to Solon was already the law in Athens, and he merely codified or collected it. One reason for believing this is that there are many religious ordinances mixed up with his civil laws, and these, certainly, could not have been innovations, for it is not easy for a lawmaker to change religious practices.

* From the Greek *ekklesia* comes our word "ecclesiastic," the derivation being by way of the meaning, an "organized body."

Solon's laws were considered so fair and desirable that almost all of them endured, despite rapidly changing conditions, for five hundred years. When Solon was through with his work, he himself was so satisfied with what he had done that he proclaimed that the law was not to be altered for one hundred years, and he bound the Athenians to this by an oath. This was not a surprising procedure, for the Greeks, in contrast to the Romans, did not consider lawmaking a normal function of government. They did not believe that laws should be changed with any frequency. Indeed, it was dangerous to propose a new law in Athens, for if the law turned out within a year to have been ill-advised, its proponent could be prosecuted. Naturally, this did not stimulate progress in the development of the Greek legal system. In Solon's case, he had the courage to institute his wide reform laws only because he had been given dictatorial powers.

Solon's restrictions on lawmaking did not last forever. In time, *nomothetai* were appointed who revised and recodified the laws; and eventually there was an annual amending process. The existing laws were voted on, section by section, and the popular debates, earlier mentioned, took place. Amendments were proposed, advocates were appointed to defend and contest the proposed amendments, and decision was by open vote. It was not a very healthy way for laws to be made.

III: The Aftermath to Solon

Once Solon had completed his reorganization job and retired from office, the criticism began, and there was plenty of it. Solon himself is reputed to have said that it was difficult "in great affairs to satisfy all sides," and so, perhaps to escape the rancor which his laws had aroused and to avoid incessant arguments about what he had done, he left the country and traveled extensively for ten years. When he returned he found that Athens was again in a state of turmoil and unrest.

The changes which Solon had made in the constitution of the state had left the nobles very dissatisfied, and their plots and connivings brought on a civil commotion in the course of which Pisistratus, an old friend and possibly a relative of Solon, managed to seize power and to establish himself as a despot. Solon died in 558

B.C., too soon to see the worst of what followed. For, while the rule of Pisistratus was benevolent, that of his two sons, who succeeded him, was far from benign. When one of the sons, Hipparchus, was assassinated in about 514, the people thought that they could breathe easier, but they soon found the single rule of Hippias was worse than his joint rule with his brother. A revolt broke out, Hippias was deposed about 510, and the dynasty of the tyrants came to an end.

While the rule of the Pisistratus family had caused much discontent and discomfort, their period was not one of national decline; on the contrary, there was great commercial prosperity, and the artistic accomplishments of Athenians in this period were astounding. Furthermore, this era of arbitrary rule served the purpose of cutting down the power and importance of the aristocrats, thus paving the way for more rapid strides toward wider democracy.

But there was not to be immediate peace after Hippias's death, for two leaders, Isagoras and Cleisthenes, contended for control. Isagoras was made archon in 508, whereupon his rival appealed to the people, promising them wide political reform if they would support him. Isagoras was overthrown, and when Cleisthenes came to power he did something quite remarkable in a politician—he remembered his campaign promises. He may, indeed, be called the true father of Athenian democracy, for while Solon had effected many reforms in the structure of the state, it was Cleisthenes who gave them their final stability after the interlude of the tyrants; and he reinforced these reforms with further innovations of his own.

The final pattern of Athenian government, after Cleisthenes, was one in which the ultimate sovereignty did in fact and in practice rest with the citizens themselves, through their Assembly (the *ekklesia*) and through the juries. The *boulê*, as a council of delegates, carried on most of the detail of government, but major decisions were under the control of the people. Cleisthenes also broadened the franchise, and did so in a way to break up somewhat the political significance and power of the clans, for his redivision of the electorate crossed clan divisions and instituted a partially territorial system.

Once control had been revested in the Assembly, the people realized that they must be alert in order to keep their power in the state. Therefore, they provided for annual rotation of office, and many positions in the state were filled by lot. Most positions could be held only once, the major offices were made elective, and every official was held accountable at the end of his year's term. He could be questioned and even made to stand trial if his acts were complained of. These methods made it impossible for a permanent bureaucracy to form, or for any group to gain control of the reins of government. It is certainly true that alertness is necessary to maintain a democracy, for power corrupts any group which is permitted to rule too long, but the Athenians weakened their state by being overanxious about the dangers of power. There was a rule that the archons or governors be elected for annual terms, but upon retirement they automatically became members of the Council of the Areopagus (the Senate). Here they carried great weight and threatened to become so influential that they might end by running the state. So, whereas the archons had previously been elected, after 487 they were appointed by lot, with the result that able and popular men were selected only by accident, and the street sweeper or the garbage collector might become an archon by drawing the lucky number. Naturally enough, the Council of the Areopagus gradually lost its power because the retired archons who became councilors were no longer men of ability but the casual winners of a lottery. In 462 B.C., to reduce the powers of the Council of the Areopagus still further, most of its functions were transferred to the Assembly and the juries. The archons were then replaced as political leaders by the ten *strategoi*, or generals, chosen by vote and permitted to be reelected. When this change came, retired *strategoi* were not automatically made members of any council but just returned to private citizenship, so that no professional or permanent class of politicians arose even then.

The Greek system of rotation in office gave short political experience to a large number of citizens, but it prevented the development of technicians who might have raised Greek law and statesmanship to higher levels because they had received the benefit of training by adopting public work as a profession.

After Solon's reforms, the judicial system of Athens continued to revolve around the popular jury. This was far different from the kind to which we are accustomed. The juries did not deliberate as ours do. Sitting under a temporary chairman selected by lot, they merely voted on whatever was presented to them, without discussing it among themselves before their decision. From the general body of citizens an annual *heliaea* of six thousand men was drawn by lot, and these were divided into ten dicasteries or juries of about five hundred men each, leaving a residue for vacancies and substitutions. In some important cases the jury was even extended to include one thousand or even twenty-five hundred men. No juror could serve more than one year, nor could jury duty be a part-time job, for the court "calendars" were so crowded that the jurors were in almost constant attendance. Bribery was an ever-common danger, so the panel was usually not selected until just before a case came on for hearing.

Not all cases came to jury trial. Some minor cases were tried before judges who circulated among the counties of Attica just as some American judges still go on circuit. Other cases went before public arbitrators chosen by lot* from among the citizens aged sixty years or over, who acted for small fees.

No sharp distinction was made in Athens between civil and criminal cases, except that the victor in a civil case was left to himself to enforce the judgment of the court. In a criminal case, on the other hand, the state enforced the judgment against the defendant. There were many criminal cases, one reason being that there was no public prosecutor, and everyone could start a prosecution by making an accusation. In fact, it was so easy that a class of sycophants or blackmailers arose who made a business of threatening to bring false accusations, but a complainant who failed to support his accusations was fined or lashed.

We are somewhat horrified to read of the brutal punishments the ancient peoples administered, but we are likely to forget that cruel and inhuman punishments were handed out until comparatively recently by our own courts. The Greeks were astoundingly enlightened in their punishment in comparison with their contemporaries. They did use branding and flogging, and they did impose the death penalty, but they had none of the refined tortures so prevalent in the Near East. They imposed fines, disenfranchisement, exile, and confiscation of property, but even imprisonment was practically unknown. And after all, perhaps imprisonment is the cruelest of all punishments but death. You might well prefer to be flogged than to languish a year in jail.

Evidence was generally presented in writing, and the witnesses, before Solon's time, were obliged to swear to the truth of their

* You will gather by this time that almost every office and function was filled by lot, nonsensical as it seems.

statements. Solon held that the oath would no longer be obligatory, and this may have been because perjury had grown so common. False swearing and evasive oaths did not seem to arouse much general comment, although some of the philosophers railed against such dishonesty. As far as the public was concerned, it enjoyed some particularly clever evasion in a lawsuit. There is a famous story of a sly cheat who was accused of misappropriating money which he held in trust. He went to court with the money hidden in his staff. As he had to swear that he did not have the money in his possession, he handed the staff to a friend just before he took his oath.

There was little similarity between an Athenian trial and one under our system. But one Greek trial practice, also found among many ancient peoples, was much like a practice still employed in our own courts. A group of people (compurgators) would make oath that the defendant was innocent of the claim or charge, or that the plaintiff was justified in his suit. Such testimony, backed by nothing whatever in the way of fact, was listened to and given considerable attention, and this does seem somewhat idiotic or, at least, primitive. Yet we introduce "character witnesses" in many lawsuits, who testify to the good character and reputation of one party or the other. We do not always allow such testimony, but we frequently do, and it is testimony which often affects a jury. However, we allow cross-questioning of these witnesses and of all witnesses, so that the party against whom they are testifying can have an opportunity to bring out facts which might discredit the testimony of the witnesses.

It is one of the essential characteristics of our court system that, when there is a jury in a case, the jury is the sole judge of the facts while the judge is the sole judge of the law. For a simple illustration, let us take a murder case. The judge will charge the jury that, if it finds that the defendant did kill the deceased and that he did so intentionally and with malice aforethought, the jury must hold him guilty of murder in the first degree. But, the judge will say, if the jury finds that either the defendant did not kill or he killed in self-defense, then the jury must hold the defendant innocent; and the court goes further and states that, if the defendant did kill, and not in self-defense but in the heat of the moment and without previous intention, it is murder in the second degree; etc. The judge thus determines what facts would support a criminal charge, and the jury determines whether these facts actually existed.

The Greek system was quite different, for the jury was really both judge and jury. The judge, elected by lot, merely presided at the meeting, and the jury decided both the facts and the law. That made justice depend not on any certainty of law but on the whim of the particular jury which was sitting. Each case was treated as a new situation. The lack of professional judges who might collect precedents and turn them into rules, the absence of a true bar of advocates, and the unwieldy size and uncontrolled nature of the juries made the development of an enduring, orderly, or scientific system of law difficult, if not impossible.

The litigant usually tried his own case, using whatever knowledge of the law he might have, if any. There were *exegetai,* or interpreters of the law, present at the trial to expound the law to the jurymen, but they had no more than an advisory capacity and were of small use to the litigants themselves. But the practice of hiring an orator to help the litigant with his case came more and more into vogue. For, as the juries were not technically trained, a well-couched oration and an intriguing argument might win a case. Therefore, the speeches made by the litigants were of the utmost importance—more important than the law. So a litigant would ask an orator to prepare an address to the jury for the client to read, or the orator read it in his client's behalf and in his name. Thus, the great names of what might be called the Greek bar are not those of lawyers, as such, but of orators. Of these the most famous was Demosthenes, whose renown at the bar was equal to his fame as a statesman. We have several of his orations delivered on behalf of others, and they are masterpieces of clarity and persuasiveness.

Another noted legal orator was Hyperides, famous for his defense, in about 340 B.C., of Phryne, a courtesan accused of profaning the Eleusinian mysteries. Dramatic tricks were practiced by the orators, and Hyperides used one which became famous. At the climax of his appeal to the jury, he snatched the gown from Phryne's shoulders, exhibiting her lovely bosom to the court, a gesture which the jury found irresistible.

There is an amusing story of a Greek trial which may be fiction but illustrates the reasoning capacity of the Greeks. Protagoras, a teacher of oratory, made a contract with a pupil on a contingent basis. Protagoras was not to be paid until his pupil had won his first case as an orator or lawyer. Some time after the student had finished his studies, Protagoras asked for his fee, and the student refused to pay because he had not yet won his first case. So Protagoras sued him. At the trial the teacher claimed that he could not lose the case because if he won he would get a verdict against the pupil, whereas if he lost the pupil would have won his first case and the teacher would be entitled to be paid. The pupil, on the other hand, reasoned that he could not lose because if he won he would not have to pay Protagoras, whereas if he lost he would not have won his first case and therefore would not have to pay. It is said that the court adjourned the case for a hundred years.

The Greeks did not begin to have the scientific approach to law which we shall find among the Romans. Their laws were badly organized and haphazardly contrived. Yet they amassed an astounding body of law, much of it enlightened and interesting. They learned the venture system from their Babylonian neighbors, created business groups and trading syndicates, and financed expeditions through a banking system which might almost be called modern. Commercial contracts existed in many forms, and the Greeks knew many of the mechanisms and contrivances of business which we use today. They even created corporations of certain limited kinds, chiefly religious, and these are the ancestors of our great business corporations.

When you buy a piece of real estate today, you have the title searched, or obtain an abstract of title from the seller. This is no recent contrivance: the Greeks had an excellent system of land recording through which the title to land could be checked before buying it. A record has been found at Tenos, dating about 200 B.C., which contains some fifty entries of land transfers, and they are in a standardized form which would be intelligible to any modern title-searcher. They also had leases, and the forms of these leases are astonishingly well developed. Much of this craftsmanship in real-estate matters, however, may have been borrowed from the advanced civilizations of Egypt and Mesopotamia, where real-estate practices had developed to a high degree of perfection at an early date.

There was not much freedom for women in Greece. The father had enormous power over his daughter, as was the case among all patriarchal people; and this control shifted to the husband when she married. In later periods, these controls were somewhat loosened, but this partial emancipation of women was accompanied by a decline in the respect and kindness with which they were treated. In all Greek history the men had far the better of the matrimonial bargain. While there was never any polygyny, there was never any need of it. Husbands used female slaves as concubines, and prostitution flourished. Homosexuality, also, was accepted socially.

But, for that matter, there was not much freedom, in the true sense, for any Greek. In the first place, there was never any thoroughgoing democracy at any time. Even after the reforms of Cleisthenes, no more than twenty or thirty thousand freemen controlled the state, and they ruled over six times that many who were disenfranchised or enslaved. Moreover, even the freemen had no "freedom" as we understand the word. The theory of individual liberty was absolutely unknown. Man was a slave to the state, and the amount of regimentation was remarkable. The individual city-states prescribed dress, regulated speech, and imposed restrictions of many kinds on conduct. In some cities it was forbidden to shave one's beard. The education of youth, rigorously controlled in Sparta, was by no means free from control in Athens and elsewhere. Religion was obligatory, and, as I have said, one could not choose one's own. Failure to participate in a religious festival was punished at Athens with a fine. Despite the "democracy" of Greece, the idea that there were fundamental rights of men was hardly known.

CHAPTER 5

Lycurgus

"Or who would not have such children as Lycurgus left behind him . . ." PLATO: SYMPOSIUM

I: Man or Myth

HISTORY ATTRIBUTES the creation of a totalitarianism in Sparta to Lycurgus. The government which he is said to have created might well have been a model for the corporate state of Mussolini, for the Russian dictatorship, and for National Socialist Germany.

It has been guessed that he lived somewhere between 900 and 600 B.C., but as is the case with Moses, Homer, and Solon, we do not really know whether Lycurgus was a man or a myth. Plutarch, his fervent admirer, did an excellent profile of him in his *Lives,* but even Plutarch says: "There is so much uncertainty in the accounts which historians have left us of Lycurgus, the lawgiver of Sparta, that scarcely anything is asserted by one of them which is not called into question or contradicted by the rest. Their sentiments are quite different as to the family he came of, the voyages he undertook, the place and manner of his death, but most of all when they speak of the laws he made and the commonwealth which he founded. They cannot, by any means, be brought to an agreement as to the very age in which he lived."

But even if Lycurgus is a myth, there still is good reason to believe that the system of government attributed to him did actually exist in Sparta; and what does it matter if it were the design of one man or of many anonymous lawmakers? There is a good chance that a man named Lycurgus did exist, even if he has been given credit for the work of others. So let us see what Plutarch, his biographer, has to say about him; though Plutarch himself had some difficulty deciding between the conflicting stories about the man whom he so greatly admired.

I shall not detail the pedigree which Plutarch gives for Lycurgus except to mention that Hercules was his ancestor. What is most interesting in Plutarch's profile is the melodrama which he describes. He says that Lycurgus's father was the King, and when the old man died Lycurgus's elder brother took the throne. But then the new King died also, and Lycurgus succeeded. However, the Queen Mother, Lycurgus's sister-in-law, was pregnant, and if the child turned out to be a boy then the infant would be the rightful king. It was the Queen Mother herself who suggested to Lycurgus that if her child turned out to be a boy she would kill him and marry Lycurgus.

This plan did not appeal to Lycurgus's noble heart, although he made believe that he had fallen in with it for fear that the angered woman might do harm to her own infant when it was born. When the child did turn out to be a boy, Lycurgus had it brought to him and immediately proclaimed the infant King of Sparta, to the great annoyance of the child's mother, who, a woman scorned, proceeded to plot against the man she had sought as a husband. Lycurgus can hardly be blamed for concluding that a protracted absence from Sparta was indicated.

There is a sort of repetitious character about the careers of many of the great historical personages. At some stage in his life each is reported to have gone into seclusion or to have retired by traveling and so picked up much information of later use in the particular contribution to society which the great man was to make. And thus Lycurgus, says Plutarch, went off to Crete, where he studied the somewhat totalitarian system there in operation, and he also went to Egypt, and as far as Spain in one direction and the Indies in the other. There is a parallel with Solon's travels in this story, but a great difference in the materials which each brought back to Greece for use in civil affairs. When Lycurgus finally returned to Sparta, the country was in bad shape. He was heartily welcomed, and he had a new bag of tricks with him.

II: Lycurgus Creates a Nazi State

Did the Germans fall prey to National Socialism because they were essentially different from other people? That is a question we ask ourselves frequently. The answer probably is that, given the right conditions, Nazism could have happened anywhere. Perhaps we have proof of that in the case of Sparta; for the Spartans were at first no different from the other groups of Hellenes which invaded the peninsula. Their final homeland was the small state of Laconia, and Sparta was its capital. Another group of Greeks who had arrived in Laconia first were subjugated and made into serfs or "helots" by the Spartans. This was not at all unusual, for the ancient Greeks fought among themselves more often than any other people, with the possible exception of the Irish.

So there was no difference between the Spartans and the other Greeks until the reforms which are attributed to Lycurgus. Sometime between 900 and 600 B.C., Laconia was turned into a military state. We do not have any clear account of how Lycurgus achieved so radical a change in the Spartan constitution. He may have been given dictatorial powers, or he may have had such powerful persuasiveness that he sold the magnates and the citizens the idea of "strength through joy" and all the rest of the authoritarian hokum which made Sparta the most powerful military state in Greece but destroyed her arts and crafts and corrupted her soul.

There was now not one king but two, just as there were later to be two consuls in Rome. The kings did not seem to have a great deal of power, and the government lay chiefly in the hands of a *Gerousia*, or Senate of old men, sixty years of age or over, twenty-eight of them plus the two kings. These were conservative old gentlemen of property who had to be of the class of *homoioi*, or "equals," and must have served their terms of military service. These elderly senators were elected by a method strangely similar to some of our television programs. A group of candidates would file in front of an audience, which registered its approval by applause. Whoever got the most applause was thereby elected to the Senate.

There was also an Assembly (the *Appella*) to which all free males over thirty were eligible. In theory the *Appella* was the more important legislative and executive body, but in practice it was virtually powerless against the Senate. The Assembly could not initiate any legislation—it could only accept or reject laws which were submitted to it by the *Gerousia;* and if the *Gerousia* objected to any veto exercised by the Assembly, it had only to hold that the veto was dishonestly arrived at, and then the law was deemed passed.

So the old men of the Senate had things their own way, and they had a powerful enforcement agency to do their bidding. There was an order of secret police, called the *Krypteia*, a sort of

Gestapo which later acted under orders of special officers called "ephors," and their special duty was to ferret out and punish treachery among the helots. Once a year the *Krypteia* had an especially good time; this was purge time, when a Spartan was permitted to kill any helot whom he suspected of insubordination.

Of course, the *Krypteia* was a necessity. You cannot run a police state without police, and they must be secret, cruel, and ruthless. The helots lived a hard life, were bound to the soil, and had to pay heavy tribute to their masters, who did not work because they had to keep themselves fit for military duties. Nor was it easy to escape the eye of the Spartans and their Gestapo, for the helots, like the Jews in Nazi Germany, were obliged to wear recognizable costumes. Now the helots were themselves Greeks, for the most part, and they had spirit. They did not take their subjugation supinely and rebelled frequently. So the *Krypteia* had to be ever vigilant, and it saved the state from disaster on many an occasion by a slaughter of aroused helots.

Lycurgus's great objective was military proficiency. To this end he desired all Spartans to be free for military duty, and he concluded that this might best be done by eliminating luxury. So he caused the land to be divided equally, and no man had enough land to be able to accumulate much wealth. Not content with this, he made all the men eat together in large groups, where the food was regulated. And, to discourage trade as a competitor of military activity, he permitted no gold or silver to be used as currency. Lycurgus established a new currency of iron, and, as Plutarch observed, ". . . to lay up twenty or thirty pounds there was required a pretty large closet, and, to remove it, nothing less than a yoke of oxen. With the diffusion of this money, at once a number of vices were banished from Lacedaemon; for who would rob another of such coin?"

Nor did Lycurgus stop there in his campaign against luxury. All needless and superfluous arts were prohibited, and manufacturing was permitted only of simple articles of household and military use. You might construct a simple kitchen table, but not a fine lamp or a carved chest. As Sparta had nothing to trade, foreign merchants avoided the country, and there were no longer any luxuries to buy. Plutarch calls attention (with commendation) to the fact that one article of great practical value was produced by the Spartans. This was a drinking cup eagerly purchased by soldiers, for its color "was such as to prevent water, drunk upon necessity and disagreeable to look at, from being noticed; and the shape of it was such that the mud stuck to the sides, so that only the purer part came to the drinker's mouth."

A man in Sparta began to be a "Spartan" at birth, for, instead of being given his first bath in water he was bathed in vinegar to make him tough. In early infancy every Spartan was taken by his father to certain officials who inspected the child. If he were found in any way defective or weak, he was disposed of promptly, for Sparta would tolerate only the strong and straight. A young Spartan who passed this preliminary test was pretty much left alone until he was seven, but then began a long and arduous period of training. He was taken away from his parents and put in residence in a public school.

This was no country boarding school life. There was some play, but plenty of order and discipline. Reading and writing were taught, but more important subjects in the curriculum were pain and courage. Young Spartans went barefooted and generally played naked, and after they were twelve they were permitted no underwear and were allowed only one coat a year. A bath was frowned upon, and a Spartan was not permitted to relieve a distaste for his own aroma by using perfumes or ointments. He slept on sharp-edged rushes, which he had to break off with bare hands.

Homosexuality was not frowned upon in Spartan schools, but rather accepted as normal and even desirable. It was the custom for a youth in school to acquire a lover from among his friends; and these relationships were considered so normal that a lover might often be punished because his playmate had been found wanting in some duty. Nor was homosexuality exclusively a male prerogative.

But this universal interest in what we consider unnatural practices did not seem to deprive the Spartans of their desire for the opposite sex. The girls were raised rigorously and in a way designed to enable them to bear better children, and both girls and boys danced naked in processions and festivals. Such exposures apparently induced the young men to seek brides as soon as they could, but they did so under severe handicaps. A husband was not permitted to live with or even consort openly with his wife until he was thirty years old. So the procedure was that a young man would carry off a bride, and at this point we must quote again our useful Plutarch: "After this, she who superintended the wedding comes and clips the hair of the bride close round her head, dresses her up in man's clothes, and leaves her upon a mattress in the dark; afterwards comes the bridegroom, in his everyday clothes, sober and composed, as having supped at the common table, and entering privately into the room where the bride lies, unties her virgin zone, and takes her to himself; and after staying some time together, he returns composedly to his own apartment, to sleep as usual with the other young men."

Despite the handicaps to marriage which this strange system presented, propagation was encouraged. Marriage was compulsory or nearly so. If you did not marry, you were obliged, on certain occasions, to parade naked with other bachelors and to sing a song of disgrace. And if, by any chance, you produced no children, it was your duty to permit your wife to consort with some other man who might produce progeny by her; for it was thought absurd that a man should wish to hold a wife exclusively to himself when he was not doing his duty of producing more soldiers for the state. On the other hand, certain rewards were offered for ample production. A father who had three boys was exempt from military service, and if he produced four he was discharged from all burdens to the state.

Our very use of the word "Spartan" indicates the character of the training which the young men of Sparta underwent, and it is understandable that this state defeated Athens and that its armies were invincible so long—until its downfall in 371 B.C. at the hands of Thebes. Sparta was the most intensely military state of ancient times, and its renown increased in later ages. Plato gave support to many Spartan ideas in his *Republic*, and Plutarch followed him in fervent admiration of the efficiency and purity of the Spartan system. However, we cannot be sure that all the complimentary things said about Sparta were well based, for Aristotle, in contrast, speaks of corruption, bribery, greed, deceit, and decadence in Sparta. But it is the picture painted by Plato and Plutarch which has come down to us, a picture agreeable indeed to the totalitarians of today.

III: The End of Lycurgus

LYCURGUS did not have too easy a time instituting his radical laws. On one occasion he was pursued by irate capitalists who threw stones at him. Lycurgus managed to outrun all but one of his pursuers, who caught up with him and knocked out one of his eyes. Lycurgus, however, took this youth into his house and, by his own example of quietness and modesty, made a rabid convert of him. And so, by good example and perseverance and persuasiveness, his whole program was effected, and the time came when the great lawgiver felt that he had done all that could be done and that his laws were safe. But he still feared that the system which he had instituted might be changed after he was no longer there to protect it. So, the story goes, he called a meeting of the two kings, the Senate and the Assembly, and told them that he intended to visit the oracle at Delphi; and he made them all take an oath that they would not change his laws until he returned.

Then he did go to the oracle. He asked whether his laws were good and sound, and he received the full approbation of the oracle. Satisfied then that he had done a good job but still fearing that his work might be undone if he gave the Spartans any opportunity to be relieved of their oath, he decided that he would bind Sparta by never returning. To make doubly sure, he starved himself to death.

CHAPTER 6

Socrates, Plato, and Aristotle

I: Socrates, the Gadfly

"The time has arrived, Glaucon, when, like huntsmen, we should surround the cover, and look sharp that justice does not steal away, and pass out of sight and escape us; . . . if you see her first, let me know."

SOCRATES, ACCORDING TO PLATO IN THE REPUBLIC

IF YOU had been walking along the streets of Athens on a winter's day about the middle of the fifth century before Christ, you might have seen a pair of bare feet coming across the cold ground. As your eyes lifted to see what poor devil of a man was reduced to such extremity, you would have taken in a single tattered garment which swelled out over a large potbelly, the whole crowned by a strikingly ugly face. A long beard and a bald pate framed ungainly features, of which a rude nose and thick lips would have impressed you most strongly. You would probably have said to yourself that this was an unfortunate but unpleasant-looking tramp, and you might have passed him by and been lucky. But had you by any chance stopped, perhaps to ask your way to the nearest Athenian equivalent of a saloon, you would have been sorry. For you would have been seduced into a conversation by Socrates. This unkempt and unprepossessing individual, who was the wisest man of his age and perhaps of all time, was also a very annoying person. He accurately termed himself a gadfly.

Only a casual question or chance remark was needed to open the sluice gates to a flood of dialectic that could completely submerge the unfortunate victim. Here was a man so adept and relentless in his use of the probing word that he was well called the father of cross-examination.

This strange and wonderful creature does not appear to have sprung from a particularly unusual background. All that might be considered odd is that his father was a sculptor and his mother a midwife. Perhaps that combination did it. Socrates followed his father's profession for quite a while, did his stint in the army with credit, and discharged his other civic duties conscientiously. But something was brewing in him. As he put it himself, he was far more attracted to his mother's profession than his father's, but he wanted to be a midwife to the mind. So he gave up sculpting and adopted his chosen trade, to the everlasting benefit of humanity but to the great discomfort of his wife, Xanthippe. She has been unfairly treated by posterity, for her name has become synonymous with "shrew." After all, her husband gave up work and spent all his time in street-corner conversation.

That was his life. He might have had a school at some time; if he did it was no organized institution but consisted of a group of pupils who followed him around to listen to his arguments. Generally he just collared anyone who happened to be handy and started a conversation. He would prefer to buttonhole someone who thought he was an expert; showing up experts was his greatest pleasure. That is all Socrates wanted to accomplish. His militant thesis was that an appreciation of our ignorance is a prerequisite to learning. And you could not turn the tables on him. Socrates was quick to assert his own ignorance. The oracle of Apollo had called him the wisest man in the world, and Socrates agreed with the oracle—but he agreed only because he was so certain of how little he knew.

He loved to induce someone to set up a hypothesis so that he could break it down by questioning. It was cross-examination developed to the highest degree of perfection and directed toward the search for truth. On one occasion, narrated by Plato in his *Dialogues,* Socrates has a discussion with a young man named Charmides. The young fellow admits that he is a "temperate" person, and Socrates asks him to define "temperance." Charmides replies that he thinks it means "quietness." So the dialogue goes on, with Socrates as the narrator:

"Are you right, Charmides?" I said. "No doubt some would affirm that the quiet are the temperate; but let us see whether these words have any meaning; and first tell me whether you would not acknowledge temperance to be of the class of the noble and good?"

"Yes."

"But which is best when you are at the writing-master's, to write the same letters quickly or quietly?"

"Quickly."

"And to read quickly or slowly?"

"Quickly again."

"And in playing the lyre, or wrestling, quickness and sharpness are far better than quietness and slowness?"

"Yes."

"And the same holds true of boxing and in the pancratium?"

"Certainly."

"And in leaping and running and in bodily exercises generally, quickness and agility are good; slowness, and inactivity, and quietness are bad?"

"That is evident."

"Then, I said, in all bodily actions, not quietness, but greatest agility and quickness is noblest and best?"

"Yes, certainly."

"And is temperance a good?"

"Yes."

"Then, in reference to the body, not quietness but quickness will be the higher degree of temperance, if temperance is a good?"

"True," he said.

"And which," I said, "is better—facility in learning, or difficulty in learning?"

"Facility."

"Yes," I said; "and facility in learning is learning quickly, and difficulty in learning is learning quietly and slowly?"

"True."

"And is it not better to teach another quickly and energetically, rather than quietly and slowly?"

"Yes."

"And which is better, to call to mind, and to remember, quickly and readily, or quietly and slowly?"

"The former."

"And is not shrewdness a quickness or cleverness of the soul, and not a quietness?"

"True."

"And is it not best to understand what has been said, whether at the writing-master's or the music-master's, or anywhere else, not as quietly as possible, but as quickly as possible?"

"Yes."

"And in the searchings or deliberations of the soul, not the quietest, as I imagine, and he who with difficulty deliberates and discovers, is thought worthy of praises but he who does so most easily and quickly?"

"Quite true," he said.

"And in all that concerns either body or soul, swiftness and activity are clearly better than slowness and quietness?"

"Clearly they are."

"Then temperance is not quietness."

Charmides may have started off on the wrong foot, but it did no good for him to start over again. Each time he did, Socrates exposed the absurdity of the proposition stated.

This is the method of teaching in most law schools today. The professor engages a student in argument by stating the facts in an actual or fictitious case and requesting an answer to the problem presented. There ensues a Socratic conversation, to which the rest of the class often listens with amusement not shared by the victim.

That was Socrates's method—with one important difference. He rarely bothered to straighten out the confusion into which he had thrown his victim. He satisfied himself with convincing him of his inability to cope with a problem. And he purposely took mean advantage; for as we have seen with Charmides, he would fasten on any unusual or critical term, insisting on a definition—and nothing is more devastating in argument. We all use terms loosely and with our own nebulous meanings. If a victim said that something was "not fair," Socrates would ask what was meant by the word "fair." Now, you try to define such a word, and let a relentless mind harass you as you fumble with it!

Socrates left no writings behind, and our information about him comes chiefly from Xenophon and from Plato, who was Socrates's pupil. We do not know how accurately Xenophon reported Socrates, and we do not know the extent to which Plato may have put his own pet words into Socrates's mouth, but from the two we get a good picture of the man and his ideas.

Suppose your own city were managed by a group of butchers,

bakers, and candlestick makers elected for one year; and suppose the people were so jealous of their control of the government that they never re-elected the same man to the same office. Each year you would have a new group of incompetents, wholly inexperienced in municipal administration, running the city affairs. That was the case in the Athens which Socrates knew, and it astounded and horrified him. He once asked a pupil whom he would engage to mend a shoe; and the pupil naturally answered, a shoemaker. Then Socrates asked: "Who should mend the ship of state?" That is why Socrates was no Athenian democrat.

Socrates, born about 470 B.C., lived to see his country go through a period of greatness, despite the handicaps of an inefficient government. But he lived also to see the defeat of Athens by Sparta, after which a police-state government was set up with Spartan assistance. This short-lived Athenian regime, known as the government of the Thirty Tyrants, did attempt to substitute efficiency for the old Athenian sloppiness in administration. Socrates certainly sympathized with this objective, but he did not hesitate to continue to criticize freely, whatever the danger to himself.

This criticism by Socrates was forgotten, however, when the tyranny was overthrown and the democrats again came into power. The new leaders remembered only that Socrates was a friend of some of the reactionaries and that he had been a bitter critic of the old democratic system. Even his large and enthusiastic following did not protect him against the enmity of the democratic leaders, who considered him public enemy number one. As they did not wish to bring the political issues into public discussion or to give Socrates an opportunity to defend his political views, charges which evaded the real issue were laid against him in 399, when he was eighty years old. He was accused of "corruption of the young" and "neglect of the gods when the city worships and the practice of religious novelties." The jury which tried the case consisted of five hundred and one citizens, and the prosecutors were Anytus, a democratic politician, Meletus, a young and obscure poet, and Lykon, an equally obscure rhetorician.

It may be that his persecutors hoped that Socrates would evade the whole business and flee the country, and it does not seem that they intended to have him executed, even though they asked for the death penalty. Socrates himself gave them no alternative but accepting defeat or getting rid of the gadfly. In his trial he berated his accusers. He had no fear of dying, and he insisted on the truth being triumphant or on falling with it. His concluding speech, reported by Plato, accused the prosecution of eloquence, while he disclaimed any himself. He reviewed the whole course of his life, justifying his conduct and methods. Finally, he implored his accusers and the jury not to do themselves the great injustice of convicting him.

The jury's verdict was a conviction by a majority of about sixty, but this was not necessarily the end for Socrates. For custom allowed the convicted man to suggest an alternative punishment for himself. If Socrates had suggested anything reasonable, even a moderate fine, the jury would probably have permitted this to take the place of the death penalty, but Socrates would not compromise. The alternative to punishment which he suggested was a nominal fine, which angered the jury into decreeing the death penalty. And even then, when the execution of the death penalty had to be postponed for a month because of a religious festival, his friends arranged for Socrates's escape from prison. But the old gentleman refused to escape, insisting that the law must be obeyed and that an escape on his part would tend to do just what he had been accused falsely of doing—it would impair the morals of youth. When the hour came, he drank the fatal hemlock, amidst his sorrowing friends, cheerful to the last and exchanging words of encouragement for their tears.

Those who follow Socrates will not accept a custom or a law merely because it has a long beard. They will not accept a theory until it has been tested by reason and subjected to careful, critical analysis. Antiquity and hallowedness will not be permitted to stand against reason and logic. Socrates undoubtedly was the original "man from Missouri."

II: The Gadfly's Pupil

"The makers of laws are the majority who are weak; they make laws and distribute praises and censures with a view to themselves and their own interests; and they terrify the stronger sort of men, and those who are able to get the better of them, in order that they may not get the better of them." PLATO: GORGIAS

AFTER THE DEATH of Socrates a sad and disillusioned young man of twenty-eight named Aristocles (we know him as Plato) left Athens in disgust. As a boy he had witnessed the utter defeat of his country at the hands of Sparta and had seen a tyrannical government installed under the direction of the enemy. When that horror had finally been overthrown, he had seen it replaced by an extremist government of the left, almost as cruel and undesirable as the occupation government. When the new leaders murdered Socrates, the most illustrious citizen of Athens and Plato's teacher for eight years, the young man had had enough.

Of course, that was not the only reason that Plato left Athens and stayed away so long. He was certainly also concerned about his own skin. The extreme democrats were on the rampage, and it was well known that Plato had been a disciple of Socrates, but any fear that he may have had was secondary. Before he left, he said that there was no hope of decent government in Athens until "either philosophers became kings or kings philosophers."

It was with this idea in mind that he established his famous Academy in 387 B.C. on his return to Athens. This remarkable school continued for nine hundred years, until it was destroyed by the Byzantine Emperor Justinian. It was remarkable in the scope of its curriculum, for it covered all the known sciences, philosophy, government, and law. It was more remarkable because it did not give instruction by rote or by the ordinary lecture method. It was a school for research, and Plato's favorite method of instruction was to set problems for his students to solve. It was a "project" method of education much like that now used by some of our modern schools. To this intellectual workshop Plato brought the critical reasoning which he had learned from Socrates, and he added to it method and organization in thinking. He was not satisfied to stop at the destruction of false premises but insisted that sound premises must be determined.

One of the most interesting aspects of this school was its function as a legislative drafting bureau. In recent decades such bureaus have been established in our country to assist legislators. Before that, the legislator, often not a lawyer himself, had to draft his own bill or get what assistance he could, where he could. As a result, many bills were badly planned and worse worded, to the endless confusion of the courts and the public. With an official drafting bureau at his service, an American legislator can have professional bill-draftsmen dash off a measure for him, with confidence that it will probably be a better job than it would if he had done it himself. Much more than two thousand years ago, Plato established such a legislative drafting bureau in his Academy. He and his assistants were frequently asked to draft laws for various Greek cities; and Plato himself was several times commissioned to advise on legal problems and matters of state and to participate in government reorganizations.

As for Plato's bent in matters of law and government, we have already learned that he was an antidemocrat. That becomes most clear in his writings. His many *Dialogues* are conversations between characters representing conflicting points of view. Plato's favorite literary character was Socrates, but the extent to which Plato was being biographical in quoting his old teacher is debatable. The *Dialogues* cover a multitude of subjects, but two of these are of particular interest to us, the *Republic* and the *Laws*.

Plato explained that he wrote the *Republic* in order to discuss "justice," and that he thought it easier to ferret out the true meaning of "justice" by discussing it in terms of the conduct of a state rather than the conduct of individuals. But his real reason seems to have been a desire to design what he thought to be an ideal state. Apparently he submitted his *Republic* as the ultimate product of his governmental workshop and legislative drafting bureau. What Plato produced was a misbegotten child, but its value lies largely in the fact that he started many generations of men to thinking constructively about government reform. About two thousand years after Plato, Sir Thomas More designed what he thought to be the ideal state and gave it the name of "Utopia." The search for utopias has been fruitless, but it has been a boon to mankind that men have devoted themselves to the proposition that all cannot be perfect as it is, and everything can be improved.

Unfortunately, Plato's progressive approach produced a reactionary result. He was the first totalitarian philosopher, inspired perhaps by his fervent admiration for the Spartan civilization which had defeated Athens. His own country had been democratic and weak. The Spartans had been authoritarian and strong. There is Spartan philosophy in the *Republic*, where, in the ideal community, there were three classes of citizens: the common people, the army, and the "guardians." The common people did all the work, a program satisfactory to any totalitarian system. The army was the protector of the state against external enemies, but it was also the police force, and we clearly see a police state in a pattern with which we have become familiar. The guardians were the elect. They were an especially trained and educated class; they constituted an aristocracy of brains and ability.

The education of the guardians was directed to bring out what Plato thought to be the best qualities for governors of a state. This was done by teaching them "gymnastics" and "music." "Gymnastics" did not mean merely turning somersaults and doing handsprings; it included everything having to do with physical fitness. "Music" was an even more comprehensive term, including all that goes into what might now be called "culture." The object of this specialized training was to produce cultured gentlemen. They were not to do any ordinary work, for Plato, like many of the Greeks, thought that one could not absorb enough culture unless full attention were devoted to it; the Spartans had a similar idea, but they wanted their gentlemanly class left free of outside occupation so that it could devote itself exclusively to military activity. Plato's concept of the "gentleman" was not far from that of the nineteenth-century English, whose upper-class young men were often carefully trained to devote themselves to public service.

So far, so good; for the production of cultured and physically sound gentlemen might be a worthy object. However, the education of his special class was to be very closely directed. There were to be no self-governing schools where educational theories would be experimented with. A careful curriculum was to be laid out and rigidly adhered to, and it was to contain only such things as Plato himself thought it best that the guardians should learn. For example, Plato happened not to like plays, so he prohibited them completely.* Many subjects were to be barred in the Republic, and many individual books of which Plato did not approve for one reason or another. For example, the ancient classics of Homer and Hesiod were to be prohibited, because in those books the gods were often displayed as doing unconscionable and unworthy things, and there were other stories in Homer and Hesiod which Plato thought might give wrong ideas to the youth in his ideal state.

In no direction did Plato seem ready to allow details to be worked

* Hitler did not like modern art and insisted on imposing his own feeble concepts of art on all of Germany. Stalin and his cohorts made it clear that the composers of Russia would have to toe the line and produce only music acceptable to the ideology of the state, whatever that might be Control of education and of the arts is essential to totalitarianism, and it is inevitable that the special tastes of the top totalitarian be imposed on the people.

out as reason might suggest in the future. He did not permit certain types of music to be taught because they might either relax the hearer or make him sorrow, which he thought undesirable. Even diet was carefully detailed. For some reason, fish could not be eaten in his imaginary state, and meat could be eaten only when roasted.

The guardians were to live a thoroughly communal life. They were to have only small houses, and they were allowed no property beyond the actual necessities; specifically, they were permitted no gold or silver, an idea which seems certainly to come direct from Lycurgus. The guardians were even to have women and children in common, in which direction Plato went even further than Lycurgus had gone. But women were granted social and economic equality, in theory at least.

Plato saw that the class of guardians would have to maintain its social standing and its capacity and ability, so he provided for eugenic marriage, that its virtues might be perpetuated. As progeny fell below the best standards, they were to be relegated to the common class; and Plato did provide that whenever someone from the lower classes showed unusual ability he should be permitted entry into the ranks of the guardians. Thus, by occasionally taking in new blood and spewing out the unsatisfactory products, the guardian class was to be kept at par. In arranging his eugenic marriages, Plato planned to resort to a fraud. The system was, in theory, that mates should be selected by lot. However, the rulers were to trick the young people by forcing the draws, so that those whom they wished particularly to see as parents of future guardians would meet each other in what appeared to be a fair lottery.

The children were to be raised by the state. They were to be taken away from their parents at birth, and the close relationships of family life were to be unknown. Every male of a previous generation was to be addressed as "father" and every female as "mother," while every male of the same generation was to be called "brother" and every female "sister." This is a primitive throwback. In many primitive societies no other relationships were recognized than those of father, mother, brother, and sister.

Naïve though it may seem, Plato imagined that the two lower classes would be satisfied always to be managed by the ruling class. He believed that it could all be so arranged if one great lie were adopted as truth, namely, that God had created three distinct types of people: one type, made of gold, fit to rule; another, made of silver, fit for military work; and a third, made of brass or iron, fit only to do manual work. Plato was probably unduly optimistic about the chances of even the men of gold being satisfied with their lot, for they were all required to be grave, decorous, and courageous.

At any rate, Plato finally arrived at his definition of justice in a state, and it is a neat but not very satisfying definition, namely, that justice exists in a state when everybody does his job and does not interfere with anyone else. And the state was to determine each man's job.

Plato was given an opportunity by the young dictator of Syracuse to put his ideal state into operation, but they soon fell out and the venture came to nothing. No serious attempt was ever made to institute a state anything like Plato's until our own era, in which the totalitarians have had something of the sort in mind. However, the principal value of Plato's idealistic *Republic* is that it initiated constructive thinking in matters political and legal. His own great weakness was his overwhelming interest in the Spartan state of Lycurgus.

Plato himself later rejected the state of the *Republic*, not because he had any quarrel with his own basic idea but because he saw ways in which his ideal state, in his own estimation, could be improved. So he wrote his *Laws*, in which another ideal state is described.

In his *Laws* Plato sets the scene in Crete, and that state is confronted with the problem of organizing a colony. Thus, Plato gave himself a chance to establish a new, basic constitution. In it he dropped many of his pet theories of the *Republic*. He abandoned communism as impractical, but he outlawed commerce, so that the whole economic basis of the state was agriculture, and he imposed a 100-per-cent excess-profits tax on incomes over a specified amount. The government was not to be as oligarchic as that of the *Republic* —there was to be qualified democracy. But there was to be the same fascist flavor in the matter of education. The minister of education was the head of the state, and education was made the most important governmental and civic activity, but there was to be severe censorship of ideas and even punishment for questioning, which is difficult to understand as the influence of Socrates was the most important factor in Plato's own development.

Plato's discussions of "justice" have given food for thought to many a subsequent philosopher. He related it to human virtue, and this, in turn, he attached to the idea of perfection in man. To establish what is virtue, Plato used the Socratic method of setting up hypotheses to shoot at, and he came to these conclusions: Virtue has to do with goodness, and being truly good involves being truly human, i.e., being natural. Thus he reaches his own variety of the "natural-law" theory: if man followed his true nature, he would be good, for justice is innate in the human soul. In his *Republic* he offered the thesis that the best education would produce justice. In his *Laws* he concluded that a perfect lawgiver, regulating life in every detail, is the best answer to our social needs—a thesis which leads in a straight line to the modern totalitarian "leadership principle."

Despite his fall from the straight line of Socrates's independent thinking, Plato comes down to us as a logician unequaled in his time and unsurpassed since, and he remains a truly great figure not only in the history of philosophy but also in the field of law. In one way he went further than his old teacher, Socrates. He took a positive as well as a negative line in his reasoning. Socrates applied one test: Is the proposition sound? Plato applied a double test: Can the opposite be refuted and can the proposition itself be defended against refutation? Socrates emphasized the necessity of questioning; Plato, the necessity of building upon the truth elicited from questioning. As both reasoning and scientific method are necessary to the development of law, Socrates and Plato must be given equally honored positions in the hall of fame of legal philosophy.

III: The Gadfly's Pupil's Pupil

"Good law means good order."

ARISTOTLE: RHETORIC

WHO WAS THE GREATEST—Socrates, Plato, or Aristotle? I would not attempt to answer that. Aristotle probably should have been, having learned all that Plato had to teach, and Plato had learned all that Socrates had to teach. At any rate, Aristotle probably had the greatest influence on European thought. Though not as inspired as Socrates and Plato, he was systematic, and he perfected logic, the most useful tool of the lawyer, the jurist, and the philosopher. Socrates pried out the rules of logic by his practical method of questioning to turn up absurdities of reasoning. Plato went one step further and applied a certain amount of method to his reasoning, not being content to rely on mere destructive questioning. But it was Aristotle who perfected the reasoning process by working out the mechanics of the syllogism. He reduced reasoning to simple formulas which are as self-evident as the simple propositions of geometry. Under Aristotle's rules it is apparent that this reasoning is sound:

All men are animals.	(Called a "major premise.")
I am a man.	(Called a "minor premise.")
Therefore, I am an animal.	(The "conclusion.")

It is equally obvious that the following is unsound and one should cry *Non sequitur* ("It [the conclusion] does not follow"):

All men are animals.
A horse is an animal.
Therefore, I am a horse.

To get at the truth of reasoning, it was merely necessary to determine whether a minor premise was properly related to a major premise and whether the conclusion naturally followed from that relationship. Of course, the premises must be correct to begin with. Starting with a major premise such as "All men are angels," there is no telling what sort of conclusion might emerge.

Some of the syllogisms are more complex than the one stated above, but Aristotle made their construction clear; and his syllogistic reasoning is the weapon of judge and lawyer today.

Aristotle was born in 384 B.C. of a family which had practiced medicine for generations. His father was hereditary physician to the King of Macedonia. Aristotle drifted to Athens at the age of eighteen and entered Plato's Academy, where he studied twenty years until Plato's death. A few years later he started his own pedagogical career, for he was appointed tutor to the young Prince Alexander of Macedonia, whom we know as Alexander the Great. Alexander later became a strong propagandist for Greek, particularly Athenian, civilization, and it may be that he learned to love it through his contact with Aristotle, but nothing whatsoever is known about the depth of the relationship between the two men.

In 335 Aristotle returned to Athens, where he organized a school of his own, the Lyceum, and spent considerable time on brilliant and voluminous writings in many varied fields for twelve years. But the enormous empire which Alexander had welded together collapsed at his death. Athens was again free. That meant trouble for

Aristotle, who was known to have been closely associated with the Macedonian court. The rebellious Athenians, after throwing off the foreign yoke, went witch-hunting and indicted Aristotle among others. It was difficult to make a charge of treason against him, so they made it "impiety." Unlike Socrates, Aristotle did not stay to defend himself. He fled to Chalcis, where he died a year later. For the second time, Athens had persecuted her then most illustrious son.

Aristotle's name bears the same blot as Plato's. He gave comfort to the totalitarians. He exalted the state and, in his *Politics,* advocated slavery. Like Plato, he saw the ideal state as one built for gentlemen of culture, who could not waste their precious time in trade, mechanics, or husbandry. They were to own the property, in Aristotle's state, but it was to be worked by slaves while their masters had leisure for the finer things of life. Slavery, according to Aristotle, is a natural institution; some people are born to be slave, others free. There are superior races, he said, of which the Greeks are naturally the most superior; others are inferior, particularly the southern races, which are intelligent but not too spirited. All this is highly reminiscent of Alfred Rosenberg and the Nazi theories of race, and is also material for our own rabid segregationists.

Aristotle railed against "usury," by which he meant, as did the Old Testament, the lending of money at interest. Landowners have never liked the practice of lending money at interest, and Aristotle favored the landholding, aristocratic classes. For the same reason, perhaps, and taking support from Aristotle as well as from the Old Testament, the medieval Church in Europe opposed "usury," for the Church was itself a great landowner.

Aristotle professed to prefer democracy to oligarchy, and oligarchy to tyranny. His democracy, however, took the aristocratic form which his description of an ideal state indicates. To tyrants he gave sound advice. To perpetuate themselves, he advised that they must cut down any persons of exceptional merit; censor assemblies, discussions, literature, and education; employ spies, including women and slaves; impoverish their subjects; sow quarrels; keep the people busy at great projects like the building of the pyramids; and keep them at war.

Aristotle's and Plato's ideal states were very similar, except that Aristotle had no use for communism, objected to the communistic flavor of the state of the *Republic,* strongly advocated private property, and abhorred the proposed abolition of the family.

Aristotle's contributions to pure reasoning were so monumental that they dwarf his mistakes of judgment and political theory. Furthermore, he propounded a legal theory which, however much it may be criticized, continues to have enormous influence upon the law and legal processes. This is the theory of "natural law."

Aristotle has sometimes incorrectly been given credit for inventing this theory. Actually, it was an old Greek idea that the universe was an ordered and orderly one governed by a sort of cosmic law, and Aristotle did not by any means "discover" the concept that there were laws higher than those made by men. But Aristotle first discussed "natural law" in detail and with elaboration; the philosophical school of the Stoics later picked it up; Cicero took it over from the Stoics; and it thus came into the Roman law, and from the Romans into our own system.

The division which Aristotle made between "man-made" law and "natural" law was simple enough, but he was not too clear in his exposition of the latter. He sometimes referred to natural law as an ideal law, and sometimes as law to be found in the natural order of things. Upon this confusion later jurists piled further confusion, until now, when someone mentions the term "natural law," he must define it with great care, for it means wholly different things to different people.

Let us first consider the Stoics, the philosophers who adopted this concept as Aristotle had propounded it. They said that man-made laws could be adjudged as good or bad by the extent to which they happened to conform to a set of absolute laws which were to be found in nature. According to the Stoics, it was the job of society to organize itself to live in an ideal state in which the natural laws could exercise full play. That seems reasonable enough, if you happen to know what the laws of nature may be, but the Stoics failed to define them.

Nor did the Roman philosophers of the law do much to clarify the matter when their turn came. The natural-law theory had many ardent and powerful exponents in Rome. Among them was Seneca (about 3 B.C. to A.D. 65), a Spaniard who became an eminent Roman statesman and acquired great wealth in spite of his Stoicism. (He had the misfortune to become the tutor of Nero; that villainous Emperor decided one day to order his tutor to commit suicide, and Seneca obediently complied.) Another great Roman Stoic was Epictetus (about A.D. 60 to 100), actually a Greek slave. The most eminent follower of the Stoic philosophy was the Emperor Marcus Aurelius. Though himself not a Stoic but an adherent of the New Academy, Cicero was the most important supporter of the theory of natural law. It will later be shown how deeply Roman jurisprudence was affected by the concept of natural law; how the Christian Church writers adopted the idea both from Aristotle and from the Romans and built it into the canonical legal system; and how the later, Continental writers on law used variations of the same concept in their thinking and writing. An enormous amount of legal literature has been produced on the concept of natural law—or rather "concepts" of natural law, for there have been so many variations that the term itself is now about as indefinite as the words "liberal" and "democratic."

It is still used frequently in the public press. A Senator will say that something is demanded by "natural law"; a conservative economist, a sociologist, or a churchman will say that "natural law" requires this or that. In all probability no two of these four are talking about the same thing.

Thus there are the theologians and jurists who conceive of natural law as law ordained by God. Grotius, the great Dutch jurist, went so far with the theory of natural law as to proclaim in his *De Jure Belli et Pacis*: "The law of nature is so unalterable that it cannot be changed by God Himself." Some believe that all law is in the Scriptures or elsewhere, readily seen and absolutely binding. In contrast to these "fundamentalists," men like St. Thomas Aquinas conceived of natural law as ordained by God but appreciated through man's "natural reason." This is, apparently, the theory of the Catholic Church today. It is an interesting theory and an elevating one, but it does not always help very much in practice, for one may differ as to what natural reason may be composed of. Natural reason may have justified the Spanish Inquisition in one century and condemned the burning of heretics in another. Some churchmen take natural law to be absolute justice, directed or required by God, but admit that we never know just exactly what it may be.

There are philosophers who base their theory of natural law upon the best in man. Some of these believe that it is the ultimate law common to "enlightened man," but they are not always clear who the enlightened among men may be. Are educated and high-minded Mohammedans enlightened, or only good Christians? Others of this general group believe that natural law *is* actually current among the enlightened, while some see it as that which *should be* current among the enlightened.

There have been those who saw natural law as the rules which would be in effect in a "state of nature." To many of these, that original state of nature was a lovely condition in which human beings were amiable, gentle, and ethical. The idea was possibly promoted by the Garden of Eden legend. However, not all thinkers have arrived at the conclusion that man in his original state was an admirable character.

The difficulty is not only in disagreement as to meaning. Even granting any one definition, men do not often agree upon the details. Thomas Jefferson, for instance, wrote into the Declaration of Independence that there are "laws of nature," but what are these laws? Do they include the sanctity of private property, as Locke said, or do they include the absolute right of a majority to interfere with property? Do they include the "law of supply and demand" when related to labor as a commodity, or do they include the right of the individual to work and to be compensated even when there is no work to be done? Do they support the laissez-faire theory of the Adam Smith economists, or the extreme collectivism of communism? You can see that not much is accomplished by using the term "natural law" as anything but an indefinite ideal.

Nevertheless, the concept of natural law, while it has led many jurists astray in their thinking, has been of great benefit to society in one way. It has given us the general theory that there is a "higher law" and that, when justice is not done by ordinary law, the higher rules of morality and ethics can be applied to give justice. Jurists may argue over definitions of natural law, but the idea that abstract principles of justice should be applied when a particular law is inadequate is a benign one. However, there must be some degree of consistency in the law, so that people may know how to act and what their rights and duties are. If abstract principles rather than fixed law are to determine these things, then the abstract principles must be made clear. The greatest weakness of Greek law was that it never clearly defined the abstract principles of justice. Thus, "justice" was always uncertain.

Aristotle, in popularizing the concept of natural law, did not give us any clarification. But he gave us stimulus.

I have selected Aristotle's theory of natural law as his principal contribution to jurisprudence. Others may disagree, for his influence on subsequent thinking in the law was great, and by no means confined to his exposition of a natural-law theory. Among his other contributions to jurisprudence was a theory of "equity," a branch of jurisprudence which, as we shall see, came to important fruition in the development of the Roman and later the English law. While Aristotle said that legal justice had a mechanical or arithmetical quality, the equitable was a better form of justice.

PART THREE

THE ROMANS

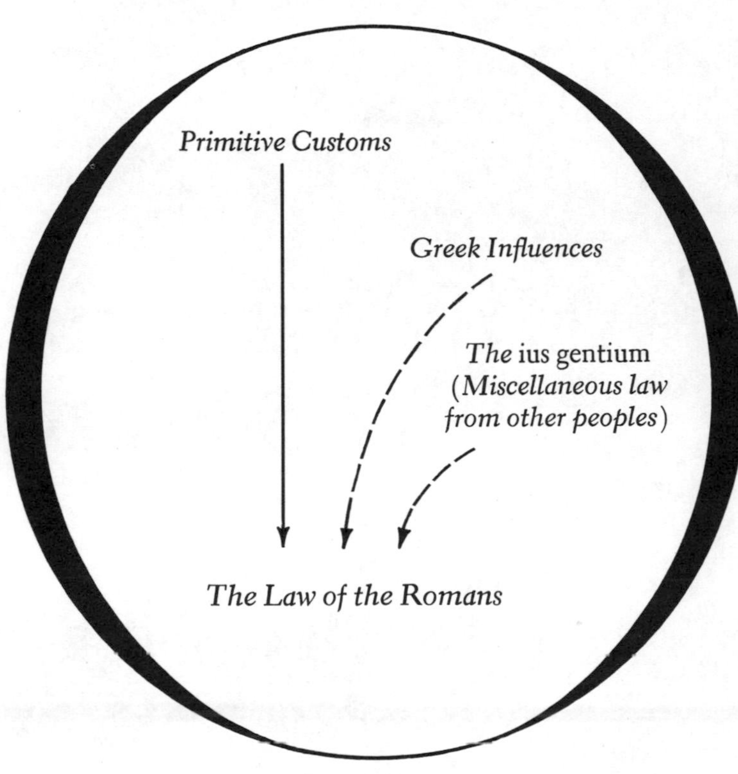

THE CHIEF BASIC SOURCES

CHAPTER 7

The Ten Men

"The safety of the people shall be the highest law."

CICERO: DE LEGIBUS

I: Appius Claudius Crassus

A DIGNIFIED ROMAN magistrate sat in his study, hearing a case which had been brought before him. His name was Appius Claudius Crassus, and he was a proud man, for he was a member of the aristocratic Claudian clan and was one of the Ten Men, the *Decemviri*, who had been appointed to rule the Roman state absolutely for a year. He was by nature a headstrong and vain man. It was unusual for him to hear this sort of case; it was a minor matter about title to a slave, and Appius would ordinarily have left such a trifling thing to a lesser magistrate. But this was a case which he was anxious to have come before him: *Marcus Claudius versus Virginius.*

The plaintiff, Marcus Claudius, stated that he had the girl Virginia in his custody and claimed her as his slave and property. His story was that Virginia was the daughter of one of his female slaves and, therefore, was herself born his slave. He claimed further that Virginia had been stolen from his house and passed off as the daughter of the wife of Virginius, the defendant. The story was completely false, but Marcus had a number of perjured witnesses to substantiate his claim.

Virginius then had his say. He was a worthy and respected citizen and a centurion, and he swore that Marcus's story was a pack of lies and that Virginia was his own free-born daughter. Then Virginia's mother took the stand and weepingly contradicted Marcus also, swearing that Virginia was her own child; and finally the beautiful Virginia herself testified that Marcus's claim was wholly false. But Appius listened with impatience, for his mind had been made up long before the case started. The whole thing had been rigged by Appius himself. Marcus bore the Claudian name only because he was a protégé and hanger-on of the Claudian family, under Appius's direct protection, and the magistrate had framed the story with Marcus. It had been agreed that, when Virginia was awarded to Marcus as his slave, he was to turn her over privately to Appius, who had long desired her for her beauty.

Appius gave judgment that Virginia was the property of Marcus, but the melodramatic climax to this story is that Virginius, rather than have his daughter pass into the hands of these villains, stabbed her to death in front of Appius. The people of Rome, already angered by the misrule of the Ten Men, heard of the tragic result of this trial, seized Appius, and dragged him off to prison, where he died ignominiously. Thus, legend has it, ended the wicked life of Appius Claudius Crassus.

Now Appius was a rascal, but, to do him justice, he must be listed among the eminent characters of the law. For the Committee of Ten of which he was chairman had been given absolute power to rule the Roman state only in order to do a specific job without interruption or interference. That job was to compile, codify, and reduce to writing the Roman law.

II: The Roman Government

BEFORE recounting the story of the Roman law and the men who made it, it would be well to review quickly the Roman government of the republican era, from the overthrow of the Tarquins, the last dynasty of kings, in about 500 B.C., until the accession of Augustus, the first Roman Emperor.

The Roman Republic was administered on a system not unlike our own. The distinctions between the branches of government were not as clear, but there was an executive and what might be called, by loose analogy, and upper and a lower legislative house, an arrangement which was almost classic in the development of a clan-based government; we have seen it in operation in Greece. Theoretically, sovereignty rested in the people through the Assembly, the lower house, which at first was open only to the upper class, the patricians, but was later opened to all citizens. The people were said to have *maiestas* (whence our word "majesty"), implying that they had the right to make *leges,* or laws (whence our word "legislation"), and the magistrates—the executives—were said to have *imperium* (whence our word "imperial"), the delegated right to govern.

Theoretically, sovereignty lay in the people, but the fact is that the Republic which succeeded the Tarquin monarchy was no democracy. The Republic was similar to that of Attica in Greece. The mass of the people, although they were not slaves as in the case of Attica, had almost no voice in government. The patricians, the clan members, ran the state, and the very word *patricii* indicates the condition of Roman society. *Patricii* signified being born of a legal father, or being legitimate.

If you were not a member in good standing of one of the old clans, you were a plebeian; and that meant you were incapable of producing legal offspring. You were then a mongrel, and your children would be mongrels, and not permitted to participate in government. Even after the plebeians gained most of the rights which had formerly been the exclusive possession of the aristocrats, the latter still considered that theirs were the only "true families," just as some Back Bay dowager in Boston may feel that the only "real families" are those she would invite to dinner. But, in Rome, the social distinction remained extremely important, for being a patrician always carried with it special rights and privileges of great value.

The untouchables of India are believed to be the descendants of the original inhabitants, who were conquered by the Hindus. It may be that class distinction in Rome similarly dated back to the foundation of the city, and that the plebeians were originally a conquered people, the class coming to be amplified by immigrants, refugees, transported captives, etc. At any rate, the distinction between the two classes was an ancient one. We know also that a third class appeared at an early date, the *equites;* these were men of wealth and power who were granted an intermediate social position. Their name, deriving from *equus* ("horse"), indicated the fact that they had enough money to mount themselves as knights.

You have seen the letters "SPQR" on the Roman *fasces* or emblem. These letters stand for *senatus populusque romanorum,* "the Senate and the people of Rome." In the early Roman period, the *populus romanus* consisted only of the patricians and the equites. The plebeians were hardly considered "people," and certainly not part of the "Roman people." But they were not to be kept down. Their numbers grew rapidly through immigration, especially as

Rome's conquests widened, and through the desertion of dependents and servants of the aristocrats. The city became packed with plebeians, their mass voice gradually became a power to be reckoned with, and it was inevitable that they be recognized as part of the *populus romanus*.

The founders of the Republic intended to prevent the return of the hated monarchy, but they had no interest whatever in making any more concessions to the plebeians than were absolutely necessary. To take the place of the king, they created the office of *praetor* or magistrate, and they elected two praetors as joint heads of the state, each being able to veto the other. The praetors were elected for an annual term, and, while there was no "constitutional" reason for not re-electing them, custom entitled the praetors to only one term. These two praetors were later given the name of *consul*, and other praetors were elected as judicial magistrates, so my subsequent use of the title "praetor" will refer only to the magisterial praetors. The word "praetor" probably came from *prae-itor*, or leader. The word "consul" may have arisen because of the duty of the consuls to "counsel" with the Senate, but the earlier title of praetor seems to have been born out of the leadership principle. The praetors (the consular praetors) were the leaders in war.

While the wartime powers of the consuls were almost absolute, they were far from absolute rulers in times of peace. They were obliged to consult with the Senate, which in its earliest form might be described as the council of the heads of families or the council of city fathers. Consular powers were further restricted by the legislative control of the lower house, the Assembly. Within these restrictions the consuls stood in the shoes of the former king, but now there were four shoes. The consuls were elected by the people in assembly. But the people could not nominate anyone of their own choice. They could vote only for such candidates as had passed the test of heavenly approval, established through the taking of auspices by the priestly officials. Through these auspices it was easy enough to rig an election.

In addition to the magisterial praetors, other magistrates were elected with various duties, the *quaestores*, *aediles*, and others; and the position of *censor* was created to take over from the consuls the work of directing a census—the censor came later to have important additional powers, including the right to remove senators for cause. And there was another vitally important official, the *tribune*.

The office of tribune was created after a successful strike of the plebeians which demonstrated the extent of their power when they were sufficiently aroused to use it. The part of the tribune in Roman government was most peculiar, and it is difficult for us to see how any government that included the tribune system could function. The tribunes were elected by the people without any participation by the Senate, and their special function was to protect the gradually increased rights and privileges of the commoners. A tribune could prevent an arrest, interfere with court procedure, and do many other direct acts in protection of the plebeians, but his most astounding right was his veto. He could say "*Veto*" ("I forbid") to almost anything, including the enactment of legislation or the enforcement of a law. He could negative a measure passed in the Senate and could even enjoin the consuls from action.

The Romans were practical men. The tribunes afforded great protection to the common people, but they did not control the state. The tribunes were often patricians themselves and not infrequently ignored the interests of their constituents. Moreover, each tribune could act independently, and thus one could frustrate another. At first there were only three tribunes; the number was eventually raised to ten, and the upper classes always managed to get control of enough of them to check any important action in the people's behalf. Furthermore, the tribunes had no power outside of the city of Rome itself. So the patricians and the equites continued to run the state, and there was rarely much chance for any strong democratic movement to gain momentum.

There was always an Assembly of the people, but here we come to a strange contrast between the Greeks and the Romans. The Greeks were enthusiastic participants in public affairs; they were jealous of their rights and were quite willing to attend public meetings frequently to discuss government and law. On the other hand, although the upper classes in Rome produced what may be considered the most remarkable governmental and legal system of all time, the lower classes were amazingly lazy about doing anything to rectify the wrongs done them. There was an occasional civil commotion in which the plebeians won rights or secured some protection against domination by the patricians, but then the usual sequel was that the plebeians would lapse into inattentiveness and lose some of the ground they had gained, or the patricians would find some clever way of getting around a mechanism which had been designed to protect the plebeians. The men who led the plebeian party were usually rich men themselves, and they rarely had the true interests of their social class at heart. Their interest was generally in exerting enough pressure on the socially elite classes so that they could get their own fingers into whatever pie might appeal to them. The Assembly was called into action only at the instance of a tribune, and it was unwieldy when it met. In contrast, the Senate, which the patricians controlled even after equites and rich plebeians were admitted, met frequently and functioned easily and efficiently.

There were actually three successive kinds of Assembly. During the period of the kings there was the Curial Assembly, an assemblage of the heads of families which represented the thirty semi-religious *curia* or wards into which the original tribes had been divided. After the fall of the monarchy, the Curial Assembly gradually lost most of its power to the Centurial Assembly, in which the soldiers voted by "centuries," divisions originally of one hundred men. The Centurial Assembly came to hold ultimate authority to grant *imperium*, to select the magistrates, to judge cases of capital crime, and to decide upon war or peace. It held ultimate legislative power also but did not initiate legislation. It merely voted "Yes" or "No" on measures proposed to it by the Senate or magistrates.

Although the whole people, plebeians included, came to participate in the Centurial Assembly, it remained under the control of the patricians and conservative propertied classes, for the centuries voted by an artificial division. At the top of the voting body were eighteen centuries of patricians and equites. The remaining citizens were divided into classes by wealth. The wealthiest groups had the most centuries, and the great mass of the unpropertied class was represented by only one century. However, the plebeians began to hold assemblies of their own which eventually developed into the Tribal Assemblies, which held some legislative powers as early as 357 B.C. In the Curial Assembly the people were grouped according to clans; in the Centurial Assembly, according to wealth; in the Tribal Assembly, according to residence. Gradually the power of the Tribal Assembly increased until by 200 B.C. it had become the chief legislative body in the Roman state; but, although the "tribes" of which the aristocratic families were members were the smallest numerically, they had equal vote. Thus, even in the Tribal Assembly the patricians retained control.

Despite the gradual enfranchisement of the plebeians, the Senate, under upper-class control, remained supreme in many important ways. Initially it had no legislative function itself, but had the right to refuse recognition to any *leges* not properly introduced for passage by an Assembly.

Membership in the Senate was for life or good conduct. Upon leaving office, consuls and censors became senators, and the consuls and censors were authorized to appoint additional senators whenever necessary to bring membership up to the standard of three hundred. The permanence of the Senate gave it practical power beyond its technical function in the state. In addition, the Senate controlled foreign policy, war, government of colonies and provinces, the distribution of lands, and the administration of the treasury. It also had the power in emergencies to decree the *senatus consultum ultimum*, establishing martial law and making the consuls dictators. The Senate was actually the only truly deliberative legislative body at any time in Rome. One way of describing a democracy is as a "government by discussion," but it was only the upper legislative house, the Senate, which had this democratic function in Rome.

III: The Twelve Tables of the Ten Men

ONE OF the great obstacles to bettering the condition of the plebeians was that Roman law was still oral and in the private custody of the patrician priests, upon whose good faith one had to rely to get justice. The scales of justice were more than once weighted against a commoner because he did not know the law, and so a clamor for written laws arose and eventually could not be resisted. In 451 B.C. the Senate appointed the Ten Men, the *Decemviri*, to collect the laws and put them into writing. They produced ten tables or chapters of law which were so well received that most of the Ten Men were reappointed for another year to finish their work; they then added another two chapters, and the whole is known as the *Code of the Twelve Tables.*

It may well be that the story is wholly legendary, and that the laws of the Twelve Tables were in fact gradually assembled. But let us take the story as it is recorded by the Roman historians, for the fact is that the Code did exist.

We are told further that the Ten Men who drafted the Code were turned out of office in the middle of their second term because power had gone to their heads. Legend has it that it was the incident of Appius and Virginia which precipitated the upheaval.

The reverence of the Romans for the Code of the Twelve Tables is comparable only to the veneration which the English-speaking world gives to the Magna Charta. Only fragments of this Code exist, but a fair knowledge of its entire substance is ascertainable, for it is mentioned frequently in the writings of Roman jurists. It was a far broader and more explicit body of law than the Magna Charta. It was not extracted from a king for the benefit of preferred classes of subjects; it came from the upper classes for the benefit of the whole people of Rome. It is largely procedural, that is, a good deal of its content deals with how actions may be started and how they are to proceed, but it also contains much substantive law.* In theory, at least, the Code gave equality to all classes.

It was not a moral code like the Ten Commandments, and it was primitive for the most part. It was a mixture of three sources, and one purpose of the Twelve Tables was to reconcile them. There was the law which had sprung up among the common people of Rome who did not have the use of the clan customs and had to find some way to settle their own differences. There were also legal customs borrowed from other peoples. There is a story, incidentally, that the Senate sent a delegation to visit Greece and study the laws of Solon, and that the *Decemviri* incorporated a good deal of Greek law in the Tables. But the largest source of Roman law was to be found in the legal customs of the patrician clans.

Of the many streams of influence which produced our law, the Roman is one of the most important. In turn, it owed much to the Greeks, especially to the Greek philosophers, whom cultured Romans read avidly. And it was at Rome in later eras that the Jewish influence started to play its part in the ultimate creation of our system. But our debt to the Romans is quite unusual. They made a science of law; they ran a veritable law factory; and they worked out so many of our human, legal problems that their own system needed little alteration to be adapted to modern necessities. So it is impor-

* The term "substantive law" may need explanation. The law is divided into two kinds, "procedural" and "substantive." Procedural law covers the rules under which one establishes one's rights, either by litigation or otherwise. How to start a lawsuit and how to proceed with it, or how to get a clerk to issue some certificate—those are matters of procedural law. Substantive law covers the rest of the law, including such things as what rights one has against a trespasser, who gets the property when a man dies, what is the penalty for theft, etc.

tant to glance at the deepest roots of the Roman system, the clan customs.

The Roman clan was called a *gens* (plural, *gentes*) and its members were called *gentiles.* It was quite similar to the Greek clan and was, in one sense, a state within itself, often comprising thousands of persons. Clans were self-governing and had a body of customs which had the force of law; these were called the *ius gentilitatis* ("the law of the *gentiles*"). The elders of the clan, the heads of the individual families, acted as a sort of legislature and court, and the judicial power within the clan was absolute; its members could be punished even with banishment or death. The head of the clan served as chief judge, chief priest, chief executive, and military commander. In most respects the Roman clans followed what might be called the standard tribal pattern; they did, however, have sub-clans or *domi.* A *domus* (from which derives our word "domicile") occasionally broke off and made itself independent of the parent clan. You could tell an aristocrat by his name if you were a Roman, for the clan names were known to everybody. For example, Publius Claudius Pulcher would have been recognized as Publius of the Pulcher branch or *domus* of the Claudian clan.

When the patrician tribes joined to form the city of Rome (the initial Roman state), they brought their *ius gentilitatis* or clan law with them. This was a personal law, applying to those who belonged to the clan. The rights which patricians had under their clan law were the most important and basic rights in Roman society. They included the right to vote, the right to take auspices and to occupy the position of priest (an extremely important office, since the priests were the custodians of the law), and the right to have contracts recognized and enforced. They also included *dominium,* the right over property, *conubium,* the right to contract a legal marriage, and the right to use the *legis actiones,* the formal legal remedies for the enforcement of rights in the courts. Thus, certain persons in the state could enforce a contract and others could not, and only a patrician could bring a lawsuit in the early days. Until the lower classes fought for and obtained a liberalization of the law, they simply had no rights.

As in any patriarchal system, the father had enormous power over the family. In the later Roman eras, the father's power was called *patria potestas.* (The word *patria* did not have the significance of "paternity" but rather of "protection" and "authority"; *potestas* meant "power.") In all domestic matters the father's word was law, a situation common to patriarchal systems, as among the early Jews. He could order corporal punishment and even death; he could select a wife for his son or a husband for his daughter; he could demand that a child be divorced; he could adopt children if he wished; and he could grant to others the right to adopt his own child. The explanation of the extraordinary power given to a father in a patriarchal system is that the primitive family needed to be governed by concentrated executive authority in what were perilous times. That such powers were continued long after the safety of the family no longer required them is not astounding. Man has a habit of retaining old customs long after their usefulness has ceased.

There was a gradual emancipation from the power of the *paterfamilias*, the head of the family. In the first place, the father had no control in any matter which affected public law. A son in military service or even in civil service could hardly be subjected to his father's command. But the father's absolute *dominium* over the family property was one of the last of his privileges to fall.

The right of *conubium* (a word which is the obvious ancestor of our "connubial") was eventually extended to all classes, and it was an important right, for one could not produce a legitimate family without the right to engage in a "legal" marriage; and citizenship was impossible to an illegitimate child.

There were two kinds of Roman marriage: that in which *manus*, or "control," passed to the husband or the head of his family; and that in which *manus* remained with the bride's father. Under a patriarchal system, when a woman marries she usually leaves her own family and joins that of her husband, passing into the control of his family. That form of marriage existed among the Romans and was called marriage *cum manu* ("with control"). But another form of marriage had developed, called *sine manu* ("without control"), under which control of the bride and of her property remained with her own family.

There were three methods of marrying *cum manu*. The first was quite similar to Greek marriage and included customs which we still carry on: the bride dressed in white and wore a crown and a veil; the groom carried her over his threshold; and the two shared a wedding cake. The second method was a marriage by purchase, which, in time, became only a token purchase. The third method was by *usus* ("use"); if you held a woman under your control for a full year, she became legally yours. This was probably an offspring of marriage by capture.

It was, of course, natural enough for marriage without control to become increasingly popular, for it was not only desirable from the bride's point of view but it also enabled her family to keep control of her property. So marriages by the *usus* method became frequent, and a clever little trick would be employed to avoid the transfer of *manus* or control to the husband. The bride would simply spend three nights a year away from her husband, breaking the continuity of his control. In time marriages were contracted which were frankly and openly *sine manu.*

Women did not have much in the way of legal rights in ancient Rome. They were under what has been called "perpetual tutelage." While she was in her father's home, a young girl was under his control. When she married, if she got out of her father's control it was only to pass into the control of her husband or his father. Although women gradually lost some of their disabilities, they were never completely emancipated. But then—how recently did we completely emancipate women!

As for marriage morals, the early Romans were hardy and austere, and good family men. Although divorce was easy, it was rarely used. But the single standard of morality did not last long. Female slaves were poured into Rome from the conquered provinces, and, as the Empire grew and prosperity increased, morals generally relaxed and promiscuity became more and more the rule rather than the exception. Learning homosexuality from the Greeks, the Romans almost outdid their preceptors. Even the great Caesar was once called the "Queen of Bithynia." Conservative statesmen railed against the decline in morality, but it did no good. Divorce had now become so easy that it was necessary only to send a wife a "bill of divorcement," or simply to order her to take her belongings and go home.

A divorced spouse could and frequently did marry again. It was not until the Christian Church exercised full influence in the Byzantine (Eastern Roman) Empire that restrictions were put on divorce and remarriage. But these restrictions, at first harsh, were later moderated frankly on the theory that it was better to permit divorce than to encourage murder.

IV: The Legis Actiones

THE *legis actiones*, or lawsuits, which for so long only patricians could use, were of five types.

Let us go into court and see how one of them worked. Suppose you and your friend Henry had a dispute as to the ownership of a cat. You would haul Henry before a magistrate, and there a strange play would be enacted. Henry and you would each be armed with a stick, and you would both hold on to the cat and make believe that you were tearing it away from each other. You could not avoid that pantomime, for each step in a Roman legal proceeding was formal and had to be taken with historic exactness. This first step was a hangover from the primitive days of self-help. Then the magistrate, unconsciously reflecting the development of the next historical stage in the growth of the legal process, would intervene to ask you to state the case. He would act as though he were merely an arbitrator. So Henry and you would let go of the cat, or one of you would, and you both would give your versions of the situation. The next step, if you were using the *sacramentum* procedure, consisted of a wager made before the magistrate, and the magistrate would be asked to decide who won the wager. If the amount of money involved was more than one thousand "asses"—which were coins, not beasts—then the law provided that the loser of the wager would pay a fine of five hundred asses, and if the amount of value of the thing in dispute was less, then a fine of fifty asses.

But a case was not actually tried by the magistrate. Having determined that an action properly lay, the matter was referred to a judge (*iudex*), generally selected by the parties themselves. In a way, the function of the judge was similar to that of our jury—he determined the facts. Modern "rules of evidence" do not permit certain kinds of testimony, such as "hearsay evidence," but a *iudex* in Rome could listen to anything he wished, even rumor.

When the judge had given his decision, the case was over; the winner was left to collect or enforce the judgment as well as he could. It was not until later times that the magistrates came to render some help in effecting judgments, and they then did it generally by holding the judgment-debtor in custody until he either paid up or worked off the debt.

Manus injectio was another of the *legis actiones,* and was rather primitive. If you owed a man money, he could seize you by the throat and shout loudly that you owed him the money, and how the debt arose. He could then drag you before a magistrate and have you confined for sixty days. During this period you would have to be taken three times into the open market place, where the debt was loudly proclaimed. This was to give some friend or relative an opportunity to come forward as a *vindex* (from which comes our word "vindication") and deny that the debt was due, or deny the legality of the proceeding. If the *vindex* turned out to be wrong, he was fined double the amount of the debt. If no *vindex* came forward, or one were proved wrong, and you did not pay up, your creditor could have your person. He could sell you as a slave, if he cared to, or even kill you. In fact, if there were more than one creditor, the law expressly gave them the right to cut you up and divide the parts. But such extreme measures were not often used; you would probably be given an opportunity to work off the debt.

There were three other *legis actiones* with formidable names: *pignoris capionem* (an attachment of a pledge), *iudicis arbitrive postulationem* (a demand for a special arbitrator), and *condictionem* (a demand for a special framing of the dispute).

The magistrate had the right to say which of the five remedies could be used. They were all extremely formal. It is characteristic of an era of unwritten law that legal proceedings be much more formal than in later stages of development, and so the ritual of the *legis actiones* was far too complex for the average citizen to learn or remember. As this ritual was not written down, a Roman who faced a lawsuit generally went to a priest to get instruction; there were no "lawyers" to help him.

CHAPTER 8

Appius Claudius Caecus and the Gracchi

"As for the Gracchi, the greatest detractors and their worst enemies could not but allow that they had a genius to virtue beyond all other Romans . . ."

PLUTARCH: LIVES

I: Another Appius Claudius

THE CLAUDIAN FAMILY produced many eminent men in Rome who made up for the discredit cast on the family name by Appius Claudius Crassus. Among them was Appius Claudius Caecus, who caused the building of the great aqueduct which bears his name, and also that superhighway, the Appian Way, which he named after himself to save posterity the trouble. But these physical accomplishments pale before the contributions of Appius Claudius Caecus to the cause of liberty for the Roman commoners.

He was elected a censor in 312 B.C. and kept the job illegally for five years. The censor had the right to fill vacancies in the Senate, and Appius used his five years as censor to good advantage. It had always been the practice to fill senatorial vacancies with safe and responsible members of the best families in Rome, but Appius scandalized his friends by appointing many men of low social standing and considerably diluting the aristocratic character of the Senate. He also tampered with the Tribal Assembly in an attempt to destroy upper-class control of that lower house. The Tribal Assembly voted by tribes, and the patricians controlled the majority of the tribes. But Appius found a way to break that monopoly. He distributed the landless citizens among the several tribes in such a way as to give the common people numerical control of most of them. The outcry at this measure must have been heard in China, but the patricians could do nothing about it at the moment. Later on, in 304, they turned the tables by causing all the plebeians to be allocated to the four urban tribes so that their concentrated votes again counted little against the more numerous rural tribes, which were controlled by patricians.

As the priests were still the only lawyers in Rome, it was most important for the plebeians to break through the monopoly which the patricians had on these jobs. Therefore, when Appius opened up the priesthood to plebeians, he made it possible for them to acquire legal advice and assistance from members of their own class. To help further, Gnaeus Flavius, the clerk of Appius, published full information about the *legis actiones,* so that, thereafter, anyone could learn the rituals and requirements if he cared to and thus protect himself against the trickery which his previous ignorance had made possible. Somewhat later, in 253 B.C., Tiberius Coruncanius was elected *pontifex maximus,* or chief priest, as the first plebeian to hold this important office, and he went one step further —he offered public instruction in the *legis actiones.*

The dikes were now open, and many public offices were successively opened to plebeians. By 287 B.C. the Senate had even lost its previous right to veto measures passed by the Assembly, and it looked as though the common people of Rome were certain to come into their full rights. But it did not come about as easily as that!

II: Tiberius Gracchus

By the time of the final destruction of Carthage, in the second century B.C., there was theoretically little legal distinction between patrician and plebeian. Rome was a democracy, on paper. But practice did not conform to theory, and the upper classes still ran the state. The patricians and equites controlled the Senate, and the Senate had regained power and controlled the government, in defiance of law and almost without check.

However, strains were beginning to show. The magistrates were often restless under senatorial control, and the people were highly dissatisfied with the power of the classes of wealth. The government, not satisfied with Rome's already enormous conquests, was disinterested in the domestic economy and was concerned only with foreign enterprises. Farming became more and more unprofitable, for the free farmer had to compete with slave labor and with grain imported cheaply from Egypt and elsewhere. Great landowners grew greater by buying up small farms. Both artisans and farmers, as in Athens before Solon's time, migrated to the cities, where they formed a noisy rabble which became an annoyance to the Senate. Easy wealth, extracted without too many scruples from the conquered provinces, enervating contact with the luxuries of the East, the spread of Greek learning, and the inability of Rome to defend itself against the weakening effect on morals and morale of certain of the Greek philosophies—these and other factors tended to change the political and social fiber of the Roman people and to presage eventual disintegration.

In the meantime, Roman power grew, and the interest of the Romans in their law grew with it. What Coruncanius had started by offering public instruction in the *legis actiones* took hold rapidly. The law fascinated the Romans, and many studied it. Professional lawyers appeared and gave further instruction, and it was not long before many of the plebeians, as well as patricians, knew the laws of Rome thoroughly. About 200 B.C., Sextus Aelius Paetus Catus published what may have been the first lawbook in Western Europe, the *Tripertita* or *Ius Aelianum*. After that, writing on the law became frequent, and public interest in law mounted. Not all patricians were disinterested in the welfare of the plebeians. There was always a rather strong liberal group, and early in the second century it began to cry loudly for agrarian reform, which seemed essential for the safety of the state.

Rome now contained many men of fabulous wealth, and the small farmer upon whose strength and virility the state had been built had almost disappeared. He was now to be found in the city, discontented, impoverished, and almost at the point of insurrection. In this emergency Tiberius Gracchus was elected a tribune in 133 B.C., at the age of twenty-eight. He had already shown enough ability, both in the army and in civil affairs, to mark him for greatness; and he was one of a small group who felt that the safety of Rome demanded restoration of the land to the small citizenry. He immediately proposed legislation to frustrate the grasping landlords.

He dug up an old law limiting the amount of public land any citizen might hold, and insisted on strengthening and enforcing it. He suggested further that indigent citizens be put back upon the land, and that the state lend them the money to resume farming. This sort of radicalism horrified the capitalists, and they organized to oppose the proposed measures with all their great force. They put pressure on another tribune, a close friend of Tiberius's, named Marcus Octavius, who finally succumbed to their seductions and announced that he would veto Tiberius's proposals.

Tiberius tried in every way to persuade Marcus to change his mind. Finding him adamant, he did something previously unknown in Rome and yet apparently wholly legal. He issued an edict preventing any magistrate from exercising his functions until the proposed legislation was either approved or rejected by public vote.

The capitalists were so furious that they conspired to murder Tiberius. When that failed and a public election was held to vote on the bills, they ran off with the balloting urns. Tiberius then demanded action from the Senate. He asked that Marcus resign his tribuneship and, when he refused, proposed that the public vote on whether Marcus should remain a tribune. This proposal was probably entirely illegal, but Tiberius, determined not to let the people's cause be frustrated, forced a vote, and, after Marcus again refused to resign, the people deposed him.

It was clear sailing after that, and Tiberius's laws were enacted. A commission consisting of Tiberius, his brother Gaius, and his father-in-law was appointed and began the gigantic task of enforcing the new agrarian laws. But Tiberius did not live to see much result from his work. The capitalists finally succeeded in having him murdered.

III: Gaius Gracchus

WHEN HIS BROTHER was assassinated in 132, Gaius Gracchus decided it was best to make himself inconspicuous for a while. The Agrarian Commission carried on for three years with a substitute appointed to take the place of Tiberius. Then it just petered out, and the whole reform movement seemed to have come to nothing.

In 123 B.C., Gaius was elected a tribune, and he decided to carry on with his brother's agrarian project. He saw, however, that the power of the Senate must be broken in order to achieve these reforms, and he proposed a series of laws to that end. Recalling the Marcus Octavius situation, he first suggested that any official discharged by the people should never again be permitted to hold public office. He suggested further that no Roman might be banished by a magistrate without legal trial; that no one could be compelled to serve in the army until seventeen years of age; that soldiers should be clothed at the cost of the state; that the public lands were to be distributed among the poor citizens; and he proposed many other laws tending to increase the safety and power of the plebeians and to cut down the strength of the Senate. One of the most important of these measures, all of which were enacted, was the opening of the panels of judges to persons of equite rank—previously all judges had been patricians.

The one regrettable measure instituted by Gaius was the creation of a relief system, to take care of the impoverished Roman masses. He intended this as a temporary expedient, and his humanitarian motive was praiseworthy, but the dole, once created, remained with Rome for good. It was a palliative, not a cure for the social ills, and its unhappy results were twofold. The very existence of the dole retarded the reform movement, for the people were reasonably content as long as they got free subsistence. Also, the dole became a political football, and many a rascally politician ingratiated himself with the people by distributing corn.

Gaius went ahead with the agrarian reform, but he failed to be re-elected as a tribune just when he was getting well under way. The capitalists had been as much enraged by Gaius's measures as they had by his elder brother's, and they were anxiously awaiting an opportunity to stop all this "radicalism." Therefore, when Gaius lost his office as a tribune, the Senate ordered his arrest. Gaius was slain in a riot which followed this decree, and so ended the democratic "revolt of the Gracchi."

But others picked up where the Gracchi had left off. Another democratic revolt broke out ten years after the death of Gaius Gracchus, led by Gaius Marius, an illiterate man of humble birth who came to power as the result of a scandal over a Roman military defeat in Numidia which was investigated by the Senate about as the United States Congress investigated Pearl Harbor. Marius led a new campaign into Numidia and restored Roman prestige by a victory. Upon his return, he plunged into domestic politics, and his hatred of the patricians made him follow somewhat the Gracchi pattern of reform. But L. Cornelius Sulla, another able general, succeeded Marius as virtual dictator of Rome and undid all that Marius had started. Then the political wheel took another turn, and Pompey the Great drove the state in a liberal direction again. But the best known of the Gracchi imitators was Julius Caesar, who adopted many planks from their program, including an extension of the right to vote, an allocation of farms to the poor, and a general democratization of the government.

CHAPTER 9

Cicero

"Law is nothing else but right reason, calling us imperiously to our duty, and prohibiting every violation of it." CICERO: ORATIONES PHILIPPICAE

I: How the Roman Law Factory Worked

THE IRRITATED American citizen will sometimes cry out: "There are too damned many laws in our country." But when he sees something happen which seems unjust and there is no redress for it, he is likely to cry, with equal anguish: "There ought to be a law." So it is all a matter of whose shoe the foot pinches. Each of us is in several minorities, but we are all in the majority as to most things which require, or seem to require, regulation by law. A certain amount of bargaining and dealing between groups, each having its own selfish interests, produces some pork-barrel legislation, it is true, but it also acts to temper the severity of what might otherwise be extreme majority action against minorities.

It is through legislation that we do most of our current reforming, and that is the quickest and most direct way to change the laws in a democracy. The Romans used this method occasionally, and *leges* (laws) were enacted by an Assembly with the consent of the Senate, or *plebiscites* by an Assembly alone, but the fact is that the magnificent structure of Roman law was built without benefit of much legislation. There were a number of other methods by which changes were made in the law or by which new rules of law were added. One of them was by way of the *senatus consulta* (senatorial decrees). These were in no sense laws in themselves, but, in those periods when the Senate happened to be powerful, its recommendations to a magistrate as to how he should conduct his office or interpret the law were usually adopted.

But a far greater body of law was made by the magistrates themselves. In sending a case to a judge for trial, a magistrate might have to decide whether some rule or law applied to the facts in the particular litigation. In doing this, he had to interpret the law, and he sometimes amplified, restricted, or extended it. Then, if other magistrates followed this precedent, the interpretation eventually became just as firmly established as the original law.

One reason we have so many lawsuits in our own courts is that a rule of law is rarely complete to the last detail. There may be seven decided cases which have determined how seven separate sets of facts fit into a particular rule of law. Yet an eighth set of facts, slightly different, may come along, and we then do not know how the rule of law would apply to this new set of facts until a judge interprets the rule all over again. It might be useful if our judges could issue decrees from time to time stating just how they would interpret rules of law if certain kinds of facts were to be brought before them, but our law is so massive and intricate that such a procedure would be quite impractical. It was not impractical, however, in Rome, where the laws administered by the early praetors or chief magistrates were comparatively simple. Thus these magistrates did get into the custom of stating in advance of their annual term of office how they would interpret the law. There came to be a system about it, each successive magistrate usually basing his interpretative *edict* on those of his predecessors, perhaps adding some innovations of his own. So the law grew by this pyramiding process.

There was one further method of creating law. When the priests lost their monopoly of expounding the law, there gradually developed a corps of lawyers and professors of law. Many were practicing lawyers who gave advice to clients, but without fee, for it was considered improper to receive fees from clients—they got their emoluments by indirect methods. Others were just wise men of the law whose studied opinions gave them such reputations that the magistrates could not well ignore their opinions. The magistrates themselves were frequently men of no legal training and anxious to have guidance from experts.

The opinions of such experts were known as *responsa prudentum*, or "answers of the learned in the law," and they had a peculiar character. The jurists who gave these opinions used the same kind of rationalization which the Jewish sages used in interpreting the laws of the Pentateuch. They would never admit that they were suggesting any change in the law or any variance from it. They fitted old rules of law, somehow, to new sets of facts, using every trick of rationalization to find a proper answer to a problem without seeming to make new law. Then another form of pyramiding took place. A change actually effected by such an opinion would be accepted by other jurists as a new premise for further rationalization; and thus opinions were built on opinions, and the law grew without anyone's claiming or admitting that anything new had been added. This was the way in which, so much later, the common law grew in the English system, and it was a healthy method of growth.

The jurists made the law more flexible. In doing so, they recognized that the *ius civile* (the civil law) was really only a translation of custom into law, and, therefore, however rigid it might seem to be, it was necessary to fit it to change, as the customs and institutions of society changed. New principles of law, established by these intelligent rationalizations of the Roman jurists, often found themselves included, sooner or later, in a praetorial edict; and, once there, they were generally firmly fixed in the law.

The work of the jurists was made easier by the fact that the statute law itself was brief and concise and left ample room for interpretation. So they interpreted and stretched, using the dialectic which they had learned from the Greek philosophers such as Socrates, Plato, and Aristotle; they treated the law as a living thing, requiring constant re-examination and restudy in the light of changing sets of facts.

Eventually, however, the responses of the jurists began to lose their virility; they grew stale, stuffy, and compendious. Much effort was given merely to collecting and arranging the existing law. It became apparent that a further advance in legal principles and institutions would have to come through means other than the originality of the jurists. Reform was then frequently accomplished much more certainly and quickly through legislation, such as the group of laws known as the *Leges Corneliae*, of which L. Cornelius Sulla was the author or sponsor. Finally, the Emperor Augustus limited the number of *jurisconsults* who were entitled to give responses, and thus limited the response system.

Many of the early jurists who made law through their *responsa* deserve places in the legal hall of fame, and among them were several members of the remarkable Scaevola family. Publius Mucius Scaevola, a *pontifex*, was a lawyer and jurist of note. His son, Quintus Mucius Scaevola, was the most famous of the family. He was an adherent of the Stoic school of philosophy, and in his voluminous writings he injected into Roman jurisprudence large parts of the Aristotelian concept of natural law which the Stoics had adopted from the Greek philosopher. It was from an uncle of Quintus, with the same name, that Marcus Tullius Cicero, the greatest of the Roman lawyers and a jurist of eminence, learned much of his law and absorbed much liberal philosophy.

II: Cicero the Lawyer

PLINY describes certain Roman lawyers walking hurriedly through the streets with piles of documents in their hands, their fingers covered with rings and a hired claque of applauders following them so that the public might be impressed by their importance and seek to hire them. They were the ambulance chasers of the Roman bar, and there were plenty of them, for anyone could hold himself out to be a lawyer. But the Roman lawyers were not all like that. Many were men who would have held their own with the best of our day and perhaps surpassed them. In cross-examination these men were often astoundingly astute and effective, and they prepared their cases with care. Perhaps no Roman lawyer ever exceeded Cicero in these characteristics, and what made him superlative, indeed, was his capacity as an orator; for oratory was far more important in trials than it is now. You can picture Cicero standing on a little dais in the Forum arguing an important case, with thousands below listening to him pluck at all the strings of his seductive oratorical harp, feeling the temper of the crowd, molding it to his purposes, and using it as a moral support for his case.

The first case which brought him to public attention was *The State versus Sextus Roscius*, in which Cicero defended a young man who had been unjustly accused of having murdered his own father. It was a case which took courage to handle, because the complainant was a pet of Sulla, the dictator, and the defendant's father had been Sulla's enemy. The deceased's estate had been sold for a small sum of money to Lucius Chrysogonus, a friend of the dictator's, and, when young Sextus dared to criticize the sale, Chrysogonus, sure that Sulla would stand behind him, caused Sextus to be accused and tried for his father's murder. It may have been that Cicero trembled in his boots when he began his oration at the trial, but he gathered his courage together and, in a masterpiece of pleading, careful to absolve Sulla of any possible implication of guilt, laid on to Chrysogonus heavily, proving by inference that the complainant himself had been guilty of the murder. He secured the acquittal of Sextus, perhaps because the public, listening to his brilliant oratory, was so well convinced that Cicero's cause was right.

But it became apparent to friends of Cicero that he had gone too far and that Sulla was angered at this young upstart. After winning another case which chalked up another black mark against him on Sulla's ledger, he journeyed to Greece, where he consorted with philosophers and writers and added much to his learning and understanding. On his return he entered politics, in which he rose rapidly to prominence, but continued with his career as a lawyer. In 70 B.C. he represented the people of Sicily in a famous case which added greatly to his stature. It was not unusual for a Roman governor to enrich himself in the provinces by all sorts of chicanery and venality, but Verres, the Governor of Sicily, had gone beyond what even Romans took for granted as a governor's privilege. That the people of Sicily prosecuted him for his malfeasance in office indicates that he must have been extraordinarily avaricious. Cicero prepared his case with unusual care and presented the facts with such forcefulness, and accompanied by such persuasive oratorial fireworks, that Verres was doomed. From this time on, Cicero was recognized as the ablest lawyer in Rome, and whenever he had a case to argue in the Forum there was a crowd waiting there to listen to his entertaining brilliance.

In 66 B.C., Cicero was elected a praetor, but his political ambitions were not to be satisfied with even this high office. It seemed to him that association with Pompey offered the greatest hope for advancement, so he joined political forces with him and was rewarded with election as consul in 63. During his term of office his most noteworthy service to the state was his destruction of the conspiracy of Catiline, and his orations against that conspirator are among the treasures of Roman literature. For these services Cicero was hailed by the people as *parens patriae*, or "father of his country," but he did not hold on to the favor of Rome very long. His proceedings against some of Catiline's accomplices had been quite irregular, and there was some danger that he might be prosecuted for these irregularities after the end of his term of office as consul, so he exiled himself for five years.

On his return to Rome he might have lived out his life usefully and died in bed, but these were difficult times for politicians—the political parties were changing so rapidly—and Cicero's political judgment in his last years was most unfortunate, or else his luck was bad. In the strife between Pompey and Caesar, he took the side of the former and made Caesar his enemy. After Caesar's assassination, Cicero again might have repaired his fortunes. He did select what turned out to be the winning side in the struggle for Caesar's mantle, but in siding with Octavian he made an enemy of Mark Antony. It was more than Cicero could anticipate that Octavian would sit calmly by while Antony's supporters wrought murderous vengeance on poor Cicero for having been their leader's enemy.

In his political career he was not so sagacious as in the practice of the law, but his reputation stands as a lawyer of most unusual talents. He was hailed in his own time as the leader of the Roman bar, and he is respected by posterity as one of the greatest lawyers of all time. Can our modern trial lawyers end a summary to the jury any better than Cicero did, in defending Titus Annius Milo, who had killed Clodius in a quarrel?—

"Shall this man, born for his country, die in any other land except his country's? or, as it may perchance turn out, for his country? Will you preserve the monuments of this man's courage, and yet allow no sepulcher containing his body to exist in Italy? Will anyone by his vote banish this man from this city, when all other cities will gladly invite him to them if he is driven out from among you? Oh, happy will that land be which shall receive him! Ungrateful will this land be if it banishes him; miserable if it loses him.

"However, I must make an end. Nor, indeed, can I speak any longer for weeping; and this man forbids me to defend him by tears. I pray and entreat you, O judges, when you are giving your votes, to dare to decide as you think just. And, believe me, [Pompey] will be sure greatly to approve of your virtue, and justice, and good faith; who, in selecting the judges, selected all the best, and wisest, and most fearless men whom he could find."

III: Cicero the Jurist

It is not as a lawyer, however, that Cicero has had his most important influence on subsequent generations of lawyers. He was a jurist and a philosopher in the law, and his writings on legal subjects have been of utmost importance. His approach was Stoic or Platonic, for he wrote of an ideal system of law. Into his system he brought much of the Greek philosophy which he had acquired in his years of study and travel in Greece and the theories he had learned from his law professor, Scaevola. His system of law was never adopted or emulated, but his theses affected subsequent Roman and European legal thinkers to an extent that is difficult to overestimate. They were prompted by his writings to think more constructively, and not merely to accept previously existing rules as "divine" or "natural."

Cicero was not only a philosopher in the law but is given credit for discovering or promoting several important legal innovations. Among these was the importance of determining "intention," in contracts and in torts. In primitive systems a contract was taken at its face value and interpreted within its four corners. New areas of judicial lawmaking opened up when men began to ask themselves: "What was the intention of the parties in making this agreement?" Cicero was probably not the first to have asked that question, but he brought into prominence this new approach to the interpretation of the wording of agreements. Similarly, in primitive societies a man was held to responsibility for an act, regardless of how he came to commit it. Cicero applied the element of intention to torts also, with the result of an intelligent expansion and elaboration of the law of personal injuries. We do not now ordinarily hold a man so responsible for an unintended act as for one which he did willfully. Before Cicero's time the distinction was by no means clear. And in the same area of law, Cicero insisted on another principle which we accept readily but which was obscure before his time: that a distinction must be made between penalties and damages—that a man must sometimes be held to damages for his acts but not necessarily be punished for them.

Cicero's great affection for the Greek dialecticians and rhetoricians reflected itself in his writings; and, through his writings, he brought these Greek philosophic influences to bear upon the reasoning of later Roman legal lights. It was largely through him that the concept of "natural law" came into the thinking of Roman jurists.

CHAPTER 10

Augustus

"The obscure name of Octavianus he derived from a mean family in the little town of Aricia. . . . The illustrious surname of Caesar he had assumed as the adopted son of the dictator. . . . It was proposed in the Senate, to dignify their minister with a new appellation: and after a very serious discussion, that of Augustus was chosen, among several others, as being the most expressive of the character of peace and sanctity, which he uniformly affected."

GIBBON: DECLINE AND FALL OF THE ROMAN EMPIRE

I: The Reformer

THE EMPEROR AUGUSTUS, absolute ruler of the entire Western civilized world, sat unhappily in his study. His digestion bothered him, but that was something he was used to, for he had been ailing for years, and though he was to reach an advanced age, he was an old man at thirty-five. What bothered him far more was the moral condition of the Roman people. The sturdy old patrician families had degenerated and were producing few children, and those who did now carry on the fine old names spent their time in carousing and elaborate dissipation. Drinking, extravagance, prostitution, perversion, and gambling were the rule with aristocratic young Romans, and any attention to the serious side of life was the exception. Augustus realized that if no stop were put to the rapidly increasing social degeneration, the Roman Empire would decline and fall.

Augustus made up his mind to bring the people back to their senses. The good example which he and his wife and a few other conservatives had set had accomplished nothing, so he determined to legislate vice out of existence. He devised the so-called *Julian Laws,* which limited extravagance and the luxuries to which people of means were addicted, and provided that weddings, which had recently become scandalous displays, must now be modest and moderate. They also provided that women could no longer go about as freely as had become the custom—they were now permitted to go to some of the public games only if they were properly chaperoned.

And, of course, something had to be done about adultery, so the Julian Laws established public trials for any woman caught in adultery. Illicit sex relations had become so prevalent that many saw no point in marriage. The laws therefore directed that all men under sixty and all women under fifty must be married, the penalties for not marrying being that unmarried persons within these ages could not inherit from anyone outside their own families, and that such unmarried women could not go to any public games. If a woman did not remarry within six months after the death of her husband or after a divorce, she was to be punished. And no aristocrat was to be permitted to marry an actress, a freedwoman, or a prostitute, nor could any daughter of a senator marry an actor or a freedman.

In order to give some incentive to reform, Augustus's laws provided rewards for producing children. The taxes on a woman's property were to be decreased with each child she produced. After the third, she paid no taxes at all, and her property was freed from the control of her husband. If two men sought the same job, the one with the more children would get it.

That is a rough summary of the laws which Augustus caused to be enacted in his fight against the decadence of Rome. But he discovered that you cannot legislate people into morality; Augustus's attempt was a complete failure. A situation similar to that arose in the United States during the Prohibition era. What the Romans could not do openly, they did surreptitiously. And they became peculiarly adept at finding ways in which to evade some of the particularly restrictive Julian Laws.

But he was not a failure in other directions. He saved the state from anarchy. The last "democratic" movement in Rome had been led by Julius Caesar, who, despite his personal ambition, certainly was democratic in his political point of view. But the cause of democracy was a losing one. Democracy could not be applied effectively in so heterogeneous an empire, and the constant internal disorders made it inevitable that dictatorship would result. There are indications that Octavian (Augustus) did not actually want all the power that was given to him, but it seemed evident that Rome was due for monarchy and that Octavian was the man who could bring peace. When he had finally defeated his rival Antony, in the squabble which followed Caesar's death, Octavian, then the sole master of the state, had received honor after honor from the Senate, including the title of "Augustus" by which we know him. He was given imperial status, which had been denied to Caesar, and he ruled as a dictator, though cleverly insistent on retaining all the old forms of the democracy. His has been called the Golden Age, and it was an era of peace and prosperity for the whole Mediterranean world. Rome itself was largely rebuilt and beautified, and the grandeur of the Empire was something to behold. What would have happened to Rome if a man of Octavian's caliber had not attained dictatorial power is difficult to guess. He must be given credit for having governed with considerable wisdom, and for having welded a lot of dissident elements into one powerful state.

Augustus left no child to succeed him, and selected Tiberius to take his place. Tiberius was not the most desirable choice, but not a bad one either. However, on his death came a succession of three pitiful emperors. First there was Gaius, known as Caligula or "Little Boots," mad and vicious; then came Claudius, who deserves some sympathy for his frailties but not much respect; and finally Nero, as ludicrous as he was villainous. With Nero, Rome had had enough of the royal family, and the army stepped in to elect General Galba, in A.D. 68.

II: The Changes Under Augustus

THE ROMAN LAW had grown with great vigor because the jurists had been able to express their opinions freely and thus to assist in the widened application of laws. But Augustus concluded that there were so many jurists in Rome, uttering so many conflicting opinions, that one often could not get a clear idea of what the law meant. This uncertainty was distasteful to Augustus. Moreover, it is probable that he desired to create a means for permitting himself to exert a more direct influence on the interpretation and development of the law. He decided to limit the number of jurists whose opinions could be offered to the courts. He licensed these selected jurists to give opinions *ex auctoritate sua*, or with imperial authority, so that they really spoke as the mouthpiece of the Emperor. That made for clarity and helped undo a lot of confusion, but it may have slowed the progress of the law for the moment.

Two of the first jurists to be licensed were Marcus Antistus Labeo and Gaius Aetius Capito; and these two founded rival schools of legal interpretation (the "Proculian" and the "Sabinian"), each of which had a large following of eminent men. The influence of these schools of law lasted for about two hundred years and greatly stimulated the study of law. There were many other law schools also, even in distant parts of the Empire, and many independent legal thinkers who adhered to neither of the great schools.

These new jurists did much to clarify and improve the old laws, but they had little opportunity to create new law. The lawmaking function passed almost entirely into the hands of the Emperor. He had given the state a somewhat Oriental character, though he had maintained the form of the Roman Republic. In one way or another he combined all the important functions of government in himself, and he did it, for the most part, not by assuming such functions arbitrarily but by assuming the offices which carried the functions with them. When he was all through with his clever indirect aggregation of power to himself, the Roman government looked about the same as it had for centuries. But the extent of his power might be illustrated by comparing his government to a cabinet government in which the President is also the Secretary of State, Secretary of War, Secretary of everything else, Chief Justice of the Supreme Court, and the legislature. He was even made head of the state religion, as *pontifex maximus*, and was virtually deified. His word was law, and his law was almost theocratic.

CHAPTER 11

Hadrian and Julian

"His vast and active genius was equally suited to the most enlarged views, and the minute details of civil policy."

GIBBON, ON HADRIAN, IN DECLINE AND FALL OF THE ROMAN EMPIRE

I: Hadrian

PUBLIUS AELIUS HADRIANUS ascended the imperial Roman throne in A.D. 117. Gibbon says he was, "by turns, an excellent prince, a ridiculous sophist, and a jealous tyrant." Nevertheless, he compares more than favorably with most Roman emperors. Gibbon also says that Hadrian "encouraged the arts, reformed the laws, asserted military discipline, and visited all his provinces in person." This last item of credit which Gibbon accords him was an extraordinary performance. Roman emperors were all too prone to sit in luxury in the capital or in some magnificent villa by the sea while the administration of the provinces was left to the caprice of delegated lieutenants. Hadrian braved the hot winds of the desert and the snows of the north, caring nothing for his own comfort, and traveling perhaps thousands of miles by foot to examine the administration of his Empire at first hand and to institute such improvements in the field as his observations might determine.

In 121, four years after his accession, he started on a five-year inspection tour which took him through Gaul, Spain, England, Mauretania, Asia Minor, Greece, the Greek islands, and Sicily, before he returned to Rome. After a short stay, he visited Africa, then Greece again, Asia Minor, Arabia, Syria and Palestine, and Egypt. Wherever he went he examined and studied and reformed. One of his most interesting reforms was the nationalization of the postal service. Rome had no other emperor like him, in the extent to which he sacrificed his own comfort to the end of perfecting the efficiency of government. It is no wonder that, as Gibbon admits, "The Empire flourished in peace and prosperity" during his reign.

Hadrian's interest in the law was constant and active. Many reforms are attributed to him, among them one which seems odd today but was logical enough in his age. He made it a crime falsely to accuse anyone of being a Christian. In Hadrian's day Christians were still persecuted for their religious beliefs, and Christians were considered enemies of the state. Hadrian's law might, therefore, be compared to the current American rule of law that it is a slander falsely to accuse another of being a Communist.

The Emperor busied himself considerably with the substantive law, but he was also intensely interested in the operation of the courts themselves. He himself was the Roman Supreme Court, he sat long and often to do justice, and he insisted on just administration in the lower courts. It is said that he almost always took the part of the lowly against the great and the poor against the rich. But his most intense interest in matters of law was his concern over the confusion which lawyers and jurists found in the vast accumulated and unco-ordinated body of magistrate-made law.

As life changed and Roman society grew more complex, Roman laws became more detailed and involved. A steady stream of magistrate-made law had poured out over the centuries, to which was added the enormous volume of opinion of the jurists. As the Roman mind struggled constantly for orderliness, many attempts were made to codify and organize the great and growing body of the law; and from this instinct for orderliness came a mass of commentaries and other attempts—largely unsuccessful—to co-ordinate the law. The confusion persisted; indeed, it was not completely settled until codification under the Emperor Justinian, who ascended the throne in A.D. 518.

But Hadrian is responsible for making order in one branch of the law, the praetorian law or, as we call it, "equity."

II: Equity

EQUITY is a vital part of our own legal system, and we have the Romans to thank for having laid a broad groundwork for our own equitable principles. An understanding of the nature of this branch of the Roman law requires a review of its history.

In the United States the same law is applied to aliens as to citizens. Aliens cannot vote and are denied a few other privileges; but their rights are the same as any citizen's. That was not so in Rome. There were two kinds of law. There was, to begin with, the *ius civile*, or civil law, which applied to citizens only; aliens had no rights under it. A distinction later came into existence between hostile aliens (*hostes*) and friendly aliens (*peregrini*). The *peregrini* were permitted to use the customs of their own nations or tribes to some extent, and some of them even came under the special legal protection of patricians and were called *clientes*.

But all roads led to Rome, foreigners jammed into the city, and the problem of how to treat these new *peregrini* under the law was a pressing one. What would happen if there were a dispute between two aliens of different nationality? Or one between an alien and a Roman citizen? These problems had to be solved, and they could not be solved by applying the civil law to the *peregrini*. For one thing, the old legal forms were still entangled with religious practices, and the *peregrini*, who did not subscribe to the Roman religion, could not take part in the religious ceremonies.

No legal problem, or any problem of administration, could stump the Romans long, and they found a way out of the apparent impasse. They appointed a new kind of praetor or magistrate and called him the *praetor peregrinus* to distinguish him from the ordinary urban magistrate who administered the civil law. This new magistrate determined the law applying when aliens were involved and the civil law could not be used. He applied what he called the *ius gentium*, the "law of foreigners."* It was also referred to as the "law of nations," but this last term is misleading, for it had no relation to international law. It was the law which the praetor supposed was common to all or most of the nations, general principles of law which were almost universal. That gave him a good deal of leeway in building up a system of law for the *peregrini*.

He had still further leeway when the concept of "natural law" came in from Greece, by way of Cicero and other Romans who actively propounded the theory. Once he could conjure with a *ius naturale*, there was almost no limit to the magistrate's ability to find law to fit situations. Unfortunately, the frequent Roman use of the term *ius naturale* as synonymous with *ius gentium* resulted in a

* This should not be confused with *ius gentilitatis*, the law of the clans and the ancestor of the *ius civile* or civil law.

good deal of confusion among later jurists. Obviously, some rule could be part of the *ius gentium* in the sense of being a universal custom, without being "natural law." For example, slavery was a universal custom in Roman times, yet it is difficult to believe that many jurists would have contended that it was an institution countenanced by natural law.

But all such reasoning with a "law of nations" and a "natural law" was just rationalizing. The *praetor peregrinus* attempted to do what we call "equity." He reasoned by whatever means he could to find a fair result. The Roman word *aequitas*, from which we derive "equity," had the meaning "reasonableness," and the *praetor peregrinus*, not being bound by any single code of law, was free to be reasonable as he saw it. He looked around him and took over many rules of law which he found in use elsewhere. In commercial cases, for example, he found that there were all sorts of general customs of the trades, which he recognized as having legal validity because of their universality. The English judges, many centuries later, applied this same principle in taking over commercial customs as part of the "law merchant."

We are not certain of the relationship of the *ius gentium* and the *praetor peregrinus*. But what we believe may have happened was that the *ius gentium*, at first applied only to foreigners, turned out to be more flexible and useful than the old civil law to which the citizens were subjected, so the idea began to spread that the *praetor peregrinus* was restoring the law to some imagined, pristine ideal. Then the urban magistrates, who had been confined to the civil law, began to introduce ideas and concepts from the *ius gentium* into their own work, thus rescuing the civil law from its former rigidity, and, once this process had started, it was impossible to keep it in check. In time the *ius gentium* came to be applied as much to citizens as to foreigners. There were now two sets of laws, side by side, the civil law and the *ius gentium*. The latter stepped in when justice was required to "do equity," just as, in our own law, equity steps in when the law itself is too harsh or is inadequate to do justice.

The impact of the practices of the *praetor peregrinus* on the civil law was felt first in procedural law. To understand what happened one must realize that the praetors, as magistrates, were only preliminary judges. We have somewhat the same thing in our own criminal procedure in a magistrate's court, where the magistrate will consider what is brought before him and decide whether or not to hold the accused man for trial by a higher criminal court. Similarly, the Roman magistrate heard the parties to a proposed civil action, and then decided whether one of them had an action which could be tried. The original actions were the *legis actiones* already discussed, but they were few in number and hedged with restrictions and formalities. The procedure before the *praetor peregrinus* was far different. Not bound by the strict rules and formalities of the civil law, he developed what was called the "formula." This was a very informal way of getting cases placed before judges. The *praetor peregrinus* would hear the parties; there were no written procedures but only oral pleadings. He would then prepare in writing a formula which would present the case to the trial judge, the *iudex*. The plaintiff did not have to comply with any ritual or make any set gestures or recite any fixed language, as was the case with the *legis actiones*. If the *praetor peregrinus* thought the applicant had a case based on the abstract principles of justice which he administered, or based upon the edict which he had published in advance of office, he issued a formula.

The common formula was simple. It named the judge who was to try the case; it included the statement of facts; it recited the issues to be determined by the judge; any technical defenses and special pleas were named; and, finally, it told the judge what judgment he was to give if he found certain facts to be true. Then the parties proceeded to the judge, who tried the case. Examples of such formulas are given by various Roman writers, and they usually use their own forms of "John Doe" and "Richard Roe." Their most usual fictitious characters were Aulus Agerius, or "AA," and Numerius Negidus, or "NN."

Here is an illustration of the recitation of issues in a formula. In the case of the dispute over the cat discussed in the section on the *legis actiones* (see page 98), under the formulary procedure the magistrate might have instructed the judge: "If you find that Joe originally owned this cat, and that Henry unjustly took possession of it, then decide for Joe. But if you find that Joe did not originally own the cat, or that it was rightfully taken by Henry, then decide for Henry."

The formula was so simple a procedure compared with that of the *legis actiones* that the urban praetors came gradually to use it themselves, and it became employed almost to the exclusion of the *legis actiones*. In fact, by the time of Caesar or Augustus, the formula became by law the only method of procedure available, the old *legis actiones* being dropped entirely. Thus, the procedure of the *praetor peregrinus* finally supplanted that of the urban praetor, and the *ius gentium* was wholly free to be applied to Romans as well as foreigners.

Great numbers of Romans made themselves reasonably familiar with the rudiments of law. It was almost a necessity for senators and those who expected to enter public life. However, legal training or experience was not required for any office; and often neither the magistrate, before whom an action at law first came on summons, nor the judge, who eventually tried the issues, knew any law at all. To guide him the magistrate had his *edict*, which he had prepared on the basis of his predecessor's. The judge had no such precise guidance as an edict, and he had to be particularly careful, for he was held responsible for making improper decisions. Naturally, the judge took advice from jurists in order to be certain that he would not get himself tangled up.

At this state in the development of Roman procedure, there was no appeal from a judgment. The only recourse which an injured litigant had was against the judge who rendered an improper decision.

When it came to enforcing the judgment rendered, the successful party had to start an entirely new action before the magistrate to get an order to execute the judgment on either the person or the property of the judgment-debtor. Personal attachments* were frequent, but a judgment-debtor could usually avoid an attachment of his person by making an assignment of his property for the benefit of creditors, a procedure somewhat like our bankruptcy proceeding. Attachments of property resulted in a public auction of the property attached.

Somewhere along the line the praetors began to use *fictions* to give relief or to do equity, and here is one way they did it. Suppose AA was the heir of his brother and thus entitled to his brother's property. But suppose that he had not yet qualified properly as the legal heir, and in the meantime NN had run off with the deceased's slave. If the magistrate had followed the strict letter of the law, he

* "Attachment" is the taking into custody of a person or his property for the purpose of holding him or it as security for the payment of a judgment, or, in the case of property, of selling it to satisfy the judgment. In our system a sheriff or marshal takes custody. In Rome it was the judgment-creditor, the successful litigant, who did the attaching.

could not have given AA any relief, for he was not yet his brother's legal heir and thus could not bring an action against the taker of the slave. But the magistrate, knowing that AA was really his brother's heir, would stretch his powers in presenting the case to a judge. In his formula he would direct the judge to hold that the property belonged to AA *if* the judge found AA entitled to the property *if* he were his brother's heir. That was using a fiction in order to do equitable justice.

By this method, new rights and new remedies were invented. Persons who were "equitably entitled" to property received it, though the law on its face did not recognize any rights but those of the "legal owner." An example of an equitable claimant might be someone to whom the property had been pledged as security for a debt and who had lost immediate possession of it. The praetor would instruct the *iudex* to find that it should be given to the claimant *if* he would have been entitled to it, in the circumstances, *if* he had been the legal owner.

Gradually, through the use of fictions, by frank stretching, or even by changing the principles of the formula, the praetors, assisted by the opinions of jurists, were able to make what had originally been formal and restrictive law fit almost all the intricate legal situations to be encountered in the increasingly expanding Roman Empire.

The *interdict,* in a limited way somewhat similar to our injunction, was a useful invention, devised after the legal system was freed from the old rigidity. It was used as an order to leave things *in statu quo* until the issues in dispute could be determined. It was actually the commencement of an action. In one sense our injunction is the last historic development in the treatment of wrongs. First there was self-help, then social justice; now there was something new—an effort to prevent wrongdoing instead of merely punishing it or giving damages for it.

The formulary system did not last through all the history of Roman jurisprudence. It was supplanted in Hadrian's time by a new legal process called the *cognitio,* from the term *causa cognitio,* "after investigation." Just as the *legis actiones* had given way to the formula system, so the latter gave way to this new system which was even less restricted by form and formality. The praetors simply investigated the circumstances and stated a relief according to law or current theory, without confining themselves to a formula. A trial system resulted which is much closer to that which we know in modern times. The *iudex* continued to be part of the process, though no longer as a dignified judge but only as a minor official, almost as a clerk. Written pleadings were submitted, and time was given to formulate answers and replies. Furthermore, a system of appeals was created: from a magistrate to a higher magistrate, and from him to an official called the praetorian prefect. The appeal could go no higher, except to the emperor himself if he gave permission. This is similar to our right to go to the Supreme Court of the United States on *certiorari* proceedings—that is, with the Court's own permission in instances where it deems the final appeal permissible.

While these developments were taking place, "equity" came gradually to be merged in law, which meant that the law took over the *ius gentium*. And with time the general concept of the *ius gentium* approached even more closely to a concept of "natural law" as the Stoics conceived it. That is, to find a basis for their own decisions, the praetors no longer had to seek out rules of law applied by the civilized world in general—they merely did what seemed to them to be dictated by "natural law."

III: Julian

THE EDICTS by which the praetors had announced their versions of the law had become extremely voluminous as the law grew, and the application of the *ius gentium* and the *ius naturale* to the civil law had made room for much difference and doubt, and had led to uncertainty and conflicts of opinion. So, as the edicts had become unwieldy and often unsatisfactory, the Emperor Hadrian created a legal reform commission to codify and fix the praetorian edict once and forever. As chairman of the commission he selected one Salvius Julianus. Julian was an African by birth; beyond that we know little about him. He had been a legal adviser to the Emperor, and his work was so valuable that the Senate awarded him twice the usual salary for that job. We know also that he was the head of the Sabinian school of law and that his *Digesta* of ninety volumes was a systematic arrangement of the entire civil and praetorian law—a monumental work.

Julian and his fellow commissioners attacked the enormous body of praetorian law, now including the *ius gentium*, and studied it piece by piece, rejecting and refining and producing a complete praetorian code which was to fix this branch of law beyond any further doubt as to what it comprised and how it might be interpreted. When they had finished their work and produced the *Perpetual Edict,* that spelled the end of lawmaking by the praetors. It did not, however, completely stop the development of the law, for jurists and legal writers continued to amplify or interpret the rules stated in the Perpetual Edict of Julianus. Finally, in the reign of Alexander Severus (222-235) the last growth of equity through this process ceased; thereafter the law grew only through imperial statutes or revisions, and equity as a living and growing principle of Roman law ceased to be.

CHAPTER 12

The Big Five and the Roman Law

"Justice is the constant and perpetual will to allot to every man his due." ULPIAN

I: Gaius

ONE DAY, in the early Middle Ages, a young monk sat disconsolately at his bare table. He had a fervent desire to make a copy of the letters of St. Jerome—a highly creditable undertaking—but he had no parchment to write on. Suddenly he recalled some old sheets of manuscript lying in the corner of the library. They had been cast aside because the old Latin writing with which they were covered seemed of no consequence, but had not been thrown away because old manuscripts were sometimes written over, if one had the energy to prepare them for it. So the young monk ran to the library, bundled the sheets in his arms, and took them back to his cell. With a knife, some soap and water, some sand and a bleaching agent, he began to scrape, and wash, and sand, and scrub, and finally he had erased enough so that he could go forward with his cherished undertaking and spread the word of the wise St. Jerome.

Fortunately, however, the good monk had forgotten one sheet of the old manuscript, which remained by itself for centuries, its original writing undisturbed. For this leaf was discovered at Verona in 1740 by Scipio Maffei, an Italian scholar and author, who recognized it as a legal manuscript, decided that it was part of some commentary on Justinian's *Institutes*, and published a translation of it into Italian. He knew of the St. Jerome manuscript, which had been preserved over the intervening years, and he knew that it was a *codex rescriptus* or palimpsest, a written-over manuscript; but he saw no connection between it and the single leaf which he had translated. It was left to another scholar, one Haubold, to discover that the single leaf was not part of a commentary on the *Institutes of Justinian* but an older work by Gaius, one of the greatest of the Roman jurists and teachers.

In the same year Barthold Georg Niebuhr, the Prussian Ambassador to the Pope and a famous student of Roman history, spent a few days in the library at Verona on his way to Rome. He examined the St. Jerome palimpsest and, suspecting that something of interest lay under the overwriting, obtained permission to infuse nutgall into one of the pages to bring out the underwriting. Niebuhr, who was a historian and an expert on old manuscripts, recognized it as part of a commentary on Roman law and sent his results to von Savigny, the leading German jurist of that day. Von Savigny identified the underwriting immediately as a work of Gaius, and his conclusion was found to be correct when, after careful and laborious treatment, the entire palimpsest was restored. What the eager young monk of the Middle Ages had written over was the only copy which has ever been discovered of the *Institutes of Gaius,* one of the most important legal works of all time.

Almost nothing is known about Gaius himself. It is believed that he lived in the second century under three emperors, Hadrian, Antoninus Pius, and Marcus Aurelius, that he was born in Greece, and that Gaius was his first name—although it may have been merely a pen-name or nickname. He was a person of no eminence whatever in his own day. It is most likely that he was merely an obscure law teacher, perhaps in the provinces, but he came to be the law teacher of the Romans for centuries after his death. For three hundred years his *Institutes** was the standard textbook for law students in the Roman Empire.

This book was not an original work. Gaius did not try to make any new law or to shed any new light on legal theories. What he intended was to compile the law in such fashion that students could absorb it easily. What is remarkable about the work is its comprehensiveness, its clarity, and the orderliness with which he presented the subject. It is so well done that great parts of it would still serve as an adequate textbook in law schools today. Nor is it all dry and prosaic. Gaius knew the art of making his subject interesting, and

* Its full title was *Institutionum iuris civilis commentarii Quatuor*.

he included historical material as well as rules of law. It contains so much of value to the legal historian that it has justly been called the most important source of our knowledge of the older Roman law.

II: Papinian, Paul, Ulpian, and Modestinus

No ROMAN WRITER seems to have mentioned Gaius for two hundred years after his death, although students continued to use the *Institutes,* but in the fifth century Gaius had come into his own as a recognized authority in the courts. In A.D. 426 the Emperors Theodosius II and Valentinian III enacted a *Law of Citations* under which they provided that the opinions of only five jurists could be cited as authority in any legal matter, and Gaius was one of the big five. The other four were Papinian, Paul, Ulpian, and Modestinus.

While Gaius was admitted to these sacred ranks, he was not given quite the standing of Papinian, for the Law of Citations ruled that if the big five disagreed on any point, then the opinion of Papinian must prevail unless two of the others were against him. This ruling merely supported the general contemporary opinion that Papinian was the greatest of the Roman jurists, an opinion shared by moderns.

Aemilius Papinianus was probably born in Syria, about A.D. 146. It is astonishing how many of the most eminent Roman jurists were born in the provinces. It rather dispels the theory that some peculiarity of the Roman blood produced their astounding body of jurisprudence. Papinian studied law under Quintus Cervidius Scaevola, a contemporary of Gaius and, in contrast to the latter, eminent in his own day. Thus Papinian had the best possible legal training, and he took advantage of his opportunity; it was not long before he himself was teaching law, and he became, through his own merit, a "counsel to the fiscus," a job somewhat akin to that of Privy Purse in modern England.

In 193 his great chance came. His close friend, Septimus Severus, was elevated to the imperial throne, and the new Emperor promptly made Papinian *Magister Libellorum,* which might be translated as "Master of Petitions." It was part of his work to pass upon the petitions of commoners who wished to be raised to the status of equites, but the office had far more importance than that. The *Magister* had functions similar to those of the Chancellor of Great Britain. He was later made *Praefectus Praetorii,* or General of the Guard, a position which had long since lost its military significance; the *Praefectus* was now the assistant to the Emperor and his virtual vice-regent.

In this position, fully supported by his imperial friend and master, Papinian devoted himself to the public welfare and to the development of the law. But he might have guessed that there would be trouble after his friend's death, for the Emperor's two sons, Caracalla and Geta, were vicious young men who did not wait for their father's death to cause turmoil. The two of them, together with Papinian, accompanied their father to England, and it is said that both sons plotted the Emperor's death but were frustrated by Papinian's alertness. Severus did die in England in 211, and in accordance with his wishes the legions proclaimed his two sons joint Emperors. As they had always hated each other, and each knew the other to be thoroughly unscrupulous, they both rushed to Rome, but separately and both well guarded. In Rome they lived apart and met only in public, each with a bodyguard. Finally their mother took a hand, and Caracalla agreed to meet his brother in her presence to talk things over, whereupon, as Gibbon describes it: "In the midst of their conversation, some centurions, who had contrived to conceal themselves, rushed with drawn swords upon the unfortunate Geta. His distracted mother strove to protect him in her arms; but, in the unavailing struggle, she was wounded in the hand, and covered with the blood of her younger son, while she saw the elder animating and assisting the fury of the assassins."

This foul deed only prompted Caracalla to further excesses, and it is estimated that some twenty thousand suspected followers and supporters of Geta were then murdered by his order. Among these was Papinian. Caracalla had directed him to write an explanation and apology for the murder of Geta. Papinian refused, and Caracalla's men slew him with an ax.

Papinian's greatness cannot be set down by reference to individual opinions or any single series of acts related to the law. His greatness lay in the fact that, in his vast number of opinions and other writings, he exemplified the Roman approach to law. The Romans excelled in extracting principles from facts, and in establishing general rules instead of specific answers to particular sets of facts. Papinian was always more interested in getting to the principle than to the particularity. He was ingenious, courageous, and profound, forever searching for theory and principle and the broad rule.

Julius Paulus (Paul) was a master logician and a clever writer, his interest lying not so much in finding principles as in differentiation and subtlety. He ranks as one of the big five, but not upon the same plane as Papinian.

Domitius Ulpianus (Ulpian), however, ran close behind Papinian. He was also an Easterner, probably born in Syria. Like Papinian, he showed his merit early and, when still quite young, became an assessor in the auditorium of Papinian and a member of the Imperial Council. After Papinian's death Ulpian fared well under Caracalla, whose madness apparently did not deeply affect this jurist. He was made *Scrinorum Magister* (Master of the Records), at the same time that Paul held the job formerly occupied by Papinian, Master of Petitions; but, what is more important, he produced a gigantic volume of legal writings in this hectic period. Somehow he managed to find enough peace and quiet to do an amazingly large amount of constructive work.

The successor to Caracalla was no improvement. He was the half-mad Heliogabalus, the sun priest who had been made Emperor. He did not last long, and then came another short reign, that of Macrinus, under whom Ulpian fell into disfavor and was banished from Rome. Then, when young Alexander Severus came to the throne, Ulpian's fortunes rose again. He became the young man's confidant and intimate, and virtually his regent. But life was hazardous in those days if you were at the top of the heap—in 214 Ulpian was murdered by fanatical soldiers in the very presence of the Emperor.

Ulpian was not so original a thinker as Papinian, but his writings were remarkable for their clarity and their orderly exposition, and they had enormous influence. When a later emperor, Justinian, directed that the opinions of the great jurists be collected and coordinated, more references were made to the work of Ulpian than to any other jurist. He was the author of many legal maxims and sayings which are still in use today, and he may well be regarded as second only to Papinian.

The last of the big five was Herennius Modestinus, a pupil of Ulpian, born in Greek-speaking Dalmatia. He was the author of special treatises, and he was perhaps the last of the great original thinkers in the Roman law. From here on the story of Roman law is one of looking backward, of lack of progress. After 300 there was a sharp decline in the character and quality of Roman jurisprudence. Partly responsible for this was the shift of the center of the Empire to the Greek-Oriental East.

III: Torts and Criminal Law

IN THE TREATMENT of torts, the Romans retained a number of primitive ideas, but even some of these often have a good deal to recommend them. Today we try to satisfy for a tort by restitution when it is possible. If your neighbor takes your pig, our law makes him return it to you. When it is not possible to give restitution—that is, if the neighbor has eaten the pig—our law grants you damages. But the Romans operated on a different theory.

In the early days, when a culprit was caught red-handed, you were entitled to hold him a prisoner until he ransomed himself, and the Roman penalty for a tort probably descends from this original right of self-help. For the Roman system imposed a penalty on a tort wrongdoing. If your pig was taken, you were entitled not merely to restitution but to a penalty which would be twice, thrice, or even four times the value of the pig, depending on the circumstances of the incident. If you did not see Antonius take your pig, the penalty was only twofold. There was a wrong, but there was no danger of social conflict because you were not there and could not have started a fight. But, if you had seen the act and had resisted Antonius, then the penalty would be threefold, for there was violence. Now, if you had learned that Antonius had taken the pig, and you and a party of friends had pursued him, and, in spite of it, Antonius got away with the pig, then the penalty was fourfold, for this was a highly violent situation indeed. There is a good deal of logic in increasing the penalty when there is an increase in the degree of violence involved in the wrongful act.

But the Romans did not confine relief to situations in which there was violence or a threat of violence. Suppose you lent your horse to Antonius to plow his field, and Antonius entered the beast in a horse race. That would be a tort because Antonius had put your property to improper use. He had exceeded his authority, and you had an action against him. It made a difference, however, whether or not Antonius knew that he was exceeding his authority, for the Romans, prompted by Cicero, had made the discovery that "intent" was important in determining whether one should be liable for an act.

Our word "injury" comes from the Roman *iniuria*, which means an injury to a person himself, in contradistinction to a *furtum* ("conversion") of his property. The treatment of *iniuria* was considerably more primitive than is our own. There was, for instance, no action for damages for a multilation: the relief was on the eye-for-an-eye principle. If the injury was less than mutilation, then damages were awarded. The theory behind such damages was not, as it is today, compensation for pain and suffering. The Romans, not understanding that concept, gave damages for an impairment of dignity. Damages for libel and slander were awarded under the same concept. If an injured person died, the action died with him, on the ground that his dignity died with him. Perhaps the basic reason for this rule was that, the injured one being dead, there was no longer any danger of a personal attempt to redress the wrong.

Eventually the meaning of an *iniuria* was extended to almost any "unlawful conduct," so that the rule which based damages on impairment of personal dignity no longer limited legal actions. Suppose Antonius took the horse he had borrowed from you, and beat it so hard that it died. There might be no intention to impair your dignity or to subject you to public disgrace, so, under the old rules, you would have had no right to damages. But the new principle was direct and simple: he had killed your horse wrongfully, and he had to pay. If he did not settle voluntarily, he had to pay twice the highest value of the horse during the previous year.

In some respects the Roman tort law was very well developed. Careful distinction was made between types of liability which are very close to each other in fact, and the capacity of the Roman jurist for classifying and distinguishing was truly remarkable. What we might generally classify as "negligence" they divided into several parts. Their category which is closest to our "negligence" was *improvidentia.* A man who practiced javelin throwing at a place where he knew people might pass was guilty of *improvidentia.* And the Romans had discovered "contributory negligence." The passer-by who knew that the javelin thrower frequently practiced at a certain place was guilty of contributory negligence if he did not watch out for flying javelins.

There was another kind of negligence, called *culpa* ("carelessness" or "culpability"), which the Romans divided into two classes. There was *culpa lata,* or "gross negligence," such as putting a flower pot on a window sill in such a manner that it might easily fall and hit a passer-by on the cranium. And there was *culpa levis,* or minor carelessness, such as leaving the flower pot on a table in such a position that a child could reach it and knock it over. The distinction is that a flower pot placed on a window sill is dangerous intrinsically, while a flower pot on a table is dangerous only if improperly placed and if there is a young child around who might upset it. A legal system which could make such sharp distinctions was advanced indeed.

One more example of the high state of philosophic accuracy to which the Romans developed their jurisprudence: they held people responsible in many ways as the indirect cause of an injury. To illustrate, an innkeeper was responsible for the thefts of his servants; and a householder was responsible if something thrown out of his window injured a passer-by. The Roman law permitted actions for defrauding creditors, malfeasance in office, corruption of slaves, malicious prosecution, willful fraud, duress, and many more kinds of human misconduct.

Many crimes in Rome were covered by specific statutes, including treason, adultery, homicide, forgery, embezzlement, kidnaping, and bribery. In a criminal case, we protect a defendant by presuming him innocent until he is proven guilty. There was no such presumption in the Roman law. On the other hand, there was no presumption of guilt, either.

IV: Contracts

In contrast to the Greeks, the early Romans held a contract to be sacred. The word "sacred" is purposely used here, because it was not so much the promise to do something which was held binding as the ritual which went together with that promise—that ritual had religious origin or was supervised by priests who gave the procedure religious sanction. These early contracts were not in writing but were effected through an elaborate process of acting. There might be the weighing of copper in scales in front of a specified number of witnesses, the various parties to the transaction being required to make certain formal recitations and gestures. So important were these formalities that any deviation from them made the contract invalid.

It was inevitable that these formalities would decrease as the growing complexities of life in Rome made more and more contracts necessary and the old forms became more and more cumbersome and hindering. It was not long before it was possible to make a contract involving practically no ritual. All that was essential was that one party say, "*Spondesne?*" ("Do you so promise?") and for the other to reply, "*Spondeo*" ("I promise"). This form of contract was called a "stipulation." It was not the only form, but its simplicity made it popular.

Written contracts came in through the influence of the commercial East, but to the Romans it was not the writing that made the contract valid: it was the promise, which the writing merely recorded. It may seem odd that they did not recognize a contract between deaf mutes, but this was logical enough. Deaf mutes could not make a promise; therefore, how could their promise be reduced to writing!

We have what are called bilateral or mutual contracts, as when you promise to build a house for me in exchange for my agreeing to manufacture some hats for you—a promise for a promise. The Romans had no such bilateral contracts in any simple form. They would have had to have two separate contracts, one covering the building of the house and the other the manufacture of the hats. Nor did the Romans know our contract for the benefit of a third party—to illustrate, your agreeing with me that, if I pay you a hundred dollars, you will build a chicken coop for Henry. But they got around this difficulty by having penalty contracts which produced almost the same result. B could say to A: "If you do not pay C, will you pay me?" Then, if A answered, "*Spondeo*," there was a binding contract, so that if A broke it by not paying C, he would suffer the penalty of having to pay B.

Our common law has made much of "consideration," the requirement that something, either a thing or a promise, must be given for another's promise in order to bind it. This concept has led us to a lot of nonsense: documents which recite that "for one dollar and other considerations," or words to that effect, somebody promises something. That "one dollar" is rarely passed, and the consideration is often purely fictitious. Yet lawyers have become so impressed with the necessity of consideration that even where a contract contains mutual promises and, therefore, does not need any further consideration, you will see this same business of "one dollar and other considerations" recited in a preamble to the agreement.*

* It may be that lawyers should abandon old forms and usages which no longer seem to make sense, but we fear to. I must confess that, in my own practice, I go on using a lot of old phraseology which I feel sure I could simplify and improve. But how do I know! I might miss some peculiar significance in a phrase which has already been passed on by the courts. To say that, like the rest of my kind, I lack courage is not quite fair. To exercise what you might

The Romans avoided all this "consideration" confusion. They held that a promise was binding, even if nothing was given for it, provided that the proper formalities had been observed. They recognized some reasonable limitations to this general rule, and two of them are obvious enough—you could not get damages for breach of a contract which it was impossible to perform, and you could not enforce a contract which was against "public policy."

We have a general law of contracts, applying to any kind of contract, even though we also have some rules which apply to particular kinds of contracts. The Romans had no general law of contracts at all; they dealt only with particular kinds. There was only a law of *nexum*, a law of *stipulatio*, a law of *depositum*, etc.*

Interest was known from an early day, but there was always some clamor against it and always agitation against moneylenders. Legislation failed to prevent it, so that, eventually, interest was legalized at 12 per cent. Justinian reduced it to 8 per cent on ordinary business loans, and specified rates from 4 to 12 per cent for other circumstances. Compound interest was rarely allowed, and Justinian proscribed it completely. The general rate of interest was 6 per cent, and this is still generally the interest allowed by American law. Interest was not allowed after it had equaled the amount of the principal.

Business life in Rome was complex, in many ways resembling modern conditions. Therefore, a great many of the more difficult or intricate legal problems arising out of commercial life were known to the Romans and solved by their clear-minded jurists. The Romans knew the intricacies of deposit or bailment, pledge, mortgage (*hypotheca*),† and many other contract involvements, some com-

---

call courage in this direction would be not at my own risk but at the risk of my clients.

* The specific Roman contracts may be divided into several categories. There were the *nexum* and *mancipium*, used to transfer property. Then there were the so-called "real contracts": *mutuum*, or loan; *commodatum*, or loan for use of something to be returned; *depositum*, or deposit; and *pignus*, or pledge. There were also "literal contracts": entries in a seller's books of sale. There were also "consensual contracts": *emptio venditio*, or sale; *locatio conductio*, or hire; *societas*, or partnership; and *mandatum*, or agency. Finally, there were special contracts, called *stipulatio*. There were eventually, in addition, what are called "innominate contracts," enforceable because they had been part performed.

† "Bailment" implies putting property in another's hands as a custodian, usually for a special purpose, so that the bailee has duties of an almost trust nature. A warehouseman is a bailee, for example. "Pledge" and "mortgage" both carry the implication of giving property to another as security for some act or promise, usually a promise to pay money.

plications of which still plague our jurists. They knew actions for the return of money or property paid over or delivered by mistake, for an illegal reason, without good reason, or without getting a reasonably expected return. They knew what we call "unjust enrichment"—they devised the maxim "It is in accordance with natural equity that no one become richer by reason of someone else's loss." There are indeed very few concepts of recovery of money or property which the Romans did not discover and develop, scientifically and with precision. The Roman answer to some current problems would not always be the same as the modern one, but the jurists found ways to make business work and to enable commerce to be undertaken on a grand scale.

In the matter of leases of lands, our law is based somewhat on inheritances from the feudal system. Therefore, there are some differences between our ideas in this province and those of the Romans, but there are few essential differences. For example, the Roman, just as we do, presumed that if a tenant remained after the expiration of his lease, he had renewed his tenancy. One rule the Romans had is foreign to us. Whatever personal property the tenant brought onto the land was deemed to be security for the payment of rent.

V: Corporations, and Business Law

ROME became a big business center, and it was natural enough for legal mechanisms to develop enabling big business to be done. Julius Caesar was a member of several trading syndicates; and men of great wealth, like Crassus, were interested in many widespread ventures. Some of these were single, joint ventures, perhaps for an expedition to trade in foreign ports. Others seem to have had more permanent character and to have extended to successive ventures over a considerable period of time.*

* There were various kinds of business associations. The simplest was the *societas unius re,* a contract to administer one thing jointly. Then there was the *societas omnium bonorum,* a contract to administer all property jointly and to be responsible for each other's debts. This might be called a superpartnership. There was also the ordinary partnership, or *societas bonorum quae ex quaestu veniunt,* under which both partners made a contribution to the business. The equivalent of our "joint venture," or partnership for a single venture, such as one trading voyage, was called the *societas negotiationis alicuius.* It was very frequently used. Some syndicates were enormous; they contained many members and were managed almost as modern corporations are. Some were almost the

There were no business "corporations" as we know the term. But the corporate entity was present in many public and semipublic bodies, such as unions or guilds of craftsmen, called *collegia.* At various times these *collegia* grew to such numbers and had such power or influence in the community that measures were introduced to suppress them. Another variety of semipublic corporation in Rome was the *universitas.*

Roman big business required banking, and some of the money-lending businesses grew to such importance that they might be classed as private banks. Money was borrowed on mortgage or other security and sometimes without security on the general credit of the borrower. Syndicates of bankers were formed, just as in modern times, to finance some of the great commercial ventures of stock companies and individuals.

Strange to say, despite the magnitude of business in the developed Roman world, the Roman law is found wanting in a few of the ordinary business forms and practices which we find so necessary to commercial life. A great part of our own commercial law came from Oriental, and frequently from Jewish, sources. The "law merchant" arose gradually as commerce increased in Western Europe, and may be traced largely to the customs of maritime merchants. Many of these practices were wholly unknown to the Romans. For example, they had a law of "bills and notes" but none of "negotiable instruments." That is, they knew and used promissory notes, written promises to pay money, but they did not know anything about such notes which might be passed by endorsement or by delivery from one person to another, free of any defenses which the original maker might have had against the original payee.

Nor did the Romans have any true bankruptcy law, but only a rudimentary procedure which we would find unsatisfactory. We have found it necessary to permit people to go through bankruptcy without legal disgrace. It does your reputation no good to go bankrupt, but the law does not treat you differently after bankruptcy. In Rome a man forced into involuntary bankruptcy by his creditors suffered *infamia,* or disgrace, and lost many civil rights and privileges.

Insurance was an infant science in Rome. Life insurance was unknown, but the Romans did use commercial insurance of the kind

---

equivalent of our "joint stock associations." These issued *partes* or *particulae*—shares—were usually managed by equities but occasionally by freedmen, and were directed by a board.

which we call "bottomry"; their form was to lend money on a ship which was to go on a trading voyage, with the agreement that the loan would be canceled if the ship went down. That is not exactly insurance, but it works the same way.

In most phases of commercial intercourse, however, the Roman law was well developed. There was a sound and workable law of sales, agency, suretyship, and hiring.

VI: Roman Property Law

WHEN a piece of property belonged to an entire family, transferring it to someone else became a very serious matter and necessarily entailed much formality. In any primitive society, particularly before the use of writing, transfers of property were quite formal. The *paterfamilias* was the actual owner of all the family's property (he had *dominium* over it). However, he held it not merely for his own use but as a sort of trustee for the whole family. Since the family subsistence and welfare depended somewhat upon the preservation of this property, transfers were discouraged. But barter and trade came along to make transfers out of the family more frequent, and as new kinds of personal property were devised something had to be done to make transfers easier.

This problem faced the Romans at an early period. As it is easier to get around an old institution by an ingenious device than it is to destroy the institution, the Roman jurists conceived the idea of dividing property into two kinds. We divide property into real and personal property,* and our laws regarding them differ. The Roman division was typical of a patriarchal society similar to that described in Chapter 1. It made no difference whether the property was "real" or "personal." The only criterion was the importance of the property to the family. Under early Roman law, property most needed for the family's subsistence, such as land, horses, oxen, and slaves, was called *res mancipi*, or things requiring mancipation. "Mancipation" was a process of transfer involving great ceremony and formality carried over from more primitive times. Elaborate forms were acted out by

* "Real property" includes not only the land but also houses and other things permanently affixed to the land. A plumbing fixture, for example, would be considered personal property if it could be removed without damage to the real estate (the house) but "real" if its removal would damage the property.

the parties. Uusally a large number of witnesses had to be present, and they, too, took an active part in this formal play. Mancipation was so strictly interpreted that if any error was made either in a gesture or in words the transaction was not effective.

To make transfers of some property easier, the second class, called *res nec mancipi,* or property not requiring mancipation, was devised. Such property—sheep, produce, tools—was not so important to the family's existence, and methods were found for transferring it readily. The principal method was *traditio,* which became virtually transfer by delivery. Many of the new methods, including *traditio,* were taken over from the *ius gentium.*

Business grew and very frequent transfers of property became necessary, particularly when new kinds of property came into use. In order to make transfers easier there came into use the fiction that these new types of property were not of the *res mancipi* class. Even if such property was vital to the family, the law would treat it as though it were *res nec mancipi* and, therefore, transferable without much difficulty.

The last state in the emancipation of property from primitive restrictions on transfer came when the simpler methods of transfer were gradually applied even to *res mancipi.* Under Justinian the distinction between *res mancipi* and *res nec mancipi* disappeared altogether.

Even during the period when the distinction was still maintained, various devices were invented to get around the formalities. One of these was the collusive judgment. An action at law would be brought by the proposed transferee of the property against the true owner. The latter would default in the action, and the claimant would thus get title to the property which otherwise could not have been conveyed to him except through onerous and difficult processes.

There were other ways of acquiring property. From the earliest days it could be secured through "prescription," known to the Romans as *usucapio.* If property had been held uninterruptedly for a certain period, it belonged irretrievably to the holder or occupant. This concept of acquiring property by prescription came only tardily into the Anglo-Saxon law because of the influence of the canon law, which was opposed to the idea that one could get title to someone else's property by merely sitting on it long enough.*

* As usual, the *ius gentium* was far more liberal than the *ius civile.* Under the *ius gentium* there were many ways of acquiring "title" to property. One was by

Certain rights which attach to property or its use are called "servitudes" or "easements." Complete title to property may be conceived of as a bundle of rights; the owner may grant some of these rights to another and still retain others. The rights to pasture cattle, to draw water from the owner's well, to conduct a stream over his land—these are illustrations of servitudes. The Romans distinguished between servitudes which attached to property and those which attached only because a particular person who was obligated owned the property.*

Among the difficult legal ideas which the Romans also mastered was the concept of possession. They understood that mere possession of property, even if one did not own it, gave certain rights against the rest of the world with the exception of the owner.

VII: Wills, Estates, and Trusts

THE CLAIM has been made that the right to will property is a "natural right." But this seems not to be the fact. Property is held at the sufferance of society, and whatever rights one has over property are rights granted or permitted by the community. At any rate, most of the systems from which we inherit our legal institutions were patriarchal in origin, and there certainly was no right to will property freely in any of these patriarchal systems. In patriarchal society the property usually belonged to the head of the family, but only as the representative of the whole family, and therefore the right to will property outside that family would have been abhorrent to the basic thesis of the system.

Evidence of this theory of family unity in property matters may

---

occupatio, by taking and holding an ownerless thing, such as wild game and abandoned articles. Another was *accessio*, under which an accessory thing belonged to the owner of a primary thing. There was a difficult method, known as *specificatio*, as to which the Proculian and Sabinian schools of law disagreed. The problem centered around who owned property used in the manufacture of something else. Justinian laid down the rule that if A's material was used in the manufacture of something by B, A retained title if the material could be restored, but B got title if it could not be. For example, if A's copper had been used in B's manufacture of bronze, A lost title or ownership.

* Some rights against property pass along with the land, regardless of who owns it, but others attach to it only so long as the man who has granted the right owns the property.

be found in the Roman laws of succession. The *heres,* or heir, stepped into the shoes of his predecessor, acquiring his assets and assuming his liabilities and obligations. The *heres* was thus not the equivalent of our "heir." Nor was he our "executor." He was a combination of both.* The situation was the same whether succession was by will or by intestacy. *Hereditas est successio in universum ius quod defunctus habuit* ("An inheritance is a succession to the entire legal position of a deceased man"). One of the duties of the deceased patriach was the protection of his family. Therefore, one of the duties attached to inheritance was this same duty of protection.

Sir Henry Maine drew the analogy that the family itself continued through succession, much as a corporation has continuous existence. Wealth, in the old Roman system, continued in the family even though one administrator of that family wealth died. Another succeeded to his place just as, upon the decease of a trustee of a trust, a successor trustee takes over.

One of the most important obligations of the Roman heir was to perform the *sacra,* or family rites. In many other societies—for example, the Hindu—the performance of religious rites by the heir was a prerequisite or necessity to succession. In the ancient Hindu law there was no such thing as a true will. The only way in which property could be passed outside the family was by adoption, which indicates the association of property disposition with the patriarchal identity of the family unit. Similarly, the Jewish law permitted the willing of property only when those persons who were natural heirs had died or were undiscoverable; and Athenians, after Solon, were not permitted to disinherit male descendants.

The classic Roman law of intestate succession† proceeded along patriarchal lines. First came the direct descendants and, if there were none, then the nearest relatives of the father's family, and if there were none of these then the greater family, the *domus* or *gens.* Relatives had no inheritance unless they were agnatically related, that

* The Roman idea of heirship has been carried over into the modern Continental system, where there is a functionary somewhat like our "executor," but without title to the estate, which our executor has. The "heir" has title. The Roman heir acquired what was called a *universitas iuris,* or university or universality of rights and duties.

† "Intestate" means "without a testament." Rules of "intestate succession," therefore, determine which relatives get the property if someone dies without leaving a will.

is, related on a patriarchal basis. However, there was a growing tendency under Roman law to convert the agnatic character of the family into a cognatic character. Eventually, in the later periods of the Empire, the transition was almost complete.

The earliest form of Roman will fits into the patriarchal pattern. For the will was executed or declared in the *Comitia Calata,* a special council of patricians. The testator was not permitted to will away from the regular intestate succession, and could dispose of his property elsewhere only if there were none of his clan in existence or if his clan had waived succession. The presence of a representative of each clan on the *Comitia* prevented any violation of this rule.

The modern will is not a descendant of the will of the *Comitia.* It descends from another form of will invented to satisfy the needs of the plebeian Roman who found it impossible—or at least awkward—to avail himself of the mechanism of the patrician *Comitia.* By this method the property was given, during the donor's lifetime, to the person who was to inherit it. The act, called by the familiar name of "mancipation," was very formal and ritualistic. It was public, and it had all the appearance of being an absolute, immediate gift, although there was little chance that the heir could claim it while the donor was alive, for the act was publicly recognized as not intending any gift until after death. But the formality was so great and the whole process so cumbersome that the more general method of disposing of property outside the existing family was to adopt the desired heir.

Later, the dangers in the old forms of mancipation were alleviated by the "praetorian" form of testament, based on the general mancipation form but without the attendant ritual. Wills were, by this time, written. Seven witnesses attended the making of the will, and each of the seven affixed his seal to the closed document. In the original mancipation ceremony the donee had to be present in person and consequently knew of his future inheritance. Under the new form of praetorian will the heir was not present, and the contents of the will did not need to be known to him. Secrecy had been introduced, and this was a milestone in the development of wills. Later still, wills became revocable.*

* Technically, the will could not pass legal title to the heir but only equitable title or use of the property. This last limitation was eliminated long afterwards in the Eastern Roman Empire, when actual legal title passed as it had in the old will by mancipation. This form of will, which is the more direct ancestor of the modern will, was confined to the Eastern Empire. In the Western Empire

There were other forms of wills. The *testamentum militum,* a will made orally or in writing by a soldier, with soldiers as witnesses, was popular because of its simplicity and lack of formality. Later there was also the *testamentum holografum,* a will written in the handwriting of the testator.

The almost universal use of wills in Rome may be explained by the growing feeling that the arbitrary rules of intestate descent violated natural sentiment. These rigid rules were based strictly upon the organization of the patriarchal family. It was to give property to close relatives, excluded from succession by the intestacy rules, that wills were most often employed.

One had to be a Roman citizen to make a will. Aliens, minors, incompetents, and those declared legally incapable of making a will —as a form of punishment—had no testamentary capacity. The immediate family could not be wholly disinherited, and the law eventually prescribed what shares the sons must get. However, there were various legal justifications for complete disinheritance—for example, an attempt on the testator's life, a son striking his father, or holding the testator up to public disgrace.

Codicils—amendments to wills—were used, and they were generally instructions to the *heres* as to the disposition of the property. Out of the codicil developed a mechanism somewhat like our testamentary trust. The *heres* was bound by the impositions placed upon him by an instructive codicil, and he could get out of them only by repudiating his heirship. Frequently a testator would hold his heir accountable to deliver a legacy to a third person to whom the testator had no legal right to leave any property. Such arrangements were known as *fidei-commissa,* and they were not far from our testamentary trust in operation; the main distinction was that, if the heir refused to accept the inheritance with the conditions attached to it, the whole arrangement was destroyed.

The Romans also had "family trusts," through which property could be held for generations in the same group—Justinian eventually limited them to four generations. In our own law we do not permit trusts to last in "perpetuity," and it is interesting to see that the Romans had already learned that it was not wise to let families perpetuate their wealth mechanically for too long. There is probably a direct relationship between the Roman concept of a family trust

the old will of mancipation continued to be used and was carried on in parts of Europe even during the Middle Ages.

and the entailing* of estates under the feudal law of medieval times.

The trust, as we know it, is an institution peculiar to the English system. It necessitates separating ownership into legal title and beneficial interest. That is, the donor of the trust might transfer property to NN (the trustee and legal owner) for the purpose of paying the income to KK (the beneficiary). This division of ownership into two parts was unknown to the Roman law except in connection with wills, and it is likewise unknown to the modern Romanesque or civil law of the Continent and Latin America. However, through the "foundation," which was somewhat like a corporation, the Roman law accomplished almost everything which our *inter vivos* trust could accomplish. "Foundations" are used in some Romanesque countries today in the same manner. The idea of the foundation came from Greece, where it was used somewhat extensively. Generally, the foundations were used for charitable purposes. A group would organize a foundation with self-perpetuating managers. The Romans also had something close to our trust in their "mandate." It arose when, for example, AA instructed NN to do some act. In so far as it involved property belonging to AA or to which he had a right, a trust relationship may be said to have resulted.

One of the best illustrations of the modern character of Roman law is to be found in the law of guardianship. An infant child was in *tutela* ("tutelage") or guardianship. He could bring an action if he were wronged, but he could not be sued for breach of contract. On the other hand, the law did not permit the child to be unjustly enriched because others could not sue him. These are present-day rules. The child was also protected against the avarice or misconduct of a guardian. The *tutor* could no more despoil his *pupillus* ("ward") than he could today. The *tutor* was obliged to put up a bond for the faithful discharge of his duties, and he was held strictly accountable for breaches of his obligations. He could even be prosecuted criminally for fraudulent acts. The Romans released male children from guardianship at fourteen and females at twelve, but, on the other hand, they gave children the right to repudiate contracts up to their twenty-fifth year.

* "Entailing" an estate means providing that it may pass only to the grantee and the heirs of his body. If such heirs fail, then the property reverts to the grantor. We do not permit "estates tail" any longer.

CHAPTER 13

Justinian

"The precepts of the law are these: to live honorably, to injure no other man, to render to every man his due."
JUSTINIAN: INSTITUTES

I: The Balkan Emperor

WHEN JUSTIN I ascended the throne at Constantinople in 518 as Emperor of the Romans, a far different Empire was commended to his care than that which had obeyed the commands of Augustus or Hadrian. Various disintegrative forces, including the unmanageable weight of the vast territories of the Empire as well as the gradual Hellenization of the Eastern provinces, had separated the two halves of the Empire long before the West fell to the onslaughts of the barbarians in 476. In the East, the name and pomp of the Roman Empire was to continue for yet another thousand years, but its glitter hid weakness and decay, and its Roman forms disguised but faintly the Greek-Oriental character of this Byzantine Empire, which had neither the vigor of old Rome nor the genius of old Greece.

Justin had emigrated from what is now Bulgaria to enlist in the Imperial Guards, and had risen quickly in the Roman service, becoming tribune, count, general, senator, and commander of the guards. When the Emperor Anastasius died, Justin took advantage of a confused political situation to cause himself to be elevated to the throne, where he reigned nine years. He was an able general but woefully inexperienced in public administration when he became Emperor at the age of sixty-eight; it was to his credit, however, that he recognized his own deficiencies and delegated much of the management of the state to carefully selected subordinates. Of these, the most important was his young nephew, Upravda, whom he had made his personal heir and removed from Bulgaria to Constantinople.

Uprauda, known to history by his adopted name, Flavius Ancius Justinianus, or Justinian, succeeded so well as his uncle's chief deputy that he was named as the heir, and upon his uncle's death in 527 he ascended the throne without any serious opposition. He was, though only for a few years, to unite East and West and to give the Empire an appearance of resurgence and energy.

The times were difficult. To defend against the dangers which beset the Empire on all of its frontiers, whenever diplomacy or bribery did not forestall an attack, Justinian dispatched two exceptionally able generals, Belisarius and Narses. Their bravery and capacity not only stood between Justinian and military disaster but even reconquered Italy and reunited the old seat of empire with the East. But dangers from within also beset Justinian during his long reign, and here his own fearful and often cowardly nature was bulwarked by the exceptional intestinal fortitude of a remarkable wife. Gibbon notes that Theodora's elevation to the throne "cannot be applauded as the triumph of female virtue," and describes her as follows: ". . . painting and poetry were incapable of delineating the matchless excellence of her form. But this form was degraded by the facility with which it was exposed to the public eye, and prostituted to licentious desire. Her venal charms were abandoned to a promiscuous crowd of citizens and strangers, of every rank and of every profession: the fortunate lover who had been promised a night of enjoyment was often driven from her bed by a stronger or more wealthy favorite; and when she passed through the streets, her presence was avoided by all who wished to escape either the scandal or the temptation."

This prostitute whom Justinian raised to his side was a cruel, capricious, and vicious woman. Yet she was proud, intelligent, and a constant support to the feebler character of her imperial husband. There was a time when Justinian was ready to flee from the capital in fear of his life, but the Empress bolstered up his failing courage by refusing to go. "If flight [she said] were the only means of safety, yet I should disdain to fly. Death is the condition of our birth, but they who have reigned should never survive the loss of dignity and dominion. I implore Heaven that I may never be seen, not a day, without my diadem and purple; that I may no longer behold the light when I cease to be saluted with the name of queen. If you resolve, O Caesar! to fly, you have treasures; behold the sea, you have ships; but tremble lest the desire of life should expose you to wretched exile and ignominious death. For my own part, I adhere to the maxim of antiquity, that the throne is a glorious sepulcher." With such a woman by his side, Justinian carried on, overcoming all dangers.

Justinian was vain and unscrupulous, and his cowardice was apparent all too frequently, but he had his other side. He was at times deeply religious and public-spirited. He made Constantinople itself a city of beauty and splendor; his many public projects would receive the full commendation of posterity if it were not for the fact that they were financed by unrelenting taxation of the already impoverished masses. The balance sheet of his reign would probably show far more debit than credit except for his magnificent service to the law. When a renaissance of interest in the Roman law began to draw Europe out of the Dark Ages and to afford a base for the development of modern jurisprudence, it was Justinian's lawbooks which were studied; and his codes formed the foundation stones for the eventual structure of European and a great deal of English and American law.

II: Justinian's Codes

One of Justinian's first acts after ascending the throne was to appoint a commission to collect and codify the Roman law. Several collections of law had been made since the Perpetual Edict of Julian. In 295 one Gregorianus had published a collection of "constitutions" of the emperors from Hadrian's time to his own day, but it was an unofficial compilation. The most interesting thing about it is that it was published not in the form of a roll, which had been the ancient practice, but in *codex* form, that is, like our books today. It is from this word *codex* that our "code" derives. At about the same time as Gregorianus's work, Hermogenianus published a somewhat similar book including the recent constitutions of the Emperor Constantine; but this, too, was an unofficial work, and little is known about either the Gregorian or the Hermogenian Code, as no copies remain in existence.

In 438 the Eastern Emperor Theodosius II published a code of which far more is known. It was intended to supplant all previous compilations of the imperial constitutions or decrees. And, before that, in 426, there had appeared the Law of Citations already referred to, which gave official status to the opinions and commentary of the five great men of the law of the imperial era, Gaius, Papinian, Paul, Ulpian, and Modestinus. But these scattered efforts at collecting the law were insufficient. Then as now, a large library was needed to include all the statutes, decrees, commentaries, and other works of authority which the practicing lawyer and the judge required in their work, and, of course, there were no printing presses to multiply these works. To make them readily available to all practitioners and to accumulate the scattered law and co-ordinate it into official editions, Justinian appointed his commission.

At its head he placed Tribonianus, an eminent lawyer and magistrate whose occasional venality pales into insignificance before his gigantic accomplishment in the codification work directed by Justinian. Tribonian's nine associates were judges, ex-judges, and jurists, and it may be that they secured help also from the great law schools at Byzantium and Beirut. They devoted themselves to a study of the Gregorian, Hermogenian, and Theodosian Codes and in 529 produced a new and comprehensive Code (we know it as the *Code of Justinian*) which took the place of all previous collections of the imperial decrees.

Twenty months after that Code had been published, Tribonian found himself again the chairman of a commission, now consisting of seventeen members, to collect, edit, and co-ordinate the vast mass of commentary on the law. The commissioners worked on almost two thousand books of comment as well as a great volume of other material in producing their *Digesta* or *Pandects*. This work took three years to complete, being published in 533, and was a thorough piece of editing in which each reference to the opinion or comment of some legal authority was noted with the author's name and the book from which it was taken. References to Ulpian and Paul were the most frequent.

The same commission created a subcommission to prepare an elementary textbook. It was called the *Institutiones* (*Institutes*) and appeared also in 533. It was based largely upon the work of Gaius, with numerous additions and some changes. By this time, the original Code had already shown itself in need of revision, and a second edition was published in 534. Other additions to it were made by later supplements, called *Novellae*. After Justinian's death editions of his works came out from time to time, and in the fifteenth century there appeared a *Corpus Iuris Civilis* which purported to be a collection of all of Justinian's books, including the *Novellae*.

The various books which bear Justinian's name were not mere collections of older works. The commissioners did a great deal of clarifying, added much new material, and revised and changed much to suit their own preferences. The result was truly remarkable and perhaps the most commendable series of works ever produced in the law. However, one finds in them little of the older Roman sages, such as the Scaevolas and others of the republican era. Thus the law was modified so considerably that it might be called an adulteration of the "pure" Roman law. This may not have been entirely the fault of the commissioners, however, as it is possible that many of the most important works of the older writers had already completely disappeared.

The great service of Justinian lay not merely in the order which he brought into the law but also in the fact that he preserved, through his publications, a mass of Roman legal material which might otherwise have gone the way of so many other historical data. Without that material, it might have taken the invading Germanic peoples of Europe far longer than it did to emerge from the mire of the Middle Ages and to develop a mature legal system.

In dealing with the great Roman jurists and the Roman law in such necessarily limited fashion, I do not mean to suggest that the Romans are to be treated in passing just as a part of ancient history. For the Roman law was truly something astounding, and the men who made it still deserve the most reverent respect. The law of which Gaius, Papinian, and Ulpian wrote was not semi-primitive but one so modern that it is the constant wonder of the student. It is not astonishing that the American legal system is comprehensive and effective, for we have the wisdom of the ages behind us and the experience of many civilizations. But the Romans used few alien materials in erecting their own legal structure; they employed materials almost entirely of their own invention, and their system, with very few changes and improvements, could be used today.

PART FOUR

THE GERMAN BARBARIANS AND THE FEUDAL SYSTEM

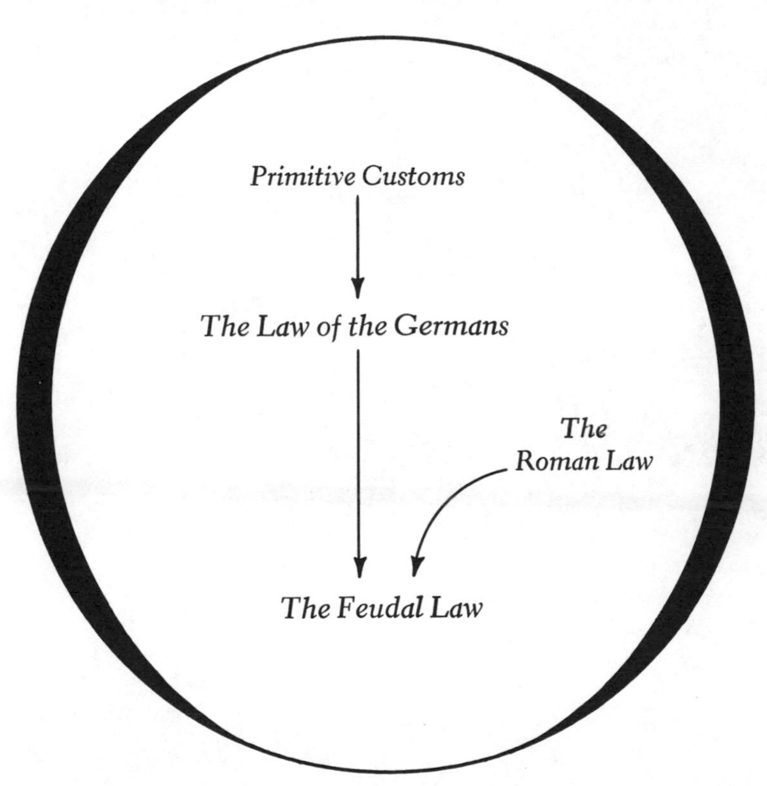

THE CHIEF BASIC SOURCES

CHAPTER 14

The German Law Speakers

"A law court shall we have and hold here every summer at the Al-ting. . . . The law speaker shall determine who may have a place on the Hill of Laws. . . . The law speaker is bound, both here at the Al-ting and at home, to say, to any who ask him thereon, what the law commands; but he is not bound any further to give folk advice in their lawsuits. . . ."

FROM THE GRAGAS, AN ICELANDIC LAWBOOK

I: The Germans

A MOHAMMEDAN who died in battle was believed to be destined to spend his time in heaven in amorous dalliance with beautiful houris, but the Germanic hero lived quite a different life in the hereafter. He was carried to Valhalla by beautiful maidens, built like trapeze artistes. But sex was secondary in Valhalla, where the heroes spent their days in fighting each other. At nightfall their wounds were healed so that they could enjoy their beer in the evening and be ready for more battle the next morning.

So valiance was worshiped in the forests of Germany, but that is not the only reason why the Romans failed to conquer but a small part of the country. The Romans thought that Germany was hardly worth the trouble of taking. Tacitus said: ". . . who would leave the softer climes of Asia, Africa, or Italy, to fix his abode in Germany? where nature offers nothing but scenes of deformity; where the inclemency of the seasons never relents; where the land presents a dreary region, without form or culture, and, if we except the affections of a native for his mother-country, without an allurement to make life supportable."

That country, so unpleasantly described, was to produce a strong stock; great nations sprang from the loins of the ancient Germans. Their descendants, both in Europe and in North America, were to add much to civilization, as well as to contribute many dreadful things to man, including astoundingly efficient means for his annihilation.

From these Germanic ancestors, the English have inherited a spirit of freedom (sometimes missing in the Germans of Germany) which had its roots in the organization of the clan, in which the assembly of the people acted as the protector of the rights of the individual. This assembly was called the *Ting* or *Thing*, and its sessions, held in the open air, were attended by all the free males. There they participated in the decisions of government and clan policy, and also in the trial of lawsuits. Tacitus tells us that, in these assemblies, ". . . accusations are exhibited, and capital offenses prosecuted. Pains and penalties are proportioned to the nature of the crime. For treason and desertion, the sentence is to be hanged on a tree: the coward, and such as are guilty of unnatural practices, are plunged under a hurdle into bogs and fens. In these different punishments, the point and spirit of the law is, that crimes which affect the state may be exposed to public notoriety: infamous vice cannot be too soon buried in oblivion. He who is convicted of transgressions of an inferior nature pays a mulct of horses, or of cattle. Part of that fine goes to the king or the community, and part to the person injured or to his family. It is in these assemblies that princes are chosen and chiefs elected to act as magistrates in the several cantons of the state. To each of these judicial officers, assistants are appointed from the body of the people, to the number of a hundred, who attend to give their advice, and to strengthen the hands of justice."

These Germans had an amazing interest in their public trials. There is an Icelandic saga, written down in the thirteenth century but apparently reflecting conditions in the twelfth, which illustrates the Germanic love of trials and disputations. The *Saga of Burnt Njal* winds its way through interminable litigation and legal wrangling. One of the chief characters was a man named Mord, whose first name was "Fiddle." This Fiddle Mord was a "great taker up of suits, and so great a lawyer that no judgments were thought lawful unless he had a hand in them." Fiddle had the misfortune to die in the middle of the saga, but there were countless others who "took up suits," among them Njal, after whom the saga is named.

Njal was "wealthy in goods," says the saga, "and handsome of face; no beard grew on his chin. He was so great a lawyer that his match was not to be found. Wise, too, he was, and foreknowing and foresighted. Of good counsel, and ready to give it, and all that he advised was sure to be the best for them to do. Gentle and generous, he unraveled every man's knotty points who came to see him about them."

There were men among the Germans who were called "lawmen" or "law speakers," and they were jurists of a primitive kind, handing down the law by word of mouth, acting as advisers to litigants in private, reciting the rules of law in public, supervising trial procedure at clan assemblies, and acting as advisers to the chief. But the disputants pleaded their own cases before the assembled people, and, when the law speakers had stated what they thought the decision should be, the people voted on it. Tacitus put it this way: "When anything is advanced not agreeable to the people, they reject it with a general murmur. If the proposition please, they brandish their javelins. This is their highest and most honorable mark of applause; they assent in a military manner, and praise by the sound of their arms."

Trials among primitive people are usually formal—anything having to do with primitive law seems always to have required the strictest adherence to prescribed forms. This becomes apparent enough in reading the *Burnt Njal*. Njal says, "So it shall be also, if the pleadings on one side are right in form, and the other wrong, that the judgment shall be given to those that are right in form." And Mord, in one court proceeding, recites these words, which are apparently the exact words which he must recite to pursue his suit: "I take witness to this, that I give notice of an assault laid down by law against Flosi, Thord's son, for that he rushed at Helgi, Njal's son, and dealt him a brain, or a body, or a marrow wound, which proved a death wound, and from which Helgi got his death. I say that in this suit he ought to be made a guilty man, an outlaw, not to be fed, not to be forwarded, not to be helped or harbored in any need. I say that all his goods are forfeited, half to me and half to the men of the Quarter, who have a right by law to take his forfeited goods. I give notice of this suit for manslaughter in the

Quarter Court into which this suit ought by law to come. I give notice of this lawful notice; I give notice in the hearing of all men on the Hill of Laws; I give notice of this suit to be pleaded this summer, and of full outlawry against Flosi, Thord's son; I give notice of a suit which Thorgeir, Thorir's son, has handed over to me." Presumably, if Mord had made a mistake in this recitation, his suit would have been defective. The Germans loved the pettifogging and hairsplitting which accompanied such a trial, and stood around applauding the clever trick of one pleader and the smart rejoinder of his opponent.

Although religion did not seem to have any prominent place in Germanic law, there were law gods. There was Thor, the War God, who was also the Lord of Justice. He was a rough-hewn and severe judge, who dispensed justice, legend has it, under the great ash tree, Ygdrasil. Forsete was another god of justice worshiped by some German tribes, and he dealt out justice in a more elegant manner, sitting in a handsome castle called Glitner, which had a silver roof supported by golden columns.

The law which the gods of justice supervised and the law speakers recited was chiefly primitive tort law. The eye-for-an-eye principle was the law, and the Germanic societies had arrived at the group stage of enforcement. It was not only the right but also the duty of the family and clan to avenge an injury, but they did distinguish between an intended and an accidental killing. If the killing was intentional, then retribution in kind was in order; but if the killing was accidental, then the killer could generally buy off vengeance through payment of a *Wergild* or reparation payment, which was graded according to the social status of the man who had been slain. But sometimes even offering *Wergild* would not prevent retribution unless the assembly recommended mercy.

In property law the ancient Germans were very primitive, recognizing no such thing as "real property." They were originally pastoral, and they held that the earth belonged to no man. The tribe or clan, when it settled for a while during its wanderings, occupied a section of land for herding and sometimes agriculture; plots were allotted to its members, and these allotments were changed annually. The crops were the property of those who cultivated them—here there was a concept of property. This system is in direct contrast with that of the Greeks, among whom the fruits of the soil were often treated communally, while the soil itself was held in strict property right. The difference can be explained by the circumstance that the Greeks were sedentary and worshiped their family gods, which were attached to the family hearth, which in turn was attached to the soil. The Germans were originally wanderers whose gods lived in Valhalla and were not in any way identified with a homestead.

Wills were unknown, except that kings sometimes divided their realms among their sons by a method which might be called testamentary. Property passed by custom and law to the son; if there was no issue, the brothers of the deceased took his property; and, if there were no brothers, then his uncle. The system was thus classically agnatic.

As there was very little commerce among the Germans, there was almost no commercial law. The first alien traders who approached them were greeted with suspicion and given no privileges, but the barbarians came to learn the advantages of barter and trade. Eventually it became possible for a visitor to trade peacefully under the protection of some eminent patron, who was sometimes rewarded by a cut in the profits. Through such escorted or protected trading ventures, some customs of trade arose, but it cannot be said that the Germans had a genuine commercial law until contact with the enlightened peoples of the Roman Empire taught them more of the benefits of commerce and of the necessity for controlling it.

Morality among the ancient Germans was very high. Marriage was held sacred, and monogamy was the almost invariable rule, although there was some polygamy among the upper classes. As part of the marriage ceremony, a dowry passed from the husband to the wife in the presence of her parents, which indicates that the Germanic marriage originated in purchase. The Germans were very practical in the selection of property for the dowry. They gave no trinkets or female ornaments, but such useful things as cattle and horses, and articles of war and of agriculture. The bride also made gifts to the groom, and the exchange of gifts seems to have constituted the entire marriage ceremony.

The high moral standards of the Germans of that day are attested to by Tacitus, who says: "Vice is not treated by the Germans as a subject of raillery, nor is the profligacy of corrupting and being corrupted called the fashion of the age. By the practice of some states, female virtue is advanced to still higher perfection: with them none but virgins marry. When the bride has fixed her choice, her hopes of matrimony are closed for life. . . . To set limits on population, by rearing up only a certain number of children, and destroying the rest, is accounted a flagitious crime. Among the savages of Germany, virtuous manners operate more than good laws in other countries."

II: The Law Speakers Lose Their Jobs

THE EMPEROR AUGUSTUS had worried over the growing decadence of the Roman people, and with good reason. Disaster was to be staved off for centuries but it was inevitable. As the Roman Empire expanded and grew ever more prosperous, the Roman metal softened. The legions, originally composed of hardy farmers led by tough aristocrats, came more and more to be composed of alien soldiers, often led by alien officers. Life was too full and too pleasant to make military life attractive for most Roman gentlemen, except for an occasional political purpose.

Large numbers of Germans were brought into the legions. Some eventually settled down in Roman territories as Romans or preferred aliens. Others returned to their own people, after a period of service as legionnaires, and took with them what they had learned of Roman military and civil ways, Roman culture, and Roman political and legal ideas. Through such returning mercenaries, as well as by actual contact with Roman arms, the Germans of the homeland began their education in civilization. A more intensive period of education followed, when, from about A.D. 300 to 700, Germanic tribes, finding the defenses of the Roman provinces softened, flooded over the greater part of the Roman Empire.

Not all the Germanic invasions were violent. Some were peaceful migrations. A number of the earliest migrations were encouraged by the Romans themselves; sometimes they took whole tribes of Germans into their service as *foederati* (note the origin of our word "confederates"). Late in the fourth century, a mass of Germans entered the Empire with permission; these were the Goths, who had been badly defeated by the Huns, and they received Roman consent to settle in the north of the Balkans. Other infiltrations occurred almost without notice until, later in the fifth century, the tidal waves began. It was not long before the Germans had spread all over Western Europe. Rome itself was sacked by Alaric the Visigoth in 410, and again by the Vandals under Generic in 455.

The migratory conquests were not all voluntary. There was tremendous pressure from the rear. Slavic peoples and Asiatic hordes were pushing the Germans, who, in turn, pushed the Romanized provincials of the West. The lure of loot was undoubtedly extremely attractive to the Germans, but they might not have advanced quite so rapidly had they not had fierce hordes at their own heels. One of these, the Huns under Attila, broke through the German mass at one period in this era and threatened to engulf all Europe.

Some historians have given us the impression that a curtain of darkness descended on Europe when the Empire was conquered by the Germans. This does not seem to be true. The invasions were certainly accompanied by various degrees of vandalism, but that word "vandalism" is an injustice to the Germanic tribe from whose name it was coined. The Romans themselves burned, ravaged, and pillaged on occasion, and such horrors were a part of the warfare of the day. It may be doubted that the Vandals were any worse than their contemporaries, and the Germanic tribes seem to have followed a universal pattern, after having run riot for a short while, of settling down rather quickly and living in peace with new neighbors. Many came as simple agrarian immigrants and brought their wives, children, herds and flocks with them, or were followed by them, and quickly fastened themselves upon the land.

The immediate effect of the Germanic conquests of the Roman Empire in the West was not so bad as the deferred effect. Considerable confusion followed immediately, of course, but Roman institutions were not destroyed to any vital extent in most areas. What brought darkness to Europe was a gradual deterioration. Eventually, people actually did forget how to read and write. Try as they might to preserve order, the Germanic kings were not up to the job. They were almost always at war among themselves; they brought on a decentralization of government and of justice which made it difficult to maintain effective management; they fathered feudalism; and they did not have the background or the experience to enable them to take advantage of the tools of government and of administration which they found at hand.

Except in the churches, the intellect of Europe went into gradual eclipse. Yet the case of civilization against our Germanic ancestors was not without counterclaim. The Germans were barbarians but not savages. Actually, they had much to recommend them over the people whom they conquered. Their personal morals and ethics were higher. They were vigorous and alert, not soft and corrupt like the Romanized provincials. They knew little of the refinements of living or of things of the intellect, but they had dignity, character, and understanding of the simple virtues—attributes which had long since become rare in the decadent Roman Empire. The very violence of their conquests, and their inability to assimilate culture quickly, created havoc, but they did not intend generally to break down what they found. The natives were not necessarily oppressed. In fact, intermarriage began immediately—an intermarriage of ways of living as well as of blood.

The tolerance of the conquerors toward the vanquished is reflected in the way in which the Germans treated the problems of government and of law. In a typical Roman province after its conquest by Germans, you would have found a rather feeble but highly cultured Latinized people ruled by strong but ignorant Germans. For a while many of the conquering German tribes did try to retain their own laws and customs, while permitting a certain degree of legal autonomy to the Latinized natives. The Lombards were the outstanding exception to the general rule. They tried hard to make the Germanic law superior to the Roman, and with considerable temporary success, but it was impossible to keep the Germanic law "pure." The general pattern in the other formerly Roman districts was two separate systems of law—that of the conquerors and that of the conquered—existing side by side.

Germanic law was meager and rough. Latin law was well developed and comprehensive. It was inevitable that the two should eventually merge and that the stronger Roman strain should eventually predominate. The Germans soon realized that their own laws could not be saved unless they were reduced to writing, and, as the Germans could not write, they called on Roman jurists or on priests of the Christian Church to write down the law. These early Germanic or Romanized Germanic codes were not comprehensive compendiums of law. There was not much to the law. These codes, known as the *Leges Barbarorum*, rarely contained more than criminal law, some brief rules of tort, and some rules of procedural law. They were written, almost always, in Latin, and thus lost in "purity," for the priests and jurists filled in gaps with their own ideas, and frequently made or suggested changes in the Germanic law.

Still, the greater part of the early *Leges Barbarorum* remained Germanically primitive. For instance, in the *Lex Salica*, the code of the Salian Franks, it is provided that if one kills a free woman after she has begun bearing children, the fine is twenty-four thousand denars, whereas if she has stopped bearing children the fine is only eight thousand denars. Yet we carry on something of the same idea today in assessing the value of a wife to a husband when he sues for damages on her death in an automobile accident. The husband is entitled to the "value of her services," a rather archaic idea not so much advanced, if at all, from the law of the Salian Franks.

The Church had, by this time, developed much law of its own, chiefly on a Roman base; and the priests were generally students of the Roman law as well as of the canon or papal law. When such men codified the German law, it was to be expected that there would be a considerable infiltration of Roman ideas. Thus, even the Lombard law came soon to be largely diluted with Roman. Many of the German kings of this era saw the advisability of having one set of laws for all the people in their domains, and the codes which they established were purposely a mixture of both legal systems. Other codes were so largely Roman that the elements of German law were lost almost completely. It made little difference whether or not these new German kings wished to preserve their own laws. They administered a society far more complex than any to which they had been accustomed, and it was inevitable that they should rely upon the assistance of Romanized advisers and agents, so the German law speakers found themselves rapidly losing their jobs.

The democratic lawmaking processes of the old Roman legal system had long since been lost, and Roman law was organized on a monarchical or imperial basis. Morevover, the Church had flourished under the Roman imperial monarchy, and had itself adopted absolutism in creating its own government, and thus felt inclined to support the monarchical system of government in Europe generally. Therefore, under the influence of the Church and of the Roman system, the Germanic states founded on the Roman provinces tended to become more and more absolute, in essence as well as in organization. The Germanic law gradually lost its democratic legislative base, and new laws came to be enacted through the fiat of kings, sometimes with the approval of a council.

The process of Romanizing the Germans was made all the easier by the conquerors' recognition of the imperial tradition, and some of the new kings subjected themselves to it frankly. Odovakar, or

Odoacer, the first German to rule Rome, did not take the title of "King" but petitioned the Emperor at Constantinople to grant him a subservient title under the Empire. His successor, Theodoric, considered himself a vassal of the Emperor to the end of his life. He took the title of "Patrician"; he maintained a Roman form of government, though under Gothic management; he used senators as agents and advisers; and he did everything he could to associate his kingdom with the Roman identity. Other kings in name likewise deemed themselves part of a continuing Empire, however independently they may have acted. So the Roman concept of empire did not die.

CHAPTER 15

Charlemagne

"The appellation of great *has been often bestowed, and sometimes deserved, but* CHARLEMAGNE *is the only prince in whose favor the title has been indissolubly blended with the name."*

GIBBON: DECLINE AND FALL OF THE ROMAN EMPIRE

I: The Birth of a New Era

PIPPIN THE SHORT had been Mayor of the Palace, or major-domo, and, like many of his forefathers, had wielded the real power while the titular King of the Franks sat on the throne as a dummy; but Pippin got tired of all that nonsense. He sent a message to the Pope asking him whether the man who held the power should not be king. The Pope had received a good deal of aid from Frankish kings, and he saw that an alliance with the Franks might be of great use to the Church, so he sent back the answer: "Rather should he have the name of king who has the power than he to whom no royal power remains." That being settled, Pippin had himself crowned in 751, and everybody was happy except King Childebert III, who had been deposed. As the Church wished to be sure that the coronation of Pippin would stick, the next Pope ratified it, and the following Pope came to France and crowned Pippin all over again. The dynasty which Pippin founded is called the "Carolingian," after Pippin's son, Charlemagne, who created a great empire.

The question of whether this new state was to be a free state or a part of some sort of Roman Empire was one which caused countless wars in Europe. The Franks felt completely independent and, indeed, rather patronizing toward the Papacy as its protectors. The Pope, on the other hand, had given Pippin the title of "Patrician of the Romans," probably intending some political significance. The Roman Empire had long before split into two parts, and the Church had, for all practical purposes, inherited the local power of the

Western emperors, but the Eastern emperor still claimed suzerainty over the Western world, and the Lombards and other obstreperous German tribes were making constant trouble for the Church. It was the purpose of the popes to make certain that the Church would have primacy in what was left of the Western Empire. They saw the opportunity to further this end by creating a new line of emperors who would be subservient to the Church.

Thus, when Charlemagne once visited Rome after an expedition to assist the beleaguered Pope, he was hailed as "Defender of the Faith" and "Patrician." On a second visit in 800 by the King of the Franks, the Pope crowned Charlemagne as "Emperor and Augustus," and did him homage. So began the Holy Roman Empire, which has been described as neither holy, Roman, nor an empire. But nothing was settled. During Charlemagne's reign there was peace between the Empire and the Church, but war broke out not long after his death and continued to harass Europe for centuries.

Charles the Great is "Charlemagne" to the French and "Karl der Grosse" to the Germans, and he is a national hero of both nations. He forged together a gigantic realm. It consisted of what is now France, almost all of what is now Germany, Belgium, Holland, Switzerland, half of Italy, and a good part of what once was Austria-Hungary. It is conceivable that France and Germany might never have separated if the Empire had not been repeatedly divided and subdivided by royal testaments. Wars usually followed these divisions, and in the resultant confusion, instead of moving closer to each other, France and Germany drew ever further apart.

II: Charles the Great

CHARLES THE GREAT was a remarkably good military leader and an excellent ruler. His capital was at Aachen, in Germany, from which point he tried to solidify his conquests and create one cohesive realm. He is said to have been dignified in mien, strong of arm, gallant in manner, and a vigorous and intelligent leader of men. He promoted literature, although he could not himself write, and he is numbered among the rulers who devoted themselves conscientiously to the development of law. In his personal life, although devoted to the Church, he was dissolute. Gibbon, in his *Decline and Fall of the Roman Empire,* wrote: "Without injustice to his fame, I may discern some blemishes in the sanctity and greatness of the restorer of the Western Empire. Of his moral virtues, chastity is not the most conspicuous: but the public happiness could not be materially injured by his nine wives or concubines, the various indulgence of meaner or more transient amours, the multitude of his bastards whom he bestowed on the Church, and the long celibacy and licentious manners of his daughters, whom the father was suspected of loving with too fond a passion."

Charlemagne's empire was a conglomerate of many nationalities governed by a confused mess of tribal and provincial law. His major problem was to bring all this confusion under control and forge a strong cohesive nation. He began by issuing a series of "capitularies": decrees made with the consent of his council, which may be termed a parliament, composed of nobles and advisers. This council was in a way a successor to the old Teutonic tribal assembly. When the Germans had settled down to a sedentary life, they found it impractical to attend tribal assembly meetings frequently, and they drifted into the habit of letting the nobles do the job for them. Thus they gradually lost any participation in government; plowing the land and getting the crops in seemed more important.

The Germanic assemblies had thus become councils of barons, and, when as strong a man as Charlemagne ruled, these councils came to be dominated by the king. Although the necessity for the consent of the people to new legislation persisted in theory, it disappeared in fact. The people did retain one function of government: they kept their popular courts. But even here the Emperor made deep inroads, for he established an *aula regis*, a royal court which stood at the head of the judicial system and created precedents which had to be followed by the provincial courts.

The influence of the Church was increasingly strong, as is evidenced by the fact that Charlemagne's civil ordinances were accompanied by religious decrees, which were almost always rules taken over verbatim from the Church. The secular capitularies were generally applicable to the whole Empire and were sent to the barons to be read in the churches and at public meetings. But Charlemagne was not satisfied merely to issue laws and hope that they might be obeyed. He sent *missi* or imperial envoys around the country to inspect the administration of justice, and some have seen in this practice an ancestor of the English jury system.

Our system of law is called "territorial"; everyone living in a country is subject to the law of that country. The conquering Germans had what is called "personal law," for it followed the person. A Lombard was subject to the Lombard law and carried it with him, figuratively, wherever he went. Even if living in Frankish territory he was under Lombard, not Frankish, law. But that system is not entirely foreign to us, for we have imposed it at times on supposedly less enlightened peoples. For a long while Americans in China were not subject to Chinese law but to American law, an imposition on the people of China.

So, when the invaders came into the Roman provinces, each tribe brought in its own law and kept it, and the confusion which came out of this practice made it necessary for special rules to be developed. Men were required to declare the tribal nationality to which they belonged. If a man had no tribe, rules were devised for deciding his nationality. A bastard who did not know his mother's tribe could adopt one of his own, and a freed slave had the same privilege. A wife took her husband's tribal nationality.

When two people of different tribal nationality had a dispute, the law of the "dominant interest" would apply. In a dispute between a guardian and his ward, this would be the law of the infant's nationality. In the case of an estate, the dominant nationality was that of the deceased. If the question were one of title to real estate, it was the law of the grantor which applied, and, in real-estate matters generally, the law of the "ancient proprietor"—that is, the oldest known possessor. In litigation, the law of the defendant applied.

The personal law was not always followed. No alien or non-Christian had any right to use his own law, with the one exception that the Jews were permitted to have their own judges administering their law. That was a carry-over of a custom which had arisen in Roman times when the Jews had, by tolerance, been treated specially. Generally, aliens were "protected," and the law of the protector was the law to which they were subjected. In all matters affecting Church or state, it was either the Church law or the territorial law which controlled, and not the personal law of a party to the dispute. The personal-law system was eventually doomed by two factors. One was the series of Charlemagne's capitularies, which applied to the whole Empire and created some uniformity of law. The other was the rapid growth of feudalism, against which personal law could not protect itself, for each feudal landholding became a partially autonomous country in which the feudal lord imposed his territorial law on the entire district, ignoring the tribal law of the inhabitants.

III: Charlemagne and the Feudal System

ROMANTIC WRITERS have given a lovely glow to the age of feudalism. They have pictured beautiful ladies rescued by gallant armored knights on proud chargers from confinement by robber barons in moated and drawbridged castles. Many a modern young girl has dreamed about those romantic days when knighthood was in flower and life was worth living. Yet the truth is that those "romantic" days were far from comfortable for even the few at the top of the social heap. They were not to be envied their use of scents (when they could get them) to hide the smells of the human body; their use of spices (when they could get them) to hide the smells and taste of spoiled food; their cold and drafty castles, verminous and without sanitation; their rough and uncomfortable furniture. Lacking medicines, they were defenseless against the assaults of disease. Whatever meager comforts and pleasures the barons and their ladies and an occasional cleric may have had, the masses lived in a miserable state. They had little comfort; they had few private rights; there was little law to protect them.

Had you lived in those days, by the laws of chance you would probably have been a serf, a slave to the soil, dependent on the will of the lord of the manor in which you toiled. With better luck, you might have been a semi-independent farmer, still largely relying upon the grace of the man in the castle; or a small craftsman or artisan dependent almost entirely on the tolerance of the big boss. With still better luck, you might have been a priest with some independence in the manor. If your luck in the draw were phenomenal, you might have been one of the pet retainers of the lord. And, if you hit the jackpot, you would have been the lord of the manor himself and boss of the works.

There was no "nationalism," there were no territorial kingdoms in the true sense, at the beginning of the feudal era. There was a King of the Franks but no King of France, and a King of the Lombards but no King of Lombardy. Nor did the feudal system create any nationality for the princes and barons who held land under a superior ruler, for feudalism ignored boundaries. One could hold a fief from several princes or several kings and thus owe allegiance to each, although one of these might be one's chief lord, entitled to first loyalty. As for the common people, the serfs and villagers, they soon lost even their identity as Saxons, Lombards, or Franks, and became identified with the manors to which they were more or less permanently attached.

There is some dispute as to the true origins of feudalism in Europe, but there is little doubt that it arose partly through fear. The Germanic invasions had brought fear to the Roman provinces—and the loose form of government which the conquerors instituted made life uncertain and living dangerous. In such times the weak are likely to commend themselves to the strong for protection, and here we have one of the roots of feudalism. The Franks and the other Germanic peoples already had a social system which was related to feudalism, for they knew vassalage and homage and the relationship of "lord" and "man." These Germanic quasi-feudal concepts made it easier for feudalism to develop, but it is probable that its deeper roots lay in certain ancient Roman institutions which the Germans found already in use in the Roman provinces. The troubled times introduced by the invasions revived their popularity.

In ancient Rome, "clients" had attached themselves to the powerful clans, in order to secure protection, giving loyalty and various kinds of service in exchange. Throughout Roman history the system of clientage persisted, even after the clans had lost their power. The later practice, called the *patrocinium*, was to attach oneself to some prominent or powerful citizen. There was also the institution of the *precarium*, by which one might deed one's lands to a patron and receive back the use of the property for life. One's heirs were then dependent on the future grace of the patron, for the returned use of the land extended only for one's own life. The conquering Franks found the *patrocinium* and *precarium* in wide use in Gaul.

The feudal idea spread quickly through the distribution of patronage by conquering chiefs. They would confiscate lands which they had taken and parcel them out among their most faithful or valuable retainers, in reward for services and to assure their continued allegiance. These would, in turn, distribute their lands in the same way to lesser lords, and these to still lower-ranking lords, until, the process being complete, the individual pieces of land were held by ultimate working tenants.

The relationship of each person to the one above him, in the hierarchy of tenancy, was that of "man and lord." The land held was at first called a *benefice* and later a *fief* or *fee* or *feud*, and the process of granting tenure was called *enfeoffment*. The Teutonic nature of a great part of the feudal system is evidenced by these words. The word "feud" is the Teutonic *fee* or *feh*, which means "wages" or "pay," combined with the Teutonic *odh* or *od*, which means "property" or "possessions." Thus, feud is "wages given for property." The word "fee" is still in our legal language, and is one of the vestiges of feudalism remaining to us. If you own land outright, you have a "fee simple."

It was Charlemagne who established the *benefice*, a grant of land in exchange for the promise of military service. As the Middle Ages became more tempestuous and life harder, most family lands were deeded to higher lords in exchange for benefices, military service being promised against protection. Primogeniture came to be recognized as the most efficient method of satisfying the conditions of the ownership of a benefice. Family settlements created primogeniture where it did not exist by original grant, and in many states the law followed practice and it became the rule.

The feudal system spread all over Western Europe, but it differed somewhat in each country. In England it reached an almost perfect state because William the Conqueror was astute enough, upon conquering England and confiscating much of its land, to demand full feudal fealty from the lords to whom he made his grants, insisting that all land was owned by him and only held in tenure by others, directly or indirectly from him.

IV: How the System Worked

Upon *enfeoffment*, when the lord made a grant of land to his man, he promised protection in return for the promise by the man to discharge certain duties to his liege lord. These feudal duties were of various kinds. Some had to do with military service. The vassal was obliged to follow his lord to battle and to bring with him such men as his status in life and the conditions of his fief warranted. In battle the vassal was obliged to surrender his horse to his lord if the latter had lost his mount, to fight beside him, and to go into captivity as a hostage when his lord was taken prisoner. An army was thus always available to the great lords, with which to defend their territories from the constant onslaughts of the Slavs, Avars, Huns, Northmen, and other invaders, and from the attacks of hostile barons. The army could be assembled rather quickly and was always in condition, for it was one of the terms of vassalage that the knights and their men attend their liege lords once every year, generally for a period of forty days, during which there was military practice.

Wars were fought in those days by armored and mounted knights and squires. There were foot troops attached to such cavalry armies, but these were used as auxiliaries only, for quick raids made foot troops almost useless. Thus, as the knights and squires had ever to be ready for war, they could spend little time in purely domestic accomplishments, and the actual farming of the land was left to serfs, bound to the land and obliged to feed not only themselves but also their masters. There were thus two classes, gentlemen and serfs. Eventually, a middle class arose, composed of merchants, tradesmen, and artisans, for the most part. There was also a wholly separate class, the men of the Church, to whom fell not only their religious duties but almost all of the clerical functions of the rather primitive society which the feudal age knew. For only churchmen could read and write.

Military duties were not the only obligations of a fief. The lord exercised civil and criminal jurisdiction over his lands and over his vassals, and held court as he wished. The tenants were required to attend these courts, as members of juries, to try their peers. These manor courts were responsible for most of the great confusion of law which grew up in Europe during the feudal age, for each manor lord was a law unto himself.

As each successor took his title to a fief, he was "invested" in a ritual which included a reaffirmation of the duties, as well as the rights, which went with the land. If a fief descended to a female, the liege lord had the right to select her husband, and he could also select the new husband of the widow of his liege man. The lord had wardship over infant heirs and could manage a fief during his ward's minority. If there were a failure of heirs, the land "escheated" to the lord.

Feudalism finally disinherited all children but the eldest male as far as real property was concerned. This was important in solidifying the feudal system of land tenure, but there was a contrasting tendency toward easier distribution of personal property. This came about chiefly through the influence of the Church. The marriage ceremony included a promise by the bridegroom to endow his wife, and there resulted from this the right of dower and similar rights giving the widow an interest in her deceased husband's property. Sometimes special rights were given to children, and later there came a tendency, also, to break down the differentiation between personal property and real property for their benefit. The net result was often that children were given a specific right in personal property, and a widow, by dower or otherwise, obtained a specific right in real property.

Among the special rights of the lord was the "relief," a grant from a succeeding tenant, usually equivalent to one year's income from the fief; and the king and the great lords were also entitled to the right of "aid," a grant by the tenants to defray the expenses of knighting the lord's oldest son, or of marrying off his daughter, or of ransoming him if he were captured in battle.

There has been much controversy over one alleged special right of the liege lord. It is called the *droit de seigneur* (the "right of the lord") and also the "right of the first night." This was the right to spend the first night with the bride of any vassal. There is little evidence that the right actually existed; if it did, the chances are that it was merely an excuse for levying a fine upon the bridegroom with which he might buy back the first night.

V: The Decline of Feudalism

When Charlemagne's empire broke up soon after his death, it was no longer necessary to reconcile the diverse nationalities which comprised his people, for the feudal system developed rapidly and created a vast number of semi-independent states and baronies, each of which virtually governed itself. The feudal law grew to such a state of mechanical perfection that the comparatively few manuals written about it served to codify it almost completely. But alongside of this feudal law, and in fields not covered by it, there developed what is generally called "customary law." Terminology in this subject is frequently troublesome, and this term is particularly vulnerable. For almost all law developed out of custom, and the feudal system itself certainly did. But the new law, growing up in the feudal localities, is specifically referred to as "customary law."

The customary law took a strange direction. It became class law.

The law of the nobles was almost wholly feudal law, and the peasants were subjected to the local law of each manor, but there was a separate law for the merchants which came out of commercial and trade customs developed by the merchants themselves. The townspeople had a sort of municipal law which was created chiefly by ordinances. The artisans had guilds and corporations in which their own customs were developed. Many of these customs were of very recent origin. Some of them grew up out of customs of trade and association in work, others out of decisions of local judges. It may seem odd to call the law produced by such decisions "customary law," but the judges did apply what they found to be custom and, if they could not find any, made rulings of their own which became "customary" after they had been followed a sufficient number of times. The judges actually made efforts to determine the existing customs, sometimes by consulting with venerable and informed persons in the community, sometimes by making general inquiries, and sometimes by consulting a higher court. Nor was it easy to create or to change a custom. For a custom to be valid, it must have been repeated often enough, it must have been public, and it must have been of long use.

No matter how well the alleged custom fitted that definition, it was not valid if it was deemed *mala* or against what might be called the public weal. At this point we meet again our old friend "natural law." The principle that a custom had to be reasonable and to conform to natural law was probably introduced by the Church. There was a technical reason for this. The people had lost the basic sovereignty which had been characteristic of old Germanic and Roman law. Their clan assemblies had passed out of existence as bodies which could sanction new legal customs. Therefore, a new form of sanction arose, through the Church, or through the king, who was considered the agent of God. If the custom was clearly reasonable, such sanction was presumed. The necessity for sanction was an excellent thing, for otherwise many more mistakes of ignorance or malice might have been made.

The customary law, developing beside the feudal law, sometimes actually changed it; and the remnants of personal law which remained after Charlemagne's death were destroyed by the growth of the feudal and customary law, for everyone in a community was held subject to one or both. The transition was not difficult. By this time the tribes had lost their essential identity, and the Germanic and other resident peoples had already mixed to a point where tribal distinctions were almost forgotten. Also, there was now a common religion.

The clan system had disappeared, except for remnants which persisted in the courts. There were no longer any assemblies to try cases, but there were lay judges in the local courts who had inherited the judicial function of the assemblies. These lay judges did not determine the issues in a trial. The presiding judge stated the issues and the law which applied, and he gave the judgment, but it had to be assented to by the lay judges in order to become a "collective judgment" and be effective. The similarity of this system to the old clan practice is clear, for the old clan trials required the assent of the assembled people to a judgment given by the chief or presiding officer. This system seems to be a crude forerunner of the modern jury system.

Other features of the old Germanic system of justice still prevailed. The ancient German court sessions were held in the open air. In the feudal era the courtrooms generally were open at one end. Sessions were usually held only from sunrise to sunset, and no judgment rendered after sunset was valid. Trials did not last beyond one day, and this custom, prevalent in England well into the eighteenth century, was inherited from the Romans as well as from Germans.

The rules of law remained somewhat primitive: compurgation of oaths was still an institution; and ordeal by various methods, decision by combat, and other ancient customs were still invoked. Trial by ordeal in the Middle Ages involved an extraordinary degree of faith in the willingness of God to intervene to protect the righteous. In the ordeal by hot irons, the iron was heated in the fire and a priest sanctified the proceeding by saying a mass over it and sprinkling it with holy water. The poor wretch who was to take the test then took communion and the priest recited, "The blessing of God the Father, the Son, and the Holy Ghost descend upon this iron for the discerning of the right judgment of God," whereupon the litigant had to carry the iron for a distance of nine feet. Then his hand was covered under seal for three days, and if festered blood were found where the iron had been, he was guilty. Or God was entreated to preserve the feet of the innocent from injury when he trod on sharp hot plowshares or seized a stone from a pot of boiling water. There was also the judgment of the cold water. If you were thrown into the water and it rejected you, you were guilty of the charge. The theory was that water had received you in baptism and, therefore, would now reject you if you were guilty. A great deal easier perhaps was the "trial by the morsel," in which a chunk of cheese and a piece of bread were put into the victim's mouth and the Lord was asked to keep him from swallowing them if he was guilty of the act charged.

Many of the duties of feudal landholding came, in time, to be dischargeable by the payment of money. The lords sought what small comforts there were to obtain, and their ladies pressed them constantly for more money. After the crusades introduced to European society the luxuries of the East, one can imagine the pressure which the lady of the manor put on her lord and master to buy silks, velvets, spices, perfumes, and jewelry. The liege lord grew more and more willing to take cash instead of service from his man. The result was a weakening of the military structure of feudal society and the increasing employment of professional soldiers. The invention of firearms spelled the death of the armored, knightly cavalry and thus destroyed the need for this specialized force.

But a force which was of greater importance in destroying feudalism was the growth of the towns. Villages grew into towns, and the townspeople developed trade. Artisans and traders banded themselves into guilds or craft unions, and these acquired money and political strength. What they could not buy in the way of privilege or release from the strictures of feudal society they finally achieved by economic pressure. New ideas of law and of legal system came into Europe by way of a renaissance of Roman law which accelerated learning and found the feudal laws and institutions distasteful. Finally, feudalism could not withstand the attack of the rapidly strengthened middle and intellectual classes.

PART FIVE

THE CHURCHMEN

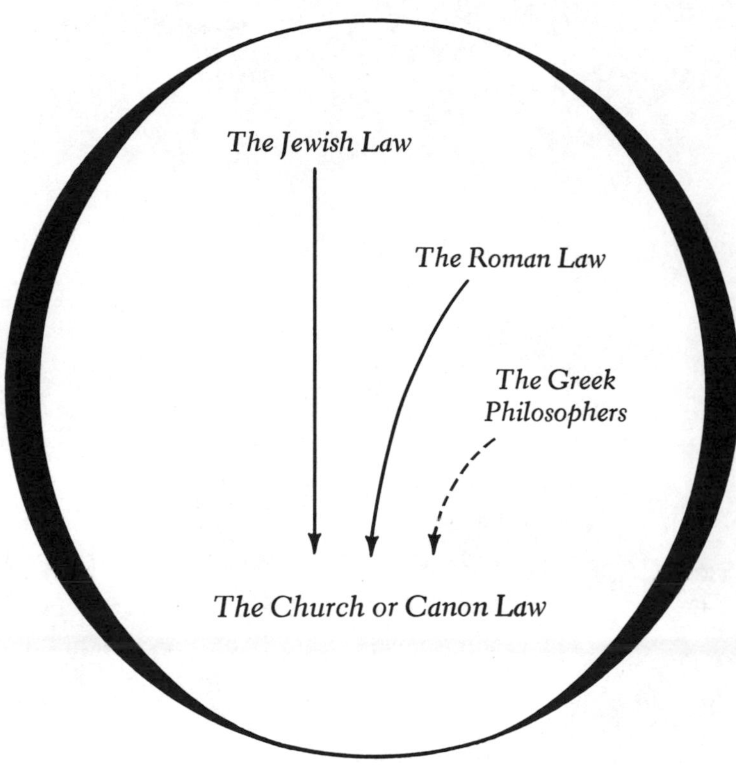

THE CHIEF BASIC SOURCES

CHAPTER 16

St. Augustine

". . . St. Augustine in many passages seems to hold that this civil state is of its nature and in its character evil." EYRE: EUROPEAN CIVILIZATION

THE CITY OF ROME had stood so long as the impregnable stronghold and center of the civilized world that the sack of the city by Alaric the Goth in 410 left the Romans dumfounded and horrified. Christianity had become the official and compulsory religion of the Empire, and whatever might happen in distant provinces, the people had felt secure in the capital, where the very presence of the pope seemed certain to shelter the faithful. Now they wondered if perhaps the new Christianity was not so powerful as the old gods of Rome. It was to allay this widespread and growing questioning of Christianity that St. Augustine (Aurelius Augustinus) wrote his *City of God,* in which he explained that the sack of Rome had not constituted a dereliction on the part of God in failing to protect his communicants but was a misfortune which had befallen the city because of human frailty and sin. The *City of God* has direct importance to the story of law, for it contains a dissertation on the position of the Church in the state which opened up a controversy not wholly ended to this day. St. Augustine insisted that the Church must be supreme within the state. He did not go as far as later Church apologists, for he admitted that there must be a division of authority and that the civil authority had its proper and independent place. However, he maintained that there could not be a good state unless the civil authority made itself subservient to the religious, and not only in matters of pure religion. He meant that the Church should determine all legal issues in which human conduct was concerned and in which morals and ethics might be involved. In later periods the Church went much further than that, proclaiming itself the ultimate authority in all of Christendom, in matters civil as well as spiritual.

The time was not yet ripe in St. Augustine's day to make this claim. It was not until 445 that a Roman emperor recognized the right of the Bishop of Rome to supremacy over all of the "Universal" Church, and that was fifteen years after St. Augustine's death. Even then the Church needed the protecting arm of the imperial authority to strengthen itself and to solidify its position. It was not until the collapse of the Western half of the Empire in the latter half of the fifth century that the Papacy could think seriously of striking for independence. Then it began to acquire a temporal domain of its own which lasted until the Papal States were abolished in 1871, when Italy was unified under Victor Emmanuel. Mussolini restored the popes to temporal sovereignty, recognizing the tiny Vatican City as the pope's dominion, and since then the popes have again functioned as temporal rulers, but the reduced size of the Church State evidences the extent of the failure of the Papacy in its long struggle for temporal supremacy in Europe. It did, at times during the Middle Ages, look as though that struggle might be won and as though all of Western Europe might come under papal sway.

Although St. Augustine was a most weighty theorist behind the temporal ambitions of the Papacy, the Church did not rely on his arguments alone. There was the more basic premise that the Bishop of Rome had inherited from St. Peter a mantle of authority granted by Jesus himself; and if that premise were accepted, then the direct vicar of Christ must be right in any controversy with the temporal arm of government. Also, the Church had inherited the imperial tradition of the Western Roman Empire. The pope is sometimes referred to as the "Supreme Pontiff," and this title, derived from *pontifex maximus*, the title of the chief priest of pagan Rome, indicates the succession. The Church had grown strong by the time of the collapse of the Western Empire and was able to weather the ensuing political storms. The Eastern emperors still had a finger in the Italian pie, for they held some territories in the peninsula, but the Lombards had established strong states in the north and in the south, and the Church found itself in fact ruling a substantial domain in the center. Control of remnants of the Western Empire by the Byzantine emperors was weakened further by subsequent events which left the popes still more independent. After the final separation of the Eastern and Western branches of the Church, the rapid conversion to the Roman Church of the barbarians who had flooded over the Western provinces, and the weakening of the Eastern Empire itself through incursions by barbarians and Saracens, the Roman Church finally found itself free and dominant.

The Roman Empire never actually died. It might be said that it merely evolved into Christian Europe. Separate states did arise, but they were united, in one sense, in their common Christianity. The Roman tradition persisted, respected by the barbarians even when they did not understand it; its law made increasing inroads on the law of the new states, and the Church acted as the catalyst in a transition from the shattered old Empire to the new Europe. However one regards the attempt of the Roman Church to attain temporal control of the Western world, its aggressive policy in this direction enabled it to imprint much of its own canon law more deeply on the civil law of Europe. Therefore, and because its own law was in many respects more benign and enlightened in the early Middle Ages than the confused local law, the practical effect on the development of European law of the papal struggle for temporal supremacy was progressive.

The crowning of Charlemagne as Roman Emperor was intended to establish a new Roman Empire in which the Church would operate side by side with—or a bit above—the civil administration of a Frankish dynasty of emperors. All was harmonious while Charles the Great was alive, but his death was soon followed by serious conflicts between subsequent emperors and popes on the issue of just where the preponderance of authority lay.

The claims of the Church to temporal supremacy were strengthened by two forgeries. One was the so-called *False Decretals* produced in the middle of the ninth century by some overzealous monk, containing what were passed off as letters written by Pope Clement I in about the year 91, in which he asserted that the pope was the supreme civil as well as religious authority on earth. The falsity of this famous document, which was used frequently to bolster papal temporal claims, was not established until the fifteenth century. But it was not so powerful a support to the Papacy as the *Donation of Constantine*. Gibbon tells the story of the Donation as follows: "This memorable donation was introduced to the world by an epistle of Adrian the First, who exhorts Charlemagne to imitate the liberality and revive the name of the great Constantine. According to the legend, the first of the Christian emperors was healed of the leprosy and purified in the waters of baptism, by St. Silvester, the Roman Bishop; and never was physician more gloriously recompensed. His royal proselyte withdrew from the seat and patrimony of St. Peter; declared his resolution of founding a new capital in the East; and resigned to the popes the free and perpetual sovereignty of Rome, Italy, and the provinces of the West. . . . The sovereignty of Rome no longer depended on the choice of a fickle people; and the successors of St. Peter and Constantine were invested with the purple and prerogatives of the Caesars. . . . In the revival of letters and liberty this fictitious deed was transpierced by the pen of Laurentius Valla, the pen of an eloquent critic and a Roman patriot." *

In the ninth century, Pope Nicholas I, a vigorous man strongly impressed with the necessity of increasing the temporal power of the Church, made good use of these two documents, but, in justice to him, he probably did not know that they were forged. Even discovery of the falsity of "the two magic pillars of the spiritual and temporal monarchy of the popes," as Gibbon describes them, did not cause the Church to abandon its claims to temporal supremacy, for the Augustinian theory persisted. Soon after the discovery of America by Columbus, Pope Alexander VI issued his bull *Inter Caetera* in which he presumed to divide the Western Hemisphere between Spain and Portugal. While the Pope was a sort of arbitrator in the colonial conflict between Spain and Portugal and actually only marked out regions in which the respective nations were to have primary rights of discovery, he did say he acted "of our own accord, not at your instance nor the request of anyone else in your regard, but of our own largess and certain knowledge and out of the fullness of our apostolic power, by the authority of Almighty God conferred upon us in blessed Peter and of the vicarship of Jesus Christ, which we hold on earth . . ."

Of the many churchmen who stoutly insisted upon the temporal supremacy of the Church, the monk Hildebrand, who became Pope as Gregory VII,† was one of the most open and aggressive. Gregory maintained the right of the pope to dictate the selection of the Holy Roman emperor; he claimed that Sardinia and Corsica, Spain and Hungary belonged to the Papacy; and he suggested to the King of Denmark that he make his kingdom a papal fief. He threatened to depose the King of France; he demanded that William the Conqueror declare himself a vassal of the pope.

The expression "going to Canossa" stems from this period, when

* *The Decline and Fall of the Roman Empire,* Chapter XLIX.
† B. 1023, d. 1085. Pope, 1073.

the Emperor Henry IV waited penitently in the snow in front of the castle of Canossa, where the Pope was a guest of Matilda of Tuscany. Henry hoped for forgiveness for his sins in fighting the Church in the matter of control of investitures.* Canossa was Gregory's greatest victory, but Henry's subservience was not sincere; it was soon repudiated, and in the last stage of this episode Gregory himself died virtually a prisoner.

Gregory's death did not end the papal struggle; it was carried on by many succeeding popes, but the end was inevitable. A growing spirit of nationalism made dictation by a "foreign despot" increasingly distasteful to the people of Europe, and the Roman Church was obliged, in the modern era, to abandon its active claims to supremacy over the state. However, the Roman Catholic Church still maintains that its own law, in some respects, is of higher force than the law of governments, and it demands obedience to it on the part of its communicants. When Archbishop Stepinac was arrested and sentenced by a Yugoslav tribunal, the Vatican declared excommunicated all who "have contributed, physically or morally, toward the consummation of the above-mentioned crimes or were necessary co-operators in them." The crimes alleged were violations of specific sections of the canon law, including the haling of a bishop before a lay judge, performing acts of violence against a bishop or archbishop, and directly or indirectly preventing the exercise of ecclesiastical jurisdiction or authority, having recourse for this purpose to any lay authority. A similar excommunication was placed upon the Hungarians who took any part in the arrest and trial of Cardinal Mindszenty.

* The term "investitures" refers to the designation of religious officeholders. Kings of the Middle Ages disputed frequently with the Papacy as to who had the right to appoint bishops, abbots, etc., within their dominions.

CHAPTER 17

Canon Law and Aquinas

"Law is a regulation in accord with reason, issued by a lawful superior for the common good."

AQUINAS: SUMMA THEOLOGIAE

I: The Growth of Canon Law

THE BUSINESSMAN who traveled across Europe in the Middle Ages could take twelve doctors of law along with him and yet not be sure that he would avoid legal difficulties. Even in one small principality he might find as many different sets of laws as there were baronies, manors, and abbeys within its borders. The laws of one village might vary considerably from those of its neighbor; and, to make it still more difficult, there was not just one local system of law, but several concurrent systems.

There was the local law, differing widely, developed in the courts and by the customs of a tiny section of territory. There was also the Germanic law, mixed up with the feudal law, in a state of considerable confusion, for no one knew exactly how much of it applied to individual territories. In addition, there were two other systems, operating side by side and rivaling each other, to either of which appeal could be made when other law was inadequate. One was the Roman law, which, as I shall describe later, came more and more to be "received" in Western Europe. The second was the canon, or Church, law which, in a sense, was even "higher law" than the Roman, particularly in matters relating to morals and ethics.

The Church had begun very early to develop its own legal system. For some time its strength was in *ecclesiae*, which were religious societies whose real purposes were hidden behind such innocuous exteriors as burial societies. These groups developed their own rules of government to determine disputes which their members brought before them for settlement, wishing not to submit themselves to the civil authorities. Like the Jews, who preferred to have their rabbis settle differences between them, the early Christians went to their priests to have their controversies judged. So a system of law gradually evolved to govern the *ecclesia* and the conduct of its members.

The early Church fathers used the Roman law, in so far as it did not conflict with Scripture and the Jewish-Christian ethical and moral principles. But the Roman law which was adopted by the Church was not always the pure or classic law.

When the Church was finally officially recognized in the Empire, its legal system came out into the open, and it began to affect the civil law materially. Then, when the Empire of the West collapsed and the popes found themselves actually temporal rulers of a remnant of the Empire, their canon law became a truly civil law as well. From this point on, the influence of the canon law grew rapidly. In the long struggle between the Holy Roman emperors and the popes, the former never went so far as to contest the right of the Church in matters of religion. Because so many spiritual factors were involved in civil law, the Church's pronouncements were frequently superimposed on the civil law of all Europe. It was as though there were a separate system of law, side by side with the law of each European nation, limited to matters of morals but available for appeal if there were a conflict between it and the civil law. In a limited way, the canon law was a system of equity law operating alongside of, or even superimposed on, the civil law.

It was inevitable that there should be a conflict between this system and the Roman system. The Roman law eventually won out, but not until canon law had made such deep inroads into the legal systems of Europe, including England, that it remains as one of the most important ancestors of our own legal system. Until that final victory of the Roman law, in the course of which the Roman law was tempered by some introduction of canon concepts, the law of the Church was almost a universal constitution for Europe.

For many centuries the papal decrees, bulls, council resolutions, and other legislative measures had accumulated into a great mass. In the eleventh century, attempts were made to codify the canon law. There were the *Decretum* of Burchard of Worms, the *Collectio Canonum* of Anselm of Lucca, and the *Decretum* of Bishop Ino of Chartres; but none of these filled the need for order. The first great codification was made about 1140 by Gratian, an obscure Benedictine monk of Bologna. He was assisted by professors of the University of Bologna. Gratian's product was respected in the Church just as the *Digest of Justinian* was among later jurists in the Roman law. It was a magnificent work of compilation and co-ordination, and virtually made a system out of canon law, although it was actually more of a textbook than a code. This *Decretum of Gratian,* as it is called, was officially sanctified by Pope Gregory IX in 1234, at which time a supplement, the *Decretals,* was adopted.

After Gratian, canon law came to be a universal subject of study at the universities where law was taught, alongside the Roman laws of Justinian. The degree of J.U.D. was given—*juris utriusque doctor,* or doctor of both lay and canon law.

In the thirteenth century, a period in which art and architecture flourished and Europe was beginning to make serious efforts to drag itself out of the darkness of the early Middle Ages, the great states began to drive toward national solidarity. France, under Louis IX (St. Louis), England under Edward I, and most of the other great European states of the West consolidated their systems of local justice, and the influence and importance of the Church courts declined as the national courts came into greater prominence. By the time of the Reformation, in the sixteenth century, the Roman Catholic Church no longer maintained its standing as a "Universal Church" with great judicial and legislative power.

In 1545 the Council of Trent assembled, attended by three hundred Church dignitaries, to reform the Church law. It sat eighteen years and legislated widely. Later, in 1582, the canon law was re-edited, at the command of Pope Gregory XIII, by a commission of cardinals and law doctors. This new codification was called the *Corpus Juris Canonici* and was the basis of canon law until the revisions of a few years ago. But the reforms of the Council of Trent did not stall the progress of the Reformation or of the nationalistic movement. The temporal jurisdiction of the papal courts was abolished, in due time, by all the great states. In England it was the domestic problems of Henry VIII which precipitated a quick change. In France the process of change started in the fifteenth century and ended with the French Revolution.

The Roman Catholic Church has apparently retired completely from the temporal juridical field, for the *Codex Juris Canonici,* the

Papal Code of 1917, establishes a code of morals and behavior merely for its own believers.

The Papacy still has its own *Cancelleria*, or Chancery, administered by the Cardinal Chancellor, a dignitary second in importance only to the Pope himself. The supreme court of the Church is the *Sacra Romana Rota*, or "Holy Roman Wheel," known as the *Rota*. Its jurisdiction is now confined to matters of Church concern alone, including such matters of morals as the annulment of marriages. But in its day, it was the most important court of Christendom, having supreme judicial authority in the system of papal courts. Its opinions fill hundreds of volumes, mostly collections of decisions and opinions of individual judges.

II: Canon Law in the Middle Ages

INHERITING the Roman tradition, the Church in the Middle Ages favored absolutism. Nevertheless, the feudal concept that the state was a personal appendage of the ruler was abhorrent to the Church, which maintained that the state was not there for the ruler but the ruler for the state. It might be put this way: The Church maintained that the ruler had the absolute right to rule but had the absolute duty to rule justly. Thus the Church tempered its support of absolutism by imposing Jewish-Christian morality and ethics on law and its administration.

The philosophy of St. Augustine had come partially into its own; and the Church used its special moral-legal function to introduce Jesus (and Moses) into European law. To do this it established all over Europe a system of courts which were comparable to our own federal courts. The Church courts were not national courts but courts of what was actually an association of states, the Christian nations of Europe. The similarity to our system ends there, however, because the Church courts did assert concurrent and superior jurisdiction in many matters of ordinary civil law.

The Church insisted on the equality of all men before the law, and it was chiefly in Church courts that one could obtain justice in an abstract sense. But the performance of the Church courts in this respect was far from perfect. The Church courts of the Inquisition practiced shocking brutalities. True, the Church did not execute its victims, for it had a saying, "*Ecclesia abhoret a sanguine*"—"The Church shrinks from bloodshed"—but it turned convicted heretics over to the civil authorities and demanded execution, generally by such means as burning at the stake, preceded by torture. But these were cruel times, and the churchmen who ordered such violence in the name of Jesus were acting with the misguided ethics of a sorry age. And, in spite of such juridical derelictions, the Church courts contributed to progress by applying a theoretically "higher law," a useful concept, however misused at times.

In criminal law it was the Church which, despite its own cruel lapses, pressed for more humane and just law. It fought the primitive system of personal vengeance and caused the substitution for it of the system of punishment by the state. It opposed the old "accusatorial" system of criminal trial, under which the injured person himself made complaint against the offender. Often the weak would fear to complain because of the danger of reprisal. The Church was largely instrumental in developing the present "inquisitorial" system, under which it is not the injured person who complains but a public prosecutor.

In matters of domestic relations, marriage, divorce, and guardianship the Church's law almost always prevailed. Its claim to moral authority was irresistible. In many respects it promoted the principle of good faith. A contract based only upon mutual promises became one which must be respected. When there was a "meeting of the minds" (a concept carried over into English and American law) there was a binding contract. The Church was somewhat instrumental in reintroducing the practice of litigants' being represented by counsel. It encouraged the use of wills and testamentary dispositions. It opposed the taking of interest (calling it by its Biblical name of "usury"), but this very opposition developed certain evasions out of which grew new legal forms, such as the limited partnership and the charging of rent.

In civil-law procedure we owe a great debt to canon law. Using the Roman practice as a base, the Church, in its own courts, developed many rules, forms, and methods which remain with us today. In trial practice the reforms of the Church were radical. Pleadings were in writing instead of oral, as among the Germans. Proof was by witnesses and written evidence, and the oath of compurgation was abandoned, as were the trial by ordeal and the judicial duel, or trial by battle.

The influence exerted by the Church also appeared in many indirect ways. The clerics, almost the only people who could read or write, were called upon to write down the laws and do all writing in connection with legal processes. They turned this virtual monopoly, consciously or unconsciously, to the promotion of the canon law. By making a slight change or giving an interpretation, by writing an annotation or a comment, they had an enormous influence in turning the rules of law toward the Christian theses pronounced by Church jurists.

Unfortunately, the Christian Church, which had been so sorely persecuted in Rome in its early years, was not averse to persecuting others when it had power, and much of the anti-Semitic legislation of the Middle Ages was either enacted or inspired by the Church. Jews had been rather well treated in Rome, but in the Christian kingdoms of Europe they were virtual slaves, without civil rights. They could not marry Christians, have Christian servants, have Christian nurses, hold public office, or hold lands. They could not appear in public in Holy Week, they could not testify against a Christian, and they were specially taxed. For centuries the Talmud (which Pope Honorius IV, in 1286, called that "damnable book," saying that "all other evils flow out of it") was condemned by the Church, and all copies of it which could be found were confiscated and burned. The year 1215, made memorable by the granting of the Magna Charta, is also memorable in the history of anti-Semitism. In that year the Fourth Lateran Council of the Church, at the instance of Pope Innocent III, decreed that all Jews must wear a badge or distinctive apparel so that they could be easily recognized, facilitating the frequent massacres of Jews.* Many later councils repeated the order.

III: St. Thomas Aquinas

Gratian's service in assembling and co-ordinating the mass of canon law was of inestimable value; but the man to whom the Church and canon law are most indebted is St. Thomas Aquinas, the thirteenth-century philosopher, the most important philosopher of the Church. It was he who most strongly emphasized the duty

* I suppose it had never occurred to the Pope that if Jesus had been living, he, too, would have had to wear a badge.

of the sovereign. "*Regnum non est propter regem sed rex propter regnum*," said Aquinas—"The kingdom does not exist for the king but the king for the kingdom." And it is largely upon the thesis of St. Thomas Aquinas that the Church jurists went so far as to pronounce that laws were of absolutely no force whatever if they were not for the common good.

From the Roman law and by reading the Greek philosophers, the Church sages knew the theory of natural law. They had considerable difficulty with the concept; there were wide differences of opinion as to what natural law was and how it manifested itself, but it was a concept which they adopted readily because natural law could certainly be ultimately considered as the law of God.

Aquinas propounded the principle that natural law might be founded by "right reason," a concept which he took over directly from the Greek philosophers, particularly Aristotle. Many Church jurists have been satisfied that this rule of right reason made it easier to determine the details of natural law. It did result in rationalizations which helped them out of such dilemmas as whether or not slavery was authorized by natural law. The answer in that case was that slavery, although not sanctioned by natural law, was accepted as part of the conventional or customary law, and that it was acceptable because it tended to curb some of the sins of man—a theory which may have been clear to a churchman but is somewhat obscure to the uninitiated.

In matters of property, the churchmen followed the Greeks. Both held that there was no natural law of property, but only conventional law. Some of the early Church writers were quite socialistic, and, indeed, it is not difficult to reconcile Christianity with socialism. Other Church jurists held that the law of God, natural law, did not comprehend private property, but the Fall of Man theory necessitated conventional laws of property, for man's sinful greed had made it necessary to curb him through laws affecting property rights. The inclusion of property rights as part of natural law was a development which came late in European legal history, with philosophers like Locke, who held property rights to be as fundamental as personal rights. The Church held that what had been given to man by conventional law could be taken away from him; and this idea made it very difficult for medieval thinkers to conceive of absolute ownership of private property.

The same distinction between God-made and man-made law

came into the political field. No absolute right to rule existed under natural law, according to the churchmen. Conventional law permitted it because it had become necessary (the Fall of Man theory again) to curb man's sinful conduct. Many of the churchmen, however, hedged a bit—though it may be called a consistent hedge—by saying that the right to rule was a divinely appointed remedy for sin. Thus they laid the basis for the theory of the divine right of kings. In any event, the Church jurists of the Middle Ages emphasized the theory that whatever the right to rule might be, it was a right which involved a trust. It was the perverted political reasoning of the seventeenth century which converted the medieval right of kings into uncurbed absolutism. The Church never abandoned Aquinas's concept of the ruler as a trustee.

Credit must go to the Church for having introduced into post-Roman Europe the idea that there is something higher than the momentary or casual law of states, a law of ultimate justice. Although this basic idea has caused and still induces some muddled thinking, it is a concept upon which much has been built, including a great part of the basic formula for our own government.

PART SIX

THE WESTERN EUROPEANS

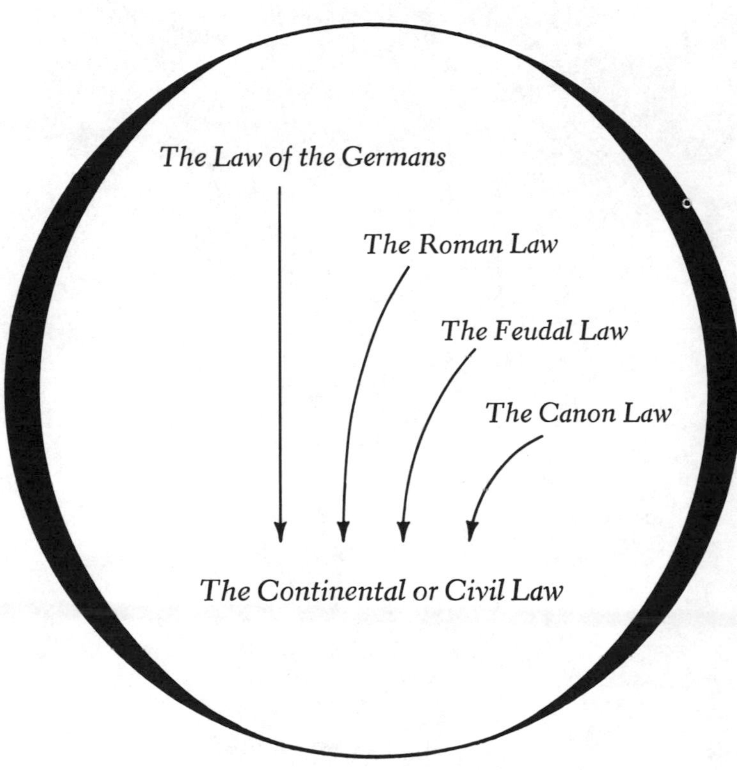

THE CHIEF BASIC SOURCES

CHAPTER 18

Bartolus

"More than any other jurist of his school, he contributed to its great work in transforming the law of the past into the law of his day." CARLO CALISSE

I: The Resurrection of Justinian

WHATEVER the degree of decadence and weakness to which the Roman people had fallen before the final conquest by the barbarians, there still remained a large intellectual class. It had access, through libraries and public records, to a great storehouse of learning, which, however, was thoroughly destroyed or neglected in the ensuing centuries. Pitifully little of it remains today.

When the barbarians came to stay, remnant law schools took refuge in churches and monasteries, where small groups listened to professors handicapped by the loss of their most valuable literary materials, who could only rely on memory to fill the gaps in their teaching equipment. It is no wonder that, although the teaching of law continued, the law itself degenerated, and what came to pass as Roman law would have been unrecognizable to Gaius, Papinian, or Ulpian. In time, it again became possible for the law schools to come into the open, and several of them, encouraged by enlightened barbarian rulers, grew into great universities. Law study gradually faltered its way back to organization and scientific method, but it still suffered from the tragic loss of the precious records of the past.

The center of law study remained in Rome until late in the eleventh century, when primacy passed to Ravenna. But, in the meantime, other schools arose where not the Roman but the barbarian law was studied. Most of these were in the kingdom of the Lombards, who had stubbornly resisted the incursions of the Roman law and insisted on a perfection of their own system. Roman law was to prove irresistible, and the Lombard battle against it was hopeless, but the schools at Mantua, Verona, Bologna, and Padua fought on for their Germanic law, which Romanists called "asses' law," and attracted many thousands of students.

Early in the twelfth century a radical change came over the Italian law schools. Although there had been some circulation of the works of Justinian after the collapse of the Western Empire, astonishingly little attention was paid to these authorities in the early centuries of the revival of law study. Scraps and pieces of historical material were used instead of the encyclopedic compilations of Justinian. But word began to come to the schools that a man named Irnerius was lecturing on Justinian's *Institutes* and *Code* at Bologna and was exalting the codified law above the crude system in use. Others quickly took up the study of Justinian, and it spread all over Italy.

We know almost as little about Irnerius as we do about Gaius. He was patronized by that Matilda of Tuscany at whose castle the Emperor Henry IV had prostrated himself as a penitent before Pope Gregory. Beyond that, we know little except that Irnerius was called "the luminary," and that he lectured in the Square of San Stefano. That he lectured in the streets was not due to any lack of respect for him by the authorities or to any Socratic lack of organization on his own part. There just were no university buildings at Bologna in his day. Indeed, the university of those times was quite unlike our conception of a university.

The university was run not by the professors but by the students. Without any official organization to manage its affairs, it had neither registered courses nor required curriculum. Each student learned from whomever he wished and arranged payment with his professors. The students exercised control over the professors, whom they fined for omitting something important or for skipping a vital paragraph of an authority. And—pleasant reverse of our modern system—the students fined teachers for coming late to class.

The student body was divided into fraternities or "nations." In contrast to the university itself, these were well organized, kept careful records, and held frequent meetings. Each was named after some national group—"English," "Saxon," "Gascon"—and these fraternities, which fought among themselves and plagued the civil authorities, were prototypes of the "corps" founded centuries later in the German universities.

Of course, the helter-skelter management of the universities by the students did not last forever. Universities multiplied rapidly, first in Italy and then elsewhere, many of them starting as law schools and later broadening their curriculums, and great masters appeared who attracted students first to one center of learning and then to another. In the course of this rapid development of higher teaching, curriculums came to be carefully supervised by university authorities. Degrees were awarded which have not changed much in form or significance in the intervening years. The degree of "bachelor" entitled the student to go on to the next rank, "licentiate," * the equivalent of our degree of "master." A master could go on to try for a doctorate, the awarding of which was accompanied by the donation of a cap, book, and ring, and which entitled the student to teach—an idea which has persisted in our own universities, where the upper grades of teaching usually require the acquisition of a doctor's degree.

The law professors of this era were known as "glossators," because they taught through glossaries, explanatory texts usually inscribed around a central text from Justinian, but without relating them to contemporary life in any way. The greatest of these glossators was Francis Accursius, a Florentine born about 1182. By the time of Accursius, the accumulation of commentary on Justinian's works had reached a point of utter confusion. It was as though the law consisted of a mass of professors' notebooks. So Accursius took all this material and blended it into a master glossary known as *The Great Gloss*, which was accepted as the embodiment of the law and cited in the courts as an authority equal to that of the actual books of Justinian.

The great contribution of the glossators was that they studied the original texts of Justinian, collected them with care, and preserved them for future generations. Thus, while the popes were fighting a losing battle for hegemony in Europe and for the supremacy of the canon law, Justinian's books spread rapidly, even to England, some in pure text and some as the core of glossaries. For about two hundred years the study of Justinian proceeded on the system of the glossators, who were now paying far more attention to the glosses, and particularly to *The Great Gloss*, than they were to the original text. These jurists and courts usually dealt with classic law, unrelated

* A lawyer in Mexico is called a *licenciado*, a derivative of the same root, but, oddly enough, *licenciado* in some other Latin-American countries means "licensed convict."

to life itself, but a new type of legal study and teaching finally came along to rescue the law from this sterility.

II: The Monarch of the Law

THE NEW PROFESSORS of law were called "practitioners" or "commentators." They cast aside the glosses; they did not devote themselves to discussing the Justinian law in the abstract, but began to apply it to the problems of life. They even adjusted it to city statutes and to the feudal and Germanic customs and the principles of the canon law. More important, they did not merely write and lecture but carried their theories and their interpretations of the Roman law into the courts where they argued cases. The actual, working law thus came to be subjected to a practical, scientific process of development. These commentators, as appeared later, had their shortcomings, but they did much to create a new veneration for the law and for justice.

The greatest of the commentators was Bartolus (1313?-1357), a brilliant man who was teaching law at the age of twenty-six, and whose writings were of dominant importance for two centuries. The Emperor Charles IV thought so much of him that he not only ennobled him but also granted him a most unusual privilege. He decreed that Bartolus and any of his descendants who might teach law should have the right to legitimize any bastard who attended their courses.*

Bartolus's approach was always practical. He realized the need to reconcile the conflicting legal systems of the day and to establish general rules of law which could be applied to the practical problems of everyday life. From the various sources, Germanic, Roman, canon, feudal, and customary law, he planned to draw a new law, universal in its application. Had he not died so young—at the age of forty-four—he might have achieved his ambition, for his talents were phenomenal and his reputation astounding. He was called

* I wonder whether the Emperor was serious about this, or whether he had his tongue in his cheek in implying that many bastards might wish to study law. Lawyers have been the butt of perhaps as many jokes as have doctors. It is said, for example, that only one lawyer ever became a saint, St. Ives, an ecclesiastical judge of Brittany in the beginning of the fourteenth century, who dispensed justice equally to rich and poor, powerful and weak.

the "monarch of the law," and his pronouncements were accepted throughout Europe as though they were legislation.

One of Bartolus's chief contributions to legal science was his work, the *Theory of Statutes,* which, though criticized in part by later generations, anticipated many modern theories of the interpretation of statute law. One of his principles was that a statute must be interpreted through its actual words, even though the inquiry were into its extent and its scope. Extraneous explanations of the meaning of a statute were rejected by Bartolus. Modern jurists have departed from this strict method of interpretation somewhat and sometimes delve into the legislative debates which accompanied the passage of the statute in order to find out what was intended by a new law.

Among his other principles of interpretation were that certain acts, such as making a will or a contract, are to be interpreted according to the law of the place where they are made; that the law of the place of performance is to govern the consequences arising from neglect or delay; and that the rules of procedure in litigation are to be those of the place of trial. These are all modern rules, and Bartolus was either the first to recognize them or the first to give them clear exposition.

So profound was his effect upon law study that subsequent teachers who followed his school were known merely as "Bartolists," and chairs were founded at universities for the sole purpose of conducting lectures on his works. It was said that *nemo jurista nisi sit Bartolista,* "no one is a jurist who is not a Bartolist."

CHAPTER 19

Luther and Calvin

"The law discovers the disease. The gospel gives the remedy."
MARTIN LUTHER

"The law of God, which we call the moral law, must alone be the scope, and rule, and end, of all laws."
JOHN CALVIN

I: The Troubles of the Church

BEFORE the time of Bartolus, the Church had been obliged to waste a good part of its energies in fighting a succession of heresies which threatened to split Europe and put an end to the chance of unifying Western Christendom. Several years after his death came the calamity which so severely weakened the power of the Church and ended all possibility of overcoming the growing strength of nationalism.

The security of the Church was attacked from two directions. There were certain powerful Italian families—Orsini, Colonna, Gaetani, Conti, and others—whose political machinations were threatening the independence of the Papacy, and the Roman people themselves were clamoring for autonomy and a civil state. To escape from these two points of pressure in Rome, the Church removed the seat of the popes to Avignon, in France, but this absence from the center of empire only further weakened the prestige of the Church and annoyed the people of Rome. When Pope Gregory XI died, the Romans insisted upon an Italian pope and forced the election in Rome of Urban VI, an Italian. However, some of the cardinals left Rome, constituted themselves a new conclave, and elected their own pope, Clement VII. There were thus two popes in office, and each claimed complete authority and appointed his own bishops and diplomats. The kings and princes of Europe took sides and increased the confusion.

Everyone hoped that the Great Schism would end with the death of one of the two popes, but, on the death of each, successors were elected, and finally a third pope was elected to make even more ridiculous and tragic this struggle which was tearing Europe apart and rapidly reducing the influence of the Church. Whatever the Church might otherwise have been able to do to retard the growing spirit of nationalism in Europe, the Great Schism prevented. And, in the midst of this turmoil, came another blow.

John Wycliffe (1320-1384), a militant English reformer, had been preaching against the venality of the prelates and advocating what might be called extreme radicalism. His *De Ultima Aetate Ecclesiae* was a book full of forebodings on the corruption of the clergy; and, in later works, he continued to fulminate against the Church and against the institution of the Papacy in particular. But, as long as Wycliffe's ideas remained in somewhat isolated England, they were not so very damaging to the Church, although on his death his works were investigated and one hundred and sixty propositions in his writings were listed for condemnation.

Many of the propositions of Wycliffe were either anarchical or communistic and extremely distasteful to the organized Church. Wycliffe had held that no man could have any right to property unless he was in a state of grace; that title to property had no value unless it came from God; that an unjust man who held property was a thief; that any person, even an ecclesiastic, could be deprived of property by the civil power if he was found to be misusing it; that inheritance gave no absolute right to property; that no one in a state of mortal sin could have any legal power; and that war was indefensible and even the ravishing of one's country must be met with humility.

When John Huss of Bohemia (1369-1415) took up Wycliffe's teachings and gained considerable ground on the mainland, the Church girded itself for a decisive battle. Huss was born in Bohemia in 1369 and studied at Prague, where he became a first-rate orator and rose to be Rector of the University. It was here that he began to propagandize as a disciple of Wycliffe; and the aroused Pope, Alexander V, asked the King of Bohemia to deny Huss his platform at the University. He was excommunicated by the Archbishop of Prague, and the Roman Curia summoned him before it for trial. Huss appealed to the religious Council of Constance, which was then in session, and appeared before it to defend himself, refusing, however, to go to Rome. His defense consisted of another attack on the Church, whereupon the Council had him imprisoned and tried to make him retract. Adamant to the last, John Huss was finally condemned by the civil authorities and burned at the stake.

This was not the end of the movement of which Wycliffe had been the inspiration and Huss the leader in Europe. The Hussites demanded the right to preach freely and according to conscience, and the Church retaliated by urging several anti-Hussite crusades. These crusades came to nothing; the burning of Huss had enraged the Czech people, to whom Huss had been a national as well as a religious leader, and they rose in arms. Finally a reconciliation between the Hussite party and the Church was effected, in 1436. The Wycliffian-Hussite heresy was over, but it presaged the far greater difficulties which were to come later with the Reformation. The radical legal philosophy of Wycliffe and Huss had no appreciable permanent effect on the law of Europe, but the very radicalism of their concepts, and the great numbers of their followers, indicated how readily the European mind was now opening itself up to new philosophic approaches to law.

II: The Humanists and the Renaissance

THE ODD NAME of "Humanism" is given to the great cultural movement, accelerating in the fifteenth century, which had as its basis a study of the ancient classics. The Bible had, of course, brought to Europe the cultural contribution of the Jews, and much of the legal literature of Rome had circulated even in the Dark Ages; but little of the Roman lay literature, and practically none of the Greek, was known in the early Middle Ages. Classic manuscripts did exist, forgotten and ignored, in monasteries and in odd corners, sometimes written over by clerics. The Arabs had brought much Greek learning with them into the Iberian peninsula, but when they were driven out, most of the manuscripts they left were destroyed or stored away and forgotten. In the Eastern Empire many more manuscripts existed, but they were not transmitted to the West until the Eastern Empire collapsed with the fall of Constantinople to the Turks in 1453. Then many Eastern scholars fled to the more hospitable regions of Western Europe, taking with them a magnificent collection of Greek and Roman literary works. Finally, the invention of the printing press by John Gutenberg (1400-1468) enabled great numbers of people to read what had previously been the privilege of but a few.

There had probably always been a few persons interested in ancient manuscripts, and in the fourteenth century many were rediscovered. Petrarch (1304-1374) dug up almost two hundred of them, including important writings of Cicero. Petrarch's friend Giovanni Boccaccio (1313-1375), best known to us as the author of the racy *Decameron,* was also an important discoverer of manuscripts. Both Petrarch and Boccaccio, after some emotional confusion due to an interest in classic paganism, adhered to the Church; and Boccaccio died repentant that he had written so pornographically in his younger days. Humanism was to seduce many a good Christian away from his faith; yet the Church itself encouraged the study of the classics, and many of the early Humanists were Church officials. Leonardo Bruni was secretary to Popes Innocent VII, Gregory XII, Alexander V, and John XXII. Gian Francesco Poggio Bracciolini, who discovered many important old manuscripts, chiefly in monasteries, was secretary to Pope Boniface IX and held other Church offices.

The geographical discoveries of the fifteenth century did much to enlarge the intellectual horizon as well, and, with the general Renaissance, Humanism came to its height. The Renaissance was *not* what its name implies, a sudden rebirth of culture. There had been an almost constant development of learning and culture in all ages in Europe after the first shock of the barbarian invasions of the Roman Empire had subsided. Even in the period of decline which we know as the Dark Ages, there had been some quiet study and a gradual enlightenment. The Renaissance did not resurrect classic literature and thought; it used these materials as a base, and built upon them the beginnings of our modern social and intellectual structures.

Cardinals devoted themselves to letters, and princes of Europe followed suit, attracting to their courts students and scholars of the classics. Princes of the Church and lay princes alike stocked great libraries and became book and manuscript collectors. Vast material for the intellect of Europe was amassed and men began to think for themselves. And so the groundwork for the Reformation was laid, for the free mind began to question dogma. For centuries there had been only one generally accepted philosophy, that of the Roman Church. Now Europeans discovered that there were other possible points of view, other basic philosophies, other ways in which to interpret life and conduct, and many were repelled by Scholasticism.* It was from the ranks of the Humanists that the greatest intellectual support for the Reformation came. Nor did the jurists escape the contamination of the new freethinking. The Humanists began to be convinced that they could think independently of the Church, and the jurists that they could apply independent thinking to the legal problems of society, free of the bonds of Roman, canon, or any other existling law. The philosophy of the law was coming into a free state in Europe.

III: Martin Luther and John Calvin

THE TWO MEN who influenced the development of law most in the sixteenth century were not lawyers. They were Martin Luther (1483-1546), a German, and John Calvin (1509-1564), a Frenchman.

Martin Luther studied law but abandoned it to go into the priesthood, where his part in establishing the Protestant movement gave more impetus to a new thinking in the law than he could have hoped to contribute as a jurist. Luther revolted against the confining orthodoxy of the Roman Church, advocating the right of every man to be his own priest. Preaching that the individual has the right to interpret the Bible for himself, he was a militant champion of freedom of religious thought, and placed personal liberty above righteousness. Faith is essential to salvation, said Luther, but he refused to assent to any dictated or ritualistic interpretation of the word of God. God's words were in the Bible, and the Bible was there for anyone to read. Luther may be likened to the Humanist jurists who rejected the mass of commentary on the Roman law and went back to that law itself to see what it meant.

"There was gunpowder packed away in Luther's doctrine of the priesthood of all believers," as Vernon Louis Parrington has said,† "and the explosion that resulted made tremendous breaches in the walls of a seemingly impregnable feudalism." It was but a short jump from religious freedom to political and individual freedom, to the concept of fundamental, basic, human rights. Luther was an intellectual ancestor of the English and French political philoso-

* Reasoning and intellectual activity limited by religious dogma.

† Parrington, *Main Currents in American Thought*, vol. I, p. 6.

phers of later periods who designed our modern ideas of individual liberty and personal freedom. These ideas do not stem from Greece and Rome, where the concept of personal freedom within the state was unknown, but from European political thinkers of the modern era.

John Calvin, too, was a religious revolutionary who believed that man should be free of the old dictation and should have direct access to the Bible; but Calvin was almost Hebraic in his insistence that righteousness was more important than love. He gave enormous importance to "the law" as found in the Old Testament. In Calvin's thinking there was little room for individualism. He created a system almost as rockbound as that from which he rebelled. It was a system which appealed to the American Puritan leaders. In early New England the conflict between the Calvinist mode of thought and that which might be called the school of Luther was the conflict between authoritarianism and liberty; this conflict had its political and legal as well as religious phase.

CHAPTER 20

Alciati and Cujas

I: Andrea Alciati

"Alciati, kindled by the Humanist movement in Italy, was the veritable inaugurator . . ."

COLEMAN PHILLIPSON

THE HUMANISTS had been belaboring the lawyers and jurists for some time. Dante called the jurists literal-minded, and he castigated them for not using philosophy in their reasoning. Petrarch accused lawyers of being venal and of ignoring the sciences. Boccaccio said that the law was no science at all. And many laymen studied law for the mere purpose of getting enough information about it to be able to blast the Bartolists, who had, by this time, become stuffy and stale. These backward-looking jurists concerned themselves with *interpretationes*, *repetitiones*, and *disputationes*, and the new world of liberal thought, and of reasoning based on critical analysis and fresh literary materials, had affected them not at all. It was time for a new leader who would apply to the law what Luther and Calvin were to apply to religion, Descartes to philosophy, and scholars such as Rabelais and Montaigne to literature. When there is a great need, someone usually does appear to lead the way. Such a one was Andrea Alciati, an Italian law student, born in the year Columbus discovered America. At the age of twenty-one he produced a book on Justinian, announced to the world that a new approach to the treatment of the law was needed, and said that he was going to establish it.

Alciati did just that in a long career as a professor of law at various French and Italian universities. His freshness of view and the innovations which he propounded were made even more palatable by the striking appearance of the lecturer and his rare ability to make seemingly dull subjects interesting and even entertaining. Students flocked to his lectures, and many of the leaders of the Humanist and

Renaissance movements, including Calvin, went to hear him speak. Even the Dauphin of France and King Francis I were occasional visitors at the lecture hall of Alciati. Among his friends and correspondents were Montagne, Erasmus, Sir Thomas More, and scores of others of the eminent men of the time. His writings were of enormous influence and gathered to him a host of followers and imitators whose enthusiasm was not lessened by the criticisms of the conservatives and mossbacks of the law.

This new approach of Alciati's was primarily a "Renaissance" in Roman law. He tried to pry out the pure Roman law from the piles of glosses and comments heaped upon it by the glossators and commentators. Alciati did not ignore the other sources of law: customary, feudal, German, Lombard, French, Italian, or canon. He believed that these had their place in the law's development, but he felt that the Roman law was the beginning from which advances in the law should be made and that a full and true understanding of the Roman law was prerequisite to any satisfactory understanding of legal processes. Such veneration for the Roman law is not difficult to understand, for no system of law until our own era was ever so complete in its development and so beautifully integrated as the Roman system. In Alciati's time no European system had even begun to approach the perfection of the Roman law.

Still, Alciati did not worship it as ultimate and perfect. He believed that it should be modified and improved not only by introducing into it the best features of other legal systems but also by whatever could be learned from such collateral sources as philosophy, philology, history, and even general literature.

Alciati was intensely interested in the Reformation, in Luther, and in the religious disputations which were current in Europe. He remained a Catholic, but he was sharply critical of the Church, hating the license of the papal court, and disapproving of the violent dogmatisms of the churchmen and the superstitions which the Church fostered in his day. He kept in close touch with events in Germany and elsewhere and had one of the most alert minds in an age of alert intellectuals. Not exclusively devoted to the law, he was a devotee of the art of cooking, and found time in his busy life to write a play and many poems and to delve deeply into philosophy, philology, history, and even medicine.

II: Jacques Cujas

"Cujas' guiding purpose was the reconstruction of what Justinian's commissioners had destroyed."

CARLO CALISSE

ALCIATI gave new direction and new stimulation to the jurists of Europe and commenced a movement which was carried to its peak by Jacques Cujas (1522-1590), a Frenchman trained by a student of Alciati's.

Had you peeked into a certain study in a university town in Europe in 1558, you would have seen a very fat little man lying on his stomach on the floor in a room littered with books, most of them lying around him. You would probably have seen him drag himself along the floor, on his belly, from book to book. That is how Cujas, the most eminent professor of law of the sixteenth century, is reported to have done his research work at home.

Unprepossessing in appearance, Jacques Cujas was one of the gigantic intellects of the law, and it is said that he was followed to and from his lectures by processions of admiring students. Although he was not an orator, and his delivery of lectures not so striking as Alciati's had been, they were so well prepared and stimulating that his listeners were enthralled. He has been considered by many as the most important figure in the history of Continental law.

He was born at Toulouse, in France, one year after Cortez had conquered Mexico. His first instructor in the law was Arnaud Ferrier, one of the disciples of Alciati, and Cujas progressed so rapidly that when only twenty-seven he was able to open a school of his own, where he carried on and perfected the Alciati methods he had learned.

Cujas inherited from Alciati a profound distate for the methods of both the glossators and the commentators. He urged his students to go to the original sources and pay no heed to commentaries built on commentaries. He went further than Alciati, holding that Justinian's commissioners had muddled the Roman law and, in compiling Justinian's books, had destroyed much of the quality of the original law. Maintaining that only by finding the roots of laws could a scientific system be built up, he sought eagerly for old manuscripts which might throw new light on the old Roman texts. But he was a tireless and intense scholar rather than a bibliomaniac, and did no work of compilation himself. His approach was essentially critical and analytical, but it would have been far more difficult for others, after him, to make any scientific compilation of the law had Cujas not lived.

Like Alciati, Cujas lived a restless life, changing from one university to another, getting embroiled in many controversies, sometimes harassed by the turmoil and bitterness of his period, reviled by professorial opponents; but always he kept the respect and veneration of his students. He invited them to his home, boarded some of them, gave them the free use of his library, lent them books and even money. His great manuscript discoveries—he accumulated about four hundred of inestimable value to scholarship—he made readily available to his pupils and to any others working on similar historical material.

Cujas kept aloof from the religious controversies of his period. When his opinion on a religious question was asked, he customarily replied: "*Nihil hoc ad edictum praetoris*"—"This has nothing to do with the edict of the praetor." In the field of the law, however, he did not dodge conflict, and the disputes between Cujas and some of his eminent contemporaries were intense. From these controversies he emerged greatly respected, and came to be recognized as the great proponent of pure, scientific method. There is a story that the professors of Germany raised their hats whenever they mentioned his name.

There were scores of eminent glossators and commentators whose names are missing from these pages. And there were contemporaries of Cujas whose stature was also great. One of the most interesting of the French jurists of this period was Charles Dumoulin (1500-1566), who was something of a throwback to Bartolus. He was an opponent of everything feudal in the law, and applied to the customary law which had developed in France the same methods which Bartolus applied to the Roman law. He found in law built upon the customs of the people a vital factor in legal development. He was a Calvinist who moved for a while to Germany to escape persecution by the Catholic Church and taught at Strassbourg and Besançon. But he was a man of courage who did not hesitate to say his mind wherever he was; he offended Calvinists as well as Catholics, and spent a term in prison as reward for his candor.

CHAPTER 21

Five Reformers

I: Gottfried Wilhelm von Leibnitz

"I have been a jurist from my youth, and in more than one court; and jurisprudence forms part of practical philosophy." LEIBNITZ

PHILOSOPHERS are to the law what abstract scientists are to industry. These scientists discover new principles or facts, or put old ones into new relationships, and then announce their achievements in formulas or scientific language which is usually unintelligible to the uninitiated. But other scientists and experimenters pick up these new materials and use them for further research and for practical use; then we have a new type of icebox or a new explosive to blow men's heads off. And so the philosophers refine reason, criticize what has long been taken for granted, postulate new principles of ethics, morals, and law, and contribute new stimulation to others who go on with the work of trying to improve the rules and customs by which men live. They may seem to be apart from the world, these scientists of the law, but they are not. Their work gradually sifts down to us until what was the unique property of a great intellect becomes the commonly accepted knowledge of the many. It is sometimes said that philosophers are never very far ahead of contemporary mass acceptance, but it is certainly true that a good deal of modern law may be traced to the influence of philosophy.

Gottfried Wilhelm von Leibnitz (1646-1716) certainly did not hold himself aloof from life. He was not only a philosopher of the first rank but a mathematician of enduring renown, and a historian and philologist of note, as well. He has, in fact, been criticized by some for having scattered his shots too much. It is said that he might better have concentrated on one intellectual field instead of dissipating his talents in many directions, but it may well be that he would not have been so great a philosopher had he not also penetrated into other fields.

He himself said, however, that when he studied law he "put everything aside for it." At the age of twenty-four he was a judge of the Court of Appeal at Mainz; and later he became an adviser to the Duke of Brunswick, in whose service he was called upon frequently for legal opinions and special counsel work. He never practiced law in the courts or in an office, but his judicial and advisory experience gave him enough practical contact with law so that he was not merely theorizing when he wrote—he knew the law in its daily work. The philosopher in him, however, was never completely obscured by any practical work. Even in his master's thesis he showed that he could not approach the law in a conventional manner. He could not resist philosophizing on such subjects as whether two absolutely contradictory statements could both be true.

In his later writings Leibnitz discussed reforms in the method of legal education, the proper divisions into which the general subject of law should be broken up, what principles should be applied in construing the meaning of wills and other documents whose meaning was not apparent on the surface, and many other subjects of practical as well as theoretical importance. But his most vital contribution to the science of law was his insistence that there must be a philosophic basis to jurisprudence. He asked, for example, how we can make any sense out of the criminal law until we have decided the true significance of such terms as "reasonableness," "responsibility," "blame," and "censure." How can we determine what to do with criminals until we are sure of the extent to which human beings should be held responsible for their actions? The criminal law, he maintained, must be based on fundamental ethical and philosophical propositions. Otherwise it is casual, arbitrary, and unintelligent.

His demand for reform reached every part of the law in which he saw sterility in the judicial mind. He belongs among the founders of the modern approach to law, one of those who rebelled against accepting laws as they are merely because they do exist.

Perhaps because of his own remarkably universal talents, he was a universalist in almost everything. He advocated a universal coinage, a universal church, a universal system of weights and measures, language, method of writing, and legal system. The basis of a universal legal system was to be the Roman law, not worshiped as perfect and ideal but, as Alciati had found it, the best basis upon which to construct a perfect system. He asked that the law be living, practical, and, above everything, clear. He had no patience with the pettifogger, the pedant, or the jurist who dealt in obscurities. He preferred a clear, bad law to an unclear, good one. In his own legal philosophy he was a supporter of natural law as interpreted and organized in relation to current events and problems.

Leibnitz also served as a statesman, but most ineffectually. He was much concerned over the dangers then pressing on Germany from Louis XIV of France in the West and both Russia and Turkey in the East. So Leibnitz tried to engineer the election of a German prince as King of Poland. When this project came to nothing, he wrote his *Projet de Conquête de l'Égypte*, in which he suggested that the French King might conquer Egypt, hoping thus to dissipate the energies of the French, but Louis XIV was not seduced by this suggestion, although many years later another Frenchman did undertake the Egyptian adventure. Napoleon Bonaparte, who wasted a good bit of France's national strength on a fruitless Egyptian campaign, did not know, until he unearthed the archives of Hanover, that an Egyptian conquest had first been suggested to the French by a German philosopher.

II: Montesquieu

> *"The laws of a country ought to bear reference to its physical character, to the climate, whether warm, cold, or temperate; to the quality of the soil, to its situation, to its size, to the kind of life led by the people, whether farmers, hunters, or laborers."*
>
> MONTESQUIEU: THE SPIRIT OF THE LAWS

ALTHOUGH Montesquieu was venerated by the generations which followed him, he is now no longer an active force in the philosophy of law or in sociology. This is because he did his work so well. His greatest gift to civilization was the formulation of ideas of vital importance in the framing of national constitutions. These ideas have been so fully adopted and so widely used that we now forget that a great mind had first to think them out and give them life.

Montesquieu (Charles Louis de Secondat) was born an aristocrat, one hundred years before the outbreak of the French Revolution, and died only twenty-five years before the Declaration of Independence. He studied law and was made a counselor of a court called the Parlement of Bordeaux when he was twenty-five. In 1716 he succeeded his uncle to the barony of Montesquieu and to a good income, and also succeeded to the post of Vice-President of the Parlement of Bordeaux, a position which his uncle had purchased and which Montesquieu later, in turn, sold to another—a practice not uncommon in that day. In 1726 he resigned this judicial office to devote himself entirely to writing and study. His three greatest books were *Persian Letters,* the *Considerations on the Greatness and Decay of the Romans,* and the *Spirit of Laws.* All three of these were published anonymously, the first two at Amsterdam and the last at Geneva.

It is no wonder that he did not dare publish them in France or under his own name. The *Persian Letters,* written while Montesquieu was quite young, purports to narrate the observations of three Persians traveling in Europe; and the book is full of dangerous passages which almost lost Montesquieu election to the French Academy. In one of the "letters" in the book, the following reference is made to the "Two Magicians": "The King of France is the most powerful prince in Europe. . . . He is a great magician. His empire extends to the minds of his subjects: he makes them think as he wishes. If he has only one million crowns in his treasure-chest and he wants two, he has merely to tell them that one crown is equal to two, and they believe it. If he has a difficult war to carry on and has no money, he has merely to put it into their heads that a piece of paper is money, and they are convinced at once. But this is no such marvel, for there is another still greater magician, who is called the Pope, and the things which he makes people believe are even more extraordinary."

It was not easy to get away with so frank a book in the France of Montesquieu's day, and the enormous success of the *Persian Letters* made it all the more remarkable that he managed to escape prosecution. Having now become a person of consequence in Paris, and being encouraged by the success of his *Letters,* he wrote the *Romans,* a work of political philosophy in which he used the Roman state as the subject of much brilliant reflection. But his greatest book was the *Spirit of Laws,* which, according to his own statement, took twenty years to prepare and write. In this book he offered a theory of "relativity," maintaining that there were no "good" laws or "bad" laws in the abstract, a proposition which ran contrary to the opinions of the day. Each law must be considered in relation to its background, its antecedents, and its surroundings. If a law fits well into this framework, it is a good law; if it does not, it is bad.

One of his illustrations related laws to government. Montesquieu divided governments into three types. The first was the republic, which might be either democratic or aristocratic (he had in mind republics such as the ancient Greek city-states, Venice, and Genoa). The second was the monarchy, by which he meant the current limited monarchies of the West. The third was despotism, as found in the absolute monarchies of the Orient. The principle behind a democratic republic, he said, is virtue or "public spirit"; that behind an aristocratic republic is moderation; that behind a monarchy is honor; and that behind a despotism is fear. Only a law which suited the principle behind the state in which it operated could be considered "good." There is, he continued, no point in considering what is good or bad in the abstract; what is important in a law is its relation to the circumstances within which it is to operate. Had he lived today, he might have said that a law in Russia which permitted imprisonment without trial was a good law; and that a law in the United States which prohibited imprisonment without trial was also a good law; for each of these laws would fit into the system within which it operates. Nor did he confine his theory of relativity to the political framework alone. He also related laws to current ideas of individual freedom, religion, manners, custom, commerce, finance, and other social and economic factors.

This theory of Montesquieu's is, of course, subject to much criticism. The principal value of the *Spirit of Laws* lies in the brilliant comments, the sly allusions, the stimulating suggestions with which his great mind interlarded the text. Montesquieu was among the foremost exponents of personal liberty, and the spirit of liberty shines through the *Spirit of Laws.*

He was a fervent admirer of the British Constitution and made its virtues clearer to the English than any of their own writers had. Actually, he idealized it, perhaps consciously ignoring the venality and the corruption then sullying the fine framework of the English government. Using the English Constitution as a basis for constructive analysis, he propounded theories which have been written into all the major democratic constitutions of our own era. He was particularly insistent on the sharp division of government into its legislative, executive, and judicial branches. If one could name a single parent to our own Constitution, it would be Montesquieu. "In the Constitutional Convention no book was more frequently quoted nor quoted with greater authority than the *Spirit of Laws*."* And Montesquieu was a parent also of the French Revolution, as important in its philosophic origin as Voltaire and Rousseau.

III: Voltaire

"Let all the laws be clear, uniform, and precise: to interpret laws is almost always to corrupt them."

VOLTAIRE: PHILOSOPHICAL DICTIONARY

TWO YEARS after the Declaration of Independence, our Ambassador to France, Benjamin Franklin, was still in Paris trying to get what support he could for the War of the Revolution. Under his plain exterior was a personality so engaging that it charmed all of Paris, particularly the ladies, who were not fooled by his prosaic exterior and recognized the magnificent old rascal as a lady-killer. One day Franklin took his little grandson with him to visit a hatchet-faced old gentleman in Paris for whom the Ambassador had profound respect, and we are told that the old man placed his hand on the lad's head and said two words: "God and Liberty." That old gentleman was François Marie Arouet, whom we know as Voltaire. Some of the leaders of the American Revolution may have read Voltaire and been much affected by him, and Franklin, as our Ambassador, gave him homage, for Voltaire's work may have had much to do with preparing our educated classes for revolt and for their determination to establish a secure and progressive government.

Voltaire was born in 1694, the son of a notary.† His father in-

* George Rossman, Chief Justice of the Oregon Supreme Court, in *American Bar Association Journal,* Feb., 1949, vol. 35.

† A notary holds an office on the Continent not to be compared with that of the man in the corner drugstore who for twenty-five cents takes your oath on a document. The French *notaire* is a superlawyer, especially trained for his work, a combination of lawyer, court clerk, and petty judge. He is a person whose dignity in a French town is less only than that of the mayor. Certain acts must be done before a *notaire;* wills, contracts, and other documents of importance are prepared by him and filed in his office just as though it were the county clerk's office; and in many other ways he performs acts which are beyond the right of the *avocat* (barrister, or court lawyer) or *avoué* (solicitor, or office lawyer).

sisted that he study law, but the boy disliked it, neglected his studies, drifted off into literary circles, took to writing political lampoons, and twice landed in jail. He was sent off to England by his family and stayed there three years, absorbing much liberal political philosophy and developing into a rabid political reformer. He became a successful author, propagandizing for legal and social reform in his sly, powerful manner.

In 1751 Voltaire went to Berlin at the invitation of Frederick the Great of Prussia and stayed for three years, a period marked by quarrels between the two which finally resulted in his virtual expulsion from the Prussian court. But his critical and satirical writings had not endeared Voltaire to the French government, and he could not get permission to return to Paris, so he settled in Geneva to continue his brilliant and provocative writing. It was only after twenty-eight years of absence that he returned to Paris, and he died there in the same year.

What has Voltaire to do with the law? Sometimes furtively and obscurely, and sometimes openly, he attacked the current foibles in government, politics, and law. His criticism was often destructive, for he had no exact thesis to offer; his great interest was in disclosing human error and in sharpening public wits to the necessity of reform.

Typical of his critical literary work is *Candide*, which satirizes the common idea that all is well with this best of all possible worlds. The theory that everything happens for the best is propounded by Dr. Pangloss as a teacher of "Metaphysicotheologocosmolonigology." It was really Leibnitz whom Voltaire was ridiculing in the character of Pangloss. The good Doctor, after going through many horrible experiences and seeing endless misfortune, still maintains that all is "for the best in this world." He says: "I am still of my first opinion, for after all I am a philosopher; and it would be unbecoming for me to recant, since Leibnitz could not be in the wrong and pre-established harmony is the finest thing imaginable like the plenum and subtle matter."

IV: Rousseau

"Good laws lead to the making of better ones; bad ones bring in worse." ROUSSEAU: CONTRAT SOCIAL

IN CONTRAST to Voltaire, Jean Jacques Rousseau had little concern with individual liberty. He was the archdemocrat, the great egalitarian.

He could hardly be held up as a model to youth. Attempts to guide him into a normal life by apprenticing him, in turn, to a notary and an engraver failed miserably; young Rousseau ran away from home and spent some years wandering about, leading a strange, hectic, boisterous, quarrelsome, disorganized, and often wretched life. During part of this time he was the lover of a young and pretty widow, Madame de Warens. But, when he finally settled down in Paris and began to produce the works which were to make him famous, he selected for his permanent mistress an unattractive woman whom he had met when she was a servant at an inn. With her, and without benefit of clergy, he had five children, and it was his boast that, as each arrived, he dispatched it promptly to a foundling home. But, as Richard Wagner's impossible character becomes of no consequence when one listens to *Die Meistersinger*, so Rousseau's moral shortcomings are of small interest to readers of the literary works which made him famous.

After some ineffectual writing, he rose to prominence with the publication of an essay, *Discours sur les Arts et Sciences,* in 1749. This astounding work promoted the thesis that savage societies were far superior to the civilized. More than one back-to-nature movement has had its roots in Rousseau's teaching, and no end of philosophers and political commentators have found his thesis intriguing.

In 1761 his novel *La Nouvelle Héloïse* appeared, to scandalize the conservatives of his day, and a year later came his most important work, his *Le Contrat Social.*

The Social Contract was antimonarchical and intended to show that all government should be with the consent of the governed—an idea which had not hitherto been popular in France or anywhere else—and Rousseau was obliged to leave France for several years. His flight took him first to Germany. At the request of the philosopher Hume, he then went to England, but his contact with Hume was marked by disputes and arguments, for the majority of which Rousseau must have been responsible, for when he left England and returned to France he continued to spend a good deal of his time quarreling with anyone he could find to quarrel with. He was a man of startling brilliance and inventiveness but a most disagreeable character, and probably insane during the latter part of his life.

Rousseau's fame grew after his death, even deeply religious people finding his basic theory attractive. It was, after all, related to the Fall of Man thesis of the Church. He maintained that man has lapsed from a previous perfect state as a primitive, and that he needs laws now only because he has abandoned his simplicity and natural goodness. Thus he believed in a "state of nature," as the Romans had, but Rousseau believed in it as a historical actuality.

Unfortunately, Rousseau was a logical prop to the dictatorship of Robespierre and could well be accepted as one of the deities of fascism and Communism. But democracy owes him much also.* In his *Social Contract* both totalitarian and democrat may find comfort.

This book was not accidentally named. It was, in large part, an exposition of Rousseau's own concept of the so-called "compact theory," the theory that there is a contract underlying the state. This had been propounded by Greek philosophers and by others before Rousseau's time, but several important political philosophers of the seventeenth and eighteenth centuries seized upon it, gave it varying form, and used it to support their respective concepts of proper government and law.

A contract does actually exist when a nation adopts a constitution as we did after the Revolution. Moreover, peoples like the ancient Jews felt themselves to have made a compact with God. In feudal society there was also a contract underlying the system. The duties between man and lord were reciprocal and were instituted by the ceremony of fealty, which held the essence of a contract. But Rousseau wrote of a more basic contract, an underlying agreement by which the individual, when society emerged from its savage state, inferentially contracted with his fellows to subordinate himself to them, to the common interest. In Rousseau's opinion, this surrender

* It has been assumed by some that many of our Founding Fathers had read and been deeply influenced by Rousseau but into a more rational variety of political credo—even that our Declaration of Independence took from Rousseau the principle that "all men are created equal." Others have doubted that those who constructed our Constitution had read much French.

was an absolute one, and the intensity with which he insisted upon the abjectness of the surrender led him into a complete disregard of any "individual rights." The majority must have its will, he said; if there is any conflict between what a majority and a minority want, that is just too bad—the minority has no "rights." He held that this was so not merely because the majority had the power to do as it pleased but also because he professed to believe that what the majority wanted was always best and for the public good.

Of course, Rousseau hedged a bit. Knowing the lack of capacity of the masses in actual practice, he was frank enough to say in his *Social Contract*: "How can the blind multitude, which often does not know what it wants because only rarely does it know what is for its own good, undertake, of itself, an enterprise so extensive and so difficult as the formulation of a system of law? Left to themselves, the people always desire the good, but, left to themselves, they do not always know where the good lies. The general will is always right, but the judgment guiding it is not always well informed. It must be made to see things as they are, sometimes as they ought to be. It must be shown how to attain the good it seeks, must be protected against the temptations inherent in particular interests; must be made to understand places and seasons, and must learn to weigh present and obvious advantage against remote and hidden dangers. Individuals see the good which they reject; the public desires the good which it does not see. Both, equally, are in need of guidance. The first must be constrained to submit their wishes to their reason, the second to learn what it is they want."

In our own day there are "social scientists" who believe that the people in general, and even our political leaders, do not know what is best for us and that government should really be directed by an "elite," the elite being, of course, such "social scientists."

V: Beccaria

> *"I owe all to French books; they have developed in my soul the feeling for humanity previously filled with eight years of fanatical education."* BECCARIA

CESARE BONESANA, later the Marchese di Beccaria, wrote only one book of note, but that one, *An Essay on Crimes and Punishments*, written when he was twenty-six years of age, was so important that it entitles him to be listed in the top rank of reformers in the law. It was an instantaneous success; it was printed first in Italian and then translated into French and English and was read avidly throughout Europe.

The shy young Italian had become incensed at the criminal and penal systems of his day. The prisons were cesspools; accused persons were held together with hardened criminals in filthy cells and compounds, old and young, males and females, being confined together, without distinction. There was no sanitation or bedding; what food was rarely provided was filthy and horrible. Torture was still employed to get evidence and to punish; secret procedure, in which the accused had no opportunity to secure counsel or to defend himself properly, was the rule rather than the exception. Punishments were extremely cruel, and there were innumerable crimes punishable by death. So, stimulated by reading such liberal philosophers as Montaigne, and by his own observations, Beccaria bitterly attacked the whole criminal and penal system with evangelical fervor. Attacking the theory that punishment must be based on vengeance, he asserted that the degree of punishment should be measured by the seriousness of the crime, and he insisted that the judicial function must be clearly separated from the legislative.

Beccaria was the father of the movement to abolish capital punishment. His great book, small in size but tremendous in import, came upon society with a strong impact and awakened many to the horror of the injustices and cruelties which they had previously accepted as inevitable because they existed. More and more, writers and social leaders took up the work which Beccaria began, and a wave of reform grew in height and in volume.

CHAPTER 22

Napoleon

"My glory is not to have won forty battles; for Waterloo's defeat will destroy the memory of as many victories. But what nothing will destroy, what will live eternally, is my Civil Code."

NAPOLEON, AT ST. HELENA

I: The Little Corporal

WAS NAPOLEON WRONG in seeking to unify Europe? We cannot have sympathy for a unification movement based on rampant nationalism and on war, but it is quite possible that, if he had produced good through evil, the world might later have thanked him for having converted the squabbling states of Europe into an association of nations. He failed in his military objective, probably for the simple reason that force cannot cement what peoples do not want, but he succeeded in one unification movement which was peaceful in its intention. As a result of his support of legal reform in France, all of Western Continental Europe eventually adopted a codified legal system, the national differences in which are relatively unimportant. The great similarity in the laws of the Western European states is due not only to their common juridical antecedents but also to the drafting of the *Code Napoléon*, used as a model by so many other nations.

This reform of codification was, in the minds of most European jurists, badly needed. England had been fortunate; after the Norman Conquest, William of Normandy had been able so closely to unify the country that a national court system was able to grow up under his successors.

On the Continent, in contrast, the armed isolationism of feudalism had led each locality and political subdivision to evolve its own legal system. Voltaire had said that if you crossed France by horse you met different systems of law as frequently as you changed horses, and so it was all over the Continent.*

Leibnitz had not been the first jurist to suggest that the law should be universal. Those who worshiped the Roman law had hoped that someday there would be a universal *lex romana,* and the canonists had dreamed that Church law could attain universal acceptance. But the national and religious wars which accompanied the Reformation made it impossible for any law of Europe to be accepted by all the nations; the best that could be hoped for was that each nation would unify its own law.

The roots of the movement for national codification went far back. Charles Dumoulin, in the sixteenth century, had urged that Frenchmen everywhere should be governed by the same law, but nothing came of it until Jean Baptiste Colbert (1619-1683), Comptroller-General under Louis XIV, persuaded his King to support the creation of a Council to draft a set of national codes. Colbert, who died so out of favor with both King and people that he had to be buried at night for fear of an "incident," deserved better of the French. He has been called the greatest minister of all times. He founded the French navy, expanded France's colonial empire, patronized its literature, arts, architecture, and sciences, and administered its finances with genius. His project for making sense out of the confusion described by Voltaire was never completed, but the Council did produce several sectional codes of considerable value. Among them were a *Commercial Code,* on which merchants were called in for advice, and a *Criminal Code,* which, while it still continued the use of torture and secret procedure, did make some reforms.

The final codifiers who worked under Napoleon's direction were far more indebted to a later Frenchman, Robert Joseph Pothier (1699-1772), who virtually did the job for them in advance, though in a different form. It was his ambition to combine the Roman law, the many customary law systems of France, and what he believed to be the laws of nature in one co-ordinated system. He produced a long series of carefully planned volumes in which he selected the most satisfactory materials out of the mass of law which he studied,

* It might be said that we have the same situation in the United States, where we have as many sets of laws as we have states and territories, plus the District of Columbia, but the analogy is not a good one. The differences in our state laws are trivial and minor in comparison with the heterogeneous mess of law which Europe had in the pre-Napoleonic era.

and readjusted them to the practical necessities of the life of his time.

Thus, when a later jurist, Jean Jacques Régis Cambacérès (1753-1824), started work on an actual codification in 1796, Pothier had done most of the ground work of research and compilation. The French Revolution interrupted Cambacérès's work, but it was resumed under Napoleon, and the association of the jurist with his Emperor was very close.

As for the credit due Bonaparte for the Code which was named after him: While he cannot be said to have contributed importantly to the detail of the work, which required minds trained in law and procedure, he did enter into the discussions frequently and sat with the commission at most of its meetings. What cannot be denied him is that the encouragement which he gave to the codifiers, and the fire of his own energy, resulted in the completion of a difficult task which might otherwise very easily have been abandoned. The *Civil Code,* to the drafting of which the entire French bar contributed, was completed in 1804, and it was followed by *Criminal, Civil Procedure,* and *Criminal Procedure* codes.

In comparison to these, the work done under the direction of Justinian was crude and unscientific and far inferior in literary quality. Napoleon's codes were translated into almost every Western and many Eastern languages, and a wave of code-making followed. The Austrian codification of 1811 and the German code, finished in 1896, are generally accepted as far superior, and the Japanese, in fashioning their code system, followed the German model. But these had the advantage of the experience of the intervening years and of the Napoleonic precedent.

II: Savigny and Jhering

"When we shall have been taught to handle the matter of the law presented to us with the same freedom and mastery as astonishes us in the Romans, then we may dispense with them as models and hand them over to a grateful commemoration of history."

FRIEDRICH KARL VON SAVIGNY: MODERN ROMAN LAW

THE MAIN DISTINCTION between the system of law now used on the Continent of Europe and that used in England and the United

States arises from this codification of Continental law. In our system, we worship precedents. What has been decided by a high court in the same circumstances becomes law in our English-based system. On the Continent, a judge has the codified law before him and it is this which he must interpret. While a good deal of case law has developed on the Continent, particularly in France, the Continental judge has been much freer in interpreting the basic law. It may be said that the growth of case laws in Europe has been a comparatively recent development.

Full discussion of this subject must wait until we take up the parallel development of the English system, but it is important to note here that students of the law differ sharply as to the merits of the two systems. Both have their advantages and disadvantages. One advantage of the Continental system is that it enables a lawyer to practice without needing to have access to tens of thousands of lawbooks. On the other hand, many lawyers point out that the law ceases to grow effectively under a code system; only by the findings of the courts can laws be adjusted and made to work in accordance with changing times and changing ideas. And, they say, how can such growth take place if judicial decisions are not considered to be part of the law?

That was the position of more than one Continental jurist who fought against codification. Outstanding among them was Friedrich Karl von Savigny (1779-1861), an eminent German, one of whose books, *The Right of Possession*, has been called by Austin, an English jurist, "of all books upon the law, the most consummate and masterly." Von Savigny called custom the real producer of sound law, claiming that law ceases to grow once it is put into the corset of a codification.*

Von Savigny was one of the modern "greats" of the law. After studying at several German universities, he toured France and parts of Germany seeking new sources of Roman law. In 1810 he became a professor of Roman law at the University of Berlin. Here he par-

* Germany, in the modern period, has produced many excellent jurists, one of whom deserves mention. Karl Joseph Anton Mittermaier (1787–1867), who was expected to die of tuberculosis when he was twenty-one but lived to a ripe old age, produced a book called *English, Scotch, and American Criminal Procedure,* which ranks among the fine legal commentaries of our age. Along with Montesquieu and Leibnitz, Mittermaier said that the law should be re-examined periodically in the light of social change, and many reforms in penal law and procedure are attributable to him.

ticipated in the creation of a *Sprachkollegium,* an extraordinary tribunal which functioned by giving special opinions on cases submitted to it by the courts. He was one of the leaders of the so-called historical school, wrote considerably on the history of the Roman law and produced an eight-volume work on the current state of the Roman law (*System des heutigen römischen Rechts*). Perhaps his greatest works were his *Recht des Besitzes* (*The Right of Possession*) and his *Vom Beruf unserer Zeit für geschichtliche Rechtswissenschaft* (*The Vocation of our Age for Historical Jurisprudence*). The latter was a protest against codification, and asserted the thesis that law is a part of national life and must be related to the condition of the national civilization and its past history, i.e., it must be a living thing. The *Recht des Besitzes* was an important and vigorous study of the rights attendant on the possession, as against the ownership, of property.

Von Savigny's influence was widespread, even extending to British jurists. As already stated, Austin was one of his great admirers.

Of the many able German jurists of the era, Rudolf von Jhering 1818–1892) stands out majestically. A lecture career brought him to quick prominence, and his voluminous writings left a deep mark on jurisprudence. In part he carried on the "historical" school of Savigny, and yet differed with him rather radically. Savigny was a strong exponent of individualism, believing that it should be the purpose of the law to leave each individual as free as possible without impairing the rights of others. Jhering was a utilitarian. He believed the law grew not through any peaceful development or according to some preordained plan, but, rather, deliberately and through conflicts.

As our own great jurist Roscoe Pound once put it: "Whereas the philosophical jurist considered that the principles of justice and right are discovered *a priori* . . . and the historical jurist taught that the principles of justice are found by experience—Jhering held that means of serving human ends are discovered by experience and fashioned consciously into laws."

CHAPTER 23

Marx and Engels

"The Communists . . . openly declare that their ends can be attained only by the forcible overthrow of all existing social conditions."

THE COMMUNIST MANIFESTO

ANY DISCUSSION of Continental Europeans must include two other Germans who were political philosophers rather than jurists. But their philosophy has had a profound effect upon the development of our own law and upon the course of world history. These two are Karl Marx (1818-1883) and Friedrich Engels (1820-1895).

Karl Heinrich Marx was the son of a Jewish lawyer of Treves who had caused his whole family to be baptized. It is not uncommon to find poverty in the background of a radical and to trace his radicalism to discontent with his lot, but such was not the case with Marx. His father was affluent, and Karl himself married a girl of social position and considerable wealth, but even in his student days he showed radical leanings. There was at that time a strong socialist movement in France, and Marx went there in order to study it at first hand. It was there he decided to make socialist propaganda his lifework, and there he met another German who was to become his lifelong friend and collaborator.

Engels was two years younger than Marx and also a man who had turned against his own class—his father was a prosperous cotton spinner. The two men threw themselves into the socialist movement with vigor and energy, and their caustic and virulent writings soon got them into difficulties with the French government, forcing them to seek sanctuary elsewhere. They found it in Brussels, where they continued to write, formed a workingmen's society, and joined a secret communistic organization which had branches all over Europe.

It was for this organization that they wrote, late in 1847, their famous *Communist Manifesto*, a magnificently written, if exaggerated and violent, document. It assailed the capitalistic system, claiming that it had reached the peak of its efficiency and was ready to die of old age. Marx and Engels expected capitalism to perish of its own weakness, and they called for a revolution of the proletariat to precipitate its fall and to institute "true democracy" on a collectivist basis.

In 1848 revolutions broke out in various parts of Germany, and Marx and Engels thought that the time had come. Returning to Germany, they joined the revolutionary movement, started a radical newspaper, and, by writings and party work, tried to fan the flames of the rebellion. But their German career came to an end when Marx was arrested by the Prussian government and tried for treason. He was acquitted unanimously by a jury, but the government forced him to leave and he again went to France, and later to England, ever the haven of the political refugee, where his friend Engels joined him. Marx lived most of the time in Soho, a poor district in London, where he kept his family alive, with considerable difficulty, chiefly by writing. At one time, strange to say, he was a contributor to the New York *Tribune*. In 1867 he published his most famous work, *Das Kapital*, and in this, as in most of his other work, Engels was his collaborator.

Socialism is as old as organized mankind; there was a form of collectivist society in the communal organizations of many primitive peoples. Marx and Engels did not even give socialism its first conscious voice. Some claim that Jesus did, extracting from his twin theses of the fatherhood of God and the brotherhood of man the whole rationale of socialist philosophy. In any event, there had been socialist agitation in Europe long before Marx discovered it as a student, but it was a moderate socialism somewhat like that of the British Labor Party and of the socialist parties of Western Europe today. It was evolutionary in its program, holding that certain social and political objectives were ideals to be approached by democratic means and as society grew ready for them. But Marx and Engels joined the extreme left wing of the socialist movement and drove it even further to the left. They were the fathers of that form of violent and aggressive socialism which captured Russia.

They expounded the theory of the class struggle, based on a materialistic conception of history and of society. They said that material, economic circumstances determined the momentary construction of the state, and that the inevitable result is the rise of a special class or classes which exploit others. Then the exploited class arises to overthrow its oppressors and to change the form of the state. Perhaps the reason Marx and Engels had no faith in growth and change through the democratic process was that, in their day, democracy had not yet advanced to its present stage. The franchise was still strictly limited, by property qualifications and otherwise, so that the wealthy upper classes actually did control the government. Marx and Engels saw no imminent possibility of overthrowing this imbalance except through revolution.

Marx's principal thesis in economics, expounded in *Das Kapital*, was that of "surplus value." He said that the true value of any product is the aggregate value of the labor which went into it; therefore, he concluded, all capitalistic surcharge on that value, including interest, rent, or other profit, is actually stolen from the workers. That is not all there is to Marxian teaching, but the materialistic interpretation of history (with its conclusion that the exploited laboring class must rise to overthrow its exploiters) and the theory of surplus value lie at the bottom of much of Marxian doctrine.

He did not believe that the worker was necessarily entitled to the direct product of his own work. He held that production was the property of society as a whole, and he did, also, grant management and direction a participating part of the value of products, but no greater share than other contributing workers. Marx distinguished between skilled and unskilled labor, holding that they contributed a different value-factor to a finished product. His theory was that the cost of producing or training a skilled laborer must be allocated as a labor-cost item, in addition to the cost of the actual labor contributed by that worker. That is all very complicated and finespun, but Marxian economics, like all theoretical economics, tried to reach an almost mathematical perfection which one does not meet in operation.

The extreme concept of economic reward advocated by Marx has been rejected today, even by Russia, and it is not even close to acceptance in Western countries which have been partially socialized. Nevertheless, socialism has had an enormous impact all over the world, and not merely in socialist states. The expanding influence of Communism, particularly in the less-developed countries, is due largely to the wide acceptance of the tenets of socialism, in opposition to capitalism or free enterprise. After all, Communists are socialists and socialism appeals far more strongly than does free enterprise to the have-not nations. To break down the illusion which is behind this point of view is our most difficult job in international relations.

In our own country, socialism has had heavy, and in some respects growing, influence. The increasing propulsion toward government intervention in human affairs and the trend toward egalitarianism and leveling may be laid at socialism's door. Indeed, socialist penetration has been so deep that a Socialist Party can make no headway in the United States. The socialist movement has been taken over and absorbed by our left-wing labor, intellectual and political groups and exercises its none too subtle influence under such shibboleth labels as "welfare state."

PART SEVEN

THE ENGLISH

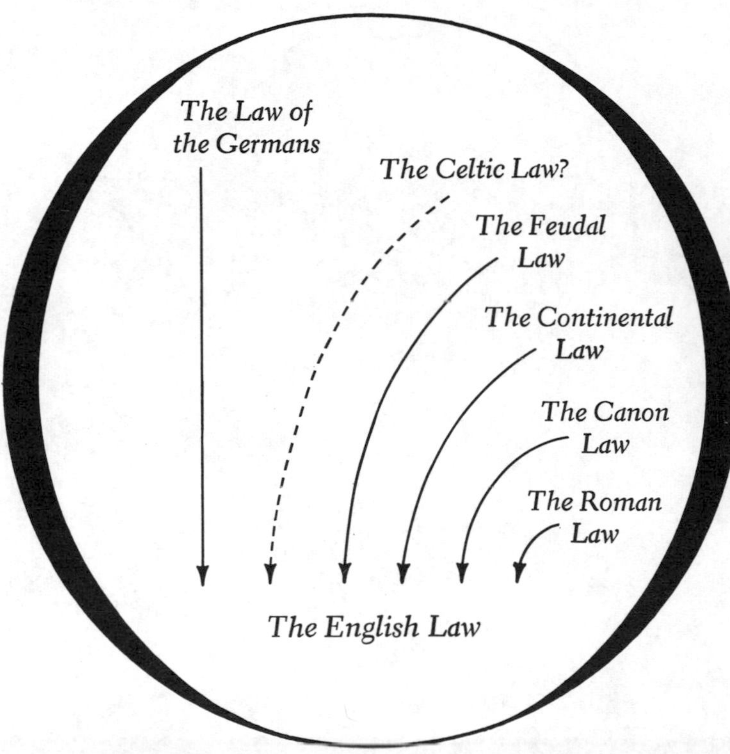

THE CHIEF BASIC SOURCES

So far, this book has been more or less chronological. But it is now necessary to drop far back in time to trace the independent origins of English law, which, mixed with much of the law as it developed on the Continent, formed the system that was the direct parent of our own.

CHAPTER 24

William the Conqueror

I: The Celts

IT IS DOUBTFUL that the Celtic law had any material effect on the development of English law. Yet I cannot resist the temptation of including some description of its interesting character and a few of its idiosyncracies. I may be excused on the ground that this may be of historical interest to many Americans of Celtic antecedents.

Diodorus, a Roman historian, tells us that the Celts were "tall, with rippling muscles and white skins; red-haired, not only naturally but they do all they can to make it redder by art. They often wash their hair in water boiled with lime, and turn it backward from the forehead to the crown of the head, and thence to their very backs, that their faces may be more fully seen, so that they look like satyrs and hobgoblins." He also said that persons of quality shaved their chins close but had mustaches which fell so low that they covered their mouths, "so that when they eat their meat hangs dangling from their hair, and when they drink the liquor runs through their mustaches as through a sieve."

The Celtic people, some of whom had crossed the Channel into England, were not savages, however Diodorus may have described them. On the European Continent the Celts were independent for some six centuries and developed a civilization of their own which, although barbarous in comparison with the Roman, was higher than that of the Germans who followed them from the East. This Celtic, Continental civilization came to an end after 50 B.C., when Caesar conquered Gaul, and the first three Roman emperors, Augustus, Tiberius, and Claudius, virtually exterminated the fraternity of Druids. For the Druids were not only the Celtic priests but also the custodians of the Celtic law and culture; it was they who handed down the Celtic traditions by word of mouth from generation to generation. We get some idea of the function of the Druids from Caesar in his *Commentaries:* "To these a large number of young men resort for the purpose of instruction, and they [the Druids] are in great honor among them. For they determine respecting almost all controversies, public and private; and if any crime has been perpetrated, if murder has been committed, if there be any dispute about an inheritance, if any about boundaries, these same persons decide it; they decree rewards and punishments; if anyone, either in a private or a public capacity, has not submitted to their decisions, they interdict him from the sacrifices. This among them is the most heavy punishment. Those who have been thus interdicted are esteemed in the number of the impious and the criminal: all shun them, and avoid their society and conversation, lest they receive some evil from their contact; nor is justice administered to them when seeking it, nor is any dignity bestowed on them." *

II: Cormac MacArt

INFORMATION concerning the Celts who inhabited England proper is very meager; they were first thoroughly Latinized by the Romans and then thoroughly submerged by the Anglo-Saxons. But the evidence is that their laws and institutions were similar to those of the Irish Celts, about whom we know much more because their independent civilization endured centuries longer. In Ireland, life was pastoral; there was little agriculture, and there were no large cities. Social organization was patriarchal and somewhat similar to that of other Indo-European peoples in an equivalent stage of growth. But the Irish did develop a legal system which compared very favorably with that of other semiprimitive peoples.

While still using self-help, they had already established a procedure for avoiding personal conflict. You could shame a debtor into submitting to arbitration. If you claimed that Fagan owed you some cattle, and he refused to settle the debt, you could go to Fagan's house, sit at his door, and refuse to eat. Fagan could not permit this. If he let you sit and starve, society would consider him so mean and reprehensible a character that he would be ostracized, so after a time

* *Commentaries,* Book VI, Chapter XIII.

Fagan would be forced to agree to go before a brehon, a Druid judge, to arbitrate the case. To this extent, the procedure was somewhat civilized. But, when the brehon had given a decision in your favor and ordered a distraint—that is, given you the right to seize enough of the debtor's property to satisfy the debt—the remaining procedure was primitive. You seized what you could, and if you could not find enough property to equal the debt you had the right to seize the debtor himself and hold him prisoner until he paid the debt.

In the Irish town of Tara a great tribal assemblage, called the *dal*, met. From this comes the name of the present Irish parliament, the Dail. In about A.D. 250, King Cormac MacArt, the first Irish lawgiver of whom we have any knowledge, reigned as chief King over the five Kings of Ulster, Leinster, Connaught, Meath, and Munster. Cormac was not royal-born, according to legend; he was raised to the throne as a youth when he showed remarkable legal ingenuity and a strong sense of justice. A neighbor was charged with permitting his sheep to eat all the woad-herb from another's field, and the judge had declared that the offender should give his sheep to the complainant in payment for the injury done to the latter's field. Cormac, sitting in the back of the courtroom, thought this unjust, and he arose to object: "Not so! for the herb is only the fleece of the earth. Therefore, let not the whole sheep be forfeited, but only the sheep's wool be sheared, to pay for the herb; for herb and wool will both grow again."

III: Early Irish Law

ONE IRISH LAWBOOK, written down in the twelfth century or perhaps earlier, gives us some idea of Irish law of earlier days. It is a short digest of the decisions of Caratnia the Scarred, a judge who held court under King Conn in the seventh or eighth century. The fifty-one paragraphs of this short work state principles of law or precedents in the most roundabout way, and in a fashion peculiarly Irish. This is typical: "23. 'I decided, Children's contracts are binding on both sides.'—'You decided wrongly.'—'I did it wisely, for here it was an exchange of goods, made openly and without overreaching.' " Thus, in each paragraph, the judge first states a decision which seems unjust or illogical, whereupon the King chides him for it, and Caratnia then explains why he made his odd decision.

St. Patrick is worshiped by the Irish not only for having driven the snakes out of Ireland but also as one of her greatest lawmen. It is said that he caused a commission to be organized as early as 440 to compile the Irish law; this work became known as the *Senchus Mor* (pronounced "Shankus Mowr") or *Great Custom*, and also as the *Code of Patrick*. Christianity had a marked effect on Irish law, and St. Patrick's Code was full of Christian spirit. It forbade the old family vengeance and insisted upon wrongs being righted by public courts, but it was easier to make laws of this kind than to enforce them in Ireland, and the Irish kept right on settling their quarrels with fists and shillelaghs.

Christianity was fervently welcomed in Ireland, and the Irish literature of about 500 to 800 may be credited to the Church. While the rest of Europe was sinking further and further into an abyss of darkness and ignorance, Irish priests, who were assiduous students of Latin and Greek, were producing wonderful illuminated manuscripts at an astonishing rate. They fostered learning and literature generally, and it was Irish missionaries who taught the Anglo-Saxons to write. The earliest English lawbooks were written in the Irish script, which was a modification of the old Roman.

During this period in which the Irish led Europe in learning, many legal textbooks and commentaries were written, of which the very ancient *Book of Aicill* is one of the most interesting. This book illustrates the love of the Irish for contention and disputation. It contains five pages of discussion on the law of pigs running into and hurting people because they have been shouted at. Whether a cause of action results depends on all sorts of facts—the age and occupation of the shouter, whether the shout was malicious, playful, etc.: " 'Idle shouting' means the doing of it for the purpose of sport, and it is not sport with respect to the pigs; and if it were, it should be considered as idleness of foul play, and there would be full fine for it. . . ."

The primitive custodian of the law was always jealous of his prerogative, and the Irish brehons were especially so. Many of their lawbooks were unintelligible to the uninitiated; the words and sentences were scrambled, so that one could not read them without knowing a code. Many of the manuscripts which have been discovered have taken as long as fifty years to decipher.

IV: Howell dda

Howell dda (the name means "Howell the Good"), a King of South Wales who dates about five hundred years after St. Patrick, ordered his Chief Justice to sit at night so that the people could have justice any time they wanted. Howell's *Code*, which he took all the way to Rome after it was compiled, for approval by the Pope, was not wholly primitive. It contained much mature law and procedure and many interesting approaches to the legal problems of that time. Did Howell perhaps have his tongue in his cheek when he included such a rule as this? "If a woman be slandered on account of a man; the first time, the oaths of seven women exculpate her; the second time, the oaths of fourteen women; the third time, the oaths of fifty women; and thence onward, for every slander, the oaths of fifty women."

And here is an interesting clause which reflects a very primitive idea: "If swine enter the house and scatter the fire about, so as to burn the house, and the swine escape; let the owner of the swine pay for their act. If the swine be burned, it is an equation between them; as being two irrational things: and, therefore, where there is an equation, by law, there is to be nothing redressed, but one is to be set against another."

This rule, however it may be rationalized by the text itself, clearly springs from the primitive urge for revenge against the thing which did an injury.

How much of the Celtic law went into the present English system is not known. Few traces have been discovered, yet the Germans may have taken over a good deal from the higher culture of the Celts when they conquered them. In all Germanic countries there are place names of Celtic origin and some indications of an absorption of Celtic culture. Few Germans realize when they sing "Die Wacht am Rhein," and few Austrians when they sing "The Blue Danube," that these two rivers have Celtic and not German names. It is possible that the Germans who invaded England had already acquired some Celtic legal customs and practices on the Continent. It is also remotely possible that some Celtic legal custom may have persisted in England during the long period of Roman rule, and that the Anglo-Saxon absorbed some of this as well.

V: The Germans

For almost four centuries England was ruled by Rome. Caesar's first invasion in 55 B.C. left little impression on the island; he stayed but a year. The Romans came again, however, in 43, this time to remain; and large numbers of Romans and Latinized provincials from the Continent followed the legions and settled permanently, bringing with them the amazing Roman talent for organization and government. England was quickly hammered into a highly civilized and prosperous Roman province, but as the Empire weakened, the hold of Rome on the distant English province loosened, and the island became an invitation to conquest. Celtic Picts and Scots from the North caused the Romans considerable trouble as early as A.D. 360 but did not gain any permanent foothold. But when the Roman Empire faded out of England entirely, between 417 and 429, the great Germanic invasions began. The Germans came not in one great migration but in successive groups of mixed subnationalities, landing at various points on the coast and fighting their way inland against a people who had relied so long on the protection of the once strong Roman arm that they were now helpless without it. Some of the local population was driven into Ireland and the mountain regions of Wales and Scotland, where their descendants still live; but many remained in the conquered territory, perhaps as serfs or subjugated inferiors, and were eventually assimilated.

The Germans did a thorough job. They destroyed the greater part of the Latin civilization which the Romans had implanted on the island. They brought their own legal customs with them, and they made England a Germanic country, governed by Germanic concepts. This Teutonization of England was not radically affected by the invasion of the Danes, who followed the Angles, Saxons, and Jutes from the Continent after the latter had settled down and grown somewhat soft in England. These Danes were also Germanic, differing not overmuch from the Anglo-Saxons in dialect and very little in customs. Warlike and in many ways more developed than their German cousins, the Danes had devised boats capable of crossing vast seas if necessary, and running up rivers with greater speed than foot soldiers could follow on shore. Bands of these Northmen raided England and gained control of a large section of the country known as the "Danelaw." The very name implies that they established their own legal system, differing from that of the Anglo-Saxons.

The word "law" itself is Danish, but, after the Danelaw was recaptured by the English under Alfred the Great (849-899) and his immediate successors of the Wessex dynasty, a merger of the two Teutonic stocks was accompanied by a rapid union of the two only slightly different systems of law. Gradually a new civilization coalesced in the new England, somewhat feudal in pattern. The king was at the head of the state, and under him were the thegns or lords who were served by tenants or underlings in exchange for protection, a system which tended toward decentralization. Justice was more and more administered by feudal lords, and some of them were churchmen, for the Church had by this time received enormous holdings of land through wills and grants, and religious officers were lords of countless manors.

VI: Anglo-Saxon Law

In all discussions of the birth and development of English institutions there are those who seek to give all possible credit to the contribution of the Franco-Normans, and other scholars who seek, equally vehemently, to discount such contributions and to show that everything came out of the unusual Anglo-Saxon character of Germanic England. The controversy seems largely unsolvable, for in many instances we do not know how a great institution originated. To present both sets of arguments: The pro-Norman party says that England came to greatness only after the Norman Conquest, while the Anglophiles answer that it did not become great until the Germanic population had had a chance to arise again out of Norman oppression. Neither argument is very convincing. The Norman civilization is claimed to have been higher than that of the Anglo-Saxons, but the latter's supporters reply that the conquerors impressed their language as the official language on England and thus prevented any expression of local culture. They say, further, that England produced no literature as good as the Anglo-Saxon until Chaucer. Actually, the merger of these two peoples and of the respective contributions which they were able to make to a new culture produced the greatest nations of modern times. There is credit enough to be shared.

When William the Conqueror arrived in England he found a well-established and co-ordinated legal system in operation, the purest Germanic system of which we have any knowledge. On the Continent the Germanic codes were adulterated, they were written in Latin, and the codifiers were Romanized clerics, willing enough to introduce innovations into Germanic law. In contrast, the laws of England were written in German, and it is difficult to trace any Latin influences in these original codes, or even any Celtic influence. The laws were German, and they stayed German without serious adulteration until the Norman Conquest. Indeed, the English have been called "the most German people on earth," the reference being to the ancient Germanic peoples who, though they liked strong leadership, were always stubbornly attached to their personal rights.

The British Parliament came to be the great defender of individual right, and the question of its origin again raises the Norman–versus–Anglo-Saxon controversy. The Anglo-Saxons did have a *Witan* or *Witenagemot*, a "great assemblage" or council, which was an outgrowth of the old institution of the tribal assembly. But William the Conqueror did not have any Parliament, and he ruled absolutely. The only group with which he associated himself in his arbitrary rule was his own council of advisers and assistants, selected by himself, and thus it seems more likely that Parliament had its roots in this council rather than in the old *Witenagemot*.

It seems equally probable, however, that the peculiarly English sense of individual right developed out of the old Germanic clan assembly, the *folkmoot*. One had certain definite rights as a member of a clan, not as an individual. But when the clans broke up or scattered in the course of the invasion and settlement of England, and there were no longer any cohesive clans to protect the individual's clan rights, the concept of "folkright" still persisted and tended to grow into the concept of actual, individual (rather than clan) rights. Royal enactments might cut down the folkrights, or modify them, but government never dared to interfere too sharply with them.

There were many codes in pre-Norman England, among them those of Ethelbert (c. 600), Edric, Ine (c. 690), Alfred (c. 900), Edward the Elder, Athelstan, Edmund, Edgar, Ethelred, and Canute the Dane (c. 1035), but all these were mere writings down of existing laws and customs and included very little innovation. In fact, written Anglo-Saxon law is very meager, covering a small amount of property law but consisting mostly of tort and criminal law. A considerable advance from purely primitive conditions is evidenced by a system of compositions which the tort law contained. You paid a *wergild* (literally, "man payment") for a killing or a *bot* (compensation) for personal injuries, and there was also a *wite*, or fine, which went to the lord and attached a kind of criminal aspect to a tort. In one respect, the Anglo-Saxon law was similar to the ancient law of Hammurabi: it made distinctions between social classes. A much higher composition had to be paid for injuring a *thegn* (thane, lord) than for injuring a *ceorl* (whence our "churl").

The Germans had formerly held land by tribes or clans, but by the time of the Conquest land in England was held in individual ownership, though sometimes on a feudal pattern. A good deal of the feudalism in England was introduced gradually by the churchmen, who, as the only persons who could read or write, administered the law. The churchmen also brought in some of the Roman law, and it may be that they introduced parts of the Jewish law of the Old Testament as well, for the canon law was then merely in the process of being formed, and its laws of marriage and domestic relations sprang largely from Jewish principles.

Although the Anglo-Saxon clan organization broke down in the confusion of nationalities during the invasions of England, the judicial function of the clan assemblies continued. The assemblies continued to exist as courts* in the counties, although clan organization was supplanted by the system of "hundreds." The people were divided into groups of one hundred families, and each tried its own petty cases. The hundred, in turn, was divided into "tithings," or groups of ten families, and each of these was responsible for order within itself. More important cases were tried in the county courts, and these county courts were generally presided over by ecclesiastics, whose influence upon the development of law must have been important. Decisions were rendered by the delegates, but it was the presiding officer who instructed them in the law. As no one but the ecclesiastics could write, the president of the court must have writ-

* This is a common pattern among peoples using the clan form of organization. We have seen it in Greece; it can be traced in the Jewish and Roman procedure; and the Germans of the Continent had it. The clan assembly was almost always not only a sort of legislature but also a court.

ten down the "dooms," or judgments, and thus had opportunity to give direction to the law.

The Anglo-Saxon court system was very primitive and its procedure was highly formalized.* In stating his claim, the plaintiff took an oath according to a formula, and the defendant, just as formally, made his denial under oath. The court then decided whether there should be proof and who should give it. There was no true trial. The evidence was not weighed, and many issues were tried by "wager of law," in which each side produced compurgators who swore for his side. It was hardly a method well calculated to ascertain truth; and after the Norman Conquest it was eliminated from the national courts, although it continued to be used in local, Anglo-Saxon courts for a long period.

William the Conqueror brought with him from the Continent the old feudal trial by duel. This was no improvement over the compurgation system. In criminal matters, the accused and accuser were obliged to fight it out themselves, except that old men, women, and children (and, later, clerics) were permitted to have "champions." In civil disputes the parties could hire champions, who had to perjure themselves to claim that they were "witnesses." Being a professional champion must have been a profitable, if dangerous, business.

VII: William Begins a New System

THE NORMAN CONQUEST was a successful contesting of a will. William the Bastard, Duke of Normandy, better known now as William the Conqueror, had several different claims to the English throne which he asserted on the death of Edward the Confessor. William's wife, Matilda, was a direct descendant of Alfred the Great (and, incidentally, of Charlemagne as well). That was not so strong a basis for his claim, however, as the alleged will of Edward the Confessor, in which he is said to have named William, his Norman cousin, as his heir. There was a contrary claim by Harold of Hastings that Edward made a deathbed will in which he named *him* to succeed, but William had still a third choice. Harold had once landed in Normandy and been imprisoned by Guy of Ponthieu, a friend of William's. There William visited the Saxon and, so William claimed, a

* It was much like the procedure described in the *Saga of Burnt Njal*. See Chapter 14.

deal was made in which Harold agreed to marry William's daughter and to support William's claim to the succession to the English throne.

None of these claims was valid, for the English throne could not be passed on by will or contract. The throne was not even hereditary; the king was elected by the *Witan*, the assemblage which had succeeded to the old tribal right to elect its chief. Furthermore, the English, having suffered first a Danish dynasty and then the rule of Edward the Confessor, who was more Norman than English, wanted no more foreigners. So, when the Confessor died, Harold stepped in and took the throne with the consent of the *Witan*. Normandy prepared for war and, at the same time, the King of Norway, assisted by Harold's own brother, also prepared an invasion.

William did not rest his case upon arms alone. A devoted supporter of the Church, he presented his case to the Pope at once, employing Lanfranc, a noted jurist, as counsel. William was fortunate that the power behind Pope Alexander II was the monk Hildebrand, one of the most fiery champions of the temporal sovereignty of the Papacy. He welcomed William's suit, for it gave the Church an opportunity to exercise what he believed to be its right to rule over princes and their disputes. A trial was held, and a strange trial it was, for Harold was not represented. A decision was rendered against Harold, he was excommunicated, and William was named a Heavenly Avenger to teach the English "due obedience to Christ's vicar" and to secure a "more punctual payment of the temporal dues of his apostle." The Pope gave William a ring, a consecrated banner, and "a hair of the prince of the apostles, to sanctify his expedition," and the Normans were thus launched in a holy war.

William collected an army composed of Normans, Frenchmen, men of Flanders, and even Germans. The weather favored him; it necessitated a long wait, during which many of Harold's defending army got tired of it all and went home to their fields and crops. William crossed the Channel in 1066, defeated Harold at Hastings, and was crowned on Christmas Day.

William, who ruled from 1066 to 1087, was a systematic and careful man, and he did not wait long to start getting his new house in order. Though he brought with him the feudal institutions which were in use on the Continent, he had the political foresight to avoid the decentralization which feudalism had introduced in the rest of Europe. William made certain that every acre of English land was held, directly or indirectly, from the king. He ordered the compilation of the famous *Domesday Book,* a survey of his entire realm made for taxation purposes, which was completed in 1086. After that, his agents had merely to look in the book to find out who owned what.

Yet William did not build a "state" as we know the term. There was no such concept, during the early Middle Ages, as that of a highly centralized government or of belonging to a geographical nation. England remained decentralized; all that William accomplished was to perfect feudalism by tying all the fiefs closely to the crown. But that was a great accomplishment, and it made possible the rapid growth of central power in later generations.

William by no means destroyed the Germanic legal system of Anglo-Saxon England, any more than the German language was destroyed by the influx of French. Rather, the two systems, Norman feudal and Anglo-Saxon, were gradually merged, just as the two languages merged to form the English tongue. Justice was done principally in the local, feudal manors, with the lord of the manor sitting as judge, but the old county courts persisted. It was here that William stepped in with an innovation which had far-reaching results. He threw out the local ecclesiastics, who had presided over the county courts, and appointed his own men to preside. The work of the courts thus came under the direction of Norman presiding judges, who were able to mold the law gradually to more alien practices. The representatives of the hundreds continued to sit in the county courts, but only as advisers, in effect, to the presiding judges.

VIII: Henry II Perfects the System

A GRADUAL CHANGE in the court system and in the law of England took place under the next three kings, William Rufus, Henry I, and Stephen, but the following ruler, Henry II, who reigned from 1154 to 1189, may be said truly to have founded the present English system. There had been some crown courts, and Henry increased their number, appointing judges who went on circuit, traveling through the provinces and holding sessions in many places. These "national" courts grew increasingly popular and gradually took the place of many of the local courts, for litigants believed that they might get surer and fairer justice from the king's court than from a local manor lord or magistrate, or even from the ecclesiastical courts which had grown up under the direct administration of the Church.

The extension of the national court system and the appointment of these *missi*, or traveling judges, by Henry II began the growth of the common law. The term implies a law common to all subjects, geographically and socially, and the circuit judges did, in fact, apply what there was of national law instead of the law which happened to be customary in any one locality. This national law was somewhat confused at first, having its chief roots both in the old Anglo-Saxon law and in the feudal law of the conquerors. As new situations arose, the judges were able to take advantage of the uncertainty of the law by either inventing solutions or borrowing from the law of the Continent. The sum total of these factors, filtered through the national court system, produced the common law.

After Henry had established his traveling judicial system, the kings found an interesting way to take trade away from the other courts. They used the concept of the "king's peace," which was well known to the Germans. Whenever possible, an action was held to invoke a breach of the king's peace and, therefore, to come properly within the jurisdiction of the king's courts rather than of the local courts. Many of the early "writs" by which actions at law were started were devised so that their very wording necessitated going to the king's courts because the king's peace had been breached. Here is an example: An action for the restoration of land which had been wrongfully taken—the writ was called *novel disseisin*—recited that the land had either been "wrongfully" taken or was "wrongfully" withheld. The term "wrongfully" implied either that force had been used or that it might be used in reprisal. Therefore, a breach of the king's peace was involved, and such an action had to be brought into the king's court.

Separate eccelsiastical courts appeared when the churchmen were deposed as presiding judges in the county courts; these ecclesiastical courts administered canon law and had jurisdiction over matters deemed to be the peculiar right of the Church, including the trial of any offense by a cleric. The expression "benefit of clergy" arose from the compromise applied by the common-law courts in the case of a crime punishable by death. If the defendant were a cleric he was given a lesser sentence. Through the Church courts a great deal of canon and Roman law came into the English legal system. The separation into Church and lay courts created a conflict of jurisdiction which continued for many centuries. Eventually, there came into use a "writ of prohibition" issued by the lay courts to prevent the Church courts from infringing upon their jurisdiction.

Henry II, a great king, made one great public error: his handling of his dispute with Thomas à Becket, the Archbishop of Canterbury, over the right of the Church to try its own priests for crimes. An ecclesiastical court had acquitted a cleric of a charge of rape, and Henry was indignant that the Church took jurisdiction in what should have been, in his view, a civil matter. He caused a Great Council to draw up and approve the *Constitutions of Clarendon,* a charter of reform which, among other things, gave the civil courts jurisdiction over clerics who were charged with civil crimes. King Henry became so incensed over Becket's obstinate refusal to ratify this charter that he chided his entourage for its failure to give him revenge against the "upstart clerk," whereupon four of his knights dashed off to Canterbury and slew the Archbishop within the Cathedral. Whatever the rights and wrongs of the controversy, the people were shocked at the murder. Becket became a national idol, and sentiment against the reform of court procedure and jurisdiction which Henry had planned was so strong that the Constitutions of Clarendon were discarded and the reform of the ecclesiastical courts was delayed by centuries. For a long period afterward, anyone who could read or write and could thus claim to be a cleric would claim the protection of the ecclesiastical courts.

One of our treasured legacies from England is the jury system. We have two kinds of juries: the *grand jury,* which indicts for crimes, and the *petit jury,* which sits in the trial of a case and determines the facts. The grand jury dates from the time of Henry II, who caused panels of twelve men, appointed by the sheriff, to be charged with the duty of accusing any persons in the locality suspected of crime. But the petit jury, although the first signs of its modern form were seen in Henry's day, had older origin. There may have been something like it in the Roman system; the Normans in their own country had taken over from the Franks some sort of inquest by a panel of freemen. A group, usually of twelve men, was appointed to make an investigation of facts in dispute. William the Conqueror used such rudimentary or casual juries during his reign. But Henry II is generally given credit for having fashioned an actual jury system. The trial jurors were called "recognitors," and they were selected as witnesses to the facts but in a way which now seems strange.

In a modern jury trial the jury is the judge of the facts. Two sets of attorneys present oral and object evidence in such manner as to convince the jury of their respective versions of the facts. The judge's part in guiding the jury is that he "charges" it; he tells what the law is, and explains that, if the jury believes one version of the facts, it must give judgment for the plaintiff, but if it believes the other, it must give judgment for the defendant. Thus the judge determines the law of the case but the jury makes up its own mind as to what the facts are.

In the ancient jury system, the jurors were "witnesses," the only witnesses. They had the duty of finding the facts, and they might do so as they pleased. They might make inquiries in open court, they might go out into the streets to find out what the facts were, or they might just guess at them. Nor did the jury have to listen to lawyers. The lawyers talked to the judge only; there were no witnesses except the jurymen themselves, and consequently no examination of witnesses, no cross-examination, and no "summing up to the jury."

The jury had to be unanimous. That is, there had to be twelve men who agreed, one way or the other. If the original twelve were not in agreement, the court did not require a new trial, but more jurors were appointed until, finally, there were twelve who could agree. Serving on such a jury was hardly as pleasant as jury service today, for if the ancient English jury were found to have made an erroneous decision, it was subject to heavy penalties. It could be "attainted" by a jury of twenty-four knights. There would virtually be a second trial, in which the knights would determine whether the original jury had been guilty of wrongful decision. By this cumbersome method, a decision might be appealed by a dissatisfied litigant.

CHAPTER 25

The Law of the Land Emerges

I: Ranulf de Glanville

WHEN HENRY II DIED and Richard Cœur de Lion succeeded him, the Chief Justiciar of England was Ranulf de Glanville, who had been sheriff three times, and three times an ambassador, an able general and a jurist of deserved renown. He had written the *Treatise on the Laws and Customs of England,** a boon to his contemporaries and a treasure to legal historians. But all this meant nothing to King Richard, whose controlling passion was his desire to fulfill a crusader's vow. Crusading was an expensive business, and Richard had to raise a large sum to hire his four thousand men-at-arms and four thousand foot soldiers and to buy and equip one hundred ships to transport the men, horses, and equipment. Richard was none too scrupulous in the way he went about his financing. He sold high offices in the kingdom to the highest bidders, made various shady deals, and resorted to kidnaping. He fired Glanville as Chief Justiciar and imprisoned him until, it is said, Glanville contributed fifteen thousand pounds as ransom. Strangely enough, Glanville accompanied King Richard on the crusade, which may be a tribute to the charm of the Lion-Hearted. Glanville died on that crusade, in the siege of Acre, to the great loss of England.

Glanville's *Treatise* is one of the most valuable books in the history of the English law. It was written chiefly to explain the complete writ system which had grown into being in the previous hundred years or so. A *writ* is the document with which a proceeding is brought in the courts, and we still use writs, if only in a limited way.

* There is some belief that Glanville's nephew, Hubert Walter, has been defrauded by history and is the true author of the *Treatise*, but Glanville is generally given credit and is entitled to it unless better evidence appears.

Our most common writ is the *summons*. It is a command to the defendant to come to court and defend the proceeding brought against him. It may be called an *order to show cause* or a *citation* or some other name, but its function is to command the defendant's presence. Some of these writs are issued by a court itself, others by the attorney for the plaintiff. An ordinary modern summons is a form that may be purchased at a stationer's, and the lawyer merely fills in the blanks and has it served on the defendant. In the ancient English system, the lawyer could not prepare the writ with which he commenced an action, but had to buy it from the chancellor or other officer of the state. A more important difference is that our summons does not always state the cause of action. A defendant today might not know what he is being sued for until his attorney asks for a "complaint." In the ancient system the writ always showed what the action was, and there was a different writ for every kind of action.

We still have some special writs, such as the writ of *habeas corpus* ("produce the body") and the writ of *certiorari* by which the Supreme Court of the United States permits appeals in certain cases from the lower courts. But in the ancient English writ system, every ordinary lawsuit had its own particular writ. Great care had to be exercised in selecting the proper writ. If a man had borrowed five pounds from you and failed to repay, you would get a writ of *debt* against him and commence an action. But if he owed the money in return for work you had done for him, and you commenced your action with a writ of debt, the defendant would *demur*, contesting the propriety of your writ. And your action would have been thrown out of court, for the proper writ for the value of services rendered was *quantum meruit*, not debt. Debt was available only when the amount owing was fixed and determined.

The question of who started the writ system brings us back to the conflict between the Anglophiles and the Francophiles, and it would seem that the honors are about even. The Anglo-Saxons had developed a writ system of a kind, but the Normans had also used a rudimentary variety. Moreover, the writ system was used by the praetors in Rome. A Roman magistrate, if he thought you had an action within the limited categories which existed, issued what was in effect a writ to a judge who would hear the facts. Probably the Church, in its own jurisprudence, brought into England the Roman, praetorial concept of the writ.

However, the writ system developed in England along lines of its own. There were only a few kinds of writ to begin with, and actions were limited to these few types in the king's courts, just as there was originally only a limited number of *legis actiones* in the ancient Roman courts. That does not mean that no litigation took place in England except under these writs, for the older Anglo-Saxon courts of the hundreds persisted and had their own procedure. But, as litigation came more and more under the jurisdiction of the king's courts, the writ system soon came to be almost universally used. As new situations arose, new writs were invented, generally issued through *assizes* or decrees.* And so, writ piled on writ until there were so many that the lawyers of the Middle Ages in England must have had the devil's own time trying to keep them straight. Glanville's book was a godsend to those who could use it to guide themselves into the proper selection of writs and through the shoals of bad pleading.

The English judges certainly borrowed from the Continent to amplify and nourish their new system; it cannot be determined exactly how much they borrowed, but we know that it was considerable. William the Conqueror's first Archbishop was Lanfranc, who had argued William's case against Harold before the Pope. Lanfranc had been a noted teacher at Padua, where a largely Romanized Lombard law was taught, and he must have taken Continental concepts to England with him. His successor, Theobald, in 1144 called over Vacarius, a celebrated professor from Mantua, to become his legal adviser, and other lay and Church law teachers were imported from the Continent, where Roman law had already made great headway and no one knew anything much about Anglo-Saxon law. These foreigners seem to have been sincere in their desire not to destroy the English law, but it was to be expected that, whenever it needed amplification, they would supply it through Roman or Romanized concepts.

The greatest benefit of the writ system was that it accompanied an abandonment of the old forms of trial by combat and by test, and substituted trial by fact and law. Glanville pointed this out in his *Treatise:* "That Justice, which, after many and long delays is scarcely, if ever, elicited by the Duel, is more advantageously and expeditiously attained through the benefit of this institution. . . .

* The word "assize," having the meaning of "sitting," was also used to designate the term or sitting of a court.

And by this course of proceeding, both the labor of Men, and the expenses of the poor are saved. Besides, by so much as the testimony of many witnesses, in judicial proceedings, preponderates over that of one only, by so much greater Equity is this Institution regulated than that of the Duel. For since the Duel proceeds upon the testimony of one Juror, this constitution requires the oaths of twelve lawful men, at least."

Glanville gives us a record of one interesting ancient English practice carried over in modified form from primitive Germanic law. In most early primitive societies a man's personal articles were buried with him for use in his afterlife. The Germans modified this practice by allocating one-third of a man's personal possessions to his heir, one-third to his wife, and one-third to the deceased; and this rule was still in effect in Glanville's time and for some time thereafter. But Christian usage had changed the practice so that the deceased's share was no longer placed in his grave; instead, the Church received it for the good of his soul.

II: Magna Charta

"John, by the grace of God, King of England, Lord of Ireland, Duke of Normandy and Aquitaine, and Count of Anjou: to the archbishops, bishops, abbots, earls, barons, justices, sheriffs, reeves, ministers, and to all bailiffs, and faithful subjects, greeting. Know that We, by divine impulse, and for the salvation of Our soul, and of the souls of Our ancestors, and of Our heirs, and for the honor of God, and the exaltation of Holy Church, and the amendment of Our kingdom, by the advice of Our venerable fathers, Stephen, archbishop of Canterbury, primate of all England and cardinal of the holy Roman Church . . . have in the first place granted to God, and by this Our present charter confirmed on behalf of Ourselves and Our heirs forever . . ." So begins the *Magna Charta*, and wicked King John signed it at Runnymede in June, 1215. Nations have not always been best served by good kings, and England was well served by John, one of her worst. Had he had not been so wicked, England would not have had the Magna Charta, and the principles which were introduced by it into English law might have been delayed for centuries.

King John ruled arbitrarily and oppressively and taxed the people heavily. He ran rampant over the feudal rights of his barons. Nor did he do anything to take the people's minds off their troubles. John's brother and predecessor, Richard the Lion-Hearted, had been a pretty arbitrary and useless ruler who had drained England heavily through taxation, but he had given the people romance and foreign conquest. John drained England even more, gave it no romance, and gave the people foreign defeats. He lost Normandy to the French and, with it, almost all of the English territories on the Continent. Defeated abroad and oppressed at home, the English had nothing but the solace of the Church to carry them through John's wicked reign, and of this too he deprived them for a time.

It began with a dispute between John and the Pope over the right to appoint the Archbishop of Canterbury. John thought to enforce his point of view by exiling all monks, and the Pope immediately replied by interdicting all of England and declaring King John excommunicated. Then the Pope threatened to depose John and to give the English throne to Philip of France. He had no such right, but John could not rely on the merits of his own case. He knew that there was so much discontent in England that his barons might join the French against him if the Pope declared a Holy War. So John capitulated and became the Pope's vassal. In John's reign England actually was a dependency of the Papacy.

But John's capitulation to the Pope did not mean that he intended reform in England. And so the barons and prelates of England began to plot against him, and not long after John's submission to the Pope they revolted under the leadership of Stephen Langton, the able new Archbishop of Canterbury. Seeing that his cause was hopeless, John met the rebels at Runnymede, near Windsor, and signed the Magna Charta, which they had prepared in advance.

The Magna Charta is frequently referred to by politicians, orators, and demagogues as the "cornerstone" of this or that, and it has often been called the "cornerstone of British liberties." It *was* a cornerstone, but its significance is often misunderstood. It was the first rock upon which the British Constitution was built, but in reality it did not grant much freedom. What it did grant was principally for the benefit of the upper classes. It was primarily a charter of rights for the barons, who had complained that certain of their feudal rights had been interfered with, and for other upper classes allied with them. The Charta refers to "freemen," a term which did not cover the ordinary Englishman but extended downward in society only to the lesser knights and the burgesses of the towns. After, as before, Magna Charta, the vast majority of Englishmen were still serfs and slaves to the land.

Thus, the Magna Charta did not, as is generally supposed, give the right of trial by jury to all Englishmen. Only the upper classes acquired the right to be tried by their peers. When the serfs were freed, centuries later, the right of trial by jury was automatically extended to them under the principles of the Charta, but this was a stretching of its express terms. Nor did the Magna Charta establish the principle of "no taxation without representation." But it contained certain clauses upon which that proposition was developed in later eras.

The Magna Charta covers a multitude of subjects and is quite a long instrument. There are innumerable clauses protecting the rights and property of the barons. One of these is rather odd at first glance: No interest is to be paid to Jews while the heir of a deceased debtor is under age, and the wife and children of the deceased are to be provided for first, before any part of a debt is paid to Jews or anyone else. The provisions referred to are not essentially anti-Semitic; the specific mention of Jews merely highlights the fact that they were the bankers and moneylenders of the age.

I shall not attempt to summarize the complex and intricate clauses of the Magna Charta, for many of them deal with feudal institutions and practices which would require many pages to explain. The document was clearly directed chiefly against certain abuses by the King and of the judicial and legal system. And it contains a provision for the supervision of its enforcement by a committee of twenty-four barons.

The Magna Charta did not have a smooth career. It would be ignored by one king and restored by another. In the time of Henry VIII of the many wives, the "cornerstone of British liberties" was castigated as the work of "certeyn traytours," and Henry paid no attention to it. And there is no mention of it in any of Shakespeare's plays—not even in his *King John*.

It was only in the course of the struggle with the Stuart kings that the Magna Charta again became the fundamental charter of the people's liberties and the basis of the English Constitution. A full recognition of its place in the English law thus came only in the modern era. The British Constitution, incidentally, is "unwritten" in the sense that it is not one cohesive instrument. It consists of a series of component parts, successively extracted from kings of England in the gradual struggle between democracy and absolutism. Liberation came slowly, class by class. As the middle classes grew in wealth and power, they combined with the barons to make further inroads into the royal power. As for the masses of common people, no one was interested in them until they finally fought for their own rights and champions were found to lead them first to emancipation and then to equality. Freedom for the masses was a comparatively recent social development in England.

III: Henry de Bracton

> *". . . we find Bracton . . . copying freely from the Roman lawbooks, though he frequently also contradicts them when English usage differed."*
>
> JAMES BRYCE

IN THE thirteenth century came the great Henry de Bracton (d. 1268), a judge of long experience whose book, *De Legibus Angliae,* was somewhat larger and more comprehensive than the *Treatise* of Glanville. For two hundred years judges and lawyers followed Bracton as Continental jurists might have followed the books of Justinian. This one book had perhaps more to do with fixing and standardizing the English law than any other single factor in English jurisprudence. It has usually been considered among the most English of English books, and yet Sir Henry Maine pointed out: "That an English writer of the time of Henry III should have been able to put off on his countrymen as a compendium of pure English law a treatise of which the entire form and a third of the contents were directly borrowed from the Corpus Juris, and that he should have ventured on this experiment in a country where the systematic study of the Roman law was formally proscribed, will always be among the most hopeless enigmas in the history of jurisprudence . . ." *

As to Maine's allegation that Bracton had foisted Roman law on the English, we do know that Bracton had read Justinian. We know also that he had used a book of Azo of Bologna, a Romanesque

* Maine, *Ancient Law*, p. 79.

jurist, as his model, and we can trace much Roman law in the *De Legibus Angliae*. But the great mass of law which he described was the law as it had actually been developed in the English courts. Careful records of many of these actual cases had been kept, and Bracton himself kept his own notebook (discovered by Professor Vinogradoff in the British Museum in 1884) full of decisions, some of which he cited as precedents. Indeed, Bracton's custom of referring to a decided case to substantiate a point of law tended to make even more certain the perpetuation of the system of "case law," of using decided cases as precedents for further determinations. At about this time the term "common law" came into wider use to distinguish general case law from all special law such as royal decrees and the local customary law which still flourished in the districts.

Bracton not only codified much of the law which had accumulated up to his time but also provided future English political philosophers and jurists with materials for the constant battle against the royal power. Centuries after Bracton's death, Sir Edward Coke led the battle against the Stuarts, who were staunch advocates of the divine right of kings. Coke himself was a devoted admirer of Bracton, in whose *De Legibus* he found ancient arguments against the absolute power of the English king. For Bracton had said that the king had two superiors, God and the law which made him king; and that, if the king had no bridle, one should be put on him. There is no law, said Bracton, of power as against right, and the king's power is restrained by the bridle of the law. He also indicated that, while the king cannot be sued, he can be petitioned, and that he must act with justice on a petition or have his power further curbed by the barons and the people.

IV: The Common Law

An enormous part of our law has been written down in the form of statutes, but a great mass of law, sometimes inappropriately referred to as "unwritten," is actually to be found in the reports of decided cases. This is the *common law*, some of it unchanged from the form in which it was originally created by early English judges.

Other legal systems have had a body of law comparable to our common law: the Jews had their commentaries on the law of the Torah, which created an underlying law; and the Romans had a "common law" consisting of a mass of juristic opinions. But the distinction between our common law and that of other systems is that ours developed almost entirely out of the decisions of judges in actual trials.

In a codified system of law, a judge may interpret the language of the written law almost as he wishes.* This is not true of the English system, which is governed by the rule of *stare decisis*, "to stand by decided cases." Once a point of law has been decided by the highest court of appeal, it is fixed law and can be changed only by legislation. But the common law has been able to grow without constant interference by legislation because judges have been able in various ways to circumvent disagreeable or obstructive precedents. The courts have been inclined to reasonable flexibility in determining what current "public policy" may be. Public policy does change as social and economic conditions change, and as the public itself changes its concepts. So judges, under the English system, have remained alert and open to being guided by changing ideas.

Sir Henry Maine has described another method by which the common law grew. He said that it was "taken absolutely for granted that there is somewhere a rule of known law which will cover the facts of the dispute now litigated, and that, if such a rule be not discovered, it is only that the necessary patience, knowledge, or acumen is not forthcoming to detect it."† Thus, by a system of rationalization, law was found where it did not exist, and all the clever devices of the logician were used to this end.

Precision was worshiped by common-law judges. They loved the maxim "It is better that the law should be certain than that it should be just." There is much to be said for the contention that an unjust law can be changed by legislation, while an uncertain one is likely to remain and to plague litigants. However, the common-law judges sometimes created uncertainty in their own decisions. Instead of confining themselves wholly to the facts before them, they might give an incidental and gratuitous opinion as to what the

* This statement, incidentally, is subject to some qualification. Naturally, a judge on the Continent cannot go flatly against some principle which has been so well established that there is no longer any doubt about it. Precedents undoubtedly do play an important part in the Continental system, but the difference is that precedents are almost ironbound in our system. Of course, even our judges do occasionally overrule themselves—our Supreme Court has done so frankly on more than one occasion.

† *Ancient Law*, p. 30.

law might be in a different set of facts. Such extraneous opinions are called *dicta,* and while the dictum of a judge does not create law, it can create doubt, which is then dispelled only when a further case decides the point about which the earlier judge speculated. And if the judge who uttered the dictum was well respected, other judges after him might continue to follow it.

So the common-law judges, using their wits, did their best to prove that the English law was sufficient to solve all problems of litigation without the necessity of legislation.

The law of each generation represents just about what society deems convenient or proper at the moment. Whether changes are made by legislation or by judge-made law, they usually reflect expediency. Justice Holmes has put it this way: "Every important principle which is developed by litigation is in fact and at bottom the result of more or less definitely understood views of public policy; most generally, to be sure, under our practices and traditions, the unconscious result of instinctive preferences and inarticulate convictions, but none the less traceable to views of public policy in the last analysis."*

The result is not always logical. Sometimes there is a clutter of old conceptions which the judges have difficulty getting around. In the present day of easy and pyramiding legislation, change can be brought about very quickly—sometimes all too quickly. In the long period of the English common law, when there was little legislation and changes in the law took place through the work of the judges in the courts, change had to be made sometimes in the face of existing, contrary law, and the ingenuity of the common-law judges in molding to suit the times was nothing short of wonderful.

A few examples can indicate the complexity of the problems which the common-law judges had to face even in simple situations out of which litigation can arise. The examples are in the area of *possession,* a much older legal concept than *ownership.* Possession of property gave certain rights to the possessor, even if he did not own the property. But before the judges could grant such rights to a litigant, they had often first to determine whether he was really the possessor. If you pursue a deer and wound it fatally, are you the possessor of the deer? Or does the second hunter, whose bullet finally brings it down, possess it? Or the third, who comes upon it while it lies prostrate, and puts an end to its life but leaves it there?

* Holmes, *The Common Law,* p. 35.

Or is it the fourth, who picks up the deer and carries it off to his house?

Here is another. You drop your pocketbook on the floor of a store. A customer sees it and picks it up. Who is the possessor of the pocketbook, the customer who found it and picked it up, or the storekeeper because the pocketbook was in his store and you have no rights in his store except for the business which brings you there? The law is filled with borderline cases in every field, and the common-law judges had to struggle to delineate the borders and to create a system which makes logical sense within itself.

There was conscious or unconscious wisdom in the common-law judges who created change gradually and without abandoning old forms unless it seemed absolutely necessary. By its gradual and painless method of change, the common law was often able to start with a very primitive or rudimentary rule of law and convert it gradually, as necessity appeared, into a modern tool. This can be illustrated through the law of "servants." The very term indicates its ancient origin, for it now covers not merely domestic help but services of many kinds. In its present meaning, it covers the services rendered by a window cleaner or a lawyer. The law of servants dates from an era in which all servants were slaves, and yet its component rules were gradually altered and amplified so that it now covers a wide field of law in a society which has no slaves.

On the Continent of Europe and generally in those countries which have adopted some form of the Romanesque law, criminal prosecutions are upon what is called the "inquisitorial system." The entire prosecution of the case is in the hands of public officials, many of whose proceedings are rigorous and secret, often taking the form of private investigation with magisterial powers and with the right to keep the accused for some time incommunicado. In contrast, the Anglo-Saxon criminal system is "accusatorial," in the sense that an accusation is made by the state, and the trial and preparations for it consist of the proof of the accusation and its defense.

CHAPTER 26

Edward I

I: The Warrior Lawgiver

WHEN HENRY III of England died in 1272, his son Edward was off on a crusade, following the romantic example set by his granduncle, Richard Cœur de Lion. In those days a throne was not always secure to the natural heir, and another prince might have rushed back to England to claim his inheritance, but Edward dallied without fear. For there was no doubt that he would be crowned king. His popularity with the people was so great that no one could have stood against him. During his father's life, whenever Edward had been given some responsibility in the management of the kingdom, he had indicated that he would be a great king.

He was tall, well built, and handsome. He loved fighting above all else, and when there was no war he fought in the tournaments. But there was another side to his nature. Edward I was moral in his domestic life in an age when morality was far from prevalent, loyal and sincere, and deeply concerned with the problems of government, conscious of his duty to his people, and eager to rule well.

Almost the first official act of the new King upon his coronation was the voluntary reproclamation of the Magna Charta, and this was but the first of a long series of steps which showed that he had a deep interest in the legal system of England and its development.

There was a Parliament in existence at Edward's accession, but it was composed only of prelates and barons designated by the king; and it was not to be expected that a Parliament so constituted would care much about improving the condition of the people in general. Actually, it did not have very much power. The king was the supreme ruler in all respects, and about all Parliament had the courage to do was occasionally to refuse consent to some monetary grant. It was Edward who took the first major step toward the development of Parliament. To his "Model Parliament" of 1295 he invited not merely the customary barons and churchmen but also two knights from every shire and two burgesses from every town. It may be that Edward realized it might be to his advantage to set a new class against the upper classes of Parliament, but the fact remains that this momentous step was taken voluntarily.

One of the few functions of Parliament at that time was the presentation of petitions to the king; these were probably the ancestors of parliamentary bills. Obviously, the petitions presented by the commoners who now had access to the king were often quite different from those submitted by the barons and the prelates. The door was open for legislative suggestions by the middle class, and, even more important, the middle class was now able to exercise more control over the national purse.

For quite a while the knights and burgesses in Parliament remained reserved, unaccustomed to their new-found authority. They usually met on the outside to discuss matters of interest to them, and they appointed a "speaker" to act as their chairman and spokesman in Parliament. Lords and Commons did not actually organize as separate branches of Parliament until the Stuart Restoration in 1660, but the outside caucus of the commoners under Edward I and later kings was the beginning of this division.

The power of the commoners in Parliament increased rapidly. They were in a position to take advantage of the constant conflict between the barons, trying to preserve their feudal rights, and the king, who was endeavoring to centralize the government and limit baronial power. Both king and barons sought the support of the middle class, which was now rapidly increasing in wealth and economic power. Middle-class representatives in Parliament solidified their own political positions by refusing permanently to ally themselves with either the king or the barons.

Also, social distinction between lords and commoners was not so strong in England as elsewhere. The rule of primogeniture, which left all younger sons without inheritance, sent a constant stream of noble blood into the middle class. Countless Englishmen of today, who are now mere commoners, are descendants of English kings and of peers. In addition, the evolution of a single English language, formed of a merger of the French of the Normans with the German of the Anglo-Saxons, tended to bring the classes closer together.

So the beginning of the modern Parliament dates from Edward's time. We can also date the clear establishment of the main branches of the judicial system from his reign. The court of judges which

Henry II had caused to sit at Westminster was the beginning of the Court of Common Pleas, whose jurisdiction in common-law cases was well drawn by Edward's day. Another court had developed out of the exercise by the king of his supreme judicial duties, the Court of King's Bench, which was, historically, the king's own court; it had civil as well as criminal jurisdiction. There also was the Court of the Barons of the Exchequer, which tried cases involving the finances of the crown and which derived its odd name from the fact that the barons sat about a checkered tablecloth. There were still other national courts, including a criminal court with an interesting name, the Commissioners of Assizes and Gaol Delivery, and countless local courts as well. The justice of the peace who fines you for speeding on a country road is a judicial descendant of an official first appointed by Edward I. Concerned over the lawlessness in the country districts, he appointed knights in each shire to be "conservators of the peace," and these functionaries became "justices of the peace" in the reign of Edward III.

Certain judicial scandals which occurred in the latter part of Edward's reign may be largely responsible for the comparatively untainted record of the English bar thereafter. These scandals broke while Edward was on the Continent, and upon his return he instituted a thorough house-cleaning. Several important judges lost their office, and Edward's job of reorganization was marred only by the fact that at the same time he expelled the Jews from England—a type of measure which was all too popular in Europe. Any public scandal or misfortune was likely to result in a persecution of Jews as scapegoats. After the scandals of Edward's reign, judges were increasingly selected from among men of legal training, who by now were rarely churchmen, but rather laymen who made the law a career.

The bar had grown rapidly. There had been no actual lawyers in England before William the Conqueror's time, but he brought with him certain *serjeants*, or "servants," of the king, some of whom became *servientes Regis ad Legem*, or "servants of the king at law." These, the first true lawyers, from whose ranks many of the early judges were recruited, increased by Edward's day into a large body of professional practitioners. In the early 1300's the Inns of Court appeared; they were guilds of lawyers who practiced around the London courts. At one time there were fourteen of these Inns, but now there are only four—Lincoln's Inn, Gray's Inn, the Inner

Temple, and Middle Temple. To these guilds law students were apprenticed, and, through the teaching of such apprentices, the Inns grew into law schools, which became so popular that the law courses at the Universities of Oxford and Cambridge were abandoned for several centuries.

The students were compelled to reside at the Inns, in an atmosphere charged with law. They held mock trials, known as "moot" trials, and, with the older lawyers, participated in almost daily trial practice and legal debate. Prominent lawyers came to give lectures, and some kept careful records of cases and arguments, which added to English legal lore. Handbooks of law were handed down, first in script and later in print, which preserved precedents for nearly three centuries, from about 1270 to 1530. These permanent records, together with the law reports which began to appear in Edward's day, helped immeasurably to create and preserve a genuine English common law which stoutly resisted any serious incursions from the Continent.

The truth is that these lawyers of the Inns were somewhat narrow in their point of view. Few knew anything about any legal system other than their own, and their rigidity of viewpoint sometimes made the common law a harsh and ruthless legal medium, saved only by the application of equity by the Chancellor's courts. Erasmus referred to the lawyers of the Inns as "a learned class of very ignorant men."

Edward I has been called the "English Justinian," a title which is hardly apt, but a good deal of very important legislation dates from his reign. Some of these new statutes were in substance not much more than codifications, or a specific writing down of laws which already existed but had not been clearly defined or clearly administered; many, however, contained new features and even new law. Although Edward himself was a thoroughly religious man, some of his laws, particularly the *Statute of Mortmain*, were directed at curbing the power of the Church and brought Edward the enmity of churchmen. So many Englishmen had sought to save their souls by making donations to the Church that it seemed as though all the land of England, sooner or later, might pass into the hands of Church corporations. So the Statute of Mortmain* prohibited such transfers without the consent of the king. The writ of *Circumspecte*

* "Mortmain" means "dead hand"—land was no longer to be transferred in such a way that it would be forever owned by a dead "hand."

Agatis was another annoyance to the Church, for it limited the jurisdiction of the Church courts to ecclesiastical matters. And Edward, by refusing to pay to the Pope the tribute promised by his grandfather, John, freed England from what had actually been a theoretical papal overlordship.

Other laws were directed against feudal privilege. His *Statute of Merchants* made it easier for merchants to collect their claims against the barons by permitting an attachment of feudal lands. He caused a compilation of land titles to be made, the *Hundred Rolls*, which was the spiritual child of the *Domesday Book*. Countless properties had been usurped by rapacious barons, and Edward insisted that every great landholder must now show proof of his original title, although anyone who could show title as far back as Richard the Lion-Hearted was considered to have valid title. Some of these statutes, and many others of importance, were included in the First and Second *Statutes of Westminster*.

Edward was a busy man. In addition to his intensive attention to domestic affairs, he conducted a series of foreign wars. Those in Wales resulted in the final defeat of Llewelyn, Prince of Wales, and spelled the end of Welsh independence. Those in Scotland were a disappointment, for he defeated William Wallace ("Scots wha hae wi' Wallace bled") but had to abandon his attempt to overthrow Robert Bruce. A French war, in which he was embroiled while fighting the Scotch, ended satisfactorily in a peace cemented by his second marriage, to the sister of the French King. Gascony was restored to English control. And Edward did not permit either affairs of state or military adventures to interfere with his duty to the country to produce progeny. By his first wife, Eleanor of Castile, he had thirteen children, and by his second, Margaret of France, two more.

II: From Edward I to the Tudors

IT MAY have been fortunate for England that Edward I, having strengthened Parliament and done so much for English law, was followed by a succession of futile kings. Parliament continued to strengthen itself, and the power of the feudal lords gradually diminished. London became the center of national life; and the lawyers became a class with increasing independence and influence. In the reign of Edward III (1327-1377) Parliament took on what was essentially its final character; though not yet legally broken into two houses, it was divided in fact, and Commons was becoming the more important house. The King, in his desire to secure the full support of Parliament in a bitter struggle with his barons, agreed to a declaration that matters which concerned king, kingdom, and the people should be considered and passed only by consent "of the prelates, earls, and barons, and the commonalty of the realm, according as hath hitherto been accustomed." Thus, in future, no law was to be passed without the consent of Commons.

The Hundred Years' War, which began in 1337, cost England much in blood and money but strengthened its budding nationalism. The Black Death, which carried off from one-half to two-thirds of the inhabitants of England, also accelerated the decline of feudalism. An era of wage economy and commerce was beginning to take the place of the age of serfdom. (The Lord Chancellor is said to sit on "the wool-sack," and his cushion is actually filled with wool. This custom dates from this period, in which the wool industry grew so important.) When the Black Death had killed so many Englishmen, the resultant labor shortage made it inevitable for the workers to begin to press for rights and advantages which had previously been confined to the upper and middle classes.

The bitter opponents of twentieth-century attempts to interfere with the laws of supply and demand in the interests of a "planned economy" may see support for their point of view in the *Statute of Laborers,* enacted in 1351. This Act compelled all those who had neither land nor money of their own to work for any employer who asked for their services, at the rate of wages in use before the Great Plague. At the same time, and in order to protect the workingman, "ceiling prices" were set upon products, which were equivalent to the preplague prices. The statute was a complete failure. The justices of the peace tried hard to enforce it, but it was generally ignored by both workers and employers, and this attempt at a managed economy did little more than increase the industrial discontent which marked the period. Of the several rebellions which took place, that of Wat Tyler is the most famous. Tyler's rebellion was a series of uprisings, the most serious of which took place in London, where young King Richard II and his entourage took refuge in the Tower of London to protect themselves from the angry mob. Peace was restored only when Wat was killed in a skirmish and the King capitulated by agreeing to abolish serfdom completely and to drop the Statute of Laborers. The King's pledges were later repudiated, but the people had tasted power, and a century later they did achieve full emancipation from serfdom.

Richard II created a packed Parliament and ruled with its assistance as a dictator, but he was forced to sign an abdication in 1399 and then was deposed by a reconvened Parliament. Parliament remained powerful through the reigns of the succeeding kings, Henry IV, Henry V, and Henry VI. It was Henry VII, the first Tudor, who ushered in a new era of power and development. He was a hardheaded and practical man, highly interested in trade and manufacture, under whose auspices England began to show signs of her coming commercial greatness. Under his rather benign reign, Parliament was content not to interfere very much, and this policy was maintained through the reign of Henry VIII and the other Tudors.

Henry VIII, somewhat despotic in temperament, was nevertheless always conscious that he ruled with the consent of Parliament. His first marriage with Catherine of Aragon (daughter of Ferdinand and Isabella, the patrons of Columbus) required the consent of the Pope because she was the widow of his elder brother, and Henry had no hesitation in asking the necessary permission. However, when Henry wished to divorce Catherine, his request to the Pope met a different response. Such divorces had been granted before, and neither the Pope nor the English prelates were shocked by the request, but the Pope, under pressure of Catherine's powerful family, refused. To extricate himself from this predicament, Henry called Parliament in 1529 and kept it in session seven years, causing successive measures to be passed that changed the structure of the Church in England. He made the clergy accept him as head of the English Church, their acceptance being qualified with the condition "so far as allowed by the law of Christ." Parliament then passed a law that no convocation of the clergy could be held without the King's consent. At this, the Chancellor, Sir Thomas More, resigned.

Sir Thomas More was the author of *Utopia*, which, like Plato's *Republic*, presented an ideal communal state. Everything is sweet and benign and lovely in this society, very moral, but nevertheless utilitarian. For example, a bride and groom must see each other naked before marriage, for, says More, no one would think of buying a horse without first taking off its saddle and bridle. It is an interesting commentary on the times that the author of this kindly and gentle book did not hesitate to burn heretics. More himself came to a violent end. He gave his client, King Henry, an opinion on the matrimonial problem which the latter did not like. Many a lawyer has lost a client who was dissatisfied with an opinion, but More lost not only his client but his head.

In 1532 Parliament passed the *Act of Annates*, a law which Henry hoped might bring the Pope to terms. It withheld payments of the first year's income from benefices, which had for long been payable to the Church. But even this did not cause the Pope to change his mind about the divorce, and Henry finally took matters into his own hands, declared himself divorced, and married Anne Boleyn, who gave birth to the future Queen Elizabeth. To settle the question of Elizabeth's legitimacy, Henry had Parliament pass the *Act of Appeals*, under which the King was made the head of all the courts of England, spiritual as well as temporal. Then a convocation was held, with the approval of Cranmer, the new Archbishop of Canterbury, at which the first marriage to Catherine was declared void and the marriage to Anne, therefore, valid and legal. But Pope Clement still refused to budge, and Henry, in anger, caused the withheld benefice payments to be paid to the crown.

This period in English history is important to the story of American law for one special reason. The first settlements in New England were by Puritan religious dissidents, and the acute religious turmoil which ultimately fathered the Puritan movement started in the reign of Henry VIII. Having emancipated himself from the spiritual control of the Pope, Henry made some attempts to popularize the new theory of religious government and to arouse the people to a feeling that they now had a national church. He had the Bible translated and published in English, and it may even be that he was genuinely affected by the spirit of the Reformation. The nationalistic spirit gradually increased, religious isolationism became popular, and Henry felt strong enough to take the last and final step of religious emancipation. The *Act of Treason and Supremacy* of 1534 made Henry the Supreme Head of the Church of England, and it became high treason for anyone to harm him or his heirs or to accuse him of being a "herectic," "tyrant," "schismatic," or "usurper" —names which his opponents had doubtless often used in private. Under this Act Henry indulged in considerable religious oppression and in a purge of his enemies.

The reign of Henry VIII was an era in which Roman law was

making enormous headway on the Continent as a result of the Humanistic movement. Pressure for the adoption of the Roman law was heavy everywhere, and it might have passed the barrier of the English Channel but for Henry's break with the Pope. A specific proposal was made by Reginald Pole that the Roman law be adopted in England, and in this period Scotland took over large sections of Roman law. But Henry did not want any part of a law emanating in any way from Rome, and the people, too, were opposed to anything "foreign." In fact, one of Henry's measures against the Roman Church was to prohibit study of the canon law. But study of the Romanesque civil law of the Continent was not discouraged, and professorships of civil law were founded at the universities.

In Mary's reign Catholicism came back to England, but Elizabeth reinstated Protestantism. Her reign was of course a great one, probably the most remarkable era of British colonial and economic expansion.

The period of the Tudors is not marked by any great advances in law. Rather, it was an era in which the national institutions were coalescing and their eventual form was beginning to appear. The Plantagenets had launched England into adolescence; under the Tudors it reached maturity. But there was still much to be done. Defendants in criminal actions were still subjected to torture and to confinement for long periods without benefit of counsel, and without the right to demand immediate trial. Various courts had seized summary powers and administered them arbitrarily. The British subject had acquired basic rights, but they were not always clearly enough defined to insure protection. Nor had the struggle of the people for the control of government been fully won. It had become clear that the king (or queen) ruled with Parliament, and that the basic law of the land was Parliament's law, yet it was only after the Stuart kings had lost their bitter fight to override this principle with that of the divine right of kings that the supremacy of Parliament was established beyond challenge.

III: Reforms and Overhauling

In 1364, during the reign of Edward III, Parliament made English the official court language of England. The king's courts still used bad Latin or old Norman French, and so ingrained was the custom of using the classic language of the courts that the lawyers of England ignored the new ordinance for almost one hundred and fifty years. This was due partly to the difficulty of translating so many technical terms from bastard Latin or old French. By the end of the War of the Roses, however, the transition was well under way, and it created a remarkable change in the jury system. Witnesses could now testify in a tongue comprehensible to them, and lawyers could address juries and be understood!

At about the same time another important change took place. Pleadings, the formal declaration of their client's position made by the lawyers at the start of a trial, had always been oral; vellum, the writing material used in legal documents, was too costly. When paper came into use, making writing materials inexpensive, lawyers began to use written pleadings more freely. Eventually it became customary for all pleadings to be written, and also for them to become formal. With all pleas made in writing, lawyers were held to greater accuracy and exactness than when pleadings had been oral.

By the seventeenth century the new form of jury, which judged the facts after hearing and seeing evidence, was firmly established; and the English then found it necessary to devise "rules of evidence." In some systems, the court hears anything it wishes to hear, but in the English and American systems there are carefully delineated rules limiting the kinds of evidence which may be offered. A judge sitting without a jury has greater latitude, for it is presumed that he will be able to distinguish the wheat from the chaff. But a jury is permitted to hear only certain kinds of evidence, presented in certain ways. For example, there is the rule against "hearsay" evidence. A witness cannot testify as to what someone else experienced, but only as to what he personally experienced. One reason for denying the admission of hearsay evidence was that witnesses were now submitted to cross-examination. The defendant's attorney should have the opportunity to see if he could trip the witness up and show that he was not really certain about his testimony.

There is much to be said against the jury system. Perhaps the most severe criticism is that juries are so often not of the desirable caliber. Today almost every busy man who gets a jury notice runs to his lawyer and asks to be excused from duty. Yet when he himself gets into a lawsuit with a technical case to present and sees in the box a jury composed of a plumber's helper, a cook, an unemployed actor, a window washer, two clerks, and six housewives who know nothing about business, he is likely to rail against the jury system. It has been suggested that the methods of selection of jurors might be improved through intelligence tests and educational qualifications. Such suggestions are met with vociferous objections by those who state that it is inconsistent with a truly democratic system to exclude anyone from the privilege of serving on juries, but this point of view is unrealistic. If morons were permitted to serve on juries, justice could not be done. A certain degree of intelligence and understanding is absolutely essential to enable a juryman to perform his judicial function. Some of our courts have therefore attempted to exclude the obviously incompetent from the lists from which panels of juries are selected.

The arguments for the jury system, however, overbalance those against it. It was certainly much safer in former days to have one's case decided by a jury of fellow men than by an appointed judge who might be influenced much more easily than a fairly chosen jury of twelve men. There is far less danger of venality in English and American judges today, but even now many judges are appointed or nominated for political reasons, and Justice might sometimes close her eyes if a jury were not there to protect the innocent. The jury system also brought the average English citizen into close contact with the courts and gave him an insight into their processes. The early use of the jury system in England may account for the fact that the English people advanced politically so much faster than did the people of the Continent.

CHAPTER 27

Elizabethan Rivals: Coke and Bacon

I: Fortescue and Littleton

"There is not pretense to say or insinuate to the contrary but that the laws and customs of England are not only good but the very best."

FORTESCUE: DE LAUDIBUS LEGUM ANGLIAE

THE ROMANESQUE SYSTEM of the Continent grew faster than the English system, for it had the Roman law to grow upon. At a time when Continental jurisprudence may be said to have become scientific, that of England was still comparatively crude. The English prevented overwhelming infiltrations by the superior Romanesque law almost solely by their proud and patriotic insularity and by the guild solidarity of the English lawyers. They rejected foreign attacks on their legal system though they did on occasion borrow freely from the Continent. They preferred bad English jurisprudence to good Continental jurisprudence, and they went steadily on their own way in developing a system that eventually turned out to be at least the equal of the one they rejected.

The earliest renowned champion of the English system was Chief Justice Fortescue (c.1394-c.1476), one of whose ancestors bore William's shield at Hastings. In about 1463 he published *De Laudibus Legum Angliae* ("In Praise of the Laws of England"). Written for laymen, it came strongly to the defense of the English system at a time when the Roman law threatened to engulf it. Pointing out defects in the Romanesque system, it asked for a patriotic support of English laws. But I wonder whether Fortescue himself did not borrow one important point from the Continental law. He said that natural law is the "mother and mistress of all laws," and that other laws must be subordinated to it. That was a concept which the Continent had taken over from Greece, by way of the Roman law, and in all probability Fortescue adopted it from either the Roman law or the Romanized canon law.

The next great name in the history of English law is Thomas Littleton. A contemporary of Fortescue, he studied at the Inner Temple, and, upon being called to the bar, he came to be an authority on real-property law. He was made a judge of Common Pleas in 1466 and remained on the bench until his death in 1481. His famous book was *Tenures,* dealing with real-property law. It is an English book, unaffected by the Roman law, held in so high esteem that it remained the classic in its field until Sir Edward Coke published his even more famous commentary upon it.

Other and lesser books appeared after Littleton,* including the *Commentaries on Reports* of Edward Plowden covering the years 1550 to 1580, the first modern law reports. Plowden pointed out that the law is in two parts, its shell and its kernel, or its letter and its sense. He said: ". . . the Fruit and Profit of the Law consists in its Sense more than in the Letter," and our courts have come increasingly to believe that a law should be interpreted according to its intended purpose rather than according to its precise and formal wording.

II: Equity vs. Common Law

THE ENGLISH PRIDE themselves on the way they "muddle through," and it is a fact that they have attained practical results with less planning and less forethought than any other people with the possible exception of the Romans. They share one other characteristic with the Romans: the tendency sometimes to solve a difficult problem by indirection instead of by attacking it head-on. So both these peoples, when their ordinary law was deemed too harsh or inadequate, left that law as it was but set alongside of it an entirely new system of law, to be used when the ordinary law failed. In the Roman law, it was the *ius gentium* which played this rescuing part, and in England it was *equity.*

* There was the *Graunde Abridgement* published about 1514 by Anthony Fitzherbert, and his *New Natura Brevium;* also, *The Doctor and Student,* published in 1518 by Christopher St. Germain.

The English equity system seems to be of local origin, although, in the course of its development, it certainly borrowed substantially from Roman law. There is a sharp distinction in the way the two systems of equity originated. The Roman equity of the *ius gentium* was an application of the "law of nations" or a supposed general or universal law. But English equity grew out of the concept of the "king's conscience." The English king had the ancient right (probably since Anglo-Saxon days) to make rules of law where none existed and thus had the right, in a sense, to "do equity." The common-law judges sometimes "did equity" without formal intervention of the chancellor, but, however ingenious the judges might be, they could not stretch the existing law beyond a reasonable point. Such limitation fortunately did not apply to the concept of the "king's conscience."

If some injury was done to you for which there was no relief under the existing writs, and if you could get access to the king, you would ask him to intervene to secure for you the justice the courts could not grant. Or you might approach a churchman who had the ear of the chancellor, who was usually himself a churchman in the early periods, and hope that he might intercede. As such applications accumulated, it was natural enough for the king to delegate to some representative the keeping of his legal conscience. He delegated it to the person most fitted for it, the chancellor, whose knowledge of the more benign Church law enabled him to determine when extraordinary relief should be granted. In this way the chancellor, and later the chancellor's court, came to take over the keeping of the king's conscience. They tried some cases themselves, but in many instances they simply intervened in a case pending in the king's common-law courts or ordered such a pending action to cease. The chancellors and their court were very likely to go to the Romanized canon law or even to the Roman law itself to find an answer to some problem for which no answer was available in English precedent.*

No one had absolute rights in equity. It was the grace of the king's conscience that gave relief if any was to be given. The appeal to the chancellor in the early days was "for the love of God and in

* I have several times mentioned the resistance of the English law to Continental influences. That resistance was chiefly in the field of the common law, although, even there, much Romanized law was taken over in the course of the years. But there was far less resistance in equity, where the chancellors were dealing with problems fresh to English law but often well known to Roman and Continental jurists.

the name of charity." Eventually, definite rules of practice and reasonably certain principles of decision were established, but the basic idea that equitable relief was to be obtained only by grace of the king persisted for a long while. And it is interesting to note that the king, by his chancellors, demanded that the plaintiff in equity come in with "clean hands." The maxim has also been put that "he who seeks equity must do equity."

Equity will often prevent a wrong, while "at law" a wrong can only be compensated by damages. The injunction, which we met somewhat similarly in the Roman law as the "interdict," is a form of preventive equitable relief. And, if you want to compel another to "specific performance" of his contract, rather than to get damages for his breach of contract, you "go into equity." You may have contracted for the purchase of a house. The owner refuses to go on with the sale. At law you can only recover damages, but if you really want the house you sue in equity to have the court compel him to give you a deed.

In our modern legal system the distinction between law and equity has almost entirely disappeared, since you can usually get equitable relief in most law courts, but the theory of equity still persists, and many cases are decided upon "equitable grounds."

During the period of Fortescue and Plowden, many English legal institutions were beginning to take the shape in which we now know them. The *Statute of Wills,* passed in 1540, in Henry's reign, permitted the disposition of lands by will. Lawyers immediately took advantage of this new statute by devising ways in which to put land into practically perpetual ownership through the use of wills, a result which was distasteful to society and was promptly stopped by the institution of what is called the *Rule against Perpetuities.*

Obviously, society cannot stand for property being held in suspended ownership or fixed ownership perpetually, for it would create an intolerable rigidity and fixedness, socially and economically. Suppose everyone with property left it, by will, so that successive trustees owned and managed it for the benefit of a succession of eldest sons. The result would be the creation of an aristocracy of property, which could not be broken. Accordingly, the law says that the "free alienation" of property, the right to dispose of it without the restriction of any trust, cannot be suspended for more than a specific period described by law. In the incredibly complex terminology of the Rule against Perpetuities: "The vesting of a future interest may not be postponed for a longer period than a life or any number of lives in being (including the life of a person *en ventre sa mère* at the time of the limitation) and twenty-one years after the dropping of the life or if there are several lives after the dropping of the last surviving life; but at the end of this period the limitation may still take effect if the person in whom the interest is to vest is *en ventre sa mère*."* Law students who first meet the Rule against Perpetuities wonder how anything so difficult could be devised by the human mind, and you may save yourself a headache by not trying to understand it. The Rule against Perpetuities in this, its common-law, form is still in operation in many of our states, but others have modified it.

The trust itself, a mechanism of wide present use and peculiarly Anglo-Saxon in form, had been developed by clever English chancery† lawyers. They prepared deeds transferring property to one person but to the "use" of another. There might be a good reason why the owner of a property would not wish his nephew, for example, to own the property, though he might wish the property to be used for the benefit of the nephew. So he would execute a deed to a third person, which gave to his nephew the "use" of the property. The ordinary common-law lawyers found this system very distasteful. With the rigidity of mind of which they were frequently capable, they rejected the "deed to a use" entirely and prevailed upon Parliament to enact the *Statute of Uses,* which converted a deed to the use of another into actual title in that other. The chancery court had approved and enforced deeds to uses. Consequently, when the common-law lawyers had caused the Statute of Uses to be enacted, the chancery lawyers invented the trust, to take the place of a use.

The strife between the common-law and chancery courts took another direction. The old system of getting a new trial through "attaintment" of a jury was cumbersome and had become unworkable. The chancery court solved the problem (which the common-law courts refused to meet) by enjoining the execution of a judgment if there appeared to be any equitable or fair reason for doing so. Thus, the successful party in the common-law court was obliged to agree to a new trial. Chancery acted in this manner, for example,

* This definition of the Rule against Perpetuities is taken from Cheshire's *Modern Real Property,* an English lawbook.

† The term "chancery" refers to the court of the chancellor, or the equity court.

if there appeared to have been fraud in the original case or if new evidence was discovered which might materially affect the result. In this and other conflicts between "law" and "equity," the latter came off the better, until gradually the respective powers of equity and law became fairly well settled.

It was inevitable that there should be conflict between the law courts and the courts which administered equity.* The chancellor's court at times overreached itself and interfered unnecessarily in the work of the common-law courts. So, in time, the principle was accepted that equity could step in only when there was no relief at law. That left a large field to equity, one important part of which dealt with cases of fraud and deceit or breach of confidence. When the trust was devised as a method of conveying and managing property, the obligations of the trustee were enforced in equity. There was no law to justify the existence of a trust, but, said the chancery court, if a man accepted a trust it would be a breach of confidence if he violated the trust and, therefore, the king's conscience would not let him benefit by his misdoing. And because the whole basis of action of the equity courts was so broad and even vague, the procedure grew to be far less formal and rigid than that of the common-law courts.

Equity almost died under the Puritan Cromwells, for the Puritans disliked it, perhaps without understanding it clearly, on the ground that it smacked of the Church and Rome, which was true enough. Fortunately, the Stuart Restoration brought back full support to the chancery court, for it is difficult to imagine what the common law would have done without equity to moderate its harshness and to fill its gaps.

English lawyers and Americans also take such pride in their legal system that they are at times inclined to overrate it. This may be true of equity. An unbiased observer might find it strange that we have one set of laws which are sometimes found to be so rigid and harsh that we require another set to "do equity"—or that we have a general system of law with so many gaps that a collateral system of law is necessary to supply the missing parts. A lawyer must sometimes ask himself, "Am I in equity or in law?" Perhaps this is another example of holding on to old concepts and practices merely

* The Court of Exchequer also had equity jurisdiction but was not a "chancellor's court."

because they have existed so long that no one stops to question them, like the pointless practice of taking off one's hat when there is a woman in a public elevator.

Long afterward, in 1876, the common-law courts were given the express right to use equity, and it was established that in a conflict between a rule of law and a rule of equity, equity was to prevail. Equity and law were then virtually amalgamated.

III: Edward Coke

"Reason is the life of the law; nay, the Common Law itself is nothing but reason."

EDWARD COKE: INSTITUTES

ON FEBRUARY 1, 1552, there was born to Robert Coke, Esquire, an eminent barrister and bencher* of Lincoln's Inn, a son who was named Edward, probably after the reigning King, Edward VI. The feudal age had passed, and England was about to emerge into its greatness, although the country was still small—the population of all England was but five million. King Edward died in young Coke's second year, and Mary Tudor ascended the throne, whereupon the already troublesome religious issue became intensified by her Spanish Catholic marriage. The country was at times in such ferment that barristers wore armor plate under their official robes. Then in Coke's sixth year, England suffered a serious setback; the French finally took and kept Calais, all that remained of English possessions on the Continent. But with the accession of Elizabeth in 1558, domestic peace seemed possible and, as it turned out, England's international position quickly took a turn for the better.

Coke had not much concern with the affairs of the world until he had passed through four years at Trinity College, Cambridge. In 1571 he went to London to enter Clifford's Inn and the Inner Temple, and was called to the bar in 1578. For more than a year thereafter Coke had not a single client, but then came an opportunity. A Lord Cromwell had started an action for slander against his vicar, claiming that the latter had accused him of sympathizing with sedition. The vicar may have seemed foolhardy to employ young Coke,

* "Benchers" were the senior lawyers in the law guilds, the Inns of Court, who acted as managers of the Inns and gave some instruction.

but it turned out to be a wise choice. After the court had declared that the vicar's defense was inadequate and had given judgment to Lord Cromwell, Coke found a serious defect in the plaintiff's pleading. When he called this to the court's attention, the case was dismissed. Coke's victory on a technical point won him renown, for England was small, there were few lawyers and few judges, and the news of the bar traveled fast among them.

The Inn made Coke a "reader," or lecturer, and his lectures were so able that his reputation increased rapidly. Then came *Shelley's case,* a litigation involving extremely difficult points of law which intrigued and confounded all the judges and lawyers of England. Coke's part in this famous action made his name even better known in legal circles. From here on his rise was rapid. He received a series of appointments to civil offices, gradually rising in stature until he came to the notice of Queen Elizabeth, who made him Solicitor-General of the Realm in 1592. The next year Coke entered Parliament, representing the city of Norfolk, and was immediately made Speaker, a position which required tact because of the imperious character of the Queen, whose temper precipitated frequent crises. Coke handled these delicate situations so well that he was recommended for the post of Attorney-General.

IV: Francis Bacon

> *"The law may be set down as good which is certain in meaning, just in precept, convenient in execution, agreeable to the form of government, and productive of virtue in those that live under it."*
>
> FRANCIS BACON: DE AUGMENTIS SCIENTIARUM

AT THIS POINT came the first of many clashes between Coke and Francis Bacon. Bacon had been born in 1561 in surroundings which promised a quicker rise to fame. His father, Sir Nicholas Bacon, became Lord Keeper of the Great Seal and a power at court, his uncle was the great Lord Burleigh, and, as a child, Francis Bacon was petted by Queen Elizabeth herself. He began studying law in 1579, was made a bencher in 1586, and served several terms in Parliament. He divided his time between his parliamentary duties and seeking the assistance and patronage of the strong.

Francis Bacon was one of the ablest men ever produced by England. He was many-sided. He was a brilliant writer, a scientist of importance, and a philosopher who must be named among England's foremost. He became a jurist of eminence, and his writings upon legal subjects emphasized system and a scientific approach. Like Leibnitz later, he pleaded for the correction of uncertainty in the law and what he called its "unprofitable subtlety." He was a historian whose work had considerable value. But, in contrast to Coke, who always managed his finances well, and, indeed, became an expert on fiscal matters, Bacon never found his income adequate. It was for this reason, and also because he did not attract clients as Coke had, that Bacon addressed himself to wealthy and powerful patrons. In Lord Essex, then the Queen's favorite, he found friendship and a willing helper.

Through Essex, Bacon hoped to become Attorney-General. When Coke was recommended for the post, Bacon intrigued through Essex to undermine Coke's chances. But the Queen had a long memory and did not forgive Bacon for his one courageous act, his opposition in Parliament to one of her pet financial bills. Though Essex's efforts delayed the appointment, Coke was made Attorney-General in 1594. Bacon's second choice had been the office of Solicitor-General, but he did not get this office either. However, the Queen, under pressure from Essex, did give Bacon something. Without appointing him to any actual office, she began to use him as one of her personal counsel, "Queen's Counsel Learned in the Law."

In time, Essex lost favor with the Queen and was accused of treason. Coke, then forty-nine, and eleven years in office as Attorney-General, prepared the case and prosecuted it. Bacon, apparently not unwillingly, joined with Coke as Counsel to the Queen in prosecuting the case against his old friend and benefactor. Essex was unanimously held guilty, and Bacon, nothing loath, accepted the Queen's request to write an exposition of Essex's crimes for the public.

V: Bacon vs. Coke

Though they worked together on the Essex case, no love was lost between Coke and Bacon. Their rivalry for the Attorney-Generalship had laid the groundwork for an enduring enmity. Neither was of forgiving character. Some time after the trial they met in the Court of Exchequer, and something which Bacon said started the following bitter colloquy:

Coke: "Mr. Bacon, if you have any tooth against me, pluck it out; for it will do you more hurt than all the teeth in your head will do you good."

Bacon: "Mr. Attorney, I respect you, I fear you not, and the less you speak of your own greatness, the more I will think of it."

Coke: "I think scorn to stand upon terms of greatness towards you, who are less than little; less than the least. . . ."

Bacon: "Mr. Attorney, do not depress me too far; for I have been your better, and may be again when it please the Queen." *

However bitterly he fought against him, Bacon always respected Coke's great ability and sagacity. Coke, on the other hand, had no appreciation of Bacon's undoubted genius, and vastly underrated his ability as a lawyer.

A new act in the drama occurred with the accession of James I in 1603. Coke was confirmed as Attorney-General; Bacon received no more than confirmation of his much inferior title of Counsel Learned. Fuel was added to the fire of Bacon's jealousy when Coke was knighted.

In 1603 Sir Walter Raleigh was accused of treason, and Coke, as Attorney-General, prosecuted this case also. The Raleigh case is hardly a credit to Coke. Lord Mansfield said of it, a hundred years later, "I would not have made Coke's speech in Sir Walter Releigh's case to gain all Coke's estate and reputation." True, Coke only used the methods and tricks of the criminal lawyers of his time; for hearsay, unsupported accusations, abuse, and invective were used freely by his contemporaries. But there was really no competent evidence against Raleigh, and in the personal exchanges between Coke and Raleigh, the prosecutor came off badly. For example:

Coke: "You are the absolutest traitor that ever was."

Raleigh: "Your words will not prove it."

Toward the end of the trial, when Raleigh asked for the last word, and the judges seemed inclined to accede to Raleigh's request, Coke

* Quoted in Lyon and Block, *Edward Coke,* in which the Coke-Bacon quarrels are described most interestingly.

sat down petulantly and had to be begged to proceed. Then his invective continued. "Thou art the most vile and execrable traitor that ever lived," he shouted at Raleigh, to which the latter replied with dignity: "You speak indiscreetly, uncivilly, and barbarously." But there were no "rules of evidence" in this trial, and poor Raleigh was undoubtedly railroaded. He was convicted, but the death sentence was commuted to imprisonment.

After several other famous prosecutions, including that of Guy Fawkes in the Gunpowder Plot, Coke was made Chief Justice of the Court of Common Pleas, the highest civil judicial office in the realm. In 1607, when Bacon finally received a high office, he was not made Attorney-General as he had hoped, but Solicitor-General. The stage was thus set for the greatest conflict between the two men, a conflict which had enormous importance in the history of the English law. For Coke now became the foremost defender of common law, and Bacon, representing the King, the great proponent of royal prerogative.

A clash came soon. Compulsory tithes were payable to the Church of England, according to an old custom of the Roman Church. Sometimes these tithes were lessened through a contract or agreement, called a *modus decimandi*, between the Church and a landowner. But the prelates often carried parishioners into the ecclesiastical courts to have the tithes ordered, and these courts did not always recognize the existence of a *modus decimandi*, were inclined to be harsh on the farmer, and preferred to impose the old standard tithes. A complaining landowner might then come to the common-law courts and ask for relief, which was granted through a "writ of prohibition." These writs annoyed the Archbishop of Canterbury, who brought the matter to the attention of the Privy Council. The Council sided with the common-law courts, and agreed that they had the right to issue the writs of prohibition.

Against this background of conflict with the Church, the *Fuller case* appeared. Fuller was a lawyer who had been prosecuted by the Church. He had aroused its enmity by defending two clients who had been imprisoned for refusal to testify in ecclesiastical courts. Fuller claimed that these courts had no right to punish by imprisonment except for certain high crimes. The matter was of such importance, involving another conflict between the common-law courts and the ecclesiastical courts, that King James called a conference between the clergy (including the Archbishop) and the judges (including Coke). Coke made an ardent defense of the common-law courts that angered King James so violently that all the judges trembled and Coke himself "fell flat on all fowrs."

The debate was inconclusive and was resumed at later hearings. Bacon was called in as one of the representatives of the prelates, and there ensued debates between Coke and Bacon in which Coke firmly insisted on the right of the common-law courts to issue writs of prohibition whenever any other court exceeded its jurisdiction. To this James finally agreed, but with extreme reluctance. Coke's victory was an important one. In effect he had argued that no one could change the laws of England except Parliament. His constant thesis was that not even the king was superior to the common law.

Coke had not invented this principle of a basic law of the land. As early as 1450, in the case of *Rous vs. the Abbot*, a court had held an English statute void because it was against the basic law of the realm, and it had become clear in the Tudor dynasty that changes in law must be made by Parliament and in accordance with the basic law. Important laws such as the Statute of Uses and the Statute of Wills, as well as those statutes enacted because of Henry VIII's marital and religious quarrels, were obviously valid only because they had been properly enacted by Parliament. But it fell to Coke to marshal the facts and precedents to establish, in his almost single-handed contest with the Stuarts, that Parliament and the basic law were superior to the king.

This thesis was involved again against a proclamation prohibiting the use of grain to make starch. The edict was well meant; there was a shortage of grain, and the use of starched linen had become so popular that great quantities of grain were consumed in this manner, instead of for food. However, in 1610 Coke held that the proclamation was, in effect, the making of a law, and since only Parliament could make a law, he held the proclamation invalid.

Coke was now a sharp thorn in the King's side; James was irked that Coke had made it so clear that the King had no legislative authority. Upon the death of the Chief Justice of the King's Bench, the highest criminal court, Bacon suggested to the King that he promote Coke to the post, out of the common-law field. This the King did, and Bacon was elevated to Attorney-General, while Coke was divorced from the common law.

Bacon and Coke had an interesting encounter in connection with the prosecution of Peacham, a Puritan clergyman accused of treason.

Bacon, as Attorney-General, prepared the case for trial. In 1614 he reported to the King that he could not get the stubborn defendant to confess. He wrote: "Peacham was examined before torture, in torture, between torture, and after torture; nothing could be drawn from him, he still persisting in his obstinate and inexcusable denials and former answers." That Bacon did not scruple at using torture is not surprising, for that horror was still in constant use in criminal cases. But the Attorney-General resorted to another practice which, while perhaps common in his day, was hardly to be applauded. Fearing that he might not get a verdict in his weak case against Peacham, Bacon approached each of the King's Bench judges privately to see whether they would decide for the crown. When he approached Coke in the same manner, that obstinate old man turned him down, informing him that it was against the law of England to question judges in advance of a trial. Bacon then avoided the King's Bench and had the case tried before the Lord Chief Baron of the Court of Exchequer, where he obtained a conviction.

There were many other matters over which Coke and Bacon met and fought, the latter always taking the side of the King's prerogative. One of these affairs was extremely important. The King asked the judges to stay a certain action until they had consulted with him, the demand being forwarded to Coke by Bacon as the King's agent, but the judges refused to comply, Coke taking the lead. Angered, James ordered a conference at which he berated the judges so severely that all but Coke fell on their knees. That staunch old supporter of the law argued with vigor that a stay would be contrary to law even if requested by the King, and, against all Bacon's arguments and the King's anger, Coke remained obdurate, though the other judges agreed to do the King's bidding.

The King acted. Coke was accused of many irregularities, he was suspended as a member of the Privy Council, and he was prevented from going on the summer circuit. He was called before Lord Ellesmere and Bacon, to report on his decisions and to confess any errors he had made in his judicial work. So he admitted five trivial errors in eleven volumes of reports covering five hundred cases.

Ellesmere and Bacon, not inclined to be arbitrary, insisted that a recitation of the charges against Coke must be drawn up. But the ire of the King overcame the objections of his counselors, and he issued a *supersedeas* on November 15, 1616, a writ which, without trial or accusation, discharged Coke from office as Chief Justice of England. At about this time Bacon finally achieved his reward for having served the King so consistently. He was appointed to the Privy Council in June of 1616; when Ellesmere resigned in 1617, Bacon was made Lord Keeper of the Seal, and in 1618 he became Lord Chancellor.

Coke was readmitted to the Privy Council in 1617, and in the next year he was again thrown together with Bacon, when both were made members of a commission to investigate the Treasury. Later he acted with Bacon on another commission appointed to investigate a second charge of treason against Raleigh, who had been permitted to leave prison in order to direct an expedition into the New World. Upon Raleigh's return, the charge was brought against him that he had illegally attacked the Spaniards, and in due course Raleigh was convicted and executed.

At the age of sixty-nine Coke started a new phase in his career. He entered Parliament again and for seven years was a leader in the battle for constitutional rights. Bacon became Baron Verulam, and then Viscount St. Albans. His fame increased, for he had published a number of books of great importance. Soon after Parliament opened in 1621, Coke was put on a commission to revise the statutes, a project which Bacon had frequently advocated. During the course of his work, Coke attacked the monopolies problem. Monopolies had been granted by the King as a royal prerogative, presumably for the public good but frequently for personal use and as a reward for service. While the controversy on monopolies was raging, rumors against Bacon crystallized into an accusation that he had been taking bribes in connection with the granting of monopolies. Formal charges were drawn against him by a committee of Commons, of which Coke was a member, and Bacon, confronted with facts which he could not deny, admitted his guilt and offered to resign. His long battle with Coke came to an end when Bacon was fined forty thousand pounds, imprisoned, and restrained from holding any further office and from again entering Parliament.

Bacon's punishment was not fully enforced. James remitted the imprisonment and assigned the fine to trustees for Bacon's creditors. Bacon's financial affairs were in a sorry state, as indeed they had always been, and the Kind had the kindness, in view of his past services, to grant him a pension of one thousand pounds a year.

Bacon thereafter devoted himself to his writing and experiments, and it is said that he died, in 1626, while conducting an experiment in refrigeration, the use of snow to preserve flesh.

Bacon's conduct had not been admirable, but we cannot condemn him too harshly in the light of the customs and circumstances of his day. Judicial offices were frequently sold, which did not necessarily mean that those who received such appointments were corrupt or incompetent, and Bacon had precedent enough for selling patronage. His misfortune was that he was caught at it.

After the Revolution of 1688, when the Stuarts were finally deposed, judges were appointed for life or good behavior, a practice which still continues in England and in our own federal courts, but not in some of our state courts. Placing judges beyond political importunities was a great step forward. Lawyers and jurists continue to debate whether judges should be appointed or elected and whether their tenure should be limited or for life. Perhaps some method of appointment may yet be devised so that both the dangers of arbitrary political appointment and the obvious weakness of the elective system may be avoided.

Though his bitterest enemy had been removed from the field, Coke was not at the end of his own troubles. In 1621 he was sent to the Tower for acts in Parliament deemed unfriendly to the King, but after seven months he was released because no legal charge could be laid against him. In 1625 James I died. Charles I, who succeeded him, was in constant need of money, but, upon his first request, Parliament gave him only 2 per cent of what he asked and refused to give more until it was informed to what use the money was to be put. Considering Coke the greatest obstacle in the way of getting co-operation from Parliament, the King disposed of the old gentleman by the simple expedient of making him a sheriff. According to law, a sheriff could not go outside his own county, and Coke thus could not attend Parliament.

Back again in Parliament after a period of exile as sheriff, Coke took a leading part in a movement for constitutional reform which was precipitated by the billeting issue. The King had been billeting soldiers in private homes, a procedure bitterly resented by the people. Opposition against financial grants to the King increased, and he made irregular attempts to raise the funds which Parliament would not give. He asked the public to make him a gift; he wanted to pawn the crown jewels; he tried to force a loan; but his expenses continued to exceed his receipts by far.

In 1628 he called a new Parliament. The elections went strongly against the government, and the Parliament which returned was one of England's greatest, with enlightened public opinion powerfully represented. Coke took the lead in demanding that governmental abuses be corrected by legislation before any funds were granted to the King. Under pressure of his commitments, Charles finally had to accede. The famous *Petition of Right* was drafted, chiefly by Coke, then in his seventy-seventh year. It provided that no person could be compelled to pay money to the state without the consent of Parliament; that no person could be imprisoned for refusing to make any such payment; that no person could be imprisoned for any crime without cause and without an opportunity to answer the charge; that soldiers and mariners could not be billeted in the houses of the people; and that no further commissions could be issued to punish persons by martial law. The Petition of Right is one of the landmarks of British freedom. With this great victory, Coke's parliamentary life ended, and he retired to continue his writings.

VI: Coke's Writings

EDWARD COKE was the greatest proponent of the English legal system and its foremost defender against onslaughts from the Continent. His own writings exalted the English law. His most important work was his *Institutes,* in four volumes. The first, published in 1628 when Coke was seventy-six, was entitled *The First Part of the Institutes of the Laws of England or a Commentary upon Littleton.* It was not an independent treatise but was, as it stated, a commentary based upon that previous authority, of whose work Coke said in his preface that it was "the most perfect and absolute work that ever was written in any humane science."

This view was contrary to that of Hotman, a famous French Romanesque jurist who had visited England in Queen Elizabeth's time. He referred to Littleton's work as a "clumsy, disorderly, and senseless piece of jargon." But Coke's opinion prevailed, perhaps because his own brilliant and energetic mind had so vastly improved upon Littleton's work. After Coke, there was small chance that the

Romanesque system would supplant the English, although the English law had not yet reached the intellectual level of the Romanesque system in many respects. It still contained absurd crudities; even in Coke's time, a case was sometimes decided by trial by battle with hired champions.

Coke's first volume covered the entire field of the common law. His second volume, published in 1641, seven years after his death, was an exposition of the ancient statutes, including Magna Charta, and Coke took the occasion to include much of his own argument concerning the supremacy of Parliament. Volume three, which appeared in 1644, was on criminal law, and volume four, appearing the same year, discussed the jurisdictions of the respective courts of England.

These were not Coke's only books. In 1614 he had published his *Book of Entries,* a manual on pleading and practice and the use of writs. His reading on *Fines* of 1592 was widely admired. In 1630 he wrote the *Complete Copyholder,* discussing "copyhold" estates, and in 1635 a *Treatise on Bail and Mainprize.** Also of enormous value were Coke's reports on cases, running from 1600 to 1616 and covering eleven volumes. Two more volumes were published after his death, in 1655 and 1658, but these do not have the same authority.

Even his bitterest enemy, Francis Bacon, held Coke's legal authority in the highest esteem. Coke's service to the common law was huge, yet it must be said that he had little interest in justice as such. His interest was so intensely in a maintenance of the common law that he did not seem to care if it resulted in hardship or injustice.

VII: John Selden

JOHN SELDEN, who carried on with the parliamentary struggle after Coke's retirement, was born in 1584, the son of a small farmer, and died one of the most highly regarded of Englishmen. Selden was a friend of all the great literati of his day, including Ben Jonson, and his own literary production was enormous. He may be ranked as a legal writer on a par with the best of the Continentals, and his

* *Copyhold* was one form of landholding. It was a tenancy at will, one which could be stopped at will, but which had been established by some custom. It was proved through a copy of a court roll. *Mainprize* was procedure for compelling a sheriff to take bail when it was proper for him to do so.

works gave evidence of intensive research and study. His *Judicial Combat* gave all the details of trial by combat, not even missing such small things as the position of the contestants on the field of judicial battle and the signals which were given to them. His *Titles of Honor* disclosed the origin of noble titles and of the insignia, rotes, investitures, and ceremonies associated with each. And, among countless other works, there was his *Marriage and Divorce among the Jews,* indicating the encyclopedic extent of his interests and learning.

Selden at times showed a courage matched only by that of Edward Coke. Both as a member of Parliament, where he did not hesitate to take the lead in movements against the royal authority, and in his writings, for which he was twice sent to the Tower of London, he indicated that he would uphold the right at any risk to his own person. He was one of the chief authors of the Petition of Right.

In one famous controversy Selden took the wrong side, influenced by the self-interest of the England which he loved. Hugo Grotius, the great Dutch internationalist, had written advocating the principle which we now accept in theory, at least, of freedom of the seas. Selden, probably believing that England's interest ran to the contrary, launched a bitter attack against this principle.

VIII: Habeas Corpus and Freedom of Speech

WE HAVE inherited much of inestimable value from the legal system developed in England, but there cannot be any doubt that two of our most valuable legacies are the writ of *habeas corpus* ("produce the body") and the right of *free speech.* The first assures us proper liberty of our persons, and the latter proper liberty in expressing our ideas.

John Selden called the writ of habeas corpus "the highest remedy in the law for any man that is imprisoned." It is a writ commanding any officer or person who is holding another in confinement to bring "the body" into court so that it may be established whether or not the confinement is legal. Sir Edward Coke maintained that habeas corpus had its origin in Article 39 of the Magna Charta, but actually the writ was of later origin. There were older, somewhat similar writs, but by the end of the Middle Ages these were no longer effective. Habeas corpus came into use in the reign of Edward I. It was then used with a writ of *certiorari*, or "privilege," to transfer cases from local courts into common-law courts. In the sixteenth century the same process was used to bring cases into the common-law courts from chancery, the Court of Requests, Admiralty, and the Court of High Commission. It was not until the end of the sixteenth century that habeas corpus was used independently.

Royalty always fought against such a use of habeas corpus. The Tudors opposed it bitterly, and its staunchest defender was old Sir Edward Coke. In 1627 there came a great test of the writ in *Darnell's case*, and the common-law judges, then under pressure from the crown, held that a writ of habeas corpus did not compel a jailer to disclose the cause or reason for the confinement of a prisoner. But the Petition of Right finally settled the matter, and the *Habeas Corpus Amendment Act of 1679* improved the use of the writ. From then on it was impossible for anyone, except in time of war, to be held in secret confinement.

The beginning of the struggle for the right of free speech took place in Parliament, where, before the time of the Tudors, a member had to be most circumspect in what he said. One whose tongue had, in the king's opinion, wagged too freely might be subjected to summary punishment. But Commons, under the Tudors, began to insist on the right to determine the extent to which members should be free to say what they pleased. There were several "free speech" clashes with Queen Elizabeth, who finally granted freedom of expression to Parliament but then proceeded to ignore her concession in fact. James I finally broke down and granted complete freedom of expression to Parliament. And when the Petition of Right was extracted from Charles I, it contained a ratification of the principle that members of Parliament could express themselves freely in debate.

It was from that right given to Parliament that the right of free speech spread to the man in the street. We now have the right to say what we please, but we are held responsible for the consequences of abusing that privilege. It is a precious right, freedom of speech, without which a truly democratic government would be impossible.

CHAPTER 28

Hobbes and Locke

I: Thomas Hobbes

"All the sentences of precedent judges that have ever been cannot altogether make a law contrary to natural equity." HOBBES: LEVIATHAN

THOMAS HOBBES (1588-1679) is said to have stirred the British intellect as much as any man before Darwin, and he had a long life to do it in—ninety-one years, a truly remarkable span in an age when sanitation and medicine were still primitive. But Hobbes was tough, physically and mentally. Although not a lawyer, he went deep into the law to learn its roots and theory. He respected ancient Bracton, had high regard for Francis Bacon, was probably most affected by Edward Plowden, and had no reverence at all for Edward Coke.

Hobbes had his own version of that troublesome concept "natural law." To many the natural state of man was a pleasant, idyllic state, such as Rousseau described, in which men were angels and lived in a harmony which was disturbed only by the mistakes of civilization. Hobbes, in his most important book, *Leviathan*, saw man in a more realistic pristine state. His "state of nature" was a sort of free-for-all, with every man for himself, a constant state of war. While a naturalist like Rousseau believed natural law to be the law of the state of idyllic nature, Hobbes considered natural law as those rules which men found necessary to curb the natural state of war. And, while he believed in natural law, Hobbes certainly felt that human beings were not wont to obey it without compulsion. He said that the laws of nature, "without the terror of some power to cause them to be observed, are contrary to our natural passions, that carry us to partiality, pride, revenge, and the like."

In pursuance of his natural-law theory, Hobbes devised his own golden rule. It was that man must be "contented with so much liberty against other men, as he would allow other men against himself." Rules so devised, he said, were the "dictates of right reason." Perhaps some of the Church fathers and Continental jurists who believed in a natural law to be disclosed by "right reason" would have agreed with Hobbes's paraphrase of the golden rule, for, like them, he identified the laws of nature with the law of God. But he insisted that the religious authority must be subordinated to the civil.

However, he also maintained that the monarch must be the head of the religion in each state. It was clear that he had no use for democracy. His animosity toward it he rationalized upon a compact theory, radically differing from that upon which Rousseau based his political discussions in his *Social Contract*. Rousseau saw a contract among the people underlying the state. Hobbes, on the other hand, saw the state as a compact between the people and their ruler. Hobbes's theory was that the people choose a ruler and, in doing so, inferentially make a compact with him. It is an artificial concept, for governments rarely come into being suddenly but usually develop by a process of evolution. But it suited Hobbes's thesis to use the compact-with-the-ruler as a major premise. From it, he arrived at the conclusion, among others, that the minority has no rights. Like Rousseau, but for a different reason, he was wholly disinterested in the majority-minority problem.

It is difficult to explain Hobbes. His thesis seems strained, and yet his arguments were extremely clever. He did not confine his position to advocating monarchy. His principle applied equally well to a parliamentary government. Whatever the form of government may be, he said, once it has been selected, the people are bound by it. But the fact is that Hobbes himself preferred the worst absolutism to the best democracy, which he considered as a form of anarchy. He saw no reason for conflict between an absolute sovereign and his people: What is good for the sovereign is, after all, he said, good for the people.

His thesis naturally led him into a distaste for anything like personal liberty, and yet he insisted, with seeming inconsistency, upon one kind. The citizen must be wholly subservient to his sovereign, he said, except that he has the right of self-defense. And he conceived the right of self-defense to go as far as justifying a refusal to fight for his country.

Hobbes was a bitter opponent of the Petition of Right, as might be expected, and when the Long Parliament met in 1641 he fled to France for fear that the government of the Commonwealth might prosecute him for his reactionary political views. However, the publication of his *Leviathan* in 1651, and his anticlerical ideas, antagonized his hosts. So he went back to England, made his peace with Oliver Cromwell, and promised to have nothing further to do with politics.

II: John Locke

"Without a notion of a lawmaker, it is impossible to have a notion of law, and an obligation to observe it."
LOCKE: AN ESSAY CONCERNING HUMAN UNDERSTANDING

THE TERM "liberal" is now much abused and confused. However, it has a distinct meaning as a label applied to a group of philosophers and jurists of the seventeenth century and later, who stimulated progressive political and juridical thought. To what extent these liberal philosophers were the product of their times, and to what extent they produced their times, is difficult to determine. The middle class was beginning to feel its full strength in the seventeenth century; religious tolerance enabled men to think for themselves; commerce widened horizons; democracy was pressing hard against what remained of absolutism; there was a general reaction among active thinkers against the remnants of medievalism. The classic societies had shown little interest in the individual, being concerned chiefly with the importance of the state. Christianity vitally concerned itself with the individual, but the medieval Church had grown intensely absolutist, both in organization and in spirit, and it was not until the birth of Protestantism that men began to feel wholly free to think for themselves.

There were offshoots from the liberal movement which reached radical ends. One of these was the extreme socialist movement fired by Marx and Engels. Another was the extreme liberal movement which found inspiration in Rousseau and worshiped majority rule at whatever cost to the individual. What might be called the main line of liberal development, however, was that which John Locke led.

Locke was born in 1632, the son of a Puritan lawyer. He did not follow his father's profession but dabbled in medicine, meteorology, chemistry, and politics until he finally found his true métier in philosophy. He became the outstanding exponent of tolerance and political liberty. He found the compact theory of Hobbes abhorrent. He held that government was a moral trust, and that, upon the violation of that trust, government rightfully could be overthrown. He believed that the people had the right to govern themselves as they wished; he concluded that there were basic human rights of which the people could not justly be deprived; and he maintained that the state is merely the expression of the people's will.

One of Locke's books, his first *Treatise on Government*, was a refutation of the theories of Sir Robert Filmer, whose *Patriarcha, or The Natural Power of Kings Asserted* was a defense of absolutism. Where Hobbes had supported absolutism on a cleverly devised basis, Filmer based it upon simple divine right. He said that God had given kingly power to Adam, that it descended from him to his heirs and so on down to the current kings. Liberty was something which Filmer despised as the cause of Adam's fall.* Such patriarchal absolutism disgusted Locke, who blasted it with his logic.

The direct influence of Locke on the founders of our government may be traced through the Declaration of Independence. The very first sentence of the Declaration makes reference to the "laws of nature" as justifying the severance from England. That Locke's particular variety of the laws-of-nature concept is intended becomes evident from other parts of the Declaration. In the second sentence the declarants hold it "self-evident" that there are "certain unalienable Rights" and that among these are "Life, Liberty, and the pursuit of Happiness." The relationship of these phrases to the following statement by Locke is not accidental: "The state of nature has a law of nature to govern it, which obliges everyone: and reason, which is that law, teaches all mankind, who will but consult it, that all being equal and independent, no one ought to harm another in his life, health, liberty, or possessions."

Immediately thereafter in the Declaration of Independence appears Locke's social contract, for the Declaration says: ". . . to secure these rights, Governments are instituted among Men, deriving their just powers from the consent of the governed. That whenever

* The theory of the Fall of Man has affected many jurists, particularly canonists who believed in a literal interpretation of the Old Testament.

any Form of Government becomes destructive of these ends, it is the Right of the People to alter or to abolish it, and to institute new Government . . ."

Locke did much to promote the clear separation of the individual major functions of government. He strongly advocated that the executive branch be wholly separate from the legislative. He maintained, further, that the legislative function must be subject to the control of the people. His writings on this subject had great influence upon constitutional thought in England and a very direct influence upon the American patriots who designed the Constitution. He gave little attention to the independence of the judiciary, and this is a rather surprising defect in Locke's political thinking. Nevertheless, Locke was an outstanding advocate of the system of "checks and balances" which was so clearly introduced into our Constitution, and it is a natural outgrowth of this system that the judiciary must be independent.

I feel that there should be appended to this section on Locke some comment on David Hume (1711-1776), a British philosopher who was the bitterest critic of the compact theory, both in the form adopted by Hobbes and in that advocated by Locke and followed by Rousseau. Hume was a skeptic and a questioner. He concluded that, while there was something to what both Hobbes and Locke had to say in their opposing compact theories, there was really a biased, political foundation to their respective contentions. Indeed, that was obvious enough, for Hobbes was rationalizing a justification for absolute monarchy, and Locke for limiting the power of the crown. Said Hume of Locke's theory: "When we assert, that all lawful government arises from the consent of the people, we certainly do them a great deal more honor than they deserve, or even expect and desire from us." * However, Hobbes was rejected and Hume was ignored by the Fathers of our country, and our own government was clearly founded upon the compact theory of Locke and Rousseau.

* "Of the Original Contract," an essay published in 1748.

CHAPTER 29

After the Industrial Revolution

I: William Murray, Lord Mansfield

"Every man who comes into England is entitled to the protection of the English law, whatever oppression he may heretofore have suffered, and whatever may be the color of his skin."

LORD MANSFIELD, IN DECIDING THE CASE OF JAMES SOMERSETT, A NEGRO

IN THE eighteenth century the rapid expansion of British trade inevitably doomed the insularity of English law. Coke and others had successfully fended off a possible complete shift to the Romanesque system, but that did not mean that all influences from the Continent were to be rejected. After the Revolution of 1688 various legal materials from the Romanized Continental law were imported into England, and sometimes in wholesale fashion. Sir John Holt, who became Chief Justice, brought in virtually the entire civil law of bailment. But it fell to Lord Mansfield to usher in modern English commercial law, largely by further importations. When he was made Chief Justice in 1756 he seized the opportunity to straighten out the mess of English commercial law, bringing in large pieces of the Continental law of quasi contract, corporations, partnerships, and agency, and shaping the amalgam into a co-ordinated and sensible system.

Lord Mansfield used the maxim *Fiat justitia ruat coelum,* "Let justice be done though the heavens fall," in the famous case of *Rex vs. Wilkes,* in 1786. Wilkes was the editor of the *North Briton,* a journal of none too good repute, who was charged with libel against the government. Failing to appear in the action, Wilkes was convicted *in absentia.* When he finally appeared and asked for a reopening of the case, he was imprisoned by Lord Mansfield's order, pending the hearing. The public was indignant and there were personal threats against Lord Mansfield himself, but that calm and dignified judge declared, "*Fiat justitia ruat coelum.*" Justice would be done even if rebellion threatened.

Events were marching rapidly toward revolution in America. Lord Mansfield aligned himself aggressively on the side of the government and argued bitterly and with intense animosity against the cause of the colonists. Thomas Jefferson recognized Mansfield as one of the most violent enemies of the colonies. Close behind as an opponent of American freedom he placed Mansfield's protégé, William Blackstone.

II: William Blackstone

> "*. . . the judges . . . are the depositaries of the laws, the living oracles, who must decide . . . according to the law of the land.*"
>
> BLACKSTONE

BEFORE American law schools developed a full course of law study, the youth who wished to become a lawyer apprenticed himself to some practitioner who immediately gave him Blackstone's *Commentaries* to read in between his duties as messenger boy and copyist. If you read Blackstone, you read the law. This veneration for Blackstone in America, which far exceeded the regard of his own countrymen, is strange in view of his bitter opposition to the American cause, but is explained by the fact that his book was of such educational importance to our lawyers. Moreover, few Americans probably knew anything about Blackstone's opinions on political matters.

Blackstone, born in 1723, was called to the bar in 1746 but fared so poorly that after seven years he gave up and went off to Oxford. He had tried with the aid of Lord Mansfield to get an appointment to a professorship of Roman law but, failing this, started a course of lectures, privately conducted, on the English law. The lectures were successful, and he finally did get a professorship at Oxford in 1758. The appointment was somewhat remarkable, for it was the first chair of English, as against Roman, law at any English university. Here he lectured well and built up, through his lecture notes, the material which he then fashioned into his *Commentaries on the Laws of England*, which was to make him the teacher of generations of American lawyers. One thousand copies of the first edition were sold in America, and fourteen hundred subscriptions were received in advance of the first American reprint in 1771. Twenty-five hundred copies were sold in America before the Declaration of Independence—a huge number of copies for a lawbook in those days.

Blackstone was elected to Parliament, but his election does not do him proud. In the England of that era seats in Parliament were often in the control of one man. Property qualifications and other restrictive political mechanisms were employed to keep the people in general from any participation in government. Of eight million Englishmen, only one hundred and sixty thousand had the vote. Blackstone was apparently selected for a seat in Parliament because he was corruptible, and his record shows that he was always willing to do the bidding of his principals, who were of the government party. He was a snob and a royalist to the point of absurdity. He said: "The king is not only incapable of *doing* wrong but even of *thinking* wrong: in him is no folly or weakness." That is quite a remarkable statement to make, considering that George II was a notoriously loose-living monarch, and his successor, George III, was at times insane.

Blackstone's snobbery included a complete contempt for the common people. As for the American colonists, he considered them beyond the pale of decent human society. But what he probably disliked most about the Americans was their insistence on "no taxation without representation." What would happen to England if the common people insisted on participation in government? Common people should have nothing to do with government! They were "virtually represented" by their betters. Blackstone felt about these upstart Americans much as Dr. Johnson did—that they were a "race of convicts" who "ought to be content with anything we may allow them short of hanging."

Blackstone's animosity against Americans did not detract from the popularity of his *Commentaries* in this country. It was worshiped as the beginning and the end of English law. But its chief claim to fame was its lucidity and the orderly fashion in which the author arranged his materials; and, in being so clear and so orderly, Blackstone avoided or slurred over the difficulties in the law, and his work was often superficial. Jeremy Bentham, the great English legal reformer, referred to Blackstone as a "formal, precise, and affected lecturer, just what you would expect from the character of his writings, cold, reserved, and wary, exhibiting a frigid pride." His bias appeared frequently, and he used the theory of natural law to justify the *status quo*. Whatever existed was proper, according to Blackstone, and he went so far as to recognize witchcraft, conjuration, enchantment, and sorcery, and held that to deny their existence was to contradict the revealed word of God. Blackstone gives a striking illustration of how the theory of natural law may be used to support whatever one happens to believe in, be one radical or deeply entrenched reactionary.

III: The English Lawyers

In England, if you needed the services of a lawyer, you might easily become confused if you did not understand the system. If you had a contract or a will to be drawn, or a corporation to be organized or a piece of property to be conveyed, you would go to a "solicitor." You would not make the mistake of going to a "barrister." Barristers are court or trial lawyers. But, in consultation with your solicitor, you might run across one odd characteristic of law practiced in England. Some difficult point of law might arise, and the solicitor would then suggest that he "brief counsel." You might wonder why the solicitor could not give you an opinion on the law, but he would explain that this is also a function of a barrister, not a solicitor. A solicitor does sometimes give opinions on questions of law, but he does so at his own peril and may be sued for negligence, while you can't sue a barrister no matter what error of negligence he may make.

Having been introduced to the work of a solicitor, you may later have a lawsuit to bring in an English court. You might then naturally visit a barrister, having learned that barristers are trial lawyers. But the barrister's clerk would inform you politiely, amazed at your ignorance, that barristers do not receive clients, and that you will have to engage a solicitor who, when he is ready, will "brief" a barrister to plead and argue the case. So you go back to your solicitor again and tell him about your troubles and about the litigation which you wish to commence. He will start to prepare the case for you, interviewing witnesses and assembling the facts for a barrister, whom he then "briefs." The barrister may advise in the preparation of the case, prepare the pleadings, and give opinions on the law involved, when he is required to.

The solicitor makes arrangements with the barrister's clerk regarding the fee, but not with the barrister himself; that would be injurious to the latter's dignity. Strictly speaking, the barrister gets no fee at all. He gets an honorarium, or gratuity. It is truly a gratuity, for the barrister could not sue for it if it were not paid. Characteristic of the English tendency to hang on to ancient customs and practices, the barrister has a pocket in the back of the gown which he wears in court, a relic of the days when his gratuity was slipped into that pocket (theoretically without his knowledge) before he entered court.

The chances are that your solicitor will have briefed a "junior," a barrister who is not yet one of the "leaders" of the bar. So the junior takes your case into court, and the solicitor sits behind him on one of the stiff, hard benches which are traditional and very uncomfortable in English courts, and occasionally consults with the trial lawyer.

But it may be that your solicitor, sometime before the trial, informs you that the other side has "taken in a silk," and advises that you take one also. "Silk" refers to one of the leaders of the bar, a "King's Counsel" or "K.C."; the expression "taking silk" refers to the process by which a junior becomes a K.C.* If the other side has taken in a silk, it usually behooves you do to so also, which runs into a double barrister's fee. The junior is not discharged but assists the K.C. and gets a fee which is two-thirds of the latter's

Not all juniors try to become leaders. A leader cannot do such work as preparing pleadings, and, as this is profitable work, most barristers cannot take the chance of cutting themselves off from this source of income. There are many barristers, indeed, who do no trial work but spend all their time preparing pleadings and giving opinions on questions of law.

The division of lawyers into two classes is very sharp. Solicitors are not "members of the bar," and judges are selected from among the barristers only. While there were barristers as long ago as the Norman dynasty, solicitors were not recognized as a separate and

* When, as now, England has a queen, "King's Counsel" becomes "Queen's Counsel," and "K.C." "Q.C."

dignified profession until recent centuries. They were, at first, just hangers on in the courts, and did clerical work.

All this is strange to us. The American lawyer is a "barrister," "solicitor," "attorney," "counselor-at-law," "advocate," and "proctor in admiralty" all rolled into one. And there is a good reason why no class division arose in the United States. There were at first no law schools in the United States. Some few men went to the Inns of Court to study, but most contented themselves with reading Blackstone in a lawyer's office in preparation for the bar. It was impossible, in such a loose system, for any divisions to arise, and there were no existing institutions like the Inns of Court, confined to trial lawyers, to perpetuate such distinctions.

IV: Adam Smith

> "*. . . for the proper performance of* ['*the duty of superintending the industry of private people, and of directing it towards the employments most suitable to the interests of society*'] *no human wisdom or knowledge could ever be sufficient . . .*"
>
> ADAM SMITH

IN SHARP CONTRAST to Mansfield and Blackstone, those two vigorous enemies of the cause of the American colonists, was a Scotsman who supported the demand of the Americans for some share of representation in their own government. He first advocated that England voluntarily surrender its authority over the colonies. But knowing that this suggestion would never be adopted, he then suggested that each colony should be allowed a number of representatives in Parliament in proportion to its contribution to the public revenue, a suggestion that horrified most of his countrymen.

Adam Smith (1723-1790) is best known to us as an economist. But Adam Smith was primarily a jurist, rather than an economist, and he was a great liberal in his day. He was a professor of jurisprudence at Glasgow from 1752 to 1764, a period which almost coincided with Blackstone's lectures at Oxford on English law. It was a time in which the lot of the workingman was still tragic. There had been another attempt at a planned economy dating from Elizabeth's time. Prices were regulated, and a labor code was enacted, called the *Poor Laws,* which included a *Statute of Artificers* and applied to workers in general. Wages were fixed annually by the justices of the peace on a scale based on the cost of living, and able-bodied men were required to work in private employment if there was any. If there was none, they were obligated to work on materials supplied by the parishes, and some of this work was given to them to do in their own homes.

Refusal to work sent one to a "house of correction," and those who could not work were cared for in "poorhouses," which were supported in niggardly fashion by local taxes and by the parish work. There were punishments for wrongful departure from work and for wrongful dismissal, and no combination either of employees or of employers was permitted.

Adam Smith was one of the few in England who called sharp attention to the "despicable condition" of the workmen. He advocated education for the common people, a terrifying idea to such as Blackstone and Mansfield; he complained that the government favored the rich against the poor; he pointed out that laws frequently continued long after they had outlived their usefulness, particularly those that were oppressive to the lowly. In his great book, *Wealth of Nations,* which is generally treated as a work on economics but is actually a commentary on the law, Smith, the liberal, noted that merchants complained about the bad effects of high wages but never complained about the disastrous effects which high prices could bring. This surely has a modern ring.

V: Jeremy Bentham

> *"The general object which all laws have, or ought to have, in common, is to augment the total happiness of the community; and therefore, in the first place, to exclude, so far as may be, everything that tends to subtract from that happiness: in other words, to exclude mischief."*
>
> BENTHAM: THE PRINCIPLES OF MORALS AND LEGISLATION

IN THE CENTURY following the Declaration of Independence an intensive movement for the reform of the English legal system took place. It was partly the result of the encouragement the impact of the American Revolution gave to liberal English minds. But it was largely due to the work of one reformer, Jeremy Bentham (1748-1832), who was called to the bar but did not practice law.

His *Fragment of Government*, published in the very year of the Declaration of Independence, brought him sharply to public attention, and he followed this success with a great many books. They are not without flaws, for Bentham lacked a sense of organization and method, but they were enormously influential, and they lit a new torch of reform which brightened the way for others to follow. So strong was Bentham's impact on current thought that by the time of his death his reform movement had already taken on considerable volume. His approach to legal and social problems is best summarized as a desire to humanize the law. He was one of the founders of the school which believes that laws should express the greatest good for the greatest number, and he cherished a bitter antipathy to Blackstone, considering that pompous jurist as a Dr. Pangloss, an advocate of the *status quo* who believed that nothing should be changed in this "best of all possible worlds."

Though the Blackstones and the other staid and comfortable British jurists were quite satisfied with the existing law, there was much room for reform in Bentham's day. The criminal law was still barbaric. One could be executed for cutting down a tree, to mention only one of the two hundred offenses for which there was a death penalty. As a result of Bentham's work, the number of crimes carrying a death penalty was drastically reduced. In addition to reforms in the criminal law, divorce laws and bankruptcy laws were enacted. Married women were freed from some of their ancient restraints, so that they could now make personal contracts and hold property independent of the control of their husbands. Very important reforms in real-property law eliminated some feudal anachronisms. One no longer needed to take title to real estate by delivery of a twig or a piece of soil, as the old law had required, but could now take title by a simple deed.

Sir Henry Maine epitomized Bentham's work as follows: "The secret of Bentham's immense influence in England . . . is . . . he gave us a clear rule of reform. English lawyers of the last century [the eighteenth] were probably too acute to be blinded by the paradoxical commonplace that English law was the perfection of human reason, but they acted as if they believed it, for want of any other principle to proceed upon. Bentham made the good of the community take precedence over every other object, and thus gave escape to a current which had long been trying to find its way outwards."*

Bentham rebelled at the smugness with which the English law was described as the perfection of wisdom. Possessing a rare ability to criticize constructively, he subjected institutions to the test of utility. And, if he found them wanting, he often had a workable change to suggest.

His influence has been far-reaching and has not yet come to an end. Jeremy Bentham, like Adam Smith, thought it was stupid of society to retain many old customs, practices, and laws merely because they were hallowed by age, and it is perhaps due to Bentham more than any other modern that we have come to question existing rules, rather than accepting them merely because they have gray hair.

There were limitations, however, to Bentham's own good sense. He knew a great deal about current English law and the legal system but comparatively little about the Roman and Romanesque systems. The insularity of his thinking and a tendency to intellectual complacency made him believe that the whole world might be ready to adopt an idealized code based on the English law as he would reform it. Moreover, he sometimes indulged in utopian nonsense. He suggested that all lawyers should be abolished, that all the law reports should be abandoned, and that every man be his own lawyer; and he wished to do away with the jury system.

Whatever his idiosyncrasies, English law began to come into its full maturity largely under Bentham's stimulus. That it could be improved still more there cannot be any doubt, for perfection has not been reached in any human institution; but, to date, no finer or more just system of law than the Anglo-American has been devised anywhere.

* *Ancient Law*, p. 65.

VI: Austin and Maine

"If we were compelled to set aside the study of Roman law, our inquiry into the origin of law and of society would be at once reduced, in great part, to vague conjecture." SIR HENRY MAINE

At least two other great Englishmen must be mentioned before passing on to the American law. One of these was John Austin (1790–1859). Studying law after a session in the army, he was admitted to the bar but practiced for only a few years, quite unsuccessfully. In 1826 he received an appointment to teach jurisprudence at University College, London, and, as his lectures did not begin until 1828, he took advantage of the waiting period to study the teaching methods of the jurists in Germany. Among the eminent Continental teachers to whom he listened was Savigny, for whom he acquired respect and veneration. Returning to London, he found his classes small but attended by several men who achieved eminence, among them the philosopher John Stuart Mill.

In 1833 he was appointed to a royal commission on the criminal law, and in the next year he lectured at the Inner Temple, but he achieved no great eminence during his life. His published works during his own life were rather modest, but Sir Henry Maine, starting to lecture just about the time of Austin's death, created intense interest in Austin's teachings, with the result that some of his lectures were republished after his death by his wife, and two volumes of fragments added.

Maine emphasized the importance of Austin's work in insisting upon analytical inquiries concerning the meaning of terms. Maine said that a philosophy of law had been made possible by Austin's work. Austin sought to distinguish between law and morals; to expose concepts of duty, right, injury, punishment, redress, liberty, and to relate these terms to sovereignty. He discussed the importance of distinguishing between rights *in rem* (rights against a thing or procedural rights) and rights *in personam* (rights against a person, or personal rights), and the necessity of fully understanding the meaning of terms such as person, thing, act, forbearance, obligation, sanction, etc. He may be said to have been the champion of the study of legal semantics.

His admirer, Sir Henry Maine (1822–1888), was appointed a professor of civil law at Cambridge at the age of twenty-five, and later lectured at the Inns of Court, these lectures becoming the foundation of a book which made him immediately famous, his *Ancient Law*, published in 1861. Despite some errors which later scholarship has disclosed, this remains a remarkable and compelling story of the birth, growth and development of legal institutions, starting with savage and barbarian customs.

From 1863 to 1869 he was a legal member of council in India and directed plans for the codification of Indian law, and he brought back with him to England a store of new knowledge to enrich his later writings and the lectures he later gave in jurisprudence and international law. His literary production was heavy and vital, including books on international law and government and further works on primitive law. His theories concerning the development of legal institutions have been subjected to much criticism, but he has certainly retained the respect and admiration of later jurists. In his political writings he was controversial, holding that democracy was not necessarily any more stable than other forms of government and that democracy does not necessarily spell progress.

PART EIGHT

THE AMERICANS

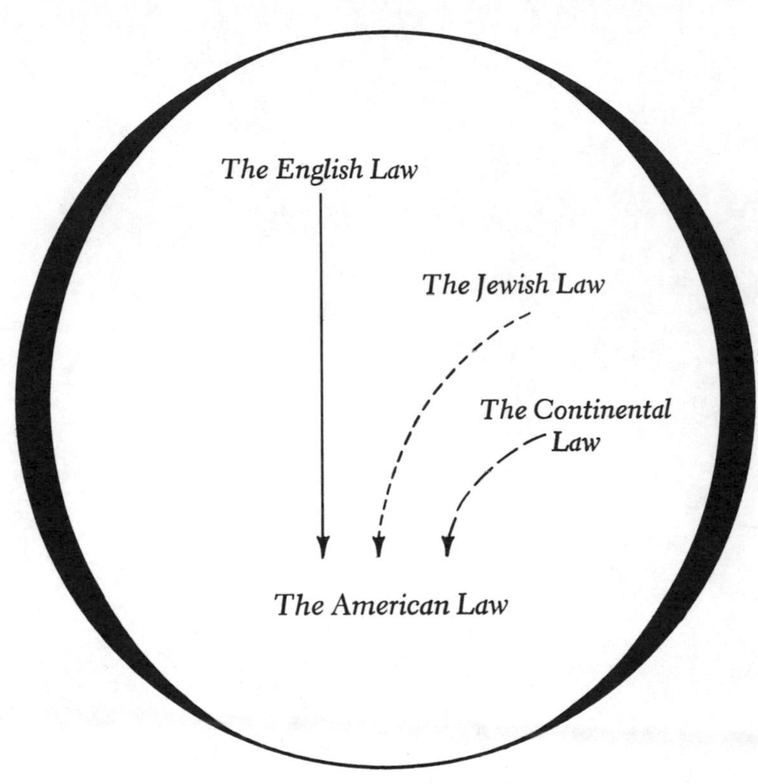

THE CHIEF BASIC SOURCES

CHAPTER 30

The Early Colonials

I: Pilgrims and Puritans

WHEN the good ship *Mayflower* arrived off Cape Cod, having aimed for Delaware Bay and missed it by quite a margin, the Pilgrims decided to land and take the chance that they might later get permission to stay in territory outside the jurisdiction of the London Company, which had granted them the right to settle in "Virginia." Of the one hundred and two persons on the *Mayflower*, only thirty-five were of the original company which had embarked at Leyden, Holland. The rest had been picked up in England. These additions were a motley lot. Some of them were rascally characters, and the Pilgrim Fathers were worried about how they might be controlled in the new settlement. Indeed, some of the "undesirable lot" had stated in no uncertain terms that they "would use their owne libertie" when they landed, and not be subject to Company rules. It was, therefore, decided to draw up an agreement for the formation of a government. This contract, signed on November 11, 1620, by forty-one men and known as the *Mayflower Compact*, contained no detail of government. It was merely an agreement to "combine ourselves together into a civil Body Politick," which was to make laws to which all would give "due Submission and Obedience."

Other Pilgrims followed the first boatload, and further settlements were made in the vicinity of Plymouth, but the great influx of settlers in New England did not come until after the Massachusetts Bay Company had been chartered in 1629 and had established a substantial colony of Puritans farther north. This new colony ex panded rapidly, for Charles I was King in England, and the Puritans were having a bad time of it. Sir Edward Coke and his colleagues had extracted the Petition of Right from Charles, but its full effects had not yet been felt, and many a harassed soul was willing to go the ends of the earth to escape from Merrie England.

It is ironical, however, that the communities established by these emigrees have contributed some of the most absurd and hateful incidents of our history. Because of what might be characterized as the abnormality of its initial political and legal development, New England deserves more attention than other colonial areas. For some understanding of these harsh people who established such an unenviable record of imprisonment, torture, and slaughter of nonconformists, it is necessary to understand the religious and political background of their emigration.

The period of the Reformation saw the creation in England of an Anglican Church independent of the Papacy. The "reform," however, went little beyond the bare fact of severance from Rome. Henry VIII had established the national Church only as a last resort, after realizing that he could neither cajole nor coerce the Pope into assisting him in solving his matrimonial problems. The existence of the liberal religious movement of the Reformation on the Continent made the transition to a national church easier. British nationalism was also growing, and "foreign domination" by the Papacy became increasingly unpalatable to Englishmen. However, the Anglican Church born of Henry's quarrel with the Roman Church was not essentially liberal either in its inception or in its development. It remained feudal, absolutist, and "Tory."

The Puritan movement started within the Church of England and had, initially, no intention of separating from it. It received its greatest impetus from those Anglicans who, during the persecutions of Mary's reign, escaped to the Continent and there imbibed some of the doctrines of Calvin. Returning to England in the friendly reign of Elizabeth, most of them remained in the Anglican Church and there sought to secure some modifications in Church rule and administration. Only a small section of the Puritan movement, at first, leaned more toward revolutionary approaches to religion and Church government. These ultimately grew into a number of sects, generally known as Separatists or Independents, who believed in a sort of Christian democracy although of course they did not use the radical term "democratic."

But the Puritans were not long satisfied with the mere severance from Rome. These "Unspottyd Lambs of the Lord" insisted upon substantial reform within the Church and upon the right to create and manage their own congregations. The Presbyterians, mostly of the propertied middle class, were strong advocates of freedom of property; the Separatists went even further, finally demanding personal liberty as well, which made them dangerous radicals in the eyes of Presbyterians and Anglicans alike.

The Puritans of Massachusetts Bay emigrated before the movement had reached this secondary stage in England. In the sixteenth century the concept of personal liberty in religion, which Luther had given to the world, had carried connotations of broader individual liberty, but it was not until the next century that these ideas actually spread into the field of politics and law. So the Puritans came to America without having been infected with any germs of personal liberty, except in religion. Moreover, these were followers of Calvin rather than of Luther. Authoritarian and narrow-minded, they wanted freedom for their own ideas but not for the ideas of others.

The Pilgrims were of a different stripe. They were Separatists who arrived in America with a simple faith in democracy, who wanted the right to self-government within the Church, and were inclined to apply the same principle to civil affairs. In contrast, the Puritan churches and communities were controlled by a handful of men strongly conscious of their power and of their membership in a ruling class.

II: The Puritan Theocrats

> *"When the people have chosen men to be their rulers, now to combine together . . . in a public petition to have an order repealed . . . savors of resisting an ordinance of God. For the people, having deputed others, have no right to make or alter laws themselves, but are to be subjects."*
>
> JOHN WINTHROP

THE COLONY OF MASSACHUSETTS BAY, which was to become the largest and most powerful colony in America, was the property of the Massachusetts Bay Company, a business corporation chartered in England. No more than twenty of the members came to America, and initially this small group firmly controlled all operations of the Company in the new land. In time deputies came to be selected by the towns and individual communities, and these grew into a lower house of the Legislature, but government never fell into the hands of the masses of people. Even when the population had risen into the tens of thousands, only a small fraction had any vote or even any indirect participation in government.

It was a strange state which the leaders of the Massachusetts Bay Company established in the New World. The charter provided that the Company might make such laws as were not inconsistent with the laws of England, but this restriction was ignored from the start. Having escaped authoritarianism in England, the settlers established it in America, and they found their inspiration in John Calvin. The Old Testament became their constitution, and a good part of the ancient tribal law of the Jews was put into actual effect. Church and state were one and the same, and the model of the state was the patriarchal, hieratical, tribal system of a primitive Jewish tribe in the wilderness.

John Cotton, the most eminent religious leader of Massachusetts, came to America at the age of forty-six to fulfill his long-cherished dream of a utopia governed by the laws of Moses, a society in which a small group of church oligarchs governed by the rules of the Old Testament. He was widely respected, and his influence upon government and law was as important as his position in the religious life of the new community. When a formal code of laws was established the code finally adopted was the *Body of Liberties* prepared by Nathaniel Ward. But Cotton had presented his own proposal, *Model of Moses His Judicials,* and although Ward's code was adopted, most of Cotton's ideas prevailed. Membership in a religious organization was necessary to first-class citizenship. Government was in the hands of a select few.

The early civil magistrates were wholly in accord with the system. John Winthrop, the first Governor, worked closely with the ministers of the church. As a magistrate, he considered himself the interpreter of the laws of God and believed that he held a stewardship from God; any disobedience to the magistrate was an offense against God. Winthrop called democracy "the worst of all forms of government," stating that "whatsoever sentence the magistrate gives, the judgment is the Lord's though he do it not by any rule prescribed by civil authority." In a system of this kind, there was no room for jury trials. There was no authority for them in Moses' code.

Nathaniel Ward, the author of the *Body of Liberties,* was slightly more progressive than John Cotton, but the difference was hardly appreciable. Born in England in 1578, and an emigrant to America in middle age, he was a lawyer who had turned to the ministry. As a political philosopher of some common sense, he saw the practical necessity of a code of laws in Massachusetts, but his proposal did little more than put the current system into writing. The government established by the *Body of Liberties* had an aristocratic foundation and perpetuated the caste system, although it did recognize some personal and property rights.

Many other ministers devoted themselves to cementing the Old Testament theocracy of Massachusetts Bay. Most eminent among them were Increase Mather and his son Cotton Mather, who did about as much as any two men could to retard the growth of liberalism; and they had their counterparts among the civil leaders. The Puritan regime produced many absurdly restrictive laws and regulations, and the literal acceptance of the Bible resulted in horrifying excesses. One of the most shocking was the wave of witch-hunting, during which the good citizens of Salem outdid themselves in what Charles and Mary Beard have termed "an experiment in demonology." Ten young girls accused a Negro slave and two old women of having bewitched them. The town went into hysterics, and within a period of four months hundreds of people were arrested and tried, nineteen were hanged, and one was pressed to death.

The managers of the Massachusetts Bay Colony consistently showed that their ideas of justice were no better than those they had complained of in England. One Ratcliffe, a mentally unbalanced servant, was whipped, had his ears cut off, was fined an impossible sum, and banished from the colony for talking loosely about the government and the church at Salem. Thomas Gray was banished, his house was torn down, and everyone was ordered to refuse him shelter. One critic of the government of the colony was put in the stocks, fined, and disenfranchised; another, who dared to say that he would appeal to England if he were punished, was put in the stocks for his effrontery.

One man who sought to organize a congregation of his own was fined and imprisoned "during the pleasure of the court." Another was convicted of "heresy" and condemned to hang if he did not leave the colony within three weeks. A woman was ordered whipped for criticism of the administration.

In 1635 a law was passed making church attendance compulsory under penalty of fine and imprisonment, and three years later every resident was made subject to a tax to support the ministers. If a recalcitrant was excommunicated and did not get himself restored to grace within six months, he was punished by fine, imprisonment, "or further." This "further" apparently included death. But there were brave souls who were willing to face persecution. Anne Hutchinson, a kindly and influential woman, began to preach a religious tenet differing somewhat from that of the established ministers; and, as she drew many people to her views, she was brought up for trial. The charge was that she had violated the Fifth Commandment in failing to honor her "father and mother." Her "father and mother" were the established authorities of Massachusetts Bay! Here is certainly an example of the perverted use of a straightforward and unambiguous phrase. The patriarchs of Massachusetts Bay Colony rationalized that because men had been enjoined by God to honor father and mother, they were enjoined to obey, without questions or complaint, the civil and religious authorities. Anne was ordered banished, and when she asked the reason, the Governor replied: "Say no more. The court knows whereof and is satisfied." *

III: Thomas Hooker

> *". . . they who have the power to appoint officers and magistrates, it is in their power, also, to set bounds and limitations of the power and place unto which they call them . . ."*
>
> HOOKER, IN A SERMON, 1638

THE COTTONS and the Winthrops represented a majority local opinion, but a revolt against absolute theocracy was growing in the Massachusetts colony. Brave souls began to drift off into the wilderness to create settlements, in Rhode Island and Connecticut chiefly, where they not only could worship God as they wished but could also have something to say in the management of their temporal affairs. One outstanding leader of insurgent emigrants was Thomas Hooker, who established a new colony in Hartford, Connecticut.

Hooker (1586-1647), a Puritan minister, had been preceded to the New World by a group of Puritans who called themselves "Mr. Hooker's Company." He himself sailed somewhat later in the com-

* Quoted in James Truslow Adams, *The Founding of New England*, p. 171.

pany of John Cotton, and became pastor of his own congregation at Newtowne (now Cambridge). But Hooker was unhappy at Newtowne and disliked the constraint and the autocratic attitude of the leaders of the Massachusetts communities. In 1636 he moved to what is now Hartford, where he preached democracy, to the horror of men such as Winthrop, with whom he had discussed the possibility of a federation of the colonial settlements. Hooker said that "the foundation of all authority is laid . . . in the free consent of the people," and when the "first written constitution of modern democracy" was established in "Conectecotte," on January 14, 1639, it was Hooker who devised its underlying *Fundamental Orders* and wrote into it his own conception of democracy. Hooker believed in that variety of the compact theory of the state which, in contrast to the Hobbes version, held that the sovereign was the servant of the people. The Orders provided for a "Generall Courte" controlled by the freemen, and for the election of magistrates by popular vote. In Hooker's Connecticut, membership in a church was not a prerequisite to a voice in government, and the foundations laid by him made Connecticut the most liberal of the colonial states.

IV: Roger Williams

> ". . . *a People may erect and establish what* forme *of* Government *seems to them most meete for their civill condition: It is evident that such* Governments *as are by them erected and established, have no more* power, *nor for no longer time, than the* civill power *or people consenting and agreeing shall betrust them with.*"
>
> ROGER WILLIAMS

ROGER WILLIAMS (1604-1684) was a protégé of Sir Edward Coke and studied law, but he gave it up and entered the ministry to become, successively, an Anglican, a Separatist, a Baptist, and a Seeker. Restless and unsatisfied with conditions in England, he emigrated to Boston, where he was no happier, for he hated the rigidity of the local church and bitterly opposed the right of the civil authorities to enforce the religious parts of the Ten Commandments. Though the people liked him, he was detested by these authorities, who resented his insistence that church and state must be separated. The mounting ire against Williams came to a head when he propounded the very unpopular theory that the colonists held their lands illegally, having taken them from the Indians, the rightful owners. Williams was accused and tried by the General Court in 1635 and held guilty of "newe and dangerous opinions against the authoritie of magistrates," but sentence of banishment was suspended until the spring, and when Williams heard that there was a plot on foot to ship him back to England, he escaped over the snow to the friendly protection of Indians in what is now Rhode Island. There he founded the Colony of Rhode Island and Providence Plantations.

Williams was a political philosopher of importance. Religious in his approach, he was attached to the New Testament rather than the Old, and became a strong advocate of equality. Like Hooker, he challenged the theory of divine right, and had no use for that variety of the compact theory of the state which viewed the compact as fixed and permanent. He fought for the free right of the people to alter their government and their laws, and he was firmly opposed to any rigid form of constitution or government.

Under Williams's influence the inhabitants of Providence drew up an agreement, in 1640, which is one of the noteworthy documents of colonial history. It provided for the arbitration of disputes. Most important, it said: "Wee agree, as formerly hath been the liberties of the town, so still, to hould forth liberty of Conscience." Willing to grant that liberty of conscience to everyone, he offered sanctuary to Jews, who established the first synagogue in the New World in Rhode Island. He opposed slavery of both black man and red, and he had frightening ideas for social and economic reform; for example, he insisted that an indentured servant was entitled to one day of rest a week.

V: The Crown to the Rescue

THOUGH LIBERALISM in politics and law might be possible in the new lands of "Conectecotte" and Rhode Island, there was yet no room for progressive ideas in Massachusetts. Complaint was made that the civil disabilities imposed on those who did not belong to the favored church were unfair. A synod met in Cambridge in 1646 to discuss the matter, but the result was the enactment of the *Cambridge Platform,* which made it abundantly clear that the state was still not to be freed of church control. Article 5 of this Platform provided: "As it is unlawful for church-officers to meddle with the sword of the Magistrate, so it is unlawful for the Magistrate to meddle with the work proper to church-officers. The acts of Moses & David, who were not only Princes, but Prophets, were extraordinary; therefore not imitable. Against such usurpation the Lord witnessed, by smiting Uziah with leprosie, for presuming to offer incense."

The Massachusetts authorities were not disposed to relent. If anything, they grew even more harsh in their insistence on subjection to authoritarian doctrine. In 1644 a law had been passed directing whipping and banishment for anyone who spoke against the orthodox theory of baptism, and a number of Baptists were severely treated under this statute. Quakers came in for even more hearty treatment. In 1656 two Quaker women, Mary Fisher and Ann Austin, were stripped naked and examined for evidence. The two women were imprisoned without light in their cells, held incommunicado for five weeks, and then banished. Several more Quakers arrived in the colony, and these were warned by Governor Endicott not to violate the religious laws on pain of being hanged. In the same year a law was enacted against Quakers—any shipmaster bringing one to the colony was to be fined, the Quaker was to be sent to a "house of correction," and any resident who continued to defend the Quaker opinion was to be fined or banished. Other New England colonies followed suit in persecuting Quakers. New Haven established the penalty of branding an "H" on the hands of male Quakers and boring the tongues of females with a hot iron.

Many were revolted by the cruelties of the authorities. Considerable indignation arose from the case of William Brend, who was put "into irons, Neck and Heels, lockt so close together, as there was no more room between each, than for the Horse-Lock that fastened them on." He was held so for sixteen hours without food after he had been whipped. The following day they took him out again and whipped him a second time with a tarred rope. The rope wore out, but they got another and "His Flesh was Beaten Black, and as into a Gelly; and under his Arms the bruised Flesh and Blood hung down, clogged as it were in Baggs." Nor is this an isolated story. There were many similar. Winthrop had been succeeded by John Endicott, a far more unpleasant character, who was eager to see the death penalty applied to recalcitrant Quakers. Death was a common penalty in these days. There were fifteen crimes for which it was meted out, among them such heinous ones as idolatry, witchcraft, blasphemy, marriage within the Levitical degrees, "presumptuous sabbath-breaking," and cursing or smiting a parent.

But there was now considerable public resentment against the theocratic thesis of men like John Eliot, who, in his *Christian Commonwealth,* claimed that the Bible was the final and entire exposition of God's word. Therefore, he said, there was no need for a legislature, for the Bible contained all the law. Moreover, Jesus was the only true king and ruler; therefore, no head was needed for the state. Eliot maintained that the citizen had no rights, but only duties. *The Christian Commonwealth* went too far even for the General Court, which suppressed it in 1661.

With the restoration of the monarchy in England in 1660, after the Puritan Revolution, the English acted against the "radicalism" and independence of the Massachusetts Bay Colony. The Puritan leaders had made it clear that they did not deem themselves subject to the laws of Parliament but only to their own law, and the British could no longer tolerate such insubordination. Emissaries sent to Massachusetts by the King ordered the cessation of killings of Quakers; and the sadism of Endicott and other New England leaders was gradually curbed. The British government further decided that the various colonies might better be joined together and administered as one. In 1684 the charter of Massachusetts Bay was revoked, and almost all of New England was thrown into one dominion and put under the management of one governor, a move that spelled the end of the arbitrary power of the Puritan religious and civil leaders.

The dominion scheme did not work out. The British were arbitrary in their management; Connecticut refused to give up her charter; and finally the Revolution of 1688 in England gave the colonists an opportunity to dissolve the dominion and to form separate colonies again.

A new charter was granted to Massachusetts in 1691, under William and Mary, which liberalized the government considerably. Property qualifications for voting replaced the Puritan practice of requiring church membership. But whatever concession to the people this new charter may have represented was undone by the increasing determination in England to exploit the colonies commercially. Various regulations forced the colonists to buy and sell only to England; they were even compelled to ship to other countries by way of England; their fiscal affairs were closely controlled. These mercantile restrictions undoubtedly proved far more offensive than such restrictive laws as those instituted by Governor Bellamont in 1698, prohibiting "Cursing, Swearing, Immoderate Drinking, Sabath Breaking and all sorts of Lewdness and Profane Behavior in Word and Action."

VI: John Wise

> *"The end of all good government is to cultivate humanity, and promote the happiness of all, and the good of every man in his rights, his life, liberty, estate, honor, etc., without any injury or abuse to any."*
>
> JOHN WISE

THE BRITISH MISMANAGED the colonies about as stupidly as they could. Political corruption in England was the order of the day, and the colonial governorships were filled, as often as not, by men badly qualified for the job. Discontent in the colonies grew rapidly, largely because of the methods of taxation employed by England and the British restrictions on commerce. It also arose through oppressive and arbitrary acts of governors. Furthermore, new Continental and English liberal ideas were beginning to spread over the world and were becoming known to the better-read colonials. Anything which smacked of absolutism was becoming abhorrent.

Not all colonial governors were tyrants; some were genuinely eager to do a good job. But the vindictiveness, arbitrariness, or lack of understanding of the majority of them provoked an increasing number of "incidents," and the angry voice of a colonial leader was now frequently heard.

John Wise, a clergyman of Ipswich, began a little revolt of his own while Sir Edmund Andros was Governor of Massachusetts Bay. Certain taxes had been assessed, and the town councils were directed to appoint commissioners to collect them. Wise influenced his flock to refuse to appoint such commissioners, and he was haled before a "star chamber" court on a charge of sedition. Wise's plea was, in substance, that he was entitled to the privileges of an English subject, but the court threw him in jail, virtually holding that he had no right to the protection of the laws of England. After his release he devoted himself to promoting the cause of liberalism.

John Wise had not read Locke, but he had read Pufendorf's* *De Jure Naturae et Gentium*, published in 1672, from which he took the theory of natural rights which that international jurist had expounded. In his writings Wise likened the Papacy and the Anglican Church to monarchical government, Presbyterianism to aristocratic oligarchism, and Congregationalism to democracy. He rejected absolutism and pointed out that one could never trust oligarchs to act for the public good as against their own. Thus he saw in democracy the only satisfactory commonwealth. His ideas spread, his writings were widely received, and the die-hards trembled in their shoes. John Wise was one of the ancestors of the American Revolution.

VII: The Zenger Case

BUT GOVERNORS CONTINUED to act high-handedly and to irritate the colonial public. In 1735 a famous trial took place in New York which is of particular importance because it established a new rule of law. Governor William Crosby, recently appointed, claimed that he was entitled to part of the compensation of the Acting Governor, Van Dam, and the dispute was brought to court. Fearing that a jury might decide against him, Crosby took the case to the Justices of the Supreme Court and, when Chief Justice Morris ruled against him, calmly removed Morris. A man named John Peter Zenger, of German birth, editor of a new paper called the New York *Weekly Journal*, commented unfavorably on the removal of Judge Morris, whereupon Crosby had Zenger imprisoned and tried for seditious libel.

Two prominent lawyers who attacked the competency of the judges sitting in Zenger's trial, because they had not been appointed with the consent of the Colony Council, were disbarred for their presumption. Then Andrew Hamilton, an eminent lawyer from Pennsylvania, made a surprise appearance in the defendant's behalf, and startled the court by asking permission to prove that the alleged libel was true. The court held that a libel existed regardless of truth, whereupon Hamilton asked the jury to take the truth or falsity of the libel into consideration. The jury was courageous enough to do so, and it discharged the defendant, thus accepting the theory that it is a defense to an allegation of libel that the state-

* See Chapter 44.

ments complained of are the truth. This case is also generally credited with establishing an important precedent for freedom of the press.

VIII: The Land and the Lawyers

THE MOST IMPORTANT FORM of property in the New World was real estate, and in the helter-skelter of colonial settlement, in the conflicts in grants, and the carelessness with which grants and transfers had been made many titles were subject to serious doubt. Some of the colonies—Connecticut notably—made it their business to rectify many of the public grants which underlay titles to land, but this did not undo all the existing title confusion. There were conflicts between the laws of England and the customs of the colonies. Primogeniture was in vogue in England, but in the colonies the custom had arisen of dividing the land among the children. To solidify this custom, Massachusetts in 1692, New Hampshire in 1693, and Connecticut in 1699 enacted laws providing for distribution among children when a landowner died intestate. The Massachusetts law was confirmed, but—illogically—the New Hampshire law was held to be against the laws of England. The Connecticut law came to test in 1717 when one Wait Still Winthrop, a descendant of the original Governor of Massachusetts, claimed his father's entire intestate estate. His sister contested under colonial law, and the case was reviewed by the Privy Council in England, which held that the laws of England must prevail. This decision threw innumerable colonial titles in doubt, and the matter was not settled until a contrary decision was made in 1745. In the meantime, the colonists had continued their own custom of division among children, and it was becoming increasingly apparent that English law would not always do for the colonies.

Colonial lawyers were not always welcomed. In Puritan New England the lawyer was not necessary for litigation, and the magistrate needed to know no law. The Bible and a few ordinances were all that he needed, and judges were not required to be men of the bar. Not until 1712 was the Chief Justice of Massachusetts a lawyer; not until 1754, in New Hampshire. In Connecticut, as late as 1698, lawyers were classed, in one law, with drunkards and keepers of disorderly houses. One reason the law was in such a bad state was that there were so few lawyers, and one reason that there were so few lawyers was that the laws were in such a bad state. It was rarely certain what the law might be, or just how much of the English law applied. Precedents were usually ignored by lay judges and even by professional judges. In 1782 the Chief Justice of New Hampshire said he did not follow precedents because "every tub should stand on its own bottom."

CHAPTER 31

The Firebrands

I: British Blunders

It does not seem fair to place all the blame for the American Revolution on the stupidities of the King of England and his minister, Lord North. The British ruling class contained plenty of Lord Mansfields and Blackstones who were rabid in their contempt for the colonists and vigorous in their support of the government's premise that the colonials were socially inferior and meant by God only for exploitation by their betters. Men like Bentham, willing to see Americans given representation in Parliament, were few and far between.

A series of laws were passed by the British Parliament—in which, of course, the colonies had no representative voice—aimed at satisfying the pocketbook of the crown or of British merchants, regardless of the effect on Americans. As early as 1733, the *Molasses Act* was passed, intended to impose heavy duties on the importation of rum and molasses into America from the French West Indies. The beneficiaries of this Act were to be the merchants of England. It was not enforced, but it helped set a pattern for future restrictive British legislation. In 1765 Parliament summarily passed the *Stamp Act*, an Act which incited the colonials to frenzy. Stamps were required on countless documents and transactions. Many were similar to today's stamp taxes on playing cards, deeds, and cigarettes, but others were applied in places where it hurt badly—for example, on all newspapers and on advertisements.

Largely at the urging of Patrick Henry, the Virginia House of Burgesses passed a set of resolutions complaining bitterly against the Stamp Tax, asserting that colonials had rights equal with Englishmen of the homeland and should not be taxed without representation. Other protests were made, and on October 19, 1765, a so-called Stamp Tax Congress, called at the instance of Massachusetts, passed similar resolutions. The stamp tax was difficult to enforce, and some London merchants, seeing the futility of this particular method of taxation, the difficulties of its enforcement, and its unpleasant effect upon trade, petitioned Parliament to revoke the law. Finally, the Act was repealed, but with bad grace, for the repeal was accompanied by a Declaratory Act which maintained the right of Parliament to make any law whatsoever for the colonies.

That was by no means the end of the story. A series of Acts, permitting quartering of British soldiers in the homes of the colonists, imposing heavy duties on imports from England, and giving the East India Company a virtual monopoly on the importation of tea into the colonies, and then a succession of laws, known as the *Intolerable Acts,* stimulated the colonists to express their indignation. Riots and violence grew more and more frequent. Indeed, revolution had actually started, though few realized it.

II: James Otis

> *"Now one of the most essential branches of English liberty is the freedom of one's house."* JAMES OTIS

ONE OF the most notable figures of the pre-Revolutionary period was James Otis (1725-1783), a plump and pleasant-looking man, but with strength and shrewdness behind his pacific exterior. Well versed in the classics and in English law and politics, this young lawyer quickly established a reputation and was engaged by Boston merchants to defend them against the operation of "writs of assistance." These were general search warrants, issued with great frequency, to enable the British government officials to enter warehouses and offices of American merchants to determine whether the laws of trade had been violated. Writs of assistance were not new in English law, but they had never been used so intensively nor so obviously directed at any one group, and the Boston merchants chafed under this oppressive use of legal process. On February 24, 1761, Otis argued a proceeding against the issuance of certain of these writs of assistance. John Adams, whose notes on Otis's speech that day have been preserved, describes it as a masterpiece. Otis rested his case upon general theories of jurisprudence, declaring that a measure which violated natural law and the British Constitution was void. Then he argued, specifically, that while a special warrant to search in a particular place for a particular purpose had justification, a general warrant, putting every citizen at the mercy of any prying, petty official, violated the fundamental rights of individuals and was against natural law and reason.* Otis lost the case, but the principle which he sponsored is now part of our law. The Fourth Amendment to the Constitution prohibits all but specific warrants.

James Otis then issued, in 1764, a pamphlet entitled *The Rights of the British Colonies Asserted and Proved,* claiming that Parliament was subject to the restrictions of the British Constitution; that Americans were as much Englishmen as were residents of England and as much entitled to their basic rights at law; and that these rights included freedom from taxation without consent (meaning representation). For a few more years Otis remained one of the foremost leaders of political and legal liberalism in the colonies, but in 1769 he received a blow in the head which made him temporarily insane, after which he disappeared from the limelight. Many have felt that if Otis had retained his mental vigor he might well have been as important as Madison and Hamilton in constructing our government and directing the course of the early Union.

III: Patrick Henry

"Guard with jealous attention the public liberty."
PATRICK HENRY

BUT ANOTHER great lawyer and orator remained to give active voice to much that needed saying. This was Patrick Henry (1736-1799), whose entire training for the bar consisted of reading *Coke on Littleton* for about six weeks. Extremely unsuccessful in several business ventures, he had turned to the law, and in spite of his lack of training and unprepossessing appearance his success was almost immediate. In three years he tried an enormous number of lawsuits and won most of them. Then came the *Maury case.*

Henry was selected to defend certain merchants against a suit brought in 1763 by an Anglican clergyman named James Maury. Anglican clergymen, in Virginia, were entitled by law to be supported by a tax on tobacco. The tax was unpopular, and it had been reduced

* Some have wondered, were Otis living today, whether he would not be fulminating against the blanket authority of the Internal Revenue Service to demand access to, and the right to comb through, one's personal records and confidential papers.

in amount and made payable in cash by an Act of the Virginia House of Burgesses. The King had vetoed this reduction, and the Anglican ministers were now suing for the difference in value between the original tobacco payment and the lesser cash payment. Young Henry had the courage to plead that the King of England had no right to veto an Act of the Virginia Burgesses, basing his contention on the compact theory, that government was based upon a contract between the people and the sovereign which could not be violated. The jury accepted his argument and gave the clergyman in the case one penny damages, and Henry's reputation was made.

In 1765 he was elected to the Virginia House of Burgesses and immediately gathered about him a group of "radical" young men. Enraged, like so many other colonials, at the Stamp Act, he brought on a series of resolutions condemning it and, when accused of treason for his actions, is said to have uttered these famous words: "If this be treason, make the most of it."

IV: Sam and John Adams

> *"I am not of leveling principles: But I am apt to think, that constitution of civil government which admits equality in the most extensive degree, consistent with the true design of government, is the best."*
>
> SAMUEL ADAMS

BY THE BEGINNING OF 1774, although ties with England were still very close, more and more colonists began to turn to the views of the minority of radicals who had proposed separation from the motherland. On May 17, 1774, the town of Providence called for a general congress to consider the grievances of the colonies and the possible formation of a union. New York followed with a similar suggestion, and finally the Massachusetts assembly, on June 17, 1774, at the instance of Samuel Adams (1722-1803), cousin of that John Adams who was to become the second President of the United States, invited the other colonies to send delegates to a great convention. Representatives were hurriedly chosen by all the colonies except Georgia, whose Governor prevented. The First Continental Congress assembled in Philadelphia.

Sam Adams was perhaps the most complete American democrat.

Although it was reported that he went to the Continental Congress in poor and shabby clothes and that a collection had to be taken for him to get him a new suit, he was a Harvard man and the son of a prosperous merchant father. His first love was the ministry, but he deserted this for the law, which, in turn he found unsatisfactory. He became what might fairly be called a professional agitator. Well read in the political and legal authorities, he knew Locke and Milton, Sidney, Hume, and Montesquieu, as well as Coke and Blackstone. He took the position that only a pure democracy made any sense, that the people must really be sovereign, and that no compromise or "mixt government" would do. His interest was not confined to politics. He believed that the law cannot be fixed and unchangeable, that it must be subject to alteration at the will of the people. The Tory system of law was obnoxious to him.

It would have been easy to predict how Sam Adams's voice would be raised in the Continental Congress. Had all the delegates been of his temper, severance from England would have been immediate. However, the list of delegates included many of the ablest conservatives of the colonies; and though there were some other hotheads, like Gadsden of South Carolina, who asked for an immediate attack on the British, there were also moderates, like Dickinson of Pennsylvania, who thought that a polite remonstrance sent to the King would solve the whole problem. Patrick Henry did his best to guide the delegates to union by declaiming, "I am not a Virginian, but an American." But the others were not swept off their feet. A plan was submitted by Joseph Galloway, a wealthy and conservative delegate from Pennsylvania, who proposed a new form of relationship with England on a dominion basis. The plan received some warm support but was bitterly opposed by Sam Adams and was eventually shelved and later expunged from the record.

A declaration was finally passed on October 14, 1774, setting forth the grievances of the colonists in dignified but restrained fashion. It did, however, include a statement of what the Americans believed were their basic rights, a statement which anticipates the premises of the Declaration of Independence: ". . . the inhabitants of the English Colonies in North America, by the immutable laws of nature, the principles of the English constitution, and the several charters or compacts . . . are entitled to life, liberty, and property, & they have never ceded to any sovereign power whatever, a right to dispose of either without their consent."

On October 20, 1774, the delegates reluctantly approved a report of a committee charged with drafting resolutions to interrupt commercial intercourse with Great Britain. The Congress had not yet reached the point of advocating severance from the mother country; but Parliament met the nonintercourse resolutions with an embargo of its own, and the issue was now clearly drawn. Massachusetts had already become embroiled in active resistance to England, and Congress promised the assistance of the other colonies. There was now no way of stopping the course of events. Blood was shed at Westminster, Vermont, on March 13, 1775; the Battles of Concord and Lexington took place on April 19, 1775. War had begun.

In an evaluation of the remarkable men who founded our government, Sam Adams's cousin, John Adams, must be ranked with Washington, Hamilton, Franklin, Jefferson and Madison, in importance and influence. He was perhaps the best constitutional lawyer among the Fathers, a very forceful man of deep convictions and unlimited courage, utterly devoted to principle. Much given to the pen, he has left us an enormous, and enormously valuable, heritage of writings which disclose, as do other contemporary accounts, that his contribution to the success of the separation from England and the establishment of a sound and workable government was perhaps second to none.

V: Washington

"Toward the preservation of your Government . . . it is requisite . . . that you resist with care the spirit of innovation upon its principles, however specious the pretexts."

WASHINGTON, FAREWELL ADDRESS

IN MAY, 1775, a Second Continental Congress assembled in Philadelphia, angered and in a mood, if necessary, to precipitate revolution. This Congress carried on through the war, and it was fortunate for the colonies that it contained, among its members, so many wise and able men, among them George Washington, Samuel and John Adams, Thomas Jefferson, and Benjamin Franklin. "Its delegates were nearly all citizens of substance and affairs. Of the fifty-six that signed the Declaration of Independence, eight were merchants, six were physicians, five were farmers, and twenty-five were lawyers—members of that learned and contentious profession against which Burke had warned his countrymen. Most of them were tutored in the arts of local politics; many had served in colonial legislatures; a majority had taken active part in agitations against British policy; nearly all were plain civilians with natural talents for political management. Among them there was no restless son of an ancient family, like Julius Caesar, eager for adventure in unsettled times; no zealot like Oliver Cromwell, waiting to direct the storm in field and forum; no professional soldier, like Bonaparte, watching for a chance to ride into power; no demagogue like Danton, marshaling the proletariat against his colleagues." *

The Congress was driven with reluctance to the extreme resort of revolt. In January, 1776, only about a third of the delegates to the Congress at Philadelphia were in favor of an actual break with England. The war had actually commenced when the Second Continental Congress met; Lexington and Concord had already been fought, and militiamen were rushing to Boston.

In a political deal to secure Southern support, George Washington was appointed Commander-in-Chief of the colonial armies. Even at this moment, independence from England was not the will of the majority. Washington himself, upon passing through New York to take up his command, assured the Assembly there that he would do everything possible to restore harmony with the mother country. Yet no one contributed as much to the success of the American Revolution as George Washington. It was not merely because of his military capacity. His dignified personality, his sincerity and honesty, a certain regal quality which caused him to be deeply respected and even venerated, made him universally acceptable as a leader even to conflicting groups. When it came to selecting the first President under the Constitution, there was never any question but that Washington would be chosen. In the political field, however, his contributions were almost solely in the effect of his character upon those with whom he worked. He contributed to the politics of the Revolution nothing original of any importance, and his own tastes were conservative. He was and remained an aristocrat. He insisted that all officers of the army must be "gentlemen."

Washington did, however, take on some of the current liberal

* Charles and Mary Beard, *The Rise of American Civilization*, p. 233.

thought; his chief political mentor in the early days was George Mason of Virginia, a scholar and a liberal advocate of states' rights. But Mason, like Washington, was a great landowner, and both were intensely interested in the protection of property. It was a natural enough consequence that Washington was probably as much concerned with the protection of property rights as with other human rights.

Much has been made by some historians of the alleged primary interest of many of the Founding Fathers in property. There can be no doubt that the protection of property was an important objective of these men, but to imply that they were crass and not idealistic in their approach to the problems of government seems wholly unjustified.*

VI: Thomas Paine

> *"The more perfect civilization is, the less occasion it has for government, because the more it does to regulate its own affairs, and govern itself . . . All the great laws of society are laws of nature."*
>
> THOMAS PAINE, THE RIGHTS OF MAN

EARLY IN 1776 Thomas Paine had fired many colonists with his demand for absolute independence, in a widely disseminated and brilliant pamphlet, *Common Sense,* the best seller of the period. One hundred thousand copies were sold in three months. Paine was an Englishman who had been in America only two years, sent here as a sort of protégé of Franklin's. He was an odd character, sour, fervently revolutionary, the editor of an obscure magazine. *Common Sense* was intended to arouse Americans, to appeal to their courage, and to induce them to make no compromise with royal government. Paine's advocacy of the extreme position in the crisis spread rapidly, although it never did convince more than a minority of Americans.

In May the Rhode Island Assembly, by Act, absolved its citizens from all allegiance to Great Britain. In June some of the Massachusetts towns voted for independence. On the fourteenth of June New Hampshire instructed its Congressional delegation to vote for

* An interesting article in this area may be found in the *Political Science Quarterly,* vol. LXXVI, No. 2, by Stanley Elkins and Eric McKitrick.

independence. In the same month Connecticut omitted the King's name from public documents and also instructed its delegates to support independence, a motion for which had already been made by Richard Henry Lee of Virginia and seconded by John Adams of Massachusetts. This resolution, passed by a bare majority on June 7, recited that the colonies "are, and of right ought to be, free and independent states," and asked for a plan of confederation. The motion was repeated on July 1, and nine colonies voted in favor of it. A committee was appointed to draft a resolution of independence. The committee consisted of Thomas Jefferson, Benjamin Franklin, John Adams, Roger Sherman, and Robert Livingston.

VII: Jefferson and the Declaration of Independence

"Were we directed from Washington when to sow and when to reap, we should soon want bread."

JEFFERSON

THE COMMITTEE appointed to draft the Declaration of Independence designated Thomas Jefferson to set it down in writing. Franklin and Adams made a number of changes in his drafts, but the eventual product was overwhelmingly Jefferson's work. Jefferson was an odd combination of aristocrat and theoretical democrat, of philosopher and practical politician. His interests were catholic, and he had a vast amount of sometimes superficial knowledge. The son of an upper-middle-class father and an aristocratic mother, he was born in 1743 on the Virginia frontier. He was something of a prodigy, and received advanced standing when he was admitted to William and Mary College at eighteen. He studied law and by 1776 had had a good deal of political experience.

Jefferson was selected to do the actual drafting of the Declaration because of his unusual felicity of expression. He was a writer of experience, grace, and power who had already distinguished himself as a literary advocate of the colonial cause in a widely read and respected work published in 1774, *A Summary View of the Rights of British America*. He was a "radical," as were Franklin, Adams, and Sherman, three of his committee fellow-members, and he threw himself into the drafting with fire and enthusiasm. The character of the document which he produced, with some assistance from his associates, bears witness to the wisdom of his selection for the job.

Jefferson claimed no originality for his work. In a defense of his method of composition, after an attack by Pickering of Massachusetts in 1823, Jefferson wrote: ". . . I know only that I turned to neither book nor pamphlet while writing it. I did not consider it as any part of my charge to invent new ideas altogether and to offer no sentiment which had ever been expressed before." Later, he wrote that he had intended "to place before mankind the common sense of the subject."

Jefferson had undoubtedly read all the English political philosophers of his era, and his mind was charged as well with the ideals and ideas of many of the great writers of history. Nor did he lack models for his actual draft. The first was his own draft of the proposed constitution of Virginia, adopted in part on June 29, 1776. The other was George Mason's *Declaration of Rights,* adopted with slight alterations by the Virginia convention on June 12, 1776; there are striking similarities between it and Jefferson's work.

Few changes were made in the instrument upon its submission to Congress by the committee. On July 4, 1776, the final draft was adopted without drama and without fanfare. It was not read publicly until several days later, and then was printed and spread all over the colonies. Actually, it was not signed until August 2.

The Declaration of Independence starts with the ethical justification of the Revolutionary cause. It contains a summary of the thought of the liberal political philosophers, that men are created equal and that there are certain inalienable rights which they possess as human beings, governments being established to assure these rights and not to deny them. The high doctrine of the first part of the Declaration was probably derived chiefly from the work of John Locke, the English philosopher who had produced the rationalization of the British rebellion of 1688 against James II, that a government is created to protect property, and that, when it fails, the people have the right to overthrow it. The second part of the Declaration recites the grievances against King George III, and concludes by declaring that, inasmuch as the British "have been deaf to the voice of justice and of consanguinity," the colonies declare themselves independent.

The first part of the Declaration of Independence is one of the cornerstones of American constitutional law, for it established as a basis for our government and our legal system the theory of equality and of basic human rights, an idea which, though by no means original, certainly did not then prevail on the Continent of Europe or in England.

The Declaration did not declare the independence of America. It declared the independence of the individual and separate colonies as virtually separate states. When union did come, it was a union of sovereign states; this, basically, is why the several states of our Union have different laws.

After the Revolution the English common law was accepted almost in its entirety, except as stubborn localisms prevailed against it and except as the state and federal constitutions modified or changed it. We still operate under a modified English system, and a great part of our current law is common law unchanged. It is not unusual for an American lawyer, when he cannot find a precedent from American court decisions to support his point, to cite an English precedent. The American judge is not bound by such a citation, but he will consider it.

A great deal of sometimes peculiar local law had developed in the separate colonies, largely because of the varied strains which made up its people. When they tore themselves away from England, some people began to call themselves "Americans," but they thought of themselves more often as "Virginians" or "Pennsylvanians." When they joined in union, it was in almost the same limited way that nations today join the United Nations Organization.

CHAPTER 32

Hamilton and Madison

I: Attempts at Union

THE YOUNG NATION which emerged from the War of Independence did not at once become one of the socially elite nations. Most Europeans thought of Americans as riffraff. Those who believed in the established order and in the sacredness of private property were horrified at the "excesses" which accompanied the military revolution. Confiscation of Tory property was widespread, and the estates of great landholders were subdivided and given to small farmers much as lands occupied by the Russians after World War II were distributed to peasants.

The moneyed classes in the colonies had not supported the war with enthusiasm. Even among those who were not outright Tories, there was little disposition to be taxed for the war. Had Washington received the necessary support, he might have ended the war in six months. As it was, hampered by lack of funds and equipment, by short-term enlistments and poorly prepared troops, it took him seven years to push to a conclusion. At the start probably a majority of Americans were against the war, and even toward the end no more than two-thirds supported it. This disunity, and chaotic postwar conditions, did not tend to create respect for the new nation abroad. In the opinion of most Europeans we were a nation of upstarts and barbarians, and not to be trusted. France, for example, insisted upon the right to try its own citizens resident in our country, just as, until very recently, we insisted on trying our own citizens resident in that "backward" country, China.

Not until we had established our Constitution, and made it work, did we achieve any international social respect. The constitutional government did not come at once but followed only upon the failure of an earlier attempt. Having freed themselves from the tyrannical rule of Great Britain, the radical leaders of the American Revolution had no stomach for a strong centralized regime. The government they created was based upon earlier, loose confederations, of which there had been several in colonial history. In 1637 the magistrates and ministers of Connecticut had proposed a union of the New England colonies; in 1643 various colonies forming Massachusetts and Connecticut met at Boston and created a federation termed a "firm and perpetual league of friendship and amity for offense and defense, mutual advice and succor," but these and similar proposals turned out to be neither firm nor perpetual. One of these earnest but fruitless efforts at union was made in 1754 by a Congress called at Albany to consider united action against the Indians. Benjamin Franklin commented to this Congress that it was surprising to him that savages such as the Six Nations of the Iroquois could organize a union whereas ten or twelve English colonies could not. Franklin's *Plan of Union* provided limited self-government through a House of Representatives for the united colonies.

On the very day that a committee was appointed to draft the Declaration of Independence, the Second Continental Congress appointed a committee, headed by John Dickinson, to draft articles of union. After the adoption of the Declaration, this committee reported and proposed *Articles of Confederation and Perpetual Union*, but its report was debated for sixteen more months and was not adopted by Congress until toward the end of 1777. It was not ratified by the states until 1781, when the war was almost over, Maryland holding out until the great states had agreed to transfer their claims to Western territories to the federal government. In the meantime, Congress acted as though the Articles had been ratified, but without any real authority.

Benjamin Franklin was the father of the Articles of Confederation. He submitted a modified version of his Albany plan to the Continental Congress in 1775. This plan received little general, public notice; Dickinson's committee did not use it as the basis for its own discussions, but much of the wording of the final Articles can be traced directly to Franklin.

II: The Articles of Confederation

THE NEW STATES were jealous of their individual sovereignty, and sectionalism was developing rapidly. The South was controlled by aristocratic planters, who were suspicious of the merchants and businessmen of the North. And in the border lands the isolated, independent backwoodsmen and small farmers were coming to distrust both North and South. It was not to be expected that these diverse groups would agree to any form of mutual government until compelled by confusion and the threat of disaster.

The Articles of Confederation, which established the first American "Constitution," created only the loosest sort of control. Each state expressly retained its own sovereignty. There was only one organ of federal government, a Congress, whose members were selected and paid by the state legislatures. The Congress voted by states, each state having an equal vote. Laws could be passed only with the consent of nine of the thirteen states, and no changes could be made in the Articles except by unanimous consent. Congress was really an association of diplomatic representatives of the individual states. It had little power, and had difficulty in using what it had. It could declare war and raise an army and provide a navy. But it could not draft; it could only request military contributions of men and money from the states. It had power to appropriate money, but not to levy taxes. It could not control domestic trade or prevent local tariffs and restrictions on commerce. The Articles provided for no executive, except that Congress could "appoint such other committees and civil officers as may be necessary for managing the affairs of the United States under their direction." Actually, a committee of thirteen, one from each state, acted as executive during interludes in the sessions. The states were most reluctant to accept any substitute whatever for the royal power.

The result was chaos. The states acted as independent nations. Some not only created foreign import tariffs but also imposed duties on imports from adjacent states. Inflated paper money was issued by some states with which debtors attempted to pay off creditors in other states. Some districts resorted to barter, because money was either scarce or too plentiful to be relied upon. Trade stagnated under local government restrictions; debtors petitioned for relief without avail. Radical schemes for reform added to the confusion.

The Continental Congress had so little power that it was dependent on local government for the safety of its own members. On one occasion eighty Pennsylvania troopers marched threateningly on the State House, where Congress sat, and the members of that august body had to fade into the night and regather in the safety of a college building at Princeton. Attendance was lax, and often there was no quorum.

Because the revolt against England had had its origin partly in objections to heavy taxation, the Continental Congress was given no taxing power. It borrowed heavily at home and abroad, issued millions in bills, and hoped that the states, on a quota basis, would redeem them. Congress printed its own paper money, and the expression "not worth a Continental" dates from those days, for the money spiraled downward in value until a Congressional paper dollar was worth only two or three cents.

III: Alexander Hamilton

"It will be of little avail to the people that the laws are made by men of their own choice if the laws be so voluminous that they cannot be read, or so incoherent that they cannot be understood; if they be repealed or revised before they are promulgated, or undergo such incessant changes that no man, who knows what the law is today can guess what it will be tomorrow."

ALEXANDER HAMILTON, IN THE FEDERALIST

THE ADOPTION of the Articles of Confederation displeased many thoughtful persons, among them Washington and Hamilton, who had anticipated the ineffectiveness of the weak central government. As it became obvious that the glaring deficiencies of the Articles were putting the life of the young nation in serious jeopardy, a strong movement for constitutional reform and for centralization of power in the federal government came into being.

Such reform came about largely through the efforts of Alexander Hamilton. He was born in 1757 on Nevis, one of the Leeward Islands in the British West Indies. His mother was the divorced wife of a Danish planter and Hamilton's father was James Hamilton, a wastrel of good family. At eleven he was a store clerk at St. Croix; at sixteen he went to New York, financed by his mother's family, and studied at Columbia University (then King's College) for three years, until his enlistment in the Revolutionary army. For six years he served in the army, and at twenty-five he was admitted to the bar, where he practiced for twenty-two years, except for his term as Secretary of the Treasury. Into his comparatively brief career was packed enormous activity and a series of accomplishments for which his adopted country is deeply indebted to him.

Hamilton was at first a royalist, but when the differences between Britain and the colonies broke out he soon became converted to the American cause. Joining a voluntary organization called the Hearts of Oak, the uniform of which bore the legend "Freedom or Death," he became, at nineteen, a captain of a company of artillery. A year later he was made aide-de-camp to George Washington. Washington found his young aide invaluable for his able writing, discretion, and military ability, but in 1781 he resigned as Washington's secretary and took an active military command, in which he showed great personal courage and military talent.

His resignation from Washington's personal service did not affect their relations; Washington seems always to have held Hamilton's opinion in great esteem, and to have been much affected by the latter's political point of view. During the war Hamilton had gained an extraordinary insight into the difficulties which the inefficiency of the government caused the Commander-in-Chief, and he became convinced of the necessity for strong centralized government.

The movement for a constitutional convention began accidentally in the spring of 1785. Representatives of Maryland and Virginia met at Mount Vernon to discuss certain waterway difficulties. In the course of their discussion many current commercial difficulties were brought to light. Pennsylvania and Delaware were invited to join in these discussions; and finally Virginia asked all the states to send delegates to a convention to be held at Annapolis in September, 1786. Actually, only five states sent delegates, but the convention at Annapolis was fruitful. James Madison was the moving spirit behind the convention, but he seems almost always to have sought a position in the background, and permitted Alexander Hamilton to take the center of the stage at Annapolis.

Though Hamilton was not yet thirty years of age, he was one of the major American leaders. His small and slight frame was no handicap, for the natural dignity of his carriage and his distinguished manner attracted immediate notice. He dominated the Annapolis convention and, with fire and resolution, called for a greater convention with wider objectives. It must be laid to the personal credit of

Hamilton that the delegates reported the necessity of such a convention to their states.

IV: James Madison

> *"The diversity in the faculties of men, from which the rights of property originate, is . . . an insuperable obstacle to a uniformity of interests. The protection of these faculties is the first object of government."*
>
> JAMES MADISON, IN THE FEDERALIST

THE GREAT Constitutional Convention at Philadelphia was called by Congress itself, under pressure of the Annapolis recommendation, on May 14, 1787, for the purpose of revising the Articles of Confederation and reporting such alterations as might be necessary to preserve the Union and to meet the necessities of government. Delegates were selected quickly by all the states except New Hampshire and Rhode Island. New Hampshire limped after the others; Rhode Island refrained altogether from sending delegates. But the delegates were not in constant attendance. Of sixty-five delegates, ten never appeared at the Convention at all, and at the session of September 17, 1787, at which the final draft was signed, only forty-two were in attendance and only thirty-nine signed the document.

The delegates were, on the whole, remarkably talented men. Seven had been governors of states. Many had served in either the Revolutionary Congress or the Congress established by the Articles of Confederation. Eight had signed the Declaration of Independence. Many were trained in war and diplomacy, legislation and administration, finance and commerce; and the average of learning in political philosophy was extremely high. George Washington was one of the delegates from Virginia, and he was unanimously chosen chairman. The conservative wing of the Revolutionary party was ably represented, but many of the "radicals" were not present. Jefferson was in Paris serving as an American minister; Patrick Henry refused to attend; Samuel Adams was not chosen as a delegate; Thomas Paine was in Europe. It may have been just as well that some of these uncompromising men were not present, for the Constitution could never have been created except as a compromise.

We are indebted chiefly to James Madison (1751-1836) for our knowledge of the Constitutional Convention. No official records were kept, but he made elaborate notes. The sessions of the Convention were held in secret behind guarded doors in an upper room of the State House. Thus the delegates did not have to make speeches directed at their constituencies, and were able to approach the problems at hand in a forthright manner. This forthrightness, however, produced a great deal of acrimony, and even anger, in some of the sessions.

A good deal of the work of the Convention was informal. There were frequent irregular sessions of delegates on the outside at which major questions were thrashed out. In these separate, small councils, the personality and persuasiveness of individual delegates counted for much. The respect of the whole group for Washington was enormous. When he took active part in the discussions, his word was of the utmost importance.

Benjamin Franklin, aged eighty-one, so feeble that James Wilson had to read his speeches for him, was always listened to with respect and veneration, even by those who disagreed with him violently. Franklin played a major catalytic role in the Constitutional Convention. "The Constitution was not his document. But without the weight of his prestige and the influence of his temper there might have been no document at all." * He was on the wrong side of almost every important controversy during the Convention, for he advocated unpopular solutions of problems, suggesting that federal executives be meagerly paid, that the central executive be more than one person, that the states be represented by population and wealth; but he was the great conciliator, and his efforts at compromise saved many a delicate situation.

James Madison, however, has been rightly called the "father of the Constitution," for it was he who seemed to have the most practical understanding of the necessities of the new government and a talent for presenting the proper compromises. Small, slim, and delicate in appearance, but with charm and grace of manner, and a quiet and sincere persuasiveness, he made men listen to him with respect. In his own quiet way, he gave more propulsion to the work of the Convention than any other delegate.

* Carl Van Doren, *Benjamin Franklin*, p. 750.

V: The Drafting of the Constitution

THE CONVENTION had been called for the purpose only of amending the Articles of Confederation. But the delegates soon came to the cold conclusion that an entirely new constitution was needed. They have been credited with establishing a government which was essentially a broad democracy. Actually the great majority of delegates had no such objective. The Constitutional Convention was almost unanimous in the opinion that democracy was dangerous. Hamilton wished to have Senators elected or appointed for life,* for he said that the people were divided into two classes, "the rich and well-born" and "the mass of people who seldom judge or determine right." Gouverneur Morris frankly wanted an aristocratic Senate of wealth to keep the lower classes down. Madison wished to see the spirit and form of popular government retained but wanted measures which would curb the ability of the masses to injure the rights of the minority. He was particularly eager to see a system of checks and balances which would make it difficult for the government to be affected quickly by popular whim.

The Revolution had been against tyranny from above, but now the delegates were concerned about the threat of a new tyranny from below. Extreme conservatives like Alexander Hamilton remarked, "The people!—the people is a great beast!" There were a few Revolutionary leaders, Jefferson, Sam Adams, and Thomas Paine among them, who went to the other extreme and wished little or no curb on popular control of government, but these three were not at the Convention, and the majority of delegates were of the stamp of James Madison and John Adams, who wanted assured protection for property.

In this, they found support in Locke, whose theory had been that unless property is protected there is no justification for a state. They followed James Harrington, an English aristocratic philosopher (1611-1677) whose *Oceana* had great effect on the thinking of John Adams. Harrington suggested an ideal constitution for England in which property was to be the fundamental reason for government,

* Even under the Labor government in England, this membership-for-life principle still applied to the House of Lords, and our democratic neighbor, Canada, appoints its Senators for life.

but there were to be some restrictions upon it, and government was not to be allowed to rest too long in the hands of any man or group of men. He advocated rotation in office and suggested a two-house legislature in which the upper would be aristocratic and the lower democratic, each having a check on the other.

The Fathers found support also in the writings of John Milton, the great English poet who had been one of the apologists for the Cromwellian revolution in England but was a republican with aristocratic leanings; in those of Sir George Savile, Marquis of Halifax, a constitutional monarchist; and in Algernon Sidney, another apologist from Cromwellism, whose advocacy of the compact theory of government did not destroy his aristocratic bias. And they found ample help in Adam Smith, whose *Wealth of Nations,* once almost a work of radicalism, was to become the bible of capitalism. For those French political philosophers who were less interested in property than in the other basic rights of man, some American leaders had little respect. They were about to make an experiment in republicanism, not in democracy. They accepted a republic almost as a compromise between monarchy and democracy. The mass of the people were apparently apathetic. In some states the majority might have turned down the Constitution, but its acceptance came about through the votes of those interested enough to vote, and these favored it.

A *Virginia Plan* was proposed by Randolph; it suggested a bicameral legislature and provided expressly that the Executive should have the right to annul state legislation deemed in violation of the Constitution. Opposed to this was the *New Jersey Plan,* proposed by William Paterson and ardently supported by several delegates, which contained some of the weaknesses of the Articles of Confederation in retaining too much power in the states. In an effort to break the jam, Alexander Hamilton proposed a third plan, indicating the leanings toward aristocracy of many delegates. What Hamilton offered was a government modeled on the British Constitution: an elective limited monarchy. He suggested two chambers, an Assembly, whose members would be elected for three-year terms by the people, and a Senate, whose members would be chosen for life or good behavior, by electors, chosen in turn by the voters. The executive officer was to be a Governor elected for life or good behavior, who would have the absolute power of veto. As an indication of the extent of federal control called for in Hamilton's plan, the governors of the states were to be appointed by the central government.

VI: The Drafting Is Finished

Hamilton failed completely in his attempt to introduce an aristocratic principle into the structure. The final compromise was a victory for the democrats, but it contained checks and balances which prevented too quick a reflection of changing public opinion. Its most important feature was that in the upper house there was to be equality of states but in the lower house representation was to be proportionate to population. This compromise settled the difficult issue of the balance of power among the small and large states. That none of the delegates seem to have been wholly satisfied with the compromise may well indicate that it was the best practical answer to the immediate problems.

Of the many compromises in the Constitution, this was perhaps the most important. Without it there might not have been a constitution, for the rights of the small states were an issue upon which the Convention might have foundered. A subordinate issue of how slaves were to be counted in establishing the apportionment of Representatives among the states was compromised by counting them at three-fifths of their actual number. The propriety of slavery as an institution was raised sharply in the Convention, but some of the cooler heads persuaded the hotter that it had best be left to the individual states.

Some issues before the Convention were easily settled. There was almost immediate agreement on the propositions that there should be separate executive, legislative, and judicial branches of government, and that a Congress should have power to tax, regulate foreign and domestic commerce, issue bills, and control a currency. The major compromises having been reached, there was comparatively little difficulty in disposing of further issues. A measure was seriously considered requiring property qualifications for voting. This was abandoned, but many of the checks and balances in the Constitution were the result of the general fear of wide democratic power.

Actually, it was not even a foregone conclusion that the United States would be a republic. It would have been almost impossible to sell the people even the most limited type of monarchy, but it was seriously proposed that Prince Henry of Prussia be invited to be King of the United States, and it is possible that Washington could have made himself king had he so desired.* In any case, the majority of delegates favored a strong Executive.

The nature of the Executive was the subject of considerable discussion, and many plans were advocated. The final decision was that there should be a single Executive, to be elected by an Electoral College. The College would act as an intermediary, and could possibly prevent the election of an Executive by ill-advised popular will.† The Executive was to hold office for a term of four years, subject to removal only by impeachment, and was given enormous power. In this comparatively democratic country of ours, the Chief Executive still has far larger powers than the King of England and his Prime Minister combined. He is in no way responsible to Congress for his acts, although there are certain specific things which he cannot do without the consent or approval of the Senate, such as making certain appointments and executing treaties,‡ but his remaining, independent powers are very great, not the least being his right of veto. These great powers are not surprising, considering that many delegates to the Constitutional Convention actually favored the appointment of a king.

* Strictly speaking, George Washington was not the first President of the United States. The first man who might have some right to be called "the first President of the United States" was Peyton Randolph, the presiding officer of the First Continental Congress. But as chairman of the Continental Congress he was actually called the "President of the Congress." The presiding officer under the Articles of Confederation, however, was called the "President of the United States, in Congress Assembled." Therefore, Thomas McKean, the first presiding officer under the Articles of Confederation, should probably be known as the "first President of the United States." There were eight other such "Presidents" before Washington. George Washington was only the first "President of the United States of America."

† The College has long since ceased to have any independent function. For all practical purposes it is only a rubber stamp, the electors voting for the candidate of their respective parties, and there is a strong current movement to abolish the institution as unrealistic. Opposition to change comes in part from a widespread reluctance to alter so old a mechanism, and partly because of the difficulty of deciding or agreeing upon an acceptable alternative—i.e., whether the popular vote is to be counted en masse or by states, etc.

‡ The restriction against the President's making treaties without the consent of the Senate has become largely ineffectual. President Franklin D. Roosevelt made many treaties during the last war, such as the one at Yalta, which have become so binding on us, illegal though they may be without Senate consent, that there is no escape from them.

The legislature was designed to insure stability of government and to prevent the rapid reflection of the opinion of the people. The Senators were to be appointed by the state legislatures, to serve for fixed terms of six years. Only one-third of the Senators were to be elected each year. The Senators were even required to be thirty years of age, five years older than the minimum requirement for Representatives, so that the radicalism of youth might not too easily show itself in the upper house.

VII: Ratification

THE FINAL DOCUMENT had not been accepted unanimously by the delegates. Some had left the Convention in anger. Others had refused to sign it, and proceeded to denounce it openly. It satisfied no one completely. Hamilton thought the federal government was not nearly strong enough. Washington, fully aware of its compromises, nevertheless strongly advocated its acceptance, saying, "I think it would be wise in the people to accept what is offered to them." Jefferson, in Paris at the time, was at first worried but later came to believe that the Constitution was a great document.

The Convention made one wise provision before submitting its work to Congress: The Constitution was to become effective upon its acceptance by two-thirds of the states. There was no legal basis for this provision, but it was a fortunate one, for unanimous aproval would have been impossible.

The campaign of ratification was a bitter one on both sides, and the opponents were almost as powerful as the protagonists. Hamilton, Madison, and John Jay wrote brilliant letters to newspapers as propaganda for ratification, which were published in *The Federalist*. Madison's may have been the most important, but Hamilton wrote the greatest number, and went into the field and stumped for adoption. Almost singlehanded, and despite bitter opposition, he persuaded the state of New York to confirm. The confirmation by New York was anticlimactic, however, because nine states—enough for absolute confirmation—had already accepted the Constitution by June, 1788; and New York acted only after Virginia, then tenth state, had approved. James Madison carried the burden in the Virginia ratification convention, overcoming the objections of many opponents, including Patrick Henry, George Mason, and James

Monroe. North Carolina and Rhode Island entered the Union only a year after ratification had been effected.

Had the confirmation of the Constitution been left to the mass of the people, then, as I have said, they might well have rejected it. It was apathy among the majority which produced ratification—in some states by slim pluralities. Constitutional conventions were established by the states to consider ratification, and the delegates to these conventions were, on the average, aristocrats and men of property to whom the new instrument of government appealed far more than it did to the people. Probably no more than one-fourth of the adult white males of the country voted for delegates to ratifying conventions. Probably no more than one-sixth of these males favored ratification—that is, about one hundred thousand people. The upper classes were the strongest proponents, the workers and farmers the most ardent opponents, of ratification.

VIII: The Bill of Rights

FAR TOO FEW people understand the difficulties which face legislators in trying to write clear and unequivocal laws, and the corresponding difficulties faced by judges in interpreting laws. The general annoyance of the public at split decisions by appellate courts is not justified. That five judges will decide one way and four the other does not indicate either that some of these judges are not competent or that the law which they have interpreted was badly drawn. It is almost impossible to write a perfect piece of legislation, and the possibilities of variant interpretation almost always exist. The *Bill of Rights,* the first ten Amendments to the Constitution, is an outstanding example of this inevitable ambiguity.

It is surprising that the Constitution itself did not include a recitation of the basic human rights which might have been anticipated from the wording of the Declaration of Independence, those rights which we now hold as our most cherished possession. It has been suggested unjustly that the framers of the Constitution were more concerned with the protection of property than with the protection of the individual. Among the protections omitted from the document were some which protected property and others, such as freedom of religion, which certainly were not in conflict with any theory of property right. The full explanation seems to be that the delegates presumed that most of the fundamental individual rights would be included in the state constitutions and thus did not have to be recited in the federal Constitution. Perhaps the delegates were so exhausted by the furious struggle to achieve agreement on the rest of the document that they were all too willing to presume the existence of certain personal rights which were by no means clear.

At any rate, there was immediate clamor for amendments when the Constitution was sent to the states for ratification. Jefferson was particularly insistent that amendments be made to include a declaration of rights, and he hoped that the Constitution would not be finally ratified without such amendments. Largely because of such complaints, the first ten Amendments to the Constitution were quickly adopted. These are called the Bill of Rights, and some of them may be traced directly to the terms of the Declaration of Independence. Twelve amendments were actually proposed, drafted principally by James Madison, and the preamble of the resolution proposing them recited: "The conventions of a number of the states having at the time of their adoption of the Constitution, expressed a desire, in order to prevent misconstruction or abuse of its powers, that further declaratory and restrictive clauses should be added, and as extending the ground of public confidence in the government will best insure the beneficent ends of its institution, be it resolved," etc.

Several measures of personal protection were actually included in the original Constitution. The most important are these: the writ of habeas corpus was guaranteed; writs of attainder were prohibited; and ex post facto laws were banned. There is also a provision which seems strange today but was important at the time. In Article III, paragraph 2 of Section 3 provides that there shall be no "corruption of blood or forfeiture" in any treason case, except during the life of the person convicted of that crime. It had been a European practice to burden subsequent generations with the guilt of one convicted of treason, a measure from which Americans had suffered during the memory of the draftsmen of the Constitution. There was also a provision for jury trial in the original Constitution but in a form not quite satisfactory to those who demanded the Bill of Rights.

The *First Amendment* to the Constitution affirmed four basic rights: freedom of religion; freedom of speech; freedom of the press; and the right to assemble peaceably and to petition the government for a redress of grievances. A monumental grant of personal liberty is represented in this single Amendment. In its few and simple words perhaps the most important protections of our democratic system are assured. The original colonists in New England had come to this country for religious freedom, but the concept of a state in which there could be no official religion and all could worship as they chose was a very recent one. There were few if any historical precedents for it—certainly not in Judea, Greece, or Rome, nor in Europe before the Reformation. The Reformation itself often had only substituted Protestantism for Catholicism as the official state religion. The First Amendment, in addition to guaranteeing the "free exercise" of religion, expressly denied to the federal government the right to establish a state religion.

Freedom of speech and of the press, and the right to assemble and complain about the government and to petition it to redress grievances—without these three rights it is doubtful whether democracy could long be supported. If the government may censor the press and prevent meetings at which grievances may be aired, totalitarianism is around the corner. These rights were not inventions of the proponents of the First Amendment. Their origins are to be found in the unwritten British Constitution. But the fact is that they had never before been written down so clearly, simply, straightforwardly, and unequivocally.

I have said that they were written down simply, yet each of the four rights granted by the First Amendment has been and continues to be the subject of extensive litigation. It is doubtful that this could have been avoided by more careful draftsmanship. A word here and there might have been improved, a few controversies might have been avoided, but not many unless the draftsmen had been able to anticipate countless possible ambiguities. This would have necessitated a monumentally long instrument, and it is often far better to express a clear generalization than to attempt to cover all details of application. Not only does such an attempt usually fail—we could never anticipate all the situations which might create ambiguities—but if we permit the courts to solve problems as they arise, the law has a chance to grow and to accommodate itself to changing public concepts.

Are there many ambiguities in the language of the First Amendment? How about freedom of religion—is anything more to be said than that we may have the "free exercise" of it? The courts have been obliged on many occasions to explain the simple words of the grant of religious freedom and to limit its apparent breadth. It is clear that there must be reasonable limits even to the free exercise of religion. Suppose a sect arises which believes that all Baptists are minions of the devil and should be killed on sight. Is this sect to have freedom to exercise its religion? This may be considered an absurd example, but it can serve to mark an extreme limit. Where should the line be drawn between rejecting freedom for such a religion and granting it to Holy Rollers? May a religion advocate the Biblical eye for an eye and tooth for a tooth? In Canada there is a Russian sect the members of which used occasionally to strip themselves naked in public. Is that to be permitted?

As an illustration: A member of the sect of Jehovah's Witnesses tried to distribute religious literature in a town in Alabama which was owned by a company, whereupon the town authorities refused permission and ordered her to leave the company's premises. She refused and was arrested as a trespasser. Did her arrest violate the First Amendment in denying freedom of religion? The answer of the Supreme Court in this case of *Marsh vs. Alabama* (1946) was that, even though the incident occurred on private property, it was in a town which had a public character, and the rights of "freedom of press and religion" were more important than the "constitutional rights of owners of property."

Other examples are to be found in the cases dealing with religious instruction in schools. Is religion still free if religious instruction in schools is compelled by law, each pupil being permitted to select his own religion? What of atheists—does not freedom of religion imply freedom to be unreligious also?

As these illustrations may indicate, the best that can be expected is for our courts to treat each new situation which arises by applying such general rules of propriety and public necessity as may appeal to them.

The First Amendment also proscribes any "law respecting an establishment of religion," and this too has given headaches to the Supreme Court. Does any direct or indirect aid to sectarian schools violate this section? That problem arose in the (1947) case of *Everson vs. Board of Education of the Township of Ewing.* A New Jersey statute authorized state reimbursement of the cost of transporting children to schools, and a taxpayer contended that this resulted in assistance to parochial schools and thus violated the First Amendment. The Court, in a five-to-four decision, held that the Constitution was not violated, but there were strong dissents. Justice Rutledge in his dissenting opinion pointed out that if bus transportation to secular schools was proper for the state then why could the state not supply schoolbooks, buildings, and even teachers? A similar problem is before the country at this writing in connection with the design of the proposed legislation to aid education. There has been bitter debate on the question of whether the benefits of this legislation should be extended to parochial schools or whether this might not be unconstitutional.

The judge's problem is no easier in questions of free speech and freedom of the press. I am free to speak my mind, but I must take the consequences, for there are limits also upon the freedom with which I may express myself. I cannot slander another without taking the consequences, and I can be sent to jail for inciting others to riot. The press suffers from similar, necessary limitations on its freedom. A newspaper cannot incite to armed rebellion against the government, but what actual words could be held to produce such a result? It would obviously be very difficult to determine the lines of demarcation.

The same is true of the fourth right given by the First Amendment, to assemble peaceably and to petition the government. When is such a meeting truly peaceful? When does it overreach by incitation, by improper purpose, by advocacy of something so strongly against the public welfare that the assembly is *per se* not peaceable?

The opportunities for judicial rationalization are many, and it would be quite possible to stretch logic into a result which would seriously curtail all the fundamental rights granted by the Constitution and the Amendments. We must rely, in our system, on the good sense of the judges, particularly the judges of the Supreme Court. Donald R. Richberg, in an address reprinted in the January, 1952, issue of the *Journal of the American Bar Association*, gave several illustrations of unfortunate judicial "stretching." There was the *Wrightwood Dairy case* in 1941 which held a dairy subject to interstate commerce although it sold milk only in Illinois; and *Wickard vs. Filburn*, which held that a farmer could be fined for raising grain on his own farm and feeding it to his own pigs, all on the ground that his acts "affected" interstate commerce. This precedent should make it possible to hold that almost any act "affects" interstate commerce.

There have been many such cases in which the Court has "gone overboard" to rationalize what seemed to be a desirable result from the majority point of view. Richberg was incensed at the increasing tendency, through such decisions, to invade the rights of and to coerce the states. He said: "It seems to me that those who contrive and strive to change our form and methods of government by devitalizing the Constitution are as much engaged in overthrowing the Government as alien and domestic fanatics who plot to overthrow the Government by a violent revolution."

Prefixing the explanation, "A well-regulated militia being necessary to the security of a free state," the *Second Amendment* gives the people the right to "keep and bear arms." However, in many states we are not permitted to either keep or without a license bear what are called "concealed weapons"—weapons, like pistols and daggers, which may readily be concealed. The Supreme Court has come to permit such restriction of this constitutional right, on the theory that the open bearing of arms is one thing, but carrying weapons which are concealed or capable of concealment involves a threat to the public peace. This theory is fortified by the explanation, given in the Second Amendment itself, that arms must be permitted to the people in order that there may be a militia.

The *Third Amendment* prohibits the quartering of soldiers in our houses except in time of war, and then only "in manner prescribed by law." We do not quarter soldiers in homes any more. But this was a practice in the eighteenth century from which the colonists had suffered grievously at the hands of the British, and the recollection of it was still with the people.

The *Fourth Amendment* was born of another specific abuse during colonial times, that which James Otis fought against so ably. It is the "my home is my castle" Amendment. "The right of the people to be secure in their persons, houses, papers, and effects, against unreasonable searches and seizures, shall not be violated . . ." This provision is made effective by the further words: "and no warrants shall issue but upon probable cause, supported by oath or affirmation, and particularly describing the place to be searched, and the persons or things to be seized." The most difficult words in this Amendment are "upon probable cause." Mere suspicion is not "probable cause." There must be sufficient evidence to indicate to the judge who signs a warrant for search or seizure that the warrant is justified. This is again a matter for the Supreme Court, in the last analysis, to determine.

The Fourth Amendment guarantees privacy in our homes and houses, and the courts have supported that privacy. But they have been presented, from time to time, with new sets of facts which have made decision difficult. A government official could not trespass on my property and break through my windows to see what I might be doing, but can he tap the telephone wire to hear what I am saying? Chief Justice Taft in the *Olmstead case* said that a telephone wire was no part of the defendant's house, but Justice Brandeis thought that such an interpretation of the Fourth Amendment was too literal, and that tapping wires was an invasion of the defendant's privacy. Using wire-tapping evidence in the federal courts was later prohibited by the Federal Communications Act.

In a 1947 case, *Harris vs. United States,* the Supreme Court, faced with a difficult set of facts, limited the constitutional protection of that Amendment more than many would have agreed was wise. Armed with a warrant of arrest based on a charge of forgery, federal officers invaded Harris's home and arrested him. Then they stayed and searched his apartment for five hours to find evidence against him, and finally found an envelope marked "George Harris, personal papers." Opening them, they found no evidence of the alleged forgery but did discover certain draft classification cards and registration certificates, possession of which by Harris was unlawful. On the basis of this evidence, Harris was convicted, not of forgery, for which he had been arrested, but for unlawful possession of the papers. In a five-to-four decision the Court held that the Fourth Amendment had not been violated, but Justice Frankfurter, in a strong dissent, said: "How can there be freedom of thought or freedom of speech or freedom of religion, if the police can, without warrant, search your house and mine from garret to cellar merely because they were executing a warrant of arrest? How can men feel free if all their papers may be searched, as an incident to the arrest of someone in the house, on the chance that something may turn up or rather, be turned up? Yesterday the justifying document was an illicit ration book,* tomorrow it may be some suspect piece of literature."

Small wonder that, in cases of this kind, there are so frequently five-to-four decisions. My own opinion is that in the Harris case the minority was right, but the issues are by no means simple.

* Referring to the earlier *Davis case.*

The *Fifth Amendment* contains a complexity of protections to the individual. It recites essential guarantees against abusive criminal procedure. First, I may not be held for a "capital or infamous crime" except on a presentment or indictment by a grand jury; the government cannot prosecute me for a serious crime unless a jury of my peers has received evidence sufficient to indicate that I really appear to have committed such a crime. Thus the government cannot put me to trial at its own instance and on flimsy evidence or none at all. An exception is made in the case of military forces in time of war or public danger, but that limitation is a necessary one.

Second, if I have been tried once for an offense, I cannot again be "put in jeopardy of life or limb" on the same charge; the government may not persecute me by trying me again and again on the same grounds. Nor, third, may I be compelled to be a witness against myself. This means that I may refuse to take the witness stand. It might seem suspicious to a jury if I did not take the stand in a criminal case against me, but the fact remains that the state must prove its case without resorting to examination or cross-examination of me, if I choose to stand on my constitutional rights.

This section of the Fifth Amendment has been the subject of extensive and bitter controversy in recent years. During Congressional and other legislative investigations, witnesses who have been asked a question regarding their possible membership in the Communist Party or their association with Communists have "taken the Fifth." There has been dispute as to the extent to which "the Fifth" may properly be used. Under it, no one can be compelled to incriminate himself. However, a Congressional investigation is not a criminal proceeding.

In the same Amendment there is a provision which has constantly plagued the courts. I may not be "deprived of life, liberty, or property, without due process of law." That term, "due process of law," is a most difficult one to define adequately. But it is one of the most important of our constitutional protections and one of the most contentiously litigated, and perhaps some examples will make it fairly clear.

"Due process" is not limited to the proper use of the actual procedure of law. Obviously, if a court or an official of government takes my property or punishes or harms me without going through the rules of procedure which may be part of the law, my constitutional right of "due process" is violated. But it goes much further than that. If a statute is arbitrary it violates the due-process requirement. If a statute is unduly harsh, it may be negated by the Supreme Court under the due-process clause of the Constitution. The standards of "arbitrariness" and "harshness" are determined by the Supreme Court, and that Court has been known to change its mind. Legislation restricting the hours of employment illustrates one area in which due process operates. A law prohibiting the employment of children under the age of eighteen for more than fourteen hours a day would not violate due process, while one prohibiting laundry workers from working more than three hours a day would. These are both ridiculous extremes, illustrating a range within which the Court must determine a line of demarcation. What is a reasonable restriction on an employer? Ten hours was once considered reasonable, but times have changed.

The breadth with which the due-process clause can be interpreted is indicated by this case. The army established an airfield adjoining the chicken farm of one Causby, and the planes which left and entered the field flew so low over Causby's grounds, and the glaring lights of the field were so annoying, that Causby lost sleep; his chickens laid fewer eggs, and some died of fright. The Supreme Court, in this case of *United States vs. Causby* (1946), held that the government had taken Causby's property without due process of law, in so far as it had taken an easement over his land without his consent and without compensation. This gives an interesting example of how the courts are obliged to suit old rules of law to new circumstances. Planes flying low over property in such a way as to interfere with the rightful use of land were certainly not anticipated by the framers of the Constitution. Yet the general principle of due process included in the Fifth Amendment has been found adequate to meet a wholly new set of circumstances.

The due-process clause is an important basic protection to the individual, in the determination of which we are entirely in the hands of the Supreme Court, which has the duty of deciding what laws may be unreasonable because they are arbitrary or harsh.

One further right is granted by the Fifth Amendment. Private property may not be taken for any public purpose "without just compensation." Occasions for the taking of private property are many. If a railroad is planned and supported by government sanction, and the survey carries the proposed line across my farm, the developers of the road will approach me to buy a right of way. If I cannot agree with them on price, they will bring an action in court under what is called the state's right of "eminent domain," its right to take over private property for a public purpose. The court will establish the fair purchase price of the right of way, and I am obliged to accept it. But the state cannot merely seize my property, for a highway or reservoir or whatever public purpose may be planned, without compensating me fairly. It can only "condemn" my property under eminent domain and then give me an opportunity to try to persuade a court that I have not been offered a fair price.

The *Sixth Amendment* goes on with my rights in a criminal prosecution—precious rights without which one might well be railroaded into prison by unscrupulous officers. The Constitution had granted a jury trial in criminal cases but had merely stated that the trial should be in the state where the crime was committed. The Sixth Amendment made many improvements in this provision. If I am prosecuted on a criminal charge, it guarantees that:

1. I must be given a speedy trial.
2. It must be a public trial.
3. I must be tried by an impartial jury.
4. The jury must be composed of citizens who reside in the district where the crime was committed.
5. The district must have been determined in advance by law and cannot be a district gerrymandered for the purpose of including me in it.
6. I must be informed of the nature and cause of the accusation against me.
7. I must be confronted with the witnesses against me, which means that I must be given an opportunity to cross-question them in an effort to break down their testimony or show it to have been false.
8. The government must grant me the means of compelling witnesses who might testify in my behalf to attend the trial.
9. And I am entitled to have the assistance of counsel.

The Amendments of the Bill of Rights are not set down in too logical an order, though not much is left out. The *Seventh Amendment* jumps to civil litigation and assures a jury trial in all cases "at common law," "where the value in controversy shall exceed twenty dollars." * It also provides that "no fact tried by a jury shall be otherwise re-examined in any court of the United States than according to the rules of common law." This latter provision was intended to make certain that the essential characteristic of a jury trial would not be lost through review by a higher court. The facts in a case are to be determined only by a jury. An appellate court may overrule the lower court on questions of law and the admission of evidence, but it cannot itself establish what the facts in the case were. That is solely the province of a jury, and thus the citizen is assured that only his "peers" will ever be able to determine facts in a litigation.

The *Eighth Amendment* skips back to criminal procedure, and prohibits excessive bail, a measure calculated to prevent the government from holding a citizen in custody unfairly. It also prohibits cruel and inhuman punishments.

The *Ninth Amendment* is a catch-all, assuring the people that if any of their personal rights have been omitted from mention in the Constitution, they shall not be deemed to have been denied or limited.

The *Tenth Amendment* is another catch-all. It reserves to the people all those rights not expressly granted to the federal government and not expressly denied to the states.

It is an amazing fact that no serious attempt has ever been made to determine what the actual rights may be which have been reserved to the people under the Ninth and Tenth Amendments. These Amendments assume that there is a possibly considerable body of such basic, inalienable rights. Yet, as far as I know, no one has been able to name a single one with authority. Nor, as far as I know, has anyone ever come to the Supreme Court and said, "This, one of my fundamental, inalienable rights, unenumerated in the Constitution or the Amendments but guaranteed me by the Ninth and Tenth Amendments, has been violated."

It is my hope that some definitive study may someday be made, perhaps by one of the foundations, to determine what some of our unenumerated inalienable rights may be. It may well appear that our laws have violated some of these rights. There is always the possibility, of course, that if such rights were asserted, the courts

* Inflation has put an excessive burden on the jury system. Twenty dollars during the Constitutional Convention would be the equivalent of many times that in our day.

might override them upon the allegedly superior applicability of general clauses in the Constitution like the "general welfare" clause.

There is a certain cynicism today among some who call themselves "liberals." The Constitution, they say, was a document framed in an era which could not have anticipated the social and economic changes of the ensuing century and a half. It contains restrictions against too rapid "progress"; it is somewhat cumbersome to amend the Constitution. This "liberalism" demands that change may be made quickly, without the confinement of a charter which is archaic in some of its terms. But I would point out, in reply to that sort of "liberalism," that the basic protections granted to the individual by the Constitution are so important that it seems wise indeed that we cannot too easily amend our fundamental charter of liberties. Whatever defects the Constitution may have, it is a truly remarkable document, and what finally made it so was the addition of the ten Amendments of the Bill of Rights.*

IX: The State Constitutions

EACH of the states has its own constitution. A few are of ancient origin, being modifications or revisions of colonial charters which were found adequate. The Second Continental Congress, concerned because some of the acting legislatures in the states were somewhat

* The term "liberal" needs some semantic discussion. Many terms of political usage have been thrown into confusion in recent decades by new and sometimes contradictory applications. The Russians, for example, refer to themselves as "democrats." A "conservative" today can be a "radical" in his opposition to "liberal orthodoxy"; and a "liberal" can be a "reactionary" in his advocacy of "statism." And so it goes. The term "liberal" now certainly has confused meanings. One might say, roughly, that there have been three basic uses of the term. The classic liberal, in the political connotations of the word in the nineteenth century and earlier, emphasized freedom and a minimum of government. In earlier decades of our century the term came also to denote those who advocated some experiment and faster progress in the settlement of social problems. There is a current type of liberal (to whom I shall hereafter refer as a Liberal, with a capital "L" to distinguish him) who has adopted the label of liberalism but advocates the solution of social problems through central-government intervention and federal compulsion. He emphasizes welfare and security, where the classic liberal emphasized individual freedom and self-reliance.

Today, some conservatives who believe themselves to be liberals (for there is no necessary inconsistency in being both a classic liberal and a conservative) call themselves "libertarians" to distinguish themselves from the current Liberals, but I find this term cumbersome.

irregular, suggested that each state create a formal government, and this was quickly done. Revisions were in order when the federal Constitution was accepted, and new states, admitted thereafter, usually modeled their constitutions more or less on the federal Constitution. These state constitutions were generally brief documents merely establishing the framework of government. It was customary to add a declaration of individual human rights, taken from the Declaration of Independence and the Bill of Rights.

State constitutions did introduce some moderate degree of social and political reform. Some declared against primogeniture and outlawed such vestiges of feudal landholding as the practice of entailing estates. Church and state were finally separated. Property restrictions on voting were somewhat lessened, though not abandoned. Yet there were no startling advances in democratic practices, and the state governments, like the federal, remained under the control of the aristocracy and the men of wealth. Few of the people voted, because they either were disqualified by property requirements or had never acquired the habit of voting, or because they felt that the men of "quality" would run the government in any event and there was no use in voting.

The paternalistic government which resulted in the states was, however, rather admirable within its limitations. It was fortunate that, in this period, the upper classes were generally well equipped to govern and were usually conscious of their public responsibility, however much they might be interested in protecting their own property rights. Nevertheless, a reaction against government by money and position was inevitable. In South Carolina one could not become Governor or Lieutenant Governor or even a member of the Council unless one was worth ten thousand pounds—a large sum of money in those days. A Senator needed a personal fortune of two thousand pounds. One could run for Representative, however, if one believed in God and "future rewards and punishments." Provisions such as these soon come under attack, and the state constitutions were gradually made more democratic, partially under the stimulus of the new states which came in from the West, bringing far more democratic charters with them. By 1809, Maryland had removed such restrictions and given the vote to virtually all male adults, and Massachusetts and New York soon followed.

X: The Dual American System

IF I COMMIT A CRIME in New York and go across the border to New Jersey, the authorities there cannot molest me unless the state of New York brings extradition proceedings. In that case, New Jersey may apprehend me for the purpose of turning me over to New York authorities if a New Jersey court permits the extradition. This looks as though the states were separate countries, and in many respects they are virtually that. The federal government is one of limited powers, and all powers not expressly vested in the federal government by the Constitution remain in the states. That leaves to the states the regulation of most of the relationships of life and most of the fields of human activity. In this great area of reserved powers, the states are almost wholly sovereign.

One limitation upon the sovereignty of the states is that the Constitution is subject to amendment at any time, and an amendment can, as it several times has, considerably restrict the state's powers. Another limitation is in Article IV of the Constitution, which requires each state to give "full faith and credit" to the "public acts, records, and judicial proceedings" of every other state. What "full faith and credit" means is not always clear until the Supreme Court makes up its collective mind on a particular issue. For example, there is still a good deal of divorce confusion in the United States. Nevada may hold that a man is resident there and grant him a divorce, but Pennsylvania may claim that there was no true residence in Nevada and thus fail to give full faith and credit to the Nevada decree.

There are other limitations in Article IV of the Constitution. Section 4 guarantees "to every State" a republican form of government. Section 2 assures to the citizens of each state "all privileges and immunities of citizens in the several States," so that a visitor to one state cannot be discriminated against by its laws.* It also provides for the extradition of persons accused of crime, though one state cannot enforce extradition against another state.

The Constitution marks out the border line between the legislative jurisdiction of the federal government and that of the states

* This provision is not so absolute as it seems to read. There are discriminations by states against visitors from other states. The test of reasonableness is applied.

only by stating general principles. Like most laws, the Constitution requires constant reinterpretation before we can know exactly how its general principles apply in practice. John Marshall, the first Chief Justice, made certain interpretations clear, and the Supreme Court has, from time to time, defined the border line, but new issues arise constantly. It is as though a geographical border had been described as "west to the Rocky Mountains." There are many mountains in the Rocky Mountain area—sometimes a parallel series of them—and there are gaps. An actual survey would have to be made to establish such a border definitely, and the survey would have to be approved by some authority. The analogy with the jurisdictional border described in the Constitution is apt, except that you can see mountains and plains and hollows easily enough if you go out on a survey mission; in contrast, the doubtful areas in a general delineation of principles do not appear until specific cases arise to bring them to light.

CHAPTER 33

John Marshall

"He [John Marshall] was not in the least concerned in the rule of the people as such. Indeed, he believed that the more they directly controlled public affairs the worse the business of government would be conducted. He feared that sheer majorities would be unjust, intolerant, tyrannical, and he was certain that they would be untrustworthy and freakishly changeable."

BEVERIDGE: LIFE OF JOHN MARSHALL

I: Some Fundamentals of Our System

LAW is inextricably associated with government, and probably the unique and most interesting part of our legal system is our constitutional law. It is difficult to discuss constitutional law without discussing government.

Our government was unique at its inception. Most of the mechanics of the state was based upon historical precedents, English and even Greek and Roman, and most of the liberal ideas translated into the personal protections in the original Constitution and in the Bill of Rights were taken from the English liberal political philosophers. There were already existing English precedents, like those contained in the Petition of Right, for some of the personal freedoms. But the peculiar construction of the whole, the selection and balance, and the very fact that, for the first time, a great written constitution had been designed and effected as a complete and finished work made the Constitution of the United States a document so unique that it served as the model for many other young nations. That we were able to produce such a remarkable, practical experiment in advanced democracy was due perhaps to two reasons. We had the opportunity to start afresh because we were a nation established by revolution and had no long-standing national government. But even more important, we were fortunate to have in the colonies the most astonishingly able set of politically minded men whom fate has ever collected together in any one country in any one era. Washington, Jefferson, the Adamses, Franklin, Marshall, Hamilton, and Madison might in themselves have been sufficient to warrant this statement, but there were so many others whose names are less familiar to the public.

It is frequently said that the Founding Fathers did not intend to create a democracy but only a republic. What they did produce may fairly be said to have been a "limited democracy." In a full democracy sovereignty is in *all* the people and government is subject to a quick reflection of their majority will. Our own government meets the test of Lincoln's famous phrase, for it is a government *by* the people, as well as *of* and *for* the people. However, although the voting franchise has been extended, ours is not a full democracy, because we have voluntarily put restraints upon our own freedom of action. For it has been part of the theory of our government that it is wise to make it a little difficult to translate the whim of the moment into action. It would be difficult for us to have a sound system of law if change could come too abruptly or too easily, and minorities would have even less protection than they now have. Although the Greeks reached astounding heights in other intellectual fields, they never developed a sound, stable legal system; and this was because they were extremists in democracy. Of course, even the Greeks did not have a full democracy; theirs was confined to the ruling classes, and the masses had no part in government. The fact is that there has never been a full democracy anywhere, except perhaps in the most rudimentary, primitive societies. No one who thinks out its fullest implications would desire a form of government in which he, as an individual, would have no protection against the possible tyranny of the majority.

England, today, is closer to full democracy in one sense than we are, despite its aristocratic, unelected upper house. When a general election is held and the public shows itself to be against the party in power, the Prime Minister resigns with his whole Cabinet, and the new government elected by the people takes immediate command, not only of the legislative machinery but also of the chief executive office and of the Cabinet. The residual veto power of the king is of no consequence, and the House of Lords has been so emasculated in its functions that its opposition to the new party in power can have no serious or deterring effect. For the Prime Minister, the chief executive officer in England, is not elected but is selected by the party in power in the House of Commons. Thus, there is only one important national election in England, an election of members of the House of Commons. In contrast, in the United States, we have three separate federal elections: for a President; for members of the Senate; and for members of the House of Representatives. There is another complication. Only one-third of the members of the Senate are up for election every two years. It is easy to see, therefore, how the executive office can be held by one party while Congress is controlled or blocked by the opposition. This has happened several times in recent history, as in the election of 1946, which left Democratic President Truman in office but gave control of both houses to the Republicans. In turn, Republican President Eisenhower was obliged to struggle with a Democratic Congress during part of his executive career.

There are other obstacles in the United States to the quick translation into action of the public will. One lies in the constitutional guarantees of certain protections to the individual and to minorities. The Constitution can be amended only by a two-thirds vote of the people, and in a somewhat difficult manner. Then, there is the Supreme Court, which has the function, among others, of protecting the people against violations of the rights granted by the Constitution, and its personnel cannot be changed quickly enough to reflect an immediate change in public point of view. If an incoming President could make majority appointments to the Supreme Court immediately, he could designate judges of the same economic and social predilections as the new party in power. But he cannot. He must wait to fill vacancies which occur through death or retirement. Thus, Franklin Delano Roosevelt was faced with a predominantly Republican Court at his accession; and the resurgent Republicans, in 1946, were faced with an overwhelmingly Democratic Court.

We have, then, a slightly qualified democracy in the United States. Sovereignty is certainly in the people, and they exercise it through responsive elected representatives. However, the machinery of government has been so set up that the public cannot always make its new will felt as quickly as it might wish. When the Republican landslide of 1946 took place, the suggestion was made that President Truman resign, a suggestion which he rejected. A British Prime Minister whose party was defeated at the polls would have to resign. The President of the United States, who has far more power, including the right to veto as well as enormous executive and semilegislative functions, cannot be forced to resign.

There is much to be said for both systems. If your party sweeps the country but is faced with the continuance in office of a President and a set of administrative officials of the discountenanced party, you are likely to see the merits of the British system. If you are of the party defeated at the polls, you are likely to feel that it is a good thing that the Constitution enables your party to retain the Presidency.

The compromise which the Fathers made has worked out surprisingly well. It was not what Rousseau or Paine and Jefferson would have preferred, for they did not see the necessity of interposing any obstacles to the immediate translation into action of the public will, although Jefferson did believe in certain rights of man, of which he held that no one should be deprived even by act of an overwhelming majority. Nor is it what Locke, Hamilton, or Washington might have preferred, for they wanted government to be as firmly as possible in the hands of an aristocracy. Maybe the middle road was the best one; at any rate, it was the only one which could be agreed upon.

Of course, it is not wholly through the intention of the Fathers that the compromise has worked so well, for they did not intend that we have quite so democratic a form of government as we have. They intended the Electoral College, which has become an anachronism, to stand between the people and the election of a President. And they planned the Senate as a semi-aristocratic house which would be more eager to protect wealth than would the popular assembly, the House of Representatives.

In a number of other ways the Fathers planned it so that the popular will should not have too free or immediate an expression, but we have found the Constitution flexible enough to mold it to fit a great variety of changes in our social and economic conditions. Yet the restraints of the Constitution have been salutory. Dictatorship by any numerical majority has not been too easy in the United States, and we have the Constitution, as well as our own good sense, to thank for it.

But the great document is by no means perfect. It contains more than one anachronism or imperfection. To give but one: the original compromise which resulted in the states' being represented equally in the Senate has created an upper house which, though no longer aristocratic, still gives states with small populations almost the same Congressional power as those with enormous populations. But, on the whole, it is a remarkable document which, regardless of the criticisms directed against it from both "Hamiltonians" and "Jeffersonians," of then and now, has served us astoundingly well.

In our self-restrained democracy, we have created a system of limited legislative powers, both state and federal. The Constitution limits not only the right of the federal government to make laws but limits the states also, and it has become the function of the Supreme Court of the United States to guard and preserve these constitutional limitations.

II: The Organization of the Supreme Court

THE BIBLE has been used to prove almost everything. Even the devil can quote Scripture. In the same way, the Constitution has been used to prove contentions and propositions much at variance with each other. Even the Supreme Court, which has had the job of being final arbiter between conflicting interpretations, has often had difficulty in making up its collective mind. And that collective mind has shown a tendency to change as the economic, social, and political leanings of its majority have changed. Nor is that an unhappy fact to contemplate, provided the judges do exercise reasonable judicial restraint. It is undoubtedly fortunate that the Constitution was written in such a way that it is susceptible of being stretched and pulled a bit. It must serve its basic purpose of being a fundamental charter containing certain restrictions and limitations on governmental power, but it must also be a living instrument which can adjust itself, reasonably but not too easily, to changes in public point of view.

Further, as noted about the Bill of Rights, not all its provisions could have been set down with exactness. In addition, the whole job of drawing up the Constitution was one of making compromises, difficult enough to arrive at without arguments over the precise meaning of a given phrase or its detailed interpretation.

We have been fortunate in having a Supreme Court which developed the power to interpret and explain and apply the terms of the Constitution, although of course the pronouncements of the Court have never satisfied everybody. One of the most controversial questions about the Constitution has been the matter of "states' rights." To what extent did the individual states surrender their sovereignty and agree that the federal law would be supreme and inviolate? Those who were the founders of the Federalist Party, the party of Hamilton and of Washington, of John Adams and of John Marshall, wished to see a strong central government. "Jeffersonians" wanted the federal government only as strong as absolute necessity demanded, and as much power as possible left to the states. The actual wording of the Constitution was a compromise between these two groups, and it was by no means clear. It was not even clear that the Supreme Court should have the right to determine the border line between federal and state power.

But the right of the Supreme Court to negate legislation, state or federal, is now so much taken for granted that few realize that it is not a right expressly granted by the Constitution. Article III of the Constitution provided for the creation of "one Supreme Court" and "such inferior courts as the Congress may from time to time ordain and establish"; but, while Section 2 details some of the Supreme Court's powers, it is conspicuously silent upon any right to pass upon the constitutionality of laws. Many of the framers of the Constitution anticipated that the Supreme Court would have this power, for there had to be some way of settling the ambiguities which surely would appear. There had been some precedents, before the adoption of the Constitution, for the exercise of such power by a court. In 1780 a New Jersey court and in 1786 one in Rhode Island had declared Acts of their state legislatures unconstitutional. Nevertheless, the dissention between the Federalists and the states' rights groups was so deep that the issue of interpretation was not permitted to come to a sharp head.

Creating an actual Supreme Court could not be avoided, however, and one of the first things which Congress did when it convened under the Constitution was to appoint a committee to bring in a bill to organize the federal judiciary. Five of the eight members of this committee had been members of the Constitutional Convention. Its chairman was Oliver Ellsworth, to whom most of the credit must belong for the wise *Judiciary Act* of September 24, 1789, the basic features of which have persisted to this day. The Judiciary Act was not without opposition. Many thought it would center all law business in the federal courts and might even destroy the state constitutions. The Act created a Supreme Court of five associate members and one Chief Justice, as well as fifteen district courts; and two circuit courts were to stand between the district courts and the Supreme Court as intervening courts of appeal. The Supreme Court had original jurisdiction over cases involving a state or an ambassador, minister, or consul. But it was also an appellate court. The judges were to be appointed by the President with the approval of the Senate; they were to hold office during life or good behavior, and could thus be removed only by impeachment.

Washington lost no time in appointing the first Supreme Court bench. The Chief Justice he appointed was John Jay of New York; the Associates were John Rutledge of South Carolina, William Cushing of Massachusetts, John Blair of Virginia, James Wilson of Pennsylvania, and James Iredell of North Carolina. All were exceptionally able men. Three had been members of the Convention, four had held high judicial offices in the states, all were ardent champions of the Constitution, and all the Associate Justices were on record as favoring judicial review of statutes. Washington had been an advocate of strong centralized government and judicial review, and his appointments reflected his views.

Perhaps the most important case which came before the Supreme Court in its early days involved the states' rights issue. It was *Chisholm vs. Georgia*, decided in 1793, which dealt with the right of a citizen of one state to sue another state in the Supreme Court. Georgia maintained that she could not be sued by a citizen of another state without her consent, refused to appear in the case, and threatened punishment by death for any official who attempted to enforce the Court's decree against her. But the Court held—only Iredell dissenting—that the action was proper. Other states protested this decision, however, and the *Eleventh Amendment* to the Constitution was enacted in 1798 to prevent such suits in the federal courts by a citizen against a state.

Jay acted as Chief Justice from the opening of the Court on February 2, 1793, to 1795, when he resigned to run for Governor of the state of New York. His successor, Oliver Ellsworth, appointed in 1796, had been a justice of the Massachusetts Superior Court and was a jurist of marked ability. In the Constitutional Convention he had been a states' rights man; it was he who had the words "national government" stricken from the draft and the words "Government of the United States" substituted. But Ellsworth was sent on a foreign mission in 1799. Upon his resignation in 1800, President John Adams commandeered his Secretary of State, John Marshall.

III: John Marshall, Federalist

JOHN MARSHALL was born in 1755 on the frontier of Virginia, and though his family was patrician its circumstances were modest. His frontier life affected him deeply, but the richest influence in his life was that of the man whom he adored and made his model, George Washington. Marshall served in the Revolution and, while still in active service, attended William and Mary College. When the war ended he hung out his shingle in Richmond, Virginia, going into competition with a remarkable group of local lawyers, many of whom were famous or were to become so.

Service in the Virginia Legislature from 1782 until the Constitution was adopted gave Marshall an opportunity to see government at work, and his experiences led him to support the party of Madison and the others who advocated a strongly centralized government, a position which he maintained at the Constitutional Convention.* Marshall's work as a delegate was principally on the judiciary article. He supported the position that the federal government should be one of enumerated powers and that, therefore, there must be a Supreme Court to determine when the government had exceeded its express powers.

There was a period in which Marshall declined many opportunities to take office, although he spent a good deal of his time in quasi-political or diplomatic activity, including the defense of the famous Jay Treaty with Great Britain and going on the "X Y Z" mission to France with Pinckney and Gerry. Finally, through the persuasion of Washington, Marshall ran for Congress as a Federalist candidate. Partly with the support of Patrick Henry, Marshall was elected by a narrow margin. During his short career in Congress, Marshall, an implacable foe of Jefferson, often found himself the strongest supporter of President Adams, who had a hostile Congress to deal with.

Adams, a left-winger in the Revolutionary period, was considered

* It is reported that Patrick Henry opposed a strongly concentrated government on the ground that the sea protected us from foreign powers, but John Marshall answered: "Sir, the sea makes them neighbors of us."

a right-winger after it. Although not as far to the right as Hamilton, he was no friend of the party of Jefferson, feeling that an aristocracy was needed for good government. He said, "There never was a democracy that did not commit suicide." He differed from Hamilton, however, in wanting to protect the small property holders as well as the great. He feared the aggression of wealth almost as much as the aggression of the poor, and he advocated a mixed government, balanced between the power of wealth and position and the power of numbers.

John Marshall had served as Adams's Secretary of State, and the departing President, as one of his last official acts, appointed Marshall to succeed Ellsworth as Chief Justice. It must have been a stirring moment when Marshall swore Jefferson in as President, for no two men could have detested each other more. Jefferson hated Marshall as an individual and because he was so strong a Federalist; and Marshall once referred to Jefferson as "the Great Lama of the Little Mountain."

Between Jefferson's election and his inauguration, the defeated Federalists and John Adams caused the *Judiciary Act of February 13, 1801*, to be passed. This amended the old Act and decreased the number of Supreme Court Justices to four, with the intention of preventing a dilution of the Federalist strength in the Court through new appointments by Jefferson. But after the inauguration, Jefferson's Republican Party restored the original number of Justices. This was not the present Republican Party, but the present Democratic Party, which changed its name from "Republican" to "Democratic" at the instance of Andrew Jackson. When it dropped the word "Republican," this was picked up by the so-called National Republican Party, which became the Whig Party. The name "Republican" was picked up again by Lincoln's party, which continues the name to this day. One reason why they adopted the name "Republican" was that the new party claimed to follow Thomas Jefferson's political ideas.

Adams's selection of John Marshall as Chief Justice was made with malice aforethought. Wishing to see Federalist policies perpetuated, he selected for the most important judicial post a wholehearted worshiper of Washington, a man who could be relied upon regardless of the political character of the Congress, the bias of the new President, or the temper of the people. Marshall was acceptable also because he was a businessman as well as a lawyer. He had wide financial interests, scattered over several states.

John Marshall did one thing for which the country is deeply indebted to him: he established certain initial principles of constitutional interpretation without which the Constitution might not have become the adaptable document it is today. A constitution cannot operate effectively for long unless it is flexible. The British Constitution is easy to change because it is "unwritten." It is more arduous to amend our Constitution, but amendments have rarely been necessary. Either by the genius of its draftsmen or by accident of fate, the wording of the Constitution gives latitude in interpretation. Thus it was all-important that the first interpretations take us along a reasonable road, for we worship precedents, and the earliest precedents were the most important.

During the crucial, initial period of constitutional interpretation, John Marshall was given a long-term opportunity to exercise his vision and his talents. He presided over the Court from 1801 until his death in 1835 at the age of seventy-seven, and, until the complexion of the Court changed toward the end of his life through appointments by Andrew Jackson, Marshall absolutely dominated it. His personality was extremely persuasive. He was tall, lean, and relaxed, and, though firm in his opinions, he was amiable and convivial. He was no flowery orator, no student, and he did not know the philosophers. He is even suspected of not having known much law, but, whatever his shortcomings, he was a man of great mental stature, and his associates recognized his incisiveness and the broad, clear approach which his mind brought to any legal problem. Lord Bryce has said that his "fame over-tops that of all other American judges more than Papinian over-tops the jurists of Rome or Lord Mansfield the jurists of England. No other man did half so much either to develop the Constitution by expounding it, or to secure for the judiciary its rightful place in the government as the living voice of the Constitution." *

Marshall's greatest ally on the Court was young Joseph Story, appointed at the age of thirty-two by President Madison. Story was a Republican, but under the influence of John Marshall he turned Federalist in spirit and Whig in party. His father had been one of the Indians of the Boston Tea Party, but whatever leanings toward modest radicalism he had as a youth he lost as he grew older. Like Marshall, he had great veneration for George Washington. Although a brilliant and profound lawyer, his knowledge of economics

* Bryce, *The American Commonwealth*, vol. I, p. 261.

and political theory was limited and his approach was legalistic. It was in this direction that Marshall found him most useful. Marshall's vision and Story's scholarship complemented each other. It is reported that Marshall would say, "Now, Story, that is the law; you find the precedents for it."

John Marshall established certain basic principles of constitutional interpretation. One of these was obvious enough: the powers of the federal government are only those which can be found, expressly or by implication, in the words of the Constitution; all other powers are retained by the states. But he added another principle: once it is established that a power has been granted to the federal government by the Constitution, that power can be interpreted broadly. The argument behind this is backed by certain explicit words in the Constitution which authorize Congress "to make all laws which shall be necessary and proper for carrying into execution the foregoing powers, and all other powers vested by this Constitution in the Government of the United States, or in any department or officer thereof."

As Lord Bryce has put it: "Congress, which cannot go one step beyond the circle of action which the Constitution has traced for it, may within that circle choose any means which it deems apt for executing its powers, and is in its choice of means subject to no review by the courts in their function of interpreters, because the people have made their representatives the sole and absolute judges of the mode in which the granted powers shall be employed." *

John Marshall may have profited by his own lack of specific learning, for it enabled him to look at problems of constitutional law from a broad point of view. He was satisfied to base his arguments upon abstract theories and upon a system of reasoning built upon the words and intrinsic meaning of the Constitution itself. Certain things seemed to him "obvious," "clear," and "beyond doubt." For such obvious premises he searched constantly, and, having found them, he drove home syllogistic conclusions.

Marshall's first great case was *Marbury vs. Madison,* decided in 1803. A *mandamus* had been asked; this is a writ or order by a court to compel a public official to do some act within his duty. The Judiciary Act of 1801 had given the Supreme Court the right to issue mandamus, but Marshall's opinion held that this part of the Act was unconstitutional. The restraint which Marshall showed in refusing to take jurisdiction in this proceeding increased public con-

* *The American Commonwealth,* vol. I, p. 369.

fidence in his fairness. This was the first time that any federal legislation had been held unconstitutional, and it was not to occur again until the *Dred Scott* decision just before the Civil War. But the principle was established that the Supreme Court had the right to pass on the constitutionality of an Act of Congress.

In 1810 came *Fletcher vs. Peck,* the first case in which the Supreme Court held an act of a state to be unconstitutional. The Georgia Legislature had rescinded a grant of land made by the preceding Legislature, and the legality of this action came before the Court. Anxious, perhaps overanxious, to base the Court's decision on constitutional grounds, Marshall's opinion rambled all over the lot, seeking justification in various parts of the Constitution for rejecting the rescinding law. His decision ended somewhat ambiguously by stating that Georgia was restrained from passing the rescinding Act "either by general principles which are common to our free institutions, or by particular provisions of the Constitution of the United States."

This unsatisfactory opinion was not clarified until the case of the *Trustees of Dartmouth College vs. Woodward* in 1819. Governor Wentworth of New Hampshire, representing George III, had given a perpetual charter to Dartmouth College in 1769. In 1815 a disagreement arose between the trustees of the college and its president, Dr. Wheelock, a son of the founder, and the latter was discharged. The Governor of the state took the side of Dr. Wheelock, and persuaded the New Hampshire Legislature to pass an Act altering the Dartmouth charter so that the trustees would be elected in some more public manner.

The college took the issue before the Supreme Court. Its case was prepared by eminent lawyers, among them the great Daniel Webster, a Dartmouth alumnus. His address to the Court is said to have ended with an emotional plea which brought tears to his own eyes and to those of John Marshall as well: "Sir, I know not how others may feel—but for myself, when I see my Alma Mater surrounded, like Caesar in the Senate house, by those who are reiterating stab after stab, I would not, for my right hand, have her turn to me and say, *Et tu quoque mi fili!* And thou, too, my son!"

John Marshall did not need any emotionalism from Daniel Webster to move him to the side of the trustees. Basing his opinion upon the premise that the college was a private institution, he declared the Act to be unconstitutional as "impairing the obligation" of a contract; the contract being the original charter granted to the college. This decision has been much criticized. Whatever its merit, it represents one of Marshall's many attempts to curb the despotic use of legislative power. Of course, the despotism which Marshall feared was that of the people. Arch-Federalist that he was, he had no sympathy with a theory which would permit a state legislature, once it had granted a property right, to retract that right and thus despoil an individual citizen. There is no doubt that John Marshall considered the security of society dependent on the sanctity of property.

In 1819, at the same Court term in which the Dartmouth College case was decided, Marshall wrote another opinion, in *McCulloch vs. Maryland*, which was a landmark in constitutional legal history. Maryland had taxed notes issued by the Baltimore branch of the Bank of the United States, the national bank which had been chartered at the instance of Hamilton in 1791. In deciding that the state had no right to tax an instrumentality created by the federal government, Marshall's opinion took advantage of the opportunity to expand his construction of the Constitution by passing on the right of Congress to establish a national bank. The opponents of the Bank had pointed out that there was no express authority in the Constitution for its creation. But Marshall, noting that Congress had authority to do such things as were "necessary and proper" to carry out the purposes of the Constitution, interpreted the words "necessary and proper" as meaning "convenient."

Marshall was not the originator of this interpretation of the Constitution. He was anticipated by Alexander Hamilton in the written opinion he gave President Washington in 1791 on the constitutionality of a national bank. Washington had had doubts and had asked Hamilton, Jefferson, and Randolph for their opinions. Jefferson was opposed, for he wished to confine the central government strictly; and Randolph's opinion was inconclusive. Hamilton strongly supported constitutionality, on the theory later to be crystallized by Marshall. Washington was persuaded, and signed the bill creating the first Bank of the United States.

In his opinion in the McCulloch case, Marshall strongly attacked the extreme variety of the theory of states' rights. He held that the Constitution did not establish a loose association of states with rights superior to the federal government's. "If any one proposition could command the universal assent of mankind we might expect it would be this: that the government of the Union, though limited in its powers, is supreme within the sphere of its action." He pointed out that the Constitution had itself left no doubt of this principle, for it read: "This Constitution and the laws of the United States which shall be made in pursuance thereof . . . shall be the supreme Law of the Land." Being supreme, he continued, the federal government must have the right to select the means to effectuate its legitimate purposes. It followed from Marshall's argument that a state could not tax an instrumentality of the federal government, for the "power to tax involves the power to destroy."

Marshall's argument was not unanswerable. Until the Civil War settled the issue, many believed the states had the right to pass on constitutionality, being ultimately superior in sovereignty to the federal government. The argument of some Southern statesmen was that the Constitution was only an amendment to the Articles of Confederation and that the Confederation was a union of independent states. Some Northerners rejoined that the Constitution does not speak of a union of states, but is established by the "people of the United States." Northerners also argued that the Declaration of Independence, drafted by Jefferson, spoke of "these United Colonies," that the Articles of Confederation created "perpetual union," and that there was no mechanism in the Constitution for the withdrawal of states.

At any rate, Marshall established the principle of the limited sovereignty of the states. Even Chief Justice Taney, appointed by Andrew Jackson, that violent Jeffersonian, held the Supreme Court the final arbiter in any dispute between the federal government and a state.

Another case in which Marshall took the opportunity to mark out some of the borders between federal and state legislative territory was *Gibbons vs. Ogden.* The state of New York had granted an exclusive right to Robert R. Livingston, Robert Fulton, and their successors to run steamboats on the waters of New York. Ogden, one of these successors, was trying to prevent Gibbons, who had steamers in the coastal trade under an Act of Congress, from operating on the Hudson between New York and New Jersey. The precise issue upon which the case turned was whether the power of the federal government to regulate commerce between the states was exclusive or merely ran concurrently with the same power in the hands of the states. Marshall, in 1824, held that a state had the right to establish regulations which might affect commerce within its borders only in so far as they did not conflict with any federal Act. He stated specifically that this right of the state was not "concurrent," but permissible only under its domestic "police power."

In the case of *Brown vs. Maryland*, decided two years later, Marshall denied the right of Maryland to tax goods introduced into the state but still in the hands of the importer in the original package. The doctrine made clear in this case—that the federal government has exclusive jurisdiction of interstate commerce—while well established in principle, has been somewhat weakened in recent times, for the Supreme Court has held, for example, that a "use tax" is constitutional, even though the property "used" in the taxing state has been shipped in interstate commerce.

Even after his retirement, Thomas Jefferson had continued to be a vociferous opponent of the constitutional theories which Marshall applied in his decisions. He said of the federal judiciary that it was a "subtle corps of sappers and miners constantly working underground to undermine our confederated fabric." However, by this time Marshall's influence in the Supreme Court had established many precedents for the theory that the states' rights were subordinate in every field in which the federal government had been given express, or even implied, powers. Irritation at Marshall's success prompted the proposal of a constitutional amendment giving to the Senate, in place of the Supreme Court, the power to hear all cases in which a constitutional issue was involved. One later proposal was to enlarge the Court to ten members—another that five out of the seven must concur in any decision adverse to constitutionality. All this is reminiscent of the unsuccessful attempt of Franklin Delano Roosevelt to remodel the Supreme Court to his own satisfaction. The difference is that President Roosevelt was able, through resignations and deaths, to fill the Court eventually with his own appointees, while neither Jefferson nor his party was able to do this until the regime of Andrew Jackson.

Through the regimes of Madison, Monroe, and John Quincy Adams, Marshall had less active antagonism to face, although these three were also Republicans and Jeffersonians. But, with the accession of Andrew Jackson, Marshall, at the end of his career, again met a bitter and powerful political enemy. Jackson had no use whatsoever for Marshall and refused in one instance to enforce a Court decision. Georgia had assumed jurisdiction over the Cherokee Indians, in violation of a federal treaty. When the matter was brought to the Supreme Court, Georgia failed to appear, and the Georgia measure was declared unconstitutional; but President Jackson, perhaps falsely, is reported to have said: "John Marshall has made his decision; now let him enforce it."

With a President openly belaboring the sacred Supreme Court, John Marshall saw fateful days ahead. He was old and tired and deeply wished to resign and retire, but he feared to do so. He felt it his duty to stick to his job and to do his part in preserving the Union and the Constitution against attacks by the new "radicals." He died in harness.

The people as a whole did not share John Marshall's Federalist theories. Until the Civil War, it is safe to say, the great majority considered the states to be a confederation and not a union. That bloody war was virtually a contest at arms over Marshall's theory, and it established, once and for all, that the United States, in accordance with that great judge's opinion, is a close union and not a loose assemblage of states.

There were other attempts to control the Supreme Court by changing its numbers, besides those referred to. In 1807 the number of Justices was raised to seven, and in 1837 to nine. In 1863 the membership was increased to ten. In 1866, Congress, annoyed at the Court during the Reconstruction period, provided that the number be reduced to seven, as soon as resignations and deaths should make it possible; but in 1869 the situation was more to Congress's liking, and the number was restored to nine, the present number, giving President Grant an opportunity to select two new Justices.

CHAPTER 34

Thomas Jefferson

"A strict observance of the written laws is doubtless one of the high virtues of a good citizen, but it is not the highest. The laws of necessity, of self-preservation, of saving our country when in danger, are of higher obligation." JEFFERSON: WRITINGS

I: The Effect of the French Revolution

FEW HISTORICAL CHARACTERS can be put into simple, neatly labeled categories. The customary picture of Lafayette is of an aristocrat who rushed over from France to fight fervently for *la liberté*. Actually, Lafayette fought *only* for the right of the colonies to separate from England. He did not fear the liberalism of the Declaration of Independence, knowing very well that the new government to be established here would be a sort of Greek democracy in which control would be in the hands of democratic-minded, but nevertheless aristocratic, gentlemen.

It was a different story when the Bastille in Paris was stormed by a mob and the newly constituted National Assembly, a month later, enacted the *Declaration of the Rights of Man*. Lafayette saw that his own country was to be ruled not by gentlemen and men of wealth but by representatives of the masses. In contrast to the situation in America at the time of the Revolution, the established order was in serious danger. Article 6 of the Declaration of the Rights of Man reads: "Law is the expression of the general will; all citizens have the right to take part, personally or by their representatives, in its formation; it ought to be the same for all, whether it protect or punish. All citizens, being equal in the eyes of the law, are equally admissible to all public dignities, places, and employments, according to their capacity, and without other distinctions than those of their virtues and their talents." Did the French really mean that the common man, the masses, were to have equal participation in government with the gentlemen of culture and the men of wealth? If so, then Lafayette wanted none of this radicalism, and he joined in the fight against the French Revolution.

The fact is that the revolt in the New World had given encouragement to the French radicals, and the Declaration of the Rights of Man was largely based upon the Declaration of Independence. And the French Revolution, having gained strength by the American precedent, in turn began to affect the American people. Although at first many American leaders, even John Marshall, warmly supported the French movement for emancipation from monarchy, the murderous activities of the Committee of Public Safety and the establishment, not long afterwards, of the Napoleonic monarchy, left little sympathy for France among "respectable" Americans. In the meantime, however, the liberal political philosophy of Thomas Jefferson had made its way into the consciousness of many in the lower classes in America, and the French Revolution had encouraged them to a more active interest in bettering their condition. The rapid growth of the Republican Party, of which Jefferson was the guiding genius, may be traced largely to the influence of the French Revolution.

II: President Jefferson

WASHINGTON was very tired of office at the end of his reluctantly accepted second term as President. The mounting criticisms of Federalist policies had distributed him, and his pride was hurt at every suggestion of personal criticism. He did not object on principle to a third term, but he did not want one for himself. In the ensuing election, John Adams of Massachusetts, a Federalist, was elected President; Jefferson, the Republican candidate, being second at the polls, was made Vice-President. Between them there was no love lost. The bitterness of the opposition to the Federalists may be illustrated by the words of an editor, a grandson of Benjamin Franklin, who, on Washington's retirement, spewed out his venom upon that great man: "If ever there was a period of rejoicing, this is the moment—every heart, in unison with the freedom and happiness of the people, ought to beat high with exultation that the name of Washington from this day ceases to give currency to political iniquity and to legalize corruption."

John Adams fared far worse than Washington. His administration was constantly assailed by the rapidly strengthening and vociferous Republicans. Re-election was impossible. After the next election was thrown into the House, Jefferson was selected as President, in preference to Aaron Burr, a brilliant lawyer without moral scruple who had become a leader of the Republican Party in the North. Bitter enemies though Hamilton and Jefferson were in their political views, the former threw his support to the latter, and this was one of the things which led to the duel in which Hamilton was killed, in 1804.

Under Jefferson came the first American legal reform movement. The Federalists had passed certain unfortunate measures in 1798, the *Alien and Sedition Acts.* The *Alien Act* gave the President authority in time of war to prescribe conditions under which aliens could be imprisoned for the public safety. The *Sedition Act* made it a crime, punishable by fine and imprisonment, to combine to oppose any measure of the government, to impede the operation of its laws, or to interfere with officers discharging their duties; it also made it a crime to publish anything which might be slanderous of the government or bring its officers into disrepute. The Alien Act was not used, but the Sedition Act was imposed with some alacrity and harshness, and opposition editors were jailed. Marshall and Hamilton denounced this law, but to no avail, and the Acts were not repealed until Jefferson became President.

Jefferson worked out an elaborate theoretical plan for the complete reform of the country. Agriculture was to be the basis of society; the federal government was to be comparatively weak; land was to be easy to acquire, and inheritance discouraged. There was to be universal education; immigration was to be limited to stocks which could be readily assimilated, and there was to be no overpopulation; slavery was to be eliminated by moving all the slaves out to a country of their own. This plan, of the school of Plato and the controlled state, though in a quite different key, contains most of Jefferson's pet concepts: egalitarianism, extreme democracy, states' rights, and agrarianism. He was influenced by the theories of a group called Physiocrats, who believed that agricultural production was the only true product of labor and considered manufacturing and banking to be sterile occupations. They believed in the minimal state, feared any delegation of power, and disliked any constitution or any fixing of laws. This appealed to Jefferson, who loved the land

and thought the country should be chiefly agricultural. Money not made off the land seemed to him a menace to society, and he disliked paper currency and all evidences of the capitalistic credit system. He mistrusted business entirely, and hoped that manufacturers would never increase.

III: John Taylor, Apostle of "Jeffersonianism"

JOHN TAYLOR AND THOMAS JEFFERSON were contemporaries and, although they were in almost full agreement in their political, economic, and social ideas, neither was a follower of the other. However, the movement which they both supported has come to be known as "Jeffersonian," and Taylor can be considered its apostle. Professor Beard has characterized Taylor's *An Inquiry into the Principles and Policy of Government* as one of the few important contributions to political science in America.

Taylor, like Jefferson, believed that the only true and sound economy was a farming economy. He hated aristocracy, both that of social position and that of economic power, claiming that it always involved exploitation and virtual theft from the true producers: the farmers. There was something almost Marxian about Taylor's critical analysis of government and of the history of governments. He claimed that governments are almost always established to support the interests of a controlling class and that the people are persuaded, through shibboleths and false principles, to accept exploitation. Taylor's thesis cannot be brushed off too easily. His theory of the social theft involved in any aristocracy is well developed and rather persuasive, but there are limitations in his reasoning which weaken his arguments seriously. In attacking the profit motive which prompts the development of business and the activities of the useful middleman, he opposed virtually all business and all production except agricultural. The state of society which Taylor envisioned would be a rather pitiful one from our point of view in this industrial age.

That Jefferson agreed with the agrarian thesis of Taylor gives some idea of the strangeness of the former's character and personality. His intellect was profound and his learning immense, yet much of what he read in volume he digested only in part. He was a theorist very likely to be led astray by the appeal of an abstract principle. There was perhaps only one field in which Jefferson was highly practical. He was a consummate politician. His dexterity in practical politics has been matched only by that of Franklin Delano Roosevelt, and the analogy to the New Deal period is often apt. During Jefferson's administration his Republican Party grew enormously in strength, owing in part to the wide appeal of his democratic ideas but also largely to his management of practical politics. The strength which his planning and adroitness gave the party helped carry it on to a long succession of victories, through the administrations of James Madison, James Monroe (the last of the "Virginia Dynasty"), John Quincy Adams, Andrew Jackson, and Martin Van Buren.

IV: Jefferson vs. Marshall

THE PEOPLE were strongly behind Jefferson's active opposition to Federalism. When he found himself faced with a staunchly Federalist Chief Justice, the President did not accept obstruction quietly. During Jefferson's administration there were a number of impeachment trials, and the President made it clear that he believed judges and officers of the state should be readily removable for misconduct or even at the whim of the Executive. Marshall felt otherwise, and was elated when Associate Justice Chase of the Supreme Court was successfully defended against impeachment and it became apparent that impeachment and removal of judges would not be easy under our system.

But the trial of Aaron Burr was the occasion of the most severe and bitter conflict between the President and the Chief Justice. Burr, one of the most fascinating characters in American history, faced disgrace and financial ruin after his bullet ended the life of Alexander Hamilton. He fled to the West, and there commenced a strange enterprise, the full details of which still remain a mystery. He met an adventurer named Blennerhassett, who had built a castle on an island in the Ohio River, and induced him to help finance the mysterious venture, apparently intended to carve an empire out of Mexican and Southern territory. An armed expedition was prepared on Blennerhassett's island. Jefferson paid little attention to the venture until an advance group of Burr's expedition was apprehended.

Then Burr was taken into custody and brought before the district court for the district of Virginia for indictment. Marshall presided at this hearing and at the subsequent trial.

In a preliminary hearing, Marshall indicated that he saw not enough evidence to prove Burr guilty of an act of treason, holding that the crime of treason was committed only when an overt act occurred. But a jury did indict him for treason, and also for a misdemeanor, an alleged plot against Spain. Burr, directing his own case, demanded that a *subpoena duces tecum* (a subpoena requiring the production of certain documents) be issued against President Jefferson. That was an astounding request, but Marshall granted it. Jefferson insisted that he need not comply with the subpoena, maintaining that the President of the United States could not be subpoenaed, but he did comply, substantially.

Burr was finally acquitted by the trial jury of the charge of treason, but Jefferson insisted that the trial be continued or resumed on the lesser charge of misdemeanor. He knew that there was no chance of conviction, but he hoped that evidence might be brought out upon which he could base an impeachment of the Chief Justice. That fervent hope came to nothing, but Marshall had to sit through this second trial knowing that he was listening to evidence which the President hoped to use for his downfall.

V: Jefferson vs. Hamilton

THE TERMS "Jeffersonian" and "Hamiltonian" have suited the convenience of those who like to use easy labels, but they are most misleading terms. It is true that Thomas Jefferson and Alexander Hamilton were on opposite sides of most of the fundamental issues which confronted our country in its initial years, but there have been few since their day who have followed either Jefferson or Hamilton completely. Perhaps the best example of this inappropriate use of terms is that the most fervent Hamiltonian of modern times, Franklin Delano Roosevelt, has been called an eminent Jeffersonian. I am, of course, making the same inappropriate use of the term "Hamiltonian" as do those whom I criticize, but it illustrates the point. For Hamilton's most important thesis was the necessity of a central government so strong that it would be almost beyond any control or check by state government, while Jefferson hated and feared centralization of government perhaps more than any other factor in political life. In that sense, Roosevelt was the most ardent follower of Hamilton since the Federalists.

The fact is that Hamilton was almost always on what turned out to be the right side, and Jefferson almost always on what turned out to be the wrong side, of every major controversy in which they took opposite views. Jefferson came to recognize the fallacy of his own violent antipathy to industrialization and, in the latter part of his life, admitted it. But the agrarianism which Jefferson partially abandoned in the last stage of his career still held many followers, particularly in the new territories of the West, where active spirits took up the fight for an agrarian economy and against "money" and "the interests." It was a long time before anything like a sensible compromise between the anti-industrial, agrarian movement and "business" appeared.

Jefferson went to an extreme in his opposition to a strong central government. Our own Civil War proved that central strength was essential. But the issue, after all, is one of degree, and it is to be doubted that even Hamilton would have approved of the extent to which our Liberals have pressed for constantly increased federal control of our lives. Certainly Jefferson would have fought this movement bitterly.

However wrong Jefferson may have been in other respects, he was our greatest humanitarian. His name couples itself naturally with the word "democratic," for his faith in humanity was constant, and his most basic and powerful thesis was the right of all classes to participate in government to the fullest extent. That we became an increasingly democratic nation through the rapid extension of the franchise was largely due to the leadership of Jefferson, and his influence upon the courts and the law has been profound.

There is a certain similarity between Jefferson and John Stuart Mill (1806-1873), the British political philosopher and disciple of Bentham and Locke, who was a socialist at heart but could not reconcile his socialism with his championship of liberty and his hatred of any form of benevolent control. Jefferson said that it was a principle "vital to republics" that there be "absolute acquiescence in the decisions of the majority." Yet he himself wrote into the Declaration of Independence his conviction that there are fundamental human rights of which no one should be deprived, and he insisted that such recitations be included in the Constitution by amendment.

That conflict, which beset both Mill and Jefferson, faces us today and ever will in a democracy. Realistically, the majority can do as it pleases, but Jefferson relied partly upon the restraints put into the Constitution and partly upon his conviction that the American majority would always be reasonable.

CHAPTER 35

Andrew Jackson

"I care nothing about clamors, sir, mark me! I do precisely what I think just and right."

ANDREW JACKSON

I: The Changing Union

BY THE TIME of the War of 1812 the United States had changed considerably in character from the country which the Fathers had known. Expansion of territory, the aggressive spirit which went into the settlement of the Western lands, the increased desire to create wealth through active means and not through a static, agrarian economy, intolerance of the old, fixed form of society, produced an atmosphere of challenge, of doubt, and of questioning, in which the humanitarian liberalism of Jefferson found increasing numbers of converts. At the same time, however, special interests were becoming more and more conscious of their special needs. The South, originally the most fertile soil for liberalism, was turning to cotton production to feed the ever-growing textile mills of the North and was centering its economy more intensively on the slave-operated plantation. The Northeast, originally the trading center of the country, was developing into the capital of manufacture and banking. Reform could not make heavy inroads in the self-interest of the new exploiters of labor in the Northeast and was losing ground rapidly among the leaders of the changed economy of the South.

A new party had arisen to take in the conservative elements. It was a motley party indeed. The Federalist Party, whatever its shortcomings, had been clear and definite in its concepts and platform. When it passed out of existence after its defeat by Jefferson's Republican Party, its remnants formed the Whig Party, joined by a confusion of interests from all sections. Characterized by a lack of clarity and by compromises, it had unity only in opposition to Jeffersonian democracy.

The Republican Party, on the other hand, while losing ground in the industrial North and the slave states of the South, found a great addition of strength from the new lands of the West. But the Republican Party itself lost much of its Jeffersonianism. The Southern leader most responsible for driving Republicanism away from the ideals of Jefferson was John C. Calhoun (1782-1850) of South Carolina, an ascetic of considerable intellectual stature, who guided his beloved South to the concept of a Greek democracy built upon slave labor. To him, black slavery in the South was no worse than the industrial slavery of the North—indeed, he thought it more kindly. Calhoun was a straddler. He took what suited him from Jefferson's creed and discarded the rest, substituting some of the principal features of Federalism. He believed that Jefferson's egalitarianism was no solution for the nation's problems, though he stoutly supported Jefferson's theory of states' rights. From the Federalists he took the principle of balanced powers; and he developed it by insisting upon a final balance by which the states had the right of veto over the federal government. Upon Calhoun's brilliant arguments and persuasive rationalization much of the Southern position which led to the Civil War was based.

From the North emerged another powerful leader to battle against the sentiment for reform and democratization, Daniel Webster. An able lawyer, he was even a better political philosopher, but with a bias which took the form of almost classic Federalism. He followed Locke, John Adams, and Hamilton; and the political philosopher for whom he seems to have had the greatest admiration was Harrington, in whose *Oceana* he found realism and practical sense. He joined Harrington in believing that power naturally and properly followed property.

Webster's reputation as a lawyer, orator, and theorist was enormous; he was respected even by those who disagreed with him. That he had ambitions for the Presidency was well known, but it eluded him. His opportunism made enemies, and he fought both the rejuvenated Jeffersonianism under Jackson and the "Greek democracy" of Calhoun. What finally may have killed any chance of political success was his stand on the slavery question. Like Lincoln later, he disliked slavery, but he decided that it should not be interfered with where it existed; it should only be opposed for extension into new territories. He supported the *Fugitive Slave Act*, and thus lost much of his support in the North.

II: Old Hickory

A MOVEMENT for greater control of the machinery of government by the people had been growing since the adoption of the Constitution, and this movement came to an almost violent head under Andrew Jackson, its perfect mouthpiece. His life was an American success story. Born of poor parents in North Carolina and brought up on the Tennessee frontier, he thus represented both the socially lowly and the independent border people. Jackson studied law in Salisbury, North Carolina, and practiced in Nashville, Tennessee, where he soon came into prominence. He was one of the draftsmen of the constitution of Tennessee; he served in the House of Representatives and in the Senate; and in 1798 he became a judge of the Supreme Court of Tennessee. When the War of 1812 broke out he joined the militia, rose to be a major-general, and beat the British at the Battle of New Orleans, which was fought after the war had ended although, because of slow communications, no one in Louisiana knew it. In 1821, when Florida was purchased, Jackson was made its Governor; and in 1823 he again entered the Senate.

The next year, Jackson ran for President against Henry Clay, John Quincy Adams, and William H. Crawford. Jackson had the most votes, but he did not have enough for election, and the contest was thrown into the House of Representatives, where Calhoun swung his strength to Adams, hoping to receive the same favor in return in 1828. Calhoun's ambitions had to be satisfied with a Vice-Presidency in the 1828 election, in which Jackson defeated Adams overwhelmingly.

Jackson's popularity was enormous; he was looked upon as a man of the people. He chewed tobacco, smoked a pipe, wore dirty clothes, and told even dirtier stories. His military career was respected, and his personality appealed to the mass of the people. He was proud and belligerent—he had once killed a man who had insulted Mrs. Jackson—and his very orneriness made him widely beloved. His election horrified the "nice people" of Washington, who were convinced that their worst fears were coming true when they saw a swarm of rough cohorts come into the capital after the election to seek their share of the spoils of office. Jackson could be suave and urbane enough when he wanted to. Many contemporaries remarked at his dignity of bearing and manner, and several distinguished foreigners were impressed by him.

Jackson has been given credit for being the inventor, though he was merely the perfector, of the "spoils system." Jeremy Bentham claimed to be the originator of the principle of rotation in office, and it certainly had been in effect in the United States before Jackson's time. However, Old Hickory adapted the principle of rotation in office to the practical necessities of an active political party, seeing no reason why he should not throw out a government official, however competent, in order to supplant him with someone who had supported the President's candidacy. Jackson did much to build up party machinery, for his wholesale rewards for political support set a precedent which enabled later politicians to solidify their organizations, and perfect that astounding, extralegal mechanism in our government—the professionally managed political party.

The people liked the change which Jackson effected. There was a growing distaste for the method of selecting party candidates by a caucus within Congress, and the political conventions which soon came to be the rule were far more pleasing to the mass of the citizens, who suffered the illusion that they were taking a more active part in selecting their representatives. Actually, they had merely exchanged politicians in Congress for politicians outside of Congress and were still voting for candidates not of their own selection but selected by political bosses. However, it was possible, I suppose, for the voice of the public to bring greater pressure to bear upon practical politicians than upon those secluded in the halls of Congress.

Jackson introduced another political innovation by changing the character of the Cabinet. Under Washington, it had been a sort of council, to which the President had invited political opponents, such as Hamilton and Jefferson, in order to get a salutary conflict of points of view. Jackson, after relying for a while on what came to be called his "Kitchen Cabinet," a group of private advisers, finally reorganized the Cabinet, in line with our current practice, as a group of party intimates.

III: Law for the Poor Man

WHEN the administration sat down to the actual business of government, it became apparent that President Jackson would be the stalwart advocate of the rights of the masses, that he would far outstrip Jeffersonian democracy. A contest over tariff problems, and another over the public sale of Western lands, brought into sharp relief the differences between the slaveholding states, the agricultural states, and the wealthy industrial states of the East. With vigor and acrimony, President Jackson took the part of the "poor" against the "rich."

His animus against the moneyed classes became more apparent when the proposal was made to grant a new charter to the second Bank of the United States, which had been chartered in 1816, during Madison's administration. Violently opposed to the Bank, Jackson vetoed the proposed bill and denounced it in no uncertain terms as the creature of Eastern capitalists. The fight against the Bank was a long and strenuous one. Its president was a Philadelphian, Nicholas Biddle, a man of ability and strength of will, who had powerful allies in Congress, among them Henry Clay, John Quincy Adams, and Daniel Webster, the last well supported by fat retainers from the Bank and from Northern industrialists. Biddle was confident that the President's veto could be overruled, but Jackson's stubborn will and the loyalty of his own squad of advisers and allies in Congress were too much even for Biddle's array of talent, and the Bank was doomed.

Jackson directed choice invective against the "rich and powerful," who, he said, were growing richer through special privilege. He declared that these rich men threatened the Union by having "arrayed section against section, interest against interest, and man against man." Declaring the Bank unconstitutional, he announced the startling theory that any officer of the government was entitled to interpret for himself the Constitution, a doctrine which gave old Chief Justice Marshall nightmares. During the Bank's remaining two years of chartered life Jackson harassed it as much as he could, refusing to permit any federal funds to be deposited in it. When it went out of existence, state banking and wildcat finance took its place; a severe depression was inevitable, and it did come to confound Jackson's successor.

Jackson was a Jeffersonian in one sense, but, like so many others, he selected from Jefferson's political creed only such elements as suited his purposes. In destroying the Bank which had been chartered in Madison's administration, Jackson acted from an intensified agrarianism and from his strong hatred of industrialists. Jefferson had come to learn that Hamilton's objective of an industrialized United States was a sound one, but Jackson's almost crackpot bias against the merchants and capitalists was irreconcilable.

IV: Chief Justice Taney

"The object and end of all government is to promote the happiness and prosperity of the community by which it is established." CHIEF JUSTICE TANEY, IN CHARLES RIVER BRIDGE VS. WARREN BRIDGE

TO JACKSON'S GREAT RELIEF, old Chief Justice Marshall died in 1835. Roger B. Taney (1777-1864) was appointed as the new Chief Justice. Taney was not one of the roughs from the West who horrified Washington society; he was a gentleman. But he had no judicial training and he had twice been rejected by the Senate when proposed for appointment, as Secretary of the Treasury and as Associate Justice of the Supreme Court. He had finally been accepted as Secretary of the Treasury, but he was an ardent follower of Jackson and it was expected that the new Chief Justice would be a wild-eyed radical. Conservatives thought the country was doomed, and Taney did start off as though he were bent on upsetting the old order entirely.

The new Chief Justice even wore trousers instead of the conventional knee breeches, but it was not only in clothing that he seemed to have ideas at variance with those of the great Marshall. Taney's very first constitutional opinion, in *Charles River Bridge vs. Warren Bridge*, in 1837, cut down the application of Marshall's Dartmouth College case, by holding that a legislative grant by a state must be construed narrowly, and that, if there is any ambiguity in the grant, it must be resolved in favor of the state. Investors saw the beginning of the end of investments, and businessmen believed that the corporate form of business was being ruined.

The sanctity of private property, that cherished tenet of Hamilton and the other Federalists, so carefully nurtured by John Marshall, was a principle continuously assailed by agrarian statesmen and politicians; and Taney was following the theory that private property is subordinate to the rights or will of the state. However, Taney was not the wild man pictured by his enemies. A period of work on the

Supreme Court bench has taken much of the "radicalism" out of many a Justice, and Taney was no exception. He was a man of intelligence and ability, and he had no intention of risking the economy of the country by too radical decisions. After a first period in which the gentlemen of economic position in the country had the jitters, they began to realize that the Supreme Court would remain respectable.

On the whole, and despite some remaining resentment against the Court from both sides of the political fence, Taney's Court did an excellent job in straddling between the radicals and the conservatives. It is possible that the comparatively weak movement for reform of the Court might have grown much stronger had not Taney and his Associate Justices found an acceptable mean in their judicial approach.

CHAPTER 36

James Kent and State Law

"My opinion is that the admission of universal sufferage and a licentious press are incompatible with government and security to property, and that the government and character of this country are going to ruin."

JAMES KENT

I: The Acceptance of English Law

THE TOTAL NUMBER of lawbooks in the United States is a close-to-astronomical figure. One reason for their mass production is that we have taken over the precedent system from the English, so that we have to keep collecting and printing the decisions of courts. And we are, after all, a rather large association of nations. There are fifty states, plus territories, possessions, and the District of Columbia, and each of these separate jurisdictions collects and prints its decided cases, in addition to which there are the decisions of the large number of federal courts and all sorts of smaller courts.

Whole forests are probably consumed annually to make the paper which goes into these lawbooks, and this deforestation would have been largely avoided had we inherited the Continental system, in which the principle of *stare decisis* does not fully obtain. This principle comes to us through the English common-law judges, who were rarely concerned with statutes. For the most part a judge made some new law of his own. He recognized and followed the principle of *stare decisis*, and held himself bound by previous decisions. But he made new law by "distinguishing" the facts before him from the facts which had been before the other judge, and our own judges still go through this same process.

Stare decisis applies only to decisions of the highest courts. For example, a judge in the Supreme Court of New York (the major trial court) does not have to follow a decision by another judge of his own court. He can differ, and the true rule of law may not be known until the case has been appealed to a higher court for final decision. In any event, as Justice Brandeis has said, the principle of *stare decisis* is not absolutely immutable. Courts, on occasion, have reversed themselves, when they thought that conditions had changed sufficiently to warrant, or when they were willing to admit that they had previously been in error.*

Remembering that we have separate legal jurisdictions in the United States, it is not surprising to find that the principle does not compel a court of one state to follow a precedent set by the courts of another. Each state may interpret its domestic law as it sees fit, and the highest court of a state cannot be overruled even by the United States Supreme Court unless the question comes under the federal Constitution. When a point of law has been settled in one state, a lawyer in another state has no assurance that his own courts will follow it, and so we have a duplication of decisions in addition to a duplication of statutes.

How much of the English law did we take over? Although the colonies originally were made subject to the English common law in their charters, the colonists identified the English law as the law of an oppressor. At best, in a community with few competent lawyers and almost no judges with legal training, the law was administered pretty much by rule of thumb.

Up to the eighteenth century, there was no desire in most areas to adopt in practice any more of the English law than was absolutely necessary. By that time, many Americans had studied law at the Inns of Court, and still others had read their Blackstone and apprenticed themselves to local lawyers for study. The caliber of the judges improved rapidly, and the bar began to have stature and significance in colonial life until, in the period of the Revolution, lawyers were almost the dominant factor in civil affairs. About the same

* The British stick far more closely to the rule of *stare decisis.* The result is that our law is perhaps more malleable or more readily changed than theirs. But the disadvantage of our departures from the strict *stare decisis* rule is that the law is left uncertain. There has in recent years been an increasing tendency on the part of the Supreme Court to reverse itself, accompanied by a feeling on the part of the bar that, in many fields of law, it is impossible to advise a client with definiteness.

time, and perhaps owing in some degree to the American adoption of Blackstone, the common law of England began to be "received" in the colonies. Parts of it were rejected because they were found to be unsuitable to American conditions, but after the Revolution the bulk of the English common law came to be law in the states.

In the first period after the Revolution, many changes in law were introduced. The law of property and of estates was brought closer to its present form. One of the most interesting developments was the enactment of special statutes under which corporations could be organized. Previously they had generally been specially chartered by the king, Parliament, or a local legislature. Now, application could be made in a way provided by statute and not requiring any special grace or privilege. Had it not been for such permissive legislation, the growth of industry and commerce might have been seriously retarded, for, if men cannot associate themselves in business organizations with limited liability, they are less likely to enter ventures embodying risk as well as possible profit. The corporation is a mechanism without which our country could never have reached the industrial primacy which it now holds.

After the Revolution, some of the social cruelties in the law were also eliminated. Debtors were now given the advantage of bankruptcy laws. The criminal law also received the reformers' attention, and much of this may be credited to the rapid spread of the powerful book of Beccaria which had shocked a complacent world into a recognition of the horrors of the old penal system.

Reform ran in another direction also. The common law had grown unwieldy and the practice of the law had become very difficult. So the movement for codification struck the United States. The Federalists, among them Justice Story, resisted this movement with all their strength, feeling that the common law was the bulwark of our society. But the codification movement was irresistible. It was not the type of codification which took place under Napoleon in France, and all over Europe thereafter, but a modest yet important form of which the *Revised Statutes of the State of New York*, adopted in 1827, were an example.* It was not long before most

* Our codifications do not have the same result as on the Continent of Europe, because of our system of *stare decisis*. Many of our partial codifications have created only a very moderate diminution in the number of explanatory and precedential cases.

states had adopted codes which included many of the rules of the common law.*

The reform movement which President Jackson started in the federal system had its counterpart in the states. There was plenty for the common man to complain about in Jackson's day. Most of the occupants of the jails were debtors, and it was generally the workingman who got into debt. It was not until 1832 that Congress passed an Act supported by Jackson abolishing imprisonment for debt, and the states all followed suit within a decade. The chief complaint of the social reformers was against capitalism, for a class had arisen which did not work with its hands but lived on the work of others. Idleness had been forgiven those who lived as landed gentry, but the idleness of those who lived on the income of stocks and bonds seemed socially unjust to the new critics. Their securities were characterized as mortgages on the future of the country, and the increasing class of wealth was castigated as nonproducers and "wastrels."

Able advocates of the people's cause arose, among them George Bancroft, the historian, who belabored monopolies and wrote of the conflict between capital and labor, "the house of Have and the house of Want." And then, as now, politicians frequently sought favor with labor, and organized labor began to make its weight felt.

II: Chancellor Kent

It was some time before there were enough American decisions and opinions to give lawyers sufficient precedents for the development of a distinct American body of common law. When James Kent was raised to the bench in 1798, he found no reported cases in New York State, and his own work in building up American law was monumental. American equity practice has its foundations largely in Kent's opinions, and his *Commentaries on American Law* may well be classed with the *Commentaries* of Blackstone (whom he worshiped)—they were for generations the two chief guides to the

* Roscoe Pound has pointed out that "a significant feature" of our system of "codification" "was that it extended certain features of the common-law system to other fields to supersede rules that had ceased to meet current moral ideas."

American law for both student and practicing lawyer. Kent himself was as vigorous a conservative in politics as he was a creator and builder in law. Actually, his political opinions were those of most of the people of the upper classes in his era, of Washington and John Adams. But Kent was particularly outspoken in presenting his completely antidemocratic point of view.*

Kent was a Yale man, better known as a Columbia professor. He was Chancellor of the state of New York from 1814 to 1824, and in this period laid the foundations for American equity practice; but perhaps his greater interest was in the common law, which he reverenced with the love of an Edward Coke, thinking it could solve all human problems without outside assistance. Kent was a Federalist and, when that party died, a Whig. Following Locke in believing that the protection of property was the chief function of government, he considered the aristocratic management of government an essential to security and progress.

In remarks made as late as 1821 at the New York Constitutional Convention of that year, James Kent expressed the opinion of a large section of the upper classes. He said that he wished the control of the Senate to remain with the propertied classes so that they would never be taxed without their consent. He opposed any expansion of the voting franchise to the unpropertied classes, saying: "The men of no property, together with the crowds of dependents connected with the great manufacturing and commercial establishments, and the motley and undefinable population of crowded ports, may, perhaps, at some future day, under skillful management predominate in the Assembly, and yet we should be perfectly safe if no laws could pass without the free consent of the owners of the soil."

III: State Law Before the Civil War

THE FEDERAL ASPECT of the new reform movement in Jackson's administration had its counterpart in the states, and in this Justice Story of the Supreme Court played a part through his writings, although he was wholly out of sympathy with the Jacksonian, demo-

* Nor was he the only literary exponent of this branch of Hamiltonianism. Fisher Ames, a Boston lawyer of agile pen, sharp wit, and incisive intelligence, ably propounded his theory that only the rich and powerful are good and that the poor and lowly are wicked and dangerous; ergo the former must have control of the state in order to be able to police the latter.

cratic movement. Story was intensely interested in the development of law, independent of its political connotations. From 1832 to 1845 he wrote a series of books which rivaled Kent's *Commentaries* as material for the American lawyer, and he laid a good part of the foundation for the later growth in our legal system.

Another period in the development of our state law lay between what might be called the Kent-Story era and the Civil War. In this period, torts and the criminal law were separated more clearly than ever before, and the system came closer to modern ideas in many ways. A step was taken in the emancipation of women from old legal restrictions. For divorce purposes, it was now held that a woman could have domicile or permanent residence differing from her husband's, an idea which would have shocked the Fathers. One interesting new legal rule appeared in the form of a new remedy, a suit by a "third party beneficiary." If you had made a contract with Smith for the benefit of Jones, Jones could now sue Smith, although he himself had no contract with him. An obvious idea to us, but it was indeed an innovation then.

Local American conditions produced some rules of law alien to the old English law. Admiralty jurisdiction over waters had formerly been determined by the "tidal rule"; that is, the federal government had jurisdiction as far as the tides flowed. This rule was changed to give the federal government jurisdiction as far as the waters were navigable. This permitted control of rivers, and the immensity of the American inland waterways made it desirable. Customs of the West produced rules as to fences and ranges and trespass by cattle; and grain elevators brought in new rules as to bailments and fungible goods.* The West also produced new mining and water rules developed out of local customs, and deeds and the conveyancing of lands underwent change in the direction of greater simplicity.

A growing liberalism showed itself in a succession of new statutes removing the religious and property restrictions on voting, holding public office, and doing jury duty. Public schools were instituted. More public-interest statutes appeared in connection with railroads, canals, and banks; labor received attention; and wages were made payable in cash. Income taxes were adopted by some states as early as 1830. The public was becoming socially conscious and grew more and more interested in ameliorating the condition of the poor.

* Fungible goods are such as can be readily mixed or confused, such as grain in an elevator, or sugar in a bin.

Life on the frontier introduced other progressive developments, such as the abolition of imprisonment for debt, the exemption of homesteads, and the further emancipation of women by granting them some separate property rights.

In line with the growing social consciousness, children were more humanely treated under the law. Parents were made punishable for cruelty to their children; and the inheritance laws were amended to give spouses and children greater security. Reformatories arose out of the new idea that perhaps criminals should be reformed and not merely punished.

Equity came with the common law from England but was adopted by the states in various doses and degrees. In some, the ideas of equity merely infiltrated the law. In others, separate equity courts were established, and a wholly separate jurisprudence developed. Separate courts were set up for the probate of wills and the administration of estates. Codes of civil procedure were adopted.

This was a period of popular control of government, and it had its effects upon the judiciary. Judges were restricted in jury cases to not much more than reviewing the evidence for the jury. Popular election of judges came to be the rule more than the exception, and judicial terms were shortened.

IV: The Romanesque States

LARGE PARTS of the United States and its possessions were first settled by Latin peoples, and it is not surprising that traces of the Romanesque legal system may be found in these sections. Many of our states which used some Romanesque law before their admission have continued parts of it. There is a comparable situation in Canada, where the Province of Quebec, settled by the French, retains its Romanesque laws and has not succumbed to the English system which surrounds it.

The first Latinized state to be admitted to the Union was Louisiana. It was a well-developed area; its capital city of New Orleans was comparable in size and importance to many of the largest cities of the Union. After the Louisiana Purchase, when Louisiana was admitted to the Union, the people of New Orleans were permitted to organize their local laws as they wished. Consequently, although much English law was introduced, particularly in procedural, business, and criminal law, Louisiana remains a predominantly Romanesque state.

The other states of Latin origin—New Mexico, California, and others—have retained only vestiges of their Romanesque law. The most generally retained institution is that of community property. By this institution, taken over from the Continental codes, property acquired by either spouse after marriage, except by inheritance or gift, is the property of both. This instittuion has been modified or varied in some of the "community-property" states.

In the year 1948 the entire United States finally succumbed to the community-property concept, in so far as the tax laws are concerned. The 1948 amendments to the Internal Revenue Code gave the full advantage of the community-property concept to all citizens, whether they reside in a community-property state or not, as to income, gift, and estate taxes. It is interesting that a Continental concept should have worked its way into our legal system at so late a date.

CHAPTER 37

Abraham Lincoln

"Discourage litigation. Persuade your neighbors to compromise whenever you can. . . . As a peacemaker a lawyer has a superior opportunity of being a good man. There will still be business enough."

LINCOLN: ADDRESS ON LEGAL ETHICS, 1850

I: Nullification

THE SUPREME COURT even today must concern itself with marking out the lines of demarcation between the rights of the states and those of the federal government. But Abraham Lincoln settled the basic issues raised by the states' rights extremists.

These issues had not been sufficiently settled even by John Marshall's work. It is probable that the mass of the people, from the first days of our Union, had supposed that they would have the right to govern themselves pretty much as they wished, without serious curtailment by the federal government, and that they would have the right to leave the Union if they ever felt themselves sufficiently discontented. Leaders in the North as well as in the South, grumbling over grievances, frequently took strong positions in favor of the rights of the individual states, and murmured about the possibility of leaving the Union.*

Some did not go so far as to recognize the right of secession, but maintained that a state might nullify a federal law which was found unacceptable. This point of view also had Northern as well as Southern advocates. Wisconsin, for example, in 1859 asserted its right to pass on the constitutionality of the *Fugitive Slave Act*, a federal measure, and to nullify it if it cared to. There were strong supporters of nullification in the North and strong opponents to it in the South.

* As late as 1861 Fernando Wood, the Mayor of New York, suggested to the City Council that it secede from the Union and become a free city.

Among these Southerners were Hugh Swinton Legaré and Alexander Hamilton Stephens. Legaré, a Charleston lawyer who contributed importantly to our political and legal literature, called himself a democrat but hated Jefferson, to whom he referred as the "holy father in democracy." Stephens, a physically feeble but mentally vigorous Georgian, became Vice-President of the Confederacy but, up to the moment of secession, opposed nullification bitterly.

The nullification issue was brought to a head more than once before the Civil War. The most interesting episode in a long history of conflict between the federal government and the states was the attempt of South Carolina to nullify the "tariff of abominations" which the South felt might ruin its interests for the benefit of the North. This was in Jackson's administration, and John Calhoun loudly proclaimed the right of the state of South Carolina to nullify any piece of federal legislation of which it disapproved. But Andrew Jackson, turning somewhat against his own Jeffersonianism, staunchly maintained that the preservation of the Union demanded that the federal government be supreme.

Nullification is now a dead issue, and so is the issue of secession, but the whole matter of states' rights is by no means settled. Even today, many believe that the federal government has usurped too much power and that some should be returned to the states. Owen J. Roberts, retired Justice of the Supreme Court, in an address as president of the Pennsylvania Bar Association on June 26, 1948, called attention particularly to the encroachments on state jurisdiction effected by federal appropriations in matters such as agriculture and schools. He said, "It would be interesting, I think, to determine how far our people generally are loyal to the spirit of the Constitution in these respects. We should at least discover whether there is a sentiment to preserve, protect, and foster state jurisdiction and state power; or whether our people prefer something more nearly approaching alien systems, wherein the states are mere administrative districts of a central government."

II: Slavery

THE STATES' RIGHTS ISSUE was one of the causes of the Civil War, but it is doubtful if the country would ever have been thrown into fraternal conflict by that alone, uncomplicated by the issue of slavery. Here again it was Abraham Lincoln who settled a great issue and determined that slavery would be outlawed in the Union. Strangely, he took this final step only when forced to it by the intransigence of the South. His initial intent had been to agree to a perpetuation of slavery in order that the Union might be preserved.

The slavery problem had been raised in the Constitutional Convention, for many delegates were worried about the inconsistency of slavery with the basic premise of the Declaration of Independence that all men are created equal. But the delegates had feared that to bring the matter to a head might wreck the Convention and prevent the adoption of a constitution. The Constitution itself mentions slavery in a back-door way. Section 9 of Article I provides that no law prohibiting the importation of slaves may be made effective before January 1, 1808,* but the opponents of slavery did not go beyond this provision that the slave importation trade might eventually be abolished.

Many Revolutionary leaders were strongly against slavery. George Washington, though a slaveowner himself, said: "Not only do I pray for it on the score of human dignity, but I can clearly foresee that nothing but the rooting out of slavery can perpetuate the existence of our Union by consolidating it in a common bond of principle." But slavery continued, and, as more and more states were admitted to the Union, there came to be a contest over which should be free and which slave.

In the early days of the Republic, slavery had been defended in the South as an institution recognized and sanctioned by the Bible and the Church. After the invention of the cotton gin in 1794, the South had a very practical reason for defending slavery. However important slave labor had been in the previous era, when cotton became king in the South slave labor seemed absolutely essential. Against mounting antislavery feeling in the North, the defense of the institution in the South increased in vehemence, and the Southern planters began to be more and more concerned about their political position in the face of the rapid rise in the number of free states. Already outnumbered by the North, the Southern states feared that the creation of new free states might endanger the vital

* In 1807 an Act was passed stopping the importation of slaves at the earliest permitted moment, January 1st of the next year.

institution of slavery. Slavery thus became to the South the foremost political issue.

The petition of Missouri for admission as a state resulted in what is known as the *Missouri Compromise,* which served to settle, for the moment, the struggle over the admission of new states. Maine was admitted as a free state in 1820, and Missouri as a slave state in 1821; and it was agreed that, thereafter, new states admitted to the Union from the Louisiana Territory above the line of 36 degrees, 30 minutes, should be free, those south of that line, slave. That satisfied both sides somewhat, but not for long.

After Missouri, Arkansas was admitted in 1836 as a slave state; Michigan, as a free state in 1837; and Florida, as a slave state in 1845. Also in 1845, Texas was admitted as a slave state, having declared its independence from Mexico. The next year, Iowa came in free; and in 1848 Wisconsin also. In 1848 came the Mexican War. The slave states, which had welcomed Texas, heartily approved of the Mexican War, for they saw the possibility of carving out further slave states from the southern parts of the country expected to be taken from Mexico. Some in the North thought the whole Mexican War just a slaveholding conspiracy.

The acquisition of vast territories from Mexico brought the slavery issue to a climax. After a long series of debates in Congress, a second great settlement was reached which again temporarily eased the tension. The *Compromise of 1850* provided that California was to be admitted as a free state; no more restrictions were to be put upon any other states to be carved out of the rest of the former Mexican territory; the border between Texas and the Territory of New Mexico was to be fixed. The slave trade, but not slavery, was to be prohibited in the District of Columbia and teeth were to be put in the old Fugitive Slave Act of 1793. That Act had provided for federal enforcement of the recapture of fugitive slaves. In 1842 the Supreme Court had enraged the Southerners through its decision in *Prigg vs. the Commonwealth of Pennsylvania.* Justice Story had held that a Pennsylvania fugitive slave Act was unconstitutional because only the federal government had the right to enact legislation of that kind. Thus, since only federal agencies could enforce any fugitive slave law, the slave states insisted, as part of the Compromise, that federal marshals and their deputies be ordered to enforce the old Act of 1793 on penalty of severe fine. However, many of the Northern states virtually nullified the Fugitive Slave Act by passing "personal liberty" laws, which materially increased the anger of the South.

The present Republican Party was born in the presidential campaign of 1856. It consisted chiefly of enemies of the expansion of slavery; but only a few of its members were outright abolitionists. It was a Northern party only. Lincoln was one of its founders, but its first nominee for President was General John Frémont, who ran against ex-President Fillmore, nominated by the American (Know-Nothing) Party, and Buchanan, nominated by the Democrats. Buchanan was elected, but the Republicans showed considerable strength.

III: The Dred Scott Case

AN EVENT had already taken place which presaged the inevitable conflict. In 1854 Congress had repealed the Missouri Compromise and opened all of the Louisiana Purchase territory to slavery. Then came the tragic decision of the Supreme Court in the *Dred Scott case*, handed down in 1857. Scott was a slave who had been taken to Illinois, then to territory where slavery was forbidden by the Missouri Compromise, and then back to Missouri, a slave state. Scott sued for his freedom on the ground that he had been taken twice to free soil. The Supreme Court, predominantly Southern, Democratic, and proslavery and presided over by Chief Justice Taney—now eighty-three but still vigorous—decided against Scott on three grounds. First, Scott was not a citizen and could not sue—an argument which seemed to beg the question. Second, Scott was a resident of Missouri and, therefore, Illinois law could not affect him—an argument which may have some justification. As a third ground for its decision, the Court held that the Missouri Compromise was unconstitutional, since it might deprive a citizen of "property" (i.e., a slave) "without due process of law." This last was, at the very least, highly questionable.

There was a bit of scandal about the Dred Scott decision. It was suspected, and has subsequently been proved, that President Buchanan consulted with one or more of the Supreme Court Justices in advance of the decision and was assured of the result. Perhaps that has happened more than once in our history, but the impropriety of it is evident.

Lincoln was horrified at the Dred Scott decision but went only as far as to suggest that the Supreme Court might reverse itself. The decision caused great jubilation in the South, where the states' rights enthusiasts were willing enough to see the Supreme Court supreme when the result pleased them, and so fortified the South in its position that compromise seemed almost impossible. The issue which concerned the nation was not the abolition of slavery but its extension into the territories. It was not so much the slavery issue which brought on the war as the political implications of the struggle to make new states slave or free. The South, throughout this period, feared that its over-all political position in the federal government might be fatally weakened if slavery were restricted in new states.

IV: Lincoln and Slavery

ABRAHAM LINCOLN was not elected by a majority vote of the people. He came into office only because the Democratic Party had split within itself. He was the representative of a minority, and the ideas he espoused were in large part minority ideas. But Lincoln carefully avoided the abolitionists. He wished to preserve the Union at all costs. Although hating slavery, he admitted the right of Southern states to have it and was even willing to support fugitive slave laws if that were necessary to keep the states together. He was opposed only to an extension of slavery into territories where it did not already exist. Although he hoped that emancipation might come in time, he was not ready to precipitate it. He went so far as to support a proposed thirteenth amendment to the Constitution, passed in the last days of Buchanan's administration, which was intended to perpetuate slavery in the existing slave states. Slavery was eventually abolished by a *Thirteenth Amendment* passed during Lincoln's administration, but the earlier, proposed thirteenth declared: "No amendment shall be made to the Constitution which will authorize or give to Congress the power to abolish or interfere within any state with the domestic institutions thereof, including that of persons held to labor or service by the laws of said state." *

* The proposed slavery-perpetuation amendment was ratified by Ohio, Maryland, and Illinois but was, of course, abandoned with the start of the Civil War.

V: Reconstruction

LINCOLN and the North freed the Negro, but to this day the Negro does not have the actual equality in the South to which, as a citizen, he is entitled by law. Even if the South had been permitted to reconstruct itself, it is unlikely that he would have been treated as the equal of the white. Some of the Southern states enacted so-called Black Codes which indicate their approach to the Negro problem. The *Black Code of Mississippi*, established by a series of laws in 1865, prohibited whites and blacks from intermarrying. It provided for special labor contracts between white employers and black or mulatto employees, under which, during a period of contract service, the employees would be almost like slaves—statutory rewards were established for the return of colored runaways. All Negroes and mulattoes under eighteen whose parents had not the means or the willingness to support them must be apprenticed, and the master or mistress of the apprentice might "inflict such moderate corporal chastisement as a father or guardian is allowed to inflict on his or her child or ward at common law." If the apprentice fled, the master or mistress could recapture him or her, and continued refusal of the ward to work led to imprisonment. All Negroes over the age of eighteen without "lawful employment" were to be deemed vagrants and to be fined or imprisoned—with the neat addition that, if the vagrant could not pay the taxes levied, that proved even more solidly that he was a vagrant and, therefore, he could be hired out to anyone who would pay the tax. It provided that no colored person could carry a firearm of any kind (the Bill of Rights notwithstanding) nor even a bowie knife, nor utter any "seditious speeches" or make any "insulting gestures." Other states enacted similar statutes, some more gentle, others, like Louisiana, as harsh.

Admitting that the whites of the South had a severe problem in controlling the natural amount of vagrancy following the freeing and economic dislocation of a multitude of slaves, such codes did not indicate any apparent intention to work for the eventual social freedom of the Negro. Yet the situation was undeniably worsened by the mess the North made in imposing its own ideas of reconstruction on the South. The Southerners neither hated nor feared the Negro until "reconstruction" was imposed on them. Southerners saw their legislatures packed with illiterate Negro dummies, bossed by carpet-bagger politicians from the North; they saw Negroes who could not read or write sit on juries in "white" cases; they saw ignorant mulattoes injected into prominent governmental offices, even into a governor's chair, manipulated from behind the scenes by rascally and venal Northerners. They grew to hate not only the Northerners who imposed such conditions upon them but also the ignorant tools of their new masters.

Lincoln, aware of many of the problems involved, had intended a quick reconstruction which would enable the South to start governing itself as soon as possible. In a proclamation of December 8, 1863, he provided that, as soon as enough of the population of each rebellious state took an oath of allegiance to the Union to equal the voting population of 1860, it could organize itself and the military would be withdrawn. Congress, however, took the position that reconstruction was a legislative, not an administrative, matter; and in 1864 it passed the *Wade-Davis Bill* containing Congress's own program for reconstruction, a bill which Lincoln refused to sign.

When Lincoln died, Andrew Johnson tried his best to continue his predecessor's policies. His own *Amnesty Proclamation* of 1865 followed Lincoln's of 1863 rather closely, but there was furious opposition in Congress to anything looking like indulgence to the South. It was led by men such as Charles Sumner of Massachusetts and the ailing, crabbed, but brilliant Thaddeus Stevens, who wanted all rebels disenfranchised and the whole white South punished.

A Freedmen's Bureau had been established to help the emancipated slaves and refugees. In 1866 a new bill enlarging the powers of the Bureau was passed by Congress but vetoed by the President on the ground that it was both inadvisable and unconstitutional; but Congress later passed a supplementary bill over his veto. In the same year the *Civil Rights Act* was enacted to give all Negroes citizenship, this being deemed necessary because the Dred Scot case had said they were not citizens. This Act was passed over Johnson's veto, interposed because he had specific detailed objections to its wording and because he felt it was premature, inadvisable, and even unconstitutional. Continued doubts about the Act prompted the eventual adoption of the Fourteenth Amendment to the Constitution. In the meantime, Congress refused to seat any Congressmen from the Southern states, proclamations of amnesty notwithstanding.

Encouraged by the elections of 1866, Congress passed, over Johnson's veto, a series of harsh *Reconstruction Acts* which instituted military governments in the rebel states. So bitter became the contest between Congress and the President that the Congressional leaders took the first opportunity to bring on the first (and last) impeachment of a President of the United States.

Johnson had carried Lincoln's Cabinet over into his own administration and, with it, Secretary of War Stanton. The latter turned out to be a thorn in the President's side, opposing him constantly, openly, and violently. In 1867, over Johnson's veto, Congress had passed the *Tenure of Office Act,* intended to insure the tenure of persons appointed with the advice and consent of the Senate, until the Senate itself consented to removal. When Stanton refused to resign, Johnson removed him, and the main charge at the impeachment trial was that this had violated the Tenure of Office Act. Johnson's defense was partly that the Act did not apply to an appointee of a previous President—otherwise an incoming President could not appoint his own Cabinet if the Cabinet of the defeated administration chose to hold on. The final vote of the Senate was thirty-five for conviction and nineteen for acquittal—short of the two-thirds vote required to remove the President.

But conditions in the South were frightful. Emancipation of the slaves had destroyed about four million dollars' worth of property, and wealth of all sorts had been lost in the war and its aftermath. Many homes had been destroyed and great plantations ruined. The agrarian economy, so long dependent on slavery, was at a standstill; business in general had virtually stopped. Worst of all, freedom had come suddenly to hordes of uneducated Negroes who were entirely unready for it. It would have been difficult enough for them to adjust slowly to their new freedom, but it was made doubly difficult by the influx of carpetbaggers from the North, and the anxiety of the Northern politicians to punish the whites of the South and, to that end, to elevate the Negro to equality politically and socially before he was prepared for it.

In 1868 the *Fourteenth Amendment* was adopted, providing that all persons born or naturalized in the United States are citizens and cannot be deprived by a state of their rights as citizens. No person may be deprived of life, liberty, or property without "due process of law," and all persons are to have equal protection of the laws. The Negro was to have equality. But things were not to go so easy for the Northern planners. A game had begun between Northern legislators and the people of the South, and as the North invented a new way to assure the Negro of equal treatment the South found a way to avoid it.

The Ku Klux Klan was organized in 1867 or before, and spread rapidly, to terrorize the Negro and prevent him from asserting the rights which were his by law. Congress took immediate cognizance of this and other secret orders such as the Order of the Camelia, and enacted various measures intended to protect the Negro. One was the *Fifteenth Amendment*, which specifically provided that the right to vote should not be denied by reason of race, color, or previous condition of servitude. It is interesting to note that New Jersey first refused to ratify this Amendment and later changed its mind, while New York first ratified and then rescinded its ratification. There followed a number of *Civil Rights Acts*, one of the most important being the so-called *Ku Klux Klan Act* of 1871; its actual title was *Act to Enforce the Fourteenth Amendment*. Various sections of all these Acts were held unconstitutional by the Supreme Court, but the battle went on.

In 1875 the *Civil Rights Act* was passed, directed against discrimination by innkeepers, public carriers, and others engaged in serving the public, but the Act was tested by the *Civil Rights Cases* in 1883, in which the Supreme Court held it unconstitutional because it sought to enforce social rights rather than legal rights. But the next year came the Supreme Court's decision in *Ex Parte Yarborough*, which held that a Negro was entitled to relief against interference with his right to vote in a federal election. The appellants in this case, who had beaten a Negro to prevent him from voting, argued that the controlling federal laws were unconstitutional, but the Court, in a stirring opinion, sustained the lower court which had convicted the appellants and sentenced them to imprisonment.

VI: Equality for the Negro

THE NEGRO remained largely disenfranchised in the South. Constitutional guarantees of equality were taken none too seriously. There were always the shotgun and Judge Lynch, used only rarely, but the threat of danger hung over the head of any Negro with courage enough to try to vote. And the threat of force was not the only deterrent. Some states enacted election laws under which a registrant had to be able to read a section of the state constitution or a statute, or to explain a section when read to him by election officers—some of whom did not read very clearly. Other states required the payment of a poll tax or the ownership of property to enable one to vote, but the whites were protected against all these limitations by what was called a "grandfather clause." If the registrant had voted or had a father or grandfather who had voted in 1867 he could vote even if he had no property, had not paid a tax, and could not read or understand the Constitution. The Supreme Court vitiated these grandfather clauses, but some of the other mechanisms for making voting difficult or well-nigh impossible for Negroes continued in use.

Another mechanism was available to the Southern politician. There was really a one-party system in the South. The Republican Party was only technically present in most districts, so the real election was the primary of the Democratic Party. The ruse was employed of permitting Negroes to vote in the election if they had the courage, but of not permitting them to participate in a primary. This was destroyed by the Supreme Court in *Nixon vs. Herndon*, known as the *Texas White Primary case*, in which Justice Holmes rendered an opinion holding that a Texas statute excluding Negroes from a primary was unconstitutional; and the more recent cases of *Classic vs. United States* and *Smith vs. Allwright* establish even more clearly the right of Negroes to vote in the primaries, but any who attempt it risk retaliation.

The South had also effectively solved the problem of keeping Negroes off juries in "white" cases. A Negro is by law just as much entitled to be called for jury duty as is a white man, and the Supreme Court has so held, but the Court can rarely do anything if a jury clerk accidentally happens to leave all Negro names off the jury list.

Abuse of the Negro is not, of course, confined to the South. In Northern cities he is in practice restricted to ghettoes; he is rarely to be found in the "best" hotels or restaurants; and certain types of employment are barred in practice to him except in his own districts. All this is not because of law but because even Northern whites do not always willingly accept the Negro as a social or economic equal. But sentiment for social and economic emancipation of the Negro has been increasing rapidly. Recent social measures of the federal government, among them the Fair Employment Practices Commission, have made some headway against racial discrimination, and some of the Northern states have begun to enact antidiscrimination laws which attempt to assure equal treatment in employment for all minority groups.

The struggle for "civil rights" has intensified in the past decade or so. The Negro is coming to be well organized and able to exert heavy pressure through the vote and by direct actions, such as "sit-ins" and "freedom rides" which precipitate issues requiring local court action, on appeals from which the Negro is able to bring these issues to the attention of higher courts and often to the Supreme Court. The *School Segregation cases* (*Brown vs. Board of Education*) were perhaps the most important and contentious of the Supreme Court cases. Here the Court reversed itself and abandoned the old "separate but equal" schooling principle* and held that the schools must be integrated. It said that separating Negro children from white "generates a feeling of inferiority as to their status in the community. . . ."

Many, even strongly against segregation, were shocked that the Court, as two writers expressed it, had "cited as authority college professors, psychologists, and sociologists," and asked: "Should our fundamental rights rise, fall or change along with the latest fashions of psychological literature?" † Indeed, it does seem regrettable that the Court, to justify its position, saw fit to use such "authorities" as the Swedish socialist Dr. Gunnar Myrdal, whose book *An American Dilemma* was cited by the Supreme Court as one basis for its ruling. In this very book, Dr. Myrdal had said the American Constitution is "impractical and unsuited to modern conditions." This was a strange citation indeed to support a ruling on a constitutional question.

Except for the most intensely prejudiced sections in the South, the majority of the American people are in principle in favor of complete equality for the Negro. They are conscious, too, of the unfortunate impact of the existence of the issue upon other nations, particularly the African and other nonwhite nations. A complicating factor in the situation, however, which concerns many, is the extent to which the federal government should force various types of "integration" upon the states. The issue of states' rights is heavily involved, and an effort to compel Southerners perhaps too quickly to abandon old habits and customs may well bring about sharp and

* Held in *Plessy vs. Ferguson* (1896), 163 U.S. 537.

† Cook and Potter, in an article in the *American Bar Association Journal* of April, 1956.

perhaps bloody conflicts, the effects of which may take many years of education to undo.

The growing belligerency of some of our Negro youth intensifies the danger of conflict. One can understand the resentment which underlies this belligerency, but race relations are not likely to be improved by it. The battle for social equality cannot be won overnight, and it is to be hoped that both races will exercise tolerance and patience.

In the long run, obviously, the whole problem will be solved by what has been called "miscegenation," a process which, whether desired or not by whites or Negroes, seems inevitable.

VII: Equality for the Indian

THE NEGROES are not the only maltreated minority in the United States. The story of our relations with the Indians is a pitiful one—one solemn treaty after another broken, one injustice after another done to the original inhabitants of the land. Does the Fourteenth Amendment really mean that anyone born in the United States is a citizen and must receive equal treatment with other citizens—that he may not be deprived of property without due process of law? We have been depriving the Indians of property without due process of law—unless there is deemed to be special "process" relating to Indians—from colonial times up to the very recent day when the last groups of free Indians were pushed into the last finally contracted, wasteland reservations.

The famous case of *Cherokee Nation vs. Georgia,* decided by the Supreme Court in 1831, established the legal status of Indians in the United States. The Cherokee Indians of Georgia had set themselves up as an independent nation. But Georgia then declared all the Cherokee lands to be owned by the state and held all Indian laws inoperative. The Indians appealed to the Supreme Court, and John Marshall, in his opinion denying them relief, said that the Indians were not foreign or independent nations but were "domestic dependent nations" in a condition of "pupilage." The decision denied the right of the Cherokee Nation to sue the state of Georgia in the federal courts. Marshall did not attempt to determine whether or not the Indians had valid grievances; he decided the case on a technical consideration of the words of the Constitution. The decision, however justified under sound constitutional law, was regrettable in so far as it made easier further aggressions against Indian rights by the states.

In 1832, in the case of *Worcester vs. Georgia,* Marshall made it clear, however, that, though the Cherokee Indian Nation had no right to use the federal courts against the state of Georgia, it was a "distinct community occupying its own territory, with boundaries accurately described, in which the laws of Georgia can have no force, and which the citizens of Georgia have no right to enter but with the assent of the Cherokees themselves or in conformity with treaties and with the Acts of Congress."

It is a sad aftermath of the controversy between Georgia and the Cherokees that, in 1835, the remaining Cherokees, the Creeks, and some other Indians were removed to Indian Territory west of the Mississippi. They were given five million dollars and the costs of removal in exchange for their Eastern lands, but they were not given much say about moving. These Indians, pushed into their last reservation, selected because it seemed particularly undesirable to white settlers, had some satisfaction, at least, when, many years later, oil was discovered on their lands. Neighboring whites were enraged that such a piece of luck had come to the red man. Had they had any intimation about what lay beneath the soil of Oklahoma, you may be sure that the last reservation would have been located in some other part of the country.

It was not until the *Dawes Act* of 1887 that the Indians were granted the protection of the laws of the United States and permanently allotted lands in the West.

VIII: Equality for Orientals

WE HAVE NOT been very kind to any of the colored races in our midst. It is not only the "black" Negroes and the "red" Indians whom we have suppressed, but also the "yellow" Orientals. The constitution of the state of California, adopted in 1879, classed persons of Chinese birth with idiots and felons. Section 1 of Article II of that constitution read that all citizens of the United States, whether by birth or by naturalization, may vote, "*provided,* no native of China, no idiot, or person convicted of any infamous crime . . . shall ever exercise the privilege of an elector in this state." There was also a special Article XIX headed "CHINESE" which permitted the Legislature to act against dangerous "alien" vagrants, paupers, etc. It also prohibited any corporation organized in California from employing any "Chinese or Mongolian," and it further prohibited the employment of any Chinese on any public work except as punishment for crime. It proceeded in some detail, reciting: "The presence of foreigners ineligible to become citizens of the United States is declared to be dangerous to the well-being of the state, and the legislature shall discourage their immigration by all the means within its power. . . . The legislature shall delegate all necessary power to the incorporated cities and towns of this state for the removal of Chinese without the limits of such cities and towns, or for their location within prescribed portions of those limits. . . ."

These provisions of the California constitution have been repealed; but they illustrate the fact that we have not always taken seriously the injunctions of the Declaration of Independence and the Constitution relating to the equality of man. In fact, the federal government has followed the California precedent in establishing Oriental exclusion. The Chinese were given the right to immigrate to the United States by the *Burlingame Treaty* of 1868, but they came in such numbers that a deep anti-Chinese feeling arose among the people of the West Coast. Pressure was put upon Congress to exclude further Chinese immigration, and, in 1880, a treaty was negotiated which empowered the United States to restrict Chinese immigration whenever it seemed to threaten the welfare of the country. Under permission of this treaty, the *Chinese Exclusion Act* of 1882 was passed suspending further Chinese immigration.

Though the Chinese problem had been thus summarily settled, a great influx of Japanese to the West Coast prompted the so-called *Gentlemen's Agreement* with Japan of 1908. By this agreement, President Theodore Roosevelt "saved face" for Japan. It provided that the Japanese government would issue emigration visas only for such as wished to join a spouse, parent, or child already in the United States or to take control of a business already there.

The Oriental immigration problem was finally settled by the immigration laws of 1917 and 1921. The first created a literacy test. The second established a quota system. The numbers of aliens permitted to immigrate each year was to be no more than 3 per cent of those of such nationality who resided in the United States according to the census of 1910. In 1924 a new *Immigration Act* revised the quota system, basing it on the nationalities of the inhabitants of the United States in 1896. Thus the Oriental problem came to an end, for, thereafter, only 100 Chinese and 100 Japanese immigrants were allowed entry in each year. The arbitrary result of this revised quota system was very odd: 51,227 Germans can be admitted each year, but only 3,954 Frenchmen; 28,567 Irishmen from the Free State but only 34,007 from all of Great Britain and Northern Ireland; only 473 Hungarians, but 5,982 Poles; only 131 Spaniards, but an unlimited number from the Republic of Haiti.*

There are still alien land laws in California which prevent anyone who is not eligible for citizenship from holding land. I find it rather difficult to distinguish these laws of the state of my birth from the Nazi laws which prevented a Jew from holding property. There have been cases in the California courts in which, in order to avoid this law, a Japanese has taken title to real estate in the name of an infant son who was born an American citizen, and the land has been confiscated by the state. The basis of the decisions is that a "fraud" has been committed against the people of California. The result apparently is that the people of California will be richer by more than a million dollars in confiscated properties.

Immediately upon the outbreak of war with Japan in 1941, residents in the continental United States of Japanese ancestry were swept up and thrown into concentration camps. Large numbers of these were American citizens not by naturalization but by birth. It was presumed that they were all potential enemies of the nation, though no similar action was taken against American citizens of German, Austrian, Hungarian, Italian, Rumanian, or Bulgarian ancestry, nor even against American citizens by naturalization who had been born in those countries. It was the Japanese-Americans only who were singled out for the special concentration camp treatment. That such an act was unconstitutional apparently bothered very few.

The people of the West Coast and the military explain that the situation was critical, that no one could tell which yellow-skinned Americans were loyal and which not, and that we could not take

* Certain countries were excluded from the quota system, and their nationals are admitted without restriction of number, among them Canada and the independent Latin-American countries.

any chance but had to corral them all. That may be credible. It is true that some of our yellow-colored citizens were also subjects of the Emperor, because they had what is known as "dual nationality." However, it is regrettable that so radical a step was deemed necessary and that so many loyal American citizens were put to discomfort and unhappiness and deprived of their civil liberties merely because they were not of the color of the majority.

We fought two great world wars within the space of a comparatively few years. In support of each, we enunciated great principles and ideals directed at the improper subjugation of peoples, maltreatment of minorities, and discrimination. It enraged us when the Germans discriminated against their Jews and other minorities, and the very words "concentration camp" have become words of horror. But the concentration camp is an ancient institution, and we have not been averse to its use. True, we do not murder the inmates, or torture them, or starve them, but the mere fact of concentration, involving the forced abandonment of home, business, and freedom, is itself an unwarranted cruelty.

It must seem strange to many people of other countries that we, who maintain our idealism so steadfastly in argument, abandon it when it comes to some of our own minorities. For there is an old history of minority oppression in our country. We give lip service to the equality guaranteed by the Constitution, but we do not always practice that equality.

CHAPTER 38

The Age of Laissez Faire

I: Laissez Faire

THE END of the Civil War marked the beginning of a period, lasting well into the twentieth century, in which growing interest in the protection of rights of property was accompanied by a minimum of social consciousness. The West was open, and anyone who wished, and had the energy, could migrate westward, purchase a homestead cheaply, and build a new life in territories still virgin. It was not until great industrial cities arose, stimulated by growing markets and the rapid development of science and mechanics, that the resultant industrial peonage and the concentration of poverty focused the attention of thoughtful men on the necessity for social reform. Such reformers were few because the leaders of the East were too busy with the rapid growth of industry. The South had suffered so severely in the war and its aftermath that it would be decades before there would be any resurgence of energy in that region. And in the West, where opportunity beckoned everyone, there were few such problems.

It was an era of enormous increase in industrial development, the time of the growth of the Big Business baronies. It culminated in what has been called "The Gilded Age"; Professor Parrington called it "The Great Barbecue." America was the land of opportunity; it was not difficult to persuade millions of peasants to emigrate from Europe to fill the needs of the vast and still expanding American industries.

The story of the great expansion in business has been told frequently enough. Banking, industrial, and communications empires, comparable to great feudal holdings, and new dynasties of wealth and power, came into being, many of them created by men without scruple, who used the venal politicians of the day to their own ends, contemptuous or negligent of the public welfare.

President Grant, in whose administration there were scandals no less unpleasant than those of the Harding administration, and Presidents Garfield, Hayes, and Arthur were all of the party of Lincoln. But the party had lost its initial idealism after the death of the Great Emancipator and become a compromise association of diverse self-seeking groups; there was little room in it for reform in the period of industrial growth. Things were going too well. There was too much money being made, too much financial whoopee. Grant, who started life as a Democrat, ended as a full partisan of power, and the Republican Presidents who succeeded him were disinclined to interfere with the generally prosperous, and to them satisfactory, condition of the country.

The Democratic Party, from among whose ranks some social-mindedness might have been expected as an inheritance from Jefferson and Jackson, was prostrate after the Civil War, and it, too, contained dissident and conflicting elements. It was apparent that there was little to choose between the parties, except on a sectional basis, for both contained some of the most reactionary groups in the nation as well as some of the few progressives. Many saw how slight was the hope of progressive legislation through association with either of the great parties, and from time to time new political movements arose. But each such movement came to an early end, leaving the field again to the two major parties, whose professional leaders, combined with "business," had no interest in stirring up the country.

II: Henry George

> *"The equal right of all men to the use of the land is as clear as their equal right to breathe the air— it is a right proclaimed by the fact of their existence."*
>
> HENRY GEORGE: PROGRESS AND POVERTY

THOUGH there were often very few to listen, strong voices did cry out, from time to time, against the complacency of society. One of these, remembered now only by students, was that of Henry George (1839-1897), whose formula for social reform was simple.

He advocated a *single tax*, one upon real estate, and that measure, he believed, would solve all our economic and social problems.

George started with the premise that the land belonged to the people and could not be permanently alienated. But he did not advocate any equal distribution of land. He recognized that land had to be exploited, and that the immediate user of it must be protected in his use. But he conceived of the proper use of land as renting it to the highest bidder by focusing the taxing power solely upon the land. His claim was that the worst or only serious monopoly in our society was the land monopoly. Let me explain it this way. Smith owns a piece of land that is more valuable than other land of the same character and size near by, perhaps because it happens to be on a main traffic artery or in a district which is especially desirable. George concluded that the landlord, who received a higher rent for this piece of property than did the landlord of a comparable piece of less value, was receiving "unearned increment." The landlord was benefiting by something either existing as a natural geographical factor or created by society. He had done nothing to warrant his getting this added income.

A concentration of taxes on rent, according to George, would solve the basic problem of land monopoly, from which the major social evils, in his opinion, derived. His theory was an oversimplification which cannot stand up against careful analysis, but he was aggressive and effective in his propaganda, and his work had profound effect upon the political and social thinking of his and later generations. It called sharp attention to the fact that there might be such an element in economic life as "unearned increment" income, resulting in the unfair exploitation of the work of others and the inequitable division of the sum total of production. It was the first heavy assault against the philosophy of *laissez faire*.

III: Labor

Though the country remained, on the whole, complacent, the movement for social change grew steadily. New ideas came from abroad, sometimes with an influx of laborers from across the sea, radical agitators among them. American intellectuals began to write and to philosophize on a more broadly humanitarian basis and seeking to stimulate social reform. Preachers, here and there, began to battle the new Mammon from their pulpits. But it was not until recent decades that the horse began to gallop, whipping along by a strong movement for a sociological approach to the law. Intellectual leaders played a strong part, but labor accelerated the reform movement through its own organized efforts. It found it necessary to organize to protect itself against the rapacity of the new industrial overlords; once organized, it exerted strong pressure not only for the alleviation of industrial ills but also for sociological reform in general. Organized labor had not always acted in the public interest, but without its participation the reform movement might never have achieved such quick results.

There was little labor organization at the time of the Civil War, no national federation. Much needed to be done for the workingman, but little could be done until there was an organization strong enough to make its pressure felt. Manufacturers did not hesitate to exploit labor. The South had frequently called the industrial slavery of the North colder and more heartless than the Negro slavery of the South; and there was much to the point. The enormous improvement in working conditions gradually accomplished in the past hundred years was extracted bit by bit, by pressure from labor and sympathetic, social-minded groups. This improvement was not entirely due to agitation, however. The rapid development of production in the United States made reform possible. For it is impossible to use or consume more than a nation produces. No amount of legislation, for example, could, by itself, improve the economic conditions of the people of the Congo. An increase in production or productive capacity would be a necessary concomitant.

One W. H. Sylvis saw the necessity of organization and, in 1866, formed the National Labor Union; but it had disappeared by 1872. It was not easy to organize labor in those days. As wages were small, labor could not accumulate great funds for its cause, and opposition was constant. Government was unsympathetic, and employers penalized those who showed any sympathy with unionism. But another great union appeared, the Noble Order of the Knights of Labor, an organization made secret in order to protect its members from punishment by employers. It had none too clear a set of purposes, however, and it suffered from opposition by the craft unions because, like the present CIO, it welcomed the unskilled as well. It died early, principally because of the organization in

1886 of the American Federation of Labor, a craft organization, by Adolph Strasser and Samuel Gompers. The Federation survived its initial difficulties, and grew in strength until it had the power to challenge those legislators who were still unwilling to take any step against the interests of wealth and power. The Federation carefully refrained from creating a separate labor party, using the indirect but effective method of supporting the more co-operative candidates for office.

The fight of labor was for unionization, for collective bargaining, for better wages, and for better working conditions. In the period after Lincoln the mere idea of unionism was held in abhorrence by industry, and almost every attempt at collective bargaining ran against arrogant obstruction. Great strikes were frequent, and some were bloody. Troops were often called to assist the entrenched employers, and gangs of strikebreakers were hired like professional armies to terrorize and intimidate striking labor. The railway strike of 1877 was accompanied by bloodshed.

Public sympathy took a long time in coming to the side of labor. In consequence, the courts were not too friendly in their attitude, and the mere suspicion of "radicalism" often caused a serious miscarriage of justice. In 1886 there was serious rioting in Haymarket Square in Chicago, started admittedly by anarchists. After the riot a meeting of labor sympathizers was held in a public hall, and everything was peaceful until, at the end of the meeting, policemen entered threateningly. A bomb was thrown, and its explosion killed one of the policemen and maimed others. It was never proved who threw the bomb, but eight anarchists were arrested, tried, and convicted of murder on the grounds that they had incited the thrower of the bomb. It was not shown that the real criminal had actually been incited by the defendants, but the court held that of no moment. Seven of the defendants were condemned to death, the other to jail.

The public was greatly aroused by the crime, which was horrible enough, but unconcerned as to whether or not the defendants were really guilty. It was sufficient that they were anarchists. Four were hanged and one committed suicide. The other death sentences were commuted to life imprisonment, but when, six years later, Governor Altgeld of Illinois pardoned the three in prison, even quasi-liberal Theodore Roosevelt censured him as the protector of murderers. The trial was actually one of the most unfortunate in our history, for there was no proof that the defendants had any connection with the crime. Incidents such as these increasingly embittered reformers and laboring men.

One of the most famous cases of this type was the later conviction for murder, in 1916, of Thomas Mooney and Warren K. Billings. A bomb had been thrown during a preparedness parade in San Francisco; Mooney and Billings were arrested with several others, but they were the only ones tried. Billings received life imprisonment and Mooney a death sentence, which was later commuted to life imprisonment after President Wilson, in response to a considerable amount of liberal clamor that the trial had not been fair, appointed an investigating commission, which reported considerable doubt as to guilt. Liberals continued to press for the release of Billings and Mooney, but they were not finally pardoned until 1939. The case was similar to that of the Haymarket bombing, in so far as the conviction of the defendants was probably caused as much by public indignation against labor agitators as anything else.

Similarly, in 1920, Nicola Sacco and Bartolomeo Vanzetti were convicted of murder in Massachusetts in a case which aroused a furor among liberals. At the trial much evidence was received to show how radical the defendants were, and Judge Thayer, who presided, was accused of prejudice because of this. So great was the remonstrance against what seemed a miscarriage of justice that Governor Fuller appointed the president of Harvard, the president of M.I.T., and Judge Robert Grant to review the case. The panel reported that the conviction was proper, but criticized the trial judge for indecorum. Some of the intelligent public still believes that the trial was unfair, but Sacco and Vanzetti, protesting their innocence to the last, were executed.

The major objective of organized labor throughout this long period was, of course, recognition of the right to unionize and of the right of collective bargaining. President Cleveland was the first President to admit that he saw any propriety in unionization, and it was because of his efforts that Congress, in 1888, took the first important step toward playing any part in industrial controversies; a federal commission was created to offer mediation in labor-capital disputes. Cleveland went further: he caused several of the great strikes to be investigated, and his investigating board reported, in the serious Pullman strike of 1894, that the company had been wrong, and recommended that unions be recognized. The mere fact that a government-appointed body should have had the temerity to say that a great corporation was wrong in a strike was an important step forward. But compulsory recognition of unions and of collective bargaining did not come into our law until the period of the New Deal. In the meantime, labor fought on, increasing steadily in power and winning more and more of the public to its side.

One of the mechanisms of the law which caused organized labor enormous discomfort was the injunction. The conviction of Eugene V. Debs, later Socialist candidate for President, for violating a broad, blanket injunction during the Pullman strike, sharpened the issue.

There is an old rule at common law that any combination in restraint of trade may be enjoined, and, from the first breath of unionism, reactionary capitalists have loudly contended that a union was *per se* an organization in restraint of trade. That was all right as far as the state courts were concerned, but the federal law was statutory, so that the federal courts could not use the common-law power of injunction. Thus, in 1890, the anguish of the industrial leaders at the passage of the *Sherman Anti-Trust Act,* directed against monopolies, was somewhat assuaged by the thought that labor unions might also be enjoined under the Act. And so the courts thought also. Injunctions against labor unions by state courts continued to be used, and now the federal courts believed they had a mandate in the same direction. The injunctions were employed mainly to prevent picketing and boycotting, the strongest labor weapons in a strike.

Two of the leading labor injunction cases were *Truax vs. Corrigan* and *Duplex Printing Press Company vs. Deering,* both decided by the Supreme Court in 1921. The Truax case concerned itself with a state statute. Arizona had passed a law prohibiting the use of injunctions in labor disputes, and the specific question before the Court was whether this law was constitutional if it prevented the granting of an injunction against all kinds of picketing. The Court held that the law was unconstitutional and that it violated the Fourteenth Amendment, because it gave unequal protection of the laws. The reasoning of the Court was that, had it not been for the Arizona statute, the employer in this case, because of the nature of the picketing, would have been entitled to an injunction. Therefore, it said, the Arizona statute discriminated against an employer who happened to have a strike in his plant.

The Duplex case involved an interpretation of the *Clayton Act,* an amendment to the Sherman Act passed during President Wilson's administration. President Gompers of the American Federation of Labor had prevailed upon Congress to include in the Clayton Act a provision that unions were not to be deemed in restraint of trade and, therefore, could not be enjoined in a labor dispute. The Clayton Act contained a statement which astounded some of the great industrial magnates: that ". . . the labor of a human being is not a commodity or article of commerce." The Sherman Act had directed itself against "monopoly" and "combination" and against "restraint," but none of these vital terms had been defined, an omission which permitted the courts to include labor unions within its terms. The Gompers clause in the Clayton Act was intended to put an end to the free use of injunctions against unions. But the Supreme Court, in the Duplex case, materially cut down the efficacy of the Gompers clause.

The Duplex Company employed, among a large number of employees, fourteen members of a union whose national membership was some sixty thousand. The company refused to grant the union's demand for a closed shop, and the fourteen members of the union struck. The issue before the Court was that the entire national union organized a carefully planned secondary boycott to prevent the company from selling its presses. The Court held that the anti-injunction provisions of the Clayton Act did not apply, reasoning that the Clayton Act spoke only of disputes between an employer and employees, whereas here the courts were dealing with a secondary boycott engineered by a union of sixty thousand members against a company which employed only fourteen of them. Justices Holmes, Brandeis, and Clarke dissented.

But the law changes as public opinion changes. Until the New Deal, injunctions against labor unions were common. President Taft, in his inaugural address of 1909, expressed the then prevailing point of view. He said: "Take away from the courts . . . the power to issue injunctions in labor disputes, and it would create a privileged class among the laborers and save the lawless among their number from a most needful remedy available to all men for the protection of their business against lawless invasion. . . . The American people . . . insist that the authority of the courts shall be sustained, and are opposed to any change in the procedure by which the powers of a court may be weakened and the fearless and effective administration of justice be interfered with."

The struggle of labor for recognition and reform was a long one. One great forward step was taken when the federal government was induced in 1884 to give official recognition of the problems of labor by creating a special Bureau of Labor Statistics, and by 1913 we had a Department of Labor with a Cabinet officer as its head. Organized labor pressed for the abolition of oppressive practices, such as the giving of wages in goods and credits and so enslaving the worker; against the use of criminal labor in penitentiaries to compete with free labor; against the practice of bringing in foreign labor under contract; against too free immigration;* against unsafe and unsanitary working conditions; against the lack of legal responsibility of the employer for injuries sustained in the course of employment; for better schools and the extension of educational facilities; for municipal ownership of public utilities; for the principle of equal pay for equal work; for the popular election of Senators; for woman suffrage; and for much else. Agitation for these reform measures appeared not only on the federal scene but also in the states.

Any help from the two major parties was reluctantly given, under great pressure. Yet the ground was gradually laid for more accelerated reform. In 1912 the so-called Pujo Committee, created by Congress to investigate "the money power," reported an enormous concentration of wealth and financial control in New York City. It named a small number of banks and banking houses, and showed how extensive was their hold on transportation and on great corporations important to the public welfare. The Committee in its final report said, "The financial control of American industry rests, therefore, in the hands of a small number of wealthy and powerful financiers . . ." The investigation gave material of war to the reformers. It gave President Wilson something to think about; and his establishment of the Federal Reserve System was perhaps largely attributable to the report of the Pujo Committee.

* A position which many economists believe to have been highly ill-advised.

IV: Political Reform

It took some time to arouse large numbers of the people against the injustices of the industrial era, but many writers began to take up the attack on the selfishness and callousness of the new capitalism, among them Horace Greeley, Charles A. Dana, Henry Adams, Henry George, Henry Demarest Lloyd, Thorstein Veblen, Frederick Townsend Martin and Lincoln Steffens. The titles of some of their books indicate the trend of their thinking: George's *Progress and Poverty* (1879), Lloyd's *Wealth Against Commonwealth* (1894), Veblen's *Theory of the Leisure Class* (1899), and Martin's *The Passing of the Idle Rich* (1911). Even foreign writers affected the reform movement in the United States. Bryce's *American Commonwealth* (1888) exposed some of the sordid American political practices and pointed up some of our social injustices. The socialism of Karl Marx and others was introduced by German and Scandinavian immigrants and egalitarianism was expounded by the writings of George Bernard Shaw, H. G. Wells, the Webbs and others, all widely read.

Many felt that social reform would be impossible unless the government itself was reformed, and a movement to this end attained substantial results. The first step was the *Civil Service Act* of 1883. A further important step was the introduction of the Australian ballot; by 1908 all but two of the states used it. One now voted in secret and used a ballot printed by the state. Reformers then attacked the corruption accompanying the boss-controlled political nominating convention. Robert La Follette deserves most credit for his fight against these conventions. His state of Wisconsin had the first state-wide primary, a system later strongly advocated by Governor Charles E. Hughes of New York and Governor Woodrow Wilson of New Jersey. The use of the direct primary is now well established, except that some states slid partially backward by resuming conventions for the nomination of state officers.

Other measures of political reform were the initiative, the referendum, and the recall. Many states adopted the first two, and some the third. The initiative and the referendum were distinctly Jeffersonian in their effect of increasing democratic control by enabling the people to take a direct part in legislation if they cared to. The recall, a measure far more controversial, might also have received Jefferson's full support, for it enabled the people to remove public officers—it could even be used against judges—at will. Perhaps, however, the *Seventeenth Amendment* to the Constitution would have given Jefferson the greatest pleasure, for that provided for the democratization of the Senate. When Senators were directly elected by the people, the Senate then had nothing left of its original semi-aristocratic character.

V: The Theodore Roosevelt Era

> *"It is difficult to make our material condition better by the best laws, but it is easy enough to ruin it by bad laws."* THEODORE ROOSEVELT, IN A SPEECH AT PROVIDENCE, 1902

THE MOST PICTURESQUE REFORMER of the period was Theodore Roosevelt. His reforms were in fact rather meager, but his aggressive spirit and unusual capacity for personal publicity kept him before the public and spearheaded the reform movement. Often cartooned with fierce eyes glaring through thick glasses, his mouth widely exposing an expanse of denture, carrying a club with which he was ready to lambast "the interests," he actually fell far short of the progressive performance of his supposedly conservative successor, President Taft. Yet T. R. stands as a symbol of the second period of the laissez-faire era, a period in which the pressure behind the reform movement was gathering strength and energy.

That he was an aristocrat may have given added emphasis to the volubility of his championship of social reform. He came out very strongly for a redistribution of wealth, and his liking for the sliding-scale income tax was in line with his hatred of vast and perpetuated wealth. The income tax law was enacted under President Taft (in whose administration such forward-looking measures as the postal savings system and the parcel post system were also instituted), but it was Teddy who first sparked the movement. Moderate though T. R. may have been, his fighting pose and intensity inspired many liberals to carry on still further the struggle against laissez faire.

An *Interstate Commerce Act* had been enacted in 1887, but it was of so weak a nature that it was of almost no use in controlling the evils of the new capitalism. The Sherman Anti-Trust Act of 1890 was also a feeble effort. The greatest of the monopolistic combinations were created after this Act was in force. Yet attempts were made to use it. Under Harrison, there were three indictments under the Sherman Act; in Cleveland's second term, two; under McKinley, none; under T. R. and his Big Stick, twenty-five; under Taft, forty-five. Though Teddy shook his Big Stick at the trusts, he failed to get much service out of the Sherman Act. President Taft did far better, for he at least secured the technical dissolution of the Standard Oil Company and the American Tobacco Company. Woodrow Wilson was responsible for the Clayton Anti-Trust Act, which put a few more teeth into trust busting, but even this law was not too helpful in breaking up the great monopolistic combinations which seemed to many to smother free enterprise. It became clear ultimately that destruction of huge enterprises was not the answer to the problem, but that reasonable regulation might be.

To this end, the *Federal Trade Commission* was established with the right to act in instances of unfair competition and trade restraint, and this has been an extremely useful instrument for curbing improper combinations. The *Interstate Commerce Commission* was also made a regulating body, and extended in power by the *Hepburn Act* of 1906 and the *Mann-Elkins Act* of 1910.

Labor and reformers pressed even harder for social legislation, and their efforts were eventually crowned with considerable success. The states began to enact legislation to provide minimum standards in industry for women and children. Massachusetts took the lead. In 1876 its highest court held constitutional an Act which limited the work of women and minors to sixty hours a week. Some ground was made in the federal domain also. Before his appointment to the Supreme Court, Louis D. Brandeis won a victory before that Court in inducing it to hold constitutional an Oregon law prohibiting the employment of women in factories or laundries for more than ten hours per day.

It was the case of *Muller vs. Oregon*, decided in 1908. As counsel for the state of Oregon, Brandeis introduced a mass of evidence of a sociological nature to prove the law reasonable. The question was: Did the Oregon statute interfere unreasonably with the right of the individual to contract for employment as she saw fit? The leading case of *Lochner vs. New York* had held against a New York statute prohibiting male bakers from working more than sixty hours per week, for just this reason—that it interfered improperly with the right of the individual to enter into a contract of his own choice. But the Supreme Court distinguished the Oregon case from the Lochner case by stating that the former concerned the labor of women, and that women, because of their peculiar physical and social problems, might be protected against themselves even though a similar law directed against the labor of men might be an improper interference.

However, when Congress enacted a law establishing minimum wages in industry for women, the Supreme Court held it unconstitutional. In *Adkins vs. Children's Hospital,* in 1923, Justice Sutherland in his majority opinion said that this law went too far in an attempt to regulate for social purposes, and that if such a law were constitutional, so might be an oppressive law establishing maximum wages in industry. Chief Justice Taft dissented, holding that Congress had the right to legislate against social evils, and that low wages were just as vital a factor in public health as the conditions and hours of labor. Justice Holmes dissented, separately, holding that Congress had the right to forbid what was bad for people, and that such social legislation was no violation of the right of the individual to contract freely. But, while the right of Congress to legislate on hours of work remained intact, the right to legislate on wages was thus denied.

In 1906 Congress had limited the number of hours of work for trainmen and telegraphers engaged in interstate commerce, and in 1916, by the *Adamson Act,* the railroad man's day was confirmed at eight hours. It took a good deal of revolutionary thinking on the part of the Supreme Court to swallow these new forms of interference with the constitutional right of the individual to contract freely. The Constitution said that the right to freedom of contract should not be abridged by the states, and the Court had, in its history, several times held forward-looking legislation unconstitutional because it interfered with that freedom. Now a workman who wanted to contract for more than an eight-hour day could not do so. Was not his right to contract freely interfered with? The Court supported this new type of legislation by holding that the public interest was the controlling factor. The Constitution was found flexible enough to permit the Court, following changed social ideas, to reverse old trends and to accommodate itself to what was now thought socially necessary.

In 1908, under T. R., common carriers in interstate commerce were made responsible for injuries to employees occasioned by their employment. The old common-law rule was that an employer was not responsible unless through his own negligence, but the feeling grew to be that industrial accidents are an expected hazard of employment and that the workman should not be left helpless through injuries sustained while employed, even if due to his own negligence.

The efforts of the federal government to regulate child labor have failed to date. In 1916 the *Keating-Owens Act* was enacted; this was intended to proscribe child labor by preventing the shipment in interstate commerce of articles manufactured by plants using the labor of children under fourteen, or those between fourteen and sixteen for too arduous periods of work. The issue was brought to the Supreme Court in the case of *Hammer vs. Dagenhart,* in 1918, and by a five-to-four decision the Act was held unconstitutional. The case illustrates that the battle between Federalism and states' rights was still going on. Justice Day, in writing the majority opinion, said that the right of the government to regulate interstate commerce was a right to regulate commerce as such, and could not be used to enforce upon a state some social objective which the government favored. Justice Holmes, however, in his dissenting opinion, took a position John Marshall might well have taken. Holmes said that the right to regulate interstate commerce was an absolute one; that, once it had been given under the Constitution, its breadth could not be cut down; and that this was no improper interference with the rights of the states.

The next episode in the attempt to regulate child labor through federal law was a tax assessed on products produced by child labor. In 1922, in the case of *Bailey vs. Drexel Furniture Company* the tax was held unconstitutional. Chief Justice Taft said that this was a tax intended to penalize manufacturers for employing child labor and, therefore, an improper invasion of state rights.

In 1924 Congress passed a child labor amendment to the Constitution permitting Congress to legislate the regulation of child labor. This amendment failed of ratification; the states in general were unwilling to surrender this legislative right to the federal government.

VI: Reform in the States

By 1910 many states had at least a workmen's compensation law (by 1919, all had). There was a good deal of moral legislation in this period—against gambling, cigarettes, alcohol, racing, and prostitution. And women came in for better treatment, gradually acquiring equal rights with men; in industry they came to be specially protected. New causes of action came into being having to do with women: breach of promise and alienation of affection, which have now been abolished in many states. And common-law marriages—marriage by merely living together as man and wife—were recognized by many states.

In technical court procedure and in matters of litigation in general, reforms were many. Arbitration laws were widely adopted, and "small courts" were established for the trial of small claims. The suit for a declaratory judgment was devised, one which merely determined the law in a given set of facts without rendering any final judgment. This is useful in cases where parties are not ready to sue each other but one wishes to know what his rights at law may be.*

In criminal law, minors came to be better protected through the creation of special courts for their trial; the age of criminal responsibility was raised. Habitual criminals, on the other hand, were more severely treated. In many states, upon four convictions the criminal was sentenced for life. But more and more attempts were made to reform the criminal, and corrective institutions multiplied; suspended sentences became frequent; commutations of sentence grew common; and a parole system was often instituted.

In the court system in general one development was geographically necessary in America and was also demanded by a people who were largely localized in their interests. In contrast to the system in England, where judges went on circuit, most courts in the United States came to be permanently and locally fixed.

* It is interesting that the declaratory judgment came into Continental law sooner than into ours. In the German and Austrian systems it is known as *Feststellungsprozess*.

VII: Woodrow Wilson

"There has been something crude and heartless and unfeeling in our haste to succeed and be great."

WOODROW WILSON, IN HIS FIRST INAUGURAL ADDRESS

WOODROW WILSON, elected by a minority when part of the Republican Party split off into the Progressive Party of the rebellious T. R., was an unsuccessful lawyer but a successful educator who also had shown himself an able administrator as Governor of New Jersey. While originally he seemed to be a conservative Democrat, he was a profound student of politics and social jurisprudence, and his advent brought on a volume of progressive legislation which might have increased had not the World War intervened. This included the Adamson Act and the Clayton Act. Whether La Follette's *Seamen's Act*, which exempted labor from the operation of the anti-trust laws, can be called "progressive" is questionable. Current abuses by professional labor bosses have led many to believe that they should be subject to restraint by injunction. There cannot be any doubt of the progressive character of perhaps the most important measure of Wilson's regime, the creation of the *Federal Reserve System* of banking. One of its prime purposes was to decentralize the "money power" by establishing branch government banks in various cities; the idea was to get away from the "bad boys of Wall Street." And in 1916 Wilson injected the federal government into the lending business by the *Farm Loan Act*, which gave the farmer new borrowing resources at reasonable rates of interest.

During Wilson's administration, also, the *Eighteenth Amendment* (the Prohibition Amendment) and its enforcing *Volstead Act* were enacted, ushering in an era of wholesale violation of law and the building up of new industrial and commercial empires, ruled with machine guns and trigger-men. The Volstead Act (the *National Prohibition Act*), which became law in 1919, when repassed over the intelligent veto of President Wilson some months after the ratification of the Eighteenth Amendment, was held constitutional by the Supreme Court in a case remarkable in that the

Court for the first time in its history gave no reasons for its conclusion.*

During the war, Wilson advocated two highly controversial Acts: the *Espionage Act* of 1917, and the *Sedition Act* of 1918. The latter made it a crime even to criticize the administration during the war. These Acts were so strongly worded that no additional censorship law was needed to enable the Attorney-General to suppress almost anything he wished. In the war period suppression of some personal liberties was deemed necessary for the safety of the country, a general thesis with which liberals agreed in part, but the performance of the Attorney-General's office was often extreme enough to arouse considerable ire.

On the credit side, the *Nineteenth Amendment*, giving women the right to vote, was enacted during Wilson's regime, after a long suffragette struggle marked by bitterness and ridicule.

After the war and the Wilson era came Warren Gamaliel Harding. For a country hoping for calmness and peace and prosperity, he coined the word "normalcy." To Daugherty, the Attorney-General, normalcy meant securing sweeping labor injunctions, for strikes were deemed to be wholly against the public good. It was not exactly what might be called a progressive period, and yet many "social" measures were enacted. The *Industrial Rehabilitation Act* of 1920 offered assistance to states to help rehabilitate those injured in industry or occupation. The *Sheppard-Towner Act* of 1921 granted federal appropriations to states for welfare work for the benefit of mothers and infants at childbirth, but many states considered this an interference with their own province and rejected the help which was offered. Aid to agriculture was provided: rural credits were increased, co-operatives encouraged, federal control of agriculture was extended, and supervision over stockyards and grain speculation instituted. The Supreme Court went so far as to approve a measure intended to make the strong railroads carry the weak by paying part of their profits into a national fund for common financing. And the powers of the Interstate Commerce Commission were again increased.

* The *National Prohibition Cases*. Chief Justice White, in a concurring opinion (only McKenna and Clarke dissented), regretted that "the Court has deemed it proper" in so important a case "to state only ultimate conclusions without an exposition of the reasoning by which they have been reached."

CHAPTER 39

Oliver Wendell Holmes, Jr.

"While there still is doubt, while opposite convictions still keep a battlefront against each other, the time for law has not come."

HOLMES, IN A SPEECH IN NEW YORK, 1913

I: The Grand Old Man

FOR MANY YEARS there sat upon the Supreme Court of the United States a tall, handsome old gentleman, with large handlebar mustachios, a full head of white hair, clear-cut features, sharp eyes, and an alert, dignified manner. The Encyclopaedia Britannica gives him a scant forty lines of attention, while it gives his poet-physician father one hundred and forty lines. Many would argue that this treatment should be reversed, not to lessen the stature of the father but to recognize that of the son. For the younger Holmes was one of our truly great jurists, although he had his derogators as well as his adulators. In a predominantly conservative era his opinions seemed opposed to conservatism, and many believe that he gave foundation to the following era, in which the Supreme Court, after a series of appointments by Franklin D. Roosevelt, showed a strong leftist tendency.

Yet Holmes himself was far from being "radical." His personal predilections seem to have been eminently conservative. But in many instances he felt that the majority judges were deciding cases in accordance with their own social or economic bias rather than on strictly constitutional grounds. In one significant dissenting opinion he said: "There is nothing I more deprecate than the use of the Fourteenth Amendment beyond the absolute compulsion of its words to prevent the making of social experiments that an important part of the community desires, in the insulated chambers afforded by the several states, even though the experiments may seem futile or even noxious to me and to those whose judgment I most respect."

This was in the case of *Truax vs. Corrigan*, already referred to. Chief Justice Taft had said in his majority opinion: "The Constitution was intended, its very purpose was, to prevent experimentation with the fundamental rights of the individual." It was apparently with this sentence that Holmes took principal issue. He saw no reason why there should not be social experimentation, however much he or any other judge might dislike it, unless the Constitution clearly forbade it.

On the other hand, he was ever alert to the necessity of confining laws to their intent and proper scope. He showed this in his dissenting opinion in the *Northern Securities case*, delivered shortly after he had been appointed to the Court by President Theodore Roosvelt, in which he held that the Sherman Anti-Trust Act did not apply to the facts in that case. Two competing railroad groups, respectively dominated by Harriman and Hill, two of the great railroad barons of the period of national expansion, had been striving for control of the Northern Pacific Railroad. They finally composed their difficulties by creating the Northern Securities Company to hold the stock of the two competing interests; and the majority of the Supreme Court held that this mechanism was a combination in restraint of trade.

Holmes's position was awaited with interest, for his reputation as a jurist was great, and people wanted to know what this newcomer to the Supreme Court bench would have to say. What he said was most distasteful to the man who had appointed him. He hinted at the danger of judges' losing their balance because of an "accident of immediate overwhelming interest which appeals to the feelings and distorts the judgment." It was his opinion that "if the restraint on the freedom of the members of a combination caused by their entering into a partnership is a restraint of trade, every such combination, the small as well as the great, is within the Act." Thus, though trust busting might have seemed to him a desirable objective, he required that all legislative and judicial objectives must be attained under law and within the actual confines of law.

The background of Oliver Wendell Holmes, Jr., was conservative. He was born in Boston in 1841. When the Civil War broke out, young Oliver enlisted at once in a Massachusetts regiment. He fought three years, saw considerable action and was wounded three times, and attained the rank of Lieutenant-Colonel. At the end of his military service he entered Harvard Law School. Three years after graduation he received his first teaching appointment, as an instructor at the Harvard Law School. Later he became editor of the *American Law Review*, and then edited the twelfth edition of Kent's *Commentaries*. In 1880 he was made lecturer on common law at the Lowell Institute, and the lectures he gave there he converted into a book, *The Common Law*. A work of remarkable erudition and an extremely able exposition of the basis of the common law, written with great charm and simplicity, it brought him an immediate international reputation.

Holmes's teaching career was cut short in 1882 by his appointment to the Massachusetts Supreme Court, where he sat for seventeen years, ending as Chief Justice. His teaching career left its mark, however, for he carried with him in his judicial work the analytical mind of the legal scientist and the pedagogical habits of a professor.

Holmes had no political ambitions. Senator Lodge suggested to him once that he might run for Governor of Massachusetts as a steppingstone to the Senate, and Holmes replied, "But I don't give a damn about being a Senator." However, judicial elevation was something else again; and, when President Theodore Roosevelt appointed him to the United States Supreme Court in 1902, Holmes readily accepted. He was then sixty-one and might have been expected to be near the end of his career. But actually the greatest phase of his career was that which followed, and it covered a period of almost thirty years. He did not retire from the Court until 1932, when he was ninety years old, and he had lost little of his mental vigor even in his last year of office.

II: Holmes Compared with Marshall

HAD NOT A VACANCY on the Supreme Court bench permitted John Adams, in his last days of office, to appoint John Marshall as Chief Justice, the basic interpretation of the Constitution might have been far different from that which we acknowledge today. And while Justice Holmes cannot be given a position in history as important as that of Marshall, it is certainly true that, had President Theodore Roosevelt appointed someone of different intellectual bent than Holmes, the legal history of the past three decades in the United States might have been far different.

There is one interesting contrast between Marshall and Holmes. Marshall was added to a young Court, the policy of which had not yet been fixed. There was no initial minority on that Court, and Marshall became for a long period the spokesman of almost continuously unanimous opinion. However, when deaths and resignations finally enabled later Presidents to make anti-Federalist appointments to the Supreme Court bench, Marshall, to his distress, found himself in the minority. At the end of his career, he feared that the structure of constitutional interpretation of which he had been the foremost architect might fall completely.

Holmes, on the other hand, was never the leader of a majority group and found himself in the minority from the very start, but after his retirement, in 1932, Holmes's approach and point of view became for the most part that of the majority. In his quiet way, he was a rebel. Gifted with an unusually attractive literary style, with great learning and an incisive mind, he hammered away, in his opinions, to induce the Court to his theories of interpretation. In Justice Brandeis he found a ready ally, and in Justice Stone another. In the generation of Justices which followed his retirement, several were "Holmes's men" before their appointment.

III: Holmes's Approach

During his long term on the bench, two great waves of political change struck the United States, and a third impended. The first was the "Square Deal" of Theodore Roosevelt, the second the "New Freedom" of Wilson, and the third the "New Deal" of Franklin D. Roosevelt. Holmes's personal reaction to each of these movements is not clear. He was not interested in discussing his own political or social ideas, but only in what he thought to be the proper interpretation of the Constitution. The interpretation which he advocated might have been called "liberal," but he himself saw only the necessity of making the Constitution fit into a growing, changing society. As he stated in the Truax case, he believed that people had the right to experiment in government if they cared to, and he did not think the Constitution was intended to fetter them.

His approach to the law was eminently philosophical, but his philosophy was realistic and inclined to the fulfillment of a workable democratic state. He said: "This tacit assumption of the solidarity of the interests of society is very common, but seems to us to be false. . . . All that can be expected . . . is that modern legislation should easily and quickly, yet not too quickly, modify itself in accordance with the will of the *de facto* supreme power in the community, and that the spread of an educated sympathy should reduce the sacrifice of the minority to a minimum. . . . The fact is that legislation in this country, as well as elsewhere, is empirical." *

Justice Frankfurter, of the present Supreme Court, has described Holmes's approach as follows: "He scrupulously treated the Constitution as a broad charter of powers for the internal classes of society, and did not construe it as though it were a code which prescribed in detail answers for the social problems of all times." †

To quote from the words of Holmes in *Gompers vs. United States:* ". . . the provisions of the Constitution are not mathematical formulas having their essence in their form: they are organic living institutions transplanted from English soil. Their significance is vital, not formal: it is to be gathered not simply by taking the words and a dictionary, but by considering their origin and the line of their growth."

When Holmes entered the Court, a movement for some restrictive regulation of corporations and of business had already begun. The Interstate Commerce Act was invigorated, and the Federal Trade Commission, the Federal Reserve Board, the Farm Loan Board, the Federal Power Commission, the Railroad Labor Board, and the Tariff Commission were either created or refurbished in Holmes's time. Much of this regulation was abhorrent to many jurists and lawyers as contrary to the strict interpretation of the Constitution. To Holmes, such measures were in line with the desirability of experimentation, permitted by a malleable Constitution, even though he might often personally dislike some proposed

* "The Gas-Stokers' Strike," *American Law Review,* VII (1873), 583. Holmes has been much criticized for advocating an empirical approach to law. I do not believe that he meant to advocate it as much as to express a fact—the fact that the law often does grow empirically.

† Frankfurter, *Mr. Justice Holmes and the Supreme Court,* p. 28.

individual measure. He did not fear what many have condemned as "class legislation," for he recognized that class legislation was necessary and proper and that all that was important was that the transition be easy and the rights of the minority be preserved through tolerance and "educated sympathy." He did not fear words such as "socialism"; he did not fear "radicalism"; but he had no illusions about the perfect state of society, and so was willing to permit experimentation to the end that practice, and trial and error, might lead us into better ways.

Holmes frequently dug beneath some common idea or concept to find out whether it really made sense. For example, he attacked one of the most common shibboleths—that a man was entitled to do what he wished if he did not interfere with his fellow citizens. Holmes pointed out* that the individual was subjected to all sorts of regulation which had nothing to do with interference with his neighbors. Why should there not be more of such regulation if the people deemed it wise? ". . . a constitution is not intended to embody a particular economic theory, whether of paternalism and the organic relation of the citizen to the state or of *laissez faire*. It is made for people of fundamentally different views, and the accident of our finding certain opinions natural and familiar or novel and even shocking ought not to conclude our judgment upon the question whether statutes embodying them conflict with the Constitution of the United States."

Most important, to Holmes, was the necessity for judges to be careful not to stretch constitutional interpretation through their own conceptions of "public policy." Public policy can change, as it did in the case of the use of wines, which had been thought proper since the "time of the Apostles." Judges must not determine public policy in accordance with their own lights, but only in the light of what the public itself deems public policy to be.†

* In *Lochner vs. New York.*

† This is, indeed, a difficult area in jurisprudence. As I have discussed earlier, the safety of our society depends on judicial restraint. It is a function of the legislature to make changes in the law as public policy changes. When judges "interpret" an existing rule of law in the light of what they believe is current "public policy," they often actually change the original intent of a law and so do "judicial legislation." There are many who believe that, while laws must change as society changes, the alterations should come after legislative debate and by legislative action and not by judicial fiat. Yet there are many laws which require an interpretation from the judges because the law itself is, in a sense, a generality requiring specification. In such cases, society must rely on judicial restraint.

In the case of *Abrams vs. United States,* Holmes gave another example of keeping one's eye on the fundamentals. Certain "alien anarchists" had published some leaflets protesting the use of American troops in Russia after the Russian Revolution. They were sent to prison for allegedly having attempted to incite resistance to the United States while at war. Holmes expressed his own views of the defendants' political ideas rather forcefully, this time. He said their creed was one "that I believe to be the creed of ignorance and immaturity when honestly held," but he said further that the creed of the defendants was not the business of the Court. He felt that freedom of speech was the all-important issue, even if it gave license to utter beliefs which were abhorrent to the majority or to himself.

Of the political philosophers whose opinions played so great a part in the development of juridical approaches, we may fairly class Holmes as a mediator between Rousseau and Locke. Locke believed in the inalienable rights of man, Rousseau in the right of the majority to make law, however much minority "rights" might be infringed. Holmes seems to have gone with Rousseau, but with the hope that "the spread of an educated sympathy" would prevent great harm to the minority. Whatever his hopes may have been, Holmes supported the absolute rights of the majority. Advocates of absolute "natural law" and those who feel that it is to the interests of all, even the momentary majority, that minority rights be preserved, will find small comfort in Holmes. Perhaps Holmes, if he had been asked, might well have expressed the desire that minority rights be inalienably preserved; but he felt that one must deal with facts as they are, and he saw as fact that, after all, a majority could do as it wished if it wished.

IV: Louis D. Brandeis

> *"There must be power in the states and the nation to remold, through experimentation, our economic practices and institutions to meet changing social and economic needs."*
>
> BRANDEIS, DISSENTING IN NEW STATE ICE COMPANY VS. LIEBMANN

TO HAVE one particular Justice sit on the bench with him gave Justice Holmes enormous pleasure. This was Louis D. Brandeis, the first Jew to sit on the Supreme Court. His story would have been one for Horatio Alger. The son of poor immigrants, he became an outstandingly successful lawyer with a highly lucrative practice. Toward the end of his career as a private practitioner, he became a crusader for public causes, and his name figured prominently in case after case which involved the public interest or welfare. His amazing success may be attributed largely to his intensive investigations and his fine powers of analysis. But much of this work lined him up against powerful interests, and he made many enemies, so that when President Wilson appointed him to the Supreme Court there was a burst of violent opposition, and a bitter fight against his confirmation was initiated in the Senate. He was accused of unprofessional conduct and of "lack of judicial temperament." Among his opponents was President Lowell of Harvard. Seven ex-presidents of the National Bar Association wrote against him, and ex-President of the United States Taft, who was to be Chief Justice when Brandeis sat on the Supreme Court bench, said that his appointment was a "fearful shock." Most of such opposition probably arose out of a distrust of Brandeis's social ideals, which were foreign to the conservative leaders of the bar and of society.

But the Senate did confirm Brandeis, and though he did remain a radical in the eyes of the conservatives, he came to be universally respected. He remained on the bench until 1939 and, throughout his career there, was extremely careful to act with the utmost propriety, and no breath of personal criticism ever attacked him. Justice Brandeis's character and devotion to principle appeared when Franklin D. Roosevelt tried to pack the Supreme Court. Although Brandeis had sided with the New Deal so often, and as part of a minority which bitterly assailed the majority brethren for decimating the President's legislation, he strongly opposed the measure to reorganize the Supreme Court and made his position cogently clear.

Brandeis had a unique ability to collect and relate facts; to deal abstractly with the mere words of the Constitution without taking into consideration the surrounding human facts seemed fruitless to him. Some liberal Justices, in the days when the Court was predominantly conservative, criticized the majority for deciding cases with their own social bias as guidance. The criticism was a valid one, but the fact is that Brandeis himself did just this. But Brandeis's bias was clear and open, and his opinions were frequently frank rationalizations based upon his social predilections.

He brought a freshness of point of view to the Court, and there can be no doubt that he stimulated his judicial brethren even when they disagreed with him violently. Clear-minded and incisive in his reasoning, he had no overwhelming respect for precedent. He said: "*Stare decisis* is ordinarily a wise rule of action but it is not a universal, inexorable command. . . . [It] does not command that we err again." So often in the minority, he took the opportunity to write carefully prepared and documented dissenting opinions. He almost always agreed with Holmes in the result, but rarely in the approach. Holmes was much more inclined to a judicial point of view than was Brandeis, whose compelling interest lay in achieving "social justice" in the light of the particular surrounding facts—Holmes was a philosopher, Brandeis a reformer.

The influence of Justice Brandeis on the Supreme Court of our era is second only to that of Holmes.

V: Stone and Cardozo

> "*. . . courts are concerned only with the power to enact statutes, not with their wisdom.*"
>
> STONE, IN UNITED STATES VS. BUTLER

> "*Needs that were narrow or parochial a century ago may be interwoven in our day with the well-being of the nation. What is critical or urgent changes with the times.*" CARDOZO, IN HELVERING VS. DAVIS

ANOTHER JUSTICE associated with Holmes during the later part of his career as a dissenter was Harlan Fiske Stone, ex-corporate lawyer, former member of a Wall Street law firm, ex-Dean of the Columbia University Law School, ex-Attorney-General of the United States. He was nominated in 1924 for the Supreme Court by his college mate, the archconservative Calvin Coolidge; and Senator Borah, Senator Norris, and other eminent liberals violently opposed his confirmation. Much to the amazement of those who had feared Stone's conservatism, he turned out, soon after his appointment, to be clearly on the other side of the Court. Stone's association with Holmes and Brandeis was close, yet he did not follow either, maintaining an independent approach and a personal method of judicial consideration. He was a judge by temperament: a profound student, and a careful and patient man. When he later became Chief Justice, and the Court had changed its character with the introduction of many new faces and a good deal of dissension, Stone's days were not as happy as when he was free to write his brilliant dissenting opinions unencumbered by administrative work.

When Justice Holmes retired in 1932, his place was taken by Benjamin Cardozo, the second Jew on the Supreme Court. He was appointed by Hoover, and it was an appointment with which few could have any quarrel. As a justice in New York and as an author on jurisprudence, Cardozo had become perhaps the most eminent judge in the United States outside of the Supreme Court. He became a powerful addition to the minority group in the Court. His opinions, though sometimes a bit florid, were always powerfully persuasive.

That this group of men, Holmes, Brandeis, Stone, and Cardozo, overlapped in service on the Supreme Court had great impact on the course of the Court. They were all doubters of the logical form and the logical process. Cardozo said that you "can give any conclusion a logical form." Or, as Holmes put it, "the whole outline of the law is the resultant of a conflict at every point between logic and good sense—the one striving to work fiction out of inconsistent results, the other restraining and at last overcoming that effort when the results become too manifestly unjust." To quote one more jurist on the point, Lord Wright said that a judge almost always has "some degree of choice." And that choice is, often as not, determined by bias, social or philosophical. That is unavoidable. The only safeguard against its misuse is the selection of the best judges possible, a principle which has not always been observed by our Presidents.

I cannot end this chapter on Holmes, Brandeis, Stone, and Cardozo without registering my belief that all of them must have been affected strongly by the teachings of both William James and John Dewey.

William James was the exponent of pragmatism. To define briefly, and perhaps oversimply, this complex thesis: Pragmatism holds that the "truth" of human ideals and cognitions is proved only by their practical effects.

John Dewey also was a pragmatist, and he spent most of his time and energy in pedagogy, in which he introduced so many new approaches and new methods that he virtually revolutionized the science of teaching. He was the father of the school of "progressive education," an approach to education which, after a long period of popularity, has lately come into disfavor. It has been held responsible for why "Johnny can't read." John Dewey exercised a most direct influence upon our judiciary, supporting a thesis, found in the opinions of Holmes, Cardozo, and others, that the logic of the Anglo-Saxon judges is not the ordinary deductive logic in which a major premise is driven to a conclusion. He said that our judicial logic has consisted of the discovery of premises out of the "total situation," or ascertaining the "statements of general principle and of particular fact, which are worthy to serve as premises."

CHAPTER 40

Franklin D. Roosevelt and After

"Our Constitution is so simple and practical that it is possible always to meet extraordinary needs by changes in emphasis and arrangement without loss of essential form." F.D.R., FIRST INAUGURAL ADDRESS

I: The Planned Economy of the New Deal

FRANKLIN DELANO ROOSEVELT, who dealt the cards during the New Deal, aroused worship in his followers and bitterness in his opponents. No President since Andrew Jackson (or certainly since Lincoln) has caused such a tumult of feeling, and it must be left to historians of the future to evaluate the period and the man who dominated it. However, even at this short range, it is clear that it was a period of "planned economy" and one in which the power of the national government was enormously increased at the expense of the states.

It is not clear that Roosevelt initially intended to go so far in these directions. One gets the impression from reading the biographies and other materials available that he had few definite plans at the time of his inauguration. It would seem that he was determined to cure the economic ills from which the country suffered, that he adopted such mechanisms as appeared to him to be curative, and that, once having taken the path of extensive legislation, he drifted quickly into the planned-economy point of view, which brought with it an enormous increase in federal power.

Though a wealthy aristocrat by birth, he did not represent the conservative viewpoint which might have been expected of one of his class but became instead the leader of those who thought the country's ills were attributable chiefly to business mismanagement and greed, and whose chief aim was the betterment of the life of the ordinary man. Standing on such a personal platform and possessing a political adroitness not matched by anyone in our history, not even Thomas Jefferson, he was the man of the hour. His attractive personality, his rare ability to induce strong personal loyalty in those who surrounded him, his quality as an orator, his inspiring courage in the face of a tragic physical handicap, his limitless self-confidence —all these, as well as his social point of view, gave him enormous public support and affection and enabled him to stay at the top longer than any man before him.

He reached the top of the political pyramid at a most difficult and critical time. The depression which started in the administration of Herbert Hoover had brought economic chaos, and the country was conditioned to drastic reform. Far more radical voices than that of Roosevelt were being heard in the United States, and it has been justly said that, had he not been willing to go partly to the left in his early days, a more powerfully radical movement might have become a serious danger to our form of society. President Hoover and his associates had announced that there would be a short period of unhappiness, after which the law of supply and demand, if not interfered with, would restore normal conditions. That might have been true, but the country felt very sick when Franklin Delano Roosevelt took office, and it was in no mood for waiting. Those who were without jobs, who could not pay their rent, who could not sell their merchandise, who could not get their money out of banks which had failed, were not hopeful that the old capitalistic system would correct its own maladjustments. F.D.R.'s overwhelming victory at the polls was deemed a mandate to overhaul the machinery thoroughly.

He started off with vigor. No one who listened to his charming and confident voice on the radio in those dark days could forget it. The American system seemed to be flying to bits, and most of his listeners, even conservative men of business, felt that a savior had been found. There can be no doubt that the President, by quick and firm action, restored a badly shaken public confidence and gave the nation renewed hope.

It had become apparent enough that it would be necessary to close the banks in order to prevent further failures and to pave the way for legislation which might stabilize the tragically disorganized banking system. President Hoover had planned such a closing but was in the embarrassing and ineffective position of a defeated candidate for re-election and was faced with a hostile Congress. He requested the co-operation of the President-Elect, but this co-operation was refused, though banks continued to close at an alarming rate. But after his inauguration, F.D.R. adopted the plan prepared by Hoover and promptly closed the banks under an unrepealed 1917 war measure. Though capable of quick decision, F.D.R. rarely planned far in advance. Having closed the banks, he had no plan arranged for reopening them, but advisers were put to work, in collaboration with several of Hoover's Treasury officials, and a bank reform measure was finally devised and rushed through Congress as the *Banking Act* of 1933.

Legislation then began to flow from a willing Congress at a terrific rate, under the stimulus of the President and his corps of legislative advisers and draftsmen. The next important measure was the abandonment of the gold standard. Great Britain, among others, had already shaken itself loose from it. When the American banks reopened, they were prevented from paying out any gold or gold certificates. On April 5 the President issued an order under the Banking Act prohibiting all transactions in gold.* Many economists predicted that abandoning the gold standard would be against the public interest, and lawyers pointed out that these measures would constitute abrogations of the right of contract, for bonds and other contracts provided for the payment of gold, and gold could no longer be paid. But Congress, by joint resolution, declared the right to require gold payments to be against "public policy," and the Supreme Court eventually refused relief to litigants who insisted upon receiving the gold which they had been promised in public and private contracts.

It is very difficult to defend Roosevelt's abandonment of the gold

* How strangely the law can change was pointed out by L. J. Dickinson in a speech in Cleveland in 1934. He said: "A year ago, if I had $100 in gold in my pocket, I was a law-abiding citizen; if I perchance had a pint of whiskey, I was a criminal. Today, if I have the whiskey, I am a law-abiding citizen; but if I have the gold I am a criminal violating the law." The *Twenty-first Amendment*, repealing the Prohibition Amendment, had been approved in February, 1933, and sufficient states ratified it by December of the same year.

standard. The step was wholly unnecessary and accomplished nothing salutory. It put our government in the position of violating solemn contractual promises, a precedent perhaps as dangerous as that of prohibiting the holding of gold. If one kind of innocent property, gold, may be denied to us by government, why not others! Moreover, it is quite possible that some of the rapid inflation of the ensuing decades might have been avoided had the natural restraints of an exchangeable currency been available to the public.

F.D.R.'s Secretary of Labor, Miss Perkins, in her book *The Roosevelt I Knew,* has said that the President did not know much about economics; and he had never had much experience with commerce or the making of money. To fill the gaps in his own knowledge, he surrounded himself with a group of professors and young intellectuals who came to be known as the Brain Trust. Few of these had had any practical economic experience, but they had no lack of enthusiasm, proposing an endless stream of measures from which the President selected such as appealed to him. Some were directed at restoring business activity, others at the President's cherished objective of bettering the condition of "the Forgotten Man" —the underprivileged. The President himself seemed relatively unconcerned with method. He was essentially a believer in the end justifying the means. It is remarkable that, in his record-breaking administration, and despite the fact that extraordinary legislation was the order of the day, he never once proposed an amendment to the Constitution. He startled a good many Americans by stating that amending the Constitution was too cumbersome a process. Miss Perkins reports him as saying: "We have to do the best we know how to do at the moment. If it doesn't turn out right we can modify as we go along." He felt that action was all-important, and experimented endlessly in order to try to find the way to get the country's business machinery properly in motion again and to promote social justice.

Perhaps under the influence of the growing movement toward paternalism in various parts of the world, Roosevelt adopted the thesis that business cannot be trusted to manage itself and that government must step in to plan and manage. Opposed were those who felt that we were approaching dangerously close to the managed economy of an authoritarian state and also those who felt that the President's selection of advisers and assistants like Henry Wallace, Harry Hopkins, and Henry Morgenthau did not indicate that either he or his associates were qualified for the extremely delicate and difficult task of directing our complex economy. But the thesis appealed to the majority of the people and was supported by a Congress even the conservative Southern members of which were kept in line by the President's astute political management.

He himself denied that the government sought control of industrial, farming, and other economic enterprises. He said that government was now to be in "partnership" with business. It seemed, however, that the government was to be the senior partner. One of the first evidences of this tendency was the *Agricultural Adjustment Act*, enacted in 1933. Prices of farm products had dropped drastically, and farmers all over the country were in severe distress. As the law of supply and demand had created havoc at the moment, the President's solution was to make supply fit demand. Too much food was being produced, so that Act gave bonuses to farmers who plowed their crops under or slaughtered their pigs. Moreover, the Secretary of Agriculture was given the right to assess and adjust a tax upon the processors of farm products to maintain prices at the levels of the period before World War I.

The AAA was declared unconstitutional in the autumn of 1935 in a six-to-three decision of the Supreme Court. The majority opinion held that the federal government had no authority under the Constitution to regulate agricultural matters, because this was a province of the states, and that the tax imposed on the processors was unconstitutional because it taxed one group (the processors) for the benefit of another group (the farmers), by giving the latter bonuses. Justice Stone disagreed violently with the majority opinion, and Brandeis and Cardozo joined him in a dissent, indicating the belief that the majority Justices had decided against the Act essentially because they disliked it. Stone maintained that the depressed state of agriculture was a national matter and a tax to be used for its amelioration was entirely proper. Whatever the respective merits of the two conflicting opinions, the decision aroused such indignation in the President's entourage that it may have marked the beginning of a movement to remodel the Supreme Court. New legislation was later devised and enacted, however, which exercised control over agriculture and prices but escaped conflict with a Supreme Court which, by that time, was, in any event, more friendly to New Deal legislation.

It is one of the remarkable aspects of our political society that the subsidization of agriculture, which has continued in radical form ever since Roosevelt's day, has been acquiesced in by the people. Billions have been spent by the government to fill countless warehouses full of stagnant agricultural products. These have been paid for through taxes, contributed in greater part by the amazingly inert urban population.

On June 16, 1933, another piece of legislation was approved which tended toward a managed economy. The strange thing about this measure, looking at it in retrospect, is that it was so contrary to the general character of the American economic system, and yet it was no mere imposition upon the country by the President—it was enthusiastically welcomed by a great part of the business community. It was the *National Industrial Recovery Act,* the NIRA. Its stated objectives were: "to remove obstructions to the free flow of interstate and foreign commerce . . . to provide for the general welfare . . . to induce and maintain united action of labor and management under adequate government sanctions and supervision, to eliminate unfair competitive practices, to promote capacity of industries, to avoid undue restriction of production (except as may be temporarily required), to increase the consumption of industrial and agricultural products by increasing purchasing power, to reduce and relieve unemployment, to improve standards of labor, and otherwise to rehabilitate industry and to conserve natural resources."

This was a big order. The mechanism provided for its accomplishment was the creation of trade associations in each industry. Each association was to establish a code of fair trade practices which, after approval by the President, would become law in the industry. If in any industry no such code was adopted, the President would impose his own code of fair practices upon it. Under the law, uniform systems of accounting, general business practices, the use of equipment and plants, even the maintenance of a price structure, could be legislated by the codes. So far, business groups approved wholeheartedly. But they were not all so pleased with an addition made to the Act before passage which required each code to contain a clause compelling collective bargaining.

The President was also given the right to impose maximum working hours, minimum rates of wages, and other working conditions for labor. He was authorized to enjoin the importation of foreign merchandise which imperiled the maintenance of any code, a provision which came strangely from the party which had traditionally supported free trade. And the codes were to be exempt from the anti-trust laws. It was in many respects a paradoxical piece of legislation. The administration was generally opposed to business monopoly, yet the NIRA, in a sense, established and perpetuated monopoly. Starting a new and competing business in a field covered by a code was, at best, difficult.

When the NIRA was enacted, the President said: "History probably will record the National Industrial Recovery Act as the most important and far-reaching legislation ever enacted by the American Congress. It represents a supreme effort to stabilize for all time the many factors which made for the prosperity of the nation and the preservation of American standards." In this opinion he was probably supported by the business community as a whole, conservative and liberal alike. In one year, more than four hundred codes were put into effect; a new day in economic planning seemed to have dawned. But the administration of the Act turned out to be difficult; the whole plan gradually came into general disfavor, at least partly because of the degree of regulation which it imposed. And so, when the Supreme Court, in the *Schlechter case*, held the NIRA unconstitutional on the ground that it regulated *intrastate* commerce and that it delegated legislative powers to the President, the corpse of the NIRA was mourned by few. Roosevelt, however, although the decision had been unanimous, spoke of the Court acting as if still in the "horse and buggy days."

The regulatory and restrictive laws which poured from the legislative hoppers were so great in number that any detailed treatment would serve no purpose here. Among them were some like the new and improved *Food, Drug, and Cosmetic Act* and the *Securities Act* (and its later elaboration, the *Securities and Exchange Act*) which were obviously desirable deterrents to old abuses and were opposed for long by only a very small and self-interested minority.

II: Priming the Pump

THE GRAVEST problem facing the country was unemployment, and this the President attacked with promptness and vigor. Great masses of people were in actual distress, and starving people could certainly not wait for laws, either legislative or economic, to take their course. Therefore the *Emergency Relief Act* was approved in May, 1933, under which the federal government made grants to the states for issuing relief payments to the unemployed; it also authorized the purchase of surpluses in the open market for distribution through state and local authorities. This was the first of many steps which, through grants and subsidies, put the federal government into fields of activity which were clearly in the province of the states. Though the central government might not itself compete or regulate in state areas of law, the result of such subsidization was, in practice, a strong, if indirect, control by the federal government. But the immediate outcry against the Emergency Relief Act was not on this basis: it was widely condemned as a dole.

To overcome this sound objection, the President used various other measures to help the unemployed by creating new employment. Among the measures used for this purpose were the *Unemployment Relief Act* of 1933, the *Civilian Conservation Corps,* and the *Civil Works Administration*. As the executive in charge of the vast spending program, Roosevelt appointed Harry Hopkins, characterized by his biographer, Robert E. Sherwood, as "a welfare worker from the corn belt, who tended to regard money (his own as well as other people's) as something to be spent as quickly as possible." * There was bad planning, waste, and even political manipulation of relief funds, but the President was chiefly concerned with keeping the otherwise unemployed alive and seemed untroubled by the methods of administration. He soon came to advocate the theory that we could spend ourselves out of the depression and into prosperity by increasing the purchasing power of the people, and that it did not make much difference how this came about.

This was "pump priming," and it also took another form. Public works of all kinds were designed. F.D.R., for example, shared with large sections of the public a dislike of the great privately owned public-utility companies. Their history was not free from scandal, and rates were in many cases much higher than necessary, as a direct result of stock watering and fabulous private gain. More careful regulation of such companies was one answer, and was later instituted. Another was to compete with them, and this would allegedly serve at the same time to create more employment. So various great public-utility works projects were authorized. There was the *Tennessee Valley* project, to dam the waters of that river at several points, create power plants, and develop the adjacent

* Sherwood, *Roosevelt and Hopkins*.

areas. Similar projects were either organized by the federal government or supported as projects of the states under the *Public Works Administration,* including the Grand Coulee Dam on the Columbia River and another at Bonneville, nearby.

The wisdom of these public power projects has been seriously questioned. For the government to compete with private industry has distressed those who dislike extensions of government function and governmental bureaucracy. Moreover, the competition is held by many to be on an unfair basis, for private industry must pay taxes and public enterprises do not. Therefore, the comparative cost accounting is unrealistic, and it is claimed that the true net cost of public power to the taxpayer exceeds the cost of that privately supplied. On the other side of the argument are the paternalists who believe in a constant increase of governmental participation in production.

Housing also received the President's attention. An *Emergency Housing Division* was created by an Act of June, 1933, under which a *Housing Corporation* was authorized to buy land, build houses, and finance local projects. A *Resettlement Administration,* created in 1935 to attempt to improve rural housing conditions and to increase employment, built a model city in a mining region of West Virginia and conducted other municipal experiments. All together, under the Public Works Administration, in the course of one year, more than seventeen thousand projects were approved and received allotments of funds. Much of this was "pump priming" intended to stimulate business. It involved the theory of deficit spending, under which even the possibility of balancing the national budget was abandoned, and these New Deal measures rapidly enlarged the public debt. This alarmed many but was supported by those who were mistakenly confident that the aggregate spending would restore good business.

III: Social Justice

AMONG the many "reform" measures enacted by a willing Congress at the instigation of Roosevelt were some which had a purely social purpose. Of this type was the *Social Security Act,* which was the first of what may come to be a long series calculated to protect the people "from the cradle to the grave." The direct motivation for such legislation is obviously benign, but there is a strong body of feeling that it may lead to overcentralization and to paternalism of an extreme nature, create a monumental bureaucracy, be over-costly, and enervate the public. It is difficult to know where to draw the line that separates desirable "reform" of our social system from what would, in fact, endanger it.

Our "social security" is, of course, a measure of paternalism. It is, in effect, an addition to the income tax, collected from the people on the theory that they are too improvident to protect themselves and that the government must take their money and protect them with it. As the system works out, following generations will have to pay a great part of the bill for the "protection" of their predecessors. Moreover, the system in operation works rather absurdly. A man can have a million dollars per year in investment income and yet receive social security, while one who works for a modest wage is by this excluded from this paternal benefit.

The most important step taken by Roosevelt in his program of "social justice" was the enactment of the *Wagner-Connally Labor Relations Act,* generally known as the *Wagner Act,* perhaps the most controversial piece of New Deal legislation. The President wanted higher wages not only because of their pump-priming effect but also because he believed that labor should receive a greater share of the income of the nation. He saw that the struggle of labor for higher wages and better working conditions would be made far easier if collective bargaining were compulsory. The NIRA, even in its brief life, strengthened organized labor considerably but it needed some further government support in its efforts to deal with capital on something like an equal basis.

The Wagner Act therefore forbade any employer to interfere with or dominate a union, compelled collective bargaining, and established a Labor Relations Board to supervise the executive machinery of the Act. There was little doubt in the minds of the majority that labor needed some such assistance from the government, and any criticism of what was called the "Magna Charta of labor" was unpopular with both the President and the people. But many critics felt that an opportunity had been missed to protect the individual worker and the public. One of the criticisms was that no safeguards were provided against arbitrary control of unions by entrenched leadership at the same time that labor organization was being strengthened. The minority suggested requiring not only democratic control of unions but also public incorporation of labor unions (so that there would be public responsibility) and public accounting of their expenditures.

Better planning of the Wagner Act and more impartial administration of it by the Labor Board and later regulating agencies might have prevented abuses which led a Republican Congress, in 1948, to supplant it with the *Taft-Hartley Act.** Among the injustices were that a labor leader could address employees at will to induce them to organization or strike, while the employer himself was prevented from exercising his right of free speech on the same subject. Unions were wholly free of responsibility; injunctions against them had been made impossible by the *Norris-La Guardia Act*, yet the Board had the virtual right of injunction against employers. Frequent strikes in basic industries did considerable damage to the general economy, but there was no legal way of stopping arbitrary abuses of power, and the President, enjoying the discomfort of "big business," showed no desire to curb such abuses.

The Wagner Act did not regulate wages and hours, because it was feared that it might then meet the same fate at the hands of the Supreme Court as had the NIRA. But the 1936 *Walsh-Healy Government Contracts Act* made certain conditions of employment prerequisite to the granting of government contracts, an effective means of regulating wages and hours in a period when so many contracts were being offered by the government.

IV: The Recession and the War

WHILE THINGS were on the upgrade, Roosevelt had said proudly: "We planned it this way." But the "recession" which came in the fall of 1936 cast grave doubt on the validity of the planned economy. It was a serious depression; by 1938, over eleven million Americans were unemployed. The President's answer to this new problem

* An indication of the arbitrary conduct of the administrating agencies was given in a 1940 decision of the Supreme Court (then overwhelmingly composed of Roosevelt appointees) that the National Labor Relations Board was not intended by Congress to have "a virtually unlimited discretion to devise punitive measures, and thus to prescribe the penalties or fines which the Board may think would effectuate its policies." But the President's own point of view is evidenced by his veto of the *Walter Bill*, which required all of the vast number of government agencies to announce the rules under which they operated and provided mechanisms of review for administrative decisions.

was to repeat the old formula, with variations—more legislation, more public works, and more pump priming. But the country remained depressed until the President's growing concern over foreign affairs finally brought relief to the business community and to the people. When Lend-Lease was implemented, the government was able to create a new prosperity by ordering munitions and equipment on a vast scale. Then, although the President's powers were enormously increased as we progressed closer to war, businessmen breathed more easily over the increased production which war preparation made necessary.

In 1940 Roosevelt was elected to his record-breaking third term. He justified this breach of precedent by declaring it his "clear duty . . . to preserve our neutrality." His fourth term was likewise justified by his conviction of indispensability, despite the injunction of Thomas Jefferson, the founder of Roosevelt's party: "If the principle of rotation be a sound one, as I conscientiously believe it to be with respect to this office, no pretext should ever be permitted to dispense with it, because there never will be a time when real difficulties will not exist, and furnish a plausible pretext for dispensation." At any rate, with our entry into war, unemployment ceased, business boomed, and many irritations were forgotten. The enormous New Deal increase in the public debt became a trifle compared with the addition brought by the war; the greatly extended administrative control of the country, with its accompanying increase in bureaucracy, became as nothing compared with the administrative machinery required to run the war.

V: F.D.R. and the Supreme Court

NOT ONLY the AAA and the NIRA, but other cherished measures of the New Deal also came a cropper when they reached the Supreme Court in the early years of the Roosevelt administration, and the President's annoyance mounted—an annoyance shared by Congress and the public, which supported his legislation overwhelmingly. But one measure which he proposed failed of adoption because it lost the President the support of many of his otherwise ardent followers. This was his proposal for remodeling the Supreme Court of the United States.

It has been an essential of our political system that the executive, the legislative, and the judicial branches of the national government should each be independent and, thus, a check on the others. Many of the best minds among the framers of the Constitution anticipated that the Supreme Court would have, as one of its functions, the right to determine the constitutionality of legislation, and this right was secured by the work of John Marshall. Without independence, the Court could not exercise this vital function. It would be subservient to other branches of government, legislative or executive, which it had become its part to check. The framers of the Constitution had seen the necessity of judicial independence by writing into that charter a provision that federal judges should hold office during good behavior or for life.

The Justices of the Supreme Court cannot be expected to be wholly objective. They cannot entirely escape their social or political predilections. It was to be expected, therefore, that the Court would, from time to time, change complexion as its membership changed. There have been times when its general tone was conservative and times when it has been liberal. Nor would a Justice always follow the bent of the President who appointed him. The late Chief Justice Stone was appointed by that eminently conservative Republican President, Calvin Coolidge; and the late Justice Cardozo was appointed by the equally conservative Republican Hoover. Justice McReynolds, appointed by the progressive Democratic President Woodrow Wilson, turned out to be a staunch conservative.

At any rate, when Franklin D. Roosevelt took office after a succession of conservative Presidents who had made many appointments to the Supreme Court, he faced a bench which, in the majority, had conservative tendencies. Four of the nine judges were outright conservatives: Pierce Butler (an eminent jurist), Willis Van Devanter (also a distinguished jurist), George Sutherland (a former Republican leader of the Senate)—these three appointed by Harding—and James McReynolds. Brandeis (appointed by Wilson), Stone, and Cardozo were usually in the minority. In between these two groups were Charles Evans Hughes, the Chief Justice, who was first appointed by Taft but resigned to run for President and was reappointed by Coolidge; and Owen J. Roberts, appointed by Hoover. Roberts at first was more likely to side with the conservatives. Hughes was perhaps slightly further to the left than Roberts, but he, too, had somewhat conservative tendencies. There were many five-to-four decisions against Roosevelt-preferred measures, and the line-up generally saw McReynolds, Sutherland, Butler, and Van Devanter stoutly on the winning side, supported by either Hughes or Roberts, or both; with Stone, Brandeis, and Cardozo on the losing side, sometimes supported by Hughes or Roberts.

Roosevelt was not alone in his irritation at the conservative nature of the Court personnel and its apparent determination to apply a conservative point of view to New Deal legislation. There was a widespread feeling in the country, and an intense one, that the Supreme Court was blocking progressive legislation because of the personal political and social views of the majority of the "Nine Old Men." Some went so far as to advocate withdrawing the Court's right to declare legislation unconstitutional or giving Congress the right to override an adverse decision as it could override a veto. But the vast majority, even those who were most bitter against obstruction by the Supreme Court, did not favor any change in its functions.

The President thought something should be done about it. He finally devised a bill for the reorganization of all the federal judicial system, which was of course directed at the Supreme Court. It provided that if any Justice should fail to retire upon reaching the age of seventy years (an age which several of the conservative Justices had already passed) the President could appoint another Justice to sit with the Court and could thus enlarge the Court by a maximum of six additional members.

In sending the proposed measure to Congress, the President accompanied it with a covering message, in which he pointed out that the poor Supreme Court had a great deal of business to do, inferring that it was all too much for the Nine Old Men (or those of them who disagreed with his political premises). He frankly stated his opinion that a "constant infusion of new blood in the courts" was required by "modern complexities," and that "new facts become blurred through old glasses fitted, as it were, for the needs of another generation; older men, assuming that the scene is the same as it was in the past, cease to explore or inquire into the present or the future." Had he forgotten about old Justice Holmes, who was still alert and flexible when sitting in the Court at the age of ninety?

Like any other human institution, the Supreme Court is not perfect. George Washington made certain that the Court would strengthen the Union, by confining his judicial appointments to persons who he knew would act upon the Federalist thesis. He did not try to appoint a Court which would be a cross-section of the opinion of the country. Adams appointed Marshall as Chief Justice in a political last-ditch attempt to save the Court for Federalist principles. The Federalist character of the Court thus remained for many years after the Party itself had gone into oblivion. With very few exceptions, each President has made his appointments with the idea in mind of securing representation upon the Court for that type of political, economic, or social thought which he himself has espoused. Even Justice Holmes was appointed on this basis. It is reported that, before the appointment, Theodore Roosevelt inquired whether "Holmes was in entire sympathy with our views."

In his annoyance at the personnel of the Supreme Court during his first years in office, Franklin D. Roosevelt was reacting no differently from other Presidents, particularly Andrew Jackson. And when Roosevelt made a series of appointments calculated to change the conservative tenor of the Court he did so within his right. It was regrettable that he did not have the patience to await his opportunity to do just that, for which he could not have been criticized seriously, but, instead, precipitated the unfortunate battle to remodel the Court to suit his own ends. It was said in F.D.R.'s defense that his was not the first attempt to remodel the Court. The number of Justices had been changed several times to suit the convenience of Presidents and Congress. But the last of these changes had taken place in 1869, the number of Supreme Court Justices had been constant ever since, and both the motivation and the method of the President in attempting his remodeling of the Court found the country predominantly against him.

The Supreme Court bill was drawn in private and was sprung upon Congress and the public without warning, causing consternation among many of the President's closest advisers. Though some prominent legal lights supported it, it received the wholesale condemnation of the bar. The proposed measure was obviously intended to make the Court completely subservient to the will of the legislature or of the President. It could have spelled the end of the independence of the Supreme Court in the exercise of its essential function as guardian of the Constitution.

The bill was defeated by a small majority, but the closeness of the defeat did not measure its severity, for it came at a time when Congress was overwhelmingly inclined to do the President's bidding.

Soon after this defeat, Justice Van Devanter resigned, and this gave the President the opportunity to make an appointment which would swing the Court from a conservative to a leftward complexion, particularly as Justice Roberts now showed some inclination to side with the left side of the Court on many issues. As his appointee, the President decided upon Senator Hugo Black, a vigorous supporter of New Deal measures in the Senate, who might be presumed to be willing to carry his approval of such legislation into his duties as Justice. But to the consternation of the President and his supporters, it was discovered that the appointee had once belonged to the Ku Klux Klan. Negroes, Jews, and Catholics rushed into print to condemn Black's selection; but after he made a public disavowal of sympathy for the Klan, the Senate approved him. It must, of course, be said for Mr. Justice Black that nothing in his opinions on the Court has indicated any trace of bigotry in him.

From this point on, the Court rapidly changed its character and became prone to ratify the President's legislation. Sutherland, Butler, Brandeis, McReynolds, Hughes, Cardozo, and Stone were eventually supplanted by Reed, Frankfurter, Douglas, Byrnes (who resigned to become Secretary of State), Rutledge (deceased), Murphy (deceased), Jackson, Vinson and Clark. Other substitutions followed. The present Court consists of Chief Justice Warren (a Liberal appointed by President Eisenhower, and a man without previous judicial experience), Justices Black, Frankfurter, Clark and Douglas (holdovers from the Roosevelt-Truman era), Harlan, Stewart, Brennan (a Liberal Democrat appointed by Eisenhower), and White (President Kennedy's first appointee). While there are some very able men among the present group, it is the general opinion of the bar that the Court has lost much of its prestige as a result of many of the appointments made, successively, by Roosevelt, Truman and Eisenhower. Some of our greatest judges and jurists, for example the late Learned Hand, have been passed by in favor of appointments for political purposes or to award a political plum. Moreover, the astonishing number of dissents and the astounding number of rather quarrelsome five-to-four decisions have left the bar, in general, with a feeling of regret that the Supreme Court of today has not its proper stature. A good deal of the reverence formerly felt by lawyers for the Supreme Court has been lost.

VI: Administrative Elephantiasis

IT WAS REPORTED toward the end of 1946 that the Washington office of the Office of Price Administration was sorting its files and that these consisted of 850,000 cubic feet of records. They would have filled 106,000 four-drawer filing cabinets. If put into letter-sized folders, they would have stacked 170 miles high. At the peak of the agency's work, its records comprised 1,250,000 cubic feet. And this is only one agency of the government.

A growing tendency toward increased administrative machinery in our government was rapidly accelerated during the period of the New Deal by the creation of the great multitude of "alphabet soup" agencies. Led by President Roosevelt, the country seemed to have arrived at the conclusion that "the greatest happiness for the greatest number" required intensive and broad government regulation. The war, and its necessary accompanying regulations, intensified this. Lawyers and accountants and other specialists were kept busy by businessmen, looking up applicable regulations, keeping in touch with new ones, preparing the mass of reports and returns and other forms required by administrative law, and, in other ways, helping the businessmen and others through the maze of new law. With the end of the war came the gradual dropping of much of the wartime regulation, but a tendency in Washington persisted to retain controls as much as possible.

Each agency had its own rules and regulations. Congress would pass a law creating a new agency and giving it authority to regulate itself. Rules made by administrative officials were emitted at such a rapid rate, and changed so frequently, that neither Congressmen nor businessmen could possibly keep up with them. These administrative rules were, in effect, laws, absolute in nature and often beyond appeal. In many fields of human activity, the federal legislature had abandoned its legislative function to administrative officials.

The student of law and government can have little doubt that this was an unhealthy trend. Roscoe Pound, our foremost living jurist,* has said: "Such processes as we have been developing belong to lands which believe in government by an omnicompetent

* See pages 461 *et seq*.

superman with a hierarchy of supermen under him to whom the life, liberty, and property of the citizen are to be subordinated; who are so all-wise as to know offhand what the public interest demands in each case and need no hearing or evidence or arguments to advise them, but are to adjust all relations and order all conduct by the light of their ex-officio wisdom in a political organization of society which does not recognize private rights." As to the general way in which some of our new administrative agencies have operated, Pound commented: "The ordinary business and the ordinary man are coerced into settlements and consent decrees to their injury and in defiance of their rights. The general tendency has been to show a marked unfairness toward business and individual enterprise. More than one of these agencies has seemed to indicate a policy of pushing all business and industry and enterprise into the hands of the government and thus bringing about an economic revolution."

One mechanical improvement fortunately took place with the passage of the *Administrative Procedure Act*, a measure long studied and finally recommended by the American Bar Association to make practice before government agencies somewhat uniform, to give certain safeguards to the public, and to give protection against administrative absolutism by assuring the right of judicial review. But it seems essential that we resist permitting ourselves to be seduced into a bureaucratic paternalism. To quote Roscoe Pound once more: "We need to be vigilant that while we are combating [totalitarian] regimes . . . , we do not allow a regime of autocratic bureaus to become so entrenched at home as to lead us in the same direction."

VII: The Group Pressure System

As JUSTICE HOLMES HAS SAID, there is a natural conflict of interests in society, and class legislation is to be expected. Our own history bears this out, for we have not been free from the plague of pressure groups since the very beginning of the Union. In the most recent period, a good deal of our law has been made by the pressure of such groups upon our legislators, and it is a regrettable fact that our current groups are becoming ever more efficiently implemented for pressure.

The most obvious pressure group at the present time is organized labor. With great political strength, it makes its presence and its desires known to legislators and to politicians, both federal and state. With money to expend for the purpose, it maintains well-organized bureaus and is served by a lobby at Washington. It maintains "educational" organizations which publish and circulate propaganda of a political nature, and it is alert actively to support its favored political candidates, directly or indirectly, with money, and to supply from its own ranks a multitude of political workers. It is a rare event when labor organizations support a Republican candidate, and it may be said fairly that "Labor" is enormously influential in the Democratic Party.

Capital is also organized for pressure, although it does not directly command a very large vote. There are business organizations like the National Association of Manufacturers and the Chambers of Commerce which lobby and propagandize. In the matter of campaign contributions, an element of the greatest importance in our political system, both labor and organized capital do their bit, but the political contributions of organized labor have grown increasingly large and decisive as union treasuries have increased in size and labor leaders have taken an increasing part in the political arena. Enormous sums are spent by unions in activities, literary and otherwise, which are termed "educational" but are in fact political. The individual union member has had no choice in the matter. His labor bosses have decided for him what his compulsory contributions shall be used for. The Supreme Court has recently given a dissident union member the relief that, if he could show that part of his dues and contributions have been used for a political purpose of which he disapproved, he could sue to get a proportionate part of his money back. This is hardly a measure of practical relief against the improper use of union funds for political purposes.

There is a farmer pressure group, not organized into as huge units as in labor, but extremely effective. Various farm organizations have loud voices, funds to work with, and lobbies and active agents at Washington and in the state capitals. There are also other powerful pressure groups devoted to special interests, such as special industrial groups, served by trade associations which watch pending legislation and rush to the defense of their patrons. The number of trade associations is legion, and each has a legislative ax to grind. The bankers have their alert association; the doctors and lawyers and other professionals have their associations.

Geographical groups must not be lost sight of. There is the South, whose legislators at Washington try their best to perpetuate segregation. Religious groups are alert, as well. The Catholic Church is well organized for political pressure. Jews spring to joint action just as quickly when they are endangered or troubled by pending legislation, or when an issue like Palestine arises. Some of the Protestant sects have organizations which can act when it is necessary. And there is a rapidly growing pressure behind the Negroes, who are beginning to understand that organization is advisable in our United States in order to get political or legislative action.

The American Legion became a pressure group, joined by veterans of World War II. One could go on listing American pressure groups for pages. Much legislation is presented by them. As soon as it is, others exert counterpressure. The legislator, looking to his political fences at home and hoping to keep everyone happy, has a difficult time. And upon him is exerted a very special kind of pressure, that of his political organization, which may have an interest in conflict with that of the individual legislator's group at home.

Loud voices often make up for lack of numbers; and legislators must make an art of listening carefully to the noise to catch how many voices compose it.

CHAPTER 41

Roscoe Pound and Legal Philosophy

I: Our Law in Flux

THE REPUBLICAN VICTORY of 1946 was recorded through the swinging over of a large number of voters to a more conservative point of view. Among them were many who were in complete sympathy with the social objectives of the New Deal, and who believed that forward-looking and highly desirable social measures had been enacted under the Roosevelt administrations. But they had concluded that there had been mixed up with these magnificent pieces of legislation many measures of impractical idealism. They felt even more strongly that paternalism, based upon the theory that a group of men in Washington could direct a planned economy with precision and safety, had proved undesirable. There was a general feeling that "business" should get a "break," and that our American economy can run itself with less government control. There was also a general belief that the type of government planning which we see in an extreme form in other countries is not for us here, even in lesser quantity. We seemed to have grown weary of administrative elephantiasis.

However, among the causes of the victory of Mr. Truman in 1948 was a clear resurgence of New Dealism. The so-called "liberal" reform movement which achieved such momentum during the Roosevelt administration carried on, unabated, during the "Fair Deal" Truman administration. Indeed, it slackened only slightly during the Republican administration of General Eisenhower, and, if President Kennedy is to have his way, it will surge to even greater speed in the current administration.

I have already referred in a footnote (see page 353) to the adoption of the label "liberal" by those who have promoted and followed this movement. One must distinguish between them and the traditional or classic liberals of the nineteenth century. In this era of semantic distortion, political labels mean little. Today's Liberals believe in a planned economy and strong centralization, virtually the opposite credo of that espoused by the old liberals. One cannot understand the propulsion behind the current Liberal movement without a knowledge of the influence of the "social engineers." They have been an intellectual pressure group, comparatively small in numbers but enormous in impact. They are the educators, the "intellectuals," who have been strongly indoctrinated with socialism.

While the Socialist Party in the United States had never acquired any substantial strength, the ideas and concepts of socialism had greatly influenced many of our leading educators during the early decades of this century. The impact of their partial conversion is understood by few Americans. It was highlighted by the appearance, in 1934, of the last section of a report of a Commission on Social Studies, called the *Conclusions and Recommendations*. The Commission, organized under the aegis of the American Historical Association, had been financed to the tune of $340,000 by the Carnegie Corporation, a tax-exempt foundation whose founder, Andrew Carnegie, would have been amazed at the use to which so large a piece of his public benefaction had been put.

The *Conclusions and Recommendations* was a frank call to American teachers to use the schools to indoctrinate our youth into an acceptance of some variety of "collectivism." "Collectivism" is a soft word for socialism, and there was no doubt about what the Commission meant. It did not mince words. It gave precise instructions. Educators were no longer to teach mere individual subjects, like geography and history, but to become propagandists, "brainwashers" in effect, to establish what was referred to as a "new order." Harold J. Laski, the philosopher of British socialism, called the report "an educational program for a socialist America." *

The professional managers of the National Education Association, representing the great mass of teachers in the United States, the Progressive Education Association, and other educational groups took the report to their respective bosoms and enthusiastically supported its *Conclusions and Recommendations*. Many influential

* See Wormser, *Foundations, Their Power and Influence*, p. 146 *et seq.*, for a more detailed exposition of the *Conclusions and Recommendations* and its impact.

educators, financed in large part through grants from tax-exempt foundations, took up the challenge and produced a mass of propaganda in the form of books, pamphlets and articles to help accelerate the burial of the free-enterprise system and to bring in the new order of "collectivism." New textbooks were written and widely introduced in the schools which disparaged the capitalist system and extolled socialist concepts. Curriculums, in universities, colleges, secondary schools and elementary schools, were changed to fit the new program of social education. As Professor Counts, a leading educator, stated in his *Dare the Schools Build a New Social Order?*, the teachers were "to fashion the curriculum and the procedures of the school" in such manner as to "definitely and positively influence the social attitudes, ideals and behavior of the coming generation." New conglomerate courses were designed and called "social studies," with biased sociological objectives.

Educators were to bring in the "new order." As to what the new order was to be, this, of course required the guidance of an "elite." The "elite" were to be the "social scientists." The very term "social scientists" indicated the trend of their thinking. They attempted to attach to themselves the character of a scientific approach to the solution of social problems, the obvious fact being that true scientific methods could not be applied to what they called the "social sciences." But they were the self-assumed wise men, the "guardians" of a coming Platonic state. They indicated what they believed their position in society to be when they called themselves "social engineers." They held themselves technically and uniquely equipped to determine what is best for our people—they were the technicians, they claimed, in our politicolegal system, far better able to solve social problems than were prelates, lawyers, other professionals or ordinary businessmen.

The new movement was by no means accepted by all educators. But the "social engineers" were in a vast majority in vociferousness and influence, for they seemed to have at their command an unlimited reservoir of financial support from major tax-exempt foundations, whose professional managers were sympathetic to their objectives and methods. In contrast, educators of contrary opinion had great difficulty in finding either financial support or available media for communicating their ideas to the public. In consequence, the influence of the "social engineers" grew enormously and permeated the colleges, the secondary schools and even the elementary schools. It is a direct result of the strength of this subsidized movement that the political opinions of our youth swung sharply to the left in the ensuing decades.

Moreover, the "social engineers" came increasingly to be used by government, to act as "experts" in fields affecting law, economics and government. In the Roosevelt, the Truman and even the Eisenhower administrations, they have been an important force, bringing their "collectivist" and planned-economy theories to bear in various vital directions. As the Kennedy administration opened, we seemed to see the final flowering of the influence of these "social engineers." Professors Galbraith, Schlesinger, Heller, Samuelson and others of the same school of thought became the inner advisers of Kennedy, the candidate, and, then, of Kennedy, the President.* The proposals and advice which these members of the "elite" brought into the Kennedy administration have had a profound effect upon the nature of his legislative and economic program.

Many of our best minds, including some eminent men who supported the original New Deal, have inveighed against the trend toward the planned economy and the welfare state which the "social engineers" have promoted. As early as 1949, James F. Byrnes, successively appointed by F.D.R. to the Supreme Court and as Secretary of State, warned in an address: "We are going down the road to statism." He continued: "Where we will wind up no one can tell. But if some of the new programs seriously proposed should be adopted there is danger that the individual, whether farmer, worker, manufacturer, lawyer, or doctor, soon will be pulling an economic oar in the galley of the state," with "the federal government regimenting our lives from the cradle to the grave."

Thomas Jefferson once said: "Were not this country already divided into States, that division must be made that each might do for itself what concerns itself directly." Following this principle, Mr. Byrnes said: "We are not only transferring too much power from the individual to government, but we are transferring too many powers of state governments to the federal government." A more strongly centralized government might be more efficient, though this is subject to some doubt, but we have seen what overcentralization

* Some of the major foundations, which had so staunchly supported the "social engineering" movement, contributed directly to the personnel of the Kennedy administration from their ranks of professional managers. The most notable of these is our Secretary of State, Mr. Rusk, who had been president of the Rockefeller Foundation.

can do in other countries. That we are a union of states having a large degree of home rule may be one of the greatest safeguards against totalitarianism.

"Liberals" have pointed out that some of the states have been remiss in failing to enact desirable social legislation, and have asserted, therefore, that the federal government must step in to apply desirable reforms. But, say men like Mr. Byrnes, there is no justification for applying a national set of morals to the individual states. If we wish to preserve our limited democracy—limited in the sense that minorities have rights of which the majority are not to deprive them—the danger of overcentralization must be watched with constant vigilance.

Few of the "social engineers" have had any experience whatsoever in the market place, yet they are the advocates of a "planned economy." Their confidence in their ability to plan something as intricate and in delicate balance as our economy is astounding. Their interference can be dangerous in the extreme. To quote Thomas Jefferson again: "Were we directed from Washington when to sow and when to reap, we should soon want bread."

They are also the advocates of the "welfare state." Many of our citizens have been persuaded to support "welfare" measures and "social benefit" legislation under the illusion that someone else—"capitalists" perhaps—would have to pay for these public benefactions, forgetting that the general public itself must bear the burden of taxation which pays for these benefits. There also has been a false assumption that our resources are limitless and that deficit financing and inflation carry with them no dangers. There has, moreover, been an amazing lack of understanding that, to the extent that government plans our economy and hands out benefits, we must lose individual freedom—degrees of liberty and independence.

How far along the road to centralization, egalitarianism, collectivism, governmental paternalism and intervention in our individual affairs our "social engineers" will be permitted to drive us is anyone's guess. There are some indications that the American people are more conservative than their recent leaders, that they are not wholly sold on the capacity of an "elite" to govern us, and that youth, in particular, is perhaps beginning to turn against the paternal state. Perhaps we have learned something from the mess which the Labor government in England made of her economy and from the resurgence of British business once the socialists were out of office. Perhaps, also, we have learned something from the amazing recovery of West Germany, which insisted upon maintaining a free-enterprise economy, repudiating the advice of a group of Liberal American economists, including Dr. Heller, who is now President Kennedy's chief economic adviser.

It is high time for taking stock.

During this stock-taking we might well assess the changes in our domestic legal and political life brought about by the recent past. Have we gone too far in the direction of bureaucracy? Have we improperly unbalanced the relationship between the federal government and the states? In every war of any consequence, the people must necessarily surrender much of their freedom. There has always been a tendency, during our own wars, to cut into the powers of the states as established by the Constitution, and to make the federal government supreme even in fields which were not intended for it except perhaps in wartime. Then, as Judge Julian P. Alexander of the Mississippi Supreme Court recently said, when the war is over, "somehow the tendency has been to redistribute the cannon to the lawns of the state capitols, but to retain the new laws in Washington." *

It is natural enough that rationalizations of such aggregation of power should be offered on the ground of "national interest"; but the Constitution established certain fields in which there should be no federal interference whether there was "national interest" or not, and it is a violent stretch of the Constitution to permit the federal government to invade the rights which the states reserved to themselves, on the ground that the nation has an interest in these rights.

Our tax system badly needs a major overhauling. It is now a monstrosity, and it may fairly be said that this results chiefly from efforts to use it not merely for its basic purpose of raising revenue but also to achieve sociological objectives. In an effort to "soak the rich" the tax rates have been raised gradually until the top percentages are virtually confiscatory. But the egalitarian objective has not been attained. It is a rare citizen indeed who pays income tax at the top rate of 91 per cent. He is to be found principally among executives whose salaries have been raised to monumental figures in order to enable them, after paying exorbitant tax rates, to have take-home pay commensurate with their contribution and their responsibility.

* "States of the Union: Time to Restore Their Powers," *American Bar Association Journal*, January, 1947.

The public, of course, pays for these necessarily high salaries in an increase in the cost of products and services.

The rich are little hurt by the punitive tax rates, for there are all sorts of ways in which taxes can be minimized and even avoided legally by the wealthy. It is the middle class, the most important in our society, which suffers most under the current tax system. It has little means of legal avoidance.

That the high rates have failed of their egalitarian objective is now widely recognized, even by those who believe in egalitarianism. All that has been accomplished has been to create an Internal Revenue Code which is monstrous in its complexities. It is the product of a continuous struggle between government and the taxpayer, whose anxiety to find ways in which to minimize his taxes has made tax practice by lawyers profitable. Tax lawyers have thus invented method after method and mechanism after mechanism to save taxes, each of which has been met by discomfort on the part of the Treasury, which has sought to close up successive "loopholes" in the tax law, only to find that, in closing up one, it has usually opened others.

The complexity of our tax law is now so great that no one can conduct a business venture of any substance without having a "tax man" at his side. The waste of human energy and time on "paper work," in the preparation of difficult and elaborate tax reports, has been enormous. Moreover, the law is full of traps for the unwary. It is beset with uncertainties as well. Various sections of the law require the Internal Revenue Service to issue explanatory or controlling "regulations" which are virtually tentative, bureaucratic legislation; but the Service sometimes does not get around to completing a set of regulations before a new law comes along to amend or change the old. In the meantime, the Service is often extremely reluctant (growingly more so) to issue "rulings" to interpret the complex rules of law and to guide the applicant. It even goes so far, when it does issue a ruling, to state that it is not necessarily binding on the Service. Nor is it unusual for Congress to pass a tax law with retroactive effect. In these circumstances, steering one's way through the shoals of the tax code is precarious indeed.

Dissatisfaction with our tax system stems from these complexities and uncertainties, and also from a mass of inequities in the law. Indeed, the basic theory of the progressive tax system is unsound. Consider the logic of taxing a citizen at one rate per dollar of income for his seven hours of work per day and, if he works longer hours than this, taxing his extra income at a higher rate per dollar. This is how the system works. It penalizes extra effort and extra labor.

One aspect of our tax system is quite astounding. Our legislators seem to be utterly blind to the fact that there is an annual increase in the tax rates. This occurs through the impact of inflation. Inflation itself is caused by government action, or its failure to act, and our government has caused substantial inflation to continue for decades without interruption. Yet no attempt has been made to adjust the progressive tax scales downward to make up to the citizen for the increased taxation which inflation imposes upon him under our sliding-scale method of taxation.

A rapid decline in public and private morals has been one of the phenomena of recent decades. Sociologists and historians may attribute this to many causes, but one which is undeniable is our tax system. Revolting against its oppressiveness and harshness, against its inequities, against its nuisance and its interference with our personal affairs, Americans have come widely to cheat on their income tax returns. As one man put it, the public considers income tax prevarications as mere "white lies." Nor is this immoral attitude confined to the rich. It is found among all strata of society. As in the case of Prohibition, the public is revolting against laws which it does not like.

Another area of law is beginning to concern the public deeply. This is the extent to which the power of organized labor should be curbed. The commuter who was unable to get to his job because a few tugboatmen in New York Harbor struck and the trainmen were induced to stop operating the trains has begun to wonder whether such strikes are justified. And the citizen who has difficulty in paying the expense of educating his children because of the high income tax rates wonders why strikes at government missile bases are permitted, his concern intensified when he learns that some of the union employees on government work have been receiving fabulous wages. More than one American has been unable to understand the justice of being put temporarily out of work because of an extended steel strike which deprived his employer of raw materials, neither he nor his employer having been involved directly in any union issue.

It may be difficult, at times, to distinguish between a legitimate strike and one which is, in its net effect, against the public welfare.

But some strikes are clearly reprehensible, in so far as large numbers of workers who are not involved in a controversy may have to be laid off. The direct and secondary impact of these lay-offs results in an enormous loss in national product. Mr. Hoffa can paralyze the entire American economy with a strike of his "teamsters," but very often even a small group of workers in a key spot can cause a huge part of our economic life to come to a standstill.

"Jurisdictional" strikes are irritating and costly to the public. A building project can be held up because of a dispute between the carpenters and the masons about which should perform some section of the work. And it is difficult for the public to understand why jurisdictional quarrels should result in such expensive nonsense as compelling an employer to have finished work redone. There have been cases such as this—lamps and other contrivances manufactured solely by union labor have had to be taken down after installation and the electric wiring torn out so that members of the electrical union could replace the wiring. The public pays for the cost of such absurdities.

Unions once were the underdogs. Now many of them have palatial offices in our capital, enormous financial resources, and even banks of their own. Though the anti-trust laws prevent employers from combining "in restraint of trade," one union can strike an entire industry and last it out, though it may have a quarrel with only one of the enterprises which comprise it.

No easy solution to these problems has been found. One difficulty is that unions now have such great political power and influence that most legislators are inclined to be careful not to step on their toes. Indeed, the political power of organized labor troubles many Americans who are sincere supporters of the union movement. They are concerned not by the fact that a majority of union members might vote one way or another but rather by the fact that few unions are operated in a democratic manner and that professional labor leaders, with fat treasuries at their command, exercise such great power in our political life.

In our legal system, one factor has come increasingly into play: a trend toward uniformity of law. While uniformity may hold out the temptation to legislate nationally in fields which now belong to the states, it does seem a desirable objective that the states adjust their laws as much as possible to the end that there be as few local differentiations as possible. Our domestic differences are sometimes wide, and this is natural enough in view of the size and gradual settlement of our country, the accidents of history, and the operation of racial, religious, social, economic, and geophysical factors of all kinds.

One state treats organized labor with great kindness. Another treats organized labor with less sympathy. A divorce may be had in Reno after six weeks' residence in the state and almost on the ground that a husband has frowned at his wife; while, in other states, residence of two years is required and there is no ground for divorce except adultery. And so it goes. Even in matters of business law there will sometimes be a "New York rule" as against a "Massachusetts rule," or a "Pennsylvania rule" in contrast to an "Illinois rule." The variances of law among the states are often wide.

There is a growing movement for uniformity, however, and particularly in the field of business law. The American Bar Association has devised sets of uniform laws in various subjects, such as Partnership and Bills and Notes, and some of these uniform laws have been adopted by a majority of the states. It is only in social and political matters that the trend to uniformity has not been strong.

Even in the administration of the law by judges in deciding cases, there has been a tendency to uniformity. The American Law Institute, composed largely of professors of law, has issued a number of restatements of various fields of law, such as the law of trusts. These restatements might be classed as textbooks or commentaries, but they have had great effect in unifying the interpretation of the common law. For judges are prone to examine such a restatement and to follow its guidance if this does not run head-on into some contrary local rule or precedent.

There has also been a growing tendency to codify the law, independently of the adoption of uniform laws. Every once in a while a state will reassemble its enacted laws and issue a set of "revised statutes." While the Romanesque lawyers were priding themselves on having made order out of confusion by codifying their law, Anglican lawyers were priding themselves that their law was more flexible and living because it was not confined in formal corsets. Now it looks as though we also were heading for wider codification. But, as I have pointed out, ours differs from that of the Romanesque system in that we retain more closely the principle of *stare decisis*. After a set of laws is codified, we still need to follow the cases decided under it in order to determine by what precedents we are bound. Therefore, as a practical matter, codification results only momentarily in cutting down the mass of legal material which must be examined in order to find out what the law is on a particular point. We still need the law reports, and lawyers must still scurry through them to find out what the law is in detail.

Our law schools have improved their standards and methods immensely in recent decades. They have produced better lawyers and thus, for the most part, better legislators and judges. It may well be doubted if we have today better legislators than we had in the early eras of our Union, but, at least, our current lawyer-legislators are likely to be better trained than were those of some decades ago. Furthermore, many of the legislatures have created what are called "legislative drafting bureaus," whose function it is to draft bills which legislators wish to present. Technicians skilled in the difficult art of drawing bills properly have, on the whole, improved legislation enormously, although there is still much room for improvement in drafting.

In general, the state laws have always taken a course similar to that of the federal law. Change has taken place as social ideas have changed, as economic factors have required adjustment, as the mechanics of business and of life in general have grown more complex; and the law has had to devise means for regulating activities unknown to previous generations. Some states have lagged behind in one field and been of the advance guard in others. Sometimes the states have led the way for the federal government, and sometimes this process has been reversed.

Human institutions certainly have not grown up entirely by logic. Mr. Justice Holmes has said that experience and the "felt necessities of the time, the prevalent moral and political theories, institutions of public policy, avowed or unconscious, even the prejudices which judges share with their fellow-men, have had a good deal more to do than the syllogism in determining the rules by which men should be governed." * To quote that great judge again, "The truth is that the law is always approaching, and never reaching, consistency. It is forever adopting new principles from life at one end, and it always retains old ones from history at the other, which have not yet been absorbed or sloughed off."

Some individual principle of law which may now seem very simple to us may have been not nearly so simple to the first judge before

* Holmes, *The Common Law*.

whom came a pertinent set of facts for adjudication. The individual judge had to rely upon his own reasoning powers, but he was never free in his determinations. He was bound by whatever rules had already been established, by the frailties of his judicial contemporaries, and his own, and by the countless prejudices, pressures, and educational limitations of the society into which he had to fit his decisions. The process by which judicial reasoning, within the framework of changing social concepts, has made sense out of law is illustrated by the law governing responsibility for one's acts.

There was a time when an act made you responsible regardless of background or intention, but all this has changed. An act itself is now of no consequence in determining responsibility. Killing a man does not, by itself, make you guilty of murder. There must be other factors present to create responsibility. The nature of these other factors is stated in Justice Holmes's *Common Law:* acts are, in general, "rendered criminal because they are done under circumstances in which they will probably cause some harm which the law seeks to prevent. . . . The test of criminality in such cases is the degree of danger shown by experience to attend that act under those circumstances."

So the mere committing of an act is not intrinsically wrongful. And "wickedness" in an absolute sense is not the criterion of responsibility either. Nor, in such cases, is an actual knowledge of the consequences. The true test is: What would a reasonably prudent man, in the circumstances, anticipate to be the consequences of his act? That is not always easy to determine, for the "reasonably prudent man" is a theoretical character, encountered only in court, when the righteousness of your conduct is being tested by comparison with his. The reasonably prudent man appears throughout criminal law. The courts cannot investigate into the intelligence of each individual defendant, yet there must be universally applicable standards by which people can be deterred from wrongdoing.

The obvious next question—What is wrongdoing?—can be answered only in a practical way, by referring to a fair and acceptable standard of conduct: not what the most informed person might be expected to do, but what this theoretical average, prudent man would do. And, of course, prudence is only what society deems it to be at the moment.

One cannot be excused by a plea of ignorance of the law. It seems unfair that everyone is responsible for knowing the great body of the law—so vast that lawyers themselves know only a small part of it—yet that is the fact. But how could it be otherwise? How could you prove to the court what laws you did or did not know? Are you not to be held guilty if you had an opportunity to learn the law and didn't bother? There is no practical answer to the problem of criminal responsibility except holding the people liable for violating all existing laws. However unjust this may seem to an individual who really acted in innocent ignorance, the greater good to society comes from enforcing laws even against the ignorant.

"Intent" in criminal law, which has given judges much concern, is, by itself, of no consequence.* That you have an unfulfilled desire to murder Joe Smith is of no legal consequence. But you can be guilty without having had the intention to commit murder. If you leave a child out in the snow, assuming that someone will take him in, and the child dies of exposure, you are guilty of murder, for you should have anticipated the reasonable consequences of your act, no matter what your actual intention may have been. You had a choice—and you chose to do something which a reasonably prudent man might well have anticipated would result in death. That is murder.

Fine lines must be drawn. If you hit someone a light blow with a light stick and he dies, that is not murder, but the lesser crime of manslaughter. If it was a heavy stroke with an iron bar, it is murder, for a prudent man would anticipate that death might result. If you knew that the man you hit with the light stroke had a weak heart, that would be murder also, for a prudent man would anticipate that the victim's heart might stop. But the question of where the line should be drawn—how heavy must the stick be, or how heavy the blow, to constitute murder—that is difficult, indeed, to answer. All middle-ground cases are difficult. Justice Holmes illustrated how the approach from both ends can answer such a question. He showed that, by decided cases in Massachusetts, "if a child of two years and four months is unnecessarily sent unattended across and down a street in a large city, his parent cannot recover for a negligent injury," but "to allow a boy of eight to be abroad alone is not necessarily negligent." "The effect of permitting a boy of ten to be abroad after dark is for the jury," whereas "such permission to a young man of twenty possessed of common intelligence has no effect whatever." In

* "Intent," however, has been made a necessary degree-factor in many crimes, such as murder in the first degree.

one case it will be held negligent to allow a child of eight to be unattended on the street. In another it will not be termed negligent if the child is fifteen. But suppose the child is twelve? Admittedly it is extremely difficult to draw an exact line in such cases, but the courts must do so; and they do it, generally, by approaching from both ends.

There is much moral phraseology in the early cases—talk of "malice," "fraud," "intent," "negligence," etc. Actually, the question of responsibility for torts comes down to the simple question: When should a man be liable for harm? The standard of conduct which measures responsibility for torts has been described by Justice Holmes as follows: ". . . whether his conduct would have been wrong in the fair average member of the community, whom he is expected to equal at his peril." It is a general rule of "blameworthiness." But it is a rule which changes in its detailed application as society changes. The law sets standards and establishes criteria. It sometimes takes cases away from juries when there is a well-established, detailed principle involved, but in general leaves the factor of "prudence" to the jury. Nor do the rules remain fixed. They are often overruled when they become inconsistent with the conditions of current life.

Gradually, a structure of law was built, changed, and perfected. At various stages in this process, the judges, jurists, and statesmen of the law, and even the public, may have thought that perfection had been reached. But it never has. We are far from perfection today. Enlightenment comes slowly. The law can only follow public opinion. Public opinion will not permit the law to precede it, and public opinion controls both the legislatures and the judges.

Expediency often dictates the course of the law. What is "public policy" for the moment often determines direction. It is sometimes, to quote Mr. Justice Holmes once more, "the unconscious result of instinctive preferences and inarticulate convictions," and thus legislators and judges have sometimes bent the law to their own predilections, which they interpreted as "public policy." Horrible as it may seem to us, the ecclesiastical judge who sentenced a heretic to be burned at the stake during the period of the Inquisition was acting, as he thought, upon "public policy." Perhaps some of the sentences and opinions of our judges may seem cruel to future generations, but each generation can only do what to it seems best.

There is a constant conflict between what may be deemed justice by any abstract or reasoned standard and what is expedient. We cannot always put the ideal into action. On the other hand, it is not wise always to be "realistic" in the sense of being expedient. So we go on compromising between justice and expediency. For example, it may be unjust to hold a man responsible for violating a law of which he had no knowledge. But, as I have said, we find that expediency governs in this instance, for if ignorance of the law were a defense, it would often be impossible to prove that a man knew the law which he had violated, and society would suffer. So expediency triumphs over abstract justice. In a reverse situation, where we refuse to condemn a man caught red-handed in a murder until he has had a fair trial, abstract justice triumphs over expediency. In the criminal law there are many conflicts between justice and expediency. Which is more important, the welfare of the individual or the welfare of society? We do not always know what abstract justice might be in a given case, nor do we always know what might be expedient; we are dealing with difficult theory and with difficult complexities of fact.

We have now reached a new stage in the legal reform movement. We are beginning to interest ourselves in what might be called anticipatory reform. The law is studied with some scientific attempt at constructive analysis, in law schools, by bar associations, and by lawyers and sociologists generally. Nevertheless, reform limps, but that is because society itself limps, toward the ideal.

II: The Difficulties of Reform

It may be in the field of criminal law that reform is most needed. Our criminal law is still rather arbitrary. Philosophers have long concerned themselves with the problem of the proper theory behind the treatment of the criminal. The injured primitive wanted revenge against someone who did him wrong, but when society took over the job of handling wrongdoing it did so not with any idea of social revenge or punishment, but merely to protect itself. But with the introduction of recognizable moral ideas, the concept of punishment did come into the criminal law. One did wrong; therefore, one had to be punished. Religion has fathered the idea of punishment. One is punished for one's sins; ergo, one should be punished for one's crimes. The validity of this proposition has been questioned seriously in modern times.

It has been questioned for several important reasons. First, we have come to realize that many crimes may be attributable not to individual but to social guilt. A society which tolerates slums and poverty may have little right to condemn the individual who is turned to crime by abject poverty. On the other hand, here we come to expediency again. Failure to punish may promote crime. The answer may be not to refrain from punishment, as we might lose its deterrent effect, but rather to try harder to remove the ultimate causes which turned the individual to crime.

We have come to realize that many criminals are criminals only because they are ill, impelled by some psychosis or compelling neurosis. This faces us with a monumental problem: Where is the line of responsibility to be drawn? And if punishment is not to be meted out, certainly something has to be done to prevent recurrence by the same individual. Confinement of some sort is needed? How long? Until we are absolutely certain there will be no recurrence? How can we ever be certain? And do we really know how to treat these "sick" cases? Society must protect itself. If a man has committed a rape we cannot simply say it was not his fault because he is deeply neurotic, and let him go on to rape others. What to do is a compelling and extremely difficult problem.

Perhaps the most important criticism of the present treatment of criminals has been on the ground that the ultimate problem is the protection of society, and mere punishment does not always protect society. We still make hardened criminals out of many offenders who could be reconditioned into good citizens. Something has been done in the direction of humanizing the treatment of the maladjusted, but not nearly enough.

It is not only in this field of law that reform is needed. There are undoubtedly a vast number of legal rules which need change or improvement though we have not yet arrived at any appreciation of the necessity. We cannot be expected to know what only time will disclose to later generations. It is not easy to reform the law or give it scientific direction.

Our system of litigation (though there is none better elsewhere) could probably be improved materially. We do overhaul it periodically, and procedure and practice are being studied constantly by bar associations and other groups with the objective of improving it still further. But there are several problems connected with the litigation system to which there are no easy solutions. One lies in the fact that a rich man can hire better lawyers than a poor man, or, at least, more expensive ones. Thus, as the system is largely one of a contest between attorneys, the rich man often comes off better. It is not likely that we shall want socialization of lawyers as an answer; we are litigious enough as it is, and if litigation were financed by the state we would have to multiply the courts in order to handle all the cases. But there is hope that the cost of litigation may be cut down, and various measures to this end have been considered.

Perhaps the most interesting defect in our system is the difficulty of getting at facts scientifically through ordinary testimony of witnesses. The rules of evidence are highly technical and often produce an unfair result. The lawyer who is best able to struggle with complex rules of evidence may sometimes win a case he should lose. The atmosphere of a court can be terrifying, and judges rarely make things easier for a witness who is frightened to begin with and then gets tangled up by arguments concerning the admission of some of his testimony and by confusing instructions. The poor witness does not understand why he cannot say what he has to say in a straightforward and natural way. Our rules of evidence sometimes make testimony unreliable by forcing it into an arbitrary corset. It is extremely difficult for a witness to tell "the truth, the whole truth, and nothing but the truth," even if he has no intention of lying. Suppose you are to testify about a long conversation you had five years ago with the defendant, and the judge keeps telling you that you cannot give the substance of what was said but must give the actual language. You are likely to give summaries, nevertheless, and to give them as though they were actual sentences. If you have bias, you are likely also to distort the meaning by inflection and facial expression. A litigant can be damned by such a recital, which is almost certain to be, at least, inaccurate.

There are always conflicting opinions on the nature of reform. There are those who wish to regulate, as much as possible, and those who wish to have as little regulation as possible; those who believe that the majority should reign absolute, and those who believe the protection of the minority to be the primary concern. There are those who consider that the individual is of no consequence in comparison with the rights of the mass, and there are, opposed, those who believe that the individual and his rights are all-important. And so it goes. The reformer must tread warily. Reform is desirable, but there is much to be said for the naturally conservative process of the law which lets it lag slightly behind the social whim of the moment.

How specific should the laws be? To write down all their detail is usually impossible, as every variation of fact cannot be anticipated. Is it then better to give a mere general principle and let the courts determine all detail? How much of the law should be dictated by the will of the majority, as expressed in legislation, and how much by professionals who have studied and are equipped to pass on legal practice and theory? How much should be taken away from the lawyers and legislators entirely and given to social scientists? That is an even harder problem, which the further development of the psychological sciences will make even more difficult. How much should society plan its future? These and many other problems of principle plague the reformer of the law.

We can justly pride ourselves on our legal system. It compares favorably with those of other countries. That it may also still contain many barbarities, crudities, and stupidities warrants neither shame (for it is difficult for each generation to see its own errors) nor complacency (for there is much we can do by intelligent analysis and study). We can advance our laws only as rapidly as we advance our education. The world has so much to learn, and we with it.

III: The Aid of Philosophy

LAWYERS AND JURISTS are often criticized by members of other professions on the ground that, unlike other professions, the legal profession does little about instituting reform on a scientific basis. This is a criticism that seems unjust and contrary to fact. Let me make a comparison between medicine and law. The average physician does little about developing his science except in so far as he may accidentally make a discovery and as he may, in the very course of his daily work, perfect diagnoses, treatments, and methods. Behind him are the medical scientists, who do contribute constantly and enormously to the conscious development of medical science. From their laboratories and from those of associated scientists—biologists, bacteriologists, physicists, and chemists—come the discoveries, innovations, and progress.

It is the same in law. The active practitioner does little to advance his science, except as minor contributions may come out of his daily work. But behind him is a set of "scientists": the jurists, the thinkers in the law, who apply themselves to the development of legal science. And, as is the case in medicine, there are associated "scientists" who contribute as well: historians, economists, sociologists, and philosophers. These legal scientists deal, of course, almost entirely with premises relating to social conduct. These premises are under constant observation and criticism. Since the time of the Greeks, countless jurists and philosophers have devoted themselves to the solution of the problem of living together.

After a lapse during the eras in which Western humanity was recovering from the darkness following the decay of Roman-Hellenic civilization, interest in the scientific development of the law has rapidly and steadily accelerated. Today there are great numbers of jurists giving attention not only to what the law is but also to what the law ought to be. They seek to find out what is wrong with the law. What are the defective premises upon which rules of law have been built, and what laws are based upon no premise at all except the supposed hallowedness of age?

Out of the critical thought-laboratories of these jurists comes an increasing amount of benefit to society. This benefit filters down into the thinking of the public through the education of lawyers in law schools affected by current juridical thought and through the influence of this thought upon legislators, judges, and even politicians. It is regrettable that the jurists do not reach the public directly to any marked extent, but the public is not much interested in philosophy, and apparently the philosophy of law seems far more forbidding than it should. Jurists often have contributed to the distaste of the public for their field by writing obscurely and employing a terminology which means nothing to the uninitiated reader. Technicians in any field are prone to do this, constantly using technical terms and phrases as a sort of trade or scientific shorthand. The philosophers of the law love to throw around terms like "epistemological," "deontological norm," and "intellection." These are all useful tools of reasoning, but it is hard going to read something like this: "In its philosophical implications and significance Natural Law reflects most acutely the basic problems arising from the inescapable conflict between *a priorism* and empiricism (aposteriorism); autonomy and heteronomy; ideal (deontological) norm and (ontological) reality deviating from this norm; stability and everlasting historical change; ideal (abstract) justice and social security in the sense of positive legal certainty; ideal social control and actual social needs." *

Yet there is much for the general public to gain from discussions of ethics, morals, principles, and methods as they apply to the law, and clear and simple exposition of them could introduce laymen readily into this important field of thought. Philosophers put into conscious thought things which may be nebulous in the general mind; they thus serve a function of crystallization. As the public in the last analysis makes the law, it is lamentable that the public does not get the direct and immediate benefit of this crystallization. Legislators cannot go faster than the public will permit; they cannot violate widespread concepts; nor can judges do more than interpret the general public mores.

The public, of course, wants "just" laws. But what specific laws it advocates depends on its ideas of "justice." A brief examination of the concept of justice may bring out the importance of legal philosophy.

The Greeks introduced humanity to legal philosophy, and some of their earliest philosophers began to consider the meaning of words bearing on the law, such as "justice." At first glance, the meaning of justice may seem clear enough. But the more one thinks about the meaning of this term (and there are many other equally troublesome terms in the field of jurisprudence) the more confused one gets. There have been countless definitions of justice, and not one of them wholly acceptable.

The lawyer usually speaks of justice as a strict compliance with the law as it now is. A judge might speak of justice in the same way; but he would be able to go further, for he often fills in gaps between the obvious rules of law, gaps in which no rules have been set to cover the exact facts before him in a trial. In such a case, he may apply his own subjective idea of justice in determining what rule should fill the gap. The judge, in such a situation, will be conditioned by his own social, economic, and religious and philosophical principles. He will also take into consideration, consciously or unconsciously, the precedents set by previous cases; and again consciously or unconsciously, the judge will take into consideration the

* Anton-Herman Chroust, "On the Nature of Natural Law," in *Interpretations of Modern Legal Philosophies*, p. 70.

current public code of morals and ethics, or what is loosely called "public policy."

Lawmaking by judicial decisions is a form of law creation, but it is not under direct public control; to examine the function of the public in determining what kind of justice it wishes to see in its laws, let us forget lawyers, judges, and legislators for the moment and treat the public as though it were itself a legislature.

It wants just laws. And what is justice?

It is obviously not happiness for everyone, for a law which would make one man happy is very likely to make another unhappy, though the latter's unhappiness does not necessarily make the law unjust or unfair or inequitable.

Is it happiness for the majority? That theory has often been advanced by many, but it is not likely to appeal to a people who believe that the minority should be protected. What makes a majority happy might be very unfair to a minority; "the greatest happiness for the greatest number" is consonant with *absolute* democracy but not with American ideas of a democracy limited by assurances of protection to minorities.

The satisfaction of human interests is not an answer to the question, for interests conflict, and compromises are essential to the working of a democracy such as ours. In an absolute democracy there could still be compromises and adjustments between groups which, together, would compose a majority, but there would always be minorities whose interests would perhaps be unjustly treated. And let me point out that individual interests are often purely selfish, and the satisfaction of them might be unjust to others. Who is to say what proper and justifiable interests are?

Change the term "interests" to "wants," and you get no further in the direction of finding proper justice. Whose wants are to be satisfied? Everyone's? That is impossible. The majority's? That is not always possible, either; and, if it were, it would often deprive the minority of the satisfaction of its legitimate wants. Franklin D. Roosevelt popularized the expression "freedom from want," which seems, at first glance, to be an excellent objective of justice, yet it is only one of many factors to be taken into account in determining justice. Ask the question: Which is more important, freedom from want or freedom itself? There is no easy answer to this, except for the Russians, who believe that freedom from want is all-important and that freedom itself is of no importance.

Aristotle offered a mechanical theory of justice as the mean between two extremes. One extreme is an excess, the other is a deficiency; it is only the middle point, the mean, he said, which is virtuous or just. An interesting theory but not a very practical one; a quasi-mathematical formula does not seem to offer any real clues to the nature of justice.

Plato was one of the foremost exponents of the metaphysical concept of justice. It was one form of the natural-law concept, of which there have been many versions. Its essence, as I have pointed out, is that there is an abstract justice, either God-given or ascertainable by man's "right reason," and that laws are just or unjust in so far as they conform to or violate the pure, abstract, ultimate rules of conduct. It seems clear that there is considerable room for argument as to what the content of this absolute or natural justice may be. Hans Kelsen, an eminent jurist, has said: "But none of the numerous natural-law doctrines has so far succeeded in defining the content of this just order in a manner even approaching the exactness and objectivity with which natural science can determine the content of the laws of nature, or legal science the content of a positive legal order. Although in the intellectual history of mankind, no other problem has so passionately been discussed, and although the most illustrious thinkers, from Plato to Kant, have tried to determine the content of the natural law of justice, the whole question is today as unanswered as it ever was."

However, natural law cannot be summarily disposed of as an element in fixing the justice of American law. Confused though the term may be, it is woven into our American law and system. We do believe in certain basic human rights of which no minority should be despoiled, and the Declaration of Independence justifies these basic rights upon the concept of natural law. Loosely, we might say that natural law comprises what we believe to be well-established and fundamental rules of conduct for human beings in relation to each other. If we limit the scope of the concept to those rights and privileges and immunities which we believe to be fundamental, the concept has usefulness. In other words, if we say that we believe in a number of basic principles whether they are God-given or reason-given or not, and call those "precepts of natural law," that will do for the purpose of giving the child a name. But we are by no means too certain even of some of these basic rights, and our own ideas are subject to change. For example, is the right to private property so basic that it must not be interfered with? We do interfere with it a good deal, and we may interfere with it far more in the future.

It is not necessary, in any event, to call such basic rights, in which we believe, by the name "natural." They can be justified on the mere ground of common and general acceptance, or upon the ground that they have been found to be "fair" or "socially desirable." Yet the term "natural" has a definite utility in impressing the public with the truly vital character of whatever we believe to be our most precious personal rights.

But when we get away from these fundamental rights and simple precepts, which we accept as the main canons of our moral code, natural law or natural justice does not give us specific guidance in judging whether a proposed law would be just.

Many more theories of justice have been advanced. One is that it is or signifies peace, in the sense that it is an adjustment of conflicting interests. This theory of peace has practical value, but not much ethical value as a criterion to be applied to laws, for a compromise often produces an unethical result.

IV: Roscoe Pound

OUR MOST EMINENT JURIST has expressed his doubt as to what justice really is, saying: 'I am skeptical as to the possibility of an absolute judgment." This jurist is Roscoe Pound, whose contribution to American thinking—indeed, to world thinking—in the field of jurisprudence has been monumental. He has given no easy answers to the problems which confront lawmakers, but he has destroyed the self-satisfaction of various groups of thinkers who were convinced that their own fixed theories were irrefutable answers to all the problems of jurisprudence. But Pound is no mere iconoclast. He has propounded theories which have affected the thinking of judges and jurists perhaps more, in the current era, than anyone else, not excepting Justice Holmes.

Roscoe Pound was born in Lincoln, Nebraska, in 1870 just a few years after the admission of that state to the Union. His father was a local judge, and his mother, an unusually intellectual woman, taught her three children herself until they were ready for a university. Pound was graduated from Nebraska University at the age of seventeen. He had no intention of becoming a lawyer and, a year after his graduation, took a master's degree in botany. In 1888 he went off to Harvard Law School, but he never received a bachelor's degree in law, for he did not stay at Harvard long enough to fulfill the requirements and was not permitted to take an examination. Long afterward, Dean Wigmore of Northwestern University Law School, finding that one of the most eminent professors on his staff had no bachelor's degree in law, conferred one on him. But Pound no longer suffers from lack of degrees; he has been deluged with honorary degrees.

In 1890 Pound was admitted to practice in Lincoln, Nebraska, and he practiced there until 1901. From 1901 to 1903 he was a commissioner of appeals of the Supreme Court of Nebraska, and during the same period he was also assistant professor of law at Nebraska University. In 1903 he became Dean, a position which he held until 1907, when he transferred to a professorship of law at Northwestern University. In 1909 he shifted to Chicago University, and in 1910 was made a professor of law at Harvard. From 1916 to 1936 he was Dean of the Harvard Law School, after which he went back to a professorship, but with a roving commission. Although now advanced in years, he has by no means fully retired. Like Justice Holmes, it is unlikely that Pound will cease to be productive until his last days.

Many stories are told about Pound's prodigious memory. Apparently the man has never forgotten anything that he has ever read. He combines enormous intellectual curiosity with considerable physical vigor, and he has maintained excellent physical health despite intensive studiousness.

He was very successful in his active practice of law, but study and the calmer atmosphere of academic halls attracted him strongly. A linguist of considerable capacity, he is even able to read the old English cases in their original bastard Latin.

In 1906, in an address to the American Bar Association on "Causes of Popular Dissatisfaction with the Administration of Justice," he startled the entire bar with an original, highly critical, and constructive analysis of the American legal system. His address shattered the complacency of many leaders of the bar, jurists and professors of law, and started a movement in the United States toward what is called "sociological jurisprudence," which, under the constant leadership of Pound himself, has made enormous headway and has radically affected, sometimes directly and sometimes indirectly, the thinking of American jurists, judges, and lawyers. It has also made itself felt throughout the entire international field of Western jurisprudence. Perhaps no other man has had so profound an effect on our legal system as Roscoe Pound.

Pound and Justice Holmes had enormous respect for each other. In many ways, their approach to jurisprudence was the same, but there were some sharp contrasts between them. Holmes lived in something of an ivory tower, aloof from ordinary life. Is is said that he never read newspapers. Pound has been much closer to practical things. Holmes has been called a Darwinian, for he wanted the best man to win and had, possibly, insufficient regard for the minority. Pound, on the other hand, has felt that jurisprudence should not be that cold-blooded.

His approach is distinctly sociological. Refusing to accept any single approach to legal philosophy, he believes that no current hypothesis is reliable, as ideas and legal philosophies change radically and frequently from time to time. He trusts no definite and specific theory fully (probably not even his own).

Before his great Bar Association address, the American approach to jurisprudence was almost entirely analytical and historical, with a good deal of interest in natural-law theories. Pound used the phrase "sociological jurisprudence" in a way which shocked his listeners, and there were cries of "socialism." But Pound is no socialist. What he has fathered is a system of jurisprudence which consists of patterns of ways of living together by actual human beings and not theoretical persons.

An important part of his own thesis is the "theory of interests," first stated in 1921, that the law must determine between conflicting sets of interests. Whether that produces justice in any abstract sense is unimportant, for the law must find a way to enable people to live together. Some of these interests, Pound points out, are protected by the state and thus "rights" arise, but interests do not always result in rights. Constant reconciliation and adjustment are necessary between the interests of individuals. And there are other interests also to be taken into consideration: the social interests, or interests "involved in social life in civilized society," which might be called "ethical interests"; and "public interests," resulting from life in a political or organized society.

We get constant interpretations of social and public interest in statements of the courts as to what is "public policy." Something will be held to be against public policy because it is against the interest of the family as a social institution (for example, a provision in a will which cuts off a beneficiary's income if he fails to divorce his wife); another would be held to be against public policy because it was against the interests of government or a political institution (a provision in a contract of employment binding the employee not to vote in a national election). There are innumerable points at which public interest may be held to come into play; and an increasing number of cases are decided on a basis of public interest or an adjustment of social interests.

Let us look at some of the systems of jurisprudential thought which Pound has considered and found wanting. There is the theory of *rationalism,* espoused by many great thinkers, including Descartes, Spinoza, and Leibnitz. It had its greatest eminence in the seventeenth century, though it has had earnest advocates since. It is based upon the premise that sound principles can be ascertained only by human reason. Knowledge obtained by the senses is false or unreliable. One must seek for self-evident principles. It may be noted that Chief Justice Marshall based many of his important conclusions on some "self-evident" fact. The reasoning of the rationalist school is almost geometric. Pufendorf and Wolff and other eminent jurists followed it in seeking absolute principles established by the logical, reasoning method. The rationalists were usually advocates of "natural law." The common law itself contains elements of the rationalistic method, for it employs basic principles upon which an edifice of conclusive reasoning is built. And in the United States it was not only John Marshall who espoused a variety of rationalism but also the other architects of our government who used "self-evident" truths about the rights of man as foundation stones.

Then there is the school of the *empiricists,* who also believe in fundamental truths but take them from the perceptions of the senses. Empiricism takes items of experience and generalizes from them, in contrast to rationalism, which arrives at generalizations through reason and then deduces conclusions from these. Rationalism tests the law by what it ought to be, while empiricism derives its generalizations from actual experience. Some of the eighteenth-century British writers were particularly attached to empiricism, including Locke, Berkeley, and Hume. Despite remnants of rationalism, empiricism—the school of law-as-is—was triumphant in America in the nineteenth century.

A third great school was that of *criticism*. It is the school of Kant, who reconciled rationalism with empiricism. He said that "concepts without perception are empty" and "precepts without concepts are blind." It was *a priori* reasoning which Kant advocated. One postulated, and then tested the postulate against experience. It was a theory which many jurists found attractive and sound.

But the philosopher Hegel, in an approach which has been called *absolute idealism*, bitterly attacked the reliability of experience. Hegel denied the existence of absolutes. He said that legal factors arise out of the surrounding circumstances, and that what might be true in one situation would not be true in another. The jurist, said Hegel, had to have an eye on history; law can be explained only within its milieu. This was also a popular school of juridical approach in the nineteenth century, but it was opposed by the school of the so-called *positivists*, who held that the only reliable thing is experience, for generalities, they said, are only tentative and must be tested by experience.

Our most modern school of legal philosophy is the *pragmatic* or *relativist* school. Its most eminent recent advocate in pure philosophy was John Dewey; its most eminent advocate in the law is Roscoe Pound. It makes both generalization and experience suspect, and it is not satisfied to adjust the two by the critical method of Kant. Everything is subject to change. It is arrant skepticism, but Pound does not permit his own skepticism, and his insistence on accepting things tentatively only, to leave him ineffective. He limits uncertainty, saying that principles must have their place. They are the "ideal" factors. But they have no value independent of experience. The law arises out of human experience. In a way, he is not so far from Kantian thought, but philosophical determination is not so simple a matter for him as for Kant. Pound sees the law as a constant and flowing process of sociological adjustment.

Jurists like Pound have been troubled not only by the difficulty of defining terms as abstruse as "justice" but even by a precise definition of the simple term "law." Justice Holmes used a definition which suited his purposes: "The prophecies of what the courts will do in fact, and nothing more pretentious, are what I mean by the law." That is a practical approach; the attempt to give a theoretical definition has never been satisfactory. To understand the difficulties of defining the term, consider the problem posed by Professor Arthur L. Goodhart. He poses a "law" passed by the Netherlands government-in-exile during the war when that government was unable to effect its will in its own country. The German government of occupation did not recognize this law. Suppose, then, that an issue arose under such a law in an English court. The English court would prefer to recognize it as a law, but consider the effect upon the poor man living in occupied Holland, where the *de facto* (German) government denied that law. If he complied with the law passed by his own exiled government, he violated the law of the power in actual control of the Netherlands. If he violated the exiled government's law, he might be penalized by an English court. Is the "law" a law? Professor Goodhart contributes some help by defining law as "a rule of conduct which is recognized as being obligatory." The definition will do, as far as it goes, but it does not wholly distinguish rules of law from rules of custom, rules of morals, rules of ethics, and religious rules.

Roscoe Pound has been by no means satisfied with some of the recent developments in American law under "welfare state" pressure, and has uttered some incisive criticisms. For example, in an article in the October, 1951, issue of the *Pennsylvania Law Review*, he said: "Belief in the obligatory force of contracts and respect for the given word are going if not gone." He continued that the constitutional provision against impairment of contract "has, in large part at least, become a mere preaching. Legislation impairing or doing away with the practical means of enforcing promises is upheld in a doctrine that a power of the legislature to relieve promisors of liability is implied in the sovereignty of the state and is to be read into every contract as a tacit term thereof. This has gone along with the notable relaxation of morals in the breakdown of the feeling of moral duty to perform promises." Yet what could one expect when our government repudiated its own solemn promise to pay its creditors in gold, an action which was as immoral as it was unnecessary?

Calling attention to another alarming development in the "welfare state," Pound says that "fault" has gradually been abandoned as a basis for liability. He said: ". . . to guarantee the expected full economic and social life, the law seems more and more to be called on to find for every victim of loss and every one who for any reason cannot keep the pace of attaining his expectations, what I have called an involuntary Good Samaritan to pull him out of the ditch, bind up his wounds, set him on his way and pay his hotel bill."

He said further: ". . . under the circumstances of life in the welfare state, in which the cost of government has become enormously multiplied and all manner of heavy demands upon the already overburdened public resources appear to preclude adding any more, there is inevitable reluctance to press the idea to its conclusion by direct and immediate imposing upon government the repairing of losses and injuries without fault of anyone." An illustration of Pound's point is to be found in legislation compelling an employer to insure his employees against injury, even when the employer is without fault—the cost of this is, of course, passed on to the public.

One might summarize much of Pound's reaction to the welfare state thesis by these remarks of his: "One may look upon what has been happening in the law of contracts, the law of torts, and the law of property as indicating a continually widening circle of satisfaction of human wants. But the one conspicuous human demand which in America was the one chiefly asserted and chiefly respected, namely, the claim to liberty—to free self-assertion or self-determination—is almost disappearing."

I must conclude this section with an expression of my own satisfaction in the growing movement to question premises which we have heretofore accepted as reliable, a movement in which Roscoe Pound has been a world leader. The essential validity of a premise will not be changed by questioning. If it is sound, let us keep it. But so many premises, formerly accepted, have been successively disclosed to be false, that continued criticism is obviously healthy and highly desirable. What is perhaps even more desirable is to question even more closely any new premise which is offered as a substitute for an old one.

PART NINE

THE INTERNATIONALS

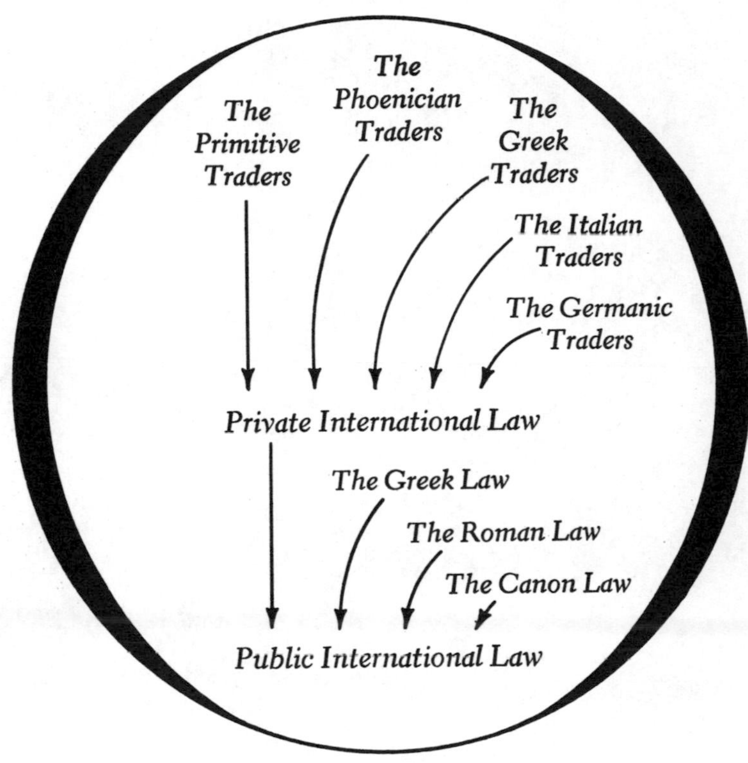

THE CHIEF BASIC SOURCES

CHAPTER 42

The Merchants

I: Private International Law

THIS IS NOT an appendix or supplement to this book but a continuation of the story of *our* law, for it is accepted that international law is part of our own law.

Ordinarily the term "international law" refers to the law of nations or the law which governs the relations of states in the society of nations, *public* international law, and I shall devote the subsequent chapters to it. But there is another kind called *private* international law. It is in one sense misnamed. It deals with the relations between citizens of different nationalities and the relations between an alien and a state, but it is "international" only in so far as some of its rules have been established by international conventions and agreements and by common practice among nations. In the United States we prefer to call this subject "conflict of laws."

Suppose an Englishman and a Swede make a contract in France by which the Swede is required to render some service in Mexico. The Swede breaks the contract and the Englishman brings an action in the courts of the United States, where both of them happen to be at the moment. What law shall the American court apply? The law of England, where the plaintiff hails from? The law of Sweden, where the defendant lives? The law of France, where the contract was made? The law of Mexico, where the contract was to be performed? Or the law of the United States, where the action is brought? In such a problem of conflict of laws the American court would apply its own rules of procedure and give only such relief to the plaintiff as its own laws permit, but it would apply the law of France in interpreting the meaning and significance of the contract. For rules of this subject provide that the *lex fori* (the law of the court) governs the procedure and remedies to be applied, and that the *lex loci contractus* (the law of the place where the contract was made) governs the interpretation of a contract. Among other rules of this type is the rule that the *lex actus* (the law of the place where a document is executed) controls documents generally, and that the *lex situs* (the law of the place where property is situated) governs litigation concerning immovable property.

There are many such rules, and they have been developed in the United States in greater detail than elsewhere because we have a unique field of application for conflict of laws here, since we are a union of states each having a considerable amount of domestic sovereignty. So conflict of laws in the United States applies not only to a conflict between the laws of two nations but also to one between the laws of two states.

Many nations have made treaties, from time to time, settling some of the difficult problems of conflict of laws, or *private* international law, but England and the United States have refused to accede to some of these treaties because of one vital difference in our approach to certain problems. In England and the United States, we base many rules upon domicile or permanent residence, whereas most of the other powers base them on nationality. If a Belgian should die while domiciled in France, his estate is governed by Belgian law, not by French law. In contrast, if a Belgian should die while domiciled in the United States, we pay no attention to Belgian law but administer his American estate entirely under our law. In reverse, if an American should die while domiciled in Belgium, we recognize their right to apply their law.

All sorts of subjects come within the province of *private* international law—the rules as to the validity of marriages and marriage contracts; divorce and separation; property settlements; guardianship; bankruptcy; commercial law; etc. And while there is a considerable amount of disagreement, most rules of *private* international law or conflicts of law are surprisingly well established. I must make the exception, of course, that no one knows how much international law is accepted behind the Iron Curtain.

The universality of acceptance of international rules is most evident in commercial and maritime law. This is not surprising; these two branches of law, however much they may now be incorporated in the domestic laws of the respective nations, had an international origin and developed almost entirely independently of the states themselves.

II: Origins of Commercial and Maritime Law

In early societies barter was difficult because the tribes were hostile to each other, but ways had to be invented to permit peaceful exchange, and man learned to give signals which indicated to stranger tribes his good intentions. We use the olive branch as a symbol of peace, and it may be that we inherit this from the primitive custom of coming to a group of strangers bedecked in foliage to show that one had peaceful intentions. There were other ways also of showing that one meant no harm, and some of these became ritualistic. American Indians smoked a "pipe of peace" as a preliminary to any exchange between tribes.

That sort of thing was all right when barter was infrequent or spasmodic, but, as trading grew more frequent, it became customary to have a neutral trading area into which men of neighboring tribes could come without fear to exchange their goods. Tribes of American Indians met on the Mississippi in this way; and African tribes, since time immemorial, have met in neutral forest places to trade and exchange. Some neutral trading posts came under the special protection of one of the neighboring tribes, but in many places the trading post was a wholly independent district in which the traders themselves governed by rules of their own making. Sometimes they set up courts to try offenders against the market customs; there were even councils of traders to regulate weights and measures and the quality of merchandise. In these market-district customs and regulations we find the beginning of a system of law, not imposed by nations but devised and imposed by traders themselves.

With the development of mediums of exchange, trade expanded more rapidly. Such mediums might be true money, although earlier forms were salt, metal, or any commodity readily acceptable to both traders. With the coming of such money, professional traders became a more distinct class. Factors and brokers arose who traded at both ends, buying from a supplier and selling to a third person. Some grew more courageous and actually invaded the neighboring territory with caravans or pack trains. Though disliked as "foreigners," they were usually welcomed for what they brought or would buy.

River and sea traffic was at first local; then peoples like the Phoenicians and Greeks carried their merchandise to far-distant lands. Successful voyagers came home and fired the imagination of their friends. Others followed where pioneers had started, and still others asked for an opportunity to take part in a venture by investing capital or risking merchandise. So the business grew and trading posts were established in remote places, some in time becoming colonies of the trader's homeland. As the ventures grew in size and the business became more complex, all sorts of mechanisms and institutions were devised, invented, or fallen into: commercial banking, commercial loans, the use of notes and bills of exchange; and customs came into being governing trade which were mutually acceptable to sellers and purchasers over vast areas and among diverse peoples.

III: The Laws of Maritime Commerce

TRAFFIC in the Mediterranean was heavy even before recorded history. The Egyptians had an extensive maritime foreign commerce. Later the Phoenicians eclipsed the Egyptians and traded as far as the British Isles and the west coast of Africa. Cities of a million or more in population were not unknown, and Alexandria, Carthage, and Tyre were huge metropolises.

On shore, all sorts of calamities and eruptions took place: revolutions, changes of dynasties, wars. Political and social upheavals disturbed domestic commerce from time to time. But maritime commerce, except in so far as it was preyed upon by pirates and by hostile ships in time of war, carried on. The merchants who plied the seas had their own laws, and they knew that these laws must be obeyed and maintained, regardless of what happened ashore, or there could be no satisfactory commerce. So for nearly five thousand years maritime law lived an independent life, created by traders and not rulers, yet observed by all.

Successively, the greatest contributions to early maritime law were made by the Phoenicians, the Greeks (chiefly by Rhodes), the town of Amalfi in Italy, Venice, Pisa, Genoa, Barcelona, England, and the Hanseatic League. Rhodes reached the height of its career about 300 B.C. Its sea code is lost to us, but it was so widely used that the law of the sea for over a thousand years was referred to as the *Rhodian Sea Laws*. As the trading centers shifted to the west, the towns of Italy came into maritime predominance, and we find the small city of Amalfi, in the eleventh century, propounding a code which had extensive application. Lost for centuries, this code was rediscovered in 1843; a copy known as the *Tablet of Amalfi* had been taken from Venice to Vienna by the Austrians. Other Italian coast towns had their own codes; few of them had much general prominence, but all conformed to general practices. Some of these Italian cities introduced new commercial mechanisms. There are examples in Genoa of the first bills of exchange and policies of insurance used in maritime commerce. And one of the earliest great commercial banks of Europe was the Bank of St. George at Genoa, founded about A.D. 1400. Its building still stands.

The *Code of Barcelona,* first established in the thirteenth century, was known as the *Consulado del Mar*. It was widely applied; for perhaps five centuries, controversies involving trade at sea were settled in countless ports by the rules of the *Consulado*. A printed edition appeared in 1494, and there were translations into several languages. The *Consulado* contained two hundred and fifty chapters, and covered more detail of law than any previous maritime code.

To the north, a new code of maritime laws grew in importance. It was the *Code of Oléron,* from the island of that name in the Bay of Biscay, then in British territory. In the thirteenth and fourteenth centuries it was used by British, Scotch, and Norman mariners. Northwestern Europe's mariners did business largely by this code for some centuries; but its use in the Baltic and northern districts ceased with the birth and growth of the Hanseatic League, which established a code of its own, based on the sea laws of Wisby, on the island of Gotland in the north Baltic. These *Sea Laws of Gotland* were, in turn, based on the Code of Oléron. Wisby was the center of northern trade for some time, until its destruction by King Waldemar of Denmark in 1361. Thereafter, the north German towns became the centers of trade.

The Hanseatic League was a confederation of many of the most important Germanic trading centers of northern Europe, with offices or branches in England and Venice and many other non-German countries, and colonies everywhere. Its influence was enormous, and its wealth helped make it one of Europe's strongest powers. Bremen was one of its most powerful units, but Lübeck might be called its capital.

The center of maritime law thus veered steadily from the eastern Mediterranean to the west and the north. In this process of change, the legal system was not altered radically or abruptly. It remained one continuous system. An illustration of the continuity of the system is found in the rules of *jettison,* the throwing overboard of cargo to save the entire venture. All merchants on board must contribute to compensate those whose cargo is lost. There have always been rules governing jettison: in the Rhodian Sea Laws, the captain is required to consult with the passengers who have goods aboard and, by a vote, secure their consent. While this system is not present in current law, it can be traced through two thousand years of successive codes. It is to be found in the Code of Amalfi, the *Consulado* of Barcelona, the Code of Oléron, the Wisby Code, and the Hansa Code. Even the thirteenth-century sea code of the Malay Islands, in a Mohammedan area, contains the same provision. The explanation of this universality is of course that the sea law was developed by merchants themselves and was not the law of territorial princes.

Maritime disputes were sometimes decided by territorial courts, applying the laws of the sea; but more usually special courts, elected by guilds of merchants, tried such cases without the supervision of territorial legal machinery. In general, the codes merely incorporated existing customs and practices and the adjudications of commercial courts. However, some contained legislated rules. This was particularly true of the Hansa Code, through which various new rules were established to cure abuses and to meet new situations.

Beginning in the seventeenth century, and prompted by the growth of nationalism, the individual nations began to adopt sea codes of their own. These were invariably an adoption of existing practices with a few modifications to suit special circumstances; but the essential change instituted was that each nation began to enforce its maritime laws in its own courts. The special maritime courts of the merchants began to disappear.

In the nineteenth century a movement started for the unification of maritime law. The *York-Antwerp Rules* of 1890 were an international codification of the rules applying to "general average." Another codification took place at The Hague in 1921.

One of the most interesting oddities of maritime law concerns the treatment of a vessel in litigation. In maritime law a vessel is treated as a defendant in litigation. In a collision, the owner of a damaged vessel may start an action for relief by "libeling" the offending ship. Originating in the remote past, perhaps in the idea of revenge against the thing which did damage, this rule has been rationalized as useful even though its original purpose has disappeared. If a man runs into you with his car, you can generally start an action by serving a summons on him; but if a ship has injured you, the owner may be in some distant place and the vessel itself may soon go off to China. Thus your chances of getting relief are small unless you can attach the ship itself. Hence the "libel" action (the term in this sense having quite a different meaning from that used in connection with "defamation").

But under American law, and generally in most of the common instances of liability, the owner of the offending vessel may surrender it and its cargo, and relieve himself of any personal liability for damages unless there is gross negligence. The vessel is treated almost as a corporation, the owner's liability being limited to the "corporate" value of the ship. The probable rationale behind this is that it enables merchants to venture with limited liability. Otherwise the risks of sea trade would be so great that few would undertake them, and international commerce would be seriously curtailed.

The theory of vengeance against an inanimate object is further illustrated in the case of an owner leasing his vessel to someone else. If the ship collides with another through the negligence of the lessee or his employees, the owner of the injured vessel may still claim against the offending ship. That the owner of the ship was not actually responsible is of no avail as a defense. The thing has caused an injury, and the thing must pay. This idea runs through much of the admiralty law. As Justice Holmes points out in his *The Common Law*, if a livery stable keeper rents out a horse and buggy which runs someone down, no one would think of claiming the right to seize the wagon. But under American law, even if the vessel injures another while under the direction of a pilot "arbitrarily and compulsorily" taken on board at a foreign port, the vessel is liable and may be libeled. The Supreme Court has declared, in the words of Chief Justice Marshall, that there may be actions against a vessel itself for an offense committed. The ship is actually treated as if it were animate.

CHAPTER 43

Gentilis and Grotius

I: Public International Law

INTERNATIONAL LAW* seems to have reached its lowest ebb in modern times. The nations do lip service to it but violate it when self-interest prompts them. Some statesmen would seem to doubt that it still exists. During the Congressional debates on Lend-Lease, Senator (later Vice-President) Barkley, President Roosevelt's spokesman in the Senate, said: "But we recognize the fact that all international law has been thrown out, and, judging by recent events, we see that it is difficult now to draw a comparison between one act of war that occurred when international law had some force and another act of war. So what is the difference, except that one may be more provocative than the other?"

But a large body of international law did exist before World War II, and I shall later speculate on how much of it has been lost.

(Public) international law governs the relations of nations. An injured citizen has no personal rights under international law, whatever his obligations. All that he can do is ask his government to make a claim against an offending nation, and when this happens the claiming government is asking reparation because of its injured dignity, not because the injured individual has any rights.

Whatever its defects and limitations, international law is no vague, nebulous thing. Many rules of international law are subject to wide dispute, either as to principle or as to interpretation, but it consists largely of rules accepted so widely and so consistently that they were presumed to have become part of the conscience as well as of the law of civilized mankind. "Narrow as may be its scope in the total complex of international relations, and in constant danger of submersion or violation by politics, it nevertheless controls a vast field of human activity and is universally invoked by governments and individuals

* In using the term "international law" in the rest of this book, I shall mean *public international law.*

affected. Few violations escape public notice, and while the sanctions necessarily differ from those of private law, they nevertheless operate with considerable efficacy. States may differ as to what is the rule of International Law, but no State would ever assert exemption from its control."*

In one sense, however, international law is still in a primitive state. Domestic societies have organized themselves so that self-help is no longer needed, but, even with the present United Nations Organization, there is still no international agency to enforce the rules of international law. An aggrieved nation, unable to secure redress otherwise, must resort to self-help, or war, or abandon its rights.

The sources of international law are, largely, custom, but the nations do not always agree on what a custom is, or when it has arisen, nor do the rules of international law always change readily in relation to changing circumstances in the way that domestic customs often do. Another source is the opinions of great international jurists whose views are often cited by international courts or commissions, but the decisions of such bodies are of more importance than the opinions of the jurists whom they cite. Finally, there are treaties and conventions. Treaties sometimes change the law, and there has been some international legislation accepted by the major nations through the many international conventions, some of which I shall refer to later.

II: Early History

IN ANCIENT TIMES war was conducted ruthlessly and without regard to any regulations, but certain usages developed which covered the conduct of states during times of peace. There were many treaties covering commercial and social intercourse and assuring merchants of safety in conducting trade. The Pharaohs entered into several treaties with their neighbors as early as the fourteenth century before Christ, and the Hebrew kings also made such compacts. And even without treaties, ambassadors were generally protected, and there was a reasonable amount of international good faith in executing engagements. But there were neither moral rules nor any form of international coercion to enforce good conduct.

The first consciousness of the rudiments of international law

* Edwin Borchard, in *American Journal of International Law*, vol. 37, pp. 46, 54.

arose in Greece, where the city-states, bound together somewhat by common customs, language, and religion, found it advisable to have an understanding. The so-called Law of the Hellenes, compounded of actual compacts and of what Aristotle called "natural law," included a large amount of regulation of the conduct between states. Ambassadors were privileged and enjoyed some extraterritorial rights. The right of asylum was recognized, especially when a political refugee sought safety in a temple. Arbitration was frequently provided by treaties, and there were elaborate rules of warfare. Declarations of war had to be formal, prisoners could not be slain but were subject to exchange or ransom, temples and embassies were inviolable, the use of poisoned weapons was proscribed, and there were many other "rules of war." But the rules of war applied only to Greek states; Athens, fighting with Persia, did not feel obligated to obey them.

Rome added considerably to international law. At first Rome acted in relation to the other city-states of Italy as did the Greek states to one another. But by the time of the Second Punic War, Rome had come to feel that there was no law but its own. Nevertheless, as it expanded, it permitted the conquered states some degree of autonomy, and, therefore, a body of law was required to govern the relation of states within the Empire. It was the *ius gentium*, the law applying to foreigners, which formed the basis of the new law which then arose. It might be called the internal international law of the Roman Empire. When there was a dispute between two states within the Empire, analogies were drawn from the *ius gentium*, which governed relations between alien individuals. But the Romans developed still more international law. The *ius fetiale*, possibly a branch of the *ius gentium*, covered the formalities which attended a declaration of war; and a *ius bellicum*, or rules of warfare, was based, like the Law of the Hellenes, partly on the concept of natural law.

Much of the confusion which characterized the development of international law in Europe in the late Middle Ages and afterwards was due to the fact that the term *ius gentium* was made interchangeable with the term "law of nations." Although the Romans built some international law on analogies from the *ius gentium*, it was never portrayed as an actual "law of nations" or international law. Obviously enough, European jurists who looked to the Roman *ius gentium*, a system of private law, to find rules of international law ran into error.

The decline of the Roman Empire put an end to international

law for the moment, and we see no further signs of it until some resurgence under the Empire of Charlemagne. But upon the decline of that new Empire, there was an agency rapidly growing in strength which was able to impress upon Western Europe the necessity of some standard of decency in the dealings between nations. This was the Church, which came to pass moral judgment on princes and nations and to impose rules of warfare upon the squabbling states. Christianity itself effected some community among the nations, overriding borders and bringing the nations into some common relationship to each other. That rules of chivalry arose and that the practices of warfare were gradually softened may be attributed chiefly to the influence of the Church.

Much of the later mature international law may be traced to the canon law, and it is through the Church law that international law traces its *ius gentium* roots, for the Church jurists were ardent students of the old Roman law. Arguing by analogy, these churchmen held that the rules and principles of the scientifically developed Roman law often were as applicable to relations between states as to relations between individuals. They were attracted to the *ius gentium* and knew of its inter- or intra-national application by the Romans, and the idea of a *ius naturale* appealed to them from a religious standpoint. In their treatises and codifications of canon law, these religious jurists frequently gave opinions on rules of warfare and of conduct among nations, basing their opinions and decisions upon general rules of Judaeo-Christian morality and ethics, and using the rules of Roman law where they seemed to fit into the Christian scheme of conduct.

Another contributing factor to the development of true international law was the maritime law which had existed in some form or other for ages. It convinced many of the necessity for laws which, in their respective fields, might transcend national borders and take precedence over national law. Maritime law was private law, but it was international or supra-national in its application. Why could there not be a supra-national public law or law of nations!

The end of the Middle Ages, and the birth of nationalism in Europe which followed it, marked the beginning of a movement which resulted in modern international law. In the sixteenth century several writers published treatises or tracts discussing either a presumed body of existing supra-national law or the necessity for developing one. Then came the great Gentilis.

III: Albericus Gentilis

"The work of Gentilis is of enduring value in the history of the law of nations." COLEMAN PHILLIPSON

ALBERICUS GENTILIS (1552-1608), the lawyer son of an Italian physician, did not practice long in his own country. His father, having adopted Protestantism, decided to escape the Inquisition and took his whole family with him first to Austria and then to England. Albericus prospered there and, except for a short period of diplomatic service abroad, remained in England the rest of his life.

Although Gentilis was eminent in his day, he was almost forgotten for about three centuries after his death, his reputation obscured by that of Hugo Grotius, the Dutch jurist who came after him, and it was not until very recent times that historians and jurists have come to appreciate his full genius. Gentilis should probably be called the father of international law, an honor which has been given to Grotius instead. Gentilis's long obscurity is partly due to the reluctance of the English to promote the reputation of an adopted son, and the dislike of the Italians for an apostate.

It was not to be expected that Gentilis would be popular with the Roman Church, and he made it even more antagonistic by a refusal to follow its accepted principles and theses in juridical matters. He was an ardent student of the Roman law and largely responsible for the resumption of the study of it at Oxford, but he repudiated the classical approach to international law—he did not see how one could always apply the principles of private Roman law to the law of nations. Nor would he follow the natural-law concept of the Church. He did believe in a natural law, but his variety was one of "natural reason," by which he meant common sense rather than God-given principle.

Gentilis never made an attempt to codify international law, but his books covered an enormous amount of material. Perhaps the most interesting thing about his work was his freedom from restraint in his thinking. He liked to treat contemporary subjects, on the theory that one must seek tentative rules from existing conditions. These rules were "tentative" because they were, according to Gentilis, subject to change as new facts and circumstances appeared. It was an astonishingly modern approach and in sharp contrast to the previous procedure of taking classic analogies.

One of the problems with which he struggled was that of "freedom of passage." He concluded that in times of peace travelers should be permitted freely to cross one country on their way to another, a principle by no means clear to his contemporaries, and he even held that obstructing peaceful passage in peacetime was a ground for war. He extended the same principle to the open seas, and denied the right of any nation to shut off any but local waters (but he left it to others to determine what "local" waters might be). We later threw ourselves into at least two wars, in 1812 and in 1917, to preserve this principle of the freedom of the seas.

In the field of diplomatic relations, Gentilis advocated the principles that embassies could not be refused, but that a ruler might reject an individual ambassador who was deemed objectionable; that the right to have embassies ceased while war was going on; that diplomatic representatives are outside the local law except for personal or business transactions; that they are entitled to undisputed passage through intervening countries; and that they are entitled to the full protection of their persons and property.

His concept of international society was that of an association of nations bound together by certain rules which were reasonable and proper because they were practical. In order better to understand international society, he studied the composition of nations themselves, and his conclusions were amazingly modern. Like St. Thomas Aquinas, he held that the state did not exist for the sovereign but the sovereign for the state. The Church had by this time become attached to the concept of the divine right of kings, and some of Gentilis's contemporaries, influenced by Church opinion, believed that only Christian princes (and some said only Roman Catholic princes) had the right to govern. But Gentilis, the radical, saw no reason why infidel states should not be considered in the family of nations, or why their princes should not be just as much entitled to govern them as Christian rulers were to rule Christian states.

His labors in the field of international law were extensive. He laid down rules for the drafting of peace treaties. He considered the problems arising out of conflicts between two states, with both of which a third had treaties of friendship. Although he opposed many of the Church's theories, he did adhere to the principle that there could be no alliance of a Christian nation with an infidel nation against another Christian nation, and condemned the alliance which Francis I had made with the Turks. He held that treaties were similar to contracts, and that misrepresentation, substantial error, or breach warranted repudiation. He maintained, however, that while breach of a treaty might also warrant retaliation, it did not form a ground for a subsequent violation of a later treaty between the nations.

Gentilis gave more attention to the rules of war than had any of his predecessors. He discussed in great detail the justifiability of war, giving prominent place to "self-defense." He insisted not only on just cause for war but also on its just conduct. One principle which he maintained that has been lost in modern society is that there must be a formal declaration of war, and he asked for a period between this proclamation and the commencing of hostilities to give time for a possible peaceful settlement.

Gentilis also maintained that certain methods of warfare should be proscribed, among them the use of assassins, poison, magic arts, serpents, and savage beasts; but he sanctioned the use of spies (at their own risk), elephants, horses, and dogs. He did sanction the destruction of fortress towns, but was against useless destruction of temples, statues, and fruit trees except in retaliation. The civilian population was to be inviolate; prisoners were not to be put to death. Anything done against barbarians, however, seemed to him lawful.

His observations on maritime warfare were sometimes very advanced. He opposed the current practice of issuing "letters of marque,"* which were invitations to legalized piracy. He had not advanced, however, to the point of condemning the seizure of private property to satisfy the obligations of the sovereign or of the state. He did consider the rules of neutrality, and maintained that the truly neutral should be protected.

In all, his greatest contribution to international law was to help free it from the chains in which it had previously been bound by religious concepts and clerical reasoning.

* A license to engage in reprisal against vessels of another nation.

IV: Hugo Grotius

". . . of whom every learned man has perhaps learned something." DR. JOHNSON

GROTIUS'S (1583-1645) renown overshadows that of all the other modern writers on international law. His service to the subject and to humanity was enormous, and perhaps the Gentilis-versus-Grotius controversy may be solved by calling the former the grandfather, and Grotius the father, of modern international law. Despite embellishments and improvements by later authorities, Grotius's *De Jure Belli et Pacis* was the standard work on international law until most recent times. King Gustavus Adolphus of Sweden carried it under his pillow on military campaigns. The Pope added it to the *Index Expurgatorius,* the list of books forbidden to good Roman Catholics, but this ban on the book acted somewhat like the prosecution of an American book by the Watch and Ward Society of Boston—its sales increased. Many editions were published, and it became a textbook at most of the universities. Unfortunately, Grotius himself got nothing out of it except two hundred free copies.

Hugo Grotius was remarkably precocious. At age seven he wrote a book of Latin poems, no mean accomplishment at any age. At twelve he entered Leyden University; at fourteen he produced another book; and at fifteen, still another. The Dutch Ambassador to France took the prodigy with him to Orléans, where Grotius continued his studies and gained his degree of Doctor of Laws. And, indeed, his earlier accomplishments had been no freak of development, for the boy began to practice law, on his return to Holland, before he was seventeen. At twenty-four he was made Advocate-General of Holland, Zeeland, and West Friesland, and in 1613 he was sent as Dutch Ambassador to England.

On his return to Holland, Grotius, a Protestant, became involved in the religious controversies wrecking Europe at that time, which were particularly severe in his country. He was convicted of treason for his religious ideas, and sentenced to life imprisonment. But through the ingenuity of his wife, he was smuggled out of prison in a packing case supposedly filled with his books. The ex-prisoner fled to France, where his exile was made somewhat easier by the friendliness of King Louis XIII, who granted him a pension, not always promptly paid, of three thousand livres a year.

Although naturalized as a Frenchman, Grotius did go back to Holland, but was soon banished again by bigotry and never returned. Holland, which claims him as her greatest jurist, repudiated him during his life. Grotius went first to Hamburg and then to Sweden, where he entered the diplomatic service, returning eventually to France as Swedish Ambassador and staying there ten years. When he retired in 1645 he made another trip to Sweden, but on his return to France fell ill and died.

Of all his works, the *De Jure Belli et Pacis*, written during his first sojourn in France and published in 1626, was his greatest. He borrowed freely and quite frankly from Gentilis, but extended the latter's work enormously. The *De Jure Belli* was a comprehensive work which is quoted to this day. It is not without many imperfections, for Grotius plowed much new ground, and his speculations and conclusions were not always sound or logical. Sometimes he went astray because, like so many other early-modern jurists, he got tangled up with metaphysical and philosophical fallacies. He based his system of international law on "natural law" as "the dictate of right reason which points out that a given act, because of its opposition to or conformity with man's rational nature, is either morally wrong or morally necessary, and accordingly forbidden or commanded by God, the author of all nature."

He accepted the Roman-based analogy that rules which bound individuals bound nations. But Grotius also granted that there is a voluntary law of nations based upon free consent and upon usages and customs. To this he gave the name of *ius gentium*, again getting mixed up with Roman concepts. He held, however, that, when there is a conflict between the *ius gentium* (or what he might have called "customary law") and "natural law," the latter must prevail.

Whatever fallacies Grotius may have been guilty of as disclosed by later criticism, his services to mankind and to his subject were great. He became interested in international law because he could not understand the barbarity with which war was waged in his generation. As he put it: "I saw prevailing throughout the Christian world a license in making war of which even barbarous nations would have been ashamed; recourse to arms being had for slight reasons or no reason; and when arms were once taken up, all reverence for divine and human law was thrown away, just as if men were thenceforth authorized to commit all crimes without restraint."

Prompted by the humanitarianism of his original interest in the field of international law, Grotius did his best to impress the world with the necessity for a higher standard of action in warfare. Whether his use of "natural law" was logical or not, he does stand as the greatest of the reformers in international law.

CHAPTER 44

The Building Period

I: Richard Zouche

"Zouche is the greatest of the earlier English school of international jurists and publicists . . ."

COLEMAN PHILLIPSON

IN THE SEVENTEENTH and eighteenth centuries a number of Englishmen and Continentals, starting with the work of Grotius, built up a fine structure of international law. Some further perfection was needed in later periods to bring it up to the comparative enlightenment of the era just before World War I, but most of the work had been done or collected by five men.

The first of the five was Richard Zouche, an Englishman of charming personality and profound learning, born in 1590, whose influence on the Continent even exceeded his popularity with his own countrymen. He sat as a judge of the High Court of Admiralty under both Charles I and Charles II, and for a while occupied the chair of civil law at Oxford from which Gentilis had lectured.

It was Jeremy Bentham who coined the term "international law." Grotius had used the term *ius gentium*, carrying with it the mistaken concept that the Romans had devised rules which were exactly applicable to the relations of states. And so we may place Zouche in his transitional role by the fact that he bettered Grotius's term and devised *ius inter gentes*, or "law between nations." In a way, Zouche went back to Gentilis, insisting that international law could not be extracted merely from classic precedents and by theorizing. He used current examples of the conduct of nations upon which to base much of his own discussion.

Perhaps it was the era in which he lived that prompted Zouche to this departure from the classicism of Grotius. In the preceding two centuries the great national states had arisen and Europe had freed itself of most of the restricting influences of feudalism and the pressure of the Church toward universal rule, so that the concepts of sovereignty and nationalism took on new meanings. Standing armies had come into vogue, and rules of military discipline had become necessary. Ambassadorial usages developed solidly, and various new factors appeared which required agreement among the nations. In Zouche's period, the bloody Thirty Years' War turned into a struggle between Catholicism and Protestantism and, at the same time, one between imperialism and nationalism. The Peace of Westphalia, which ended that conflict, laid the factual foundation for modern international law by recognizing the absolute territorial jurisdiction of the national states. And, during this same period, colonial and maritime expansion by the European powers opened up a new field of international relations.

Zouche, though not to be classed with Grotius, did contribute a better organization to the subject of international law, and he furthered the idea that it must deal with the practical as well as the theoretical. He was the founder of the "positivist" or "historical" school of international law. Zouche's great book, *De Jure inter Gentes,** published shortly after the Peace of Westphalia, reflected the new times. He was Socratic in one way, for he did not arrive at many conclusions, being satisfied to raise problems and to offer conflicting precedents and arguments. For, while he acknowledged a *ius naturale* as one of the component parts of international law, he maintained that custom was also part of it, and consent as well. He was less concerned with what the law should be than to ascertain what it actually was in practice.

II: Samuel Pufendorf

"His treatise is a mine in which all successors must dig."
SIR JAMES MACKINTOSH

PUFENDORF (1632-1694), one of the greatest German jurists, produced many notable works, on the whole somewhat dry and difficult reading but of great importance in the history of jurisprudence. Perhaps his most valuable service was in pointing out that "natural

* Its full title is *Juris et Judicii Fecialis sive, Juris inter Gentes, et Quaestionum de Eodem Explicatio.*

law" was a much-abused term, used by many merely to rationalize their own purposes. He stated the difficulty upon which I have commented several times, that, if there is any "natural law," there is no way of determining whose version is correct. Therefore, he tried to establish a different approach to "natural law." He started with no theological concepts but merely with reason and philosophy. Like Grotius, but unencumbered by the latter's largely theocratic version of the natural-law concept, Pufendorf discussed the "natural" duties of man to man and used these duties as the chief base for his conclusions as to the duties of state to state.

There are two important doctrines in international law with which a good deal of conjuring may be done. They are the doctrines of "self-defense" and of "necessity." Pufendorf took particular interest in "necessity," giving many instances of its application. He noted that this principle requires a nation to refuse transit to foreign troops if they are to be used against a friendly neighbor. Again, he pointed out that aliens must be permitted easy transit across one's borders as a general rule, but "necessity" may dictate, in some circumstances, that transit be denied them, as in the case of diseased or enemy aliens. Such a principle seems obvious enough, and you may wonder why any mention of it should be made. But principles obvious to us now were far from obvious to the generation to which they were first propounded.

Pufendorf had his say about another issue which has plagued the world for centuries—freedom of the seas. He had no doubt about the correctness of the thesis that the seas should be free. He said that no nation could have dominion over them, and that, besides, there was room enough for everyone. He did admit sovereignty over what are called "territorial waters," waters adjacent to one's own shores, but he, like Grotius, left it to others to determine the extent of such jurisdiction.

Very modern in many ways, he nevertheless recognized the legality of "booty," the practice of grabbing anything you can in enemy territory and sending it home. Pufendorf held that booty belongs to the sovereign, who may divide it among his soldiers.

Pufendorf followed Grotius for the most part. Yet his contribution to international law was an important one, for he developed a scientific approach to its problems and suggested a more systematic and useful classification and arrangement. His most bitter critic was

Gottfried Wilhelm von Leibnitz.* Author of the *Codex Juris Gentium Diplomaticus*, which helped greatly to clarify thinking in international law, Leibnitz disliked theorizing like Pufendorf's, which failed to recognize the realities of international life. What *should* be seemed to him of little practical consequence. One must, he maintained, deal with current ideas of morality and ethics, good, bad, or indifferent; and relations between states could be governed only by what they were willing to recognize as sound and practical principles. But there has always been a conflict between those who wish the law to be what it should be and those who wish to deal with it as it is.

III: Cornelis van Bynkershoek

"He who returns to his sovereign's ally . . . is deemed to have returned to his own country."

VAN BYNKERSHOEK

GROTIUS had avoided modern examples, basing his conclusions on natural law. Pufendorf, though differing in his concept of natural law, was also a "naturalist." Zouche had been a "positivist," holding that actual usage was more important than theory and using many modern illustrations to point up his thesis. Van Bynkershoek. a Dutchman (1673-1743), followed the Zouche method. He could not give much weight to abstractions predicated on "natural law," and gave almost exclusive attention to positive law and to actual practice.

In the old problem of freedom of the seas, he took the side of Grotius and Pufendorf, holding that the seas were free to the navigation of all, and that fishing rights could not be restricted on the high seas. The issue was an ancient one. Venice had claimed the Adriatic; Genoa, the Ligurian Sea; France, an indefinite area around her coast; and Norway and Denmark had laid similar claims to great stretches of open water. Spain and Portugal had gone even further. With the approval of the Pope, they had divided the western oceans. England claimed wide jurisdiction over huge bodies of open water. But eventually the theories of Grotius, Pufendorf, and Van Bynkershoek prevailed. It was Van Bynkershoek who suggested the practical solution of the delineation of "territorial waters." He pointed out that effective protection of the waters was the proper criterion.

* See Chapter 21, Section I.

Therefore, the distance of a cannon shot (a marine league, or three miles) became the maximum of territorial sovereignty off a coast.

Van Bynkershoek was not interested in producing a complete code of law. He was concerned only with the clarification of certain individual rules, among them those relating to the treatment of ambassadors, whose persons, families, and possessions, he insisted, must be fully protected. And he was deeply interested in the basis of some of the rules of war, working intensively on the subjects of blockade and contraband. He sometimes tended to a harsh view, that the necessities of war permit almost any method, saying that the virtues are noble but cannot always be insisted on. Grotius had held that a formal declaration of war was necessary, but the Japanese could have cited Van Bynkershoek for the proposition that it was not.

Before his time not much had been done to clarify the previously hazy concept of "neutrality." The Romans had considered every nation either friend or enemy. Van Bynkershoek imposed on the neutral an obligation not to assist either belligerent, and went far to protect the rights and property of neutrals who maintained such disinterest.

IV: Emmerich de Vattel

> *Vattel's* Droit des Gens *"ought to be studied by every gentleman of liberal education, and by youth, in whom the best morals should be inculcated."*
>
> JOSEPH CHITTY

VATTEL (1714-1767), a German diplomat of Swiss birth, had a critical and selective approach, though he contributed comparatively little original thinking. Before his time there had only been Grotius's *De Jure Belli et Pacis* as a textbook on international law. The writings of the other top jurists in the field had been more scattered and less co-ordinated. But Vattel's *Droit des Gens* came to be another text.

Vattel had a precise, logical, and hard mind. In many ways he anticipated Jeremy Bentham, the British reformer, for he was a utilitarian, announcing the creed of the "greatest good for the greatest number." His utilitarianism, however, had a semireligious basis; it was one to be exercised in the reflected light of God to give men a sense of fairness and equity. He held that morality can be brought to its height of perfection only through love of God.

Like so many other jurists, Vattel thought and wrote much about natural law. If the reader by this time is thoroughly confused as to the term, and disturbed by the many variations of it, let him take solace in the fact that the jurists themselves seem to have been just as confused, disagreeing so much as to the meaning and application of the term that it became almost useless. Vattel conceived of nations as moral persons, having obligations and rights; and he suggested that nations live together as a set of free individuals might in a "state of nature." He concluded, therefore, that the law of nations is merely the "law of nature," and, thus, nations are obliged to live with each other in the way man had to live in a "state of nature" before there were any nations. But this sort of theorizing hardly establishes valid premises from which further reasoning can be drawn. I have already pointed out how this "state of nature" concept confused "natural law" even further. Hobbes and Rousseau had quite different ideas about the state of man in nature, and between these two extremes were a multitude of other opinions. I wonder if even anthropologists could agree on a uniform "state of nature."

Yet Vattel arrived at many attractive conclusions. He conceived a sort of golden rule applying to the relations of the nations. His "natural law" imposed a conscience on the nations, and, while many of his conclusions were faulty, he did much to elevate the ethics of international relations.

V: Lord Stowell

> *"The truth may not always be discernible, but when it is discovered, it is according to the truth and not according to the fiction that we are to give to the transaction its character and denomination."*
>
> LORD STOWELL

LORD STOWELL (1745-1836) lived in a difficult era. Many Englishmen hated the French Revolution and its leaders bitterly, and Napoleon was perhaps the object of as much horrified disgust as Hitler was in our day. An English judge, sitting in a court which had before it cases involving foreigners and their rights, could not have found it easy to free himself of his personal prejudices and to avoid the temptation of deciding litigations in the interests of his own nation. But Lord Stowell did just that. As a judge of the High Court of Admiralty he stood carefully by accepted rules of law, never hesitating to apply them against his own countrymen.

He sat upon many prize court cases. A "prize" is a vessel captured at sea during war or a state of war, and a "prize court" establishes whether the prize was legally captured, whether the vessel or any part of the cargo may be confiscated, and any other issues which arise out of the circumstances. While such a court is a domestic court in fact, it is in theory an international court. It administers international law, but it is not unnatural that it would follow the war regulations of the country in which it sits, whether or not these violate international law. But Lord Stowell endeavored always to adhere to proper principles of law. In fact, he may be said to have "made" a good deal of the law of prize, just as Lord Mansfield is said to have "made" much of the English commercial law.

His work had a marked effect on the general development of international law, for Stowell's decisions were of universal application. In the early case of the *Maria,* Lord Stowell laid down a clear rule as to the locality of a prize court and the law which it is to administer: "The seat of judicial authority is locally here in the belligerent country, according to the known law and practice of nations, but the law itself has no locality. It is the duty of the judge sitting in an Admiralty Court not to deliver occasional and shifting opinions to serve present purposes and particular national interests, but to administer with indifference that justice which the law of nations holds out without distinction to independent States, some happening to be neutral and some belligerent." Thus he maintained the principle that a prize court is an international court.

Lord Stowell would have been unhappy to see the destruction of many sound rules of international law during the past few decades. One can imagine him sternly upholding the well-established old rules of law, regardless of the nationality of the injured party and the emotions of the moment.

In many cases involving conflict of laws, Lord Stowell established clear and logical principles. In his famous *Dalrymple case,* he had to determine whether a marriage contracted in Scotland by a British officer quartered there was valid. Lord Stowell declared that the English law must apply because the matter was brought up in an

English court. But, he continued, the English law should be that only the law of the place where the marriage was contracted could establish validity. Therefore, he said, the English law itself must retire in favor of an application of Scotch law, and so the case was decided. He applied the same principle in deciding whether a Jewish marriage was valid, investigating the rabbinical law to find the pertinent rules.

One important doctrine he clarified and laid to permanent rest. Many had claimed that the domicile in time of peace must be deemed the domicile in time of war. Stowell held otherwise, and it has become the established rule that neutrals in an enemy country in time of war must be treated for prize purposes as enemies and, similarly, that a merchant of a neutral country, having trading interests in an enemy country, must be deemed an enemy to the extent of his interests in that country. We had it as the *Trading with the Enemy Act* in World War I, and during the last war also. An American citizen, while in an enemy country, has been treated for all practical purposes as though he were an enemy alien.

International law has, since Lord Stowell's time, produced many jurists of eminence, but none of stature equal to his. Our own James Kent does deserve mention, though, as one of the strongest modern advocates of the thesis that only the consent of the nations forms the true basis for international law, a theory now almost universally accepted among jurists.

VI: The Modern Codes

THE FIRST ENACTMENT of rules of international law was the *Declaration of Paris* of 1856, a treaty between a small group of powers who asked others to join them in the establishment of fixed rules of conduct and of law. It was acceded to by almost all the maritime powers, and covered much of the law of warfare at sea; it abolished privateering, and legislated regarding contraband, blockade, etc. Then, in 1864, the *Geneva Convention* legislated on the treatment of wounded soldiers. This was signed by nine states. In 1868 the *Declaration of St. Petersburg* legislated on the use of explosive or inflammable projectiles.

In 1874 a conference was held at Brussels, called by the Russian government, to consider the conduct of war. In the meantime, the American code of warfare had been prepared for the United States government by Francis Lieber during the Civil War. It gave instructions to officers in the field and covered all sorts of questions. This code attracted wide attention and formed the basis of the work of the Brussels Conference. The Conference failed because the British government refused to ratify the convention it established, but many of the principles laid down by this Conference were later adopted. The *Declaration of Brussels* contained the principle that "the laws of war do not concede to belligerents an unlimited power with reference to the choice of means of injuring the enemy." Pillage was prohibited; open towns were not to be bombarded. There were also rules governing occupation of enemy territory, including a careful distinction between the treatment of public and private property. It contained, as well, important rules governing the treatment of prisoners.*

There followed a series of conventions and declarations of various peace conferences, starting with the First International Peace Conference of 1899, at The Hague, called by the Czar of Russia. Its important Conventions were ratified by almost all the powers. The Second Peace Conference of 1907 revised the Conventions of 1899. Hague Conventions successively covered the use of dumdum bullets; missiles ejected from balloons; gas; certain principles of sea warfare; the opening of hostilities; the status of enemy merchantmen at the outbreak of hostilities; the conversion of merchantmen into ships of war; the laying of automatic mines; bombardments by naval forces; restrictions on the right of capture in maritime warfare; and the rights and duties of neutrals.

In 1908 the *Declaration of London* provided rules governing blockade, contraband, and other aspects of naval warfare. It was an excellent and carefully worked-out convention, but the House of Lords seemed to think it was too favorable to neutrals, and England failed to ratify the Declaration.

After World War I there were a number of conferences looking

* Americans in service during the last war were carefully instructed as to their rights if they should be taken prisoner. They were told, for instance (and it is an accepted rule of international law), that they could be obliged only to give their true names and rank or else their serial number and that they did not have to answer any questions as to the state of their country or its military forces. But this is only a small detail of the very elaborate rules for the treatment of prisoners, stated at considerable length in our army field manual.

toward further international "legislation" on the rules of warfare, and in 1924, at the instance of the Assembly of the League of Nations, the Council created the Committee of Experts for the Progressive Codification of International Law. Three subjects were decided upon for treatment, and the Harvard Research in International Law prepared draft conventions on nationality, territorial waters, and the responsibility of states for damage done in their territory to the person or property of foreigners. But all this work came to little; there was too much disagreement on major points to permit any general acceptance of the conventions.

What did all these conventions and declarations accomplish? At the moment, the layman may conclude that little had been accomplished, but that is not true. Some rules of war are obsolete by general agreement or acceptance; others are so in fact; still others, which are not obsolete at all, have been violated with such persistence that they might as well be obsolete. However, an astonishing number of the rules of warfare are observed. Even the Nazis and the Japanese observed many of them; they have become too strong a part of the conscience of mankind to be violated, particularly when violation accomplishes nothing but to increase the determination of the enemy. Furthermore, some of the rules of international law applying in times of peace are rarely violated, and these rules are of great value to international society.

VII: International Law in Times of Peace

GREAT AREAS of international activity have already been covered by rules of law, but vast possible fields remain untouched. Conspicuous among these are the areas involving what is called "national policy." A trend does now exist, however, toward a greater surrender of freedom of action even in areas of political policy. It was accelerated by the creation of the League of Nations, however feeble its work may have been, and was further directed by the establishment of the United Nations, however weak an association that may be. It remains to be seen if the trend will continue, or whether there will be a retrogression and an intensification of nationalism. There are signs of both at the time of this writing.

One of the necessary results of basing international law on the old Roman law of nations was that the persons with whom it deals must be equal. The Roman law dealt with persons, and they were deemed to be equal. Therefore, by analogy, although international law dealt with nations and not individuals, the nations were treated as equals, and this concept of equality runs through international law. While unassailed in principle, this rule of equality means little when the great powers impose their will upon the weaker, as we have had occasion to see.

The persons at international law are thus the nations, but the concept of nationality is a recent one. The first European peoples of history were not nations. Kings ruled peoples, not territories. The concept of territorial sovereignty came much later in the development of feudalism, when permanent attachment to the land created a pyramidal structure, from serf to lord, and up to king. From this organization of society it was logical that the King of the Franks should become King of France.

The family of nations is rather an exclusive lot, in some ways. While its members are all equal in theory, they are equal only when so recognized. There are rules of international law by which equality of status is determined. Some states have been adopted into the family only with conditions. For example, restrictions were laid upon Montenegro, Serbia, and Rumania when they were recognized by the major powers. Similarly, Czechoslovakia, Yugoslavia, and Poland were constrained by restrictions when they were created (in the case of Poland, "re-created") after World War I. Then there are other groups of states which are almost, but not quite, full members of the family. Among these were the British Dominions, which, for all practical purposes, were wholly independent but still were not always treated like those powers which are free from an Empire association. Since the creation of the British "Commonwealth," its individual states have acquired clear independent status. Soviet Russia has been attempting, not without some success, to create for its constituent republics an international status similar to that of the British Dominions. Vassal states, protectorates and such, have a status inferior to that of other nations.

From time to time a new government comes into being, by the actual creation of a new sovereignty or by annexation or emancipation. Such a state requires "recognition" before it may sit at the family table. When such a newcomer is entitled to recognition is often a difficult question. There are some rules which apply; but it comes down, in practice, to what each other power may see fit to do.

Often when a revolution has put a new government into power, another state may recognize it as a *de facto* government until it has proved itself permanent and may be recognized as a government *de jure* (a legal government). Sometimes recognition is formal; sometimes it is by silent acquiescence. Annexations and changes of sovereignty over a section of the globe are subject to recognition or the denial of it. For example, when Italy annexed Ethiopia, some nations gave recognition while others staunchly refused it. Similarly, Russia has been using every coercive means possible to secure universal recognition of East Germany, but without success to date. On the other hand, we have given recognition to some of the satellite countries behind the Iron Curtain, though they are wholly under the control of Soviet Russia. We have even given a strange sort of recognition to the Ukraine and Byelorussia, though these are actually constituent states of the U.S.S.R. For reasons which seem to us overwhelmingly proper, we recognize the Chinese government seated on the island of Formosa as the "Chinese Government," and refuse recognition to the massive power on the mainland of China. It may well be said that the rules of "recognition" are in a state of chaos, if, indeed, any such rules remain.

Under international law a state is entitled to the right of self-defense.* From this simple right, however, odd conclusions have been rationalized. In 1807 the British justified a bombardment of neutral Copenhagen because the Danes had refused to turn over their fleet to the British, who were fighting France and Russia. In 1914 Germany justified its violation of Belgian and Luxembourg neutrality by the necessities of self-defense. The United States in 1823 announced the Monroe Doctrine on the principle of self-defense. It made clear that it would go to war if any European power sought to intervene in the Western Hemisphere, and the United States did go to war against Spain on such grounds. Austria-Hungary's ultimatum to Serbia in 1914, which precipitated World War I, was based upon her alleged right of self-defense against misgovernment in a neighboring state. The intervention of some of the powers in Russia after World War I was upon this right to defend themselves against a neighboring nuisance. The initial Russian attack on Finland and much of the strange behavior of Russia after World War II may also be laid to this odd theory of aggressive self-defense. It is conceivable

* I am getting halfway into the rules of war at this point, but there is certainly no definite line of demarcation.

that we may someday directly attack Cuba to drive out Castro and his Communists and that we shall do so on the theory of self-defense.

The defense of "national honor" has also led to strange situations. Often some isolated incident outside the control of the local government has been made the justification for a military venture, generally with some ulterior objective. Taking advantage of the murder of several Christians in Annam and Cambodia, the French, in the latter part of the last century, came to the defense of their national honor by annexing Indo-China. One of the justifications for the French war against the Bey of Algiers in 1830, and later annexation of Algeria, was that the Bey had struck a French envoy in the face with a fan. Many similar profitable protections of the national honor may be laid at the door of all the great powers, not excluding the United States. The British have been peculiarly adept at choosing local situations to further an imperialistic policy. The great powers have never been loath to rush to the defense of their honor when they deemed it assailed by a small nation with exploitable resources or good harbors.

Where maritime law ends and public international law begins is not clear. At any rate, many rules of international law govern the sea and its use, the sea itself being international, except for the narrow belt along the national coasts. Vessels are treated as though they were floating territory of their state, and the state of the craft is that of its registration, not of its ownership, each ship on the high seas sailing under some national flag and registry. In two instances, however, this runs into a conflict of laws. In case of war far different rules prevail. In foreign waters or foreign ports, by custom and general acceptance, the vessel subjects itself to the local law but is governed by its own law in so far as its own internal discipline is concerned.

To cover the whole range of international law would take volumes. There are countless points at which international conflicts might arise, and the great majority of them have been settled with some degree of uniformity. Nations have simply found it made sense to agree. For example, in the recognition of territorial changes, there are numerous rules covering the determination of boundaries, the treatment of inhabitants of annexed territories and of their property, the legality of occupation and acquisition of territory, the legality of cessions of territory, the delineation of boundaries only generally described in treaties or cessions, and many other problems.

Some rules are detailed and carefully reasoned. When a border is established as the line of a river, for example, it is not the center of the river which marks the line but the center of the main channel of the river. If the channel changes by erosion or accretion, the line changes with it, but if it is altered by sudden change of the course of the river, the old line stands.

Diplomatic agents are protected by carefully delineated rules. Consulates and embassy buildings are deemed extraterritorial—islands of the territory of the accredited power. A diplomatic agent is generally immune from process in local courts and is exempt from most direct local taxation. There are also elaborate rules as to the appointment, accrediting, and recall of diplomatic agents.

There are several areas, however, in which, while there should be international law, there is none. One of the most important is in the recognition of citizenship. There have been serious controversies between Poland and our ambassadors over the treatment of persons whom we recognize as citizens while Poland claims them as its own. The conflict arises because Poland, like many other countries, holds that nationality depends on the nationality of one's parents, or, in the case of a woman, on the nationality of her husband. We, on the other hand, claim that birth in the United States makes one a citizen here, regardless of the nationality of parents or husband. It is thus possible to have dual nationality, as many of our citizens have, including large numbers who were born in Hawaii of Japanese ancestry. In the past we have had many squabbles with other countries who have seized our citizens while within their borders and enforced military service upon them, on the ground that, under their law, these individuals were not Americans at all but nationals of the impressing country. Under present law, each country has the right, for most purposes, to determine for itself who is or is not its citizen.

Another conflict of importance relates to the extent to which a citizen of one country subjects himself to the local law if he resides in a foreign state in time of peace. South America holds to what is called the *Calvo Doctrine*, that, in assuming residence within a foreign land, an alien must take the law as he finds it. England and the United States, on the other hand, claim a sort of international "natural law." We hold our citizens entitled to certain fundamental rights, wherever they may be. If one of our citizens is treated unconscionably by some other nation, it is no defense for that nation to point out that it treats its own citizens just as badly. There is a clear distinction between this stand, which we have constantly, but ever more feebly, maintained, and the "extraterritoriality" which we have sometimes imposed on weaker nations such as China. In that case we do not admit that any local foreign law governs our citizens. But in all other situations we do recognize that the local law is binding in so far as it does not impinge on what we believe to be the fundamental rights of human beings.

VIII: Individual Claims

ALTHOUGH the rules of international law govern the conduct of nations, it is usually the individual who is injured by the breach of these rules. Yet he has, strictly speaking, no rights at all, under the law.

When a national of a power victorious in war has sustained some injury at the hands of the defeated enemy or its nationals, his chance of recovery depends on whatever deal is made at the peace table. However, if a claim arises in times of peace, there are pretty clear rules to govern it. This is true even though the individual is not recognized as a claimant. It is a strange system, and perhaps one of the gravest weaknesses of international law is that it is a law of nations only in which individuals, as such, have no rights.

The injured person may obtain redress through his own government's taking up his case with the government at fault. But the other *government* must be at fault; it is not enough that its national is at fault. The United States has no claim against Sweden if a Swedish citizen stole my watch in that country. It has a claim only if I have been denied justice, if the Swedish government failed to try to apprehend the criminal, or if, having been brought to trial, he is discharged without a genuine attempt at conviction having been made. When I have been denied justice, then my own government has a claim, based not upon the fact that its national has been injured but on the fact that the claiming government has suffered an injury to its dignity.

It follows from this peculiar reasoning that a government can present a claim only for an individual who was its national both at the time the injury took place (otherwise its dignity would not have been impaired) and at the time the claim is made (otherwise it would be making a claim for someone not entitled to its protection). Thus, unless special machinery is established, a large group of individuals without a protecting government are left without any means of making international claims, for there are now in the world vast numbers of "stateless" persons, and every country has its refugees, with no government of their own to protect them.

Claims are often settled by direct negotiation or by the mediation or friendly intervention of another state acting as arbiter. Frequently, however, claims commissions are established. Some of these, whether established by peace treaties or by conventions, have been boards representing both nations involved, generally with a neutral sitting as chairman; such commissions have considered either cross-claims of both sides or only the claims of one nation. In some instances, when a lump-sum, aggregate settlement of all claims has been agreed upon, another commission has then been established by the recipient of the settlement to determine how it should be distributed among its own claimants.

CHAPTER 45

The First "Big Three"

"The law speaks too softly to be heard amid the din of arms." GAIUS MARIUS, IN PLUTARCH'S LIVES

I: Directions

UNTIL 1914 there had been a steady development in international law. Hoping that someday we might have permanent peace, men had sought, meanwhile, to lessen the horror of war and the tragedies of its consequences. But hate breeds evil, and the hate engendered by World War I introduced a retrogression in international law. More severe than the immediate consequences of this were the later, World War II, results.

In preface to this story of the breakdown of international law, let me say that I have no use for the school which holds that international law, as applied to war, is no longer of any consequence because of the emergence of so-called "total war." I am not sure that there has been any change in warfare which might necessitate new rules of law, except that new and more horrible weapons have been invented. I do understand, of course, that the more vicious of the totalitarians have made war in a way which seems new to us. But it is not, in fact, new at all; they have merely gone back to more primitive ways and have re-advanced the thesis that what is good for the state is "good," and that no ethical restraints on self-interest should be recognized. That has been made clear in both Nazi and Communist writings. These systems have propounded the thesis that the desirable end justifies any means, however horrible. Those who say that rules of war are no longer needed are, in fact, acquiescing in this evil doctrine in the name of "practicality."

Must we fight evil with evil? Sometimes, in reprisal, we must, but there are ethical limits. If the enemy should torture prisoners to secure military information, our reprisal should be severe, but not to the extent of torturing enemy prisoners. Torture in retaliation might be rationalized as proper but could hardly be countenanced by decency. It seems clear that if the nations which hope for a better world do not maintain the standards of morality and ethics they preach, we shall sink to the level of barbarism we deplore.

II: The Old Rules of War

BEFORE WORLD WAR I the rules of warfare were in great measure well defined and clear. You will find most of them, but slightly changed, in the war manuals issued by the services at the beginning of World War II.* Most were based on treaties or international conventions or the repeated opinions of authorities.

Underlying these rules were three great principles. The first was *military necessity*, permitting a belligerent to apply any amount and kind of force to compel complete submission of the enemy, except as it was limited by the other two principles, *humanity* and *chivalry*. "The right of belligerents to adopt means of injuring the enemy is not unlimited," said the *Rules of Land Warfare*, which is replete with the limitations civilized nations had imposed upon themselves.

As far as specific weapons were concerned, the old rules were behind the times; the nations had not gotten around to a full agreement on the propriety of some. Poison gas was proscribed only as a result of World War I and then not by unanimous agreement of the powers. And World War I had not been concerned with rocket bombs, atomic bombs, or even modern flame throwers. The recitation of "dumdum bullets" and "explosives discharged from balloons" as prohibited weapons was pitiful. The latter proscription had already been interpreted, before World War II, as failing to exclude "the use of modern military aircraft against armed forces or defended places."

From the great number of detailed rules, I shall select those which seem most important to my story. Among these are the rules which prohibited bombardments of undefended places. Paragraphs 45 to 48 of the *Rules of Land Warfare* state:

"45. Bombardment of undefended places forbidden.—The attack or bombardment, by whatever means, of towns, villages, dwellings,

* *Rules of Land Warfare*, War Department Basic Field Manual FM 27-10 (1940); and *Tentative Instructions for the Navy of the United States Governing Maritime and Aerial Warfare* (May, 1941).

or buildings which are undefended is prohibited (H.R., art. 25).*

"46. Use of balloons.—The addition of the words 'by whatever means' was for the purpose of making it clear that the bombardment of these undefended localities from balloons or airplanes is prohibited.

"47. Defended place defined.—Investment, bombardment, assault, and siege have always been recognized as legitimate means of warfare, but under the foregoing rule (par. 45) their use is limited to defended places which certainly will include the following:

a. A fort or fortified place.

b. A town surrounded by detached forts, which is considered jointly with such forts as an indivisible whole.

c. A place that is occupied by a combatant military force or through which such a force is passing. The occupation of such a place by sanitary troops alone is not sufficient to make it a defended place.

"48. Throwing projectiles from aircraft on combatants and defended places.—There is no prohibition of general application among the great powers against the discharge of authorized projectiles from aircraft against combatant troops or defended places."

These rules were amplified by others suggesting the warning of civilian inhabitants before a bombardment.

The longest section of the *Rules of Land Warfare* was devoted to prisoners of war. It covered such areas as who may be treated as prisoners; the obligations placed on prisoners themselves; the effects which they must be permitted to retain; their evacuation from the front; what information must be given to the enemy by prisoners; proper methods of internment; requirements for humane treatment of prisoners; hygienic laws; treatment of the ill; religious freedom; work which they may be compelled to do; wages they are to be paid for such work; correspondence to be permitted; parcels they may receive; right to make complaints; punishments permitted; treatment on attempts to escape; right to counsel in trials; repatriation; wills; and much else.

The treatment of the sick and wounded and of the dead was covered carefully. The spy was recognized as a necessary evil, but it was accepted that he took his own risks and could be executed if caught

* "H.R." refers to certain "Hague Rules."

and convicted. There were rules such as guaranteed safe-conduct to a *parlementaire* advancing under a white flag. And there were elaborate rules for the proper conduct of troops of occupation and of an occupying military government.

The naval rules included other regulations which had special application to the sea. Contraband was defined and its seizure permitted. Blockade was defined. The right of visit and search of neutral vessels was treated at some length, as well as the determination of when either enemy ships or neutral ships may be captured. There were also rules as to the treatment of the captured vessel, its crew, passengers, and goods, and when a prize may be destroyed. Undefended places might not be bombarded, and there were restrictions against the use of automatic contact mines.

To the naval rules were appended certain aerial rules, admittedly somewhat behind times. They were based, in general, on the naval rules, but had not been properly distinguished, specified, or elaborated by the beginning of World War II.

There was one important distinction between sea and land rules. Private enemy property found at sea was subject to seizure and confiscation, even when on neutral ships. But private property of enemies on land, when of an innocent nature, was inviolable. If it were seized and expropriated for any proper military purpose, adequate compensation had to be paid to the owner.

III: Sea Warfare in World War I

WORLD WAR I opened up a new era which undermined some established principles of the laws of war.

The first serious breakdown of old rules started with the system of blockade used by both sides in World War I. Both Germany and England declared blockades wider than they could make wholly "effective." The old rule had been that a blockade—which involves preventing the passage of neutral ships—was illegal except to the extent that it was "effective." This word had been defined to mean that the blockading vessels must be in sufficient local strength to assert actual control of the whole area declared blockaded. As stated by Secretary of State (later President) Monroe, the blockading vessels "should be stationary and not a cruising squadron and placed so near the entrance of the harbor or mouth of the river as to make it evidently dangerous for a vessel to enter." But, obviously, stationary blockading ships would be easy prey; therefore, both Germany and Britain proceeded to violate the old rule, declaring blockades of the entire enemy coasts and even of large areas of the sea without being able to blockade "effectively" within the meaning of the old rule.

The old concept of a blockade, dating from sailing-vessel days, certainly did not make sense in 1914. On the other hand, the concept of an "effective" blockade might still have been retained had there been some modern definition of what comprised effectiveness. While the British blockade was not effective within the strict meaning of the old rule, it was so effective in practice that the Germans decided to repudiate the old and well-established rule that a merchant ship could not be sunk without warning, and then only after the safety of passengers and crew had been assured. The Germans claimed that their ruthless measures were a proper retaliation for the "illegal" British blockade and for the alleged British violation of international law in arming merchantmen. They added that the submarine was comparatively weak on defense and could not give warning to an armed ship which might sink her. Because of the unrestricted submarine warfare, the British proceeded, as the United States later did, to arm all merchantmen.

The Germans, during World War I, came pretty close to the concept of "total war." Acts such as the violation of Belgian neutrality, for which there was no excuse except self-interest, the long-range bombardment of civilians with "Big Berthas," and the unrestricted submarine warfare presaged the greater liberties which were to be taken with the law in the next World War, in the interests of "expediency." That theory of expediency was found by the Allies to be abhorrent when used in World War I by the Germans, but our side did not hesitate to adopt it, on occasion, also. Asquith, in 1915, said that Great Britain would not be hampered by "juridical niceties"—that is, by law. In the period between World Wars I and II, considerable progress was made in studies and negotiations looking toward the restoration of broken rules and even their improvement. But the fact is that the new practices in sea warfare were here to stay—they were repeated in World War II.

IV: Wilson, Clemenceau, and Lloyd George*

PRESIDENT WILSON arrived in France for the peace negotiations, full of idealism and enthusiasm for a new world in which there would be no war. This new world was to be built on fair dealing and on honest covenants openly arrived at. Its spirit had been injected into the Fourteen Points, which the world had seemingly accepted as the skeleton of the proposed settlements. But the President soon found that he was to deal with hardheaded, practical, and nationalistic-minded men whose ideas of a settlement differed radically from his own. Not only did they insist upon the execution of secret agreements which violated some of the Fourteen Points, but it was also made clear that they deemed their immediate national interests far more important than any ephemeral plans for an international utopia which the President might have. Lloyd George and Clemenceau considered Wilson an idealistic and wholly impractical professor who had been useful as a propagandist in time of war but was badly suited for negotiating a peace.

David Lloyd George was a strong nationalist, caring for little except the best advantages which his country could extract from the peace, and succeeding so well that close to a million square miles, the lion's share of the spoils, were added to the British Empire. Clemenceau was an even more fervent nationalist, but his efficiency was somewhat hampered by his hatred of Germany, so intense that he was apparently willing to sacrifice many possible gains in exchange for a vengeful and punitive peace. Against these two, President Wilson, devoted to his League of Nations concept and hoping that it would, in time, cure the ills which he saw being created by an imperialistic peace, was helpless. His idealism could have prevailed, perhaps, had he refused to compromise and had he appealed to the conscience of the world, but he did not. He remained at the peace table and rapidly lost his chips.

In his reply to the German delegates' objections to the draft of

* I use the term the "Big Three" at the head of this chapter to refer to Wilson, Clemenceau, and Lloyd George. One could refer to a "Big Four" or a "Big Five," but the Italians and Japanese actually played a subordinate role. In the same way, I shall later refer to the "Second Big Three," as the representatives of England, Russia, and the United States, the parallel situation being that China and France played comparatively minor parts.

the Treaty of Versailles, Clemenceau said: "In the view of the Allied and Associated Powers the war which began on August 1, 1914, was the greatest crime against humanity and the freedom of peoples that any nation, calling itself civilized, has ever committed." This premise was used in the Treaty itself to justify holding Germany "responsible" for "all the loss and damage" to which the victors and their nationals "have been subjected as a consequence of the war imposed upon them by the aggression of Germany and her allies." Whether the premise was correct or not is beside the point. I fear that the precedent was established that a "guilty" nation cannot receive the normal protections of international law. That seems a dangerous principle to establish as long as we have no disinterested means of determining guilt, for the victor will always attribute guilt to the vanquished; after winning an aggressive war against Finland, Russia attributed guilt to Finland, and complete innocence to herself. There is a further danger in the principle. It is all too easy to derive from it the conclusion that innocent citizens of defeated states are entitled to no rights; this rationalization was virtually incorporated in the Treaty of Versailles.

It had been an established rule of international law that incidental damage sustained because one happened to be in the path of warfare was not recoverable, even by a citizen of a victor state. But the Treaty held Germany responsible for *all* damage, of whatever kind, sustained during the war. Collecting reparations from the defeated nation was an old and accepted practice, but, after almost every modern war, there had been claims commissions established to settle the claims of individuals of one side against the other, independent of national or bulk reparations. The rules were rather well settled, protecting the citizens of the loser as well as of the victor. But the Treaty of Versailles created the precedent that the private citizen of the victor might recover for all loss whatsoever (even if not justified under old rules of law) whereas the citizen of the loser could make no claim against the governments of the victors. It was, of course, impossible for the victors to collect in full—Germany could not begin to pay the total cost of the war to the nationals of the Allies—and no serious attempt to collect in full was made, but the precedent had been set that the nationals of the defeated nations were to have no rights against the victors, however justified their claims.

From this principle it was a short step to confiscation of the private property of enemy nationals. The Treaty rationalized this departure from an accepted rule of law by giving the enemy nationals a claim against their own governments for the value of property confiscated by the victors. The United States did not take full advantage of the opportunity given by the Treaty, for Congress found it distasteful,* but many of the Allied powers did.

It is regrettable that a stronger stand was not made by us against the innovations of the Treaty. The United States had been the staunchest supporter of the theory that private property should not be confiscated in a war. Hamilton had said: "No powers of language at my command can express the abhorrence I feel at the idea of violating the property of individuals, which, in an authorized intercourse, in time of peace, has been confided to the faith of our government and laws, on account of controversies between nation and nation. In my view every moral and every political consideration unite to consign it to execration." He said further that it was "inconsistent with the notion of property" to take it away "without any personal fault of the proprietor."† Chief Justice Marshall, in one case, although admitting that a sovereign could confiscate private enemy property, said: ". . . it is not believed that modern usage would sanction the seizure of the goods of an enemy on land, which were acquired in peace, in the course of trade." And on February 8, 1917, just before we entered the war, Secretary of State Lansing, with the approval of President Wilson, stated: "The Government of the United States will in no circumstances take advantage of a state of war to take possession of property to which international understandings and the recognized law of the land give it no just claim or title. It will scrupulously respect all private rights alike of its own citizens and of the subjects of foreign states."

Professor Borchard of Yale, one of our foremost authorities on international law, has said that the rule that innocent property is not subject to confiscation "was not adopted in any sudden burst of humanitarian sentiment, but was the result of an evolution of centuries. It rests upon a sound development in political and legal theory which was deemed natural and incidental to the evolution of civilization . . ."‡

* We did not ratify the Treaty of Versailles but made our own treaty with Germany, in which we reserved whatever rights Versailles would have given us.

† *Hamilton's Works* (Lodge edition, 1885), vol. 4, p. 343.

‡ Borchard, "Enemy Private Property," *American Journal of International Law*, vol. 18, p. 523.

V: The League of Nations

The peace after World War I was made on the theory that there were good and bad nations. Therefore, as the victors were naturally the good nations, it was only necessary to impose harsh territorial penalties, semi-permanent reparations and disarmament upon the losers, and to cement the alliances of the victors, and perpetual peace was assured. That was the theory of most Allied leaders. It was not the theory of President Wilson, who realized that a nation could be very bad today and very good tomorrow, and that even one's best friends could turn up in jail next week. So he conceived the noble idea of a League of Nations which would devote itself to uplifting the standards of international morality and preserve peace. Against hardheaded and "realistic" negotiators at the peace table, Wilson was forced to make concession after concession in the terms of peace in order to get general consent to his League, which he believed to be more important than anything else.

So we got a League and, at the same time, a set of peace treaties which distressed many enlightened historians and thinkers of the following period. The peace was a peace of vengeance, but the world had not realized that this is an unsound peace. It has not learned this lesson yet. Vengeance wreaked on a nation punishes the innocent with the guilty, and the sons for the sins of their fathers. It breeds hate and a determination to exact retribution. And our friends of today are not always our friends of tomorrow— among the "good nations" of World War I were Japan and Italy; and among the "good nations" of World War II was Russia.*

The League offered hope, but that hope was slim. It was attached to and virtually made a guarantor of the status created by the peace; it was made more slim by the refusal of the United States to join; it was made fallible and weak by the "Great Power" system.

Whatever its handicaps, the League might have worked had the United States been willing to join. But we did not. We were still unwilling to embroil ourselves in the quarrels of Europe as a permanent policy. Apparently we were disgusted that Europe had shown so little disposition to give up age-old imperialistic concepts

* For a full discussion of the subject, see Wormser, *The Myth of the Good and Bad Nations.*

and the secret plotting and bargaining which go with them. We were disturbed that the League was to perpetuate the violations, in the Treaty of Versailles, of the Fourteen Points of President Wilson, which this country had found so acceptable and desirable. Finally, we were annoyed that the President had not taken the country into his confidence and, ignoring Congress, had made a one-man peace. Perhaps the League might have performed better if we had joined it, but we did not join, the others had to carry on without us, and they did not carry on very well.

Germany had been condemned for her "imperialism." Yet the era immediately after World War I (even before Germany's resurgence) was one of the most imperialistic of history. France's territorial acquisitions were second only to those of the British Empire, though a poor and disgruntled second. Italy was unhappy that her friends allowed her so little, and soon cast her eyes on possibilities of expansion. Japan received great numbers of Pacific islands; and she began planning very soon indeed to go into one of the most radical programs of imperialistic expansion in the modern era.* The Great Powers did not appear very sincere in their opposition to imperialism. They just did not like other people's imperialism.

The rest of the world was never wholly impressed with the good intentions of the Great Powers. There was considerable discomfort at the whole "Great Power" idea. One of the weaknesses of the League was that it attempted to perpetuate this concept. The League was virtually controlled by Great Britain, France, Italy, and Japan. Conspicuously absent was Russia, just coming out of the throes of a revolution. After some years it was impossible to keep Russia out of the ranks of the great any longer, and she was given a permanent seat in the controlling League body which she held until she was thrown out in 1939 as a "bad" power, because of her war of aggression against Finland. Eventually Germany also was admitted as a Great Power, even though still under armament limitations. In the meantime, other nations resented being treated as minor leaguers. Brazil showed her displeasure by resigning completely. China, far greater in population and area than Japan, did not see why she should not be a Great Power.

Then came the violent defections. Germany resigned in 1933;

* In addition, the Big Three gave Japan a piece of the mainland of China, our ally, a precedent followed by Roosevelt and Churchill later in their concessions to Russia.

Hitler had come to power and was laying plans which would brook no interference by any League. Japan resigned in the same year; there had been criticism of her imperialism in China. The League had done nothing to curb Germany's apparent aggressive intentions; it had done nothing to curb Japan's even more obvious intentions. So, when it ordered sanctions against the aggression in Ethiopia by Italy, the weakest of the big boys, Italy, in righteous indignation, also pulled out of the League. By the time Russia was ousted in 1939, the political importance of the League had waned almost to a shadow.

VI: The World Court

In the meantime, the League had accomplished much in spheres outside the purely political. Various commissions had begun to study and report on fields of international interest and concern. Most important, a World Court had been established. The *Permanent Court of International Justice* was established by the League of Nations on December 13, 1920, to adjudicate

"(a) the interpretation of a treaty;
(b) any question of international law;
(c) the existence of any fact which, if established, would constitute a breach of an international obligation;
(d) the nature or extent of the reparation to be made for the breach of an international obligation."

It was to have fifteen judges, no more than one from any single country. Fifty-seven states signed the protocol of the Court, but only fifty ratified it. The United States and Russia were conspicuously absent. The United States signed, but the motion to ratify was defeated in 1935 in the Senate by a vote of fifty-two to thirty-six, a two-thirds majority being required. Despite our rejection of the Court, it (and its United Nations successor, the International Court of Justice) has always contained an American judge. Our first was John Bassett Moore; the next, Charles Evans Hughes; then Frank B. Kellogg; then Manley O. Hudson; and now Philip C. Jessup.

John Bassett Moore deserves to be mentioned as perhaps the greatest international jurist the United States ever produced. He died in 1947 after a long and distinguished career of service to his country. He served on many commissions centering in the Department of State, as an Assistant Secretary of State and as Counselor to the Department. He was the authority on international law, a subject which he taught at Columbia University for many years; and his great work, *Digest of International Law,* in eight volumes, became the major reference book on the subject. Moore was convinced that World War I was unnecessary and disagreed bitterly with President Wilson on the handling of the problems which brought us into the war. He had no faith in the League of Nations. But when, to his surprise, he was appointed to the bench of the World Court, he worked hard at the task and became the most important of the judges.

The Court decided thirty-two cases, in which twenty-four nations were concerned, and all its judgments were observed. In so far as matters were submitted to its jurisdiction, the Court made an excellent record. Its judges were, on the whole, able men who did their jobs earnestly and with a minimum of political implication. But the great weakness of the World Court was the great weakness of the League—the unwillingness of the powers to use it fully for its intended purposes.

The League continued in existence during World War II, but as an ineffectual and dying enterprise. Russia would never have anything more to do with it, and any new world order would have to include Russia. So the League just waited for the inevitable *coup de grâce,* which came in the meeting at Yalta, and in the Dumbarton Oaks Conference which followed it.

CHAPTER 46

Hitler and the Second "Big Three"

I: The New Dispensation

TO SAY that the international law of war is in a state of flux is to put it mildly. Many of its major rules have been battered so much that no one really knows which are left, or what changes may be deemed permanent. A few years ago many people held that all discussions of the rules of warfare had become academic. Expressing great faith in the U.N., they looked forward to a "new dispensation"; we would no longer need any rules of warfare.

They argued that bringing on a war would now be the gravest of international crimes. Therefore, how can there be rules of warfare? How can there be rules as between a criminal and the policeman who is pursuing him? The international criminal (a nation) will be condemned in advance, and will be an outlaw. Neither the criminal nation nor its criminal leaders can expect worse punishment for additional acts against ethics than for the crime of commencing a war, which will be the equivalent in ordinary criminal procedure of murder in the first degree. All that will save the criminal from dire punishment will be victory, by whatever method.

So, faced with the probability of ruthless warfare on the part of the criminal nation, what is the international policeman to do? This final question was rhetorical, the obvious answer being that he must not be bound by any rules of chivalry in tracking down and apprehending a man condemned of murder in the first degree. The argument may seem logical enough, but are the premises sound? Will we ever have an organization capable of outlawing war, or of judging "aggression" fairly? We are a long way from it at the moment.

There is that other school, to which I have alluded, which believes that in "total war," a phenomenon of our era, the old rules of international law have no serious place. But, as I see it, we should make every effort to restore decency to the world. We shall have to be realistic in the sense of being prepared to use weapons and methods which are distasteful to us, if we are forced to it by an enemy. But we should steel ourselves against unnecessary acquiescence in a deterioration in law.

II: Adolf Hitler, the Lawmaker

"The law and the will of the Führer are one."

GÖRING

IT IS SAD indeed to be obliged to list Adolph Hitler as one of the important makers of international law. But rules of international law come into being by use and acceptance, and several particularly nasty rules of international law have come into being through use by Hitler and acceptance by others, including ourselves.

Our fall into Hitler's ideological trap commenced with the dangerous rule of *reprisal*. It is a well-established rule that, if the enemy violates a rule of warfare, we may retaliate, though not excessively. Paragraph 358 of the *Rules of Land Warfare* describes the limits:

". . . Reprisals are acts of retaliation resorted to by one belligerent against the enemy individuals or property for illegal acts of warfare committed by the other belligerent, for the purpose of enforcing future compliance with the recognized rules of civilized warfare.

". . . Reprisals are never adopted merely for revenge, but only as an unavoidable last resort to induce the enemy to desist from illegitimate practices. . . .

"The acts resorted to by way of reprisal need not conform to those complained of by the injured party, but should not be excessive or exceed the degree of violence committed by the enemy. . . ."

Reprisal does not condone the offense and abandon the old rule. But it does, in effect, often change that rule. For if there is sufficient, continued use of the illegal method, there results a change in law through general acquiescence.

The specific cause of our entry into World War I was the German unrestricted submarine warfare, which we characterized as inhuman and wholly illegal. Yet a few days after Pearl Harbor, the American Chief of Naval Operations sent these instructions: "Execute unrestricted air and submarine warfare against Japan." Admiral Nimitz, in an affidavit read to the International Military Tribunal, admitted that there had been unrestricted American submarine warfare against the Japanese, justifying it because of "Japanese attacks on United States bases and on armed and unarmed ships . . . without warning or declaration of war." Reminiscent of the German arguments in World War I, he stated further that "Japanese merchantmen were usually armed and always attacked submarines by any available means when feasible," and he admitted that American submarines did not rescue enemy survivors "if undue hazard to the submarine resulted" or if it were prevented from accomplishing its mission. According to a report in the New York *Times* of February 3, 1946, the U. S. Navy, commenting on unrestricted submarine warfare, announced that we had sunk 1,194 Japanese vessels and had refused to rescue from the waters 276,000 Japanese nationals.

Perhaps we may make a show of maintaining that the old rules of no sinkings without warning are still in effect and that our abandonment of them was merely momentary and by way of reprisal, but it is unlikely that anyone will take such a position seriously. It is more likely that the position taken by the German authorities in World War I will now be accepted universally, and this is a striking example of a change in law through violation, reprisal, and acquiescence.

There are some who feel that any criticism of our own conduct or that of our allies should be repressed, that we should never admit any derelictions of our own, for it might give comfort to the totalitarians. I have no sympathy with this point of view. It is important that we do not blind ourselves to our own errors and shortcomings. Hitler, of course, made his law as he went along. His view was that anything was "legal" if it seemed advisable from Germany's point of view, or might further his maniacal schemes. So, as it suited him, he ordered pillage, plunder, wanton destruction, devastation, murder, extermination, enslavement, deportation and crimes of unearthly horror, crimes in violation of every rule of human decency. He was the high priest of the cult of total war; his only rule was that there are no rules when your own country's welfare is at stake.

But to detail the frightful violations by the Nazis of rules of law and decency would serve no useful purpose here. *The vital problem is: What has happened to international law? Hitler could not make new international law all by himself—it would take acquiescence by others in his new practices. What I am interested in discovering is the extent to which we have permitted ourselves to acquiesce in new and undesirable practices. We have defeated and repudiated Hitler, but in some ways he seems to have half-persuaded us.*

I have suggested that, while expediency may sometimes override law, the extent to which this may be countenanced ethically is difficult to determine. The totalitarians believe that law must fall completely before national expediency. We are revolted by that concept, and yet we have also, on occasion, permitted expediency to guide us. For example, before our entrance into World War II we began to ignore the rules governing neutrality. President Wilson, in a statement to the Senate on August 19, 1914, just after the outbreak of World War I, had warned against "that deepest, most subtle, most essential breach of neutrality which may spring out of partisanship, out of passionately taking sides. The United States must be neutral in fact as well as in name . . ." His aim was to observe the rules of neutrality. They have been expressed by one of the foremost authorities on international law in this way: "Since neutrality is an attitude of impartiality, it excludes such assistance and succor to one of the belligerents as is detrimental to the other, and, further, such injuries to the one as benefit the other. But it requires, on the other hand, active measures from neutral states. For neutrals must prevent belligerents from making use of their neutral territories, and of their resources, for military and naval purposes during the war." *

Both Presidents Wilson and Roosevelt had made campaign pledges to keep us out of war. However, as Professor Beard points out in his *President Roosevelt and the Coming of the War, 1941*, Roosevelt repeatedly violated international law in his eagerness to assist the Allies. It is part of Professor Beard's thesis that the United States virtually made war on Germany, before she declared war on us, by military support of the Allies, including the reconditioning of British war vessels in our ports, the Lend-Lease Bill, the contribution of overage destroyers, and the convoying of ships. In its anxiety

* L. F. L. Oppenheim's *International Law* (6th ed. by Lauterpacht, 1940), p. 516.

to enter the war to save the "democracies,"* our administration was disposed to ignore rules of international law on the theory (of which Hitler was the most active exponent) that the end justifies the means. During the successive steps by which we entered into the conflict, Roosevelt was careful to rationalize each step, to give at least the appearance of justification under law.

Certainly the overwhelming majority of the American people were enraged at the barbarism of Hitler and prayed for the victory of the hard-pressed Allies, and it may well be that England would have gone down to defeat—with dire results to us—had it not been for prompt action in assistance. It is conceivable that the American people were not conscious of an actual danger to them and that the President was extraordinarily wise in believing that we had to help the "democracies" even at the risk of war. It may be "realism" to applaud Roosevelt's intelligence and courage in having taken the steps which he did to assure the success of the "democracies," but is it not also applause for the theory of the end justifying the means? As Professor Beard has said, "At this point in its history the American Republic has arrived under the theory that the President of the United States possesses unlimited authority publicly to misrepresent and secretly to control foreign policy, foreign affairs, and the war power."

III: The Atom Bomb

It is difficult to resist the pull of expediency. Once having succumbed to its attraction, we can be led along ethically dangerous paths. When World War II brought in new weapons and new uses for these weapons, the old rules of law were inadequate to give us full guidance in using them, and we were obliged, therefore, to decide for ourselves to what extent these innovations could be properly employed. Whether we went too far, and on an indefensible basis of pure expediency, is a problem which has been much disputed. In our defense it must be said, of course, that we were driven to an anger of white heat by the horror of Nazism and by the conduct of the Japanese. But the natural desire for vengeance may have motivated us to exceed the proper bounds of reprisal.

* I put "democracies" in quotes because Soviet Russia was included in the term.

If the enemy uses poison gas, we are legally permitted to use it also. If the enemy uses buzz bombs against the civilian population of London, we are justified in dropping bombs on the citizens of Berlin and Nuremberg. But are we justified in using something so horrible and devastating as an atom bomb, if the enemy has not used it?

The atomic bomb presents a double question: whether it should be used in any case; and, if it is, whether it may be used to bomb unfortified places. Perhaps all the rules about bombing unfortified places should be revised. In so-called total war all the essential combatants do not wear uniforms, and the instrument maker may be a more important cog in the military wheel than the infantryman. We do not always have clearly definable military objectives. Should we admit that all objectives are military, and that the purpose of war is to crush the enemy however one can? But we must call a halt somewhere. If no distinction is to be made between a factory and a fort, then why distinguish between the factory and the homes of factory workers? Why not mow down all the enemy population we can find, and by whatever means we may? There is no end to the horror opened up by the logic of justification of the atomic bomb.

It is doubtful that the world will ever return to the old rule that bombings of civilian populations are prohibited. The use of the atomic bomb has been called justified because it brought the war with Japan to a quicker end. Its use has also been rationalized on a legal basis—that the use of an atomic bomb is no worse in principle than the use of any other type of bomb, that the mere extension of the scope of the devastation does not make it different in nature. This argument presupposes, though it is certainly subject to question, that the indiscriminate use of any bomb against civilians is permissible under international law as it existed before World War II.

The official attitude of the administration which authorized the use of the bomb is expressed in *On Active Service in Peace and War*, the memoirs of our wartime Secretary of War, Henry L. Stimson, written by him and McGeorge Bundy: "Stimson believed, both at the time and later, that the dominant fact of 1945 was war, and that therefore, necessarily, the dominant objective was victory. If victory could be speeded by using the bomb, it should be used; if victory must be delayed in order to use the bomb, it should *not* be used. So far as he knew, this general view was fully shared by the

President and all his associates . . . no effort was made, and none was seriously considered, to achieve surrender merely in order not to have to use the bomb." *

It is difficult for me to distinguish such a point of view from the basic point of view of Hitler that the end justifies the means. It is difficult for me to understand the morality and humanity of drawing no line, and of not attempting to draw one, between the method a civilized nation may use and the method that aligns it with those who, like Hitler and the Russians, believed national self-interest should not be curbed by any legal or ethical hindrance whatsoever.

Norman Thomas has gone so far as to say that the destruction of Nagasaki "was the greatest single atrocity of a very cruel war. No condemnation of war criminals or assessment of reparations will be just in the eyes of God or history, which ignores that fact." Similar protests were made by many. Bernard Shaw in a letter to the London *Daily Express* suggested to the judges at Nuremberg that "after dropping atomic bombs on helpless civilians without warning we are hardly in a moral position to hang anyone."

A report of Protestant church leaders deplored the "irresponsible" atomic bombings of Hiroshima and Nagasaki, and suggested that the United States rebuild the two cities in repentance.† The report said in part:

"As American Christians, we are deeply penitent for the irresponsible use already made of the atomic bomb. We are agreed that the surprise bombings of Hiroshima and Nagasaki are morally indefensible. They were loosed without specific warning, under conditions which virtually assured the deaths of 100,000 civilians. . . . Even though use of the new weapon last August may well have shortened the war, the moral cost was too high.

"All things considered, it seems necessary to include in any condemnation of indiscriminate, excessive violence not only the use of atomic bombs in August, 1945, but the policy of wholesale obliteration bombing as practiced at first by the Axis Powers, and then on a far greater scale by the Allies."

* Page 629.
† New York *Times*, March 6, 1946.

IV: The Atlantic Charter and Territorial Changes

RETALIATION in time of war is difficult to control. We fought the most vicious and ruthless enemies any nation has ever been called upon to fight. It is comparatively easy to justify excesses in retaliation for the offenses of our enemies. *However, when retaliation takes place after the conclusion of peace, then we may well wonder if we have not become infected with the virus brought to birth in the horrible political laboratories of the totalitarians.*

The desertion by President Wilson, under pressure from the practical politicians of Europe, of the high principles which he introduced into his Fourteen Points had its counterpart in the desertion by President Roosevelt of the high principles contained in the Atlantic Charter.

Article "Second" of the Atlantic Charter provided that there should be no territorial changes without the "freely expressed wishes of the peoples concerned." But it had become "expedient" to buy Russia's assistance in the war against Japan, and so Roosevelt, in addition to recognizing acquisitions of territory of the enemy, committed the United States to a recognition of the acquisition by Russia of 40 per cent of Poland, Bessarabia, privileges in China which amounted to sovereignty of the northern provinces, and (tacitly) acquiesced in the absorption of the three Baltic nations. In an effort to make up for the violation of the Atlantic Charter in the case of Poland, Roosevelt agreed to compensate Poland by granting her an extensive dividend out of German territory, in which there would be no more opportunity for the inhabitants to express their desires than for those in the Polish provinces granted to Russia.

Review what has happened with our consent in Europe and Asia, and contrast it with Article "Third" of the Charter: "They respect the right of all peoples to choose the form of government under which they will live; and they wish to see sovereign rights and self-government restored to those who have been forcibly deprived of them." The repudiation of these words does not augur well for the future of international relations. The *London Economist* in its issue of July 27, 1946, said: "Having abandoned principle for what they thought was policy, the Western Powers are now left with neither principle nor policy."

V: Mass Expulsions

FROM the moral lapse which consented to the transfer of territories against the wishes of the inhabitants (including even territories belonging to our own allies) to acquiescence in the mass expulsion of vast populations was an easy step. Roosevelt, expressly in some instances and tacitly in others, agreed that future minority problems could be solved simply by throwing out the minority which might cause trouble. Here, again, a procedure advocated by the lawmaker Hitler was followed by us as proper modern procedure. Forced annexation of territories against the will of the inhabitants is an old, if immoral, thing, but mass expulsion of the inhabitants, regardless of age, innocence, or guilt, from lands on which they and their ancestors have lived for centuries is a new refinement. There were such expulsions of many millions of Germans from eastern Germany and from the Sudetenland in Czechoslovakia, but this cruelty was not confined to enemy nationals. Poles were driven out of that section of Poland granted to Russia, for example. Forced deportation of whole peoples or large groups of people, most of them innocent of wrongdoing, has never had the support of international law.

It is not only the nations behind the Iron Curtain which have treated populations ruthlessly. It is a sad reflection on the era that that most civilized of countries, France, has, for example, followed a similar course where it suited her. The twelve thousand inhabitants of the German town of Kehl, who were evacuated during hostilities, were ordered by the French not to return to their homes.*

The argument given to support such expulsions is that the Germans and Japanese had done the same thing and much worse. But, away from the emotions of the immediate period, historians are not likely to support such retaliation, for the retaliation is, in fact, against not a government but, for the most part, innocent individuals. It is not the type of retaliation to which one might ordinarily expect the United States government to lend sympathy; it is an indication that international law his indeed fallen into one Nazi ideological trap.

* New York *Times*, April 3, 1949.

It did not help for the agreements at Yalta and Potsdam to provide that "any transfers that take place should be effected in an orderly and humane manner." How can mass expulsions be orderly and humane!

VI: Devastation

A LONG OCCUPATION of Germany was anticipated, but no adequate provision had been made for the occupation. The result of our insistence on unconditional surrender was the disappearance of the government of Germany itself. There was no authority which could repair and co-ordinate the already severely shattered public economy, except that of the occupying powers, and these were disposed to let the Germans stew in their own juice. No effort was made to establish a central government. The country was divided into zones of occupation and each was assigned to a respective major victor, the United States, Britain, France, and Russia, with an extra piece for Poland. The decision had not been made whether Germany was to be split into permanently separated parts, or to be made into a federated union of states, or permitted again to become a centralized nation. It was our own hope that, either as a federated or a centralized state, Germany's pieces would be put together again eventually and, in the meantime, the separate zones of occupation could be operated together under co-operative four-power management. We did not anticipate the intransigence of the French, stemming from their double desire to separate vital parts of Germany permanently for defense reasons and to secure for themselves valuable resources of Germany. Nor did we anticipate the maladroitness of the British in insisting on imposing in their zone the collectivist ideas of the Labor Party then in the process of being applied in England, or the pressure of British industrialists against permitting a resurgence of German industry in competition with Britain. And apparently the Russians were expected to sacrifice their own ideology in the territories which they and their Polish minions occupied and to surrender them cheerfully to some form of government the powers would jointly prescribe.

Our own part in this heterogeneous administration of Germany was not improved by the plan adopted by our government to guide our own occupation authorities. Its author was Henry Morgenthau,

Secretary of the Treasury under President Roosevelt. Morgenthau had expressed this plan in a memorandum to the President dated September 6, 1944, from which former Secretary of War Stimson quotes in his memoirs* as follows: "This area [the Ruhr and "surrounding industrial areas" comprising thirty thousand square miles] should not only be stripped of all presently existing industries but so weakened and controlled that it cannot in the foreseeable future become an industrial area. . . . All industrial plants and equipment not destroyed by military action shall either be completely dismantled or removed from the area or completely destroyed, all equipment shall be removed from the mines and the mines shall be thoroughly wrecked."

Germany, said Secretary Morgenthau, should be made into an agricultural country. With this thesis Secretary Hull, although in favor of stern punishment for Germany, could not agree, and Secretary Stimson was almost violent in his opposition to the plan, which he fought against with all his power. In one memorandum to the President, Stimson said: "Sound thinking teaches that . . . poverty in one part of the world usually induces poverty in other parts. Enforced poverty is even worse, for it destroys the spirit not only of the victim but debases the victor. It would be just such a crime as the Germans themselves hoped to perpetrate upon their victims—it would be a crime against civilization itself."†

But the President went into conference with Churchill at Quebec apparently determined to apply Morgenthau's plan, and Stimson wrote in his diary, concerning the President's state of mind upon leaving for the vital conference: "So far as he had evidenced in his talks with us, he has had absolutely no study or training in the very difficult problem which we have to decide, namely of how far we can introduce preventive measures to protect the world from Germany running amuck again and how far we must refrain from measures which will simply provoke the wrong reaction. I hope the British have brought better trained men with them than we are likely to have to meet them."

Stimson's fears were justified. The President and Churchill initialed a memorandum under date of September 16, 1944, the next to the last paragraph of which reads: "This programme for eliminating the war-making industries in the Ruhr and in the Saar is looking

* *On Active Service in Peace and War*, p. 574.

† *Ibid.*, p. 578.

forward to converting Germany into a country primarily agricultural and pastoral in its character." Stimson said that one reason why the President had accepted the Morgenthau Plan was that the elimination of German industrial competition would greatly benefit the industry of England.* It is a sad commentary on this tragic incident that, when Stimson chided the President later for having acquiesced in the plan to agrarianize Germany and the President denied that he had done so, Stimson read him the memorandum referred to above, which the President had initialed, whereupon: "He was frankly staggered by this and said that he had no idea how he could have initialed this; that he had evidently done it without much thought." †

The directive known as J.C.S. 1067 was eventually given to our military commander in Germany, stating that the commander should "take no steps (a) looking toward the economic rehabilitation of Germany or (b) designed to maintain or strengthen German economy . . ."

The suppression of German industry proceeded for a long period. During it, the Russians benefited by the transfer of industrial equipment to their own country. The Russians also—in control of the most important German food-producing areas, and unwilling to contribute from their production to the rest of the severed country—were glad to see that both Britain and the United States were obliged to pour into Germany, to keep the people even on a subsistence level, enormous sums of money, part of which the reactivation of the German industrial plant would have made unnecessary.

It was an almost incredible performance, and our government seems finally to have understood the mistake we made. The Marshall Plan included Germany among its beneficiaries; we united the French, British, and American zones, permitting the Germans themselves, under our supervision, to have some degree of autonomous control;

* That this point has been taken seriously appears from reports which one saw periodically in the press, of which the following from the New York *Times* of April 3, 1949, is typical: "Germany will be prohibited from producing synthetic rubber, oil, and gasoline under the British-French-American reparations accord reached in London earlier this week. . . . The synthetic rubber, gasoline, and oil plants now standing probably will be destroyed . . . it is doubtful whether Britain would care to see these synthetic industries, and particularly the rubber plants, established elsewhere in Europe. It is generally believed here that, in her concern over the future of the synthetic industries, Britain was less worried about the security problem than about markets for her natural rubber sources."

† *On Active Service in Peace and War*, p. 581.

and we decided to abandon further substantial destruction of the German industrial plant. We did come to understand that the recovery of Germany was essential to the recovery of Western Europe. In the meantime, irreparable damage had been done to the economy of Europe. And it is a factor of no little importance that the Morgenthau Plan increased many-fold our cost of occupation and the cost of our contribution to European recovery.

What was the effect of the Morgenthau-Roosevelt Plan upon international law? The plan itself has gone into oblivion. But it may stand as a precedent for the proposition that it is the right of the victor in war to devastate the economy of the vanquished.

VII: Confiscation of Private Property

THE WAR DEPARTMENT'S BASIC MANUAL, *Rules of Land Warfare*, says in paragraph 323: "Private property must be respected." And in paragraph 326 it says: "Private property cannot be confiscated." Both these rules are taken from Hague Conventions.

But the precedent set by the Treaty of Versailles has done its work well. Hardly a protest has been raised in this country over our evident purpose of confiscating the private property of German nationals wherever we may find it and however innocent of war guilt its owners may be. The confiscatory provisions of the Treaty of Versailles have been repeated in the treaties which ended World War II with the minor allies of Germany. In the case of Germany, we have not even waited for any peace treaty. We have gone so far as to exert pressure upon neutral countries to disgorge private property of Germans in those countries. We have asserted "title to German property in Switzerland by reason of the capitulation of Germany and the exercise of supreme authority within Germany . . ." The Swiss have stated officially that they were "unable to recognize the legal basis of these claims." But they have capitulated and made a compromise deal in their "desire to contribute" Switzerland's "share to the pacification and reconstruction of Europe." * It would be difficult to find precedents for the assertion of title to alien property in a neutral state, based upon the right of an occupying power.

* Letters of agreement were exchanged under date of May 25, 1946. (State Department Bulletin, June 30, 1946, 1121.)

But we have virtually abandoned the principle of neutrality. An individual nation is now no longer entitled to exercise its own judgment. If the majority of the nations enter a war, it has come to be considered by many that a nation which remains neutral is denying its duty to civilization. There are any number of persons who believe that countries like Sweden, Switzerland, and Ireland, which stayed neutral in World War II, acted immorally and unethically in so doing.

Only here and there is a voice to be heard saying that it is immoral on our part to confiscate the private property of innocent persons just because they happen to live in a country we have defeated. Several Americans did protest when it was announced in 1947 that Puccini's music had been rented to one of the Shuberts by the Alien Property Custodian. But most of those who thought that the confiscation of the copyrights to *La Bohème* and *Madame Butterfly* was going too far did not seem to have any such objections to confiscation of the property in this country of other, less famous, former enemy nationals.

Another recent development shows an even more startling tendency to adopt the principle of confiscation. During World War II, all alien property in the United States had to be recorded with the Treasury Department. We then arranged to give information from these data to Marshall Plan countries, for the purpose of enabling these governments to force their citizens to sell their American assets at the current unrealistically low rates of exchange. Our aim was to permit these governments to increase their dollar assets and thus reduce the amount of subsidization required from this country, but the effect was that we were assisting in what was virtually a partial confiscation—amounting to millions of dollars—of the property of friendly aliens.

There is one further item of confiscation which warrants mention. The Russians set no limits to themselves in reorganizing the social and economic life of an occupied territory. Do we have any grounds for objection? We ourselves caused the dissolution of certain cartels in Germany, imposing some of our own anti-trust theories on the people of another country, and, among other things, initiated a land reform and land resettlement program under which owners of more than 247 acres of land could be made to sell acreage to others.

Evil precedents take their toll. In recent decades many million dollars' worth of private property of American citizens has been confiscated by foreign governments, most recently by Dr. Castro in Cuba. It is rather difficult for us to become indignant at such confiscations of innocent property in the light of our own confiscations.

VIII: Booty

THE RUSSIANS have insisted on their right to claim vessels on the Danube and other vital Austrian assets as "war booty," and we stubbornly denied their right. But we have been illogical. A new principle has been introduced into international law, or, rather, an ancient principle has been revived. It is the principle of "booty" extended to reparations. Our new reparation policy was described by John B. Howard, special adviser to the United States representative on the Allied Commission on Reparations for Germany and United States delegate to the Paris Conference on Reparations, as follows: "At the Potsdam Conference the Governments of the United States, the Union of Soviet Socialist Republics, and the United Kingdom agreed upon the principles of a plan for the exaction of reparation which formed an integral part of a co-ordinated Allied political and economic policy toward Germany. The World War I conception of reparation as the maximum obtainable financial compensation in fixed sums of money for the staggering costs of war to the Allies was abandoned. The application of this conception had actually transferred much of the real burden of German reparation to the Allies, in the form of repudiated loans. Instead, the Potsdam Agreement established two major new principles. First, it was agreed that the primary objective should be the establishment of military and economic security against renewed German aggression, not the maximizing of reparation receipts. Second, it was agreed that reparation should be paid by Germany in kind, rather than in cash, the payment in kind to be made out of such German assets as would, if left under German control, constitute an economic base for future aggression by Germany but would, if received as reparation, hasten the economic recovery of the United Nations. The total amount and duration of reparation and, to some extent, the character of the reparation assets to be made available by Germany were not fixed in advance but were made dependent upon subsequent determinations to be reached by the Control Council for Germany with respect to the establishment of the German economy on a peaceful basis." *

Paragraph 321 of the *Rules of Land Warfare* reads as follows: "All movable property belonging to the state directly susceptible of military use may be taken possession of as booty and utilized for the benefit of the invader's government. Other movable property, not directly susceptible of military use, must be respected and cannot be appropriated." It is made clear by the Hague rules that all private property, even if "directly susceptible of military use," must be returned after the war, or compensation be given. There are many American precedents for the rule. In *U.S. vs. Klein,* a Civil War case, Chief Justice Chase said: "The government recognized to the fullest extent the humane maxims of the modern law of nations, which exempt private property of non-combatant enemies from capture as booty in war."

Reparations and indemnities are well-recognized penalties which the victor in war may impose on the vanquished. But there is a distinction between such penalties and "booty." "Booty" is an ancient practice; in barbaric times, a conquering army seized what it pleased. The vanquished population could hardly complain if, during the war or a subsequent occupation, the soldiers and agents of the conqueror carted off everything that could be pried loose. However, the comparatively enlightened rules of warfare which developed in the modern era put definite limits on the practice of taking booty. Booty was to be taken only during an actual state of war. Booty was to be confined, with some few exceptions, to movable state or public property which could be used for military purposes. Under no circumstances was innocent private property to be confiscated under the principle of booty. Private property was inviolate under the rules of international law before the Treaty of Versailles—no right to "booty" in any way limited the rule.

In Germany and Japan we demolished factory buildings, appropriating to ourselves and distributing to our allies the machinery and other contents of these buildings. The stated purpose of this procedure was the demilitarization of our late enemies and the rehabilitation of the victors' devasted areas. These objectives might have been sound, but the method used has resulted in the breakdown of another established rule of law. It is no answer to the illegality of our method to say that we have a new kind of warfare,

* Department of State Bulletin of June 6, 1946.

that factories are as much military equipment as cannon are. Nor is it any answer to say that the law must change as circumstances change. For we have adequate relief under the old rules of law, if we will but use them.

We had a perfect right to enforce demilitarization on Germany and Japan. We also had the right to demand reparations in kind—automobiles, railroad cars, coal, perhaps even factories and the machinery in them. But we had no right to go in and take them unless reparation had been asked and refused. Otherwise, we should be confiscating private property without compensation—something which has been prohibited by international law. We took booty, and took it illegally. We got into this peculiar violation of international law because we had decided that there should not be a quick peace. So, in order to get reparations in kind and, at the same time, effect industrial demilitarization, we took "booty." In the case of Germany there was another reason—there was no German government to deal with, and for a long while we showed little disposition to want one. That, in fact, made our violation of law all the more severe, for we were virtually in the position of a permanent occupier—we had temporarily annexed western Germany in fact, and the Germans were, therefore, in the position of individuals to whom the occupying power, as the government in fact, owed the duty of proper treatment. For us to confiscate the private property of the inhabitants of a nation which we had temporarily absorbed was doubly reprehensible.

You may consider this a tempest in a teapot and believe that it made no difference whether we demanded that a German government turn over the contents of an optical factory to us or whether we took it. But the difference lies in the contrast between acting by rules of law and doing it as we please. By the method we used, private owners of property, *regardless of individual guilt or innocence,* were pillaged and looted. Reparations collection from a nation places the burden of recompense for damage upon the whole defeated nation and spreads the loss over all its citizens. Reparations collected by pillaging individuals penalizes individuals and leaves them to their own devices to recover their losses, if they can, from their fellow citizens.

It is difficult for many to approach any subject of this kind without being affected by the emotions which World War II produced. It is easy to say, "Hitler did it to us, why should we not do it to his people!" But that means using Hitler's new concepts of jurisprudence as models upon which to revise our own, and this we did in several important respects.*

IX: Human Reparations

YASUKE HUKATE, clothed in rags and badly fed, is working as a slave in the forests of northern Siberia, while his wife and half-grown children are eking out subsistence on the tiny Hukate farm on Hokkaido. What was Yasuke's crime? In accordance with law, he was called up as a recruit of the Japanese army, obliged to leave his young wife and small children and go into training. Although he was a loyal Japanese, he did not want to go to war. But his masters sent him to Manchuria, and one day there was a battle and a rout, and he found himself captured by Russian soldiers.

Hans Schmidt, private of the Second Bavarian Infantry, dug coal in a French mine for three years after the end of the war. He did not want to dig coal. He wanted to go home to his aged parents in Lindau. But he could not go. He was a slave to his French masters. He lived in a concentration camp from which, early each morning, he was sent under armed guard to the mouth of the mine where he descended for the day, and so day passed after day while he dreamed of Lake Constance. Schmidt's crime was simply that he was born in Germany.

At Yalta, Roosevelt and Churchill agreed that prisoners of war might be used as "human reparations" to restore war damage, and there are still, at this writing, war prisoners slaving in Russia. Hundreds of thousands slaved in France† and in England for years. We have not enslaved prisoners ourselves. We would not mind enslaving the Goebbelses, Görings, and Streichers, but we could not hold the Yasukes and Schmidts in slavery. There is something in our Constitution about "involuntary servitude," and we fought a war to

* In January, 1949, six German workmen were sentenced to imprisonment by a British court for disobeying an order of the British Military Government of Germany to work at the dismantling of a plant. This is only one example of the ends to which logic based on dangerous premises may bring us. Such a decision can be justified, but the justification is not ethically attractive.

† The Bulletin of the State Department reported on March 23, 1947, that there were still 450,000 German prisoners working in France who had been transferred by the American authorities, plus 180,000 captured by the French forces.

end it within our country. Our *Rules of Land Warfare* (Par. 358) say: "Reprisals against prisoners of war are expressly forbidden by the Geneva Convention of 1929." They state further (Par. 161) that "in any case, repatriation of prisoners shall be effected with the least possible delay after the conclusion of peace." It is true that, while prisoners of war were being used as "human reparations," i.e., as slaves, there was no peace treaty in existence, but the rules say that an "armistice" shall cover the repatriation of prisoners and, if it does not, then arrangements shall be made "as soon as possible." If the enemy government is destroyed and there is none to make peace until the victor chooses to permit one to come into existence, are the rules relating to prisoners suspended at the will of the victor? It would be difficult to support that thesis.

We read about human slavery in Russia and are aghast. Yet we have consented to that slavery, in so many words, and we have done more than that. We took hundreds of thousands of German troops whom we captured and turned them over to our allies, principally to the French, to permit their use as slaves.

At the Potsdam Conference on July 26, 1945, Truman, Stalin, and Attlee said tô the Japanese people: "The Japanese military forces, after having been completely disarmed, shall be permitted to return to their homes with the opportunity of leading peaceful and productive lives . . ." When was this to take place? After they were broken and no longer useful as slaves?

Score another for Adolf Hitler, the lawmaker, who taught us that the barbaric system of converting prisoners of war into slaves is excellent for the domestic economy.

The New York *Times* quotes ex-President Hoover as saying that, under the name of reparations, men are being seized and prisoners are being worked "under conditions reminiscent of Roman slavery," and that so habituated to brutality have we become that this condition is tolerated with little protest. "And indeed," Mr. Hoover commented, "our own army officers are required to take part in that policy." *

A statement issued on March 2, 1947, by the International Labor Relations Department of the American Federation of Labor† said that the "expanding system of slave labor" is a "dire threat to the free workers of all countries" and pointed out that in Europe "nearly

* New York *Times,* October 14, 1945.
† New York *Times,* March 2, 1947.

one-third of all productive work is now being done by forced labor." "Millions of men and women from former enemy countries," continues the statement, "are still being held as slave laborers," and it calls a spade a spade by saying that the crimes committed by the Nazis are no excuse "for the crimes being perpetrated today, especially in the name of democratic and peace-loving peoples."

It has been argued that the military prisoners were being used to reconstruct after the terrible devastation caused by the Axis powers. Presumably, therefore, the precedent is set that prisoners of war may, in the future, be used as slaves by the victor to restore damage. Again, as in the case of pillaging private property, it is an individual who is punished. I cannot understand the sanity of attributing personal guilt to *all* the citizens of a guilty nation. In this instance, human slavery is so dangerous a practice to sanction, and so susceptible of frightful abuse, that I do not understand how it can be defended.

X: The War Trials

In the ancient city of Nuremberg, an impressive court came into session, to which we sent our Attorney-General, as our representative judge, and a member of our Supreme Court, as our representative prosecutor. There were corresponding judges and prosecutors representing England, France, and Russia, and twenty-two defendants were to be tried. Indictments containing four "counts" had been drawn up. The third count covered violations of the rules of war, and, as the court sat as a military tribunal, there could be no basic quarrel with its jurisdiction on that count. Nor could its right to try defendants on the fourth count, " crimes against humanity," be doubted; it was entitled to try such of the crimes against humanity as arose out of the war or were connected with it. Moreover, the Tribunal might also be said to have been a court of the *de facto* government of Germany* and, as such, entitled to try those charged with such crimes. Indeed, trials on these two counts were highly desirable, and, had the indictment confined itself to them, the precedent of the Nuremberg trial would have been difficult to assail in the future.

But the first two counts were of a different order. Count 1

* At the time of the trials, there was no fully empowered local German government.

charged a "common plan or conspiracy" to commit other crimes alleged in the indictment, and count 2 charged "crimes against peace," defined as "planning, preparation, initiation, or waging of a war of aggression, or a war in violation of international treaties, agreements, or assurances or participating in a common plan or conspiracy for the accomplishment of any of the foregoing." These two counts reached into new judicial territory.

The "common plan or conspiracy" count introduced legal principles foreign to Continental law. Dr. Hans Ehard, Minister-President of Bavaria, pointed out in an address reproduced in the April, 1949, issue of the *American Journal of International Law*, that the "concept of the common plan" was hitherto "unknown either in the Anglo-Saxon or in any other law." General Telford Taylor, our Chief of Counsel for War Crimes, has admitted that "many European jurists view the Anglo-Saxon concept of criminal conspiracy with deep suspicion." But the second count is subject to even graver criticism.

That there was no precedent for these war crimes trials in Germany was admitted by the opening words of Robert H. Jackson, Chief Counsel for the United States at the trials, who said, "The privilege of opening the first trial in history for crimes against the peace of the world imposes a grave responsibility." The prosecution in these cases made no serious attempt to rely upon existing principles of international law. Rather, the Charter of the Tribunal, a charter drawn up by victors without regard to existing law, was held to be final. As Mr. Jackson said, "The validity of the provisions of this Charter is conclusive upon us all . . ." * Anticipating that the defendants would claim that they were being tried under *ex post facto* laws (a thing abhorrent to the English-American system and proscribed by our Constitution), Mr. Jackson said: "But these men

* The Charter might have declared that all nations were subject to the law asserted by it, but it did not. It might have proved embarrassing to the victors if similar crimes committed by their own soldiers and civilians had been subject to like prosecution. (The rather distressing story of these crimes may be found in *The High Cost of Vengeance*, by Freda Utley, and *Victors' Justice*, by Montgomery Belgion, both published in 1949.) At any rate, *the Charter was directed at the enemy alone.*

Some of the prosecutors rationalized by reference to various international treaties and declarations like the Kellogg-Briand Pact, but the approach of the Russian prosecutor, General Rudenko, was simpler. He said: "The Charter is to be considered an unquestionable and sufficient legislative act, defining and determining the basis and the procedure for the trial and punishment of major war criminals."

cannot bring themselves within the reason of the rule which in some system of jurisprudence prohibits *ex post facto* laws. They cannot show that they ever relied upon international law in any state or paid it the slightest heed." His argument thus was that the defendants need not be tried under international law because they violated it. The argument against an American accused of murder might well be that he need not be tried under American law because he violated it!*

The following section of Mr. Jackson's opening address summarizes the attitude of the victorious Allies toward existing international law: "It is true, of course, that we have no judicial precedent for the Charter. But international law is more than a scholarly collection of abstract and immutable principles. It is an outgrowth of treaties and agreements between nations and of accepted customs. Yet every custom has its origin in some single act, and every agreement has to be initiated by the action of some state. Unless we are prepared to abandon every principle of growth for international law, we cannot deny that our own day has the right to institute customs and to conclude agreements that will themselves become sources of a newer and strengthened international law. International law is not capable of developments by the normal processes of legislation for there is no continuing international legislative authority. Innovations and revisions in international law are brought about by the action of governments designed to meet a change of circumstances. . . . I am not disturbed by the lack of judicial precedent for the inquiry we propose to conduct."

Justice Jackson's statement has not impressed some of the American authorities on international law. Professor Edwin Borchard commented: "It must be, therefore, that the victors have simply availed themselves of their power as victors to judge the vanquished, and for that reason it seems unlikely, in spite of Justice Jackson's predictions, that the judgment, however just, will commend itself as an authority in international law."†

George A. Finch, Editor-in-Chief of the *American Journal of In-*

* There is a Continental rule similar to ours against *ex post facto* law—it is *nullum crimen nulla poena sine lege* (no crime, no punishment, without [existing] law). It is reported that French jurists had considerable difficulty reconciling themselves to the "aggressive war" count under this principle.

† *The American Journal of International Law*, vol. 41, p. 107. In a footnote, Professor Borchard said that the judges, in characterizing "aggressive war" as a crime, were each condemning the history of their own nation.

ternational Law, in reviewing a book on the Nuremberg trial,* made the point that he regards "as untenable, however, the argument . . . of the prosecutors and judges at Nuremberg that custom can be judicially established by placing interpretations upon the words of treaties which are refuted by the acts of the signatories in practice, by citing unratified protocols or public and private resolutions of no legal effect, and by ignoring flagrant and repeated violations of nonaggression pacts by one of the prosecuting governments† which, if properly weighed in the evidence, would nullify any judicial holding that a custom outlawing aggressive war had been accepted in international law.

". . . the prosecutors and judges at Nuremberg tend to confuse the issue in suggesting a qualification of the criminality of aggressive war according to the brutality with which it is waged or its terrible consequences. No such distinctions are made by the count in the indictment charging the planning or waging of aggressive war. Acts of brutality and terrorism were disposed of in the separate counts charging war crimes and crimes against humanity [and I believe] that the proceedings and convictions at Nuremberg on those counts were legally justifiable."‡

Mr. Finch pointed out that since World War I the urge to prevent aggressive war has been growing constantly, but he failed to see any binding agreement which really outlawed war and made individual participation in its plan and prosecution personally responsible. He called attention to the fact that the Nuremberg judgment, in its historical narrative of the basic events, makes obvious omissions which make it difficult to accept the recital as an impartial document. He noted that the annexation of Austria by Germany

* *American Journal of International Law*, vol. 41, no. 1, p. 334.

† An interesting sidelight is offered by Justice Jackson's description of the discussions with the Russians during the conference preparatory to the organization of the Nuremberg trial. The New York *Times* of August 26, 1948, reports Jackson as saying: "During the conference, the Soviet delegation suggested that 'it is quite possible that the accused would like to become the accusers in the course of the trial' and suggested provisions to exclude propaganda. The American delegate ventured the opinion that the best way to exclude such counterattacks would be to narrowly define 'aggression' so as to confine the issue to the actual attack and suggested consideration of definitions used in nonaggression pacts to which the Soviet Union was already a party. The idea was coldly received. Perhaps the reference to the Soviet nonaggression treaties was not exactly tactful."

‡ Mr. Finch elaborates further in his "The Nuremberg Trial and International Law" in the same volume, page 20.

was promptly recognized and the League of Nations failed to act upon it. The German aggression upon Czechoslovakia was not only ratified by Great Britain and France but practically imposed by them upon Czechoslovakia; thus, if the aggressions against Austria and Czechoslovakia were aggressive war, they were aggressions ratified by the Great Powers. The Tribunal omitted reference "to the vitally important part played by Soviet Russia" in the aggression against Poland. Germany certainly acted pursuant to an understanding with Russia, and there followed almost immediately a similar aggression on the part of Russia. The Tribunal held that the aggression against Poland was an international crime, and yet one of the judges was appointed by a state which participated in the crime. Furthermore, even after the aggression against Poland, the United States carefully maintained its neutrality—an act which gives the impression that no crime was committed.

Sir Hartley Shawcross, Attorney-General of England and England's prosecutor at the Nuremberg trial, has stated the results of the trial as follows:

"What is of enduring importance is that the Nuremberg trial, to which twenty-three nations directly adhered, has established beyond doubt three principles:

(I) That to initiate a war of aggression is an international crime;
(II) That the individuals who lead their countries into such a war are personally responsible;
(III) That individuals therefore have international duties which transcend the national duty of obedience imposed by particular states where to obey would constitute a crime against the nations." *

That is a fair statement of the precedent which the Nuremberg trial sought to establish, as far as it goes. But it omits important additional precedents, namely, that the victors in a war may themselves determine whether an aggression has been committed, may themselves try individuals for this new crime, may deny to the defendants the right to cite the actions of the victors as precedents for the defendants' indicted acts, and may determine strictly what laws and precedents are to form the criteria of responsibility. The vice

* "International Law: A Statement of the British View of Its Role," *Journal of the American Bar Association,* January, 1947.

of the situation lies in the fact that the victor, without check by others, may try "international criminals" as it sees fit.*

One other comment seems apt. International law has not yet recognized any rights of individuals. Yet the precedent of the Nuremberg trial recognized new duties of individuals, which, according to Sir Hartley Shawcross, override the duty of the individual to his state. The *Rules of Land Warfare* published for use by the American army in 1940 granted to soldiers the defense of *respondeat superior;* that is, a soldier could not be held accountable for what he was ordered to do by a superior officer. Paragraph 347 delineates offenses against the rules of war, including such things as refusing quarter, killing the wounded, ill-treatment of prisoners, ill-treatment of inhabitants in occupied territory, etc. But it goes on to say, "Individuals of the armed forces will not be punished for these offenses in case they are committed under the orders or sanction of their government or commanders. The commanders ordering the commission of such acts, or under whose authority they are committed by their troops, may be punished by the belligerent into whose hands they may fall." The British *Manual of Military Law* contained a similar defense. Nevertheless, German defendants at Nuremberg, and Japanese and Germans in subsequent trials, were denied the defense of *respondeat superior* which our own *Rules of Land Warfare* and those of the British declared was permitted to our own troops. It is of some significance that the American *Rules of Land Warfare* were amended *in 1944* to eliminate the material quoted above, substituting elsewhere the following: "Individuals and organizations who violate the accepted laws and customs of war may be punished therefor. However, the fact that the acts complained of were done pursuant to order of a superior or government sanction may be taken into consideration in determining culpability, either by way of defense or in mitigation of punishment. The person

* The world has been informed by the Chinese Communists that they will try such Nationalist leaders (our late allies) as they may capture, unless they "repent" and further "the People's Liberation." Their crime is that they had launched a "counterrevolutionary civil war." Quincy Wright, in the April, 1948, *Journal of International Law,* said: "Undoubtedly if an aggressor state should be victorious in a general war, the position of the leaders of the victim states would be hazardous, and the rulers responsible for the aggression would escape prosecution. It is in confidence that such a situation can be prevented, especially with the instrumentalities of the United Nations available, that the governments of the 'peace-loving states' committed themselves to the Nuremberg principles." I wonder.

giving such order may also be punished." I understand that a similar change was made in the British rules.

Are we really ready to accept this new principle? It means that the individual is obliged to put international loyalty above loyalty to his country. It means that every citizen is obliged to exercise his own judgment as to the conduct of his government vis-à-vis other governments. It imposes an obligation on every statesman and military leader to question whether what he is asked to do by his government, or whether what he is prompted to do for what seems to him its best interests, may not conflict with a higher duty, which he must determine somehow by himself, to international society. This does not seem realistic. It is a principle which certainly could not possibly operate in Russia, where the individual is not permitted discretion in his conduct, nor could it be possible in the United States, where duty to our own country would be deemed by any statesman or military leader to override any theoretical international duty.

I certainly do not suggest that Göring, Streicher, and other responsible German leaders should have gone without trial. The Nuremberg trial would have been wholly desirable on charges under the third and fourth counts. And what would have been the result? The following Nuremberg defendants were convicted on either or both of counts 3 and 4: Göring, Ribbentrop, Keitel, Jodl, Rosenberg, Frick, Seyss-Inquart, Sauckel, Bormann, Kaltenbrunner, Frank, Streicher, Raeder, Funk, Speer, Schirach, Neurath, and Doenitz. Fritzsche, Von Papen, and Schacht were discharged on all counts. Rudolf Hess was the only defendant convicted under counts 1 and 2 but acquitted on counts 3 and 4. He alone of the convicted defendants would have gotten off had counts 1 and 2 been eliminated.

A compromise might have made some sense. If the Allies were convinced that a precedent must be set for a new international law that plotting or assisting in a war of aggression is a crime, then a fair job could have been done of it. That would have necessitated making the court a truly international court, not a court of victors. Neutral judges could have been requested to participate. This suggestion is discarded by apologists for the Nuremberg precedent in somewhat the following fashion:

"A neutral court might be thought by many to be and to seem fairer and more impartial. Unfortunately, however, impartiality is no longer an attribute of neutrality. In other times states remained neutral in a war because they had no interest in the quarrel or no strong feelings about its merits. A state remained neutral because it wanted to. But that is no longer the case. A state can now remain neutral only if it is allowed to and it makes little or no difference whether it wants to be neutral or feels neutral. . . . When neutrality is conditioned by good fortune and not by good feeling it ceases to provide a useful touchstone for impartial judgment." *

The argument seems specious to me. It has been repeated by General Taylor: ". . . the number of truly 'neutral' countries was so small that this solution would have proved entirely unfeasible." Can it be doubted that there would have been greater weight to the trials had judges from Switzerland, Sweden, Ireland, and Turkey (and perhaps even Spain, and Germany, Austria, and Japan) sat on the bench?

More important, perhaps, would have been a willingness on the part of the Nuremberg judges to permit the defendants to contest the existence of the crimes in the first and second categories by proving the extent to which the victors themselves, though sitting in judgment, had committed aggressions and acquiesced in aggressions. It is a bit farcical to condemn acts of aggression during a period in which one of the judging powers, Russia, herself committed grave acts of aggression and the other Great Powers acquiesced in these and in some by the nation of the defendants.

I have said that the Nuremberg court sat properly as a military tribunal, judging crimes against the laws of war. If a court of *one* victor nation could try such crimes, it appears logical that a joint court of victors may try the same crimes. But this innovation, a mixed tribunal, containing judges appointed by five nations, introduced into the situation what seems to me a most unfortunate factor. The United States has now adhered to a new form of international military trial for war crimes, from which the convicted have no right of appeal whatsoever. When we try one of our own citizens in our own military courts, however summary the procedure may be, there are appeals which the accused may take, and, if there is justification, he may even appeal to the United States Supreme Court by habeas corpus. But it has been held by our Supreme Court, in the case of Tojo and other Japanese convicted by a joint military court, that there can be no appeal or judicial review of their convictions. This decision is logical enough, for I do not see how the appel-

* Peter Calvocoressi, *Nuremberg—The Facts, the Law and the Consequences,*

late court of one judging nation can overturn the judgment joined in by judges of other nations. But the unhappy result of it is that, whereas our own citizens are protected by the right of appeal, the alien who is tried by the new form of joint court has no appeal whatsoever.

On June 27, 1949, Justice Douglas of the Supreme Court handed down a long-delayed separate concurring opinion in the *Hirota case* in which he termed the rationale of the majority opinion "potentially dangerous." He characterized international military tribunals of the kind which convicted the Japanese war leaders (and presumably the Nuremberg class of trials in general) as "solely an instrument of political power." He agreed that there was no direct judicial review by the Supreme Court because of the mixed national nature of the trial courts but added that he was disturbed by just that. He said: "It leaves practically no room for judicial scrutiny of this new type of military tribunal which is evolving. It leaves the power of those tribunals absolute. Prisoners held under its mandates may have appeal to the conscience or mercy of an executive; but they apparently have no appeal to law."

Douglas suggested, however, that a prisoner held by an American official or custodian might, by writ of habeas corpus, apply to the Federal District Court of the District of Columbia to rule whether he is being properly held—this would constitute a collateral attack on the legality of the trial. I am sure that many jurists are concerned by the fact that these trial courts in which we have participated are absolute in their power and that there is no direct appeal from their determinations.

Some of the other major war trials seem to have created precedents as unfortunate as that of Nuremberg. In his dissenting opinion in the *Yamashita case*, decided by the Supreme Court in 1946, Mr. Justice Rutledge quoted Thomas Paine as follows: " 'He that would make his own liberty secure must guard even his enemy from oppression; for if he violates this duty he establishes a precedent that will reach himself.' " Rutledge also said: "It is not in our tradition for anyone to be charged with crime which is defined after his conduct, alleged to be criminal, has taken place . . ."

In the *Homma case*, decided seven days later by the Court, Mr. Justice Murphy similarly protested: "Today the lives of Yamashita and Homma, leaders of enemy forces vanquished in the field of battle, are taken without due process of law. There will be few to protest. But tomorrow the precedent here established can be turned against others. A procession of judicial lynchings without due process of law may now follow. No one can foresee the end of this failure of objective thinking and of adherence to our high hopes of a new world."

And in the same case Mr. Justice Murphy said: "Either we conduct such a trial as this in the noble spirit and atmosphere of our Constitution or we abandon all pretense to justice, let the ages slip away and descend to the level of revengeful blood purges. Apparently the die has been cast in favor of the latter course. But I, for one, shall have no part in it, not even through silent acquiescence."

These two judges dissented from the decisions of the majority in denying a writ of habeas corpus to Yamashita and Homma after trials which, had they been so conducted against a citizen of the United States, would certainly have aroused public protests.

The trial rules in the Japanese war-criminal cases, as laid down by General MacArthur, permitted introduction of evidence of a character which no domestic American court would permit, not even a military court trying our own soldiers. The enemy generals were, therefore, tried under conditions which would have violated the basic constitutional rights of defendants had they been our own nationals.

That strange results ensue from the ill-conceived war trials is apparent from the statement attributed by the New York *World-Telegram* of December 21, 1948, to Joseph B. Keenan, prosecutor on behalf of the United States against Tojo and other major Japanese war criminals. Mr. Keenan is reported to have said that he would have nolle prossed the case against Shigemitsu. "He was quite different from any other accused in that it clearly appeared he opposed the war against the United States, the British Commonwealths and the Netherlands. He voiced his opposition at a time when it was dangerous as a Japanese for him to do so. . . . The Allied court held that since he believed the war to be unwarranted and aggressive, he was guilty of an offense in joining the cabinet long after the war decision was made. With this conclusion I disagree." Mr. Keenan is reported further to have asserted that Shigemitsu was tried at the insistence of the Russians, who promised to disclose certain pertinent documents at the trial which were never, in fact, disclosed.

Major Ben Bruce Blakeney, of the U. S. Air Forces, counsel to

General Umerzo in the Tokyo war trials, argued the insufficiency of the indictment of the Japanese "war criminals" before the International Military Tribunal. It is difficult to read his argument, published in the August, 1946, issue of the *American Bar Association Journal,* without being convinced of how tragic an error has been made by the United States in consenting to the form and method of the war trials. He termed the "observing of legal forms, while ignoring the essence of legal principles," to be "the supreme atrocity against the law." He pointed out that the defendants were accused of the crime of starting a war, but that no such crime exists; that international law has not recognized "just" wars as against "unjust wars"; that there has never in the history of civilization been a trial on the charge of "planning and waging of war"; that the victorious Allies might well have taken summary action against individuals, whether proper action or not, but that in presuming to act against them under law they were inventing their own law for the purpose; that there is no such thing, legally, as a "crime against peace"; that no treaty or covenant (such as the Hague Conventions, the League Covenant, the Geneva Protocol, the Pact of Paris, etc.) made war a crime; that even the Charter of the United Nations does not make war a crime, for the veto may be exercised by a Great Power, which may then resort to war with full legality; that one of the nations sitting on the Tribunal had been expelled from the League for waging aggressive war in Asia and Europe but had hardly considered war to be "illegal"; that war and the making of it are attributable to nations and not to individuals; that, even though guilt can be attributed by inference to a nation under any treaty, pact, or covenant, there is in none of them any basis for holding a premier, foreign minister, chief of staff, or other individual personally responsible; that, if violations of the admitted rules of war are charged, procedure exists for prosecution through ordinary military commissions of a quite different character than this so-called "Military" Tribunal; that a killing is no more illegal in war if the war is "unjust" than if it is "just," else all Japenese soldiers would be guilty, and not only superior officers; that the bombing of Pearl Harbor is not different in essence from the atomic bombing of Japan; etc.

It is a powerful indictment of the indictment.

There have been several protests against the conduct of other "war-crimes" trials in which lesser Nazis have been tried. Judge Charles F. Wennerstrum, of the Iowa Supreme Court, who acted as an American judge in one of the Tribunals, is reported by the New York *Times* of February 25, 1948, to have said that "justice has been denied" in some German war-crimes trials. He stated that "the prosecution has failed to maintain objectivity aloof from vindictiveness," and "any man should have a chance for appeal—that's justice."

And considerable indignation has followed disclosures concerning the methods by which the defendants in the Malmédy massacre cases were tried. Senator Langer, in introducing a resolution for a Congressional investigation of the conduct of war trials, said: "We cannot have a double standard of justice, one brand for use at home and another for export. We must get at the bottom of this shocking deviation from American principle in American-occupied areas and we must correct the situation." The Federal Council of Churches of Christ in America, the American Civil Liberties Union, and the *Christian Century*, among others, have protested earnestly against methods which are alien to the United States. Judge Van Roden, summarizing the conclusions of the Simpson Commission, appointed by Secretary of the Army Royall to investigate, said: "Statements admitted as evidence were obtained from men who had first been kept in solitary confinement for three, four, and five months. Confined between four walls, without windows, they had two meals a day shoved in to them through a slot in the door. They were not allowed to talk to anyone. They had no communication with their families, nor with any minister or priest. Solitary confinement proved sufficient in some cases to persuade the Germans to sign prepared statements." He said, further: "The Malmédy massacres . . . actually happened. . . . But . . . because some wicked Germans did it, are we right to say that all Germans we lay our hands on are wicked and should be destroyed? That is not the way of thinking that I learned in my church."

The Simpson Commission had found that "investigators customarily put black hoods over the heads of defendants, punched them in the face with brass knuckles, kicked them, and beat them with rubber hoses";* and Judge Van Roden said also that defendants faced investigators in American uniforms seated around a black table with a crucifix in the center and only two candles providing light. Such "sham courts" would impose a death sentence and then again try to wring a confession from the defendants.

* Quoted from the New York *Times*, March 2, 1949.

Are these methods American?

In April, 1949, a Nuremberg court, consisting of three American judges, held nineteen of twenty-one defendants guilty of crimes within the categories of the original Nuremberg trial. The defendants had either signed direct orders for war crimes or had been in administrative posts under which they had been carried out. One judge, Leon W. Powers, dissented bitterly, stating that he would have freed thirteen of the nineteen.*

"It is argued that the defendants are guilty of all those crimes of which they received knowledge," said Judge Powers. "The theory is that if a defendant knew of a crime anywhere in the government and remained on his post of duty, he thereby approved the crime and became guilty of it.

"It is a strange doctrine to be advanced by lawyers representing American justice."

Powers pointed out that the "reason for existence" of all the war-crimes trials was "to encourage respect for rules of warfare." Therefore, "any suggestion of constructive or collective fault, no matter how disguised, would punish those who did not personally violate the rules equally with those who did and thus destroy not only respect for rules but also the whole legitimate purpose of the trial."

This was a court composed solely of American judges. Would we wish to have precedents like this established, not only in international law, but for our own courts?

XI: What Is Left?

How MUCH of international law is left? Well, the rules in times of peace are still with us. As to the rules of war, the principles of humanity and chivalry have received serious blows; and new precedents have been contributed, the effect of which upon the law of the future cannot now be foreseen. What concerns me is that either we have sought to justify immoral conduct on our own part on the ground that others have been more immoral or else we have caught a milder dose of the same disease and are unaware of it. I fear that future violators of international decency may be able to point to precedents established by us to justify otherwise indefensible actions.

We may then record the following as new rules of warfare:

* Quoted in the New York *Times*, April 14, 1949.

1. Unrestricted use of submarines is permitted.
2. Any type of weapon may be used.
3. Bombing of civilian populations is permitted.
4. Devastation of nonmilitary cities is permitted.
5. Upon the conclusion of hostilities and the annexation or occupation of territory by the victors, the local population may be expelled and its property confiscated.
6. After hostilities have ceased, the victor may continue the devastation of occupied territory to any extent deemed advisable.
7. The victor may take as booty, and in lieu of reparations, whatever may be useful to its economy or may impair either the military or competitive economic potential of the defeated country.
8. Private nonmilitary property of enemy civilians may be confiscated at will, wherever found, after hostilities have ceased.
9. The victor may retain prisoners of war as human reparations for such period as it sees fit.
10. Under rules established by them and through a court of their own representatives, the victors may try military, government, and industrial leaders of the vanquished country, after the war has been concluded, for any crimes designated by the indictment, whether *ex post facto* or not, and the accused has no appeal from the judgment.

The argument is made by some apologists that acts of which we have been guilty, or have condoned, which are the product of retributive anger in the course of a war against a horrible enemy, cannot become the basis for, or be extended to, "rules of law." To me this seems unrealistic reasoning. A precedent is a precedent, and those which we helped to create may well be turned, in the future, against enemies decidedly more innocent than the Germans of World War II.

XII: The Eichmann Supplement

THE EICHMANN TRIAL in Israel may be said to have been a logical supplement to the unsound Nuremberg precedent. Adolf Eichmann, one of the worst of the Nazi torturers and executioners, was kidnaped, on May 11, 1960, by Israeli agents in Argentina, taken aboard an Israeli airliner, and removed to Israel, where he was imprisoned. He was brought to trial on April 11, 1961. His conviction was assured, and no one could grieve over the fact itself, for no punishment could possibly have been severe enough to match his guilt. But the method used to apprehend him and to try him for his crimes created extremely unfortunate precedents in international law.

The first of these precedents is that any country may safely kidnap a citizen of a second country while residing in a third. The Argentine government protested bitterly against the kidnaping, and the issue was brought before the United Nations Security Council. Argentina demanded the return of Eichmann and asked reparations. The Council, in a fumbling resolution, ignored the demand for Eichmann's return but "requested" the government of Israel "to make appropriate reparation in accordance with the Charter of the United Nations and rules of international law." All that was expected and all that was given was an apology by Israel. The resolution implied that if the same thing happened again, i.e., if Israel should kidnap another resident in Argentina, this might be deemed to endanger peace, but, apparently, any nation is now entitled to one such kidnaping with no more risk than to be required to apologize.

It is understandable that horror at Eichmann's inhuman acts should have caused universal satisfaction that this beast was apprehended and brought to task. But it is regrettable that some jurists should try so hard to support procedure which so clearly violated sound rules of law and practice. In a long article in the April, 1961, issue of the *American Journal of International Law*, Professor Helen Silving, of the University of Puerto Rico, rationalized the position of Israel both as to the kidnaping and as to the issue of assuming jurisdiction over Eichmann. The fine-spun reasoning of her article is hardly convincing. A kidnaping is a kidnaping, and I do not see how international law can countenance one committed in times of peace in the territory of a friendly state. It is even more difficult to accept the rationalization which is offered by Professor Silving and others to support Israel's right to try Eichmann.

It is a basic rule that a defendant be tried only in the jurisdiction where he committed a crime. It is also basic that he be not tried under an *ex post facto* law, but only under law existing at the time his acts were committed. Yet Eichmann was tried in Israel, where he committed no crime, under an Israeli statute enacted some years after his acts, and by the courts of a state which was not even in existence when his acts were committed.

Professor Silving offered the principle of "inexigibility of law abidance" or "inexigibility of a different conduct" to justify Israel's assumption of jurisdiction. "The principle of inexigibility," she said, "implies that in exceptional situations, in fairness and equity, it cannot be 'morally' demanded or expected of a person that he abide by the law." Applying the same principle to nations, she added: "However narrowly conceived, the 'principle of inexigibility' undoubtedly applies to the Eichmann case. . . . Within the 'inexigibility' test, it is moreover demanded that the intensity of Israel's 'interest' in trying him was so great as to outweigh any unusual considerations of international law."

That is a big stretch—to apply the principle of inexigibility to the law of nations. One of the bases of the rule that a defendant in a criminal case must be tried in the jurisdiction where he is alleged to have committed a crime is that he is presumed to have had knowledge of the law and moral standards applied in that jurisdiction. Another state, another jurisdiction, would be inclined to apply not only its own laws but also its own standards of morality to the facts in issue. The world does not think alike on moral problems. For example, Russia does not have the same moral standards as do we. What might, to the rulers of Soviet Russia, come clearly within some rule of inexigibility might horrify us. Who is to determine, then, whether the principle of inexigibility does apply in a particular case? If each nation is to determine this for itself, in relation to the apprehension and trial of an alleged criminal whose acts were committed outside that nation's borders, international law, in this area, becomes a shambles. Suppose, for instance, that Communist Russia manages to kidnap an American citizen while he is residing in England, and tries him in Russia for an alleged trumped-up crime "against the Russian state" committed in the United States. What, then, is to prevent Russia from alleging inexigibility, under the Eichmann precedent, and claiming that the alleged crime against the Russian people brought the case under Professor Silving's rationalized exception to the basic rule of international law that the defendant can be tried only in the jurisdiction where he committed an alleged crime.

It was understandable that Israel wished to see Eichmann tried and also to use the occasion to bring the story of Nazi horror to full light. But it was not necessary to use the arbitrary methods employed. Eichmann could have been tried in Germany, by a German court, under German law, as hundreds of Nazi criminals have been tried and convicted. Some have said that Germany did not want to try Eichmann. This may well be so, but the issue could have been forced. If Israel had publicly demanded such a trial, Germany could not possibly have refused, and there would have been a public trial, with vast attendant publicity.

It is distressing to me that, as a result of the Nuremberg and Eichmann precedents, substantial protections of international law may have disappeared. If both these precedents are to receive approving recognition, then not only can victors in a war try a citizen of the vanquished under new law imposed by the victors, *ex post facto*, but a nation, even in peacetime, can kidnap a resident of a friendly state and try that resident, under *ex post facto* laws of its own design, and in a jurisdiction where no crime was committed.

XIII: The Creation of the U.N.

When the results of the Dumbarton Oaks Conference, held in August, September, and October of 1944, were made known, we were told that a new era had dawned. There was to be a new League, bigger and better than the last, which was to make aggressive war impossible and which would institute a new rule of law and ethics in international relations. But it had not started well. It was utterly clear that the smaller powers were to have little or nothing to say and that the new League was to be controlled by the "Big Five": by Russia, England, China, and the United States (the conferees at Dumbarton Oaks), plus France. And it was apparent that Russia would not be easy to deal with, for it had insisted, and we had conceded, at Yalta that two of its major constituent states, the Ukraine and Byelorussia, were to be treated exactly like Canada and the other British Dominions. Russia had originally insisted that each of her soviet states should be treated like an independent country.

When the San Francisco Conference started on April 25, 1945, to consider the Dumbarton Oaks proposals and to establish the United Nations Organization, two things soon became apparent. One was that there was to be a Communist bloc, composed of Russia,

Byelorussia, Ukraine, Czechoslovakia, and Yugoslavia. Another was that, despite the passionate opposition of independent smaller powers, the Conference would have to accept the dictates of the Big Five, which, at the time, really meant the "Big Three"—Russia, England, and the United States, for China was hardly in a position to exercise much independence, and France was not yet one of the fully elect. That this system could not work was clear enough from the method by which the veto power was introduced to prevent any possibility of serious action against one of the Great Powers. There were many who recognized this but hoped that the U.N. would constitute a sort of international debating forum in which recalcitrant nations could be put to shame, a hope that has turned out to be futile.

Let us examine the mechanism of the United Nations. The major units established in the Charter are the Assembly, the Security Council, the Economic and Social Council, the Trusteeship Council, the International Court of Justice, and the Secretariat. The Assembly is composed of representatives of all member states. Its main function is debate. It may make recommendations to the Security Council within the scope of the Charter, but it cannot consider any matter which is currently being considered by the Security Council. It may study various things, and receive reports. It is to have annual sessions and such special sessions as occasion may demand. In the Assembly, voting on anything important is by the two-thirds rule.

Article 13 of the Charter of the U.N. charges the Assembly with "encouraging the progressive development of international law and its codification," and steps have already been taken to follow this charge; but it will be a long pull, and it has small hope of success. Russia has made it clear that it considers our old concepts of international law to be "capitalistic"; that it does not honestly believe in any "rights of man"; and that private property is a wholly "bourgeois" idea. Subsidiary committees and branches, such as the Economic and Social Council, also may contribute suggestions as to changes in and codifications of international law, for they deal with what former Secretary of State Acheson has called "those basic levels where the root causes of international disorders have their origins."

The Security Council is permanently in residence, is to be ready to meet promptly at any time, and is to have frequent meetings. Its decisions are final. It consists of eleven members, of which the Big Five are permanents. Six others are elected periodically by the Assembly. But voting is set up so that the Big Five will control. On "procedural matters" there must be seven affirmative votes cast. On "substantive" matters the affirmative vote must also be seven, and must include all of the Big Five. This is the so-called "veto" provision. Nothing of substantive matter can be settled without the unanimous consent of the Big Five. That means, of course, that, if any issue arises which endangers the peace of the world and one of the Big Five is involved, it may stop any action by exercising its veto. So we have a new league which can act against one of the Big Five powers only with its own consent. And the United States has until recently been as insistent on the right of veto as the Russians have. We are inclined to charge the Russians with a lack of desire to co-operate in reforming international relations, but we have not shown any readiness to subject ourselves to the control of the majority. It seems clear that there can be no effective international agency to preserve peace unless the Great Powers are willing to subject themselves to it.

In case of a dispute, the Council takes the lead. The parties to the dispute are enjoined to arbitrate, conciliate, mediate, or otherwise try to settle their grievances; and the Security Council shall urge them to it. The Council may investigate a dispute; even the Assembly may call a dispute to the attention of the Council; and a nonmember may also bring a dispute to it if it agrees to be bound to a peaceful settlement.

If the Council finds that peace is endangered or has already been broken, it can recommend action. "Peaceful" measures, such as sanctions, breaking off diplomatic relations, or severing commercial relations, may be tried; or even warfare; and there is provision for the creation of an international police force. But it must be remembered that all such measures, peaceful or forceful, are subject to the veto. Furthermore, there is an interesting reservation: every nation is entitled to act in self-defense. But self-defense is the cry of almost every aggressor; it is easy enough to create a military border incident which requires armed "resistance" in the interests of "self-defense."

Regional peace arrangements and conferences are permitted as long as these do not conflict with the United Nations and its purposes. This reservation was made, in part, to permit inter-American organizations.

The Assembly has arrogated to itself, quite illegally, some of the powers of the Security Council. This took place on the occasion of United Nations endorsement of our intervention in the Korean conflict. The Russian delegate to the Council made the mistake of walking out and thus gave the Assembly an opportunity to pass its "Uniting for Peace" resolution, which stated that when the Council did not act and the peace was endangered, the Assembly might take the necessary action by a two-thirds vote. However, the heavy influence which we originally exercised in the Assembly has turned into a comparatively feeble one, through the admission of so many new states in the past decade, most of which seem to have at least "neutralist" tendencies. Indeed, many of our former friends seem to have acquired an unsympathetic attitude.

Despite this and despite the veto power which Russia has exercised so very frequently in the Council, our foreign policy seems to be largely based upon co-operation with the U.N. This and our various other treaty entanglements have deprived us of considerable freedom of decision and of movement. It has also produced some rather odd results. For example, our entry into the Korean War was called a "police action" by President Truman. It was actually a making of war without a declaration of war, but Mr. Truman's fiction that we were acting for the United Nations as policemen enabled him to violate the Constitution, which requires the consent of Congress to a declaration of war.

Since the creation of the United Nations Organization, there has been a constant succession of aggressions and small wars. The record of the U.N. as a peacemaker and a protector of the innocent has been pitiful. The aggressors have been allowed the fruits of their aggression. Citizens of the United States have had their property confiscated in many sections of the world, and some of them have been imprisoned and tortured; some Americans still languish in Chinese and other prisons. Neither the United Nations Organization nor our own government, handicapped as it is by reliance on the false value of the U.N., have succored them. Once an American President said: "Perdicaris alive, or Raisuli dead." Now we merely send a note which is ignored and the Raisulis stay living and our Perdicarises stay imprisoned.

Economic and social co-operation is pledged and also the betterment of the condition of humanity. The members agree to promote "universal respect for, and observation of, human rights and fundamental freedoms for all, without distinction as to race, sex, language, or religion." This difficult job is left to the Economic and Social Council. How all nations are to agree on what "human rights" are is difficult to imagine. We maintain that totalitarian states like Russia and its satellites do not recognize some of the most basic "human rights." On the other hand, the Russians may well point out that the "democracies" do not give that human equality which, allegedly, is given in Russia, regardless of "race."

The Charter looks forward to the gradual enlightenment and emancipation of countries not yet self-governing. That is a magnificent objective, but evidently does not apply to any countries under Soviet domination. Moreover, one may well question what "enlightenment" newly emancipated nations may expect under United Nations tutelage. Communists hold hundreds of key posts in the various U.N. agencies and departments. Odd as it may seem and tragic as it has been, we once suddenly discovered that many of the U.N. posts allotted to American citizens were occupied by American Communists.

While China is certainly a Great Power today, her seat on the Council is occupied by the Chinese Nationalist government situated on Formosa, for we have steadily, and rightfully, refused to permit the substitution of the rapacious Chinese Communist government to take its place. So we have a rather strange assortment of holders of the veto power.

XIV: The International Court of Justice

THE CHARTER might just as well have continued the old World Court of the League of Nations, but the Russians felt a little delicate about this, having been thrown out of the League; so the new Court, the International Court of Justice, was created. Actually, it varies in few important details from the old Court. It consists of fifteen judges and is so organized that one-third of the Court will be elected every three years. The method of election is slightly involved but seemingly fair enough. The initial designations were characterized, however, not so much by a selection of those most eminently fitted for the work as by political considerations, and the personnel of the Court is hardly the best that could have been selected. Submission to the Court is not mandatory, but, to date, most of the United Nations have agreed to it. The judges have a nine-year term and are required to make their work exclusive. They are kept in permanent session except for a vacation period which they may determine. They are bound by certain ethical restrictions, but a judge may sit when his own nation is involved. In fact, if any party to a litigation has no representative on the bench, it may designate one as a temporary judge.

The kind of law that this Court administers is carefully stated: recognized agreements; international customs well accepted by civilized nations; "the general principles of law recognized by civilized nations"; judicial opinions; and opinions of the "most highly qualified publicists." The last (carried over from the old Court) may be a joker in Russia's favor, because Russian academies and courts are turning out theories of law which would be somewhat odd to the rest of the world—yet these would come, presumably, from one of the highest and most "qualified" sources.

The Court has an opportunity to make some new law through its judicial decisions if they are accepted as precedents, for it is provided that the Court may, with the consent of the parties to a dispute, decide *ex aequo et bono*, that is, according to the general principles of equity and justice. The Court may also give certain advisory opinions when called upon. Its decisions are to be given by majority vote; and the reasons for a decision must be given, dissenting judges having the right to express the reasons for their dissent.

One great defect in international law is continued. Individuals have no place before the Court; only nations may come before it. Nations may appear voluntarily, as issues arise. But the Charter of the International Court of Justice also provides that nations may bind themselves to compulsory jurisdiction of the Court in disputes arising under or involving questions of international law.

The overwhelming wish of the nations was for absolute, compulsory jurisdiction by the Court, but some of the larger powers, the United States among them, refused to permit compulsory jurisdiction to be written into the Charter for fear that it might prevent its acceptance. The United States by Senate resolution, passed by a vote of sixty to two, accepted the *ipso facto* jurisdiction of the Court in international disputes with any other state which also accepted compulsory jurisdiction. The resolution limited our acceptance by excluding any "matters which are essentially within the domestic jurisdiction of the United States," and an amendment proposed by Senator Connally added the words "as determined by the United

States." But the Charter itself excluded from United Nations attention any "matters which are essentially within the domestic jurisdiction of any state . . . ," so even this is not too serious a reservation. Besides, at this writing, Russia and its satellites are absent from the list of those who accepted compulsory jurisdiction of the Court. Pressure by Liberal groups to rescind the Connally amendment has been unsuccessful to date.

Another amendment, proposed by Senator Vandenberg, also reserved "Disputes arising under a multilateral treaty, unless (1) all parties to the treaty affected by the decision are also parties to the case before the Court, or (2) the United States especially agrees to jurisdiction."

The relief granted by the Charter, if a nation refuses to recognize a Court decision against it, is somewhat feeble. The matter may be referred to the Security Council, which may, "if it deems necessary, make recommendations or decide upon measures to be taken to give effect to the judgment." With the veto power still in effect, that relief can hardly be relied upon.

There have been several previous attempts to create a sensible international arbitration or court system. The Permanent Court of Arbitration was established at The Hague by the International Convention of 1899 and continued in the next Convention of 1907. It was not truly a court but rather a system of arbitration. It was not overburdened with work, being infrequently referred to, but its record was good. And the Court established by the League, though it suffered also from insufficient attention, did its job well. There is some feeble hope that, in spite of the deficiencies of the United Nations, the new Court may improve upon the record of past courts and establish a more active and virile system of international adjudication.

XV: U.N. and the Future of International Law

THE LEAGUE OF NATIONS was a compromise, and an ineffective one, largely because it started as an alliance of victors to enforce an artificial peace created by tragically ill-designed peace treaties. The United Nations, at present writing, looks as though it may go the way of the League. Again created by victors in a war, it was erected upon the illusion that the Soviets would co-operate to construct a peaceful world. The major power defeated in the war at the conclusion of which this new organization was devised has not yet been admitted as a member, and great sections of its territories have been swallowed up by Russian imperialism. Russian intransigence has frustrated all attempts to make the U.N. work effectively. Now a multitude of small, new nations have been added to the voting roster, countries many of which have merely some of the trappings but not the substance of civilized states. Some of these are easily swayed by Russian oratory, threats and benefactions to oppose the Western powers which seek to make sense out of the world. The constant allegations of "colonialism" and "imperialism" against these Western powers, while the brutal Russian colonialism and imperialism is treated with respectful silence, is distinctly disheartening. The "neutralist" failure to insist upon self-determination for the Germans, the Hungarians and other peoples in Europe leaves one rather ill. The growing support for the admission of Communist China into the U.N., in the face of the fact that the U.N. itself is still actually at war with mainland China—for the Korean War has not been terminated, there is only an armistice—is shocking. The tendency to accept as *fait accompli* and unremediable the Communist absorption of vast territories during the very existence of the U.N. gives little promise that morality, ethics and principle are to govern its deliberations in the future. The United Nations is a mess.

What is to happen to international law? If one proposed solution is achieved it may disappear. No international law would be necessary if we had a world-state, in which the powers were in a position like that of the states in our Union. But there is small hope of inducing the national states to give up their own sovereignty to form such a world-state. The mechanical problems are so great that it would take a convention of statesmen with even greater vision than had the Fathers of our own country to institute it. Would the present states be the constituent states, or would new states be carved out by population or geographical convenience? Would the new states be delineated by language, race, nationality? Would the "backward peoples" have equal voice with the Western nations? The problems are many and difficult, but they are not impossible of solution, if we can find international Madisons, Franklins, Washingtons, and Hamiltons to do the job.

The concept of a world-state certainly has attraction. However, it can be no more, for the moment, than a dream for the future. Nationalism is rampant. The former vast empires of the British, French and Dutch have been broken up into a large number of individual nations of various sizes. Some were ready for independence. Others were not and, in consequence, cannot be expected to assume a truly republican or democratic character. The number of dictators extant has increased measurably and will increase further. A world debating society is possible; a union or a federation is remote indeed, if ever probable. In the meantime, efforts to create some international organization which can promote peace effectively will continue.

The League of Nations was a compromise, and an ineffective one, largely because it started as an alliance of victors to enforce an artificial peace created by an ill-designed treaty. The United Nations has similar defects. Perhaps it may be used as an opening wedge, but it does seem to be so far from what the world requires that a long period of international education must perhaps come first. No international utopia is possible, nor can an ideal world-state be created overnight. We must stumble ahead and, as the British so often have done, "muddle through." But we must begin soon to muddle through. The atomic bomb has made the world even smaller than the One World that Wendell Willkie saw.

In a better form of international organization international law might drop its concept of nations as the sole persons with which it deals. Individuals might come to have rights, not merely as their own governments may protect them on a basis of defending national honor, but because they are individuals and, as such, are entitled to a protection against violation of basic rights as citizens of the world. A start was made in this direction in the adoption by the General Assembly of the United Nations on December 10, 1948, of a *Universal Declaration of Human Rights*. It is not an international law, however. The General Assembly has merely proclaimed it to be "a common standard of achievement for all peoples and all nations, to the end that every individual and every organ of society, keeping this declaration constantly in mind, shall strive by teaching and education to promote respect for these rights and freedoms and . . . to secure their universal and effective recognition and observance. . . ."

The Declaration is an illegitimate descendant of the Petition of Right, of the Preamble to our own Declaration of Independence, and of our Bill of Rights. It is worrisome. It contains some conspicuous omissions, which represent concessions to Russian dissidence. It contains many explicit statements of right and duty, where our Bill of Rights uses generalities which have more force. It includes many very obvious principles, thus, possibly, implying that other rights we have always taken for granted are purposely omitted. And it uses technical phrases and what lawyers call "terms of art," the definitions of which are clear under American law but perhaps wholly unacceptable to the law of other nations. For example, we know pretty well what principles lie behind the injunction that no one shall be subject to *arbitrary* arrest or be held on a criminal charge without a *fair* hearing. But what do these words "arbitrary" and "fair" mean in other systems of jurisprudence? And toward the end of the Declaration comes: "In the exercise of his rights and freedoms, everyone shall be subject only to such limitations as are determined by law solely for the purpose of securing due recognition and respect for the rights and freedoms of others *and of meeting the just requirements of morality, public order, and the general welfare in a democratic society* [my italics]." But what are these just requirements? Unless a true court for the determination of such issues is established, I fear they are only whatever the government of a state wishes them to be. Much of the American bar, while favoring *a* declaration, is highly critical of the one prepared by the U.N. Assembly.

The Assembly has also brought forth a declaration against "genocide," the crime of mass killings, and it illustrates the effect of Russia's participation in the determinations. While mass killings for racial or religious reasons are denounced, genocide directed against groups of political enemies is not. Still other legal problems are under study, among them a proposal to formulate the law recognized by the Nuremberg trials. It is not difficult to predict that there will be considerable difficulty in persuading Russia to accept as binding upon herself the principles and rules applied in the war trials, and that the problem of establishing a disinterested method for determining war guilt will be found extremely hard to solve.

However impotent the United Nations may be in dealing with

international emcrgencies, there was alway some hope that its various commissions and study groups might serve a desirable purpose in considering and labeling the problems which someday—perhaps through a better-implemented organization—should be solved by international agreement. But a study of much of what has been produced is deeply discouraging. The strong tendency is toward international "welfare state" concepts, and the heavy concentration of Communists and Socialists upon the United Nations commissions and their staffs has produced little of encouragement to those who believe in liberty and the free-enterprise system.

The Future

In our domestic law the prospect is encouraging, provided we stem the drift toward a competely centralized and perhaps totalitarian state, and there are signs today that a growing conservatism among our youth may call a halt. There is much to be done, and we still have much to learn before we can do it, but the rising interest in the ethical aspects of domestic social problems bodes well for the future. I am of the evolutionary school, and therefore it is my hope that progress will be rapid, but not too rapid to prevent us from digesting change as we make it, not so rapid as to result in the adoption of half-understood and half-thought-out measures, the application of which may seriously impair our national life and our economy. Experimentation is necessary, for the effect of no measure can be fully understood in advance of trial, but rashness in introducing new measures may be worse than introducing none. I hope that our desire for reform will not lead us further along what has been called "the road to statism."

In international law, I am not sanguine for the future. The breakdown in international morality seems to me so severe, and the degree to which we have contributed to it so little apprehended in our country, that I fear the amount of re-education which may be necessary to bring us, as well as the rest of the suffering world, back to decency is truly formidable. In international law we have had vicious retrogression. The gradual enlightenment which came to its peak toward the end of the nineteenth century and the beginning of the twentieth has been succeeded by a depression of ethics and morality. How soon will there be recovery from this depression of the conscience of mankind?

The Future

Index

About the Author

René A. Wormser has been a member of the New York bar since 1920, engaged in general law practice and specializing to some extent in estate planning and international law. A long-standing interest in making legal matters clearly understandable to laymen led, in 1937, to the writing of Your Will and What Not to Do About It. *This was followed by* Personal Estate Planning in a Changing World, *published in 1942;* Collection of International War Damage Claims, 1944; The Theory and Practice of Estate Planning, 1944, 1948; The Myth of the Good and Bad Nations, 1954; Foundations: Their Power and Influence, 1958; Wormser's Guide to Estate Planning, 1958; *and* The Planning and Administration of Estates, 1961 *(editor). Mr. Wormser has also written numerous articles, both nontechnical and technical.*

Born in Santa Barbara, California, a graduate of Columbia College and Columbia Law School, Mr. Wormser now lives in Greenwich, Connecticut, with his wife and two daughters. He is the senior partner of Wormser, Koch, Kiely & Alessandroni, a New York law firm, which also has an office in London.